SCOTTISH CATHOLIC SECULAR CLERGY
1879-1989

For Pat with love

SCOTTISH CATHOLIC SECULAR CLERGY 1879-1989

Christine Johnson

Foreword by
The Right Rev. Mark Dilworth, OSB
The Abbot, Fort Augustus

JOHN DONALD PUBLISHERS LTD
EDINBURGH

ISBN 0 85976 345 5

British Library Cataloguing in Publication Data

A catalogue record for this book is available
from the British Library.

Phototypeset by Burns & Harris Ltd, Dundee, Scotland
Printed in Great Britain by Billing & Sons Ltd., Worcester

Contents

Foreword

On 4 March 1878 a papal bull restored normal government to the Roman Catholic Church in Scotland. It was a decisive turning-point in that Church's history. Catholicism after the Reformation had dwindled almost to vanishing point over most of Scotland, until in the mid-seventeenth century a slow build-up began. A bishop was appointed in 1694; from 1731 there were two bishops, and from 1827 three, each administering an extensive district with powers delegated by Rome.

It was therefore a major step in 1878 to establish six dioceses under bishops enjoying powers that were theirs by right. And not only was it the culmination of a process, but it also provided the impetus for further expansion. Priests had been increasing in number during the decades of Irish immigration and were now to increase even more as each bishop built up his diocesan structure. The number of Roman Catholics, 9 per cent of the total population in 1878, rose until in the 1960s they formed 16 per cent. Two more dioceses were created in 1947.

Dr Johnson has compiled a summary of information on every diocesan priest in Scotland since dioceses were restored. It is valuable, for the details are not easily available elsewhere; and it is authoritative, for she has written and published on Scottish Catholic history and has already produced lists of priests from 1732 to 1878, which historians have welcomed.

This book too will be welcomed, and not only by students of Roman Catholicism but by anyone interested in local history or sociology or the relations of the Churches to each other. In fact it is likely to be the standard work of reference for many years to come.

Fort Augustus, 1991   M.D.

Introduction

In 1878 the hierarchy was restored in the Roman Catholic Church in Scotland, and the three old vicariates were replaced by two archdioceses and four dioceses. The Northern Vicariate became, with minimal changes, the diocese of Aberdeen. The Western Vicariate shed its more northerly and southerly extremities to become the Archdiocese of Glasgow. The Eastern Vicariate shed its northern and south-western parts to become the Archdiocese of St Andrews and Edinburgh. From the parts so shed were created the dioceses of Argyll and the Isles in the north-west, Galloway in the south-west and Dunkeld in the Tayside area. All four dioceses came under the metropolitan of St Andrews and Edinburgh. In 1947 the Archdiocese of Glasgow was itself subdivided. New dioceses of Motherwell and Paisley were created, while northern Ayrshire was added to Galloway. The Archdiocese was thereby reduced to Greater Glasgow and Dumbartonshire, but it became the metropolitan of Motherwell and Paisley.

This book is an attempt to provide a complete *Fasti* of all Scottish secular priests ordained from 1879 to 1989 inclusive. The data is dealt with diocese by diocese. Short biographical notes are given for each priest ordained. These are followed by lists of all the priests who served in each parish. Within this framework certain limitations have been imposed. The biographical notes include only secular clergy who served in parishes. Regular clergy (members of religious orders and societies) are omitted. Priests from outwith Scotland who served exclusively as chaplains to religious houses are also omitted. Similarly the parish lists contain only those parishes which had, for however short a time, a resident secular priest. Those always served from a neighbouring parish are omitted, as are those always served by regular clergy.

The main source of information is the *Catholic Directory for Scotland*, an annual publication giving all currently serving priests and the parishes to which they are attached. It also provides ordination notices and obituaries, both of which usually give details of the priest's background, education, and, in the case of obituaries, career. The Directories are not, of course, infallible. Their accuracy depends on the diligence of contributors and errors often creep in. A priest may be listed simultaneously under two parishes or his name may be cited incorrectly. Other errors are unavoidable given the lapse of time between information being collected and the

Directory being published. Thus a man who dies in December of one year will probably still appear in the following year's issue. Again, when information is sent in, forthcoming changes may be anticipated. At best this is misleading and, at worst, it can lead to completely erroneous information being printed. Because the publication is annual it is only accurate to within a twelvemonth, and so a post given as vacant for a year may in fact just have been vacant over the December – January period. However, if one bears in mind these limitations, one can find in the Directories a remarkably full picture of the Church in Scotland.

A second source of information is Canning's *Irish-Born Secular Priests in Scotland* which gives detailed biographical notes. In spite of the duplication I have included these men in order to provide a comprehensive list. I have, however, confined myself to facts immediately relevant to Scotland. The reader interested in the Irish side is referred to Canning.

A problem arises where the Directories and Canning are not in agreement. Sometimes it is obvious from his quoted sources that Canning is correct. Where no sources are quoted it is sometimes possible to reconcile Canning with the Directories. When this fails I have generally adhered to the information given in the Directories since they are the source for Scottish-born priests. Parish and clergy lists can be cross-checked (rather as one can check accounts by using double entry book-keeping), but such a system works best when a single source is used. It may not be absolutely accurate, but the entries 'match up' better.

Occasionally notes on a priest are included under a diocese other than that of his ordination. For instance, if he never served in the diocese for which he was ordained, he is listed under the one in which he actually worked. Again, if he spent all his working life on the staff of colleges before being appointed bishop, he is listed under his episcopal diocese. Priests of the same name and the same diocese are distinguished by their ordination dates. Very occasionally a priest appears briefly in one diocese, and then, a number of years later, someone of the same name and ordination date appears for a short time under another diocese. It seems at least possible that they are one and the same, but, in the absence of any proof, such an identification cannot be assumed. Instead cross-references are given. Sometimes a priest will appear in the Directory's address list, but not under the relevant parish. This has been taken to mean that that particular man, for one reason or another, is not actually serving the parish and his name is not included in the parish lists. Another source of ambivalence is the Directory's giving a priest's address as c/o Diocesan Office. This phrase can cover anything from sick leave or retiral to further studies or missionary service and is used interchangeably with more specific entries. One final point should be noted. Although diocesan reorganisation may be authorised *de jure* in a particular year, it is always at least a year later that it *de facto* takes place.

These lists of clergy have been drawn up over a considerable period of time, each diocese being taken in turn. There are inevitably slight differences in the treatment of each. For the smaller dioceses there has been, perhaps, a tendency to include extra detail, while the sheer size of the archdioceses has made brevity essential.

By their very nature, lists consist of raw, unprocessed data, but hidden within the mass of facts are many pointers to change and development within the Church. Parish lists enable one to trace the rise and fall of populations. In the cities congregations swelled until the post-war period, when there was a general migration away from the city centre. St John's, Glasgow is a case in point: when the Gorbals were demolished the parish vanished. Clergy lists, too, provide much information. They allow one to trace changes in the education of priests, such as the different uses made of Continental and English colleges and the emergence of university education as a diocesan policy. They also allow one to discover changes in patterns of recruitment. Aberdeen diocese, at one time the cradle of vocations, now has to rely heavily on Jesuits. Dioceses with large Irish immigrant populations at one time depended heavily on short term loans of Irish priests. Most surprising of all, perhaps, is the number of priests from Germany and Belgium who came to Scotland about the turn of the century. It is to be hoped, therefore, that these lists may inspire research into specific topics of Scottish Catholic history.

Abbreviations

SJ, OSB, etc after a priest's name, indicates that he belonged to a religious order or society.

(WD), (ND), or *(ED)* after a priest's name indicates that he was ordained for a vicariate before 1879.

St A & E stands for the Archdiocese of St Andrews and Edinburgh.

Scots Colleges – shortened forms have been given in the biographical notes as follows:

Valladolid: the Royal Scots College, Valladolid.

Blairs: St Mary's College, Blairs, Kincardineshire – national seminary, later minor seminary, 1829 – 1986.

Langbank: St Vincent's College, Langbank – inter-diocesan minor seminary to supplement Blairs 1961 – 78.

St Peter's: St Peter's College, the major seminary for Glasgow archdiocese, situated at different times at Partickhill, New Kilpatrick, Cardross, Newlands; 1874 – 1985.

Chesters: Chesters College, successor to St Peter's College; major seminary for all dioceses except Aberdeen, and St Andrews and Edinburgh.

Drygrange: St Andrew's College, Drygrange – major seminary for Archdiocese of St Andrew's and Edinburgh; 1953 – 86.

Gillis College: successor to Drygrange – major seminary for Aberdeen and St Andrews and Edinburgh.

Archdiocese of St Andrews & Edinburgh

Secular Clergy

AGNEW, HENRY: Born Ireland. Educated Ireland and Irish College, Rome. Ordained Rome 1932. Lent to St A & E. St Columba's, Edinburgh 1933-34. Died Edinburgh 29 March 1934. (Canning)

AGNEW, JOHN: Born Edinburgh 1938. Educated Blairs, Drygrange. Ordained Edinburgh 1961. Methil 1961-66. C/o Diocesan Office 1966-71. On Nigerian Mission 1971-75. C/o Diocesan Office 1975-77. Hawick 1977-79. Inverkeithing 1979-88. Bonnybridge 1988-.

ALLCHIN, ARTHUR: Ordained 1892. Falkland 1908-09. No further entries.

ANDERSON, JAMES: Ordained 1945. Lochore 1946-47. No further entries.

ANDERSON, WILLIAM R T: Born Glasgow 1931. Educated George Watson's College, Edinburgh; Edinburgh University; Sidney Sussex College, Cambridge; Scots College, Rome. Ordained Rome 1960. St David's, Dalkeith 1960-61. Professor, Blairs 1961-69. Edinburgh, no parish, 1969-77. Spiritual Director, Scots College, Rome 1977-85. Professor, Blairs 1985-86. Lent to Aberdeen diocese: chaplain, Aberdeen University 1986-.

ANGUS, GEORGE: Born Aberdeen 1842. Served in Indian Army 1859-63. Educated Oxford University. Ordained for Anglican Church and served in Gloucestershire. Joined Roman Catholic church 1873, and was ordained priest in England 1876. Kensington 1876-84. Came to Archdiocese of St A & E. St Andrew's, Fife 1884-1909. Died St Andrew's 17 March 1909.

ANTHONY, WILLIAM: Born Manuel, Stirlingshire 1912. Educated Campion House, Osterley; Blairs; St Edmund's College, Ware. Ordained Edinburgh 1948. Kilsyth 1948-56. St Francis Xavier's, Falkirk 1956-64. St Columba's, Edinburgh 1964-69. Duns 1969-72. Larbert 1972-79. Sacred Heart, Grangemouth 1979-89. Retired 1989.

1

ANTON, JAMES: see Aberdeen diocese

ARCHIBALD, JOHN: Born Loanhead 1934. Educated Blairs; Propaganda, Rome. Ordained Rome 1957. Edinburgh Cathedral 1958-59. Rosewell 1959-61. Professor, Langbank 1961-63. Further studies, Rome 1963-64. Raploch 1964-65. Immaculate Conception, Bathgate 1965-67. Holy Cross, Edinburgh 1967-68. St Margaret's, Dunfermline 1968-76. Milton of Campsie 1976-.

ASHLEY, IAN: Born Edinburgh 1938. Educated Holy Cross Academy, Edinburgh; National Service with RAF; Drygrange 1960-66. Ordained Edinburgh 1966. Broxburn 1966-67. Our Lady of Perpetual Succour, Kirkcaldy 1967-69. Larbert 1969-75. Died Edinburgh 11 Sept 1975.

ASHWORTH, JOHN J: Ordained 1937. Portobello 1937-38. No further entries.

BACON, JAMES: Born and educated Ireland. Ordained Thurles 1946. Lent to St A & E. St Mary's, Stirling 1946-48. Resumed his vocation in Ireland 1948. (Canning)

BAGAN, MICHAEL: Born Edinburgh 1953. Educated Holy Cross Academy, Edinburgh; St Augustine's High School, Edinburgh; Drygrange. Ordained Edinburgh 1978. Awaiting appointment 1978-79. Hawick 1979-85. St Francis Xavier's, Falkirk 1985-87. Raploch 1987-.

BARBER, ERIC SIORDET: Born Sheffield 1893. Educated Bootham School, York; Manchester University; Beda, Rome. Ordained 1945. St Cuthbert's, Edinburgh 1945-47. Edinburgh Cathedral 1947-49. Holy Cross, Edinburgh 1949-50. Hawick 1950-55. Chaplain, St Mary's, Balnakiel, Galashiels 1955-68. Died Edinburgh 9 Nov 1968.

BARCLAY, CHARLES: Born London 1938. Educated Blairs, Drygrange. Ordained Edinburgh 1961. St Mary's, Stirling 1961-64. St John Vianney's, Edinburgh 1964-69. Catechetical Centre, Dundalk, Eire 1969-70. Professor, Drygrange 1970-78. St Andrew's, Livingston 1978-84. Our Lady of Perpetual Succour, Kirkcaldy 1984-88. On foreign missions 1988-.

BARR, DAVID MORRISON: Born Edinburgh 1942. Educated Campion House, Osterley; Drygrange. Ordained Edinburgh 1972. Whitburn 1972. St Francis Xavier's, Falkirk 1972-77. St Patrick's, Edinburgh 1977-78. Our Lady of Perpetual Succour, Kirkcaldy 1978-80. Fallin 1980-86. St Margaret's, Edinburgh 1986-89. St Margaret's, Dunfermline 1989-.

BARRETT, FRANCIS: Born Glasgow 1935. Educated Blairs, Drygrange. Ordained Edinburgh 1959. St Francis Xavier's, Falkirk 1959-63. St

Andrew's, Edinburgh 1963-67. Cowie 1967-69. Hawick 1969-70. No further entries.

BARRY, JOHN CHARLES McDONALD: Born Edinburgh 1917. Educated Fort Augustus School; Cambridge University; Fribourg University; Oscott College. Ordained 1944. Kilsyth 1944-46. Further studies, Rome 1946-49. St Cuthbert's, Edinburgh 1949-50. Polmont 1950-53. Professor, Drygrange 1953-60. Rector, Drygrange 1960-77. St Mark's, Edinburgh 1977-89. North Berwick 1989-.

BARRY, MICHAEL: Born and educated Ireland. Ordained Dublin 1942. Linlithgow 1942-44. Chaplain, Royal Navy 1944-51. In hospital 1951-52. Died Dublin 24 March 1952. (Canning)

BARRY, ROBERT E: Ordained 1938. Burntisland 1938-41. No further entries.

BATCHELOR, KENNETH STEWART: Born Dundee 1925. Educated Harris Academy, Dundee; Brechin High School; Drygrange; Beda, Rome. Ordained Elgin 1978. Edinburgh Cathedral 1978-79. Chaplain, convent of Mary Reparatrix, Elie 1979-80. Our Lady of Perpetual Succour, Kirkcaldy 1980-84. Innerleithen 1984-86. Rosewell 1986-.

BELL, MICHAEL: Born 1927. Educated Holy Cross Academy, Edinburgh; Campion House, Osterley; St Sulpice. Ordained Edinburgh 1961. Kilsyth 1961-72. Blanefield 1972-85. St Catherine's, Edinburgh 1985-89. In America 1989-.

BENNETT, GEORGE HENRY: Born Antigua, West Indies 1875. Educated Scots College, Rome 1892-1901. Ordained Rome 1898. St Patrick's, Edinburgh 1901-10. North Berwick 1910-12. Hawick 1912-18. Consecrated Bishop of Aberdeen 1918. Died Aberdeen 25 Dec 1946.

BENNETT, PETER: Ordained 1934. Linlithgow 1967-68. Chaplain, Balnakiel Convent, Galashiels 1968-69. No further entries.

BERKERY, WILLIAM: Born and educated Ireland. Ordained Edinburgh 1881. Haddington 1881-82. St Patrick's, Edinburgh 1882-83. Linlithgow 1883-85. Retired in bad health 1885. Died Ireland 21 March 1927. (Canning)

BERMINGHAM, PATRICK: Ordained 1944. St Patrick's, Edinburgh 1946-47. No further entries.

BIRNIE, JAMES K: Born Edinburgh 1913. Educated Fort Augustus School; Scots College, Rome 1931-38. Ordained Rome 1937. St Margaret's, Dunfermline 1938-40. Kelso 1940-44. West Calder 1944-47.

Hawick 1947-56. St Andrew's, Edinburgh 1956-77. Died Edinburgh 6 Nov 1977.

BIRNIE, PATRICK: Born Edinburgh 1868. Educated Blairs 1881-86; Issy 1886-87; Scots College, Rome 1887-93. Ordained Rome 1893. St Patrick's, Edinburgh 1893-95. St Francis Xavier's, Falkirk 1895-98. Jedburgh 1898-1901. Grangemouth 1901-08. Our Lady of Perpetual Succour, Kirkcaldy 1908-29. St Patrick's, Edinburgh 1929-50. Died Edinburgh 8 Feb 1950.

BLAKE, EDWARD: Born and educated Ireland. Ordained Thurles 1902. Lent to St A & E. Penicuik 1902-03. Kilsyth 1903-15. Resumed his vocation in Ireland 1915. Died Ireland 28 Jan 1948. (Canning)

BLEE, BERNARD: Born and educated Ireland. Ordained Maynooth 1934. Lent to St A & E. St Francis Xavier's, Falkirk 1934-39. Kelso 1939-40. Resumed his vocation in Ireland 1940. Died Ireland 13 Oct 1974. (Canning)

BOILSON, THOMAS: Born and educated Ireland. Gave his services to St A & E. Ordained Edinburgh 1881. St Mary's, Stirling 1881-82. Penicuik 1882-86. Our Lady of Perpetual Succour, Kirkcaldy 1886-87. No further entries. (Canning)

BONNER, JAMES: Born and educated Ireland. Ordained Maynooth 1915. Lent to St A & E. St Patrick's, Edinburgh 1915-22. Resumed his vocation in Ireland 1922. (Canning)

BOURKE, JEREMIAH: Ordained 1944. St Columba's, Edinburgh 1946-47. At Nunraw Abbey 1947-49. No further entries.

BOWDEN, THOMAS: Born and educated Ireland. Ordained Ireland 1937. Lent to St A & E. Edinburgh Cathedral 1937-39. Resumed his vocation in Ireland 1939. (Canning)

BOYD, DANIEL: Born Stenhousemuir 1938. Educated St Modan's High School, Stirling; Drygrange. Ordained Edinburgh 1961. St Ninian's, Edinburgh 1961-63. Further studies, Rome 1963-65. Ballingry 1965-66. Professor, Drygrange 1966-70. Lennoxtown 1970-79. Torrance 1979-.

BOYLAN, PATRICK: Born Broxburn 1952. Educated St Mary's Academy, Bathgate; Drygrange. Ordained Broxburn 1977. North Berwick 1977. St Francis Xavier's, Falkirk 1977-80. Further studies, Rome 1980-84. Professor, Drygrange 1984-86. Pathhead Ford 1986-.

BOYLE, DANIEL JOSEPH (1940): Born Grangemouth 1918. Educated Blairs 1929-34; Institut Libre de St Lo 1934-35. St Sulpice 1935-39;

Seminaire Limoges 1939-40. Ordained Grangemouth 1940. Further studies, Cambridge University 1940-43. St John's, Edinburgh 1943-46. Bannockburn 1946-47. Immaculate Conception, Bathgate 1947-53. Pittenweem 1953-62. Rosyth 1962-.

BOYLE, DANIEL PATRICK ALOYSIUS (1940): Born Ireland 1917. Educated Blairs 1929-34; St Lo 1934-35; Issy and Limoges 1935-40. Ordained Edinburgh 1940. Further studies, Cambridge University 1940-43. Professor, Blairs 1943-49. On leave of absence 1949-50. Spiritual Director, Valladolid 1950-52. Professor, Blairs 1952-60. Rector, Valladolid 1960-65. Rector, Blairs 1965-67. Rector, Scots College, Rome 1967-73. West Calder 1973-80. Immaculate Conception, Bathgate 1980-84. Died Edinburgh 20 Feb 1984. (Canning)

BOYLE, LIAM: Born and educated Ireland. Ordained Maynooth 1954. Lent to St A & E. Portobello 1954-58. Resumed his vocation in Ireland 1958. (Canning)

BRACELIN, JOHN: Born Whifflet 1900. Educated Blairs 1914-20; Valladolid 1920-27. Ordained Valladolid 1927. St Patrick's, Edinburgh 1927-30. Kelso 1930-35. Cowie 1935-54. St Francis Xavier's, Falkirk 1954-72. Died Falkirk 15 Dec 1972.

BRADY, HUGH: Born Ireland. Educated Ireland, Paris. Ordained Paris 1935. Lent to Dunkeld diocese: Saints Peter and Paul, Dundee 1935-36. St Cuthbert's, Edinburgh 1936-38. North Berwick 1938. Denny 1938-39. Not in Catholic Directory 1939-40. Lent to Galloway diocese: St Mary's, Irvine 1940-41. Went to serve in Ireland 1941. (Canning)

BRADY, PATRICK: Born Kilsyth 1941. Educated Blairs, Drygrange. Ordained Kilsyth 1965. St Catherine's, Edinburgh 1965-70. No further entries.

BREDIN, PATRICK J: Born and educated Ireland. Ordained Ireland 1931. Lent to St A & E. Edinburgh Cathedral 1931-36. Resumed his vocation in Ireland 1936. Died Ireland 27 May 1950. (Canning)

BREEN, JOHN: Born Ireland. Educated Blairs 1918-23; Grand Seminaire de Coutances 1923-28. Ordained Dundee 1928. Tranent 1928-29. St Peter's, Edinburgh 1929-32. Further studies, Cambridge University 1932-36. Cardinal Vaughan School, London 1936-38. Professor, Blairs 1938-42. Headmaster, Blairs 1942-46. C/o Prestwick 1946-47. Edinburgh Cathedral 1947-56. Died Edinburgh 29 Aug 1956. (Canning)

BREEN, PATRICK: Born and educated Ireland. Ordained Kilkenny 1947. Lent to St A & E. Methil 1947-49. No further entries. (Canning)

BREMNER, ALEXANDER: Born Baltimore, USA 1934. Educated Blairs, Valladolid. Ordained Valladolid 1957. Further studies, Rome 1957-60. Edinburgh Cathedral 1960-77. Peebles 1977-85. Addiewell 1985-87. Stoneyburn 1987-

BRENNAN, JAMES (1934): Born Ireland. Educated Ireland, Spain. Ordained Spain 1934. Lent to St A & E. Immaculate Conception, Bathgate 1935-37. St Ninian's, Edinburgh 1937. Our Lady of Perpetual Succour, Kirkcaldy 1937-40. Resumed his vocation in Ireland 1940. (Canning)

BRENNAN, JAMES (1945): Born and educated Ireland. Ordained for St A & E 1945. St Patrick's, Edinburgh 1945-47. Kilsyth 1947-61. Spiritual Director, Blairs 1961-66. St Mary's, Glenrothes 1966-67. Rector, Blairs 1967-74. Lent to Aberdeen diocese: Fochabers 1974-77. Denny 1977-88. Bo'ness 1988-. (Canning)

BRENNAN, JAMES (1947): Born and educated Ireland. Ordained Derry 1947. Lent to St A & E. St Columba's, Edinburgh 1947. Sacred Heart, Grangemouth 1947-48. Resumed his vocation in Ireland 1948. (Canning)

BRENNAN, WILLIAM: Born London 1937. Educated St Edmund's College, Ware. Ordained London for Archdiocese of Westminster 1962. Came to St A & E 1982. Portobello 1982-85. St Francis Xavier's, Falkirk 1985-88. Kilsyth 1988-90. Kelso 1990-.

BRETT, JAMES C: Ordained 1913. St Patrick's, Edinburgh 1920-21. No further entries.

BRODIE, CHARLES: Born Edinburgh 1919. Educated North Berwick High School; Campion House, Osterley; Blairs; Oscott College, Birmingham. Ordained 1946. St Andrew's, Fife 1946-47. Hawick 1947-50. Holy Cross, Edinburgh 1950-61. Lennoxtown 1961-67. St Mary's, Glenrothes 1967-72. Galashiels 1972-85. Fauldhouse 1985-.

BROWN, DAVID P: Born Coneypark, Banknock 1928. Educated Blairs; Scots College, Rome. Ordained Rome 1952. Addiewell 1952-53. Musselburgh 1953-55. Raploch 1955-57. Professor, Blairs 1957-73. St Magdalene's, Edinburgh 1973-76. Cowie 1976-85. Galashiels 1985-.

BROWN, GORDON RICHARDSON: Born Edinburgh 1938. Educated University of Edinburgh, Drygrange. Ordained Edinburgh 1969. Further studies, Maynooth 1969-70. Professor, Drygrange 1970-77. Rector, Drygrange 1977-84. St Patrick's, Edinburgh 1984-85. Newbattle 1985-88. Immaculate Conception, Bathgate 1988-89. Burntisland 1989-.

BRUCE, MICHAEL VICTOR: Born Kensington, London 1886. Educated

Scots College, Rome 1913-19. Ordained Rome 1918. St Peter's, Edinburgh 1919-20. Edinburgh Cathedral 1920-25. Haddington 1925-30. West Calder 1930-34. St Peter's, Edinburgh 1934-48. Died Tipperary 19 June 1948.

BURNS, MICHAEL: Born Methil 1945. Educated St Agatha's School, Methil; St Patrick's College, Buchlyvie; Drygrange. Ordained Methil 1974. St Patrick's, Edinburgh 1974-76. St John Vianney's, Edinburgh 1976-78. Rosewell 1978-83. Chaplain, Stirling University 1983-85. Further studies 1985-86. Chaplain, Stirling University 1986-89. Immaculate Conception, Bathgate 1989-.

BURNS, PETER: Born Edinburgh 1879. Educated Blairs 1893-97; Scots College, Rome 1897-1904. Ordained Rome 1903. West Calder 1904-05. Broxburn 1905-08. Denny 1908-09. Professor, Valladolid 1909-11. Balfron 1911-12. Immaculate Conception, Bathgate 1912-13. Slamannan 1913-14. Haddington 1914-17. Forces chaplain 1917-19. Lochgelly 1919-21. Duns 1921-23. Loanhead 1923-26. Dunbar 1926-32. Retired 1932. Died London 16 Aug 1947.

BYRNE, BRIAN PATRICK: Born and educated Ireland. Ordained Waterford for St A & E 1956. Bannockburn 1956-57. St Joseph's, Edinburgh 1957-58. Musselburgh 1958-60. Edinburgh Cathedral 1960-63. C/o Diocesan Office 1963-64. Nigerian mission 1964-65. Edinburgh Cathedral 1965-69. Florida, USA 1969-72. St Margaret's, Dunfermline 1972-74. Kilsyth 1974-76. St Magdalene's, Edinburgh 1976-79. Chaplain, Heriot Watt University 1979-81. Bowhill 1981-. (Canning)

BYRNE, JOHN (1919): Born and educated Ireland. Ordained 1919. Lent to St A & E. Edinburgh Cathedral 1919-26. Resumed his vocation in Ireland 1926. Died Ireland 13 Feb 1958. (Canning)

BYRNE, JOHN FRANCIS (1945): Born and educated Ireland. Ordained Derry for St A & E 1945. St Andrew's, Edinburgh 1945-56. Hawick 1956-59. Broxburn 1959-65. Jedburgh 1965-66. St Andrew's, Livingston 1966-78. Died Edinburgh 25 Feb 1978. (Canning)

BYRNE, JOSEPH: Born and educated Ireland. Ordained Glasgow for St A & E 1922. Lent to Glasgow archdiocese: Pollokshaws 1922-23. Penicuik 1923-24. St Mary's, Stirling 1924-30. Winchburgh 1930-32. Larbert 1932-36. Lochgelly 1936-38. Our Lady of Perpetual Succour, Kirkcaldy 1938-77. Died North Berwick 14 May 1977. (Canning)

BYRNE, SYLVESTER: Born and educated Ireland. Ordained Wexford 1939. Lent to St A & E. St Columba's, Edinburgh 1939-41. Resumed his vocation in Ireland 1941. Died Ireland 20 Aug 1973. (Canning)

CALLAGHAN, JOHN: Born Kilsyth 1938. Educated Blairs, Valladolid. Ordained Valladolid 1962. St Patrick's, Edinburgh 1962-67. Raploch 1967-69. C/o Diocesan Office 1969-71. Nigerian mission 1971-75. C/o Bannockburn 1975-76. Bannockburn 1976-79. Galashiels 1979-81. South Queensferry 1981-87. Bannockburn 1987-.

CAMERON, ANDREW J: see Aberdeen diocese

CANNON, PATRICK AIDAN: Born Duns 1945. Educated Campion House, Osterley; Drygrange. Ordained Hawick 1973. Currie 1973. Methil 1973-77. Nigerian mission 1977-.

CAMPBELL, JOSEPH: see Argyll diocese

CAPALDI, PAUL: Born Kendal 1947. Educated Scotus Academy, Edinburgh; Drygrange. Ordained Edinburgh 1980. Innerleithen 1980. Denny 1980-85. St Catherine's, Edinburgh 1985-86. St Margaret's, Dunfermline 1986-87. St Columba's, Bathgate 1987-89. South Queensferry 1989-.

CARDEN, PATRICK JOSEPH: Born Pumpherston 1905. Educated Blairs 1921-24; Scots College, Rome 1924-31. Ordained Rome 1931. Methil 1931-32. Rosewell 1932-33. Holy Cross, Edinburgh 1933-35. Duns 1935-38. Loanhead 1938-67. Died Edinburgh 24 Nov 1967.

CARDEN, WILLIAM G: Ordained 1946. St Francis Xavier's, Falkirk 1946-47. No further entries.

CAREY, MICHAEL: Born and educated Ireland. Joined Cistercian Order, Roscrea 1944. Ordained Nunraw 1951. Left Order and joined St A & E 1961. Bonnyrigg 1961-72. St Columba's, Edinburgh 1972-77. Kennoway 1977-79. Larbert 1979-89. Oakley 1989-. (Canning)

CARNEY, MATTHEW: see Glasgow Archdiocese

CARR, BERNARD: Born Ireland. Educated Ireland, Rome. Ordained Rome 1931. Lent to English Mission 1931-37. Lent to St A & E: St Margaret's, Dunfermline 1937-41. Resumed his vocation in Ireland 1941. Died Ireland 30 Jan 1973. (Canning)

CARRIGAN, NICHOLAS: Born and educated Ireland. Ordained Kilkenny 1919. Lent to St A & E. St Mary's, Stirling 1919-20. St Margaret's, Dunfermline 1920-23. St Patrick's, Edinburgh 1923-27. Resumed his vocation in Ireland 1927. Died Ireland 25 March 1962. (Canning)

CARROLL, DANIEL: Born and educated Ireland. Ordained Kilkenny 1936. Lent to St A & E. St Patrick's, Edinburgh 1936-37. Resumed his vocation in Ireland 1937. Died Ireland 7 Dec 1972. (Canning)

CARROLL, THOMAS: Ordained 1944. St Cuthbert's, Edinburgh 1946-47. No further entries.

CARTWRIGHT, CHARLES: Born and educated Ireland. Ordained Maynooth 1929. Lent to St A & E. St Ninian's, Edinburgh 1930-33. Resumed his vocation in Ireland 1933. Died Ireland 15 July 1967. (Canning)

CARTY, WILLIAM J: Born and educated Ireland. Ordained Maynooth 1940. Lent to St A & E. Broxburn in addresses, but not under parishes, 1940-41. Broxburn 1941-43. St Andrew's, Edinburgh 1943-44. Resumed his vocation in Ireland 1944. (Canning)

CASSIDY, MARTIN J: Born and educated Ireland. Ordained Kilkenny for St A & E 1957. St Margaret's, Dunfermline 1957-58. Dalkeith 1958-60. Dalkeith in addresses, but not under parishes, 1960-61. Florida 1961-. (Canning)

CASSIDY, MICHAEL: Born and educated Ireland. Ordained Wexford for St A & E 1954. St Francis Xavier's, Falkirk 1954-55. St John Vianney's, Edinburgh 1955-60. Tranent 1960-64. North Berwick 1964-66. St Ninian's, Edinburgh 1966-67. Pathhead Ford 1967-76. St Margaret Mary's, Edinburgh 1976-. (Canning)

CHAMBERS, ALLAN THOMAS: Born Edinburgh 1955. Educated St David's High School, Dalkeith; Drygrange. Ordained Musselburgh 1980. Edinburgh Cathedral 1980-82. St Kentigern's, Edinburgh 1982-84. Not in Catholic Directory 1984-86. Broxburn 1986-89. St Philip's, Livingston 1989-.

CHASE, CUTHBERT: Born London 1880. Educated St John's Seminary, Wonersh; Scots College, Rome; St John's, Wonersh. Ordained England 1905. St Patrick's, Edinburgh 1905-09. Edinburgh Cathedral 1909-18. West Calder 1918-22. Holy Cross, Edinburgh 1922-59. Died Edinburgh 11 March 1959.

CLAFFEY, PATRICK: Born and educated Ireland. Ordained Maynooth 1950. Lent to St A & E. St Margaret Mary's, Edinburgh 1950-54. Resumed his vocation in Ireland 1954. (Canning)

CLARKE, FRANCIS: Born Winchburgh 1945. Educated Campion House, Osterley; Drygrange. Ordained Winchburgh 1970. St Cuthbert's, Edinburgh 1970-73. No further entries.

CLARKE, PATRICK: Born Broxburn 1938. Educated Blairs, Drygrange. Ordained Edinburgh 1962. Cowie 1962-67. Nigerian mission 1967-80. Awaiting appointment 1980-81. Banknock 1981-85. Lochgelly 1985-.

COLLINS, JAMES: Born and educated Ireland. Ordained Maynooth 1933. Lent to St A & E. St Andrew's, Edinburgh 1933-35. St Patrick's, Edinburgh 1935-37. Oakley 1937-38. Joined African mission. Died Ireland 13 Oct 1977. (Canning)

COMERFORD, THOMAS: Ordained 1944. Sacred Heart, Grangemouth 1945-46. No further entries.

COMEY, NICHOLAS: Born and educated Ireland. Ordained Maynooth 1928. Lent to St A & E. Rosewell 1928-30. St Mary's, Stirling 1930-33. Resumed his vocation in Ireland 1933. Died Ireland 29 Aug 1974. (Canning)

CONNOLLY, EWEN J: Born Edinburgh 1888. Educated Blairs 1904-09; Scots College, Rome 1909-17. Ordained Rome 1916. St Francis Xavier's, Falkirk 1917-19. Duns 1919-21. Bowhill 1921-28. Addiewell 1928-37. Broxburn 1937-41. Retired in bad health 1941. Died Stoke on Trent 20 July 1952.

CONNOLLY, JAMES: Born Lumphinnans, Fife 1889. Educated Scots College, Rome 1906-14. Ordained Rome 1914. Inverkeithing 1914-17. Kelso 1917-19. Vice-rector, Valladolid 1919-46. Rector, Valladolid 1946-52. Rosewell 1952-59. Died Rosewell 26 June 1959.

CONNOLLY, PETER: Born Edinburgh 1903. Educated Blairs 1917-22; Scots College, Rome 1922-29. Ordained Rome 1928. East Calder 1929-31. Edinburgh Cathedral 1931-35. North Berwick 1935-43. St Cuthbert's, Edinburgh 1943-69. Haddington 1969-86. Retired 1986.

CONSIDINE, HUGH PATRICK: Born Edinburgh 1866. Educated Royal High School, Edinburgh 1876-81; Blairs 1881-86; Issy 1886-88; St Sulpice 1888-91. Ordained Edinburgh 1891. Edinburgh Cathedral 1891-95. Fauldhouse 1895-99. Haddington 1899-1901. St Andrew's, Edinburgh 1901-36. Died Edinburgh 22 July 1936.

CONWAY, DANIEL: Born Port Glasgow 1873. Educated Blairs 1888-92; Petit Seminaire de Notre Dame des Champs, Paris 1892-93; Valladolid 1893-99. Ordained Valladolid 1899. St Francis Xavier's, Falkirk 1899-1901. Lennoxtown 1901-03. Penicuik 1903-09. Denny 1909-10. Bonnybridge 1910-22. Died Glasgow 7 Oct 1922.

CONWAY, EDWARD M: Born Ireland. Educated Ireland, Spain. Ordained 1932. Lent to St A & E. St Andrew's, Edinburgh 1932-33. Resumed his vocation in Ireland 1933. (Canning)

CONWAY, HUGH: Born Ireland. Educated Ireland, Spain. Ordained 1918. Lent to St A & E. Lochgelly 1918-27. Resumed his vocation in Ireland 1927. Died Ireland 7 July 1978. (Canning)

CONWAY, PATRICK GERALD: Born and educated Ireland. Ordained Kilkenny for St A & E 1956. Cowie 1956-62. Returned to Ireland 1962. (Canning)

CONWAY, RICHARD: Born and educated Ireland. Ordained Kilkenny for St A & E 1945. St Mary's, Stirling 1945-46. St Patrick's, Glasgow in addresses, but not under parishes, 1946-48. St Mary's, Stirling 1948-49. Edinburgh Cathedral 1949-53. Baker City, USA 1953-. (Canning)

CONWAY, WILLIAM: Born Carfin 1941. Educated St Illtyd's College, Cardiff; Our Lady's High School, Motherwell; St Mary's College, Aberystwyth; Drygrange. Ordained Edinburgh 1968. St Francis Xavier's, Falkirk 1968-69. Further studies, Maynooth 1969-70. Further studies, Rome 1970-73. Professor, Drygrange 1973-82. Jedburgh 1982-89. Loanhead 1989-.

COOPER, NORMAN PAUL: Born Falkirk 1955. Educated St Mungo's High School, Falkirk; Drygrange. Ordained Polmont 1980. St John the Evangelist, Edinburgh 1980-82. St Francis Xavier's, Falkirk 1982-85. Edinburgh Cathedral 1985-88. Further studies (c/o Diocesan Office) 1988-89. Further studies, Virginia, USA 1989-.

COPPINGER, MICHAEL: Born and educated Ireland. Ordained Carlow for Paisley 1954. Lent to St A & E. Methil 1954-60. Returned to Ireland 1960. (Canning)

CORCORAN, THOMAS: Born Bonnybridge 1905. Educated Blairs 1919-24; Notre Dame, Avranches 1924-25; Grand Seminaire, Coutances 1925-30. Ordained Edinburgh 1930. St Cuthbert's, Edinburgh 1930-31. Holy Cross, Edinburgh 1931-33. Rosewell 1933-34. Bowhill 1934-44. Galashiels 1944-72. Rosewell 1972-79. Retired 1979.

CORDUFF, JAMES: Born and educated Ireland. Ordained Maynooth 1937. Lent to St A & E. Methil 1938-40. St Columba's, Edinburgh 1940-45. Forces chaplain 1945-48. Returned to Ireland 1948. Died West Linton 8 May 1974. (Canning)

COSTELLOE,-: Ordained 1897. St Patrick's, Edinburgh 1897-98. No further entries. (Possibly same as 'Costello, Maurice' in Canning)

COSTIGAN, WILLIAM P: Born and educated Ireland. Ordained Kilkenny 1886. Lent to St A & E. St Mary's, Stirling 1901-03. West Calder 1903-04. Resumed his vocation in Ireland 1904. Died Ireland 31 Jan 1933. (Canning)

COUTTENIER, OCTAVE: Ordained 1893. St Andrew's, Edinburgh 1904-05. Edinburgh Cathedral 1905-07. Chaplain, Little Sisters of the Poor,

Edinburgh 1907-19. Jedburgh 1919-21. Kelso 1921-30. Kclso in addresses, but not under parishes, 1930-31. No further entries.

COX, KENNETH CHARLES: Born Argyll 1911. Educated South London College; Royal Polytechnic; Osterley; Oscott College. Ordained 1943. Dalkeith 1944-45. St Mary's, Stirling 1945-48. Not in Catholic Directory 1948-49. Our Lady of Perpetual Succour, Kirkcaldy 1949-51. Sick leave 1951-53. No further entries.

CRAMPTON, PATRICK: see Crampton, Walter Patrick

CRAMPTON, WALTER PATRICK: Born Perth 1914. Educated St Edmund's College, Ware. Ordained Edinburgh 1940. Sacred Heart, Grangemouth 1940-41. St Andrew's, Fife 1941-45. Methil 1945-46. Professor, Blairs 1946-53. Professor, Drygrange 1953-55. Selkirk 1955-67. Camelon 1967-87. Retired 1987.

CREANOR, JOHN: Born Shotts 1941. Educated Blairs, Drygrange. Ordained Fauldhouse 1965. Portobello 1965-69. St Patrick's, Edinburgh 1969-76. Innerleithen 1976-84. St Andrew's, Livingston 1984-.

CULHANE, GEORGE: see Dunkeld diocese

CULHANE, STEPHEN: Born Ireland. Educated Ireland, Rome. Ordained Rome 1884. Lent to St A & E. St Patrick's, Edinburgh 1884-87. St Margaret's, Dunfermline 1887-89. Resumed his vocation in Ireland 1889. Died Ireland 4 April 1920. (Canning)

CULLEN, JOHN: Born Bathgate 1936. Educated Blairs, Drygrange. Ordained Edinburgh 1960. Musselburgh 1960-62. Bursar, Drygrange 1962-63. Our Lady of Perpetual Succour, Kirkcaldy 1963-65. No further entries.

CUMMINS, JAMES: Ordained 1942. St Cuthbert's, Edinburgh 1942-45. No further entries.

CUNNINGHAM, PATRICK: Born and educated Ireland. Ordained Maynooth 1940. Lent to St A & E. Addiewell 1940-42. Methil 1942-48. Denny 1948-54. Resumed his vocation in Ireland 1954. (Canning)

CURRAN, HENRY: Born Haddington 1921. Educated Fort Augustus School; St Peter's, Wexford; All Hallows, Dublin; St Edmund's, Ware. Ordained 1945. East Calder 1945-47. Our Lady of Perpetual Succour, Kirkcaldy 1947-49. St Mary's, Stirling 1949-52. Lochgelly 1952-58. Portobello 1958-62. Denny 1962-65. Kelso 1965-71. Cowie 1971-76. Cowie in addresses, but not under parishes, 1976-77. Methil 1977-78. C/o Diocesan Office 1978-81. Died Haddington 28 Feb 1981.

CURRAN, JOHN DOMINIC: Born Edinburgh 1904. Worked for British Transport Hotels. Educated Beda, Rome. Ordained Rome 1967. St Margaret Mary's, Edinburgh 1967-68. Rosewell 1968-69. Camelon 1969-73. Chaplain, Sisters of Charity, Musselburgh 1973-77. Died Edinburgh 19 Dec 1977.

DALRYMPLE, JOCK JAMES: Born London 1957. Educated Ampleforth College; Oxford University; followed career in marketing; educated for priesthood Beda, Rome. Ordained North Berwick 1986. Musselburgh 1986-.

DALRYMPLE, JOHN: Born North Berwick 1928. Educated Ampleforth College; Scots College, Rome. Ordained Rome 1954. Professor, Drygrange 1955-57. Edinburgh Cathedral 1957-60. Professor, Drygrange 1960-64. Spiritual Director, Drygrange 1964-70. Chaplain, St Andrew's University 1970-74. St Paul's, Edinburgh 1974-76. St Ninian's, Edinburgh 1976-85. Died Florida 4 Sept 1985.

DALY, CHARLES: Born and educated Ireland. Ordained Maynooth 1914. Lent to St A & E. St Patrick's, Edinburgh 1914-15. St Peter's, Edinburgh 1915-18. Lent to Dunkeld diocese: St Mary's, Dundee 1918-20. Resumed his vocation in Ireland 1920. Died Ireland 19 Feb 1941. (Canning)

DALY, EUGENE: Born and educated Ireland. Ordained Kilkenny for Liverpool 1947. Lent to St A & E. Newtongrange 1947-50. Resumed his vocation in Liverpool diocese. (Canning)

DAVISON, LAURENCE: Born Edinburgh 1920. Educated Fort Augustus School; Coutances; Bordeaux; All Hallows, Dublin; St Edmund's College, Ware. Ordained 1943. Edinburgh Cathedral 1943-58. Dunbar 1958-67. Lochgelly 1967-69. St Cuthbert's, Edinburgh 1969-89. Retired 1989.

DAVITT, THOMAS: Born Edinburgh 1899. Educated Blairs 1913-20; Scots College, Rome 1920-27. Ordained Rome 1926. Immaculate Conception, Bathgate 1927-30. Bo'ness 1930-39. Immaculate Conception, Bathgate 1939-69. Died Ireland 29 Sept 1969.

DAWSON, JUSTIN: Born 1904. Entered Benedictine Order, Buckfast Abbey. Ordained 1942. Left Order and was accepted for St A & E. St Columba's, Edinburgh 1950. Broxburn 1950-65. Falkland 1965-76. Died Falkland 19 March 1976.

DAY, AIDAN J: Born and educated Ireland. Ordained Wexford for St A & E 1951. Sacred Heart, Grangemouth 1951-52. Dalkeith 1952-53. No further entries. (Canning)

DEERY, LEO: Born and educated Ireland. Ordained 1947. Lent to St A & E.

St Patrick's, Edinburgh 1947-48. Polmont 1948. Resumed his vocation in Ireland 1948. (Canning)

DELANEY, PATRICK: Born and educated Ireland. Ordained Maynooth 1937. Lent to St A & E. St Ninian's, Edinburgh 1937. Served in dioceses of Menevia, Leeds. Resumed his vocation in Ireland 1942. (Canning)

DELANEY, RICHARD: Born Edinburgh 1887. Educated St Patrick's School, Edinburgh; Blairs 1902-06; Scots College, Rome 1906-13. Ordained Rome 1912. Immaculate Conception, Bathgate 1913-16. Slamannan 1916-19. Linlithgow 1919-24. Tranent 1924-36. St Margaret's, Dunfermline 1936-65. Died Dunfermline 31 July 1965.

DENNIS, JAMES KENNEDY: Born and educated Ireland. Ordained Kilkenny for St A & E 1934. Edinburgh Cathedral 1934-36. St Francis Xavier's, Falkirk 1936-38. Penicuik 1938-41. Left priesthood; went to Canada. (Canning)

DE SOUZA, ACHILLES: Ordained 1968. Portobello 1971-72. No further entries.

DEVANE, MICHAEL J: Born and educated Ireland. Ordained Ireland 1941. Denny 1941-48. St Cuthbert's, Edinburgh 1948-52. Blanefield 1952-64. St Pius', Kirkcaldy 1964-88. Retired 1988. (Canning)

DEVANEY, THOMAS: Born and educated Ireland. Ordained Maynooth 1930. Lent to St A & E. Edinburgh Cathedral 1930-34. Resumed his vocation in Ireland 1934. Died Ireland 22 April 1968. (Canning)

DEVLIN, (Anthony) BRIAN: Born Irvine 1960. Educated St Columba's High School, Dunfermline; Drygrange. Ordained Dunfermline 1985. St Margaret Mary's, Edinburgh 1985. St Ninian's, Edinburgh 1985-86. No further entries.

DEVLIN, GERARD: Ordained 1946. St Columba's, Edinburgh 1957-58. St Francis Xavier's, Falkirk 1958-59. No further entries.

DICK, BARRINGTON DOUGLAS: see Galloway diocese

DOBRINA, VINCENT: Ordained 1939. Polish chaplain for Stirlingshire; at St Francis Xavier's, Falkirk 1949-55.

DOHERTY, FRANCIS J: Born Cowie 1927. Educated Blairs; Oscott College, Birmingham. Ordained Edinburgh 1951. Our Lady of Perpetual Succour, Kirkcaldy 1951-62. St Francis Xavier's, Falkirk 1962-65. Broxburn 1965-67. C/o Diocesan Office 1967-68. Portobello 1968-70. Lennoxtown 1970-72. C/o Diocesan Office 1972-73. St Francis Xavier's, Falkirk

1973-78. St Mark's, Edinburgh 1978-79. C/o Diocesan Office 1979-80. St Mark's, Edinburgh 1980-81. St Paul's, Edinburgh 1981-82. St Mark's, Edinburgh 1982-85. St Margaret Mary's, Edinburgh 1985-89. Retired 1989.

DOHERTY, PATRICK: Born Edinburgh 1862. Educated Blairs 1879-82; St Edmund's College, Douay 1882-84; Scots College, Rome 1884-89. Ordained Rome 1889 and died there 23 June 1889.

DOHERTY, PHILIP: Born Cowie 1931. Educated Blairs, St Sulpice. Ordained Edinburgh 1955. St Cuthbert's, Edinburgh 1955-61. Denny 1961-62. Our Lady of Perpetual Succour, Kirkcaldy 1962-72. Gorebridge 1972-85. Cowdenbeath 1985-.

DONAGHUE, ALEXANDER: see O'Donaghue, Alexander

DONATI, PETER (Pietro): Born Edinburgh 1904. Educated Blairs 1919-24; Propaganda, Rome 1924-26; St Kieran's College, Kilkenny 1926-30. Ordained Kilkenny 1930. St Francis Xavier's, Falkirk 1930-34. Falkland 1934-39. Linlithgow 1939-40. Forces chaplain 1940-43. St Margaret's, Dunfermline 1943-45. Lennoxtown 1945-51. Blanefield 1951-52. Gorebridge 1952-63. Peebles 1963-77. Retired 1977. Died Edinburgh 10 Nov 1983.

DONLEVY, JOSEPH: Born Edinburgh 1861. Educated Blairs 1877-81; Valladolid 1881-87. Ordained Valladolid 1887. Edinburgh Cathedral 1887. Lennoxtown 1887. St Mary's, Stirling 1887-89. Our Lady of Perpetual Succour, Kirkcaldy 1889-90. Portobello 1890-1924. Died Portobello 20 March 1924.

DONNELLY, JOHN J: Born Edinburgh 1907. Educated Blairs 1922-26; Scots College, Rome 1926-32. Ordained Rome 1932. St Mary's, Stirling 1932-34. Professor, Blairs 1934-42. Our Lady of Perpetual Succour, Kirkcaldy 1942-47. Armadale 1947-76. Died Armadale 30 Dec 1976.

DONOGHUE, JAMES: see Donoghue, Matthew James

DONOGHUE, MATTHEW JAMES: Born Bathgate 1917. Educated St Joseph's College, Dumfries; St Mary's College, Oscott; Coutances Seminary. Ordained Edinburgh 1939. Further studies, Cambridge University 1939-43. Professor, Blairs 1943-56. Kilsyth 1956-58. North Berwick 1958-72. St Margaret's, Edinburgh 1972-86. Retired 1986.

DOONAN, BERNARD: Born Denny 1940. Educated Drygrange. Ordained Denny 1969. Portobello 1969-72. Professor, Drygrange 1972-86. St Mark's, Edinburgh 1986-87. South Queensferry 1987-89. Kilsyth 1989-.

DORRIAN, GERALD: Born Edinburgh 1904. Educated Blairs 1919-25;

Coutances 1925-30. Ordained Edinburgh 1930. Lennoxtown 1930-31. St Cuthbert's, Edinburgh 1931-33. Armadale 1933-37. Methil 1937-65. Retired 1965. Died Musselburgh 14 July 1970.

DOWLING, GEORGE: Ordained for the Franciscan Order 1872. Served in London, Glasgow etc. Left the Order and was accepted for St A & E. Edinburgh Cathedral 1883. St Patrick's, Edinburgh 1883-84. Our Lady of Perpetual Succour, Kirkcaldy 1884-89. St Francis Xavier's, Falkirk 1889-90. Dunbar 1890-92. Died Dunbar 21 April 1892.

DOWNEY, MICHAEL: Born and educated Ireland. Ordained Ireland for St A & E 1921. St Patrick's, Edinburgh 1921-24. St Mary's, Stirling 1924-26. No address given 1926-27. St Mary's, Stirling 1927-28. Bonnybridge 1928-38. Kilsyth 1938-55. Died Kilsyth 24 Dec 1955. (Canning)

DOYLE, PATRICK: Born and educated Ireland. Ordained Wexford 1926. Lent to St A & E. St Patrick's, Edinburgh 1926-29. Resumed his vocation in Ireland 1929. Died Ireland 18 March 1968. (Canning)

DUFFY, ANTHONY LEONARD: Born Edinburgh 1947. Educated Holy Cross Academy, Edinburgh; Drygrange. Ordained Edinburgh 1973. St Cuthbert's, Edinburgh 1973-81. St Paul's, Edinburgh 1981-84. St Mary Magdalene's, Edinburgh 1984-89. St Cuthbert's, Edinburgh 1989-.

DUFFY, AUGUSTINE: Born and educated Ireland. Ordained Maynooth 1942. Lent to St A & E. St Ninian's, Edinburgh 1943-49. Resumed his vocation in Ireland 1949. (Canning)

DUFFY, VINCENT: Born and educated Ireland. Ordained Cavan 1944. Lent to St A & E. Linlithgow 1946-51. Resumed his vocation in Ireland 1951. (Canning)

DUTHIE, CHARLES J: Born 1841. Educated Marlborough College, Wilts; Edinburgh Academy; Trinity College, Oxford. Was ordained for Anglican Church. Became Roman Catholic 1888. Educated for priesthood Scots College, Rome. Ordained Rome 1890. Edinburgh Cathedral, as secretary to Archbishop, 1890-91. North Berwick 1891-1910. Died North Berwick 29 Aug 1910.

EARDLEY, BERNARD: Born Broxburn 1874. Educated Blairs 1890-93; Petit Seminaire de Notre Dame des Champs, Paris 1893-95; Scots College, Rome 1895-1900. Ordained Rome 1899. St Patrick's, Edinburgh 1900-01. St Columba's, Edinburgh 1901-03. Balerno 1903-04. No address given 1904-05. Blackburn 1905-06. Left the diocese. Died West Indies 4 Oct 1928.

EARDLEY, STANISLAUS: Born East Calder 1911. Educated Blairs 1925-30; St Lo 1930-31; Grand Seminaire, Coutances 1931-36. Ordained

Edinburgh 1936. Methil 1936-37. St Patrick's, Edinburgh 1937-43. Innerleithen 1943-48. Burntisland 1948-51. Went to France for sake of health, serving there as priest, 1951. Died Warrenpoint 6 June 1964.

EASSON, DONALD: Born Tomintoul 1864. Educated Blairs 1877-81; Valladolid 1881-87. Ordained Valladolid 1887. Edinburgh Cathedral 1887-89. Linlithgow 1889-97. Vice-rector, Valladolid 1897-99. Died Valladolid 7 March 1899.

EDIE, MARK THOMAS WILLIAM: Born Leith 1958. Educated St Augustine's High School, Edinburgh; Drygrange. Ordained Edinburgh 1983. St Margaret's, Dunfermline 1983. St Mark's, Edinburgh 1983-86. No further entries.

EGAN, DANIEL P ('Patrick Peter' in Canning): Born and educated Ireland. Ordained Ireland 1921. Was affiliated to St A & E. Edinburgh Cathedral 1921-24. Not in addresses 1924-25. St Cuthbert's, Edinburgh 1925-29. Polmont 1929-30. Our Lady of Perpetual Succour, Kirkcaldy 1930-32. Left priesthood. (Canning)

ENGELEN, THOMAS: Born Pilling, Lancs 1918. Educated Blairs; Coutances; Bordeaux; All Hallows, Dublin; St Edmund's College, Ware. Ordained 1943. St Andrew's, Fife 1943-46. Hawick 1946-47. Fauldhouse 1947-48. St Margaret Mary's, Edinburgh 1948. Lochgelly 1948-49. St Margaret's, Dunfermline 1949-50. Newtongrange 1950-53. Gorebridge 1953-54. St Joseph's, Edinburgh 1954-57. St John's, Edinburgh 1957-59. Kennoway 1959-69. St Andrew's, Fife 1969-87. Retired 1987.

FALCONER, JAMES PATRICK: Born Armadale 1925. Educated Blairs, Oscott College. Ordained Edinburgh 1950. St Margaret's, Dunfermline 1950-51. St Peter's, Edinburgh 1951-58. Denny 1958-61. Holy Cross, Edinburgh 1961-67. Lennoxtown 1967-70. Blanefield 1970-72. St Mary's, Glenrothes 1972-74. Died Edinburgh 23 May 1974.

FALLON, MICHAEL: Born Edinburgh 1945. Educated Holy Cross Academy, Edinburgh; Blairs; Campion House, Osterley; Drygrange; St Peter's. Ordained Edinburgh 1977. Our Lady of Perpetual Succour, Kirkcaldy 1977-79. St Columba's, Edinburgh 1979-80. Currie 1980-81. Ratho 1981-85. Our Lady of Perpetual Succour, Kirkcaldy 1985-88. Newbattle 1988-.

FALLON, PATRICK MURRAY: Born Loanhead 1937. Educated Campion House, Osterley; Drygrange. Ordained Leith 1968. Lent to Aberdeen diocese: Aberdeen Cathedral 1969. St Ninian's, Edinburgh 1969-79. Fallin 1979-80. Spiritual Director, Drygrange 1980-86. Spiritual Director, Gillis College 1986-88. Our Lady of Perpetual Succour, Kirkcaldy 1988-.

FERGUSON, WILLIAM: Born Cowie 1933. Educated Blairs, Valladolid. Ordained Edinburgh 1957. Bonnybridge 1957-65. St Ninian's, Edinburgh 1965-66. C/o Diocesan Office 1966-69. No further entries.

FERRARI, JAMES: Born Denny 1931. Educated Campion House, Osterley; Drygrange. Ordained Edinburgh 1960. St Francis Xavier's, Falkirk 1960-61. St Andrew's, Edinburgh 1961-63. Edinburgh Cathedral 1963-68. Broxburn 1968-79. Rosewell 1979-86. Linlithgow 1986-.

FERRIGAN, THOMAS: Born Edinburgh 1881. Educated Blairs 1895-1900; Issy 1900-02; St Sulpice 1902-05; St Peter's 1905-06. Ordained Ghent 1906. Lennoxtown 1906-09. Sick leave 1909-10. Broxburn 1910-11. West Calder 1911-12. Oakley 1912-14. Winchburgh 1914-15. Forces chaplain 1915-20. St Columba's, Edinburgh 1920-22. Balerno 1922-24. Methil 1924-31. Inverkeithing 1931-37. Rosyth 1937-62. Died Edinburgh 25 April 1962.

FINNIGAN, JAMES I: Born Ireland. Educated Ireland, Spain. Ordained Salamanca 1927. Lent to St A & E. Catholic Directories have him under two parishes simultaneously: St Patrick's, Edinburgh and Armadale 1928-30. He is at St Patrick's in addresses and in Canning. Resumed his vocation in Ireland 1930. Died Ireland 20 Dec 1966. (Canning)

FISCHER, LAURENCE WALLS: see Galloway diocese

FITZGERALD, RICHARD J: Born and educated Ireland. Ordained Ireland 1905. Lent to St A & E. Edinburgh Cathedral 1907. St Mary's, Stirling 1907-09. Resumed his vocation in Ireland 1909. (Canning)

FITZSIMMONS, GERARD MICHAEL: Born Edinburgh 1959. Educated St Augustine's High School, Edinburgh; Drygrange. Ordained Edinburgh 1984. St Mary's, Stirling 1984-85. Further studies 1985-87. St Andrew's, Livingston 1987-.

FITZSIMMONS, WILLIAM C: Born Kelty 1934. Educated Blairs, Valladolid. Ordained Valladolid 1958. St Ninian's, Edinburgh 1958-61. St Francis Xavier's, Falkirk 1961-62. Died Glasgow 22 March 1962.

FLANAGHAN (Flanagan), PATRICK: Born and educated Ireland. Ordained Monaghan 1931. Lent to St A & E. St Patrick's, Edinburgh 1931-33. Resumed his vocation in Ireland 1933. Died Ireland 20 May 1974. (Canning)

FLYNN, ANTHONY: Born Winchburgh 1905. Educated Blairs 1918-24; Coutances 1924-30. Ordained Edinburgh 1930. St Patrick's, Edinburgh 1930-33. Penicuik 1933-36. Camelon 1936-67. Retired 1967. Died Bangour 12 Feb 1968.

FLYNN, THOMAS W: Born Fauldhouse 1941. Educated Scotus Academy, Edinburgh; Drygrange. Ordained Fauldhouse 1976. St Patrick's, Edinburgh 1976-81. Dalkeith 1981-85. Kennoway 1985-.

FOLEY, DANIEL: Born Denny 1927. Educated Blairs; St Mary's College, Oscott. Ordained Edinburgh 1951. Bo'ness 1951-53. Dalkeith 1953-58. Nigerian mission 1958-64. C/o Diocesan Office 1964-65. St Mary's, Stirling 1965-69. Slamannan 1969-77. Newbattle 1977-85. St Columba's, Edinburgh 1985-.

FOLEY, JOHN: Born Ireland. Educated Ireland, Rome. Ordained 1885. Lent to Glasgow Archdiocese: Sacred Heart, Glasgow 1885-88. Lent to St A & E; later got exeat to remain there. St Patrick's, Edinburgh 1888-89. Balfron 1889-90. Blanefield 1890-92. Strathblane 1892-99. Dunbar 1899-1902. Our Lady of Perpetual Succour, Kirkcaldy 1902-08. Sacred Heart, Grangemouth 1908-13. Bo'ness 1913-30. Retired 1930. Died Musselburgh 5 June 1946. (Canning)

FOLEY, LAURENCE: Born and educated Ireland. Ordained Kilkenny 1943. Lent to St A & E. Rosewell 1943-52. Resumed his vocation in Ireland 1952. Died Ireland 26 Jan 1961. (Canning)

FOLEY, PATRICK: Born and educated Ireland. Ordained Wexford 1948. Lent to St A & E. Cowdenbeath 1948-49. Resumed his vocation in Ireland 1949. (Canning)

FORREST, ANDREW ALEXANDER: Born Farnborough 1933. Educated Blairs, St Sulpice, Drygrange. Ordained Edinburgh 1959. St Margaret's, Edinburgh 1959-64. St Mary's, Stirling 1964-67. Polmont 1967-73. C/o Diocesan Office 1973-75. Larbert 1975-79. Kennoway 1979-85. Cowie 1985-87. St Joseph's, Edinburgh 1987-.

FORSYTH, JOHN: Born Portobello 1861. Educated Blairs 1879-81; Douay 1881-83, returning home in bad health; Scots College, Rome 1883-85, returning home in bad health; St Peter's 1886-88. Ordained Edinburgh 1888. St Francis Xavier's, Falkirk 1888-89. St Cuthbert's, Edinburgh 1889-1942. Died Edinburgh 2 June 1942.

FOX, JOHN COLLINS: Born Leith 1925. Educated Campion House, Osterley; Drygrange. Ordained Edinburgh 1960. St Margaret's, Dunfermline 1960-66. St Ninian's, Edinburgh 1966-76. St Mary's, Stirling 1976-80. Burntisland 1980-83. Died Edinburgh 17 June 1983.

FOYLAN, PETER: see Dunkeld diocese

FRANCE, SAMUEL: Born Edinburgh 1889. Educated Blairs 1903-07; Scots College, Rome 1907-16. Ordained Rome 1914. Our Lady of Perpetual

Succour, Kirkcaldy 1916-17. Haddington 1917-24. St Margaret's, Dunfermline 1924-26. St Francis Xavier's, Falkirk 1926-28. Died Dublin 5 Jan 1928.

FRANKLIN, ALBERT EDWARD: Born Lee, Kent 1868. Educated Scots College, Rome 1905-09. Ordained Rome 1908. Edinburgh Cathedral 1909-13. Tranent 1913-24. Portobello 1924-52. Retired 1952. Died Edinburgh 11 Feb 1955.

FRASER, JAMES C D: Born Edinburgh 1850. Educated Circus Place Preparatory School, Edinburgh; Edinburgh Academy; Edinburgh University; Trinity College, Glenalmond. Ordained for Episcopalian Church. Served in Worcestershire, Banchory-Ternan. Became Roman Catholic 1902. Educated for priesthood Scots College, Rome 1902-04. Ordained Edinburgh 1905. Greenhill Gardens 1905. Died Fort Augustus 2 Jan 1906.

FRIEL, JAMES: Born Lennoxtown 1933. Educated Blairs, St Sulpice. Ordained Edinburgh 1956. Professor, Blairs 1956-61. Professor, Langbank 1961-66. Spiritual Director and Procurator, Blairs 1966-69. Edinburgh Cathedral 1969-74. St Mary's, Glenrothes 1974-87. Christ the King, Grangemouth 1987-.

FUSCO, JOHN: Born Portobello 1908. Educated Holy Cross Academy, Edinburgh; Blairs 1923-26; Scots College, Rome 1926-32. Ordained Rome 1932. St Mary's, Stirling 1932-36. Innerleithen 1936-39. Forces chaplain 1939-46. Oakley 1946-53. Cowdenbeath 1953-58. St Ninian's, Edinburgh 1958-76. Pathhead Ford 1976-85. Retired 1985.

GAFFNEY, JAMES: Ordained 1931. Lennoxtown 1931-36. No further entries.

GAFFNEY, LIAM (Thomas William): Born and educated Ireland. Ordained Maynooth 1947. Lent to St A & E. St Ninian's, Edinburgh 1947-53. Resumed his vocation in Ireland 1953. (Canning)

GALLACHER, PETER: Born Craighead, Milton of Campsie 1923. Educated Blairs; Oscott College, Birmingham. Ordained Lennoxtown 1946. St John's, Edinburgh 1946-50. Blackburn 1950-52. Rosewell 1952-59. Holy Cross, Edinburgh 1959-64. Rosewell 1964-67. Slamannan 1967-69. C/o Diocesan Office 1969-70. Chaplain, Poor Clares' Convent, Edinburgh 1970-87. Methil 1987-.

GALLACHER, WILLIAM: Born Falkirk 1939. Educated Blairs, Drygrange. Ordained Denny 1962. St Ninian's, Edinburgh 1962-65. Raploch 1965-67. C/o Diocesan Office 1967-68. Cowdenbeath 1968-69. Linlithgow 1969-70. No further entries.

GALLAGHER, ANTHONY REDMOND: Born and educated Ireland. Ordained Dublin for St A & E 1933. St Margaret's, Dunfermline 1933. Methil 1933-36. Cowdenbeath 1936-39. St Margaret Mary's, Edinburgh 1939-43. Lochgelly 1943-58. C/o Diocesan Office 1958-59. Rosewell 1959-65. Died Ireland 17 Feb 1965. (Canning)

GALLAGHER, EDWARD: Born Glasgow 1939. Educated St Ninian's High School, Kirkintilloch; Blairs; Scots College, Rome. Ordained Rome 1963. St Patrick's, Edinburgh 1964-69. Whitburn 1969-74. Edinburgh, not serving a parish, 1974-86. Oakley 1986-89. St Margaret's, Edinburgh 1989-.

GALLAGHER, JAMES: see Gallagher, William James

GALLAGHER, RICHARD: Born Ireland. Educated Ireland, Paris. Ordained Paris 1929. Lent to St A & E. Lochgelly 1929-37. Resumed his vocation in Ireland 1937. Died Ireland 1 Sept 1976. (Canning)

GALLAGHER, ROGER: Born Falkirk 1908. Educated St Kieran's College, Kilkenny 1925-27; Scots College, Rome 1927-34. Ordained Rome 1933. Edinburgh Cathedral 1934-36. Penicuik 1936-38. Selkirk 1938-39. Cowdenbeath 1939-53. Rector, Drygrange 1953-60. St Patrick's, Edinburgh 1960-67. Fauldhouse 1967-70. Died Fauldhouse 27 Oct 1970.

GALLAGHER, THOMAS EDWARD: Born and educated Ireland. Ordained Kilkenny 1935. Edinburgh Cathedral 1935-43. North Berwick 1943-48. Fauldhouse 1948-67. Retired 1967. Died Bournemouth 21 Dec 1969. (Canning)

GALLAGHER, WILLIAM JAMES: Born and educated Ireland. Ordained Dublin for St A & E 1942. Bo'ness 1942-48. St Patrick's, Edinburgh 1948-60. Bonnyrigg 1960-. (Canning)

GALLIGAN, THOMAS: Born and educated Ireland. Ordained Maynooth 1931. Lent to St A & E. Bonnybridge 1931-35. Resumed his vocation in Ireland 1935. Died Ireland 5 Oct 1961. (Canning)

GEARY, PATRICK: Born and educated Ireland. Ordained Maynooth 1913. Lent to St A & E. Broxburn 1913-17. Broxburn in addresses, but not under parishes, 1917-18. Resumed his vocation in Ireland 1918. (Canning)

GEMMEL, RODERICK: Born Glasgow 1917. Educated Blairs; All Hallows College, Dublin. Ordained Edinburgh 1941. St Andrew's, Fife 1941-43. Addiewell 1943-46. Lent to Argyll Diocese: Rothesay 1946-49. Lennoxtown 1949-58. St Margaret's, Edinburgh 1958-63. Died Edinburgh 31 Jan 1963.

GEMMELL, DAVID: Born Oakley 1953. Educated St Columba's High School, Dunfermline; Drygrange. Ordained Oakley 1978. St Kentigern's, Edinburgh 1978-82. Edinburgh Cathedral 1982-86. Pastoral Director, Gillis College 1986-.

GIBBONS, JOHN: Born Dunfermline 1927. Educated Campion House, Osterley; St Edmund's College, Ware. Ordained Edinburgh 1955. Edinburgh Cathedral 1955-61. Nigerian mission 1961-66. Died Nigeria 11 Jan 1966.

GILBRIDE, PATRICK MICHAEL: Born and educated Ireland. Ordained Maynooth 1942. Lent to St A & E. Cowdenbeath 1942-48. Resumed his vocation in Ireland 1948. Died Ireland 26 April 1973. (Canning)

GILCHRIST, EDWARD THOMAS: Born and educated Ireland. Ordained Dublin 1938. St Ninian's, Edinburgh 1938-39. Kilsyth 1939-40. St Margaret's, Dunfermline 1940-41. Lennoxtown 1941-49. Lochgelly 1949-51. Burntisland 1951-58. Newtongrange 1958-71. Newbattle 1971-77. Retired 1977. (Canning)

GILLAN, IAN THOMSON: Born Stonehaven 1915. Educated Aberdeen University, Edinburgh University, St Sulpice. Ordained Edinburgh 1953. St Andrew's, Fife 1953-64. Chaplain, St Andrew's University 1964-70. Musselburgh 1970-72. Jedburgh 1972-73. No further entries.

GILLON, THOMAS: Born Ratho 1878. Educated Blairs 1893-97; Petit Seminaire, Paris 1897-98; Scots College, Rome 1898-1903. Ordained Rome 1903. St Mary's, Stirling 1903-10. St Patrick's, Edinburgh 1910-13. Sacred Heart, Grangemouth 1913-18. Hawick 1918-24. Linlithgow 1924-34. Spiritual Director, Scots College, Rome 1934-40. Retired 1940. Died Edinburgh 10 May 1942.

GLACKIN, JOHN: Born and educated Ireland. Ordained Maynooth 1927. Lent to St A & E. St Margaret's, Dunfermline 1927-33. Resumed his vocation in Ireland 1933. (Canning)

GLANCEY, LAWRENCE ALEXANDER: Born Broxburn 1917. Educated Blairs; Ushaw College; Scots College, Rome; All Hallows College, Dublin; St Edmund's College, Ware. Ordained 1943. Further studies, Oxford University 1943-46. St Andrew's, Edinburgh 1946-48. Chaplain, Good Shepherd Convent, Edinburgh 1948-50. St Columba's, Edinburgh 1950-55. St Peter's, Edinburgh 1955-61. St Magdalene's, Edinburgh 1961-70. St John Vianney's, Edinburgh 1970-79. East Calder 1979-84. Immaculate Conception, Bathgate 1984-88. Dunbar 1988-.

GLANCY, LEO: Born Musselburgh 1939. Educated Blairs, Drygrange. Ordained Edinburgh 1963. St Francis Xavier's, Falkirk 1963-68. C/o

Diocesan Office 1968-71. Nigerian mission 1971-75. C/o Diocesan Office 1975-76. Edinburgh Cathedral 1976-80. Currie 1980-86. Haddington 1986-88. Spiritual Director, Gillis College 1988-.

GLANCY, WALTER JOSEPH: Born Newark, New Jersey, USA 1914. Educated Blairs 1926-32; Oscott College, Birmingham 1932-38. Ordained Edinburgh 1938. Further studies, Cambridge University 1938-41. St Margaret Mary's, Edinburgh 1941-42. Immaculate Conception, Bathgate 1942-45. St Columba's, Edinburgh 1945-50. St Andrew's, Edinburgh 1950-56. St Peter's, Edinburgh 1956-80. Died Edinburgh 27 Feb 1980.

GLASHEEN, MICHAEL: Born and educated Ireland. Ordained Thurles 1880. Lent to St A & E. Haddington 1880-81. Dunbar 1881-84. St Patrick's, Edinburgh 1884-86. No further entries. (Canning)

GLASS, CHARLES: Ordained 1946. Broxburn 1946-47. No further entries.

GORDON, ERIC: Born Edinburgh 1914. Educated Blairs 1930-34; Seminary of St Lo 1934-35; Coutances 1935-39; St Kieran's College, Kilkenny 1939-40. Ordained Edinburgh 1940. Portobello 1940-42. Hawick 1942-45. St Margaret's, Dunfermline 1945-51. Addiewell 1951-52. Pittenweem 1952-53. C/o Diocesan Office 1953-54. St Mary's, Stirling 1954-57. Balerno 1957-66. Currie 1966-69. Retired 1969. Died Edinburgh 7 April 1970.

GORDON, HUGH: Born Inverness 1910. Educated Stonyhurst; St Mary's College, Oscott 1932-37. Ordained Edinburgh 1937. Lent to Aberdeen diocese: St Mary's, Inverness 1937-38. Portobello 1938-40. Forces chaplain 1940-44. St Mary's, Stirling 1944-49. Selkirk 1949-55. St Andrew's, Fife 1955-69. St Margaret's, Edinburgh 1969-72. Portobello 1972-80. Linlithgow 1980-86. Chaplain, Little Sisters of the Poor, Edinburgh 1986-.

GORDON, JOHN: Born Port Glasgow 1936. Educated Drygrange. Ordained Kilsyth 1965. St Cuthbert's, Edinburgh 1965-72. St Andrew's, Livingston 1972-74. Military chaplain 1974-76. No further entries.

GOULDBOURN, FRANCIS L: Ordained 1946. St Margaret's, Dunfermline 1946-47. No further entries.

GRACE, PIERCE: Born and educated Ireland. Ordained Kilkenny for St A & E 1939. Musselburgh 1939-53. Falkland 1953-58. St Mary's, Glenrothes 1958-69. Died Glenrothes 1 Feb 1969. (Canning)

GRADY, JAMES: see Grady, Patrick

GRADY, PATRICK JOSEPH: (entered as `James' in 1949 Directory). Born Broxburn 1921. Educated St Mary's School, Bathgate; Blairs; Oscott. Ordained 1945. Further studies, Cambridge University 1945-48. Edinburgh Cathedral 1948-59. Chaplain, Little Sisters of the Poor, Edinburgh 1959-66. St Kentigern's, Edinburgh 1966-81. Edinburgh Cathedral 1981-.

GRANT, WILLIAM: Born Braemar 1877. Educated Blairs 1891-95; Notre Dame des Champs, Paris 1895-96; Issy 1896-98; St Sulpice 1898-1901. Ordained Paris 1901. Broxburn 1901-02. Galashiels 1902-04. Bo'ness 1904-13. Polmont 1913-23. Duns 1923-30. Balerno 1930-41. Innerleithen 1941-43. Chaplain, Dominican Convent, Hawick 1943-60. Died Hawick 29 Nov 1960.

GRAY, GORDON JOSEPH: Born Leith 1910. Educated Holy Cross Academy, Edinburgh; St Joseph's College, Mark Cross 1927-29; St John's Seminary, Wonersh 1929-35. Ordained Edinburgh 1935. St Andrew's, Fife 1935-41. Hawick 1941-47. Rector, Blairs 1947-51. Consecrated Archbishop of St A & E 1951. Made Cardinal 1969. Retired 1985.

GRAY, JOHN (1901): Born London 1866. Educated Scots College, Rome 1898-1901. Ordained Rome 1901. St Patrick's, Edinburgh 1902-05. St Peter's, Edinburgh 1905-34. Died Edinburgh 16 June 1934.

GRAY, JOHN ALLAN (1902): Born Mill of Park, Banffshire 1873. Educated Scots College, Rome 1898-1902. Ordained Rome 1902. St Francis Xavier's, Falkirk 1902-06. Selkirk 1906-16. Forces chaplain 1916-19. North Berwick 1919-26. St Margaret's, Dunfermline 1926-29. St Andrew's, Fife 1929-55. Died St Andrew's 26 June 1955.

GREEN, PATRICK: Born Ireland. Educated Ireland; Blairs 1881-84; Douay 1884-87; Scots College, Rome 1887-91, returning home in bad health. Ordained Edinburgh 1891. Professor, Blairs 1891-94. St Patrick's, Edinburgh 1894-96. St Margaret's, Dunfermline 1896-98. Linlithgow 1898-99. Lent to Glasgow Archdiocese: Holy Family, Kirkintilloch 1899-1901; St Patrick's, Glasgow 1901-04. St Francis Xavier's, Falkirk 1904-06. Galashiels 1906-08. Edinburgh Cathedral 1908-12. Loanhead 1912-16. Cowdenbeath 1916-19. Immaculate Conception, Bathgate 1919-24. Sick leave 1924-26. Chaplain, Little Sisters of the Poor, Edinburgh 1926-44. Retired 1944. Died Musselburgh 6 July 1950. (Canning)

GREENAN, THOMAS: Born Edinburgh 1956. Educated Langbank, Blairs, Valladolid. Ordained Portobello 1980. Holy Cross, Edinburgh 1980-81. St Andrew's, Livingston 1981-86. On mission in St Salvador 1986-.

GRIFFIN, PATRICK (1927): Born Ireland. Educated Ireland, Paris.

Ordained Paris 1927. Lent to St A & E. St Francis Xavier's, Falkirk 1928-34. Resumed his vocation in Ireland 1934. Died Ireland 8 March 1940. (Canning)

HALLORAN, BRIAN: Born Aberdeen 1935. Educated Blairs, Drygrange. Ordained Edinburgh 1959. Armadale 1959-67. St Margaret Mary's, Edinburgh 1967-72. Portobello 1972-77. St Andrew's, Livingston 1977-78. Methil 1978-87. St Andrew's, Fife 1987-.

HAMILTON, WILLIAM DOUGLAS: Born Edinburgh 1907. Educated George Watson's College, Edinburgh; worked in father's silversmith business; studied for priesthood Beda, Rome, studies being interrupted by military service, 1939-48. Ordained Rome 1948. Edinburgh Cathedral 1948-56. Chaplain, Poor Clares, Edinburgh 1956-70. Retired 1970. Died Edinburgh 31 July 1974.

HAND, GERARD ROBERT: Born Edinburgh 1949. Educated Holy Cross Academy, Edinburgh; Drygrange. Ordained Edinburgh 1973. St Andrew's, Livingston 1973-77. Further studies, Rome 1977-79. Professor, Drygrange 1979-86. Professor, Gillis College 1986-.

HANLON, THOMAS: Born Slamannan 1927. Educated Blairs; Scots College, Rome. Ordained Rome 1952. Loanhead 1952-53. Further studies, Rome 1953-55. Professor, Drygrange 1955-68. Chaplain, Sacred Heart Convent, Edinburgh 1968-75. Polmont 1975-.

HANNAN, JOSEPH: Born Ireland. Educated Ireland, Blairs, Valladolid. Ordained Edinburgh 1879. St Patrick's, Edinburgh 1879-81. Loanhead 1881-84. St Patrick's, Edinburgh 1884-87. Denny 1887-91. St Francis Xavier's, Falkirk 1891-93. Immaculate Conception, Bathgate 1893-99. Lennoxtown 1899-1903. Died Glasgow 27 May 1903. (Canning)

HARKIN, PETER: Born Ireland. Educated Ireland, Paris. Ordained Paris 1930. Lent to St A & E. Tranent 1930-32. Resumed his vocation in Ireland 1932. (Canning)

HAROLD, JAMES GEORGE: Born and educated Ireland. Ordained for St A & E 1922. St Patrick's, Edinburgh 1922-23. Kilsyth 1923-28. Bowhill 1928-34. Our Lady of Perpetual Succour, Kirkcaldy 1934-38. Hawick 1938-42. Peebles 1942-53. St Ninian's, Edinburgh 1953-58. Musselburgh 1958-72. Retired 1972. Died Ireland 10 May 1973. (Canning)

HART, DOMINIC: Born Denny 1882. Educated Blairs 1895-1900; Scots College, Rome 1900-06. Ordained Rome 1905. St Francis Xavier's, Falkirk 1906-08. Our Lady of Perpetual Succour, Kirkcaldy 1908-12. Slamannan 1912-13. Jedburgh 1913-17. Loanhead 1917-23.

Inverkeithing 1923-30. Hawick 1930-38. Lochgelly 1938-43. Retired 1943. Died Edinburgh 22 April 1965.

HART, JAMES: Born Edinburgh 1890. Educated Blairs 1905-09; Scots College, Rome 1909-17. Ordained Rome 1916. St Mary's, Stirling 1917-18. Inverkeithing 1918-19. Kelso 1919-21. Cowie 1921-35. Chaplain, Poor Clares, Edinburgh 1935-40. Mount Alvernia, Edinburgh 1940-41. Gourock, not attached to parish, 1941-43. West Calder 1943-44. Chaplain, Little Sisters of the Poor, Edinburgh 1944-47. Died Edinburgh 2 Sept 1947.

HARTIGAN, PATRICK: Born and educated Ireland. Ordained Maynooth 1889. Lent to St A & E. St Patrick's, Edinburgh 1889-92. Resumed his vocation in Ireland 1892. Died Ireland 2 July 1937. (Canning)

HEALY, JOSEPH: Born Newmains 1904. Educated Blairs 1918-23; Scots College, Rome 1923-30. Ordained Rome 1930. St Patrick's, Edinburgh 1930-32. Edinburgh Cathedral 1932-35. St Francis Xavier's, Falkirk 1935-36. East Calder 1936-78. Died East Calder 19 Jan 1979.

HEALY, LIAM: Born and educated Ireland. Ordained Kilkenny for St A & E 1956. Loanhead 1956-58. St Cuthbert's, Edinburgh 1958-64. Immaculate Conception, Bathgate 1964-70. St Columba's, Bathgate 1970-84. Armadale 1984-88. Dalkeith 1988-. (Canning)

HEANEY, JAMES: Born and educated Ireland. Ordained Kinnoull 1911. Lent to St A & E. St Mary's, Stirling 1911-16. Resumed his vocation in Ireland 1916. Died Ireland 16 Nov 1954. (Canning)

HEFFRON, SAMUEL A: see Galloway diocese

HENDRIE, ROBERT: Born Laurieston, Stirlingshire 1938. Educated Blairs; Scots College, Rome. Ordained Rome 1962. Portobello 1962-65. Broxburn 1965-69. St Mark's, Edinburgh 1969-71. Professor, Drygrange 1971-81. C/o Diocesan Office 1981-83. Burntisland 1983-84. Pittenweem 1984-.

HENERY, WILLIAM W: Born Grangemouth 1914. Educated Campion House, Osterley; Blairs; St Edmund's College, Ware. Ordained Edinburgh 1948. St Cuthbert's, Edinburgh 1948-55. Military chaplain 1955-60. Bonnybridge 1960-67. Banknock 1967-81. St Kentigern's, Edinburgh 1981-84. East Calder 1984-87. Died Grangemouth 28 April 1987.

HENNESSY, FRANCIS: Ordained 1937. St Margaret's, Dunfermline 1937-38. St Patrick's, Edinburgh 1938-39. No further entries.

HENNESSY, THOMAS: Born Plymouth 1934. Educated Blairs, Drygrange. Ordained Edinburgh 1959. Bowhill 1959-67. St Ninian's, Edinburgh

1967-69. Armadale 1969-77. St Catherine's, Edinburgh 1977-80. Kelty 1980-88. Armadale 1988-.

HENRY, DAVID: Born Edinburgh 1939. Educated Blairs, Drygrange. Ordained Edinburgh 1962. St Patrick's, Edinburgh 1962-64. Further studies, Rome 1964-67. St Kentigern's, Edinburgh 1967-68. Methil 1968-73. Bonnyrigg 1973-77. Dalkeith 1977-81. Leven 1981-89. Jedburgh 1989-.

HENRY, JAMES: Born Drem 1946. Educated Holy Cross Academy, Edinburgh; Scots College, Rome. Ordained Currie 1970. St Mark's, Edinburgh 1971-74. Professor, Blairs 1974-77. Professor, Drygrange 1977-84. Rector, Drygrange 1984-86. Rector, Gillis College 1986-87. Died Edinburgh 16 Oct 1987.

HESSION, MICHAEL JOHN: Born Ireland. Educated Ireland, St Peter's. Ordained Kilkenny for St A & E 1921. St Patrick's, Edinburgh 1921-22. Lennoxtown 1922-24. Our Lady of Perpetual Succour, Kirkcaldy 1924-25. No further entries. (Canning)

HIGGINS, PETER GEORGE: Born Portobello 1905. Educated Blairs 1921-24; Scots College, Rome 1924-31. Ordained Rome 1931. St Cuthbert's, Edinburgh 1931-35. Linlithgow 1935-39. St Ninian's, Edinburgh 1939-53. St Joseph's, Edinburgh 1953-56. Hawick 1956-86. Retired 1986.

HOBAN, FREDERICK: Born Perth 1861. Educated Blairs 1875-81; Scots College, Rome 1881-87. Ordained Rome 1886. Edinburgh Cathedral 1887-88. Ratho 1888-89. Penicuik 1889-90. Loanhead 1890-1901. Haddington 1901-08. Broxburn 1908-34. Died Edinburgh 16 Feb 1934.

HODGSON, REGINALD JOHN JOSEPH: Born Cupar 1915. Educated St Joseph's College, Dumfries; Seminary of Coutances; St Kieran's College, Kilkenny. Ordained Kilkenny 1940. St Peter's, Edinburgh 1940-53. Jedburgh 1953-56. Bowhill 1956-69. Chaplain, Balnakiel Convent, Galashiels 1969-70. C/o Diocesan Office 1970-72. C/o Gatehouse of Fleet 1972-86. Chaplain, Brothers of Charity, Gattonside 1986-.

HOGAN, RICHARD: Born Glasgow 1873. Educated Blairs 1887-92; Scots College, Rome 1892-98. Ordained Rome 1897. St Patrick's, Edinburgh 1898-1902. Lochgelly 1902-16. Denny 1916-28. Died Denny 13 April 1928.

HOGAN, THOMAS: Born and educated Ireland. Ordained Thurles 1943. Lent to St A & E. Lochgelly 1943-47. Resumed his vocation in Ireland 1947. (Canning)

HOLDEN, FRANCIS: Ordained 1939. Camelon 1950-61. Edinburgh

Cathedral 1961-62. Innerleithen 1962-72. St John the Baptist's, Edinburgh 1972-.

HOLDEN, PATRICK: Ordained 1934. St Ninian's, Edinburgh 1934-36. No further entries.

HOLLAND, WILLIAM: Born Ireland. Educated Ireland, Paris. Ordained Paris 1902. Lent to St A & E. St Margaret's, Dunfermline 1902-04. Immaculate Conception, Bathgate 1904-05. Lent to Glasgow Archdiocese: St Patrick's, Dumbarton 1905-08. Resumed his vocation in Ireland 1908. Died Ireland 13 Dec 1950. (Canning)

HOLOHAN, JOHN J: Born and educated Ireland. Ordained Kilkenny 1940. Lent to St A & E. St Francis Xavier's, Falkirk 1940-41. Sacred Heart, Grangemouth 1941-45. Resumed his vocation in Ireland 1945. (Canning)

HOLUKA, RYSZARD: Born Irvine 1949. Educated Holy Cross Academy, Edinburgh; Drygrange. Ordained Edinburgh 1974. St Kentigern's, Edinburgh 1974-80. St Peter's, Edinburgh 1980-85. Sacred Heart, Edinburgh 1985-86. Virginia, USA 1986-.

HORGAN, PATRICK: Born and educated Ireland. Ordained Maynooth 1910. Lent to St A & E. St Mary's, Stirling 1910-11. Died Stirling 17 March 1911. (Canning)

HORNE, IAIN: Born Edinburgh 1959. Educated St Augustine's High School; worked as internal auditor, Common Services Agency; educated for priesthood Drygrange. Ordained Edinburgh 1985. St Margaret's, Dunfermline 1985. Denny 1985-86. No further entries.

HYLAND, EDWARD: Born Ireland. Educated Ireland, Spain. Ordained Maynooth 1940. St Patrick's, Edinburgh 1940-54. Penicuik 1954-67. St Patrick's, Edinburgh 1967-88. Retired 1988. (Canning)

JACKSON, MICHAEL: Born and educated Ireland. Ordained 1943. Immaculate Conception, Bathgate 1943-47. St Mary's, Stirling 1947-49. Whitburn 1949-50. St Ninian's, Edinburgh 1950-52. Portobello 1952-54. Methil 1954-55. Duns 1955-57. St Margaret Mary's, Edinburgh 1957-63. Slamannan 1963-67. Penicuik 1967-. (Canning)

JOHNSTON, MICHAEL HARRY: Born Galashiels 1951. Educated Langbank, Blairs, Drygrange. Ordained Portobello 1975. Edinburgh Cathedral 1975. Denny 1975-77. Professor, Blairs 1977-86. Further studies, Rome 1986-89. Duns 1989-.

JOYCE, JOHN (1896): Born Fountainhall 1871. Educated Blairs 1887-91; Scots College, Rome 1891-97. Ordained Rome 1896. St Patrick's,

Edinburgh 1897-99. Lennoxtown 1899-1901. Tranent 1901-13. Winchburgh 1913-14. Falkland 1914-16. Kelso 1916-17. No address given 1917-20. Not in Directories 1920-22. Went to Glasgow Archdiocese: Our Holy Redeemer, Clydebank 1922-24. Leave of absence 1924-30. No further entries.

JOYCE, JOHN B (1899): Born Inverkeithing 1874. Educated Blairs 1888-92; Valladolid 1892-99. Ordained Valladolid 1899. St Patrick's, Edinburgh 1899-1902. Kelso 1902-09. Fauldhouse 1909-23. Musselburgh 1923-36. Died Edinburgh 21 Nov 1936.

JOYCE, KIERNAN: Born and educated Ireland. Ordained Edinburgh 1919. Lent to St A & E. St Mary's, Stirling 1919-20. St Cuthbert's, Edinburgh 1920-28. St Columba's, Edinburgh 1928-30. Resumed his vocation in Ireland 1930. Died Ireland 5 April 1973. (Canning)

JUDGE, STEPHEN: Born Edinburgh 1935. Educated Blairs, Valladolid. Ordained Valladolid 1958. St Ninian's, Edinburgh 1958-62. St Columba's, Edinburgh 1962-69. Holy Cross, Edinburgh 1969-72. St Gregory's, Edinburgh 1972-85. St Peter's, Edinburgh 1985-89. Camelon 1989-.

KEENAN, JOSEPH: see Dunkeld diocese

KELLY, ANTHONY: Born Kelty 1904. Educated Blairs 1919-24; St Lo 1924-25; Grand Seminaire, Coutances 1925-30. Ordained Edinburgh 1930. St Ninian's, Edinburgh 1930-33. Innerleithen 1933-36. Larbert 1936-43. Rosewell 1943-52. Dalkeith 1952-65. Died Edinburgh 13 Feb 1965.

KELLY, BERNARD: Born Ireland. Educated Ireland, Paris. Ordained Paris 1934. Lent to St A & E. Rosewell 1934-37. St Patrick's, Edinburgh 1937-39. Selkirk 1939-40. Resumed his vocation in Ireland 1940. Died Ireland 2 June 1974. (Canning)

KELLY, CHARLES J: Born and educated Ireland. Ordained Kilkenny for St A & E 1941. St Columba's, Edinburgh 1941-42. Further studies, Oxford University 1942-45. St Columba's, Edinburgh 1945-46. St Columba's, Edinburgh in addresses, but not under parishes, 1946-47. Chaplain, St Teresa's Residential Nursery, Aberdour 1947-49. Further studies, Edinburgh, 1949-50. Our Lady of Perpetual Succour, Kirkcaldy 1950-56. Jedburgh 1956-65. St Mark's, Edinburgh 1965-77. Armadale 1977-84. Died Ireland 8 Oct 1984. (Canning)

KELLY, DANIEL: Born Ireland. Ordained 1912. Lennoxtown 1918-22. Denny 1922-27. Kelty 1927-30. Selkirk 1930-38. Hawick 1938-42. Retired 1942. Died Glasgow 25 May 1943. (Canning)

KELLY, MICHAEL: Born Kelty 1905. Educated Blairs 1918-23; Grand Seminaire de Coutances 1923-28. Ordained Dundee 1928. Edinburgh Cathedral 1928-29. Tranent 1929-30. Edinburgh Cathedral 1930-32. South Queensferry 1932-37. Addiewell 1937-47. Denny 1947-77. Retired 1977. Died Milford 9 March 1978.

KELLY, PATRICK: Born Kilsyth 1935. Educated Blairs, Drygrange. Ordained Edinburgh 1959. St Ninian's, Edinburgh 1959-66. Camelon 1966-67. St Margaret's, Dunfermline 1967-72. Musselburgh 1972-85. St John Vianney's, Edinburgh 1985-.

KELLY, PAUL: Born Brighton 1946. Educated Brighton, Hove and Sussex Grammar School; Oxford University; worked in National Library of Scotland; educated for priesthood Beda, Rome. Ordained Edinburgh 1985. St Mary's, Bathgate 1985-87. St Margaret's, Dunfermline 1987-.

KELLY, THOMAS (1925) (2): see Glasgow Archdiocese

KELLY, THOMAS A (1926): see Dunkeld diocese

KELLY, WILLIAM RICHARD: Born and educated Ireland. Ordained Dublin 1939. Methil 1939-42. Methil in addresses, but not under parishes, 1942-47. No further entries. (Canning)

KENNEDY, JOHN: Born and educated Ireland. Ordained Maynooth 1936. Lent to St A & E. Edinburgh Cathedral 1936-37. Resumed his vocation in Ireland 1937. (Canning)

KENNY, HARRY (Henry): Born Edinburgh 1883. Educated Blairs 1897-1902; Issy 1902-04; Scots College, Rome 1904-08. Ordained Rome 1907. West Calder 1908-11. Broxburn 1911-13. Addiewell 1913-28. Cowdenbeath 1928-32. Winchburgh 1932-45. Died Winchburgh 23 Dec 1945.

KENNY, JOHN: Born and educated Ireland. Ordained Kilkenny 1936. Lent to St A & E. St Ninian's, Edinburgh 1936-37. Resumed his vocation in Ireland 1937. (Canning)

KERR, EDWARD NORMAN: Born Edinburgh 1917. Educated Daniel Stewart's College, Edinburgh; Campion House, Osterley; St Edmund's College, Ware. Ordained Edinburgh 1953. St Cuthbert's, Edinburgh 1953-56. C/o Diocesan Office 1956-58. No further entries.

KERR, FRANCIS (1937): Born Ireland. Educated Ireland, Paris. Ordained Paris 1937. Lent to St A & E. Kilsyth 1938-39. St Ninian's, Edinburgh 1939-40. Went to Nottingham diocese. (Canning)

KERR, FRANCIS (1970): Born Edinburgh 1939. Educated Drygrange. Ordained Edinburgh 1970. St Francis Xavier's, Falkirk 1970-72. Edinburgh Cathedral 1972-78. Chaplain, Little Sisters of the Poor, Edinburgh 1978-86. North Berwick 1986-89. St Peter's, Edinburgh 1989-.

KERR, JOHN: Born and educated Ireland. Ordained Maynooth 1933. Lent to St A & E. Immaculate Conception, Bathgate 1933-38. St Cuthbert's, Edinburgh 1938-43. Resumed his vocation in Ireland 1943. (Canning)

KERR, PHILIP JOHN: Born Edinburgh 1956. Educated Holy Cross Academy, Edinburgh; St Augustine's High School, Edinburgh; Scots College, Rome. Ordained Edinburgh 1979. St Margaret's, Dunfermline 1979. Further studies, Rome 1979-80. St Francis Xavier's, Falkirk 1980-82. Professor, Drygrange 1982-86. Vice-rector, Gillis College 1986-.

KERRISK, JOHN M: Born and educated Ireland. Ordained 1943. Blackburn 1943-48. Whitburn 1948-49. St Mary's, Stirling 1949-64. Our Lady of Lourdes, Dunfermline 1964-72. Died Dunfermline 19 Aug 1972. (Canning)

KIELT, BERNARD: Born and educated Ireland. Ordained Maynooth 1932. Lent to Liverpool Archdiocese 1932-36. Lent to St A & E. Rosewell 1937. St Cuthbert's, Edinburgh 1937-38. Resumed his vocation in Ireland 1938. (Canning)

KIERNAN, ANTHONY: Born Broxburn 1921. Educated Blairs; Oscott College, Birmingham. Ordained 1946. Dalkeith 1946-47. Lochore 1947-56. St Andrew's, Edinburgh 1956-61. Camelon 1961-66. Jedburgh 1966-69. Kennoway 1969-77. St Andrew's, Edinburgh 1977-89. St Catherine's, Edinburgh 1989-.

KILROY, THOMAS: Born and educated Ireland. Ordained Maynooth 1930. Lent to St A & E 1934. Our Lady of Perpetual Succour, Kirkcaldy 1934-35. Resumed his vocation in Ireland 1935. (Canning)

KIRKE, TERENCE: Born Ireland. Educated Ireland, Paris. Ordained Paris 1931. Lent to St A & E. St Francis Xavier's, Falkirk 1932-33. Resumed his vocation in Ireland 1933. (Canning)

KRUGER, KARL-HEINZ: Born Berlin 1924. Refugee to Britain 1939. Arrested and deported to Canada as an alien 1939. Returned to Scotland 1940. Became Roman Catholic. Educated Blairs; St Edmund's College, Ware. Ordained Edinburgh 1949. St Ninian's, Edinburgh 1949-50. Further studies, Cambridge University 1950-53. St Cuthbert's, Edinburgh 1953-54. Professor, Blairs 1954-55. Further studies, Institut Catholique, Paris 1955-57. Professor, Drygrange 1957-70. Christ the

King, Grangemouth 1970-87. Kilsyth 1987-89. Died Kilsyth 24 May 1989.

KUPPERS, HENRY: see Glasgow archdiocese

LAUGHTON, HERBERT R: Born 1864. Educated St Paul's School, London; St Thomas's Seminary, Hammersmith; English College, Rome. Ordained Rome 1890. Served at St James', London 1890-1906. Came to St A & E. St Andrew's, Fife 1906-24. Died St Andrew's 20 Aug 1924.

LAWSON, ALISTAIR: Born Bathgate 1941. Educated St Mary's School, Bathgate; Scotus Academy, Edinburgh; Drygrange. Ordained Edinburgh 1966. Rosewell 1966-67. St Mary's, Stirling 1967-76. St Peter's, Edinburgh 1976-77. C/o St Kentigern's High School, Blackburn 1977-78. Whitburn in addresses, but not under parishes, 1978-82. West Calder 1982-.

LEAHY, JAMES W: Born and educated Ireland. Ordained Dublin 1925. Lent to St A & E. St Columba's, Edinburgh 1925-27. Resumed his vocation in Ireland 1927. Died Ireland 4 March 1970. (Canning)

LECKIE (Leck), JAMES: Born and educated Ireland. Ordained 1946. Lent to St A & E. Methil 1946-47. St Cuthbert's, Edinburgh 1947-48. Resumed his vocation in Ireland 1948. (Canning)

LEE, THOMAS: Born and educated Ireland. Ordained Waterford 1886. Served in Liverpool Archdiocese 1886-89. Edinburgh Cathedral 1889-90. Our Lady of Perpetual Succour, Kirkcaldy 1890-92. No further entries. (Canning)

LEYDEN, CHARLES: Born and educated Ireland. Ordained Monaghan 1931. Lent to St A & E. Broxburn 1931-36. Resumed his vocation in Ireland 1936. (Canning)

LOFTUS, WILLIAM P: Born Bonnyrigg 1905. Educated Campion House, Osterley; Beda, Rome. Ordained Rome 1958. St Peter's, Edinburgh 1958-66. Chaplain, Convent of Mary Reparatrix, Elie 1966-73. Jedburgh 1973-81. Died Jedburgh 23 Nov 1981.

LOGAN, VINCENT PAUL: Born Bathgate 1941. Educated Blairs, Drygrange. Ordained Edinburgh 1964. St Margaret's, Edinburgh 1964-66. Further studies 1966-67. St Margaret's, Edinburgh 1967-69. Rosewell 1969-73. Chaplain, Daughters of Charity, Rosewell 1973-77. Ratho 1977-81. Consecrated Bishop of Dunkeld 1981.

LOGUE, ANDREW: Born Ireland. Educated Ireland, Paris. Ordained Maynooth 1902. Edinburgh Cathedral 1902-05. Resumed his vocation in Ireland 1905. Died Ireland 19 Sept 1948. (Canning)

LOGUE, DANIEL: Born Ireland. Educated Ireland, Paris. Ordained Paris 1934. Lent to St A & E. Edinburgh Cathedral 1934. Bannockburn 1934-35. Lent to Glasgow Archdiocese: Newmains 1935-36. Lent to English Mission 1936-48. Resumed his vocation in Ireland 1948. (Canning)

LONG, JOSEPH: Born Hamilton 1874. Educated St Mary's School, Hamilton; Mount St Mary's, England; Waterford. Ordained Waterford 1901. Edinburgh Cathedral 1902-09. Dunbar 1909-16. Loanhead 1916-17. Inverkeithing 1917-23. Fauldhouse 1923-30. St Francis Xavier's, Falkirk 1930-33. Spiritual Director, Blairs 1933-41. Retired 1941. Died Ireland 17 Jan 1952.

LOUGHLIN, EUGENE W: Born and educated Ireland. Ordained Cavan 1940. Lent to St A & E. Methil in addresses, but not under parishes, 1940-41. St Mary's, Stirling 1941-44. Burntisland 1944-46. Burntisland in addresses, but not under parishes, 1946-47. Resumed his vocation in Ireland 1947. (Canning)

LOWRIE (Lowery), JOHN: Born Ireland. Educated Ireland, Rome. Ordained Rome 1934. Lent to St A & E. Portobello 1934-37. Resumed his vocation in Ireland 1937. (Canning)

LYLE, JOHN STEVENSON: Born Ireland. Ordained 1889 for St A & E. St Francis Xavier's, Falkirk 1889-90. Not in Directory 1890-91. St Francis Xavier's, Falkirk 1891-92. Hawick 1892-1912. Peebles 1912-19. Died Dunninald near Montrose 12 April 1919. (Canning)

LYNAGH, DESMOND EDWARD: Born Falkirk 1941. Educated St Aloysius' College, Glasgow; Drygrange. Ordained Falkirk 1964. Further studies, Cambridge University 1964-66. Methil 1966-69. Professor, Blairs 1969-75. Procurator, Blairs 1975-77. St Kentigern's, Edinburgh 1977-78. Chaplain, Stirling University 1978-83. St Margaret's, Dunfermline 1983-84. Bonnybridge 1984-88. Denny 1988-.

LYNCH, EDWARD: Born and educated Ireland. Ordained Maynooth 1941. Lent to St A & E. Broxburn 1942-47. Our Lady of Perpetual Succour, Kirkcaldy 1947. Resumed his vocation in Ireland 1947. (Canning)

LYNCH, FRANCIS J: Born Ireland. Ordained 1851. Lent to St A & E. Oakley 1879-86. Resumed his vocation in Ireland 1886. (Canning)

LYNCH, GERARD: Born and educated Ireland. Ordained 1944. Dalkeith 1944-47. St Ninian's, Edinburgh 1947-58. Our Lady of Perpetual Succour, Kirkcaldy 1958-64. Duns 1964-65. Gorebridge 1965-68. C/o Diocesan Office 1968-69. Galashiels 1969-70. Hawick 1970-77. Cowdenbeath 1977-78. Edinburgh Cathedral 1978-87. Died Nunraw 29 July 1987. (Canning)

LYNCH, JOHN J: Born and educated Ireland. Ordained Carlow for St A & E 1935. St Ninian's, Edinburgh 1935-38. Kelty 1938-71. Died Edinburgh 17 April 1971. (Canning)

LYNCH, PATRICK C: Born and educated Ireland. Ordained Carlow 1931. Kilsyth 1931-32. Our Lady of Perpetual Succour, Kirkcaldy 1932-34. Dunbar 1934-36. Blackburn 1936-48. Whitburn 1948-49. Lochore 1949-61. St Mark's, Edinburgh 1961-65. St Margaret's, Dunfermline 1965-84. Died Dunfermline 14 Nov 1984. (Canning)

LYNG, PATRICK: Born and educated Ireland. Ordained Kilkenny 1940. Lent to St A & E. St Ninian's, Edinburgh 1940-43. Sick leave, Ireland 1943-46. Archdiocese of Perth, Australia 1946-47. Died Australia 18 May 1947. (Canning)

LYONS, PETER: Born and educated Ireland. Ordained Ireland 1939. St Francis Xavier's, Falkirk 1939. Our Lady of Perpetual Succour, Kirkcaldy 1939-43. Falkland 1943-49. Bo'ness 1949-69. Lochgelly 1969-85. Banknock 1985-. (Canning)

McALLISTER, BERNARD JAMES: Born Bo'ness 1939. Educated Blairs, Drygrange. Ordained Edinburgh 1963. Methil 1963-65. St Francis Xavier's, Falkirk 1965-78. Slamannan 1978-86. Gorebridge 1986-.

McALLISTER, CHRISTOPHER: Born Lochgelly 1909. Educated Blairs 1924-30; St Lo 1930-31; St Sulpice 1931-36. Ordained Edinburgh 1936. Addiewell 1936-40. Bannockburn 1940-87. Retired 1987.

McALLISTER, DESMOND JOSEPH PATRICK: Born Edinburgh 1940. Educated St Joseph's College, Mark Cross, Sussex; Scots College, Rome. Ordained Rome 1964. Lennoxtown 1964-65. Munich, Germany 1965-69. No further entries.

McALLISTER, JOHN: Born Leith 1932. Educated Blairs, St Sulpice. Ordained Edinburgh 1955. St Francis Xavier's, Falkirk 1955-60. Leave of absence 1960-61. Nigerian mission 1961-66. Edinburgh Cathedral 1966-69. St Paul's, Edinburgh 1969-79. Lennoxtown 1979-87. St Ninian's, Edinburgh 1987-.

McANAA, PATRICK: Born Airdrie 1856. Educated Blairs 1874-76; Petit Seminaire de St Riquier 1876-77; Scots College, Rome 1877-83. Ordained Rome 1881. Broxburn 1883-84. Edinburgh Cathedral 1884-87. Penicuik 1887-89. Haddington 1889-98. Died Haddington 25 Nov 1898.

MACARDLE, JOSEPH FRANCIS: Born and educated Ireland. Ordained Kilkenny for St A & E 1928. Edinburgh Cathedral 1928-30. Musselburgh

1930-32. Dunbar 1932-34. Kelty 1934-35. Leave of absence 1935-36. Broxburn 1936-39. Denny 1939-41. Bonnybridge 1941-45. St Cuthbert's, Edinburgh 1945-52. Bonnyrigg 1952-60. Retired 1960. Died Ireland 10 Feb 1973. (Canning)

McCABE, GERALD: Born and educated Ireland. Ordained Kilkenny for St A & E 1947. Immaculate Conception, Bathgate 1947-61. Kilsyth 1961-68. Gorebridge 1968-72. Our Lady of Lourdes, Dunfermline 1972-. (Canning)

McCABE, JAMES: Born and educated Ireland. Ordained Maynooth 1940. Lent to St A & E. Immaculate Conception, Bathgate 1940-47. Resumed his vocation in Ireland 1947. (Canning)

McCABE, JOSEPH: Born 1914. Educated Blairs 1927-32; St Edmund's, Old Hall Green 1932-38. Ordained Edinburgh 1938. St Mary's, Stirling 1938-40. Lochore 1940-44. Bowhill 1944-56. St Joseph's, Edinburgh 1956-77. Kelso 1977-80. Retired 1980. Died Loanhead 9 Sept 1984.

McCABE, MICHAEL: Ordained 1953. Musselburgh 1963-70. No further entries.

McCABE, WILLIAM AUGUSTINE: Born West Calder 1895. Educated Blairs 1910-15; Scots College, Rome 1915-22. Ordained Rome 1922. St Patrick's, Edinburgh 1922-23. St Peter's, Edinburgh 1923-26. St Patrick's, Edinburgh 1926-28. Balerno 1928-30. Lochore 1930-36. Loanhead 1936-38. Bonnybridge 1938-49. Lennoxtown 1949-79. Died Leith 13 Feb 1979.

McCAFFREY, DANIEL: Born and educated Ireland. Ordained Maynooth 1929. Lent to St A & E. St Patrick's, Edinburgh 1930-31. Resumed his vocation in Ireland 1931. Died Ireland 6 Feb 1951. (Canning)

McCALLUM, JAMES: see McCallum, John

McCALLUM, JOHN: Born Denny 1914. Educated Blairs 1926-31; Scots College, Rome 1931-38. Ordained Rome 1938. St Columba's, Edinburgh 1938-39. Immaculate Conception, Bathgate 1939-41. St Margaret's, Dunfermline 1941-43. Our Lady of Perpetual Succour, Kirkcaldy 1943-44. St Ninian's, Edinburgh 1944-47. Slamannan 1947-53. Stoneyburn 1953-61. Whitburn 1961-72. Retired 1972. Died Denny 14 April 1977.

McCANN, DAVID HUGH: Born Burntisland 1937. Educated Blairs, Drygrange. Ordained Edinburgh 1960. Galashiels 1960-62. Cowdenbeath 1962-65. Nigerian mission 1965-67. C/o Diocesan Office 1967-70. Musselburgh 1970-72. Bonnybridge 1972-77. Chaplain, Daughters of Charity, Rosewell 1977-80. Kelso 1980-85. Lochore 1985-87. St Patrick's, Edinburgh 1987-88. Peebles 1988-.

McCANN, THOMAS: Born Denny 1898. Educated Blairs 1913-19; St Peter's 1919-20; Scots College, Rome 1920-26. Ordained Rome 1925. Broxburn 1926-30. Broxburn in addresses, but not under parishes, 1930-31. Burntisland 1931-36. Polmont 1936-75. Died Polmont 14 May 1975.

McCARTHY, FLORENCE: Born Ireland. Educated Ireland, Leeds. Ordained Edinburgh 1890. Edinburgh Cathedral 1890-93. Fauldhouse 1893-95. Died 28 Sept 1895. (Canning)

McCARTHY, SEAN: Born and educated Ireland. Ordained 1954. Lent to St A & E. St Ninian's, Edinburgh 1954-57. Resumed his vocation in Ireland 1957. (Canning)

McCARVILLE, THOMAS: Born and educated Ireland. Ordained Maynooth 1940. Lent to St A & E. Kilsyth 1942-47. Resumed his vocation in Ireland 1947. (Canning)

McCAULEY (McAuley), JAMES: Born and educated Ireland. Ordained 1947. Lent to St A & E. Broxburn 1947-49. Resumed his vocation in Ireland 1949. Died Ireland 1 Sept 1974. (Canning)

McCLAFFERTY, MANUS: Born and educated Ireland. Ordained Maynooth 1933. Lent to African mission 1933-43. Lent to St A & E: St Andrew's, Edinburgh 1943-45. Resumed his vocation in Ireland 1945. Died Ireland 20 Aug 1953. (Canning)

McCLELLAND, WILLIAM: Born Bridgeton 1907. Educated Blairs 1923-28; Scots College, Rome 1928-35. Ordained Rome 1934. Holy Cross, Edinburgh 1935-38. St John's, Edinburgh 1938-71. Died Edinburgh 5 Jan 1972.

McCOLGAN, (James) EDWARD: Born and educated Ireland. Ordained Kilkenny for St A & E 1943. Portobello 1943. St Patrick's, Edinburgh 1943-46. St Francis Xavier's, Falkirk 1946-49. Methil 1949-54. St Andrew's, Edinburgh 1954-56. Died Edinburgh 4 Feb 1956. (Canning)

McCONNACHIE, GEORGE: Born Castletown, Glenlivet 1875. Educated Blairs 1888-92; Valladolid 1892-99. Ordained Valladolid 1899. Linlithgow 1899-1900. No further entries.

McCONVILLE, TIMOTHY BERNARD: Born Corbridge, Northumberland 1958. Educated St Augustine's High School, Edinburgh; Napier College, Edinburgh; North Staffordshire Polytechnic. Career in computer studies. Educated for priesthood Drygrange, Gillis College. Ordained Edinburgh 1987. St Francis Xavier's, Falkirk 1987-.

McCORMACK, PATRICK: Born Ireland. Educated Ireland, Paris. Ordained Paris 1929. Lent to St A & E. Broxburn 1930-31. Resumed his vocation in Ireland 1931. Died Ireland 28 Sept 1969. (Canning)

McCULLAGH, MICHAEL COLUM: Born Ireland. Educated Blairs; St Edmund's College, Ware. Ordained Edinburgh 1947. Portobello 1947-53. St Margaret's, Dunfermline 1953-65. Lennoxtown 1965-67. Milton of Campsie 1967-76. Stoneyburn 1976-87. Musselburgh 1987-. (Canning)

McDANIEL, PATRICK: see Dunkeld diocese

McDANIEL, PETER: Born Dundee 1864. Educated Blairs 1877-81; Valladolid 1881-87. Ordained Valladolid 1887. Our Lady of Perpetual Succour, Kirkcaldy 1887. St Patrick's, Edinburgh 1887-88. Lennoxtown 1888-92. Dunbar 1892-99. Immaculate Conception, Bathgate 1899-1912. Lennoxtown 1912-16. Lochgelly 1916-35. Died Edinburgh 22 Dec 1935.

MACDERMOTT, JAMES: Born Edinburgh 1863. Educated Royal High School, Edinburgh; Mount St Mary's, Chesterfield. In Jesuit Novitiate, Roehampton, studying and teaching, 1882-94. Educated for priesthood Scots College, Rome, returning home in bad health; St Peter's. Ordained 1898. Edinburgh Cathedral 1898-1901. Died Edinburgh 1 April 1901.

McDERMOTT, JOSEPH: Born and educated Ireland. Ordained Maynooth 1941. Lent to St A & E. St Patrick's, Edinburgh 1941-46. Resumed his vocation in Ireland 1946. (Canning)

MACDONALD, JAMES (1903): Born Lennoxtown 1880. Educated Blairs 1893-98; Scots College, Rome 1898-1904. Ordained Rome 1903. Broxburn 1904. Edinburgh Cathedral 1904-07. Slamannan 1907-12. Kelso 1912-16. Duns 1916-19. Bannockburn 1919-33. St Francis Xavier's, Falkirk 1933-38. Died Falkirk 6 June 1938.

McDONALD, JAMES (1940): Ordained 1940. St Cuthbert's, Edinburgh 1941-45. No further entries.

MACDONALD, JAMES ANTHONY (1989): Born Glasgow 1942. Educated St Mungo's Academy, Glasgow; Drygrange; Gillis College. Ordained Edinburgh 1989. St Ninian's, Edinburgh 1989. Denny 1989-.

MACDONALD, SAMUEL: see Argyll diocese

McDONNA, THOMAS: Born Glasgow 1870. Educated Blairs 1883-87; Valladolid 1887-94. Ordained Valladolid 1894. Edinburgh Cathedral 1894-97. Lennoxtown 1897-99. Talla Reservoir 1899-1905. West Calder 1905-06. Armadale 1906-12. West Calder 1912-18. No address given 1918-20. No further entries.

McELHENNEY (McElphiney), JOSEPH: Born Ireland. Educated Ireland, Paris. Ordained 1927. Lent to St A & E. Edinburgh Cathedral 1927-30. West Calder 1930. Portobello 1930-31. Immaculate Conception, Bathgate 1931-33. Joined Carmelite Order in Ireland 1933. (Canning)

McEWAN, WILLIAM JOSEPH: Born Glasgow 1919. Educated Blairs; Oscott College, Birmingham. Ordained Lennoxtown 1946. Polmont 1946-47. No further entries.

McFADDEN, PATRICK JOSEPH: Born and educated Ireland. Ordained Kilkenny for St A & E 1955. Fauldhouse 1955-56. Our Lady of Perpetual Succour, Kirkcaldy 1956-58. Nigerian mission 1958-59. Galashiels 1959-60. Bo'ness 1960-61. C/o Diocesan Office 1961-62. Edinburgh Cathedral 1962-66. Tranent 1966-67. C/o Diocesan Office 1967-69. St Margaret's, Edinburgh 1969-72. Chaplain, Sisters of Charity, Musselburgh 1972-73. Retired to Ireland 1973. (Canning)

McFARLANE, FRANCIS J: Born Edinburgh 1902. Educated Blairs 1918-23; Grand Seminaire de Coutances 1923-28. Ordained Dundee 1928. St Mary's, Stirling 1928-30. Rosewell 1930-33. Denny 1933-37. Methil 1937-38. Oakley 1938-41. Immaculate Conception, Bathgate 1941-43. Sick leave 1943-45. Lent to Glasgow Archdiocese: Baillieston 1945-47. No further entries.

MACFARLANE, MALCOLM WILLIAM: Born Streatham Hill, London 1920. Educated Blairs; Coutances; St Peter's College, Wexford; All Hallows College, Dublin; St Edmund's College, Ware. Ordained 1943. Further studies, Cambridge University 1943-45. St Margaret Mary's, Edinburgh 1945-46. St Patrick's, Edinburgh 1946-48. Holy Cross, Edinburgh 1948-49. St Francis Xavier's, Falkirk 1949-58. Falkland 1958-65. Stoneyburn 1965-76. Died Ireland 5 Feb 1976.

MACFARLANE, PETER: Born Bannockburn 1906. Educated Blairs 1920-25; Scots College, Rome 1925-32. Ordained Rome 1931. St Peter's, Edinburgh 1932-35. Fauldhouse 1935-36. Burntisland 1936-40. Forces chaplain 1940-46. Broxburn 1946-67. Died Broxburn 30 July 1967.

McGARRIGLE, ROBERT GEORGE: Born Alloa 1939. Educated Campion House, Osterley; Drygrange. Ordained Stirling 1968. St Kentigern's, Edinburgh 1968-74. Kilsyth 1974-81. Holy Cross, Edinburgh 1981-83. Chaplain, St Andrew's University 1983-87. Camelon 1987-89. No further entries.

McGARRY (McGarrie), GERARD: Born and educated Ireland. Ordained Dublin 1938. St Patrick's, Edinburgh 1938-41. Penicuik 1941-54. Cowie 1954-65. Methil 1965-77. Leven 1977-81. Died Leven 19 Oct 1981. (Canning)

Note: 1942 Directory gives his name as 'William'; Canning lists him as 'William Gerard'.

McGARRY, WILLIAM: see McGarry, Gerard

McGARVEY, THOMAS: Born Uddingston 1896. Educated Blairs 1913-19; St Peter's 1919-20; Scots College, Rome 1920-26. Ordained Rome 1925. St Patrick's, Edinburgh 1926-30. Polmont 1930-36. Lochore 1936-49. Bonnybridge 1949-56. Kilsyth 1956-72. Retired 1972. Died Kilsyth 6 Oct 1987.

McGEE, JAMES EDWARD: Born and educated Ireland. Ordained Carlow for St A & E 1955. Broxburn 1955-59. St John the Baptist's, Edinburgh 1959-60. Cowdenbeath 1960-62. Rosewell 1962-65. Denny 1965-69. Pittenweem 1969-84. Died Glasgow 17 Sept 1984. (Canning)

McGEOWN, JOHN (1933): Born Flemington 1906. Educated St Kieran's College, Kilkenny; Scots College, Rome 1927-34. Ordained Rome 1933. St Francis Xavier's, Falkirk 1934-35. St Peter's, Edinburgh 1935-39. Bo'ness 1939-43. St Margaret Mary's, Edinburgh 1943-76. Died Waterford 16 Dec 1977.

McGEOWN, JOHN (1938): Born and educated Ireland. Ordained Kilkenny 1938. Rosewell 1938-42. St Andrew's, Edinburgh 1942-43. Slamannan 1943-47. Dunbar 1947-58. Cowdenbeath 1958-72. Sacred Heart, Grangemouth 1972-79. Retired 1979. Died Ireland 12 July 1986. (Canning)

McGETTIGAN, JOHN: Born Ireland. Educated Ireland, Paris. Ordained Paris 1928. Lent to St A & E. St Patrick's, Edinburgh 1928-30. Kilsyth 1930-38. Resumed his vocation in Ireland 1938. Died Ireland 9 Jan 1977. (Canning)

McGETTIGAN, PATRICK: Born Fauldhouse 1868. Educated Blairs 1883-86; Valladolid 1886-93. Ordained Valladolid 1893. St Patrick's, Edinburgh 1893. Edinburgh Cathedral 1893-98. Tranent 1898-1901. Musselburgh 1901-23. Edinburgh Cathedral 1923-47. Died Peebles 1 June 1947.

McGHEE, CHARLES: see Glasgow Archdiocese

McGILLIGAN, JOHN: see Galloway diocese

McGLOIN, PATRICK: Born and educated Ireland. Ordained Maynooth 1934. Lent to St A & E. Our Lady of Perpetual Succour, Kirkcaldy 1934-39. Slamannan 1939-40. Resumed his vocation in Ireland 1940. Died Ireland 11 Aug 1972. (Canning)

McGLYNN, JAMES: Born and educated Ireland. Ordained Maynooth 1909. Lent to St A & E. St Francis Xavier's, Falkirk 1909-13. Resumed his vocation in Ireland 1913. Died Ireland 9 Feb 1958. (Canning)

McGOVERN, MATTHEW: Born Netherburn, Lanarkshire 1925. Educated Drygrange. Ordained Bothwell 1977. St Mark's, Edinburgh 1977-78. St Peter's, Edinburgh 1978-80. St Mary's, Stirling 1980-82. Died Stirling 20 Feb 1982.

McGOVERN, MICHAEL: Born and educated Ireland. Ordained Waterford for St A & E 1935. St Patrick's, Edinburgh 1935-38. Lochore 1938-40. Linlithgow 1940-80. Died Edinburgh 4 July 1980. (Canning)

McGRAIL, JOHN: Born and educated Ireland. Ordained Kilkenny 1925. Lent to St A & E. Edinburgh Cathedral 1925-26. Rosewell 1926-28. Resumed his vocation in Ireland 1928. Died Ireland 17 Sept 1961. (Canning)

McGRAIL, JOSEPH P: Born Edinburgh 1873. Educated Blairs 1886-92; Scots College, Rome 1892-98. Ordained Rome 1898. Edinburgh Cathedral 1898-1901. St Francis Xavier's, Falkirk 1901-02. Dunbar 1902-09. Kelso 1909-12. Methil 1912-24. Immaculate Conception, Bathgate 1924-39. Died Bathgate 9 March 1939.

McGRAIN, JOHN: Ordained 1911. St Columba's, Edinburgh 1930-31. No further entries.

McGRATH, ALPHONSUS BENEDICT: Born and educated Ireland. Ordained Maynooth 1942. Lent to St A & E. Falkland 1942-43. Methil 1943-45. Lent to Birmingham diocese 1945-50. Resumed his vocation in Ireland 1950. (Canning)

McGRATH, JOHN PATRICK: Born South Queensferry 1921. Educated St Mary's School, Bathgate; Blairs; Coutances; All Hallows College, Dublin; St Edmund's College, Ware. Ordained 1944. St Mary's, Stirling 1944-45. St Margaret's, Dunfermline 1945-46. Addiewell 1946-49. St Margaret Mary's, Edinburgh 1949-51. C/o Diocesan Office 1951-52. No further entries.

McGREGOR, THOMAS P: Born Leith 1901. Educated Blairs 1915-20; Valladolid; St Kieran's College, Kilkenny. Ordained Ossory 1926. Lent to Glasgow Archdiocese: Longriggend 1926-28; St Patrick's, Coatbridge 1928-29. Haddington 1929-31. Sick leave 1931-32. Methil 1932-33. St Margaret's, Dunfermline 1933-37. Edinburgh Cathedral 1937-42. St Francis Xavier's, Falkirk 1942-47. East Calder 1947-48. Innerleithen 1948-52. Whitburn 1952-53. Peebles 1953-54. Retired 1954. Died Glasgow 2 Nov 1969.

McGUIGAN, PATRICK: Born and educated Ireland. Ordained Derry 1947. Lent to St A & E. St Margaret's, Dunfermline 1947-49. Resumed his vocation in Ireland 1949. (Canning)

McGUINNESS, DANIEL: Born Lochgelly 1925. Educated Blairs; St Edmund's College, Ware. Ordained Edinburgh 1949. St Margaret Mary's, Edinburgh 1949-50. Further studies, Cambridge University 1950-53. Loanhead 1953-56. Immaculate Conception, Bathgate 1956-64. Galashiels 1964-69. Jedburgh 1969-72. Whitburn 1972-88. Haddington 1988-.

McHUGH, (Patrick) IGNATIUS: Born and educated Ireland. Ordained Maynooth 1909. Lent to St A & E. St Patrick's, Edinburgh 1911-14. Resumed his vocation in Ireland 1914. (Canning)

McHUGH, JAMES: see Galloway diocese

McHUGH, JOHN: Born and educated Ireland. Ordained Kilkenny for St A & E 1935. Our Lady of Perpetual Succour, Kirkcaldy 1935-37. St Francis Xavier's, Falkirk 1937-40. Burntisland 1940-48. St Patrick's, Edinburgh 1948-62. Chaplain, Good Shepherd Convent, Edinburgh 1962-64. Retired 1964. (Canning)

McHUGH, PATRICK: Born and educated Ireland. Ordained Maynooth 1914. Lent to St A & E. St Mary's, Stirling 1914-17. Inverkeithing 1917-18. Broxburn 1918-19. Resumed his vocation in Ireland 1919. Died Ireland 6 Nov 1964. (Canning)

McILLHARGIE, (McIlhargey) MANUS: Born Ireland. Educated Ireland, Spain. Ordained Salamanca 1932. Lent to St A & E. Musselburgh 1932-37. Armadale 1937-41. Broxburn 1941-45. Died Ireland 4 Nov 1945. (Canning)

MACINTEE, CHARLES: Born Ireland. Educated St Mary's College, Dundalk; Carlow College; St Peter's. Ordained Glasgow 1890. St Francis Xavier's, Falkirk 1890. Died Falkirk 27 May 1890.

MACINTYRE, J ANDREW: Born Glasgow 1872. Educated Blairs 1890-92; Valladolid 1892-99. Ordained Valladolid 1899. Kilsyth 1899-1900. Edinburgh Cathedral 1900-01. Immaculate Conception, Bathgate 1901-02. Cowdenbeath 1902-16. Dunbar 1916-26. Sick leave 1926-27. Peebles 1927-29. Oakley 1929-37. Died Oakley 6 Jan 1937.

McINTYRE, JOSEPH: Born Bathgate 1948. Educated St Mary's High School, Bathgate; Drygrange. Ordained Bathgate 1976. Holy Cross, Edinburgh 1976-80. St Francis Xavier's, Falkirk 1980-82. Kilsyth 1982-85. Kelso 1985-.

McKAY, EDWARD: Born Stirling 1906. Educated Blairs 1921-24; Scots College, Rome 1924-31. Ordained Rome 1931. Our Lady of Perpetual Succour, Kirkcaldy 1931-34. Cowdenbeath 1934-35. Kelty 1935-38. Holy Cross, Edinburgh 1938-42. Kilsyth 1942-44. Polmont 1944-45. Sick leave 1945-46. Lent to Glasgow Archdiocese: St Teresa's, Glasgow 1946-47. No further entries.

McKEAN, BRIAN MICHAEL: Born and educated Ireland. Ordained Edinburgh 1967. St Patrick's, Edinburgh 1967-74. Chaplain, St Andrew's University 1974-79. No further entries. (Canning)

McKEE, JOHN (1906): Born Balerno 1881. Educated Blairs 1896-1901; Scots College, Rome 1901-07. Ordained Rome 1906. Edinburgh Cathedral 1907-08. Professor, Blairs 1908-23. Camelon 1923-29. Our Lady of Perpetual Succour, Kirkcaldy 1929-34. Broxburn 1934-37. Died Broxburn 18 June 1937.

McKEE, JOHN (1936): Born Edinburgh 1912. Educated Blairs 1926-29; Scots College, Rome 1929-31; Oscott College, Birmingham 1931-36. Ordained Edinburgh 1936. Further studies, Cambridge University 1936-39. St Peter's, Edinburgh 1939-40. Professor, Blairs 1940-54. Peebles 1954-63. St Margaret's, Edinburgh 1963-69. Retired 1969. Died Norwich 27 July 1986.

McKEESICK, PETER: Born Dalkeith 1915. Educated Campion House, Osterley; St Edmund's College, Ware. Ordained 1954. St Cuthbert's, Edinburgh 1954-61. St Mark's, Edinburgh 1961-69. Died Edinburgh 2 April 1969.

McKENNA, PATRICK: Born and educated Ireland. Ordained Monaghan 1931. Lent to St A & E. St Columba's, Edinburgh 1931-33. (Address is given as St Patrick's presbytery). Resumed his vocation in Ireland 1933. Died Ireland 29 April 1970. (Canning)

MACKENZIE, COLIN: see Aberdeen diocese

McKENZIE, KENNETH: see Aberdeen diocese

McKEOGH, SAMUEL: Born and educated Ireland. Ordained for St A & E 1890. Edinburgh Cathedral 1890-92. Linlithgow 1892-93. No further entries. (Canning)

McKEON, PETER: Born and educated Ireland. Ordained Monaghan for St A & E 1935. St Columba's, Edinburgh 1935-38. St Ninian's, Edinburgh 1938-39. Duns 1939-52. St John Vianney's, Edinburgh 1952-70. Fauldhouse 1970-85. Retired 1985. (Canning)

McKINNON, JAMES: Ordained 1956. Raploch 1957-64. Whitburn 1964-69. C/o Diocesan Office 1969-70. No further entries.

MACKINNON, MALCOLM: Ordained 1914. Lochgelly 1942-43. (This is probably the Malcolm MacKinnon of Argyll diocese who retired to Barra in 1940).

McLAUGHLIN, BERNARD: Born Balerno 1891. Educated Blairs 1905-11; Scots College, Rome 1911-18. Ordained Rome 1917. St Patrick's, Edinburgh 1918-26. North Berwick 1926-33. Methil 1933-37. Musselburgh 1937-58. Died Musselburgh 22 Feb 1958.

McLAUGHLIN, HENRY: Born Edinburgh 1946. Educated Scotus Academy, Edinburgh; Scots College, Rome. Ordained Rome 1971. Edinburgh Cathedral 1972-76. St Ninian's, Edinburgh 1976-84. On mission in El Salvador 1984-.

McLAUGHLIN, JOHN HENRY: Born Ireland. Educated Ireland, Drygrange. Ordained Edinburgh 1965. Musselburgh 1965-70. No further entries. (Canning)

McLAUGHLIN, THOMAS J: Born Grangemouth 1913. Educated Blairs 1927-31; St Lo 1931-32; Grand Seminaire de Coutances 1932-37. Ordained Edinburgh 1937. Possibly St Mary's, Stirling 1937 (his name appears under both Stirling and St Cuthbert's, Edinburgh). St Cuthbert's, Edinburgh 1937-41. Falkland 1941-43. Bo'ness 1943-49. St Mary's, Stirling 1949-82. Died Stirling 26 Aug 1982.

McLAUGHLIN, WILLIAM: Born Fauldhouse 1906. Educated Blairs 1923-26; Propaganda, Rome 1926-31. Ordained Rome 1931. Portobello 1932-34. Lent to Aberdeen diocese: St Mary's, Inverness 1934-35. Kelso 1935-39. Forces chaplain 1939-45. St Columba's, Edinburgh 1945-85. Died Edinburgh 16 March 1985.

McLEAN, MURDOCH: Ordained 1950. Cowdenbeath 1950-51. No further entries.

McMAHON, JAMES: Born Lochgelly 1919. Educated St Columba's High School, Cowdenbeath; Blairs; Grand Seminaire de Coutances; All Hallows College, Dublin. Ordained Cowdenbeath 1942. Further studies, Cambridge University 1942-44. Our Lady of Perpetual Succour, Kirkcaldy 1944-47. Polmont 1947-48. C/o Diocesan Office 1948-52. St Ninian's, Edinburgh 1952-56. Kelso 1956-65. Addiewell 1965-85. Retired 1985.

McMAHON, JOSEPH: Born Dundee 1929. Educated Campion House, Osterley; Drygrange. Ordained Edinburgh 1960. St John Vianney's,

Edinburgh 1960-64. Hawick 1964-69. Broxburn 1969-72. Bonnyrigg 1972-73. C/o Diocesan Office 1973-74. Portobello 1974-75. Chaplain, Good Shepherd Convent, Edinburgh 1975-77. Chaplain, Heriot Watt University 1977-79. St Magdalene's, Edinburgh 1979-84. Burntisland 1984-89. Sacred Heart, Grangemouth 1989-.

McMAHON, PATRICK: Born Perth 1863. Educated Blairs 1875-81; Issy 1881-82; Scots College, Rome 1882-88. Ordained Rome 1888. St Francis Xavier's, Falkirk 1888. Dunbar 1888-90. Penicuik 1890-92. Lochgelly 1892-1902. West Calder 1902-03. Chaplain, Poor Clares' Convent, Edinburgh 1903-35. Edinburgh address, no parish, 1935-38. No further entries. Not in obits.

MACMANUS, FRANCIS: Born Edinburgh 1869. Educated Blairs, France. Ordained Paris 1895. In various (unspecified) parishes 1895. Edinburgh Cathedral 1895-1900. Bannockburn 1900-19. St Mary's, Stirling 1919-49. Retired 1949. Died Whitburn 1 April 1955.

McMANUS, JOHN ('Bernard' in Canning): Born and educated Ireland. Ordained Kilkenny 1926. Lent to St A & E. Lennoxtown 1926-30. Resumed his vocation in Ireland 1930. Died Glasgow 24 Aug 1952. (Canning)

McMASTER, ARCHIBALD: Born and educated Ireland. Ordained Maynooth 1910. Lent to St A & E. St Francis Xavier's, Falkirk 1910-17. Resumed his vocation in Ireland 1917. Died Ireland 20 Aug 1957. (Canning)

McMEEL, JOHN JAMES: Born and educated Ireland. Ordained Derry for St A & E 1945. St Andrew's, Edinburgh 1945-54. St Patrick's, Edinburgh 1954-62. Musselburgh 1962-65. Duns 1965-69. St Paul's, Glenrothes 1969-. (Canning)

McMULLAN, JOSEPH: Born Denny 1940. Educated Blairs, Drygrange. Ordained Edinburgh 1965. Cowdenbeath 1965-66. St Margaret's, Edinburgh 1966-69. Immaculate Conception, Bathgate 1969-74. St Margaret's, Dunfermline 1974-82. St Peter's, Livingston 1982-.

McNALLY, ANTHONY JOSEPH: Born Edinburgh 1932. Educated Blairs, St Sulpice. Ordained Edinburgh 1955. Methil 1955-62. Larbert 1962-63. C/o Diocesan Office 1963-65. Nigerian mission 1965-66. C/o Diocesan Office 1966-67. Bonnybridge 1967-72. Burntisland 1972-80. St Peter's, Edinburgh 1980-85. Musselburgh 1985-87. Rector, Gillis College 1987-.

McNAMARA, JAMES: Born Edinburgh 1934. Educated Drygrange. Ordained Edinburgh 1962. St Margaret Mary's, Edinburgh 1962-67. Military chaplain 1967-69. C/o Diocesan Office 1969-70. No further entries.

MACNAMARA, MICHAEL BERNARD: Born Edinburgh 1940. Educated St Joseph's College, Mark Cross, Sussex; Drygrange. Ordained Edinburgh 1964. Fauldhouse 1964-67. Armadale 1967-69. St John Vianney's, Edinburgh 1969-70. No further entries.

McNAMARA, PATRICK: Born and educated Ireland. Ordained Kilkenny for St A & E 1886. Lent to Dunkeld diocese: Immaculate Conception, Dundee 1886-87. Edinburgh Cathedral 1887-88. Lochgelly 1888-92. Penicuik 1892-1903. Kilsyth 1903-38. Died Ireland 14 Aug 1938. (Canning)

McNAMEE, BERNARD: Born and educated Ireland. Ordained Maynooth 1912. Lent to St A & E. Edinburgh Cathedral 1912. Lochgelly 1912-17. Resumed his vocation in Ireland 1917. Died Ireland 4 April 1945. (Canning)

McNAY, JOHN WILLIAM: Born Grangemouth 1911. Educated Blairs 1926-32; Oscott College, Birmingham 1932-38. Ordained Edinburgh 1938. St Cuthbert's, Edinburgh 1938-47. Jedburgh 1947-53. Oakley 1953-86. Retired 1986.

McNICHOLL, DANIEL J: Born and educated Ireland. Ordained Derry 1949. Lent to St A & E. Addiewell 1949-51. Resumed his vocation in Ireland 1951. (Canning)

McNULTY, MICHAEL: Born and educated Ireland. Ordained Kilkenny for St A & E 1936. Edinburgh Cathedral 1936-37. Lochgelly 1937-40. Selkirk 1940-49. Whitburn 1949-50. Blackburn 1950-81. Retired to Ireland 1981. (Canning)

McNULTY, PATRICK: Born and educated Ireland. Ordained Dublin for St A & E 1939. St Francis Xavier's, Falkirk 1939-46. St Columba's, Edinburgh 1946-52. Duns 1952-57. C/o Diocesan Office 1957-58. Kilsyth 1958-61. Lochore 1961-72. Died Ireland 1 June 1972. (Canning)

McNULTY, THOMAS: Born Chicago, USA 1933. Educated Blairs, St Sulpice. Ordained Edinburgh 1956. Our Lady of Perpetual Succour, Kirkcaldy 1956-63. Larbert 1963-69. St Columba's, Edinburgh 1969-72. Duns 1972-84. St Kentigern's, Edinburgh 1984-.

McOSCAR, JAMES: Born and educated Ireland. Ordained Edinburgh 1890. St Patrick's, Edinburgh 1890-92. Broxburn 1892-96. Linlithgow 1896-97. Slamannan 1897-1903. Jedburgh 1903-13. Retired 1913. Died Ireland 28 Jan 1932. (Canning)

McSORLEY, DANIEL: Born Ireland. Educated Ireland, Paris. Ordained Paris 1932. Lent to St A & E. St Cuthbert's, Edinburgh 1933-37.

Rosewell 1937-38. Resumed his vocation in Ireland 1938. Died Ireland 4 May 1979. (Canning)

MAESTRI, FEDELE: Born Glasgow 1938. Educated St Ninian's High School, Kirkintilloch; Drygrange. Ordained Edinburgh 1963. St Ninian's, Edinburgh 1963-65. Our Lady of Perpetual Succour, Kirkcaldy 1965-67. Holy Cross, Edinburgh 1967-69. No further entries.

MAGUIRE, BRIAN C: Born and educated Ireland. Ordained Maynooth 1928. Lent to St A & E. Denny 1928-33. Resumed his vocation in Ireland 1933. Died Ireland 20 Aug 1959. (Canning)

MAGUIRE, JAMES (1906): Born Loanhead 1882. Educated Blairs 1896-1901; Issy 1901-03; St Sulpice 1903-06. Ordained Edinburgh 1906. St Margaret's, Dunfermline 1906-08. Cowdenbeath 1908-13. Kelty 1913-26. Lennoxtown 1926-30. Kelty 1930-31. Methil 1931-33. St Margaret's, Dunfermline 1933-36. St Andrew's, Edinburgh 1936-39. Consecrated Coadjuter Bishop of Dunkeld 1939. Died Dundee 10 Oct 1944.

MAGUIRE, JAMES ANTHONY (1959): Born Loanhead 1932. Educated Campion House, Osterley; Drygrange. Ordained Edinburgh 1959. Edinburgh Cathedral 1959-61. Ballingry 1961-65. Bonnybridge 1965-67. No further entries.

MAGUIRE, ROBERT MILLER: Born Glasgow 1948. Educated St Mungo's Academy, Glasgow; Langbank; Blairs; Edinburgh University; Scots College, Rome; Drygrange. Ordained Cambuslang 1977. Denny 1977-80. Edinburgh Cathedral 1980-81. Sick leave 1981-82. No further entries.

MALLOY, JOHN BERNARD: see Dunkeld diocese

MARTIN THOMAS: Born Linlithgow 1910. Educated Blairs 1926-30; Institut Libre, St Lo 1930-31; Grand Seminaire, Coutances 1931-36. Ordained Edinburgh 1936. Burntisland 1936-38. Immaculate Conception, Bathgate 1938-39. Innerleithen 1939-41. Balerno 1941-48. North Berwick 1948-58. St Catherine's, Edinburgh 1958-85. Gorebridge 1985-86. Retired 1986. Died Lasswade 14 June 1988.

MASON, GEORGE ST LAWRENCE: Born and educated Ireland. Ordained Carlow 1891. St Patrick's, Edinburgh 1891-92. Lennoxtown 1892-94. Slamannan 1894-97. Peebles 1897-98. Talla Reservoir 1898-99. Fauldhouse 1899-1909. Innerleithen 1909-30. Retired 1930. Died Ireland 28 April 1939. (Canning)

MAXWELL, JAMES FRANCIS: Born Ireland. Educated Ireland, Oscott College. Ordained Newry for St A & E 1927. Denny 1927-28. Kilsyth 1928-30. Edinburgh Cathedral 1930-31. Penicuik 1931-33. North

Berwick 1933-35. Sick leave 1935-39. Immaculate Conception, Bathgate 1939-40. St Anne's, Edinburgh 1940-41. Sick leave 1941-51. Lent to Paisley diocese: St Charles', Paisley 1951-54. Not in Directories 1954-56. Chaplain, Elie Convent 1956-65. Retired 1965. Died Ireland 17 Oct 1979. (Canning)

MEADE, JOHN L: Ordained 1892. St Patrick's, Edinburgh 1902-05. No further entries.

MEEHAN, WILLIAM: Born and educated Ireland. Ordained Maynooth 1925. Lent to St A & E. Our Lady of Perpetual Succour, Kirkcaldy 1925-30. St Margaret's, Dunfermline 1930-32. Resumed his vocation in Ireland 1932. Died Ireland 6 Aug 1946. (Canning)

MELLON, EDWARD: Born Edinburgh 1884. Educated Blairs 1898-1903; Scots College, Rome 1903-09. Ordained Rome 1908. St Peter's, Edinburgh 1909-15. Our Lady of Perpetual Succour, Kirkcaldy 1915-16. Selkirk 1916-24. Hawick 1924-30. South Queensferry 1930-32. St Columba's, Edinburgh 1932-35. St Margaret's, Dunfermline 1935-36. St Andrew's, Edinburgh 1936-39. Retired 1939. Died Edinburgh 1 Sept 1951.

MELLON, WILLIAM HENRY: Born Edinburgh 1877. Educated Blairs 1892-96; Issy 1896-97; Scots College, Rome 1897-1903. Ordained Rome 1902. Edinburgh Cathedral 1903-04. Balerno 1904-16. St Margaret's, Dunfermline 1916-24. Lennoxtown 1924-26. St Columba's, Edinburgh 1926-35. Consecrated Coadjutor Bishop of Galloway 1935. St Andrew's, Dumfries 1936-44. Succeeded as Bishop of Galloway 1943. Died Dumfries 2 Feb 1952.

MIFSUD, JOSEPH: Ordained 1970. St Ninian's, Edinburgh 1971-72. No further entries.

MILEY, EDWARD IGNATIUS: Born Edinburgh 1873. Educated Blairs 1887-92; Scots College, Rome 1892-98. Ordained Rome 1897. St Margaret's, Dunfermline 1898-1902. Linlithgow 1902-12. Armadale 1912-16. Balerno 1916-22. Bonnybridge in addresses, but not under parishes, 1922-23. Bonnybridge 1923-28. Died Edinburgh 5 July 1928.

MILEY, THOMAS: Born Edinburgh 1871. Educated Blairs 1885-89; Valladolid 1889-94. Ordained Valladolid 1894. Professor, Blairs 1894-1905. St Patrick's, Edinburgh 1905. St Ninian's, Edinburgh 1905-38. Died Edinburgh 28 Dec 1938.

MILLIGAN, HUGH: Born and educated Ireland. Ordained Wexford 1924. Lent to St A & E. Penicuik 1924-25. Lent to Glasgow Archdiocese: Holy Redeemer, Clydebank 1925-28. Retired to Ireland in bad health 1928. Died Ireland 30 July 1952. (Canning)

MITCHELL, ALEXANDER JAMES: Born Edinburgh 1944. Educated Holy Cross Academy, Edinburgh; Drygrange. Ordained Edinburgh 1968. Cowdenbeath 1968-69. Denny 1969-74. Nigerian mission 1974-84. St Philip's, Livingston 1984-89. St Mark's, Edinburgh 1989-.

MOFFATT, VINCENT: Born Edinburgh 1928. Educated Holy Cross Academy, Edinburgh; Campion House, Osterley; Scots College, Rome. Ordained Rome 1959. Professor, Drygrange 1960-71. C/o Diocesan Office 1971-74. No further entries.

MOHAN, EDWARD: Born and educated Ireland. Ordained Wexford for St A & E 1932. St Margaret's, Dunfermline 1932-35. Jedburgh 1935-47. Addiewell 1947-65. Dalkeith 1965-88. Retired 1988. (Canning)

MOLONEY, PHILIP: Born Ireland. Educated Ireland, Rome. Ordained Rome 1906. Lent to St A & E. Lochgelly 1906-09. Went to South Africa for his health. (Canning)

MONAGHAN, ANDREW GEORGE: Born Bathgate 1941. Educated Blairs, Drygrange. Ordained Bathgate 1964. St Francis Xavier's, Falkirk 1964-73. St Cuthbert's, Edinburgh 1973-75. Chaplain, Sacred Heart Convent, Edinburgh 1975-85. Chaplain, St Joseph's Hospital, Rosewell 1985-.

MONAGHAN, JAMES: Born Bathgate 1914. Educated Blairs 1929-33; Valladolid; St Kieran's College, Kilkenny. Ordained Edinburgh 1940. St Andrew's, Edinburgh 1940-42. St Margaret Mary's, Edinburgh 1942-47. Chaplain, Little Sisters of the Poor, Edinburgh 1947-59. Holy Cross, Edinburgh 1959-. Consecrated auxiliary bishop of St A & E 1970. Retired as bishop 1990.

MONAGHAN, THOMAS M: Born Ireland. Educated Blairs, France, Ireland. Ordained Carlow 1882. Dunbar 1883. Our Lady of Perpetual Succour, Kirkcaldy 1883-86. Broxburn 1886-90. Ratho 1890-95. East Calder 1895-1929. Died Edinburgh 29 April 1929. (Canning)

MOONAN, LAWRENCE: Born Bonnybridge 1937. Educated St Modan's High School, Stirling; Drygrange. Ordained Edinburgh 1960. Lochore 1960-61. Rosewell 1961-62. Further studies, College du St Esprit, Louvain 1962-66. St Margaret's, Edinburgh 1966-67. St Andrew's, Fife 1967-69. Oxford University 1969-71. C/o Diocesan Office 1971-72. Bolton, Lancashire 1972-84. No further entries.

MOORE, THOMAS J: Born and educated Ireland. Ordained Kilkenny 1919. Lent to St A & E. Portobello 1919-24. Lent to Glasgow Archdiocese: Longriggend 1924-26. St Peter's, Edinburgh 1926-29. Resumed his vocation in Ireland 1929. Died Ireland 5 April 1948. (Canning)

MORGAN, FREDERICK JOHN: Ordained 1957. St Margaret's, Dunfermline 1958-60. Methil 1960-61. Larbert 1961-62. Naval Chaplain, becoming Vicar General of Royal Navy, 1962-84. Oratory School, Reading 1984-.

MORGAN VAUGHAN F J: see Morgan Frederick John

MORIARTY, FRANCIS: Born and educated Ireland. Ordained Maynooth 1954. Lent to St A & E. Denny 1954-58. Resumed his vocation in Ireland 1958. (Canning)

MORRISON, EDWARD: Born Lochgelly 1891. Educated Blairs 1905-11; Versailles Seminary 1911-15; Institut Catholique, Paris 1915-16. Ordained Paris 1916. Edinburgh Cathedral 1916-17. Broxburn 1917-18. St Mary's, Stirling 1918-19. Slamannan 1919-23. Polmont 1923-26. Loanhead 1926-36. Fauldhouse 1936-48. Died Fauldhouse 17 Feb 1948.

MULHERN, JAMES: ('John' in Canning). Born Ireland. Educated Blairs; Propaganda, Rome. Ordained Rome 1905. Edinburgh Cathedral 1905. Galashiels 1905-06. St Patrick's, Edinburgh 1906-10. Lochgelly 1910-13. Lochore 1913-30. Lennoxtown 1930-36. Died Glasgow 6 May 1936. (Canning)

MULLAN, GEORGE: Born Dunfermline 1862. Educated Blairs 1875-81; Issy 1881-83; St Sulpice 1883-86. Ordained Paris 1886. Edinburgh Cathedral 1886. St Francis Xavier's, Falkirk 1886-87. Slamannan 1887-89. St Margaret's, Dunfermline 1889-1903. St Columba's, Edinburgh 1903-26. St Francis Xavier's, Falkirk 1926-29. Died Falkirk 4 Dec 1929.

MULLAN, (Edward) JAMES: Born and educated Ireland. Ordained Letterkenny 1917. Lent to St A & E. Immaculate Conception, Bathgate 1917-18. St Patrick's, Edinburgh 1918-20. St Mary's, Stirling 1920-23. Resumed his vocation in Ireland 1923. Died Ireland 11 Dec 1960. (Canning)

MULLAN, JOHN D: ('Desmond' in Canning). Born and educated Ireland. Ordained Maynooth 1946. Lent to St A & E. Burntisland 1946-48. Resumed his vocation in Ireland 1948. (Canning)

MULLEN, THOMAS: Born Cowdenbeath 1939. Educated St Columba's School, Cowdenbeath; St Patrick's College, Buchlyvie; Drygrange. Ordained Cowdenbeath 1977. St Mary's, Bathgate 1977-85. Kilsyth 1985-87. Lochore 1987-.

MULLIGAN, WILLIAM: see Aberdeen diocese

MULLINS, DENIS: Born and educated Ireland. Ordained Dublin 1940. Lent to St A & E. St Patrick's, Edinburgh 1940-41. No further entries. (Canning)

MULVEY, MICHAEL: Ordained 1908. St Francis Xavier's, Falkirk 1922-23. St Margaret's, Dunfermline 1923-24. No further entries. (But see p 315)

MULVIHILL, THOMAS: Born and educated Ireland. Ordained Maynooth 1892. Lent to St A & E. St Patrick's, Edinburgh 1892-94. Chaplain to Lord Bute 1894-95. Went to New Zealand for his health 1895. Died there 1906. (Canning)

MURDOCH, CHARLES: Born Kintewline, Blairs 1870. Educated Blairs 1884-88; St Edmund's, Douay 1888-89; Scots College, Rome 1889-95. Ordained Rome 1894. St Patrick's, Edinburgh 1895-98. St Mary's, Stirling 1898-1901. Loanhead 1901-12. Immaculate Conception, Bathgate 1912-19. St Francis Xavier's, Falkirk 1919-26. Died Aberdeen 1 Sept 1926.

MURNIN, MICHAEL: Born Bannockburn 1901. Educated Blairs 1915-20; Valladolid 1920-27. Ordained Valladolid 1927. St Ninian's, Edinburgh 1927-30. Jedburgh 1930-35. Bannockburn 1935-40. Forces chaplain 1940-46. Winchburgh 1946-56. Bonnybridge 1956-84. Retired 1984. Died Lasswade 2 March 1988.

MURPHY, ALEXANDER C: Born Lincoln City 1928. Educated Campion House, Osterley; St Edmund's College, Ware. Ordained Edinburgh 1956. Fauldhouse 1956-59. Sacred Heart, Grangemouth 1959-61. Dalkeith 1961-68. C/o Diocesan Office 1968-69. No further entries.

MURPHY, DANIEL: Born and educated Ireland. Ordained Maynooth 1914. Lent to St A & E. St Patrick's, Edinburgh 1914-15. Kilsyth 1915-23. No further entries. (Canning)

MURPHY, EDWARD J: Born and educated Ireland. Ordained Maynooth 1945. Lent to St A & E. Camelon 1945-50. Resumed his vocation in Ireland 1950. (Canning)

MURPHY, JOHN (1880): Born and educated Ireland. Ordained Thurles 1880. Lent to St A & E. St Mary's, Stirling 1880. Kilsyth 1880-85. Linlithgow 1885-89. Lent to Birmingham 1889. Resumed his vocation in Ireland 1889. Died Ireland 25 Dec 1917. (Canning)

MURPHY, JOHN J (1924): Born and educated Ireland. Ordained Dublin 1924. Lent to St A & E. Edinburgh Cathedral 1924-25. Resumed his vocation in Ireland 1925. Died Ireland 4 Dec 1955. (Canning)

MURPHY, PHILIP: Born East Calder 1895. Educated Blairs; Propaganda, Rome 1914-20. Ordained Rome 1920. St Peter's, Edinburgh 1920-23. St Patrick's, Edinburgh 1923-25. Penicuik 1925-26. Polmont 1926-29. Camelon 1929-36. Tranent 1936-69. Died Tranent 6 Nov 1969.

MURPHY, WILLIAM: Born and educated Ireland. Ordained 1919. Lent to St A & E. Inverkeithing 1919-20. Cowdenbeath 1920-23. Resumed his vocation in Ireland 1923. Died Ireland 8 Nov 1975. (Canning)

MURRAY, IAN: Born Lennoxtown 1932. Educated Blairs, Valladolid. Ordained Valladolid 1956. Lochore 1956-61. St Columba's, Edinburgh 1961-63. Vice-rector, Valladolid 1963-70. Chaplain, Stirling University 1970-78. Cowdenbeath 1978-85. St Ninian's, Edinburgh 1985-87. Rector, Valladolid 1987-.

MURRAY, JOSEPH: Born Saltcoats 1944. Educated St Michael's College, Irvine; Drygrange. Ordained Saltcoats 1974. St Mark's, Edinburgh 1974-79. St Francis Xavier's, Falkirk 1979-80. C/o Diocesan Office 1980-81. In Directories as being at St Patrick's, Edinburgh 1981-82 (under parish and addresses) and also at Lennoxtown 1981-82 (under parish only). No further entries.

MURRAY, THOMAS F P: Born and educated Ireland. Ordained Maynooth 1948. Burntisland 1948-51. St Margaret's, Dunfermline 1951-53. Resumed his vocation in Ireland 1953. (Canning)

MYERS, JAMES LAWRENCE: Born Lennoxtown 1952. Educated St Ninian's High School, Kirkintilloch; Blairs; Valladolid. Ordained Lennoxtown 1976. Portobello 1976-78. Nigerian mission 1978-82. Our Lady of Perpetual Succour, Kirkcaldy 1982-85. Peebles 1985-88. Whitburn 1988-.

NEILSON, ANGUS MONCUR JOSEPH: Born 1923. Educated Blairs; Oscott College, Birmingham. Ordained Edinburgh 1946. Cowie 1946-49. Methil 1949. Kingussie Sanatorium 1949-50. Chaplain, Good Shepherd Convent, Edinburgh 1950-51. Sick leave 1951-54. Chaplain, Balnakeil Convent, Galashiels 1954-55. St Cuthbert's, Edinburgh 1955-58. C/o White Fathers, Uganda 1958-68. C/o Diocesan Office 1968-69. Slamannan 1969. Selkirk 1969-77. Our Lady of Perpetual Succour, Kirkcaldy 1977-84. Died Kirkcaldy 16 Dec 1984.

NELSON, PETER J: Born Edinburgh 1932. Educated Blairs; St Edmund's College, Ware. Ordained Edinburgh 1956. St Andrew's, Fife, studying at University 1956-60. Leave of absence 1960-61. [Further studies?] Oxford 1961-62. Galashiels 1962-64. [Further studies?] Paris 1964-67. St Andrew's, Edinburgh 1967-68. Professor, Drygrange 1968-72. No further entries.

NICHOLSON, JAMES F: Born Leith 1931. Educated Blairs; Oscott College, Birmingham. Ordained 1954. St Columba's, Edinburgh 1954-55. Cowdenbeath 1955-60. St John the Baptist's, Edinburgh 1960-72. Lochore 1972-85. St Gregory's, Edinburgh 1985-.

O'BRIEN, EAMON: Born Ireland. Educated Ireland, Ware. Ordained Ware 1951. Loanhead 1951-52. St Margaret Mary's, Edinburgh 1952-62. Methil 1962-68. St Andrew's, Edinburgh 1968-71. Kelso 1971-77. Selkirk 1977-87. East Calder 1987-. (Canning)

O'BRIEN, FRANCIS: Born 1876. Educated St Edmund's College, Douay; Blairs 1891-94; Valladolid 1894-1902. Ordained Valladolid 1902. St Francis Xavier's, Falkirk 1902-03. Slamannan 1903-07. Oakley 1907-12. Linlithgow 1912-19. Cowdenbeath 1919-28. Denny 1928-47. Died Denny 2 Dec 1947.

O'BRIEN, KEITH MICHAEL PATRICK: Born Ireland. Educated Edinburgh University, Drygrange. Ordained Edinburgh 1965. Holy Cross, Edinburgh 1965-66. Cowdenbeath 1966-72. Kilsyth 1972-74. Immaculate Conception, Bathgate 1974-78. Spiritual Director, Drygrange 1978-80. Rector, Blairs 1980-85. Consecrated Archbishop of St Andrew's and Edinburgh 1985. (Canning)

O'BRIEN, LAURENCE: Born and educated Ireland. Ordained Derry 1947. Lent to St A & E. St Francis Xavier's, Falkirk 1947-49. Resumed his vocation in Ireland 1949. (Canning)

O'CONNELL, DENNIS (Denis): Born and educated Ireland. Ordained Thurles 1941. Lennoxtown 1941-49. Methil 1949-50. St Columba's, Edinburgh 1950-54. Spiritual Director, Blairs 1954-57. St Margaret Mary's, Edinburgh 1957-60. St Gabriel's, Middlesex 1960-61. Stoneyburn 1961-65. Rosewell 1965-72. Kilsyth 1972-87. St Mary's, Glenrothes 1987-. (Canning)

O'CONNOR, MICHAEL: Born and educated Ireland. Ordained Kilkenny 1935. St Francis Xavier's, Falkirk 1935-37. Methil 1937-38. Not in Directories 1938-39. Falkland 1939-41. Armadale 1941-47. Newtongrange 1947-58. Lochgelly 1958-67. Broxburn 1967-86. Retired 1986. (Canning)

O'DOHERTY, ANTHONY: Born and educated Ireland. Ordained Maynooth 1913. Lent to St A & E. St Patrick's, Edinburgh 1913-15. Lennoxtown 1915-16. St Mary's, Stirling 1916-18. Resumed his vocation in Ireland 1918. Died Ireland 9 Feb 1960. (Canning)

O'DONNELL, BERNARD: Born Ireland. Educated Ireland, France. Ordained Buncrana for St A & E 1941. Burntisland 1941-42. St Columba's, Edinburgh 1942-45. Dalkeith 1945-52. St Cuthbert's, Edinburgh 1952-53. Slamannan 1953-63. Gorebridge 1963-65. Cowie 1965-71. Died Stirling 24 Jan 1971. (Canning)

O'DONOGHUE, ALEXANDER H: Born Edinburgh 1887. Educated Blairs

1900-05; Valadolid 1905-06; Scots College, Rome 1906-13. Ordained Rome 1912. Edinburgh Cathedral 1913-16. Professor, Blairs 1916-24. Galashiels 1924-44. Died Galashiels 14 April 1944.

O'FLAHERTY, JAMES: Born and educated Ireland. Ordained Derry 1917. Lent to St A & E. Edinburgh Cathedral 1917-19. Resumed his vocation in Ireland 1919. Died Ireland 11 May 1947. (Canning)

O'HANLON, BERNARD: Born Niddry 1893. Educated Blairs 1907-13; Scots College, Rome 1913-20. Ordained Rome 1920. St Patrick's, Edinburgh 1920-21. Penicuik 1921-23. Cowdenbeath 1923-24. Balerno 1924-26. Kelty 1926-27. Professor, Blairs 1927-37. South Queensferry 1937-69. Retired 1969. Died Saltcoats 7 June 1974.

O'HANLON, JAMES: Born Denny 1913. Educated Blairs 1926-31; St Lo 1931-32; Grand Seminaire, Coutances 1932-37. Ordained Edinburgh 1937. Further studies, Cambridge University 1937-41. Professor, Blairs 1941-43. St Mary's, Stirling 1943-45. Dalkeith 1945-46. Professor, Blairs 1946-54. Raploch 1954-84. Chaplain, St Joseph's Hospital, Rosewell 1984-85. Chaplain, Nazareth House, Lasswade 1985-86. Died Edinburgh 27 Feb 1986.

O'KANE, EDMUND: Born and educated Ireland. Ordained Thurles 1880. Lent to St A & E. St Mary's, Stirling 1880-81. St Patrick's, Edinburgh 1881-84. Kelso 1884-86. Jedburgh 1886-88. Resumed his vocation in Ireland 1888. Died Ireland 16 Nov 1941. (Canning)

O'KEEFE, THOMAS: Born and educated Ireland. Ordained Maynooth 1911. Lent to St A & E. St Margaret's, Dunfermline 1911-13. Lochgelly 1913-14. Resumed his vocation in Ireland 1914. Died Ireland 1 Feb 1973. (Canning)

O'KELLY, SEAN: Born Ireland. Educated Ireland; Scots College, Rome. Ordained Rome 1962. St Cuthbert's, Edinburgh 1963-65. Vice-rector, Scots College, Rome 1965-73. Rector, Scots College, Rome 1973-81. Died Rome 17 Feb 1981. (Canning)

O'LEARY, MICHAEL: Born and educated Ireland. Ordained Maynooth 1909. Lent to St A & E. Immaculate Conception, Bathgate 1909-12. Edinburgh Cathedral 1912-16. Resumed his vocation in Ireland 1916. Died Ireland 2 Jan 1937. (Canning)

O'LEARY, PATRICK: Born Ireland. Educated Ireland, Paris. Ordained Paris 1932. Lent to St A & E. Musselburgh 1937-39. Broxburn 1939-40. Slamannan 1940-43. Resumed his vocation in Ireland 1943. Died Ireland 19 Oct 1972. (Canning)

OLIVER, LEONARD ANDREW: Born Edinburgh 1949. Educated Scotus Academy, Edinburgh; Drygrange. Ordained Edinburgh 1976. St Andrew's, Livingston 1976-81. C/o Diocesan Office 1981-82. No further entries.

O'MAHONY, LIAM: Born and educated Ireland. Ordained Maynooth 1951. Lent to St A & E. Burntisland 1951-55. Hawick 1955-56. Resumed his vocation in Ireland 1956. (Canning)

O'MEARA, MAURICE: Born and educated Ireland. Ordained Waterford 1936. Lent to St A & E. Lennoxtown 1936-41. Lennoxtown in addresses, but not under parishes, 1941-43. Resumed his vocation in Ireland 1943. (Canning)

O'NEILL, HENRY: Born and educated Ireland. Ordained Maynooth 1933. Lent to St A & E. St Patrick's, Edinburgh 1933-38. Resumed his vocation in Ireland 1938. (Canning)

O'RAW, WILLIAM: Born Kilsyth 1876. Educated Blairs 1890-93; Petit Seminaire de Notre Dame des Champs, Paris 1893-95; Scots College, Rome 1895-1900. Ordained Rome 1900. Edinburgh Cathedral 1900-02. Broxburn 1902-04. Lochgelly 1904-05. No address given 1905-06. No further entries.

O'REGAN, PATRICK: see Argyll diocese

O'REILLY, DANIEL: Born and educated Ireland. Ordained Kilkenny 1930. Lent to St A & E. St Mary's, Stirling 1930-33. Resumed his vocation in Ireland 1933. Died Ireland 24 Sept 1961. (Canning)

O'REILLY, FRANCIS: Born and educated Ireland. Ordained Maynooth 1891. St Patrick's, Edinburgh 1891-92. Resumed his vocation in Ireland 1892. Died Ireland 28 July 1924. (Canning)

O'REILLY, JAMES T: Born Ireland. Educated Ireland, Rome. Ordained Rome 1938. Lent to St A & E. Blackburn 1940-43. Resumed his vocation in Ireland 1943. (Canning)

O'REILLY, MICHAEL: Born and educated Ireland. Ordained Maynooth 1939. Lent to St A & E. St Cuthbert's, Edinburgh 1941-45. Resumed his vocation in Ireland 1945. (Canning)

O'SULLIVAN, PATRICK: Born and educated Ireland. Ordained Kilkenny for Liverpool Archdiocese 1947. Lent to St A & E. Lochgelly 1947-48. Lochgelly under addresses, but not under parishes, 1948-49. No further entries. (Canning)

O'SULLIVAN, TIMOTHY: Born and educated Ireland. Ordained Maynooth

1933. Lent to St A & E. Addiewell 1933-36. Resumed his vocation in Ireland 1936. (Canning)

O'SULLIVAN, WILLIAM: Born and educated Ireland. Ordained Kilkenny for Liverpool Archdiocese 1947. Lent to St A & E. St Cuthbert's, Edinburgh 1947-49. (Canning)

OWENS, KENNETH JOHN: Born Grangemouth 1961. Educated St Mungo's High School, Falkirk; Glasgow University; Scots College, Rome. Ordained Grangemouth 1989. St Mary's, Bathgate 1989-.

PAUL, GEORGE: Born Dalavich, Argyll 1958. Educated St Mary's School, Bathgate; worked in the Civil Service; educated for the priesthood Drygrange, Gillis College. Ordained Bathgate 1987. St Andrew's, Livingston 1987. Kilsyth 1987-88. No further entries.

PAUL, JOHN: Born Bathgate 1956. Educated St Mary's Academy, Bathgate; Drygrange. Ordained Bathgate 1985. St Margaret's, Dunfermline 1985-86. Edinburgh Cathedral 1986-.

PAYNE, JAMES: Born Bowhill 1904. Educated Blairs 1918-25; Coutances 1925-30. Ordained Edinburgh 1930. St Patrick's, Edinburgh 1930-34. St Columba's, Edinburgh 1934-38. Dunbar 1938-47. West Calder 1947-73. Retired 1973. Died Musselburgh 3 Dec 1974.

PAYNE, JOSEPH: Born Lochgelly 1874. Educated Blairs 1887-92; Issy 1892-94; St Sulpice 1894-97. Ordained Paris 1897. Linlithgow 1897-98. St Patrick's, Edinburgh 1898-1901. Bo'ness 1901-03. His health gave way 1903. He spent the winter in the Canaries, coming home 1904. Died East Calder 19 June 1904.

PAYNE, MICHAEL ALOYSIUS: Born Bowhill 1903. Educated Blairs 1916-21; Issy 1921-25; St Sulpice 1925-26. Ordained Dundee 1926. St Francis Xavier's, Falkirk 1926-30. Innerleithen 1930-33. Bannockburn 1933-35. Sick leave 1935-36. Chaplain, Dominican Convent, Hawick 1936-43. Died Hawick 21 May 1943.

PHELAN, JAMES: Born and educated Ireland. Ordained Waterford for St A & E 1938. St Columba's, Edinburgh 1938-40. Methil 1940-41. St Andrew's, Edinburgh 1941-43. Larbert 1943-57. St Patrick's, Edinburgh 1957-58. Innerleithen 1958-62. Pittenweem 1962-69. Bo'ness 1969-88. Retired 1988. (Canning)

PHILLIBEN, MICHAEL BERNARD: Born Haddington 1944. Educated St Modan's High School, Stirling; Blairs; Drygrange. Ordained Stirling 1968. St Ninian's, Edinburgh 1968-69. Immaculate Conception, Bathgate 1969-70. No further entries.

PORTELLI, JOSEPH: Born Gozo, Malta 1949. Educated Sacred Heart Seminary, Gozo. Ordained Gozo for Gozo diocese 1974. Came to Scotland 1976. In bad health 1976-81. Kilsyth 1981-82. St Ninian's, Edinburgh 1982-83. St Francis Xavier's, Falkirk 1983-85. Was incardinated into St A & E 1985. Dunbar 1985-88. St Pius X, Kirkcaldy 1988-.

POSTLETHWAITE, GERARD JOSEPH BASIL: Born Warrington 1950. Educated Xaverian College, Manchester; entered Benedictine Order, Ampleforth; Oxford University. Ordained as secular priest Edinburgh 1983. St Ninian's, Edinburgh 1983-85. St Mary's, Stirling 1985-86. Slamannan 1986-89. El Salvador mission 1989-.

POWER, THOMAS WILLIAM: Born Denny 1927. Educated Campion House, Osterley; St Edmund's College, Ware. Ordained Edinburgh 1956. St Andrew's, Edinburgh 1956-58. St Columba's, Edinburgh 1958-61. Edinburgh Cathedral 1961-66. Chaplain, Little Sisters of the Poor, Edinburgh 1966-77. St Joseph's, Edinburgh 1977-87. Lennoxtown 1987-.

PRICE, PATRICK JOSEPH: see Rice, Patrick Joseph

PRUNTY, JAMES: Born and educated Ireland. Ordained Maynooth 1950. Lent to St A & E. Methil 1950-54. Resumed his vocation in Ireland 1954. (Canning)

PURCELL, JOSEPH: Ordained 1934. St Patrick's, Edinburgh 1939-40. No further entries.

PURCELL, MICHAEL: Born Rosewell 1956. Educated St David's High School, Dalkeith; Drygrange. Ordained Rosewell 1981. Edinburgh Cathedral 1981-82. St Mary's, Stirling 1982-84. American College, Leuven, Belgium 1984-87. St Mark's, Edinburgh 1987-88. Kelty 1988-.

QUIGLEY, EDWARD: Ordained 1938. Further studies, Cambridge University 1940-42. Professor, Blairs 1942-43. St Patrick's, Edinburgh 1943-44. Kelso 1944-56. Winchburgh 1956-85. Retired 1985. Died Linlithgow 18 Dec 1989.

QUIGLEY, WILLIAM F: Born Leith 1894. Educated Blairs 1909-14; Propaganda, Rome 1914-20. Ordained Rome 1920. St Mary's, Stirling 1920-24. Broxburn 1924-26. Balerno 1926-28. Blackburn 1928-30. Inverkeithing 1930-31. Kelty 1931-34. West Calder 1934-44. Died Rosewell 25 July 1944.

QUILLE, PATRICK: Born and educated Ireland. Ordained Kilkenny for St A & E 1936. Bonnybridge 1936-38. Immaculate Conception, Bathgate 1938-39. St Andrew's, Edinburgh 1939-40. Further studies, Oxford

University 1940-42. St Andrew's, Edinburgh 1942-46. Chaplain, Good Shepherd Convent, Edinburgh 1946-48. St Peter's, Edinburgh 1948-56. Edinburgh Cathedral 1956-82. Retired 1982. Died Ireland 1 Aug 1984. (Canning)

QUINLAN, JOHN M: Born and educated Ireland. Ordained Cashel 1891. Lent to St A & E. Broxburn 1891-92. St Patrick's, Edinburgh 1892-95. St Margaret's, Dunfermline 1895-96. Broxburn 1896-1901. Resumed his vocation in Ireland 1901. Died Ireland 14 March 1950. (Canning)

QUINN, GEORGE: Born Ireland. Educated Ireland, Paris. Ordained 1933. Lent to St A & E. Immaculate Conception, Bathgate 1933-34. St Francis Xavier's, Falkirk 1934-35. Resumed his vocation in Ireland 1935. (Canning)

QUINN, JAMES: see Paisley diocese

QUINN, PATRICK (1932): Born and educated Ireland. Ordained Carlow for Birmingham diocese 1932. Lent to St A & E; later got exeat to remain there. Our Lady of Perpetual Succour, Kirkcaldy 1941-42. Addiewell 1942-43. Portobello 1943-52. Innerleithen 1952-58. Burntisland 1958-72. Cowdenbeath 1972-77. Slamannan 1977-78. Died Slamannan 2 Jan 1978. (Canning)
Note: entered as 'William' in 1943 Directory.

QUINN, PATRICK (1949): Born and educated Ireland. Ordained Derry 1949. Lent to St A & E. Bannockburn 1949-51. Resumed his vocation in Ireland 1951. Died Ireland 10 March 1967. (Canning)

QUINN, THOMAS: Born Ireland. Educated Ireland, Paris. Ordained Paris 1933. Lent to St A & E. Immaculate Conception, Bathgate 1934-35. Resumed his vocation in Ireland 1935. (Canning)

QUINN, WILLIAM: see Quinn, Patrick (1932)

RADIN, JAMES D: Born Edinburgh 1933. Educated Blairs, Oscott College. Ordained Edinburgh 1957. Sacred Heart, Grangemouth 1957-59. Fauldhouse 1959-64. Tranent 1964-66. St Margaret's, Dunfermline 1966-70. No further entries.

RAE, JAMES: Born Edinburgh 1926. Educated Blairs, Oscott College. Ordained Edinburgh 1951. St Mary's, Stirling 1951-61. St Peter's, Edinburgh 1961-69. Currie 1969-80. Portobello 1980-.

RAFFERTY, KEVIN: Born and educated Ireland. Ordained Kilkenny for St A & E 1957. Linlithgow 1957-67. Dalkeith 1967-77. North Berwick 1977-

86. Broxburn 1986-. Consecrated auxiliary bishop of St A & E 1990. (Canning)

RAINEY, BRENDAN: Born Ireland. Educated Rome. Ordained Rome 1936. Lent to St A & E. Edinburgh Cathedral 1936-42. Resumed his vocation in Ireland 1942. (Canning)

RAMSAY, DANIEL: Born and educated Ireland. Ordained Maynooth 1913. Lent to St A & E. St Patrick's, Edinburgh 1913-14. Lochgelly 1914-16. Lennoxtown 1916-18. Immaculate Conception, Bathgate 1918-20. Penicuik 1920-21. Resumed his vocation in Ireland 1921. Died Ireland 27 Feb 1955. (Canning)

RAMSAY, JOHN CHARLES MAULE: Born London 1926. Educated Eton; Beda, Rome. Ordained Rome 1959. Hawick 1959-64. St Cuthbert's, Edinburgh 1964-70. St Catherine's, Edinburgh 1970-71. Edinburgh, no parish, 1971-74. Denny 1974-75. Spiritual Director, Scots College, Rome 1975-77. Lent to Aberdeen diocese: Tomintoul 1977-78. Winchburgh 1978-79. St John Vianney's, Edinburgh 1979-85. Winchburgh 1985-.

RATTRIE, ROBERT JOHN: Born Edinburgh 1883. Educated Mount Melleray Seminary, County Waterford; Issy 1903-04; Scots College, Rome 1904-09. Ordained Rome 1908. St Mary's, Stirling 1909-14. Slamannan 1914-16. Armadale 1916-25. Died Whitburn 5 Oct 1925.

REGAN, MATHEW I: Born and educated Ireland. Ordained 1934. Lent to St A & E. St Andrew's, Edinburgh 1935-36. St Margaret's, Dunfermline 1936-37. Resumed his vocation in Ireland 1937. Died Ireland 28 Sept 1963. (Canning)

REGAN, MICHAEL BRIAN: Born London 1955. Educated St Aloysius' College, London; Stirling University. Ordained London 1982. St Andrew's, Livingston 1982. St Margaret's, Dunfermline 1982-85. Further studies, Paris 1985-88. Edinburgh Cathedral 1988-.

REGAN, WILLIAM: Born Ireland. Educated Paris. Ordained Paris 1931. Lent to St A & E. St Andrew's, Edinburgh 1931-36. Resumed his vocation in Ireland 1936. (Canning)

REID, HENRY: Born Lochgelly 1937. Educated Blairs, Drygrange. Ordained Edinburgh 1961. St Cuthbert's, Edinburgh 1961-63. Bursar, Drygrange 1963-66. St Peter's, Edinburgh 1966-74. St Andrew's, Livingston 1974-82. On leave 1982-83. No further entries.

REYNOLDS, ROBERT: Born Ireland. Educated Ireland, Salamanca. Ordained 1908. Lent to St A & E. St Francis Xavier's, Falkirk 1908-10. Resumed his vocation in Ireland 1910. Died Ireland 29 Oct 1917. (Canning)

RHATIGAN, THOMAS: Born and educated Ireland. Ordained Kilkenny for St A & E 1947. St Cuthbert's, Edinburgh 1947-48. Further studies, Cambridge University 1948-51. Chaplain, Good Shepherd Convent, Edinburgh 1951-62. Edinburgh Cathedral 1962-68. Loanhead 1968-82. St Mary's, Stirling 1982-. (Canning)

RICE, PATRICK: Born Whifflet 1897. Educated St Mungo's Academy, Glasgow 1908-12; Mount St Michael, Dumfries 1912-19; St Kieran's College, Kilkenny 1919-21; Scots College, Rome 1921-25. Ordained Rome 1924. St Patrick's, Edinburgh 1925-26. Edinburgh Cathedral 1926-28. South Queensferry 1928-30. No address given 1930-31. No further entries.

RIORDAN, JAMES: Born and educated Ireland. Ordained Maynooth 1924. Lent to St A & E. St Patrick's, Edinburgh 1924-26. Resumed his vocation in Ireland 1926. (Canning)

RITTER, HENRY F: see Aberdeen diocese

ROBERTSON, DAVID: Born Banffshire 1867. Educated Blairs; Scots College, Rome. Ordained Rome 1895. Linlithgow 1895-96. St Mary's, Stirling 1896-98. St Francis Xavier's, Falkirk 1898-1901. Jedburgh 1901-03. St Margaret's, Dunfermline 1903-16. Lennoxtown 1916-24. Selkirk 1924-28. Died Edinburgh 29 Feb 1928.

ROBINSON, JOHN GEORGE: Born Edinburgh 1941. Educated Campion House, Osterley; Drygrange. Ordained Edinburgh 1972. Portobello 1972. Holy Cross, Edinburgh 1972-76. Edinburgh Cathedral 1976-81. Galashiels 1981-84. Melrose 1984-87. Selkirk 1987-.

ROBSON, STEPHEN: Born Carlisle 1951. Educated Carlisle Grammar School; Lanark Grammar School; Edinburgh University; Napier College, Edinburgh; Drygrange. Ordained Carlisle 1979. Edinburgh Cathedral 1979. Our Lady of Perpetual Succour, Kirkcaldy 1979-81. Professor, Blairs 1981-86. Holy Cross, Edinburgh 1986-88. Duns 1988-89. No further entry.

ROCHE, ALFRED P: Born and educated Ireland. Ordained 1878. St Patrick's, Edinburgh 1888-89. Edinburgh Cathedral 1889-90. Tranent 1890-98. No address given 1898-1902. Selkirk 1902-06. No further entries. (Canning)

ROCHE, RICHARD: Ordained 1923. Our Lady of Perpetual Succour, Kirkcaldy 1927-31. No further entries.

RODGERS, GEORGE EDWARD: Born Musselburgh 1937. Educated Campion House, Osterley; Drygrange. Ordained Musselburgh 1969. Our

Lady of Perpetual Succour, Kirkcaldy 1969-77. Bonnybridge 1977-84. Duns 1984-88. Inverkeithing 1988-.

ROGERSON, JOHN: Born Edinburgh 1923. Educated Fort Augustus School; Blairs; St Edmund's College, Ware. Ordained Edinburgh 1947. Broxburn 1947-50. St Peter's, Edinburgh 1950-51. St Margaret's, Dunfermline 1951-67. Selkirk 1967-69. South Queensferry 1969-81. Blackburn 1981-.

ROONEY, GERARD PAUL: Born Ireland. Educated Langbank, Blairs, Drygrange. Ordained Burntisland 1974. St Peter's, Edinburgh 1974-76. St Paul's, Edinburgh 1976-81. Professor, Drygrange 1981-82. No further entries. (Canning)

ROONEY, WILLIAM: Born Edinburgh 1857. Educated Blairs 1873-77; St Edmund's, Douay 1877-79; Scots College, Rome 1879-85. Ordained Rome 1884. Edinburgh Cathedral 1885-86. Vice-rector, Scots College, Rome 1886-91. Denny 1891-1902. Galashiels 1902-24. St Andrew's, Fife 1924-29. Peebles 1929-41. Died Peebles 25 May 1941.

ROURKE, PATRICK J A: Born and educated Ireland. Ordained Dublin for St A & E 1941. St Margaret's, Dunfermline 1941-45. Bonnybridge 1945-57. Duns 1957-64. Holy Spirit, Stirling 1964-. (Canning)

RYAN, JAMES: Born and educated Ireland. Ordained Maynooth 1919. Lent to St A & E. Edinburgh Cathedral 1919-21. Resumed his vocation in Ireland 1921. Died Ireland 12 Nov 1964. (Canning)

RYAN, JOHN: Born and educated Ireland. Ordained Maynooth 1944. Lent to St A & E. Dalkeith 1944-53. Resumed his vocation in Ireland 1953. (Canning)

RYAN, MICHAEL: Born and educated Ireland. Ordained Dublin 1924. Lent to St A & E. St Patrick's, Edinburgh 1924-25. Resumed his vocation in Ireland 1925. Died Ireland 1 June 1961. (Canning)

SADDLER, BRIAN WILLIAM: Born Edinburgh 1944. Educated Campion House, Osterley; Drygrange. Ordained Edinburgh 1969. St Francis Xavier's, Falkirk 1969-70. St John Vianney's, Edinburgh 1970-72. Our Lady of Perpetual Succour, Kirkcaldy 1972-78. St Andrew's, Livingston 1978-82. On leave 1982-83. No further entries.

SAUNDERSON, WILLIAM: Born and educated Ireland. Ordained Kilkenny for St A & E 1906. West Calder 1906-08. New Zealand 1908-23 and from 1924. In bad health. Died Musselburgh 17 July 1946. (Canning)

SAVAGE, THOMAS: Ordained 1944. St Cuthbert's, Edinburgh 1945-47. No further entries.

SCOTT, BRYAN (Brian): Born and educated Ireland. Ordained Kilkenny 1942. Lent to St A & E. Rosewell 1942-43. Edinburgh Cathedral 1943-47. Resumed his vocation in Ireland 1947. (Canning)

SCOTT, JAMES: Born and educated Ireland. Ordained 1919. Lent to St A & E. St Francis Xavier's, Falkirk 1919-22. Immaculate Conception, Bathgate 1922-27. Resumed his vocation in Ireland 1927. Died Ireland 10 Aug 1972. (Canning)

SHANNON, HUGH DESMOND: Born Sheffield 1945. Educated Fort Augustus School, Drygrange. Ordained Edinburgh 1970. St Joseph's, Edinburgh 1970-76. St Paul's, Edinburgh 1976-78. C/o Diocesan Office 1978-79. St Andrew's, Livingston 1979-82. No further entries.

SHARPLEY, CHARLES: Born and educated Ireland. Ordained Maynooth 1925. Lent to St A & E. St Francis Xavier's, Falkirk 1925-26. Edinburgh Cathedral 1926-30. Address Cathedral House, but not under parish, 1930-31. No further entries in Directories. Retired in bad health 1933. (Canning)

SHEAHAN, PHILIP: Born and educated Ireland. Ordained Maynooth 1889. Lent to St A & E. St Mary's, Stirling 1889-96. Resumed his vocation in Ireland 1896. Died Ireland 19 Sept 1943. (Canning)

SHIELS, ANDREW: Born Falkirk 1921. Educated Osterley; Oscott College, Birmingham. Ordained 1954. Gorebridge 1954-55. St Columba's, Edinburgh 1955-62. Portobello 1962-68. Kilsyth 1968-71. Kelty 1971-80. West Calder 1980-84. Died Falkirk 12 Oct 1984.

SHIVERS, PATRICK: Born Ireland. Educated Blairs; Petit Seminaire de St Riquier; Douay; Issy; Scots College, Rome. Ordained Rome 1883. St Mary's, Stirling 1884-87. Hawick 1887-92. Our Lady of Perpetual Succour, Kirkcaldy 1892-98. Linlithgow 1898-1902. Denny 1902-16. Died Denny 12 Oct 1916. (Canning)

SIMPSON, DANIEL: Born Edinburgh 1921. Educated Osterley; St Edmund's College, Ware. Ordained Edinburgh 1955. St Columba's, Edinburgh 1955-57. Nigerian mission 1957-.

SINNOTT (Synott), GERALD: Born and educated Ireland. Ordained Carlow 1926. Lent to St A & E. Rosewell 1926-30. Rosewell in addresses, but not under parishes, 1930-31. Resumed his vocation in Ireland 1931. Died Ireland 6 Feb 1957. (Canning)
Note: given as 'John' in 1927 Directory.

SINNOTT, JOHN: see Sinnott, Gerald

SLATTERY, JOHN: Born and educated Ireland. Ordained Maynooth 1907. Lent to St A & E. Broxburn 1908-10. St Patrick's, Edinburgh 1910-11. Joined Redemptorist Fathers 1911. Died Clapham 7 March 1956. (Canning)

SLOAN, MICHAEL: Born Ireland. Educated Campion House, Osterley; Drygrange. Ordained Kilkeel 1974. St Francis Xavier's, Falkirk 1974-79. St Mark's, Edinburgh 1979-83. Holy Cross, Edinburgh 1983-85. Hawick 1985-. (Canning)

SMITH, ANTHONY: Born Ireland. Educated Ireland, Paris. Ordained Paris 1938. Lent to St A & E. Lochgelly 1940-42. Burntisland 1942-44. Resumed his vocation in Ireland 1944. (Canning)

SMITH, BERNARD A: Born and educated Ireland. Ordained Maynooth 1912. Lent to St A & E. St Patrick's, Edinburgh 1912-13. St Francis Xavier's, Falkirk 1913-16. Immaculate Conception, Bathgate 1916-17. Resumed his vocation in Ireland 1917. (Canning)

SMITH, BRENDAN: see Motherwell docese

SMITH, JAMES: Born Edinburgh 1956. Worked as electrician. Educated for priesthood St Patrick's College, Buchlyvie; Drygrange; Gillis College. Ordained Edinburgh 1989. Broxburn 1989-.

SMITH, JOHN: Ordained 1973. Denny 1988-89. Denny in addresses, but not under parishes, 1989-.

SMITH, PETER: Born and educated Ireland. Ordained Maynooth 1940. Lent to St A & E. Our Lady of Perpetual Succour, Kirkcaldy 1940-41. Oakley 1941-46. Linlithgow 1946. Resumed his vocation in Ireland 1946. (Canning)

SMITH, STANISLAUS JOSEPH: Born Newtongrange 1914. Educated Holy Cross Academy, Edinburgh; Campion House, Osterley; Scots College, Rome. Ordained Rome 1952. Cowdenbeath 1953-55. Musselburgh 1955-58. St Cuthbert's, Edinburgh 1958-61. Immaculate Conception, Bathgate 1961-69. Bowhill 1969-81. Died Bowhill 26 May 1981.

SMITH-STEINMETZ, ALFRED: Born Oakley 1881. Educated Scots College, Rome 1899-1906. Ordained Rome 1905. St Patrick's, Edinburgh 1906-12. North Berwick 1912-19. Oakley 1919-29. St Margaret's, Dunfermline 1929-33. No further entries.

SMITH-STEINMETZ, ALISTAIR: Born Edinburgh 1877. Educated St Cuthbert's College, Ushaw 1897-99; Scots College, Rome 1899-1903. Ordained Edinburgh 1903. St Francis Xavier's, Falkirk 1903-04. Galashiels 1904-05. In London 1905-07. No further entries.

SMYTH (Smith), PETER: Born and educated Ireland. Ordained Cavan 1944. Lent to St A & E. Sacred Heart, Grangemouth 1946-47. St Cuthbert's, Edinburgh 1947-52. Resumed his vocation in Ireland 1952. Died Ireland 26 Jan 1974. (Canning)

SOMERS, RICHARD: Born and educated Ireland. Ordained 1945. Broxburn 1945-46. Further studies, Oxford University 1946-48. Polmont 1948-50. St Cuthbert's, Edinburgh 1950-55. St Francis Xavier's, Falkirk 1955-56. St Ninian's, Edinburgh 1956-58. Lennoxtown 1958-64. Blanefield 1964-70. Tranent 1970-. (Canning)

STAPLES, FRANCIS: Born and educated Ireland. Ordained Maynooth 1947. Lent to St A & E. St Margaret Mary's, Edinburgh 1947-48. Resumed his vocation in Ireland 1948. (Canning)

STUART, ALEXANDER: Born Glenlivet 1860. Educated Blairs 1872-77; Scots College, Rome 1877-83. Ordained Rome 1883. Edinburgh Cathedral 1883-85. Vice-rector, Scots College, Rome 1885-86. St Patrick's, Edinburgh 1886-88. St Columba's, Edinburgh 1888-1903. Edinburgh Cathedral 1903-23. Died Edinburgh 20 Sept 1923.

STUART, JOHN L (1895): Born Glenlivet 1870. Educated Blairs 1884-88; Scots College, Rome 1888-95. Ordained Rome 1895. Lennoxtown 1895-97. Edinburgh Cathedral 1897-98. St Francis Xavier's, Falkirk 1898-99. Sick leave 1899-1906. Cathedral House in addresses, but no mention under parishes, 1906-07. Edinburgh Cathedral 1907-08. Haddington 1908-14. Forces chaplain 1914-20. Immaculate Conception, Bathgate 1920-22. West Calder 1922-30. Fauldhouse 1930-35. St Columba's, Edinburgh 1935-45. Retired 1945. Died Musselburgh 15 Feb 1947.

STUART, JOHN (1896): see Dunkeld diocese

STUART, ROBERT L: see Aberdeen diocese

SWEENEY, ANTONY: see Dunkeld diocese

SWEENEY, JOSEPH: Ordained 1935. Lochore 1944-46. No further entries.

TABONE, LORETO: Born Gozo, Malta 1948. Educated Sacred Heart Seminary, Gozo. Ordained for Gozo diocese 1974. Came to St A & E 1976. St Columba's, Edinburgh 1977-79. Broxburn 1979-87. Cowie 1987-.

TAYLOR, CHARLES: Ordained 1910. Cowdenbeath 1925-27. Lochgelly 1927-29. Stirling under addresses, but not under parishes, 1929-31. No further entries.

THOMSON, FRANCIS: Born Edinburgh 1917. Educated Edinburgh University; Cambridge University; St Edmund's College, Ware. Ordained Edinburgh 1946. Kilsyth 1946-48. Further studies, Rome 1948-49. St Andrew's, Fife 1949-52. St Cuthbert's, Edinburgh 1952-53. Professor, Drygrange 1953-60. Rector, Blairs 1960-64. Consecrated Bishop of Motherwell 1965. Retired as bishop 1983. Biggar 1983-87. Died Glasgow 6 Dec 1987.

THOMSON, JAMES: Ordained 1963. St Margaret Mary's, Edinburgh 1963-67. Immaculate Conception, Bathgate 1967-69. Cowie 1969-72. Fallin 1972-79. Chaplain, St Andrew's University 1979-83. No further entries.

THORNHILL, RICHARD: Born and educated Ireland. Ordained Maynooth 1914. Lent to St A & E. St Patrick's, Edinburgh 1914-17. St Francis Xavier's, Falkirk 1917-25. Resumed his vocation in Ireland 1925. Died Ireland 1 May 1962. (Canning)

TONER, STEPHEN DAVID: Born Kilmarnock 1956. Educated Scotus Academy, Edinburgh; University of Alberta, Edmonton; Drygrange. Ordained Edinburgh 1983. Edinburgh Cathedral 1983-85. Musselburgh 1985-86. No further entries.

TONNER, JAMES F: Born Ireland. Educated Blairs; Scots College, Rome. Ordained Rome 1908. Lennoxtown 1909-15. Winchburgh 1915-29. East Calder 1929-37. Died East Calder 28 May 1937. (Canning)

TORSNEY, NICHOLAS: Born Bathgate 1926. Educated Blairs; Scots College, Rome. Ordained Rome 1950. St John's, Edinburgh 1950-57. Died Stirling 16 April 1957.

TRACEY, JAMES GERARD: Born Lennoxtown 1961. Educated St Ninian's High School, Kirkintilloch; Drygrange; Gillis College. Ordained Lennoxtown 1988. Musselburgh 1988. Holy Cross, Edinburgh 1988-.

TURNER, JAMES: Born Edinburgh 1896. Educated Campion House, Osterley 1930-32; St Edmund's College, Ware 1932-37. Ordained Edinburgh 1937. St Andrew's, Edinburgh 1937-50. St Patrick's, Edinburgh 1950-60. Died London 28 Feb 1960.

TURNER, MICHAEL JOSEPH: Born Penrith 1855. Educated Blairs 1867-72; St Edmund's, Douay 1872-73; Issy 1873-75; St Sulpice 1875-76; Blairs 1876-77; St Sulpice 1877-78. Ordained Edinburgh 1879. Edinburgh Cathedral 1879-82. Cramond 1882-87. South Queensferry 1887-90. Kilsyth 1890-1903. Lennoxtown 1903-12. St Francis Xavier's, Falkirk 1912-19. Peebles 1919-27. Retired 1927. Died Edinburgh 14 Dec 1928.

TWEEDIE, JOHN G: Born Armadale 1926. Educated Blairs; St Edmund's College, Ware. Ordained Edinburgh 1949. Edinburgh Cathedral 1949-70. St Magdalene's, Edinburgh 1970-73. St Francis Xavier's, Falkirk 1973-.

URQUHART, JOHN: Born Bowhill 1934. Educated Blairs, Valadolid, Drygrange. Ordained Edinburgh 1959. St Joseph's, Edinburgh 1959-70. Galashiels 1970-72. Chaplain, Balnakiel Convent, Galashiels 1972-75. Galashiels 1975-79. St Paul's, Edinburgh 1979-84. St Margaret's, Dunfermline 1984-89. Larbert 1989-.

WALLS, MICHAEL J: Born and educated Ireland. Ordained 1935. Lent to St A & E. St Mary's, Stirling 1936-37. Resumed his vocation in Ireland 1937. (Canning)

WALSH, ANDREW: Born and educated Ireland. Ordained 1939. Lent to St A & E. Edinburgh Cathedral 1939-43. Resumed his vocation in Ireland 1943. Died Ireland 9 Dec 1973. (Canning)

WALSH, JAMES BERNARD: Born Ireland. Educated Ireland, Paris. Ordained Paris 1939. St Ninian's, Edinburgh 1939-44. Haddington 1944-69. Immaculate Conception, Bathgate 1969-80. Retired to Ireland 1980. (Canning)

WALSH (Walshe), JOHN: Born and educated Ireland. Ordained 1947. Lent to St A & E. Our Lady of Perpetual Succour, Kirkcaldy 1947-51. Resumed his vocation in Ireland 1951. (Canning)

WALSH, MICHAEL: Born and educated Ireland. Ordained for St A & E 1947. St Patrick's, Edinburgh 1947-51. St Margaret Mary's, Edinburgh 1951-52. C/o Diocesan Office 1952-53. Not in Directories 1953-58. Lochgelly 1958-67. Dunbar 1967-85. Retired to Ireland 1985. (Canning)

WALSH, THOMAS: Born Ireland. Educated Ireland, Paris. Ordained Paris 1933. Lent to St A & E. St Ninian's, Edinburgh 1933-35. Resumed his vocation in Ireland 1935. (Canning)

WALSHE (Walsh), MAURICE: Born and educated Ireland. Ordained Maynooth 1951. Lent to St A & E. Broxburn 1951-55. Resumed his vocation in Ireland 1955. (Canning)

WARD, DOLTY: Born South Queensferry 1904. Educated St Eunan's College, Letterkenny; Scots College, Rome. Ordained Rome 1930. St Patrick's, Edinburgh 1930-33. Haddington 1933-44. Sacred Heart, Grangemouth 1944-72. Innerleithen 1972-76. Died Innerleithen 18 Feb 1976.

WARD, JOHN (1927): Born Edinburgh 1901. Educated Blairs 1918-21;

Scots College, Rome 1921-28. Ordained Rome 1927. St Cuthbert's, Edinburgh 1928-30. Duns 1930-32. Blackburn 1932-36. Dunbar 1936-38. Sacred Heart, Grangemouth 1938-44. Dalkeith 1944-52. Portobello 1952-72. North Berwick 1972-77. Died Haddington 11 Oct 1977.

WARD, JOHN (1934): Born Edinburgh 1910. Educated Blairs 1924-28; St Lo 1928-29; Grand Seminaire, Coutances 1929-34. Ordained Edinburgh 1934. St Mary's, Stirling 1934-35. Lent to Aberdeen diocese: St Mary's, Inverness 1935-37. Denny 1937-38. Duns 1938-39. Forces chaplain 1939-41. St Francis Xavier's, Falkirk 1941-42. Holy Cross, Edinburgh 1942-48. Balerno 1948-57. Larbert 1957-72. Musselburgh 1972-84. Retired 1984. Died Edinburgh 11 May 1986.

WARD, JOSEPH AUGUSTINE: Born Edinburgh 1899. Educated Blairs 1913-15; Scots College, Rome 1915-22. Ordained Rome 1922. Broxburn 1922-24. Lennoxtown 1924-26. Leave of absence 1926-27. St Columba's, Edinburgh 1927-28. Selkirk 1928-30. Blackburn 1930-32. Duns 1932-35. Sick leave 1935-37. No further entry.

WATT, THOMAS: Born Glasgow 1912. Educated Campion House, Osterley 1930-32; Oscott College, Birmingham 1932-38. Ordained Edinburgh 1938. Holy Cross, Edinburgh 1938-39. St Andrew's, Edinburgh 1939-41. Kilsyth 1941-42. Edinburgh Cathedral 1942-43. Lennoxtown 1943-45. Hawick 1945-46. No further entries.

WELSH, FRANCIS: Born Motherwell 1932. Educated St Joseph's School, Motherwell; Technical College, Stafford; Atholl Crescent College of Domestic Science, Edinburgh; Drygrange. Ordained Linlithgow 1981. St Cuthbert's, Edinburgh 1981-86. Denny 1986-88. Sick leave 1988-.

WELSH, WALTER: Born Stirling 1886. Educated Blairs 1900-03; Valladolid 1903-05; Propaganda, Rome 1905-12. Ordained Rome 1912. St Patrick's, Edinburgh 1912-18. Sacred Heart, Grangemouth 1918-38. St Francis Xavier's, Falkirk 1938-54. Died Edinburgh 12 March 1954.

WHEELER, WILLIAM: see Galloway diocese

WHELAHAN, MICHAEL: Born Edinburgh 1889. Educated Blairs 1905-07; Valladolid 1907-16. Ordained Edinburgh 1917. Our Lady of Perpetual Succour, Kirkcaldy 1917-24. Haddington 1924-25. Armadale 1925-32. Cowdenbeath 1932-36. Lennoxtown 1936-49. Died Lourdes 11 Sept 1949.

WHITE, HUGH GOLDIE: Born Bathgate 1940. Educated Drygrange. Ordained Bathgate 1963. Further studies, Rome 1963-66. North Berwick 1966-67. Rosewell 1967-68. Professor, Drygrange 1968-79. Chaplaincy, London 1979-82. Loanhead 1982-89. Virginia, USA 1989-.

WHITE, JAMES: Born and educated Ireland. Ordained 1932. Lent to St A & E. St Patrick's, Edinburgh 1932-35. Resumed his vocation in Ireland 1935. (Canning)

WIGGINS, ROBERT: Born and educated Ireland. Ordained Maynooth 1936. Lent to St A & E. St Andrew's, Edinburgh 1936-37. (Canning)

WILSON, WILLIAM: Born Portobello 1908. Educated Blairs 1924-28; St Lo 1928-29; Coutances 1929-34; Oscott 1934. Ordained Edinburgh 1934. St Cuthbert's, Edinburgh 1935-36. St Mary's, Stirling 1936-46. Edinburgh Cathedral 1946-47. St Margaret Mary's, Edinburgh 1947-49. Falkland 1949-53. Whitburn 1953-61. Ballingry 1961-87. Retired 1987.

WOOD, JOHN D: Born Newcastle on Tyne 1879. Educated Blairs 1893-97; Scots College, Rome 1897-1904. Ordained Rome 1903. Broxburn 1904-05. St Patrick's, Edinburgh 1905-06. St Francis Xavier's, Falkirk 1906-09. Penicuik 1909-26. Rosewell 1926-42. Died Rosewell 12 Nov 1942.

WOODS, HENRY: Born Edinburgh 1853. Educated Blairs 1870-74; Douay 1874-76; Issy 1876-77; Scots College, Rome 1877-82. Ordained Rome 1881. Edinburgh Cathedral 1882. St Francis Xavier's, Falkirk 1882. Edinburgh Cathedral 1882-84. Denny 1884-87. Fauldhouse 1887-90. Broxburn 1890-91. St Francis Xavier's, Falkirk 1891-95. St Patrick's, Edinburgh 1895-98. Our Lady of Perpetual Succour, Kirkcaldy 1898-1902. Chaplain, Poor Clares Convent, Edinburgh 1902-03. Chaplain, Little Sisters of the Poor, Edinburgh 1903-07. Sick leave 1907-09. Falkland 1909-14. Oakley 1914-19. Chaplain, Little Sisters of the Poor, Edinburgh 1919-21. Retired 1921. Died Musselburgh 23 April 1936.

WOODS, JOHN: Born and educated Ireland. Ordained Kilkenny 1942. Lent to St A & E. Edinburgh Cathedral 1942-49. Resumed his vocation in Ireland 1949. (Canning)

WYNNE, STEPHEN: Born Edinburgh 1930. Educated Holy Cross Academy, Edinburgh; Scots College, Rome. Ordained Rome 1958. St Joseph's, Edinburgh 1958-59. Lennoxtown 1959-61. Sacred Heart, Grangemouth 1961-70. No further entries.

Parishes

ARCHBISHOPS: 1864-83 John Strain (ED). 1885-92 William Smith (ED). 1892-1900 Angus MacDonald (WD). 1900-28 James Smith (ED). 1929-50 Andrew J McDonald OSB. 1951-85 Gordon Gray (St A & E). 1985- Keith O'Brien (St A & E)
Auxiliary Bishops: 1917-30 Henry Grey Graham (Glasgow). 1970-90 James Monaghan (St A & E). 1990- Kevin Rafferty (St A & E).

ABERDOUR – ST TERESA'S RESIDENTIAL NURSERY: CHAPLAINS
1948-49 Charles J Kelly.

ADDIEWELL
Heads: 1913-28 Henry J Kenny. 1928-37 Ewen J Connolly. 1937-47 Michael Kelly. 1947-65 Edward Mohan. 1965-85 James A McMahon. 1985-87 Alexander Bremner.
Assistants: 1933-36 Timothy O'Sullivan. 1936-40 Christopher McAllister. 1940-42 Patrick Cunningham. 1942-43 William Quinn. 1943-46 Roderick Gemmell. 1946-49 John McGrath. 1949-51 Daniel McNicholl. 1951-52 Eric Gordon. 1952-53 David P Brown.
From 1987 served from Stoneyburn.

ARMADALE
Heads: 1906-12 Thomas McDonna. 1912-16 Edward Miley. 1916-25 Robert J Rattrie. 1925-32 Michael Whelahan. 1932-33 vacant. 1933-37 Gerald Dorrian. 1937-41 Manus McIlhargie. 1941-47 Michael O'Connor. 1947-76 John J Donnelly. 1976-77 vacant. 1977-84 Charles J Kelly. 1984-88 Liam Healy. 1988- Thomas Hennessy.
Assistants: 1928-30 James I Finnegan (possibly). 1959-67 Brian Halloran. 1967-69 Michael B Macnamara. 1969-77 Thomas Hennessy.

BALERNO: 1903-04 Bernard Eardley. 1904-16 William Mellon. 1916-22 Edward Miley. 1922-24 Thomas J Ferrigan. 1924-26 Bernard O'Hanlon. 1926-28 William Quigley. 1928-30 William Maccabe. 1930-41 William Grant. 1941-48 Thomas Martin. 1948-57 John Ward (1934). 1957-66 Eric Gordon. From 1966 served from Currie.

BALFRON (Blanefield, Strathblane)
The location of this Mission was changed several times between 1889 and 1912.
Balfron: 1889-90 John J Foley.
Blanefield: 1890-92 John J Foley.
Strathblane: 1892-99 John J Foley. 1899-1911 served from Lennoxtown.
Balfron: 1911-12 Peter Burns. 1912-51 served from Lennoxtown.
From 1951 Blanefield was a separate parish (see below)

BALLINGRY
Head: 1961-87 William Wilson.
Assistants: 1961-65 James A Maguire. 1965-66 Daniel Boyd.
From 1987 served from Lochore.

BANKNOCK: 1967-81 William W Henery. 1981-85 Patrick Clarke. 1985- Peter Lyons.

BANNOCKBURN
Heads: 1900-19 Francis J Macmanus. 1919-33 James MacDonald (1903).

1933-35 Michael Payne. 1935-40 Michael Murnin. 1940-87 Christopher McAllister. 1987- John Callaghan.

Assistants: 1934-35 Daniel Logue. 1946-47 Daniel Joseph Boyle (1940). 1949-51 Patrick Quinn. 1956-57 Brian P Byrne. 1976-79 John Callaghan.

BATHGATE – IMMACULATE CONCEPTION

Heads: 1876-88 Thomas O'Carroll (ED). 1888-93 Patrick Morris (ED). 1893-99 Joseph Hannan. 1899-1912 Peter McDaniel. 1912-19 Charles Murdoch. 1919-24 Patrick Green. 1924-39 Joseph P McGrail. 1939-69 Thomas Davitt. 1969-80 James B Walsh. 1980-84 Daniel Patrick Boyle (1940). 1984-88 Lawrence Glancey. 1988-89 Gordon R Brown. 1989- Michael Burns.

Assistants: 1901-02 J Andrew MacIntyre. 1904-05 William Holland. 1909-12 Michael O'Leary. 1912-13 Peter J Burns. 1913-16 Richard Delaney. 1916-17 Bernard A Smith. 1917-18 James Mullan. 1918-20 Daniel Ramsay. 1920-22 John Stuart. 1922-27 James Scott. 1927-30 Thomas Davitt. 1930-32 Joseph Campbell (Argyll). 1931-33 Joseph McElhenney. 1932-33 Andrew J Cameron (Aberdeen). 1933-34 George Quinn. 1933-38 John Kerr. 1934-35 Thomas Quinn. 1935-37 James Brennan (1934). 1937-38 Thomas A Kelly (1926) (Dunkeld). 1938-39 Thomas Martin. 1938-39 Patrick Quille. 1939-40 James Maxwell. 1939-41 John McCallum. 1940-47 James McCabe. 1941-43 Francis McFarlane. 1942-45 Walter Glancy. 1943-47 Michael Jackson. 1947-53 Daniel Joseph Boyle (1940). 1947-61 Gerald McCabe. 1954-56 Robert L Stuart (Aberdeen). 1956-64 Daniel McGuinness. 1961-69 Stanislaus Smith. 1964-70 Liam Healy. 1965-67 John Archibald. 1967-69 James Thomson. 1969-70 Michael B Philliben. 1969-74 Joseph McMullan. 1974-78 Keith O'Brien. 1977-85 Thomas Mullen. 1985-87 Paul Kelly. 1988-89 Joseph Millar (Kiltegan Fathers). 1989- Kenneth J Owens.

BATHGATE – ST COLUMBA'S: 1970-84 Liam Healy. 1984-87 served from Immaculate Conception, Bathgate. 1987-89 Paul Capaldi. From 1989 served from Immaculate Conception, Bathgate.

BLACKBURN

Heads: 1905-06 Bernard Eardley. 1906-28 served from Armadale. 1928-30 William Quigley. 1930-32 Joseph Ward. 1932-36 John Ward. 1936-48 Patrick C Lynch. 1948-50 served from Whitburn. 1950-81 Michael T McNulty. 1981- John Rogerson.

Assistants: 1940-43 James T O'Reilly. 1943-48 John M Kerrisk. 1950-52 Peter Gallacher.

BLANEFIELD: see also Balfron

1951-52 Peter Donati. 1952-64 Michael J Devane. 1964-70 Richard Somers. 1970-72 James P Falconer. 1972-85 Michael Bell. 1985- William Forrester SJ.

BO'NESS
Until 1890 served from Linlithgow.

Heads: 1890-92 Henry Kuppers (Glasgow). 1892-1901 served from Linlithgow. 1901-03 Joseph Payne. 1903-04 vacant. 1904-13 William Grant. 1913-30 John Foley. 1930-39 Thomas Davitt. 1939-43 John McGeown (1933). 1943-49 Thomas J McLaughlin. 1949-69 Peter Lyons. 1969-88 James Phelan. 1988- James K Brennan (1945).

Assistants: 1942-48 William James Gallagher. 1951-53 Daniel F Foley. 1960-61 Patrick J McFadden.

BONNYBRIDGE
Heads: 1910-22 Daniel Conway. 1922-23 vacant. 1923-28 Edward Miley. 1928-38 Michael Downey. 1938-49 William MacCabe. 1949-56 Thomas McGarvey. 1956-84 Michael Murnin. 1984-88 Desmond Lynagh. 1988- John Agnew.

Assistants: 1931-35 Thomas Galligan. 1936-38 Patrick Quille. 1938-40 Andrew J Cameron (Aberdeen). 1941-45 Joseph MacArdle. 1945-57 Patrick J Rourke. 1957-65 William Ferguson. 1960-67 William Henery. 1965-67 James Anthony Maguire. 1967-72 Anthony McNally. 1972-77 David McCann. 1977-84 George Rodgers.

BONNYRIGG
Heads: 1952-60 Joseph MacArdle. 1960- James Gallagher.

Assistants: 1961-72 Michael Carey. 1972-73 Joseph McMahon. 1973-77 David John Henry.

BOWHILL
Until 1921 served from Lochgelly.

Heads: 1921-28 Ewen J Connolly. 1928-34 James George Harold. 1934-44 Thomas Corcoran. 1944-56 Joseph Maccabe. 1956-69 Reginald J J Hodgson. 1969-81 Stanislaus Smith. 1981- Brian P Byrne.

Assistant: 1959-67 Thomas Hennessy.

BROXBURN
Heads: 1877-84 John Carmichael (ED). 1884-1908 William O'Neill (ED). 1908-34 Frederick Hoban. 1934-37 John McKee (1906). 1937-41 Ewen J Connolly. 1941-45 Manus McIlhargie. 1945-46 vacant. 1946-67 Peter Macfarlane. 1967-86 Michael O'Connor. 1986- Kevin Rafferty.

Assistants: 1883-84 Patrick McAnaa. 1886-90 Thomas Monaghan. 1890-91 Henry Woods. 1891-92 John Quinlan. 1892-96 James McOscar. 1896-1901 John Quinlan. 1901-02 William Grant. 1902-04 William O'Raw. 1904 James MacDonald (1903). 1904-05 John D Wood. 1905-08 Peter Burns. 1908-10 John Slattery. 1910-11 Thomas J Ferrigan. 1911-13 Henry Kenny. 1913-17 Patrick J Geary. 1917-18 Edward Morrison. 1918-19 Patrick McHugh. 1919-22 John McGilligan (Galloway). 1922-24 Joseph A Ward. 1924-26 William Quigley. 1926-31 Thomas McCann.

1930-31 Francis McCormack. 1931-36 Charles Leyden. 1936-39 Joseph MacArdle. 1939-40 Patrick O'Leary. 1941-43 William J Carty. 1942-47 Edward Lynch. 1945-46 Richard Somers. 1946-47 Charles Glass. 1947-49 James McCauley. 1947-50 John Rogerson. 1950-65 Justin Dawson. 1951-55 Maurice Walshe. 1955-59 James Edward McGee. 1959-65 John F Byrne (1945). 1965-67 Francis J Doherty. 1965-69 Robert Hendrie. 1966-67 Ian Ashley. 1968-79 James Ferrari. 1969-72 Joseph McMahon. 1979-87 Loreto Tabone. 1986-89 Allan T Chambers. 1989- James Smith.

BURNTISLAND
Heads: 1931-36 Thomas McCann. 1936-40 Peter Macfarlane. 1940-48 John McHugh. 1948-51 Stanislaus Eardley. 1951-58 Edward T Gilchrist. 1958-72 Patrick Quinn. 1972-80 Anthony McNally. 1980-83 John C Fox. 1983-84 Robert Hendrie. 1984-89 Joseph McMahon. 1989- Gordon R Brown.
Assistants: 1936-38 Thomas Martin. 1938-41 Robert E Barry. 1941-42 Bernard O'Donnell. 1942-44 Anthony Smith. 1944-46 Eugene Loughlin. 1946-48 John D Mullan. 1948-51 Thomas F P Murray. 1951-55 Liam O'Mahoney. 1983-85 James Maher SDB.

CAMELON: see Falkirk, St Mary of the Angels

CAMPSIE: see Lennoxtown (also Milton of Campsie).

COWDENBEATH
Heads: 1902-16 J Andrew MacIntyre. 1916-19 Patrick Green. 1919-28 Francis P O'Brien. 1928-32 Harry J Kenny. 1932-36 Michael Whelahan. 1936-39 Anthony R Gallagher. 1939-53 Roger Gallagher. 1953-58 John Fusco. 1958-72 John McGeown (1938). 1972-77 Patrick Quinn. 1977-78 Gerard Lynch. 1978-85 Ian Murray. 1985- Philip Doherty.
Assistants: 1908-13 James Maguire. 1920-23 William Murphy. 1923-24 Bernard O'Hanlon. 1925-27 Charles Taylor. 1934-35 Edward McKay. 1942-48 Patrick Gilbride. 1948-49 Patrick Foley. 1950-51 Murdoch McLean. 1953-55 Stanislaus Smith. 1955-60 James F Nicholson. 1960-62 James E McGee. 1962-65 David McCann. 1965-66 Joseph McMullan. 1966-72 Keith O'Brien. 1968-69 William Gallacher. 1968-69 Alexander Mitchell.

COWIE
Until 1921 served from Bannockburn.
Heads: 1921-35 James Hart. 1935-54 John Bracelin. 1954-65 Gerard McGarry. 1965-71 Bernard G O'Donnell. 1971-76 Henry Curran. 1976-85 David P Brown. 1985-87 Andrew Forrest. 1987- Loreto Tabone.
Assistants: 1946-49 Angus Neilson. 1956-62 Patrick G Conway. 1962-67 Patrick Clarke. 1967-69 Francis Barrett. 1969-72 James Thomson.

CRAMOND: 1882-87 Michael J Turner. From 1887 served from South Queensferry.

CURRIE
Until 1966 served from Balerno.
Heads: 1966-69 Eric Gordon. 1969-80 James Rae. 1980-86 Leo Glancy.
Assistants: 1973 Patrick Cannon. 1980-81 Michael Fallon.
From 1986 served by Augustinians.

DALKEITH – ST DAVID'S
Until 1944 served by Jesuits.
Heads: 1944-52 John Ward. 1952-65 Anthony Kelly. 1965-88 Edward Mohan. 1988- Liam Healy.
Assistants: 1944-45 Kenneth Cox. 1944-47 Gerard Lynch. 1944-53 John Ryan. 1945-46 James O'Hanlon. 1945-52 Bernard O'Donnell. 1946-47 Anthony Kiernan. 1952-53 Aidan J Day. 1953-58 Daniel Foley. 1958-60 Martin J Cassidy. 1960-61 William R T Anderson. 1961-68 Alexander C Murphy. 1967-77 Kevin Rafferty. 1977-81 David J Henry. 1981-85 Thomas Flynn. 1985-88 Albert Gardner WF.

DALKEITH – ST LUKE'S: see Newbattle

DENNY
Heads: 1877-84 William O'Neill (ED). 1884-87 Henry Woods. 1887-91 Joseph Hannan. 1891-1902 William E Rooney. 1902-16 Patrick Shivers. 1916-28 Richard Hogan. 1928-47 Francis O'Brien. 1947-77 Michael Kelly. 1977-88 James K Brennan (1945). 1988- Desmond Lynagh.
Assistants: 1908-09 Peter Burns. 1909-10 Daniel Conway. 1922-27 Daniel Kelly. 1927-28 James F Maxwell. 1928-33 Brian C Maguire. 1933-37 Francis McFarlane. 1937-38 John Ward. 1938-39 Hugh Brady. 1939-41 Joseph MacArdle. 1941-48 Michael J Devane. 1948-54 Patrick Cunningham. 1954-58 Francis Moriarty. 1958-61 James P Falconer. 1961-62 Philip Doherty. 1962-65 Henry Curran. 1965-69 James Edward McGee. 1969-74 Alexander Mitchell. 1974-75 John Ramsay. 1975-77 Michael H Johnston. 1977-80 Robert M Maguire. 1980-85 Paul Capaldi. 1985-86 Iain Horne. 1986-88 Francis Welsh. 1988-89 John Smith. 1989- James A MacDonald (1989).

DUNBAR
1877-81 served from Haddington.
Heads: 1881-84 Michael Glasheen. 1884-88 Patrick Griffin (ED). 1888-90 Patrick McMahon. 1890-92 George Dowling. 1892-99 Peter McDaniel. 1899-1902 John Foley. 1902-09 Joseph P McGrail. 1909-16 Joseph C Long. 1916-26 J Andrew Macintyre. 1926-32 Peter J Burns. 1932-34 Joseph MacArdle. 1934-36 Patrick C Lynch. 1936-38 John Ward. 1938-47 James Payne. 1947-58 John McGeown (1938). 1958-67 Laurence

Davison. 1967-85 Michael J Walsh. 1985-88 Joseph Portelli. 1988-
Lawrence Glancy.
Assistant: 1883 Thomas Monaghan.

DUNFERMLINE – OUR LADY OF LOURDES: 1964-72 John M Kerrisk.
1972- Gerald McCabe.

DUNFERMLINE – ST MARGARET'S
Heads: 1867-79 Francis McKerrell (ED). 1879-87 Joseph B Hare (ED).
1887-89 Stephen Culhane. 1889-1903 George Mullan. 1903-16 David
Robertson. 1916-24 William Mellon. 1924-26 Samuel France. 1926-29
John Allan Gray (1902). 1929-33 Alfred Smith-Steinmetz. 1933-36
James Maguire. 1936-65 Richard Delaney. 1965-84 Patrick C Lynch.
1984-89 John Urquhart. 1989- David M Barr.
Assistants: 1895-96 John Quinlan. 1896-98 Patrick Green. 1898-1902
Edward Miley. 1902-04 William Holland. 1904-06 William Mulligan.
1906-08 James Maguire. 1909-13 Antony Sweeney (Dunkeld). 1911-13
Thomas O'Keefe. 1919-20 John Stuart (Dunkeld). 1920-23 Nicholas
Carrigan. 1923-24 Michael Mulvey. 1927-33 John Glackin. 1930-32
William Meehan. 1932-35 Edward Mohan. 1933 Anthony Gallagher.
1933-37 Thomas McGregor. 1935-36 Edward Mellon. 1936-37 Matthew I
Regan. 1937-38 Francis Hennessy. 1937-41 Bernard Carr. 1938-40
James K Birnie. 1940-41 Edward T Gilchrist. 1941-43 James McCallum.
1941-45 Patrick J Rourke. 1943-45 Peter Donati. 1945-46 John
McGrath. 1945-51 Eric Gordon. 1946-47 Francis L Gouldbourn. 1947-
49 Patrick McGuigan. 1949-50 Thomas Engelen. 1950-51 James
Falconer. 1951-53 Thomas F P Murray. 1951-67 John Rogerson. 1953-
65 Michael McCullagh. 1957-58 Martin J Cassidy. 1958-60 Frederick J
Morgan. 1960-66 John Fox. 1966-70 James D Radin. 1967-72 Patrick
Kelly. 1968-76 John Archibald. 1972-74 Brian Byrne. 1974-82 Joseph
McMullan. 1979 Philip Kerr. 1982-85 Michael Regan. 1983 Mark T Edie.
1983-84 Desmond Lynagh. 1985 Iain Horne. 1985-86 John Paul. 1986-
87 Paul Capaldi. 1987- Paul Kelly.

DUNS
Heads: 1916-19 James MacDonald (1903). 1919-21 Ewen J Connolly.
1921-23 Peter J Burns. 1923-30 William Grant. 1930-32 John Ward.
1932-35 Joseph Ward. 1935-38 Patrick Carden. 1938-39 John Ward.
1939-52 Peter J McKeown. 1952-57 Patrick McNulty. 1957-64 Patrick J
Rourke. 1964-65 Gerard Lynch. 1965-69 John James McMeel. 1969-72
William Anthony. 1972-84 Thomas McNulty. 1984-88 George Rodgers.
1988-89 Stephen Robson. 1989- Michael H Johnston.
Assistant: 1955-57 Michael J Jackson.

EAST CALDER
Heads: 1895-1929 Thomas Monaghan. 1929-37 James F Tonner. 1937-78
Joseph Healy. 1978-79 vacant. 1979-84 Lawrence Glancey. 1984-87

William W Henery. 1987- Eamon O'Brien.
Assistants: 1936-37 Joseph Healy. 1945-47 Henry Curran. 1947-48 Thomas P McGregor.

EDINBURGH – ST MARY'S CATHEDRAL

Heads: 1878-85 William Smith (ED). 1885-1903 James Donlevy (ED). 1903-23 Alexander Stuart. 1923-47 Patrick McGettigan. 1947-56 John Breen. 1956-82 Patrick Quille. 1981-82 Patrick Grady (co-head). 1982- Patrick Grady.

Assistants: 1878-85 James Donlevy (ED). 1879-82 Michael J Turner. 1882 Henry Woods. 1882-84 Henry Woods. 1883 George Dowling. 1883-85 Alexander Stuart. 1884-87 Patrick McAnaa. 1885-86 William E Rooney. 1886 George Mullan. 1886-87 Matthew Brady (ED). 1887 Joseph Donlevy. 1887-88 Frederick Hoban. 1887-89 Donald Easson. 1888-89 James MacDonald (ND). 1888-89 Joseph B Hare (ED). 1889-90 Alfred P Roche. 1889-90 Thomas Lee. 1890-91 Charles Duthie. 1890-92 Samuel McKeogh. 1890-93 Florence McCarthy. 1891-95 Hugh Considine. 1893-98 Patrick McGettigan. 1894-97 Thomas McDonna. 1895-1900 Francis McManus. 1897-98 John Stuart. 1898-1901 James Macdermott. 1898-1901 Joseph McGrail. 1900-01 J Andrew Macintyre. 1900-02 William O'Raw. 1901-02 Charles McGhee (Glasgow). 1902-05 Andrew Logue. 1902-09 Joseph Long. 1903 James Anton (Aberdeen) (possibly at Cathedral). 1903-04 William Mellon. 1904-07 James MacDonald (1903). 1905 James Mulhern. 1905-07 Octave Couttenier. 1907 Richard Fitzgerald. 1907-08 John Stuart. 1907-08 John McKee (1906). 1908-12 Patrick Green. 1909-13 Albert E Franklin. 1909-18 Cuthbert F Chase. 1912 Bernard McNamee. 1912-16 Michael O'Leary. 1913-16 Alexander H O'Donaghue. 1916-17 Edward Morrison. 1916-20 Patrick McDaniel (Dunkeld). 1917-19 James O'Flaherty. 1918-19 John McGilligan (Galloway). 1919-21 James Ryan. 1919-26 John Byrne (1919). 1920-25 Michael V Bruce. 1921-24 Daniel P Egan. 1924-25 John J Murphy. 1925-26 John McGrail. 1926-28 Patrick Rice. 1926-30 Charles Sharpley. 1927-30 Joseph McElhenney. 1928-29 Michael Kelly. 1928-30 Joseph MacArdle. 1930-31 James F Maxwell. 1930-32 Michael Kelly. 1930-34 Thomas Devaney. 1931-35 Peter Connelly. 1931-36 Patrick J Bredin. 1932-35 Joseph Healy. 1934 Daniel Logue. 1934-36 Roger Gallagher. 1934-36 James K Dennis. 1935-43 Thomas E Gallagher. 1936-37 Michael McNulty. 1936-37 John Kennedy. 1936-42 Brendan Rainey. 1937-39 Thomas Bowden. 1937-42 Thomas P McGregor. 1939-43 Andrew Walsh. 1942-43 Thomas Watt. 1942-49 John Woods. 1943-46 Matthew Carney (Glasgow). 1943-47 Bryan Scott. 1943-58 Laurence Davison. 1946-47 William Wilson. 1947-49 Eric Barber. 1948-59 Patrick (James) Grady. 1948-56 William D Hamilton. 1949-53 Richard Conway. 1949-70 John Tweedie. 1955-61 John Gibbons. 1957-60 John Dalrymple. 1958-59 John Archibald. 1959-61 James Anthony Maguire. 1960-63 Brian P Byrne. 1960-77 Alexander Bremner. 1961-62 Francis Holden. 1961-66 Thomas W Power. 1962-66 Patrick J McFadden. 1962-

68 Thomas Rhatigan. 1963-68 James Ferrari. 1965-69 Brian P Byrne. 1966-69 John McAllister. 1969-74 James Friel. 1970-73 Desmond McKeever SPS. 1972-76 Henry McLaughlin. 1972-78 Francis Kerr. 1974-75 Desmond McKeever SPS. 1975 Michael Johnston. 1976-80 Leo Glancy. 1976-81 John Robinson. 1978-79 Kenneth Batchelor. 1978-87 Gerard Lynch. 1979 Stephen Robson. 1980-81 Robert M Maguire. 1980-82 Allan T Chambers. 1981-82 Michael Purcell. 1982-86 David Gemmel. 1983-85 Stephen D Toner. 1985-88 Norman Cooper. 1986- John Paul. 1988- Michael Regan.

EDINBURGH – HOLY CROSS
Heads: 1922-59 Cuthbert F Chase. 1959- James Monaghan.
Assistants: 1931-33 Thomas Corcoran. 1933-35 Patrick Carden. 1935-38 William McClelland. 1938-39 Thomas Watt. 1938-42 Edward McKay. 1942-48 John Ward. 1948-49 Malcolm McFarlane. 1949-50 Eric Barber. 1950-61 Charles Brodie. 1959-64 Peter Gallacher. 1961-67 James P Falconer. 1965-66 Keith O'Brien. 1967-68 John Archibald. 1967-69 Fedele Maestri. 1969-72 Stephen Judge. 1972-76 John Robinson. 1976-80 Joseph McIntyre. 1980-81 Thomas Greenan. 1981-83 Robert G McGarrigle. 1983-85 Michael Sloan. 1986-88 Stephen Robson. 1988- James Tracey.

EDINBURGH – ST ANDREW'S (Ravelston)
Heads: 1901-36 Hugh Considine. 1936-39 James Maguire. 1939-50 James Turner. 1950-56 Walter Glancy. 1956-77 James K Birnie. 1977-89 Anthony Kiernan.
Assistants: 1904-05 Octave Couttenier. 1931-36 William Regan. 1932-33 Edward M Conway. 1933-35 James Collins. 1935-36 Matthew J Regan. 1936-37 Robert Wiggins. 1936-39 Edward Mellon. 1937-39 James Turner. 1939-40 Patrick Quille. 1939-41 Thomas Watt. 1940-42 James Monaghan. 1941-43 James Phelan. 1942-43 John McGeown (1938). 1942-46 Patrick Quille. 1943-44 William Carty. 1943-45 Manus McClafferty. 1945-54 John J McMeel. 1945-56 John F Byrne (1945). 1946-48 Lawrence A Glancey. 1954-56 Edward McColgan. 1956-61 Anthony Kiernan. 1956-58 Thomas W Power. 1961-63 James Ferrari. 1963-67 Francis Barrett. 1967-68 Peter J Nelson. 1968-71 Eamon O'Brien.
From 1989 served from St Margaret's.

EDINBURGH – ST ANNE'S ORATORY: normally served from Cathedral.
1940-41 James F Maxwell.

EDINBURGH – ST CATHERINE OF ALEXANDRIA (Gracemount)
Heads: 1958-85 Thomas Martin. 1985-89 Michael Bell. 1989- Anthony Kiernan.
Assistants: 1964-65 James McHugh (Galloway). 1965-70 Patrick Brady. 1970-71 John Ramsay. 1977-80 Thomas Hennessy. 1985-86 Paul Capaldi.

EDINBURGH – ST COLUMBA'S

Heads: 1888-1903 Alexander Stuart. 1903-26 George Mullan. 1926-35 William Mellon. 1935-45 John L Stuart. 1945-85 William McLaughlin. 1985- Daniel Foley.

Assistants: 1896-98 Barrington Douglas Dick (Galloway). 1901-03 Bernard Eardley. 1920-22 Thomas J Ferrigan. 1925-27 James W Leahy. 1927-28 Joseph A Ward. 1928-30 Kieran Joyce. 1930-31 John McGrain. 1930-31 Patrick O'Regan. 1931-32 Kenneth McKenzie (Aberdeen). 1931-33 Patrick McKenna. 1932-35 Edward Mellon. 1933-34 Henry Agnew. 1934-38 James Payne. 1935-38 Peter McKeown. 1938-39 John McCallum. 1938-40 James Phelan. 1939-41 Sylvester Byrne. 1940-45 James Corduff. 1941-42 Charles J Kelly. 1942-45 Bernard O'Donnell. 1945-46 Charles J Kelly. 1945-50 Walter Glancy. 1946-47 Jeremiah Bourke. 1946-52 Patrick McNulty. 1947 James Brennan (1947). 1950 Justin Dawson. 1950-54 Dennis O'Connell. 1950-55 Lawrence A Glancey. 1954-55 James F Nicholson. 1955-57 Daniel P Simpson. 1955-62 Andrew Shiels. 1957-58 Gerard Devlin. 1958-61 Thomas W Power. 1961-63 Ian Murray. 1962-69 Stephen Judge. 1963-64 James McHugh (Galloway). 1964-69 William Anthony. 1969-72 Thomas McNulty. 1972-77 Michael Carey. 1977-79 Loreto Tabone. 1979-80 Michael Fallon.

EDINBURGH – ST CUTHBERT'S (Slateford)

Heads: 1889-1942 John Forsyth. 1942-43 John Kerr. 1943-69 Peter Connolly. 1969-89 Laurence Davison. 1989- Anthony L Duffy.

Assistants: 1920-28 Kieran Joyce. 1925-29 Daniel Egan. 1928-30 John Ward. 1930-31 Thomas Corcoran. 1930-31 Laurence Fisher (Galloway). 1931-33 Gerald Dorrian. 1931-35 Peter Higgins. 1933-37 Daniel McSorley. 1935-36 William Wilson. 1936-38 Hugh Brady. 1937-38 Bernard Kielt. 1937-41 Thomas McLaughlin. 1938-42 John Kerr. 1938-47 John McNay. 1941-45 Michael O'Reilly. 1941-45 James MacDonald (1940). 1942-45 James Cummins. 1945-47 Thomas Savage. 1945-47 Eric Barber. 1945-52 Joseph MacArdle. 1946-47 Thomas Carroll. 1947-48 James Leckie. 1947-48 Thomas Rhatigan. 1947-49 William O'Sullivan. 1947-52 Peter Smyth. 1948-52 Michael J Devane. 1948-55 William Henery. 1949-50 John Barry. 1950-55 Richard Somers. 1952-53 Bernard O'Donnell. 1952-53 Francis Thomson. 1953-54 Karl Kruger. 1953-56 Edward Norman Kerr. 1954-61 Peter McKeesick. 1955-58 Angus Neilson. 1955-61 Philip Doherty. 1956-58 Brendan Smith. 1958-61 Stanislaus Smith. 1958-64 Liam Healy. 1961-63 Henry Reid. 1963-65 Sean O'Kelly. 1964-70 John Ramsay. 1965-72 John Gordon. 1970-73 Francis Clarke. 1973-75 Andrew Monaghan. 1973-81 Anthony L Duffy. 1981-86 Francis Welsh.

EDINBURGH – ST GREGORY THE GREAT: 1972-85 Stephen Judge. 1985- James F Nicholson.

EDINBURGH – ST JOHN THE BAPTIST'S (Corstorphine)
Heads: 1938-71 William McClelland. 1971-72 vacant. 1972- Francis Holden.
Assistants: 1943-46 Daniel Joseph Boyle (1940). 1946-50 Peter Gallagher. 1950-57 Nicholas Torsney. 1957-59 Thomas Engelen. 1959-60 James E McGee. 1960-72 James Nicholson.

EDINBURGH – ST JOHN THE EVANGELIST'S (Portobello)
Heads: 1872-81 John Smith (ED). 1881-88 Patrick Morris (ED). 1888-90 Martin Meagher (ED). 1890-1924 Joseph Donlevy. 1924-55 Albert E Franklin. 1955-72 John Ward. 1972-80 Hugh Gordon. 1980- James Rae.
Assistants: 1919-24 Thomas Moore. 1930-31 Joseph McElhenney. 1931-32 Andrew J Cameron (Aberdeen). 1932-34 William McLaughlin. 1934-37 John Lowrie. 1937-38 John J Ashworth. 1938-40 Hugh Gordon. 1940-42 Eric Gordon. 1943 Edward McColgan. 1943-52 Patrick Quinn. 1947-53 Michael McCullagh. 1952-54 Michael Jackson. 1952-55 John Ward (administrator). 1954-58 Liam Boyle. 1954-61 Thomas Kelly (1925) (2) (Glasgow). 1958-62 Henry Curran. 1962-65 Robert Hendrie. 1962-68 Andrew Shiels. 1965-69 John Creanor. 1968-70 Francis Doherty. 1969-72 Bernard Doonan. 1970-71 James J Donnelly SJ. 1971-72 Achilles de Souza. 1972 John Robinson. 1972-77 Brian Halloran. 1974-75 Joseph McMahon. 1976-78 James Myers. 1977-80 Sean Murphy CM. 1980-82 Norman Cooper. 1982-85 William Brennan.

EDINBURGH – ST JOHN VIANNEY'S (Gilmerton)
Heads: 1952-70 Peter J McKeon. 1970-79 Lawrence A Glancey. 1979-85 John Ramsay. 1985- Patrick Kelly.
Assistants: 1955-60 Michael J Cassidy. 1960-64 Joseph McMahon. 1964-69 Charles Barclay. 1969-70 Michael B Macnamara. 1970-72 Brian Saddler. 1976-78 Michael Burns.

EDINBURGH – ST JOSEPH'S (Sighthill)
Heads: 1953-56 Peter Higgins. 1956-77 Joseph Maccabe. 1977-87 Thomas W Power. 1987- Andrew Forrest.
Assistants: 1954-57 Thomas Engelen. 1957-58 Brian P Byrne. 1958-59 Stephen Wynne. 1959-70 John Urquhart. 1970-76 Hugh Shannon.

EDINBURGH – ST KENTIGERN'S (Barnton)
Heads: 1966-81 Patrick Grady. 1981-84 William W Henery. 1984- Thomas McNulty.
Assistants: 1967-68 David J Henry. 1968-74 Robert G McGarrigle. 1974-80 Ryszard Holuka. 1977-78 Desmond Lynagh. 1978-82 David Gemmell. 1982-84 Allan T Chambers.

EDINBURGH – ST MAGDALENE'S: see Edinburgh, St Mary Magdalene's

EDINBURGH – ST MARGARET'S (Davidson's Mains)
Heads: 1958-63 Roderick Gemmell. 1963-69 John McKee (1936). 1969-72 Hugh Gordon. 1972-86 Matthew J Donoghue. 1986-89 David M Barr. 1989- Edward Gallagher.
Assistants: 1959-64 Andrew Forrest. 1964-66 Vincent Logan. 1966-67 Lawrence Moonan. 1966-69 Joseph McMullan. 1967-69 Vincent Logan. 1969-72 Patrick J McFadden.

EDINBURGH – ST MARGARET MARY'S (Granton)
Heads: 1939-43 Antony R Gallagher. 1943-76 John McGeown (1933). 1976- Michael J Cassidy.
Assistants: 1941-42 Walter Glancey. 1942-47 James Monaghan. 1945-46 Malcolm Macfarlane. 1946-47 William Wheeler (Galloway). 1947-48 Francis Staples. 1947-49 William Wilson. 1948 Thomas Engelen. 1949-50 Daniel McGuinness. 1949-51 John McGrath. 1950-54 Patrick Claffey. 1951-52 Michael Walsh. 1952-62 Eamon O'Brien. 1954-58 James Quinn. 1957-60 Denis O'Connell (administrator). 1957-63 Michael J Jackson. 1962-67 James McNamara. 1963-67 James Thomson. 1967-68 John Curran. 1967-72 Brian Halloran. 1980-82 Edward Gilchrist. 1985 Brian Devlin. 1985-89 Francis J Doherty.

EDINBURGH – ST MARK'S (Oxgangs)
Heads: 1961-65 Patrick J Lynch. 1965-77 Charles J Kelly. 1977-89 John Barry. 1989- Alexander J Mitchell.
Assistants: 1961-69 Peter McKeesick. 1969-71 Robert Hendrie. 1971-74 James Henry. 1974-79 Joseph Murray. 1977-78 Matthew McGovern. 1978-79 Francis Doherty. 1979-83 Michael Sloan. 1980-81 Francis Doherty. 1982-85 Francis Doherty. 1983-86 Mark T W Edie. 1986-87 Bernard Doonan. 1987-88 Michael Purcell.

EDINBURGH – ST MARY MAGDALENE'S (St Magdalene's) (Portobello)
1961-70 Lawrence A Glancey. 1970-73 John Tweedie. 1973-76 David P Brown. 1976-79 Brian P Byrne. 1979-84 Joseph McMahon. 1984-89 Anthony L Duffy. 1989- Patrick Harrity WF.

EDINBURGH – SAINTS NINIAN AND TRIDUANA (Restalrig)
Heads: 1905-38 Thomas Miley. 1938-39 vacant. 1939-53 Peter Higgins. 1953-58 James G Harold. 1958-76 John Fusco. 1976-85 John Dalrymple. 1985-87 Ian Murray. 1987- John McAllister.
Assistants: 1927-30 Michael Murnin. 1930-33 Charles Cartwright. 1930-33 Anthony Kelly. 1933-35 Thomas Walsh. 1934-36 Patrick Holden. 1935-38 John J Lynch. 1936-37 John Kenny. 1937 James Brennan (1934). 1937 Patrick Delaney. 1938-39 Peter McKeown. 1938-39 Edward T Gilchrist. 1939-40 Francis Kerr. 1939-44 James B Walsh. 1940-43 Patrick Lyng. 1943-49 Augustine Duffy. 1944-47 James McCallum. 1947-53 Liam Gaffney. 1947-58 Gerard Lynch. 1949-50 Karl Kruger. 1950-52 Michael Jackson. 1952-56 James McMahon. 1954-57 Sean

McCarthy. 1956-58 Richard Somers. 1958-61 William Fitzsimmons. 1958-62 Stephen Judge. 1959-66 Patrick Kelly. 1961-63 Daniel Boyd. 1962-65 William Gallacher. 1963-65 Fedele Maestri. 1965-66 William Ferguson. 1966-67 Michael J Cassidy. 1966-76 John Fox. 1967-69 Thomas Hennessy. 1968-69 Michael P Philliben. 1969-79 Patrick Fallon. 1971-72 Joseph Mifsud. 1976-84 Henry McLaughlin. 1982-83 Joseph Portelli. 1983-85 Basil Postlethwaite. 1985-86 Brian Devlin. 1986-89 Kevin McEwan CSsR. 1989 James A MacDonald (1989)

EDINBURGH – ST PATRICK'S
Heads: 1870-91 Edward J Hannan (ED). 1891-1912 William Grady (ED). 1912-29 Patrick Morris. 1929-50 Patrick Birnie. 1950-60 James Turner. 1960-67 Roger Gallagher. 1967-88 Edward Hyland.
Assistants: 1877-79 Michael Corcoran (ED). 1877-82 Martin Meagher (ED). 1877-82 Patrick Griffin (ED). 1879-81 Joseph Hannan. 1881-84 Edmund O'Kane. 1882-83 James McCartney (ED). 1882-83 William Berkery. 1883-84 John Lee (ED). 1883-84 George Dowling. 1884-86 Michael Glasheen. 1884-87 Stephen Culhane. 1884-87 Joseph Hannan. 1886-88 Alexander Stuart. 1887-88 Peter McDaniel. 1888-89 Alfred P Roche. 1888-89 John G Foley. 1889-91 George Culhane (Dunkeld). 1889-92 Patrick Hartigan. 1890-92 James McOscar. 1891-92 George Mason. 1891-92 Francis O'Reilly. 1892-94 Thomas Mulvihill. 1892-95 John Quinlan. 1893 Patrick McGettigan. 1893-95 Patrick Birnie. 1894-95 Barrington Douglas Dick (Galloway). 1894-96 Patrick Green. 1894-97 James McGinnes (ED). 1895-98 Henry Woods. 1895-98 Charles Murdoch. 1897-98 [-] Costelloe. 1897-99 John Joyce (1896). 1898-1901 Joseph Payne. 1898-1902 Richard Hogan. 1899-1901 Samuel MacDonald (Argyll). 1899-1902 John Joyce (1899). 1900-01 Bernard Eardley. 1901-10 George Bennett. 1902-03 Joseph Keenan (Dunkeld). 1902-05 John L Meade. 1902-05 John Gray (1901). 1905 Thomas Miley. 1905-06 John D Wood. 1905-09 Cuthbert F Chase. 1906-10 James Mulhern. 1906-12 Alfred Smith-Steinmetz. 1910-11 John Slattery. 1910-13 Thomas Gillon. 1911-14 Ignatius McHugh. 1912-13 Bernard A Smith. 1912-18 Walter Welsh. 1913-14 Daniel Ramsay. 1913-15 Anthony O'Doherty. 1914-15 Charles Daly. 1914-15 Daniel Murphy. 1914-17 Richard Thornhill. 1915-22 James Bonnar. 1918-20 James Mullan. 1918-26 Bernard McLaughlin. 1920-21 James C Brett. 1920-21 Bernard O'Hanlon. 1921-22 Michael J Hession. 1921-24 Michael Downie. 1922-23 William A Maccabe. 1922-23 James G Harold. 1923-25 Philip Murphy. 1923-27 Nicholas Carrigan. 1924-25 Michael Ryan. 1924-26 James Riordan. 1925-26 Patrick J Rice. 1926-28 William Maccabe. 1926-29 Patrick Doyle. 1926-30 Thomas McGarvey. 1927-30 John Bracelin. 1928-30 James I Finnegan (possibly). 1928-30 John McGettigan. 1930-31 Daniel McCaffrey. 1930-32 Joseph Healey. 1930-33 Dolty Ward. 1930-33 Anthony Flynn. 1930-34 James Payne. 1931-33 Patrick Flanaghan. 1932-35 James White. 1933-36 Andrew J Cameron (Aberdeen). 1933-38 Henry O'Neill. 1935-37 James Collins. 1935-38

Michael McGovern. 1936-37 David Carroll. 1937-39 Bernard Kelly. 1937-43 Stanislaus Eardley. 1938-39 Francis Hennessy. 1938-41 Gerard McGarry. 1939-40 Joseph Purcell. 1939-40 Peter Foylan (Dunkeld). 1940-54 Edward Hyland. 1941-46 James McDermott. 1943-44 Edward Quigley. 1943-46 Edward McColgan. 1945-47 James Brennan (1945). 1946-47 Patrick Bermingham. 1946-48 Malcolm Macfarlane. 1947-48 Leo Deery. 1947-51 Michael Walsh. 1948-60 William J Gallagher. 1948-62 John McHugh. 1954-62 John J McMeel. 1957-58 James Phelan. 1962-64 David Henry. 1962-67 John Callaghan. 1964-69 Edward Gallagher. 1967-74 Brian McKean. 1969-76 John Creanor. 1974-76 Michael Burns. 1976-77 Sean Murphy CM. 1976-81 Thomas Flynn. 1977-78 David Barr. 1981-82 Joseph Murray. 1982-84 Thomas Dooley WF. 1984-85 Gordon R Brown. 1987-88 David McCann. From 1988 served by Franciscans.

EDINBURGH – ST PAUL'S (Muirhouse)
Heads: 1969-79 John McAllister. 1979-84 John Urquhart.
Assistants: 1971-75 Thomas Devane SMA. 1974-76 John Dalrymple. 1976-78 Hugh Shannon. 1976-81 Gerard Rooney. 1981-82 Francis J Doherty. 1981-84 Anthony L Duffy.
From 1984 served by Salesians.

EDINBURGH – ST PETER'S
Heads: 1905-34 John Gray (1901). 1934-48 Michael V Bruce. 1948-56 Patrick Quille. 1956-80 Walter Glancy. 1980-85 Anthony McNally. 1985-89 Stephen Judge. 1989- Francis Kerr.
Assistants: 1909-15 Edward Mellon. 1915-18 Charles Daly. 1919-20 Michael V Bruce. 1920-23 Philip Murphy. 1923-26 William A Maccabe. 1926-29 Thomas Moore. 1929-32 John Breen. 1932-35 Peter Macfarlane. 1935-39 John McGeown (1933). 1939-40 John McKee (1936). 1940-53 Reginald J Hodgson. 1950-51 John Rogerson. 1951-58 John Falconer. 1955-61 Lawrence Glancey. 1958-66 William Loftus. 1961-69 James Rae. 1966-74 Henry Reid. 1974-76 Gerard Rooney. 1976-77 Alistair Lawson. 1978-80 Matthew McGovern. 1980-85 Ryszard Holuka.

EDINBURGH – CONVENT OF THE GOOD SHEPHERD: CHAPLAINS
1946-48 Patrick Quille. 1948-50 Lawrence A Glancey. 1950-51 Angus Neilson. 1951-62 Thomas Rhatigan. 1962-64 John McHugh. 1975-77 Joseph McMahon.

EDINBURGH – LITTLE SISTERS OF THE POOR: CHAPLAINS
1881-87 Alexander Gordon (ED). 1889-99 John Shaw (ND). 1899-1903 Joseph B Hare (ED). 1903-07 Henry Woods. 1907-19 Octave Couttenier. 1919-21 Henry Woods. 1926-44 Patrick Green. 1944-47 James Hart. 1947-59 James Monaghan. 1959-66 Patrick Grady. 1966-77 Thomas W Power. 1978-86 Francis Kerr. 1986- Hugh Gordon.

EDINBURGH – POOR CLARES' CONVENT: CHAPLAINS
1902-03 Henry Woods. 1903-35 Patrick McMahon. 1935-40 James Hart. 1956-70 William D Hamilton. 1970-87 Peter Gallacher.

EDINBURGH – SACRED HEART CONVENT: CHAPLAINS
1968-75 Thomas Hanlon. 1975-85 Andrew Monaghan. 1985-86 Ryszard Holuka.

EDINBURGH – ST MARGARET'S CONVENT: CHAPLAINS
1884-87 John Lee (ED). 1898-1918 James McDonald (ND).

ELIE – CONVENT OF MARY REPARATRIX: CHAPLAINS
1956-65 James F Maxwell. 1966-73 William Loftus. 1979-80 Kenneth Batchelor.

FALKIRK – ST FRANCIS XAVIER'S
Heads: 1871-82 Alexander O'Donnell (ED). 1882-91 William Grady (ED). 1891-93 Joseph Hannan. 1893-1912 Patrick Morris (ED). 1912-19 Michael J Turner. 1919-26 Charles Murdoch. 1926-29 George Mullan. 1929-30 vacant. 1930-33 Joseph C Long. 1933-38 James MacDonald (1903). 1938-54 Walter Welsh. 1954-72 John Bracelin. 1972-73 vacant. 1973- John Tweedie.

Assistants: 1882 Henry Woods. 1885-86 Colin MacKenzie (Aberdeen). 1886-87 George Mullan. 1887-88 Joseph B Hare (ED). 1888 Patrick McMahon. 1888-89 John Forsyth. 1889-90 George Dowling. 1889-90 J Stevenson Lyle. 1890 Charles MacIntee. 1891-92 J Stevenson Lyle. 1891-95 Henry Woods. 1895-98 Patrick Birnie. 1898-99 John Stuart. 1898-1901 David Robertson. 1899-1901 Daniel Conway. 1901-02 Joseph P McGrail. 1902-03 Francis O'Brien. 1902-06 John A Gray (1902). 1903-04 Alistair Smith-Steinmetz. 1904-06 Patrick Green. 1906-08 Dominic Hart. 1906-09 John D Wood. 1908-10 Robert Reynolds. 1909-13 James McGlynn. 1910-17 Archibald McMaster. 1913-16 Bernard A Smith. 1917-19 Ewen J Connolly. 1917-23 Richard Thornhill. 1919-22 James Scott. 1922-23 Michael Mulvey. 1923-25 Richard Thornhill. 1925-26 Charles Sharpley. 1926-28 Samuel France. 1926-30 Michael Payne. 1928-34 Patrick Griffin. 1930-32 Samuel Heffron (Galloway). 1930-34 Peter Donati. 1932-33 Terence Kirke. 1934-35 George Quinn. 1934-35 John McGeown (1933). 1934-39 Bernard Blee. 1935-36 Joseph Healy. 1935-37 Michael O'Connor. 1936-38 James K Dennis. 1937-40 John J McHugh. 1939 Peter Lyons. 1939-46 Patrick McNulty. 1940-41 John J Holahan. 1941-42 John Ward. 1942-47 Thomas P McGregor. 1946-47 William G Carden. 1946-49 Edward McColgan. 1947-49 Laurence O'Brien. 1949-55 Vincent Dobrina. 1949-58 Malcolm McFarlane. 1954-55 Michael J Cassidy. 1955-56 Richard Somers. 1955-60 John McAllister. 1956-64 William Anthony. 1958-59 Gerard Devlin. 1959-63 Francis Barrett. 1960-61 James Ferrari. 1961-62 William Fitzsimmons. 1962-65 Francis J Doherty. 1963-68 Leo Glancy. 1964-73 Andrew Monaghan. 1965-78

Bernard J McAllister. 1968-69 William Conway. 1969-70 Brian Saddler. 1970-72 Francis Kerr. 1972-77 David Barr. 1973-78 Francis J Doherty. 1974-79 Michael Sloan. 1977-80 Patrick Boylan. 1979-80 Joseph Murray. 1980-82 Joseph McIntyre. 1980-82 Philip Kerr. 1982-85 Norman Cooper. 1983-85 Joseph Portelli. 1985-87 Michael Bagan. 1985-88 William Brennan. 1987-89 James Brennan CSsR. 1987- Timothy McConville. 1988-89 Albert Gardner WF. 1989- Joseph Millar (Kiltegan Fathers).

FALKIRK – ST MARY OF THE ANGELS (Camelon)
Heads: 1923-29 John McKee (1906). 1929-36 Philip Murphy. 1936-67 Anthony Flynn. 1967-87 Walter P Crampton. 1987-89 Robert G McGarrigle. 1989- Stephen Judge.
Assistants: 1945-50 Edward J Murphy. 1950-61 Francis Holden. 1961-66 Anthony Kiernan. 1966-67 Patrick Kelly. 1969-73 John Curran.

FALKLAND
Heads: 1908-09 Arthur Allchin. 1909-14 Henry Woods. 1914-16 John Joyce (1896). 1916-19 vacant. 1919-21 served from Lochgelly. 1921-34 served from Bowhill. 1934-39 Peter Donati. 1939-41 Michael O'Connor. 1941-43 Thomas McLaughlin. 1943-49 Peter Lyons. 1949-53 William Wilson. 1953-58 Pierce Grace. 1958-65 Malcolm MacFarlane. 1965-76 Justin Dawson.
Assistant: 1942-43 Alphonsus McGrath.
From 1976 served from Kennoway.

FALLIN: 1972-79 James Thomson. 1979-80 Patrick Fallon. 1980-86 David Barr. From 1986 served from Cowie.

FAULDHOUSE
Heads: 1870-87 John Grogan (ED). 1887-90 Henry Woods. 1890-93 Joseph B Hare (ED). 1893-95 Florence McCarthy. 1895-99 Hugh Considine. 1899-1909 George Mason. 1909-23 John B Joyce (1899). 1923-30 Joseph C Long. 1930-35 John L Stuart. 1935-36 Peter Macfarlane. 1936-48 Edward Morrison. 1948-67 Thomas E Gallagher. 1967-70 Roger Gallagher. 1970-85 Peter J MacKeown. 1985- Charles Brodie.
Assistants: 1947-48 Thomas Engelen. 1955-56 Patrick J McFadden. 1956-59 Alexander C Murphy. 1959-64 James Radin. 1964-67 Michael B Macnamara.

GALASHIELS
Until 1902 served by Jesuits.
Heads: 1902-24 William Rooney. 1924-44 Alexander H O'Donoghue. 1944-72 Thomas Corcoran. 1972-85 Charles Brodie. 1985- David P Brown.
Assistants: 1902-04 William Grant. 1904-05 Alistair Smith-Steinmetz. 1905-06 James Mulhern. 1906-08 Patrick Green. 1959-60 Patrick J McFadden. 1960-62 David McCann. 1962-64 Peter J Nelson. 1964-69

Daniel McGuinness. 1969-70 Gerard Lynch. 1970-72 John Urquhart. 1975-79 John Urquhart. 1979-81 John Callaghan. 1981-84 John Robinson.

GALASHIELS – BALNAKIEL CONVENT: CHAPLAINS
1954-55 Angus Neilson. 1955-68 Eric Barber. 1969-70 Reginald J J Hodgson. 1972-75 John Urquhart.

GATTONSIDE – BROTHERS OF CHARITY: CHAPLAINS
1986- Reginald J J Hodgson.

GLENROTHES – ST MARY'S: 1966-67 James K Brennan (1945). 1967-72 Charles Brodie. 1972-74 James P Falconer. 1974-87 James Friel. 1987- Denis O'Connell.

GLENROTHES – ST PAUL'S: 1958-69 Pierce Grace. 1969- John J McMeel.

GOREBRIDGE
Heads: 1952-63 Peter Donati. 1963-65 Bernard G O'Donnell. 1965-68 Gerard Lynch. 1968-72 Gerald McCabe. 1972-85 Philip Doherty. 1985-86 Thomas Martin. 1986- Bernard J McAllister.
Assistants: 1953-54 Thomas Engelen. 1954-55 Andrew Shiels.

GRANGEMOUTH – CHRIST THE KING: 1970-87 Karl H Kruger. 1987- James Friel.

GRANGEMOUTH – SACRED HEART
Heads: 1901-08 Patrick Birnie. 1908-13 John Foley. 1913-18 Thomas Gillon. 1918-38 Walter Welsh. 1938-44 John Ward. 1944-72 Dolty Ward. 1972-79 John McGeown (1938). 1979-89 William Anthony. 1989- Joseph McMahon.
Assistants: 1940-41 Walter P Crampton. 1941-45 John J Holahan. 1945-46 Thomas Comerford. 1946-47 Peter Smyth. 1947-48 James Brennan (1947). 1951-52 Aidan J Day. 1957-59 James D Radin. 1959-61 Alexander C Murphy. 1961-70 Stephen Wynne.

HADDINGTON
Heads: 1869-82 William Grady (ED). 1882-88 Martin Meagher. 1888-89 Thomas O'Carroll. 1889-98 Patrick McAnaa. 1898-99 Patrick Griffin (ED). 1899-1901 Hugh Considine. 1901-08 Frederick Hoban. 1908-14 John Stuart. 1914-17 Peter J Burns. 1917-24 Samuel France. 1924-25 Michael Whelahan. 1925-30 Michael Bruce. 1930-31 Thomas P McGregor. 1931-33 Peter Walter OSB. 1933-44 Dolty Ward. 1944-69 James B Walsh. 1969-86 Peter Connolly. 1986-88 Leo Glancy. 1988- Daniel McGuinness.
Assistants: 1877-80 John Pinkman (ED). 1880-81 Michael Glasheen. 1881-82 William Berkery. 1929-30 Thomas P McGregor.

HAWICK
Heads: 1847-87 Patrick Taggart (ED). 1887-92 Patrick Shivers. 1892-1912
  J Stevenson Lyle. 1912-18 George Bennett. 1918-24 Thomas Gillon.
  1924-30 Edward Mellon. 1930-38 Dominic Hart. 1938-42 Daniel Kelly.
  1942-47 Gordon Gray. 1947-56 James K Birnie (1945). 1956-86 Peter
  Higgins. 1986- Michael Sloan.
Assistants: 1936-38 Andrew J Cameron (Aberdeen). 1938-42 James G
  Harold. 1941-42 Gordon Gray. 1942-45 Eric Gordon. 1945-46 Thomas
  Watt. 1946-47 Thomas Engelen. 1947-50 Charles Brodie. 1950-55 Eric
  Barber. 1955-56 Liam O'Mahoney. 1956-59 John F Byrne. 1959-64 John
  Ramsay. 1964-69 Joseph McMahon. 1969-70 Francis Barrett. 1970-77
  Gerard Lynch. 1977-79 John Agnew. 1979-85 Michael Bagan. 1985-86
  Michael Sloan.

HAWICK – DOMINICAN CONVENT: CHAPLAINS
1936-43 Michael A Payne. 1948-60 William Grant. 1961-63 Thomas Kelly
  (1925) (2) (Glasgow).

INNERLEITHEN
Heads: 1877-81 Archibald Hog (ED). 1881-84 John Smith (ED). 1884-89
  Francis McKerrell (ED). 1889-98 James MacDonald (ND). 1898-1909
  James McGinnes (ED). 1909-30 George Mason. 1930-33 Michael Payne.
  1933-36 Anthony Kelly. 1936-39 John Fusco. 1939-41 Thomas Martin.
  1941-43 William Grant. 1943-48 Stanislaus Eardley. 1948-52 Thomas P
  McGregor. 1952-58 Patrick Quinn. 1958-62 James Phelan. 1962-72
  Francis Holden. 1972-76 Dolty Ward. 1976-84 John Creanor. 1984-86
  Kenneth Batchelor.
Assistant: 1980 Paul Capaldi.
From 1986 served from Peebles.

INVERKEITHING (Jamestown)
Heads: 1913-17 Antony Sweeney (Dunkeld). 1917-23 Joseph C Long. 1923-
  30 Dominic Hart. 1930-31 William Quigley. 1931-37 Thomas Ferrigan.
  1937-79 combined with Rosyth, see below. 1979-88 John Agnew. 1988-
  George Rogers.
Assistants: 1914-17 James Connolly. 1917-18 Patrick McHugh. 1918-19
  James Hart. 1919-20 William Murphy.

JAMESTOWN: see Inverkeithing

JEDBURGH: 1876-79 Patrick Morris (ED). 1879-86 Patrick McManus (ED).
  1886-88 Edmund O'Kane. 1888-98 Patrick Griffin (ED). 1898-1901
  Patrick Birnie. 1901-03 David Robertson. 1903-13 James McOscar.
  1913-17 Dominic Hart. 1917-19 served from Kelso. 1919-21 Octave
  Couttenier. 1921-30 served from Kelso. 1930-35 Michael Murnin. 1935-
  47 Edward Mohan. 1947-53 John McNay. 1953-56 Reginald J J
  Hodgson. 1956-65 Charles Kelly. 1965-66 John F Byrne (1945). 1966-69
  Anthony Kiernan. 1969-72 Daniel McGuinness. 1972-73 Ian T Gillan.

1973-81 William P Loftus. 1981-82 vacant. 1982-89 William Conway. 1989- David J Henry.

KELSO: 1878-79 John Lee (ED). 1879-82 James McCartney (ED). 1882-84 Patrick Griffin (ED). 1884-86 Edmund O'Kane. 1886-1902 served from Jedburgh. 1902-09 John B Joyce (1899). 1909-12 Joseph P McGrail. 1912-16 James MacDonald (1903). 1916-17 John Joyce (1896). 1917-19 James Connolly. 1919-21 James Hart. 1921-30 Octave Couttenier. 1930-35 John Bracelin. 1935-39 William McLaughlin. 1939-40 Bernard Blee. 1940-44 James K Birnie. 1944-56 Edward Quigley. 1956-65 James A McMahon. 1965-71 Henry Curran. 1971-77 Eamon O'Brien. 1977-80 Joseph Maccabe. 1980-85 David McCann. 1985- Joseph McIntyre.

KELTY: 1913-26 James Maguire. 1926-27 Bernard O'Hanlon. 1927-30 Daniel Kelly. 1930-31 James Maguire. 1931-34 William Quigley. 1934-35 Joseph MacArdle. 1935-38 Edward McKay. 1938-71 John J Lynch. 1971-80 Andrew Shiels. 1980-88 Thomas Hennessy. 1988- Michael Purcell.

KENNOWAY: 1959-69 Thomas Engelen. 1969-77 Anthony Kiernan. 1977-79 Michael Carey. 1979-85 Andrew Forrest. 1985- Thomas W Flynn.

KILSYTH
Heads: 1873-90 John Murphy (ED). 1890-1903 Michael J Turner. 1903-38 Patrick Macnamara. 1938-55 Michael Downey. 1955-56 vacant. 1956-72 Thomas McGarvey. 1972-87 Denis O'Connell. 1987-89 Karl H Kruger. 1989- Bernard Doonan.
Assistants: 1880-85 John Murphy. 1899-1900 J Andrew Macintyre. 1903-15 Edward Blake. 1915-23 Daniel Murphy. 1923-28 James Harold. 1928-30 James F Maxwell. 1930-38 John McGettigan. 1931-32 Patrick Lynch. 1938-39 Francis Kerr. 1939-40 Edward Gilchrist. 1941-42 Thomas A Watt. 1942-44 Edward McKay. 1942-47 Thomas McCarville. 1944-46 John C Barry. 1946-48 Francis Thomson. 1947-61 James Brennan (1945). 1948-56 William Anthony. 1956-58 Matthew Donoghue. 1958-61 Patrick McNulty. 1961-68 Gerald McCabe. 1961-72 Michael Bell. 1968-71 Andrew Shiels. 1972-74 Keith O'Brien. 1973-74 Desmond McKeever SPS. 1974-76 Brian Byrne. 1974-81 Robert G McGarrigle. 1981-82 Joseph Portelli. 1982-85 Joseph McIntyre. 1985-87 Thomas Mullen. 1987-88 George Paul. 1988- William Brennan.

KIRKCALDY – OUR LADY OF PERPETUAL SUCCOUR (St Marie's)
Heads: 1872-79 Joseph B Hare (ED). 1879-81 Patrick Morris (ED). 1881-84 Patrick Fay (ED). 1884-89 George Dowling. 1889-90 Joseph Donlevy. 1890-92 Thomas Lee. 1892-98 Patrick Shivers. 1898-1902 Henry Woods. 1902-08 John Foley. 1908-29 Patrick Birnie. 1929-34 John McKee (1906). 1934-38 James G Harold. 1938-77 Joseph Byrne. 1977-84 Angus Neilson. 1984-88 Charles Barclay. 1988- Patrick Fallon.

Assistants: 1883-86 Thomas Monaghan. 1886-87 Thomas Boilson. 1887 Peter McDaniel. 1908-12 Dominic Hart. 1915-16 Edward Mellon. 1916-17 Samuel France. 1917-24 Michael Whelahan. 1924-25 Michael Hession. 1925-30 William Meehan. 1927-31 Richard Roche. 1930-32 Daniel Egan. 1931-34 Edward McKay. 1932-34 Patrick Lynch. 1934-35 Thomas Kilroy. 1934-39 Patrick McGloin. 1935-37 John J McHugh. 1937-40 James Brennan (1934). 1939-43 Peter Lyons. 1940-41 Peter Smith. 1941-42 Patrick (William) Quinn. 1942-47 John J Donnelly. 1943-44 John McCallum. 1944-47 James McMahon. 1947 Edward Lynch. 1947-49 Henry Curran. 1947-51 John Walsh. 1949-51 Kenneth Cox. 1950-56 Charles Kelly. 1951-62 Francis J Doherty. 1956-58 Patrick J McFadden. 1956-63 Thomas McNulty. 1958-64 Gerard Lynch. 1962-72 Philip Doherty. 1963-65 John Cullen. 1965-67 Fedele Maestri. 1967-69 Ian Ashley. 1969-77 George Rodgers. 1972-78 Brian Saddler. 1977-79 Michael Fallon. 1978-80 David Barr. 1978-82 Thomas Dooley WF. 1979-81 Stephen Robson. 1980-84 Kenneth Batchelor. 1982-85 James Myers. 1985-88 Michael Fallon.

KIRKCALDY – ST MARIE'S: see Kirkcaldy. Our Lady of Perpetual Succour.

KIRKCALDY – ST PIUS X: 1964-88 Michael J Devane. 1988- Joseph Portelli.

LARBERT
Until 1932 served from Falkirk.
Heads: 1932-36 Joseph Byrne. 1936-43 Anthony Kelly. 1943-57 James Phelan. 1957-72 John Ward. 1972-79 William Anthony. 1979-89 Michael Carey. 1989- John Urquhart.
Assistants: 1961-62 Vaughan F J Morgan. 1962-63 Anthony McNally. 1963-69 Thomas McNulty. 1969-75 Ian Ashley. 1975-79 Andrew Forrest.

LASSWADE – NAZARETH HOUSE: CHAPLAINS
1985-86 James O'Hanlon.

LENNOXTOWN (Campsie)
Heads: 1866-89 John Magini (ED). 1889-99 Francis McKerrell (ED). 1899-1903 Joseph Hannan. 1903-12 Michael J Turner. 1912-16 Peter McDaniel. 1916-24 David Robertson. 1924-26 William Mellon. 1926-30 James Maguire. 1930-36 James Mulhern. 1936-49 Michael Whelahan. 1949-79 William McCabe. 1979-87 John McAllister. 1987- Thomas W Power.
Assistants: 1887 Joseph Donlevy. 1888-92 Peter McDaniel. 1892-94 George Mason. 1894-95 Thomas O'Carroll (ED). 1895-97 John Stuart. 1897-99 Thomas McDonna. 1899-1901 John Joyce (1896). 1901-03 Daniel Conway. 1903-06 Charles McGhee (Glasgow). 1906-09 Thomas Ferrigan. 1909-15 James F Tonner. 1915-16 Anthony O'Doherty. 1916-18 Daniel Ramsay. 1918-22 Daniel Kelly. 1922-24 Michael J Hession. 1924-26 Joseph A Ward. 1926-30 Bernard (John) McManus. 1930-31 Gerald J

Dorrian. 1931-36 James Gaffney. 1936-41 Maurice O'Meara. 1941-49 Edward Gilchrist. 1941-49 Dennis O'Connell. 1943-45 Thomas Watt. 1945-51 Peter Donati (serving Blanefield from 1948). 1949-58 Roderick Gemmell. 1958-64 Richard Somers. 1959-61 Stephen Wynne. 1961-67 Charles Brodie. 1964-65 Desmond McAllister. 1965-67 Michael McCullagh. 1967-70 James P Falconer. 1969-70 Alphonsus Rushe SPS. 1970-72 Francis J Doherty. 1970-79 Daniel Boyd. 1977-85 William Forrester SJ. 1981-82 Joseph Murray.

LEVEN: 1977-81 Gerard McGarry. 1981-89 David J Henry. From 1989 served from Kennoway.

LINLITHGOW
Heads: 1865-79 James McCartney (ED). 1879-83 John Lee (ED). 1883-85 William Berkery. 1885-89 John M Murphy. 1889-97 Donald Easson. 1897-98 vacant. 1898 James McGinnis (ED). 1898-1902 Patrick Shivers. 1902-12 Edward Miley. 1912-19 Francis O'Brien. 1919-24 Richard Delaney. 1924-34 Thomas Gillon. 1934-35 vacant. 1935-39 Peter Higgins. 1939-40 Peter Donati. 1940-80 Michael McGovern. 1980-86 Hugh Gordon. 1986- James Ferrari.
Assistants: 1892-93 Samuel McKeogh. 1895-96 David Robertson. 1896-97 James McOscar. 1897-98 Joseph Payne. 1898-99 Patrick Green. 1899-1900 George McConnachie. 1942-44 Michael Barry. 1946 Peter Smith. 1946-51 Vincent Duffy. 1957-67 Kevin Rafferty. 1967-68 Peter Bennett. 1969-70 William Gallacher.

LIVINGSTON – ST ANDREW'S
Heads: 1966-78 John F Byrne (1945). 1978-84 Charles Barclay. 1984- John Creanor.
Assistants: 1972-74 John Gordon. 1973-77 Gerard Hand. 1974-82 Henry Reid. 1976-81 Leonard Oliver. 1977-78 Brian Halloran. 1978-82 Brian Saddler. 1979-82 Hugh Shannon. 1981-86 Thomas Greenan. 1982 Michael Regan. 1987 George Paul. 1987- Gerard Fitzsimmons.

LIVINGSTON – ST PETER'S: 1982- Joseph McMullan.

LIVINGSTON – ST PHILIP'S: 1984-89 Alexander Mitchell. 1989- Allan T Chambers.

LOANHEAD
Heads: 1878-81 served from Dalkeith. 1881-84 Joseph Hannan. 1884-90 John Lee (ED). 1890-1901 Frederick Hoban. 1901-12 Charles Murdoch. 1912-16 Patrick Green. 1916-17 Joseph Long. 1917-23 Dominic Hart. 1923-26 Peter J Burns. 1926-36 Edward Morrison. 1936-38 William McCabe. 1938-67 Patrick Carden. 1967-68 vacant. 1968-82 Thomas Rhatigan. 1982-89 Hugh G White. 1989- William Conway.
Assistants: 1951-52 Eamon O'Brien. 1952-53 Thomas Hanlon. 1953-56 Daniel McGuinness. 1956-58 William (Liam) Healy.

LOCHGELLY

Heads: 1888-92 Patrick McNamara. 1892-1902 Patrick McMahon. 1902-16 Richard Hogan. 1916-35 Peter McDaniel. 1935-36 vacant. 1936-38 Joseph Byrne. 1938-43 Dominic Hart. 1943-58 Anthony R Gallagher. 1958-67 Michael O'Connor. 1967-69 Laurence Davison. 1969-85 Peter Lyons. 1985- Patrick Clarke.

Assistants: 1904-05 William O'Raw. 1906-09 Philip Moloney. 1906-12 William Mulligan. 1910-13 James Mulhern. 1912-17 Bernard McNamee. 1913-14 Thomas O'Keefe. 1914-16 Daniel Ramsay. 1917-18 H F Ritter. 1918-27 Hugh Conway. 1919-21 Peter J Burns. 1927-29 Charles Taylor. 1929-37 Richard V Gallagher. 1937-40 Michael McNulty. 1940-42 Anthony Smith. 1942-43 Malcolm MacKinnon. 1943-47 Thomas Hogan. 1947-48 Patrick O'Sullivan. 1948-49 Thomas Engelen. 1949-51 Edward Gilchrist. 1952-58 Henry Curran. 1958-67 Michael Walsh.

LOCHORE

Until 1913 served from Lochgelly.

Heads: 1913-30 James Mulhern. 1930-36 William McCabe. 1936-49 Thomas McGarvey. 1949-61 Patrick Lynch. 1961-72 Patrick J McNulty. 1972-85 James Nicholson. 1985-87 David McCann. 1987- Thomas Mullen.

Assistants: 1938-40 Michael McGovern. 1940-44 Joseph MacCabe. 1944-46 Joseph Sweeney. 1946-47 James Anderson. 1947-56 Anthony Kiernan. 1956-61 Ian Murray. 1960-61 Lawrence Moonan.

MELROSE: 1984-87 John G Robinson. From 1987 served from Selkirk.

METHIL

Until 1912 served from Kirkcaldy.

Heads: 1912-24 Joseph P McGrail. 1924-31 Thomas J Ferrigan. 1931-33 James Maguire. 1933-37 Bernard McLaughlin. 1937-65 Gerald Dorrian. 1965-77 Gerard McGarry. 1977-78 Henry Curran. 1978-87 Brian Halloran. 1987- Peter Gallacher.

Assistants: 1931-32 Patrick Carden. 1932-33 Thomas McGregor. 1933-36 Anthony R Gallagher. 1936-37 Stanislaus Eardley. 1937-38 Francis McFarlane. 1937-38 Michael O'Connor. 1938-40 James Corduff. 1939-42 William R Kelly. 1940-41 James Phelan. 1942-48 Patrick Cunningham. 1943-45 Alphonsus B McGrath. 1945-46 Walter P Crampton. 1946-47 James Leckie. 1947-49 Patrick Breen. 1949 Angus Neilson. 1949-50 Dennis O'Connell. 1949-54 Edward McColgan. 1950-54 James Prunty. 1954-55 Michael Jackson. 1954-60 Michael Coppinger. 1955-62 Anthony McNally. 1960-61 Frederick J Morgan. 1961-66 John Agnew. 1962-68 Eamon O'Brien. 1963-65 Bernard J McAllister. 1966-69 Desmond Lynagh. 1968-73 David J Henry. 1973-77 Patrick A Cannon.

MILTON OF CAMPSIE: 1967-76 Michael McCullagh. 1976- John Archibald.

MUSSELBURGH
Heads: 1901-23 Patrick McGettigan. 1923-36 John B Joyce (1899). 1936-37 Manus McIlhargie. 1937-58 Bernard McLaughlin. 1958-72 James Harold. 1972-84 John C Ward. 1984-85 Patrick Kelly. 1985-87 Anthony McNally. 1987- Michael McCullagh.
Assistants: 1930-32 Joseph MacArdle. 1932-36 Manus McIlhargie. 1937-39 Patrick O'Leary. 1939-53 Pierce Grace. 1953-55 David P Brown. 1955-58 Stanislaus Smith. 1958-60 Brian P Byrne. 1960-62 John Cullen. 1962-65 John J McMeel. 1963-70 Michael McCabe. 1965-70 John McLaughlin. 1970-72 Ian T Gillon. 1970-72 David McCann. 1972-84 Patrick Kelly. 1985-86 Stephen Toner. 1986- Jock Dalrymple. 1988 James G Tracey.

MUSSELBURGH – SISTERS OF CHARITY: CHAPLAINS
1972-73 Patrick J McFadden. 1973-77 John Curran.

NEWBATTLE (Dalkeith, St Luke's)
1971-77 Edward Gilchrist. 1977-85 Daniel Foley. 1985-88 Gordon R Brown. 1988- Michael Fallon.

NEWTONGRANGE
Heads: 1947-58 Michael O'Connor. 1958-71 Edward Gilchrist.
Assistants: 1947-50 Eugene Daly. 1950-53 Thomas Engelen.
From 1971 served from Dalkeith.

NORTH BERWICK
1879-82 served from Haddington.
Heads: 1882-86 Matthew Brady (ED). 1886-91 Colin C Mackenzie (Aberdeen). 1891-1910 Charles J Duthie. 1910-12 George Bennett. 1912-19 Alfred Smith-Steinmetz. 1919-26 John Allan Gray (1902). 1926-33 Bernard McLaughlin. 1933-35 James Maxwell. 1935-43 Peter Connolly. 1943-48 Thomas E Gallagher. 1948-58 Thomas Martin. 1958-72 Matthew J Donoghue. 1972-77 John Ward. 1977-86 Kevin Rafferty. 1986-89 Francis Kerr. 1989- John Barry.
Assistants: 1938 Hugh Brady. 1964-66 Michael J Cassidy. 1966-67 Hugh G White. 1977 Patrick Boylan.

OAKLEY: 1879-86 Francis J Lynch. 1886-1907 served occasionally from Dunfermline. 1907-12 Francis O'Brien. 1912-14 Thomas J Ferrigan. 1914-19 Henry Woods. 1919-29 Alfred Smith-Steinmetz. 1929-37 J Andrew MacIntyre. 1937-38 James Collins. 1938-41 Francis J McFarlane. 1941-46 Peter Smith. 1946-53 John Fusco. 1953-86 John McNay. 1986-89 Edward Gallagher. 1989- Michael Carey.

PATHHEAD FORD: 1967-76 Michael J Cassidy. 1976-85 John Fusco. 1985-86 served from Dalkeith by Edward Mohan. 1986- Patrick Boylan.

PEEBLES
Heads: 1850-83 James Clapperton (ED). 1883-1912 James McCartney (ED). 1912-19 J Stevenson Lyle. 1919-27 Michael J Turner. 1927-29 J Andrew Macintyre. 1929-41 William Rooney. 1941-53 James G Harold. 1953-54 Thomas P McGregor. 1954-63 John McKee (1936). 1963-77 Peter Donati. 1977-85 Alexander Bremner. 1985-88 James Myers. 1988- David McCann.
Assistant: 1897-98 George Mason.

PENICUIK
Heads: 1882-86 Thomas Boilson. 1886-87 vacant. 1887-89 Patrick McAnaa. 1889-90 Frederick Hoban. 1890-92 Patrick McMahon. 1892-1903 Patrick McNamara. 1903-09 Daniel Conway. 1909-26 John D Wood. 1926-31 served from Rosewell. 1931-33 James Maxwell. 1933-36 Anthony Flynn. 1936-38 Roger Gallagher. 1938-41 James K Dennis. 1941-54 Gerard (William) McGarry. 1954-67 Edward Hyland. 1967- Michael J Jackson.
Assistants: 1902-03 Edward Blake. 1920-21 Daniel Ramsay. 1921-23 Bernard O'Hanlon. 1923-24 Joseph Byrne. 1924-25 Hugh Milligan. 1925-26 Philip Murphy.

PITTENWEEM: 1952-53 Eric Gordon. 1953-62 Daniel Joseph Boyle (1940). 1962-69 James Phelan. 1969-84 James E McGee. 1984- Robert Hendrie.

POLMONT
Heads: 1913-23 William Grant. 1923-26 Edward Morrison. 1926-29 Philip Murphy. 1929-30 Daniel Egan. 1930-36 Thomas McGarvey. 1936-75 Thomas McCann. 1975- Thomas Hanlon.
Assistants: 1944-45 Edward McKay. 1946-47 William McEwan. 1947-48 James McMahon. 1948 Leo Deery. 1948-50 Richard Somers. 1950-53 John C Barry. 1967-73 Andrew Forrest.

PORTOBELLO: see Edinburgh, St John the Evangelist.

RAPLOCH: see Stirling, St Margaret of Scotland.

RATHO: 1877-81 Daniel Donnelly (WD). 1881-88 William Farquhar (ND). 1888-89 Frederick Hoban. 1889-90 Joseph B Hare (ED). 1890-95 Thomas Monaghan. 1895-1903 served from East Calder. 1903-66 served from Balerno. 1966-77 served from Currie. 1977-81 Vincent Logan. 1981-85 Michael Fallon. 1985-86 served from Winchburgh. From 1986 served from Currie.

RICCARTON – HERRIOT WATT UNIVERSITY: CHAPLAINS
1977-79 Joseph McMahon. 1979-81 Brian P Byrne. 1981-86 served from Ratho. From 1986 served from Currie.

ROSEWELL
Until 1926 served from Penicuik.
Heads: 1926-42 John D Wood. 1942-43 Bryan Scott. 1943-52 Anthony Kelly. 1952-59 James Connolly. 1959-65 Anthony R Gallagher. 1965-72 Denis O'Connell. 1972-79 Thomas Corcoran. 1979-86 James Ferrari. 1986- Kenneth Batchelor.
Assistants: 1926-28 John McGrail. 1926-30 Gerard (John) Sinnott. 1928-30 Nicholas Comey. 1930-33 Francis McFarlane. 1932-33 Patrick Carden. 1933-34 Thomas Corcoran. 1934-37 Bernard Kelly. 1937 Bernard Kielt. 1937-38 Daniel McSorley. 1938-42 John McGeown (1938). 1943-52 Laurence Foley. 1952-59 Peter Gallacher. 1959-61 John Archibald. 1961-62 Lawrence Moonan. 1962-65 James E McGee. 1964-67 Peter Gallacher. 1966-67 Alistair Lawson. 1967-68 Hugh G White. 1968-69 John Curran. 1969-73 Vincent Logan. 1978-83 Michael Burns.

ROSEWELL – ST JOSEPH'S HOME / HOSPITAL: CHAPLAINS
1973-77 Vincent Logan. 1977-80 David McCann. 1984-85 James O'Hanlon. 1985- Andrew Monaghan.

ROSYTH: Combined with Inverkeithing until 1937. 1937-62 Thomas J Ferrigan. 1962- Daniel Joseph Boyle (1940).

RUMFORD: see Polmont

ST ANDREWS, FIFE
Heads: 1884-1909 George Angus. 1909-24 Herbert R Laughton. 1924-29 William Rooney. 1929-55 John A Gray (1902). 1955-69 Hugh Gordon. 1969-87 Thomas Engelen. 1987- Brian Halloran.
Assistants: 1906-09 Herbert R Laughton. 1935-41 Gordon Gray. 1941-43 Roderick Gemmell. 1941-45 Walter P Crampton. 1943-46 Thomas Engelen. 1946-47 Charles Brodie. 1949-52 Francis Thomson. 1953-64 Ian T Gillan. 1956-60 Peter Nelson. 1967-69 Lawrence Moonan.

ST ANDREWS UNIVERSITY: CHAPLAINS
1964-70 Ian Gillan. 1970-74 John Dalrymple. 1974-79 Brian McKean. 1979-83 James Thomson. 1983-87 Robert G McGarrigle. From 1987 served by parish priest, St Andrews.

SELKIRK: Until 1902 served by Jesuits. 1902-06 Alfred P Roche. 1906-16 John Allan Gray (1902). 1916-24 Edward Mellon. 1924-28 David Robertson. 1928-30 Joseph Ward. 1930-38 Daniel Kelly. 1938-39 Roger Gallagher. 1939-40 Bernard Kelly. 1940-49 Michael McNulty. 1949-55 Hugh Gordon. 1955-67 Walter P Crampton. 1967-69 John Rogerson. 1969-77 Angus Neilson. 1977-87 Eamon O'Brien. 1987- John G Robinson.

SLAMANNAN: 1887-89 George Mullan. 1889-94 Thomas O'Carroll (ED). 1894-97 George Mason. 1897-1903 James McOscar. 1903-07 Francis O'Brien. 1907-12 James MacDonald (1903). 1912-13 Dominic Hart. 1913-14 Peter J Burns. 1914-16 Robert J Rattrie. 1916-19 Richard Delaney. 1919-23 Edward Morrison. 1923-39 served from Longriggend. 1939-40 Patrick McGloin. 1940-43 Patrick O'Leary. 1943-47 John McGeown (1938). 1947-53 John McCallum. 1953-63 Bernard O'Donnell. 1963-67 Michael Jackson. 1967-69 Peter Gallacher. 1969 Angus Neilson. 1969-77 Daniel Foley. 1977-78 Patrick Quinn. 1978-86 Bernard J McAllister. 1986-89 Basil Postlethwaite. From 1989 served from St Francis Xavier's, Falkirk.

SOUTH QUEENSFERRY: 1884-87 served from Cramond. 1887-90 Michael J Turner. 1890-1928 William Farquhar (ND). 1928-30 Patrick J Rice. 1930-32 Edward Mellon. 1932-37 Michael Kelly. 1937-69 Bernard O'Hanlon. 1969-81 John Rogerson. 1981-87 John Callaghan. 1987-89 Bernard Doonan. 1989- Paul Capaldi.

STIRLING – HOLY SPIRIT: 1964- Patrick J Rourke.

STIRLING – ST MARGARET OF SCOTLAND (Raploch)
Heads: 1954-84 James O'Hanlon. 1984-87 John McCluskey SJ. 1987- Michael Bagan.
Assistants: 1955-57 David Brown. 1957-64 James McKinnon. 1964-65 John Archibald. 1965-67 William Gallacher. 1967-69 John Callaghan.

STIRLING – ST MARY'S
Heads: 1876-79 Patrick McManus (ED). 1879-84 Francis McKerrell (ED). 1884-1919 John Smith (ED). 1919-49 Francis J Macmanus. 1949-82 Thomas J McLaughlin. 1982- Thomas Rhatigan.
Assistants: 1880 John Murphy (1880). 1880-81 Edmund O'Kane. 1881-82 Thomas Boilson. 1882-84 Donald MacKay (WD). 1884-87 Patrick Shivers. 1887-89 Joseph Donlevy. 1889-96 Philip Sheahan. 1896-98 David Robertson. 1898-99 Joseph B Hare (ED). 1898-1901 Charles Murdoch. 1901-03 William P Costigan. 1903-10 Thomas Gillon. 1907-09 Richard J Fitzgerald. 1909-14 Robert J Rattrie. 1910-11 Patrick Horgan. 1911-16 James Heaney. 1914-17 Patrick McHugh. 1916-18 Anthony O'Doherty. 1917-18 James Hart. 1918-19 Edward Morrison. 1919-20 Nicholas Carrigan. 1919-20 Kiernan Joyce. 1920-23 James Mullan. 1920-24 William Quigley. 1924-26 Michael Downey. 1924-30 Joseph Byrne. 1927-28 Michael Downey. 1928-30 Francis McFarlane. 1930-33 Nicholas Comey. 1930-33 Daniel O'Reilly. 1932-34 John J Donnelly. 1932-36 John Fusco. 1934-35 John Ward. 1936-37 Michael Walls. 1936-46 William Wilson. 1937 Thomas McLaughlin. 1938-40 Joseph McCabe. 1941-44 Eugene Loughlin. 1943-45 James O'Hanlon. 1945-46 Richard Conway. 1945-48 Kenneth Cox. 1946-48 James Bacon. 1946-49 Hugh Gordon. 1947-49 Michael Jackson. 1948-49 Richard Conway. 1949-52

Henry Curran. 1949-64 John Kerrisk. 1951-61 James Rae. 1954-57 Eric Gordon. 1961-64 Charles Barclay. 1964-67 Andrew Forrest. 1965-69 Daniel Foley. 1967-76 Alistair Lawson. 1976-80 John Fox. 1980-82 Matthew McGovern. 1982-84 Michael Purcell. 1984-85 Gerard Fitzsimmons. 1985-86 Basil Postlethwaite.

STIRLING UNIVERSITY: CHAPLAINS
1970-78 Ian Murray. 1978-83 Desmond Lynagh. 1983-85 Michael Burns. 1985-86 Andrew Campbell OSB. 1986-89 Michael Burns. From 1989 served from Cowie.

STONEYBURN: 1953-61 John McCallum. 1961-65 Denis O'Connell. 1965-76 Malcolm Macfarlane. 1976-87 Michael McCullagh. 1987- Alexander Bremner.

STRATHBLANE: see Balfron.

TALLA RESERVOIR (Construction workers' camp.)
1898-99 George Mason. 1899-1905 Thomas McDonna.

TORRANCE: Served from Milton of Campsie until 1979. 1979- Daniel Boyd.

TRANENT
Heads: 1888-90 William Farquhar (ND). 1890-98 Alfred P Roche. 1898-1901 Patrick McGettigan. 1901-13 John Joyce (1896). 1913-24 A Edward Franklin. 1924-36 Richard Delaney. 1936-69 Philip Murphy. 1969-70 vacant. 1970- Richard Somers.
Assistants: 1928-29 John Breen. 1929-30 Michael Kelly. 1930-32 Peter Harkin. 1960-64 Michael J Cassidy. 1964-66 James D Radin. 1966-67 Patrick J McFadden.

WEST CALDER
Heads: 1874-90 Anthony Goldie (ED). 1890-1912 John Murphy (ED). 1912-18 Thomas McDonna. 1918-22 Cuthbert F Chase. 1922-30 John L Stuart. 1930 Joseph McElhenney. 1930-34 Michael V Bruce. 1934-44 William Quigley. 1944-47 James K Birnie. 1947-73 James Payne. 1973-80 Daniel Patrick Boyle. 1980-84 Andrew Shiels. 1984- Alistair Lawson.
Assistants: 1895-1902 Thomas O'Carroll (ED). 1902-03 Patrick McMahon. 1903-04 William P Costigan. 1904-05 Peter Burns. 1905-06 Thomas McDonna. 1906-08 William Saunderson. 1908-11 Henry Kenny. 1911-12 Thomas J Ferrigan. 1943-44 James Hart. 1982-84 Alistair Lawson (administrator).

WHITBURN
Until 1948 served from Blackburn.
Heads: 1948-49 Patrick C Lynch. 1949-50 Michael McNulty. 1950-52

served from Blackburn. 1952-53 Thomas P McGregor. 1953-61 William Wilson. 1961-72 John McCallum. 1972-88 Daniel McGuinness. 1988- James Myers.

Assistants: 1948-49 John M Kerrisk. 1949-50 Michael J Jackson. 1964-69 James McKinnon. 1969-74 Edward Gallagher. 1972 David M Barr.

WINCHBURGH

Heads: 1913-14 John Joyce (1896). 1914-15 Thomas J Ferrigan. 1915-29 James Tonner. 1929-30 vacant. 1930-32 Joseph Byrne. 1932-45 Harry J Kenny. 1945-46 vacant. 1946-56 Michael Murnin. 1956-85 Edward Quigley. 1985- John Ramsay.

Assistant: 1978-85 John Ramsay.

BAUCHI – NIGERIA

From 1957 priests from the Archdiocese of St Andrews & Edinburgh were going out to serve in Nigeria. In 1964 the Province of Bauchi was officially adopted by the Archdiocese. The following priests have served there. (As Directory entries are sometimes misleading the dates can only be approximate.)

1957- Daniel Simpson. 1958-59 Patrick J McFadden. 1958-64 Daniel Foley. 1961-66 John Gibbons. 1961-66 John McAllister. 1964-65 Brian P Byrne. 1965-66 Anthony McNally. 1965-67 David H McCann. 1967-80 Patrick Clarke. 1971-75 John Agnew. 1971-75 John Callaghan. 1971-75 Leo Glancy. 1974-84 Alexander J Mitchell. 1977- Patrick Aidan Cannon. 1978-82 James L Myers.

Diocese of Aberdeen

Secular Clergy

ANDERSON, WILLIAM R T: see archdiocese of St Andrew's & Edinburgh

ANTON, JAMES: Born Huntly 1879. Educated Blairs 1894-98; Issy 1898-1900; St Sulpice 1900-03. Ordained Paris 1903. Lent to Archdiocese of St A & E: Edinburgh (particular mission not stated) 1903. Marydale 1903-04. Dornie 1904-06. St Peter's, Aberdeen 1906-13. Inverurie 1913-15. Fraserburgh 1915-22. Nairn 1922-30. Dufftown 1930-43. Fochabers 1943-48. Died Fochabers 14 Feb 1948.

ASHWORTH, BERNARD: Born Upper Norwood, near London, 1890. Educated St Mary's, Woolhampton. Worked in the law courts. Officer in Gunners 1914-18; invalided out due to poison gas. Married 1919. Widowed 1955. Studied for the priesthood Beda, Rome 1956-60. Ordained Rome 1960. St Peter's, Aberdeen 1960-62. Braemar 1962; left as altitude affected his health. Chaplain, Nazareth House, Aberdeen 1962-73. Died Aberdeen 31 March 1973.

AUER, BERNARD: Born Aberdeen 1882. Educated Blairs 1895-1900; Issy 1900-02; St Sulpice 1902-05. Ordained Paris 1905. Aberdeen Cathedral 1905-06. St Mary's, Inverness 1906-12. Wick 1912-14. Dingwall 1914-34. Tomintoul 1934-43. Elgin 1943-56. Retired to Banchory 1956. Died Rothesay 21 Aug 1959.

BARRY, PETER: Born Kirkwall 1944. Educated Blairs, Drygrange. Ordained Edinburgh 1969. Aberdeen Cathedral 1969-72. Dornie 1972-76. Bishop's House 1976-77. Our Lady of Aberdeen, Aberdeen 1977-83. Aviemore 1983-88. Lerwick 1988-.

BELLASIS, HENRY: From the Oratory, Birmingham. Clova 1897-98. Otherwise served in England.

BENNETT, ALEXANDER: Born Blairs 1884. Educated Blairs 1897-1902; Issy 1902-04; St Sulpice 1904-07. Ordained Blairs 1907. Aberdeen

Cathedral 1907-08. Fochabers 1908-10. Professor, Blairs 1910-18. Dornie 1918-24. Tombae 1924-49. Fochabers 1949-60. Retired to Banchory 1960, and died there 30 Nov 1961.

BEVERIDGE, JOHN: Born Methil 1952. Educated Thurso High School; Langbank; Blairs; Scots College, Rome. Ordained Thurso 1977. Alness 1977. Rome, completing studies, 1977-78. St Mary's, Inverness 1978-80. St Francis', Aberdeen 1980-85. Buckie 1985-88. Died Buckie 23 April 1988.

BIRRELL, JAMES: Born Dunfermline 1948. Educated George Heriot's School, Edinburgh; Dundee University; Drygrange. Ordained 1979. St Mary's, Inverness 1979-82. Dingwall 1982-90. Our Lady of Aberdeen, Aberdeen 1990-.

BONNYMAN, JAMES: Born Clochan, Enzie 1885. Educated Milne's Institution, Fochabers; Blairs 1901-04; St Peter's 1904-06; Issy 1906-11; St Sulpice 1911-12. Ordained Paris 1912. Aberdeen Cathedral 1912-13. Lerwick 1913. Aberdeen Cathedral 1913-14. Wick 1914-19. Ballater 1919-25. Portsoy 1925-39. Braemar 1939-41. Died Braemar 29 Aug 1941.

BOWIE, WILLIAM: Born Jersey City, USA 1892. Came to Scotland as a child. Educated Blairs 1905-11; Versailles 1911-14; Scots College, Rome 1914-17. Ordained Rome 1916. St Mary's, Inverness 1917-18. Aberdeen Cathedral 1918-19. Wick 1919-25. Aboyne 1925-32. Died Ilford 19 Aug 1932.

BRADY, JOHN: see Motherwell diocese

BRANNAN, CHRISTOPHER STEPHEN: Born Glasgow 1945. Educated St Aloysius' College, Glasgow; Glasgow University; Beda, Rome. Ordained Aberdeen 1983. Aberdeen Cathedral 1983-85. St Francis', Aberdeen 1985-.

BRENNAN, JAMES (1945): see archdiocese of St Andrew's and Edinburgh

BUTLER, GEORGE: Born Ampleforth 1906. Educated Blairs 1918-24; St Lo 1924-25; Coutances 1925-30. Ordained Ampleforth 1930. Aberdeen Cathedral 1930-37. Dornie 1937-45. Aboyne 1945-52. St Joseph's, Aberdeen 1952-66. Retired to Ballater 1966 and died there 10 May 1974.

CAMERON, ANDREW: Born Simla, India 1887. Educated Blairs 1903-05; Valladolid 1905-07; Scots College, Rome 1907-14. Ordained Rome 1913. Aberdeen Cathedral 1914-18. Aboyne 1918-19. Clova 1919-29. Fraserburgh 1929-31. Transferred to Archdiocese of St Andrews and Edinburgh. Portobello 1931-32. Immaculate Conception, Bathgate 1932-

33. St Patrick's, Edinburgh 1933-36. Hawick 1936-38. Bonnybridge 1938-40. Retired 1940. Died Musselburgh 28 July 1945.

CAMPBELL, DONALD: see Argyll diocese

CASLIN, JOHN JOSEPH: Ordained [?Ireland] 1945. Came to Aberdeen diocese 1954. Sutherland 1954-57. Brora 1957-59. Aberdeen Cathedral 1959. Tomintoul 1959-68. Inverurie 1968-69. C/o Bishop's House, Aberdeen 1969-71. No further entries.

CASSIDY, JOHN: Born Paisley 1915. Educated St Mirin's Academy, Paisley; joined White Fathers, continuing education in Autreppe, Algiers and Carthage. Ordained 1942. Taught in White Father seminaries, England, Scotland and Holland 1943-55. Nigeria 1955-57. Left the White Fathers for health reasons and came to Aberdeen diocese 1957. Aberdeen Cathedral 1957-62. Stratherrick 1962-66. Portsoy 1966-68. Retired to Aberdeen 1968 and died there 1 Oct 1975.

CATTERAL, ROBERT: Ordained for Salford 1930. Dornie 1957-58. No further entries.

CHISHOLM, DONALD: Born Glenmoriston 1860. Educated Blairs 1873-77; St Edmund's, Douay 1877-80; Issy 1880-82; St Sulpice 1882-85. Ordained Paris 1885. Glengairn 1885-88. Stratherrick 1888-90. Professor, Blairs 1890-92. Tomintoul 1892-99. Eskadale 1899-1918. Retired in Eskadale 1918 and died there 8 April 1919.

CLAPPERTON, WILLIAM: Born Fochabers 1886. Educated Aberdeen Grammar School; Ushaw; Durham University; Scots College, Rome 1907-13. Ordained Rome 1913. Vice-rector, Scots College, Rome 1913-22 and rector there 1922-40. Banff 1940-46. Rector, Scots College, Rome 1946-60. Retired in Rome 1960 and died there 19 Feb 1969.

COLLINS, CHARLES: Born Glasgow 1912. Educated Blairs 1926-31; Scots College, Rome 1931-37. Ordained Rome 1937. St Peter's, Aberdeen 1938-46. Kirkwall 1946-52. Ballater 1952-57. Tomintoul 1957-59. Banff 1959-81. Retired to Ballater 1981. Died Aberdeen 31 March 1986.

CONTI, MARIO: Born Elgin 1934. Educated Blairs 1947-52; Scots College, Rome 1952-59. Ordained Rome 1958. Aberdeen Cathedral 1959-62. Wick 1962-67. Thurso 1967-77. Consecrated Bishop of Aberdeen 1977.

COPLAND, JOHN: Born Tombae 1920. Educated Blairs; Scots College, Rome; St Peter's. Ordained Blairs 1946. St Peter's, Aberdeen 1946-48. Aberdeen Cathedral 1948-51. Portsoy 1951-64. Braemar 1964-66. St Joseph's, Aberdeen 1966-74. Keith 1974-.

COYLE, RAYMOND: Born South Shields 1938. Educated St Mary's College, Kentucky; St Mary's University, Baltimore. Ordained Princeton, New Jersey for Trenton diocese 1977. Lent to Aberdeen diocese; later was incardinated into it. Dingwall 1978-79. Aberdeen Cathedral 1979-80. Dornie 1980-89. Fraserburgh 1989-.

CRONIN, FRANCIS: Born Lossiemouth 1879. Educated Blairs 1892-96; St Peter's 1896-98; Scots College, Rome 1898-1904. Ordained Rome 1903. Aberdeen Cathedral 1904-11. Vice-rector, Valladolid 1911-18. St Mary's, Inverness 1918-28. Rector, Blairs 1928-39. Died St Leonard's- on-Sea 13 March 1939.

CUNNINGHAM, JOHN: Born Aberdeen 1931. Educated Blairs; St Edmund's, Ware. Ordained 1955. Aberdeen Cathedral 1955-59. Brora 1959-65. St Joseph's, Aberdeen 1965-66. London in bad health 1966. Stonehaven 1966-67. Stratherrick 1967-73. Nairn 1973-77. Died on his way to hospital 19 Aug 1977.

DAINE, JOHN: Ordained for Salford 1878. Clova 1881-82. No further entries.

DALTON, JOSEPH: Born Melbourne, Australia 1936. Educated Melbourne, Rome. Ordained for Leeds diocese 1977. Lent to Aberdeen diocese: 1983-90 Stratherrick. Returned to England 1990.

DAVIS, WILFRID: Born Crosshill, Glasgow 1905. Educated St Columbcille's School, Rutherglen; Blairs 1918-23; Petit Seminaire d'Avranches 1923-24; Issy-les-Moulineaux 1924-30. Ordained Blairs 1930. Buckie 1930-33. St Peter's, Aberdeen 1933-38. Kirkwall 1938-46. Banff 1946-53. Dingwall 1953-61. Nairn 1961-73. Died Inverness 20 April 1973.

DOUGLAS, EDWARD: see Glasgow archdiocese

DOYLE, ALISTAIR: Born Montrose 1937. Educated Lawside Academy, Dundee; Oscott College. Ordained Birmingham for Clifton diocese 1962. Transferred to Aberdeen diocese 1964 and was later incardinated into it. Holy Family, Aberdeen 1964-65. Aberdeen Cathedral 1965-68. Brora 1968-74. Peterhead 1974-83. Banff 1983-89. St Ninian's, Inverness 1989-.

FALLON, PATRICK: see archdiocese of St Andrews & Edinburgh

FERGUSON, ALEXANDER: Born Braemar 1888. Educated Blairs 1903-08; Propaganda, Rome 1908-14. Ordained Rome 1914. Aberdeen Cathedral 1914-30. Sacred Heart, Aberdeen 1930-40. Fetternear 1940-48. Fochabers 1948-49. Ballater 1949-52. Retired to Musselburgh 1952 and died there 2 Feb 1957.

FITZPATRICK, MICHAEL: Born Aberdeen 1936. Educated Blairs, Drygrange. Ordained Blairs 1959. Further studies, Rome 1959-63. Aberdeen Cathedral 1963-65. Brora 1965-68. Peterhead 1968-74. St Joseph's, Aberdeen 1974-79. Left priesthood 1979.

FORDE, (Patrick) GORDON: Born Buckie 1950. Educated Fochabers High School; Langbank; Blairs; Scots College, Rome. Ordained Fochabers 1975. Aberdeen Cathedral 1975. Completing studies, Rome 1975-76. Aberdeen Cathedral 1976-79. Inverurie 1979-.

FRASER, CHARLES: Born Kiltarlity, Beauly 1910. Educated Blairs 1926-29; Valladolid 1929-37. Ordained Blairs 1937. Aberdeen Cathedral 1937-45. Dornie 1945-54. Eskadale 1954-66. Braemar 1966-72. Died Braemar 20 June 1972.

FRASER, ROBERT: Born Wardhouse, Aberdeenshire 1858. Educated Blairs 1872-75; St Edmund's, Douay 1875-77; Scots College, Rome 1877-83. Ordained Rome 1882. Professor, Blairs 1883-97. Rector, Scots College, Rome 1897-1913. Ordained Bishop of Dunkeld 1913. Died Dundee 28 March 1914.

GARRITY, DENIS: see Glasgow archdiocese

GEDDES, AENEAS: Born Macduff, Banffshire 1882. Educated Blairs 1885-1900; Issy 1900-02; St Sulpice 1902-05. Ordained Paris 1905. Inverurie 1905-07. Stratherrick 1907-18. Eskadale 1918-54. Retired to Peterculter 1954 and died there 9 April 1957.

GORDON, HUGH: see archdiocese of St Andrews & Edinburgh

GOWANS, JOHN: see Glasgow archdiocese

GRADY, PATRICK: Born Bellshill 1920. Educated Our Lady's High School, Motherwell; joined White Fathers and continued his education at Bishop's Waltham, England; Hainault, Belgium; Algiers; Carthage. Left White Fathers and was accepted for Aberdeen diocese; completed his education St Peter's. Ordained Blairs 1944. St Mary's, Inverness 1944-48. Tynet 1948-51. Keith 1951-54. Sacred Heart, Aberdeen 1954-59. Fraserburgh 1959-62. Alford 1962-70. Eskadale 1970-75. Aviemore 1975-77. St Peter's, Aberdeen 1977-89. Retired 1989.

GRANT, ANDREW: Born Auchindryne, Braemar 1869. Educated Blairs 1883-86; Rue Vaugirard 1886-89; Scots College, Rome 1889-95. Ordained Rome 1894. Aberdeen Cathedral 1895-97. Wick 1897-99. Aberdeen Cathedral 1899-1902. St Peter's, Aberdeen 1902-16. Chaplain, 51st Highland Division, 1916-19. St Peter's, Aberdeen 1919-47. Retired to Portessie 1947. Died Aberdeen 2 June 1955.

GRANT, GEORGE: Born Auchindryne, Braemar 1877. Educated Braemar School; Blairs 1890-94; Notre Dame des Champs, Paris, 1894-95; Scots College, Rome 1895-1900. Ordained Rome 1900. St Peter's, Aberdeen 1901-06. Dornie 1906-11. Aboyne 1911-16. St Peter's, Aberdeen 1916-19. Aboyne 1919-25. Tomintoul 1925-30. Beauly 1930-54. Retired to Buckie 1954 and died there 6 March 1959.

GRATION, JOSEPH GEORGE: Born Keith 1941. Educated Blairs, Drygrange. Ordained Aberdeen 1965. Holy Family, Aberdeen 1965-66. Aberdeen Cathedral 1966-70. Left the diocese 1970.

HEALY, THOMAS (1939): see Glasgow archdiocese

HENDERSON, JAMES: Born Keith 1867. Educated Blairs 1880-84; Douay 1884-86; Scots College, Rome 1886-92. Ordained Rome 1891. Aberdeen Cathedral 1892-93. Kirkwall 1893-94. Strichen 1894-95. Fraserburgh 1895-97. Died Fraserburgh 28 Feb 1897.

HUNKIN, ANDREW: An Anglican, converted to Roman Catholicism. Ordained April 1974. Aberdeen Cathedral 1974. Returned to Anglican Church.

KEANE, STEPHEN ALOYSIUS: Born Paisley 1894. Educated Fort Augustus 1920-21; Campion House, Osterley 1921-22; Valladolid 1922-29. Ordained Valladolid 1929. St Peter's, Aberdeen 1929-31. Fraserburgh 1931-37. His health broke down and he transferred to Glasgow archdiocese: Mossend 1938-49. Transferred to England: Southend-on-Sea, Burnham-on-Couch, 1949-62. Retired to Glasgow 1962 and died there 14 Aug 1963.

KEENAN, PATRICK: Born Aberdeen 1880. Educated Blairs 1893-98; Issy 1898-1900; Scots College, Rome 1900-03. Ordained Rome 1903. St Mary's, Inverness 1903-06. In bad health at Cathedral and then in England 1906-08. Lent to Glasgow archdiocese: St Mirin's, Paisley 1908-12. Beauly 1912-13. Sacred Heart, Aberdeen 1913-28. St Mary's, Inverness 1928-33. Admitted to St Raphael's Hospital, Edinburgh 1933 and died there 31 Aug 1934.

KEITH, DAVID: Born Dundee 1925. Educated Blairs; St Peter's; St Sulpice. Ordained 1948. St Mary's, Inverness 1948-51. Aberdeen Cathedral 1951-53. Wick 1953-62. Aviemore 1962-74. Buckie 1974-84. Ill in Dundee 1984-85 and died there 2 May 1985.

KENNEDY, ALISTAIR (Alexander): Born Inverness 1901. Educated Blairs 1914-20; Scots College, Rome 1920-27. Ordained Rome 1926. St Peter's, Aberdeen 1927-29. Dornie 1929-37. Fochabers 1937-43. Tomintoul 1943-52. Forres 1952-75. Died Forres 25 June 1975.

KERR, ALEXANDER SPENCE: Born Fife-Keith 1893. Educated St Margaret's School, Huntly; Blairs 1907-13; Scots College, Rome 1913-20. Ordained Rome 1920. Aberdeen Cathedral 1920-24. Dornie 1924-29. Clova 1929-33. Aberlour 1933-41. Braemar 1941-62. Died Braemar 30 June 1962.

KERR, GEORGE GORDON: Born Fife-Keith 1908. Educated Blairs 1922-27; Scots College, Rome 1927-34. Ordained Rome 1933. Buckie 1934-41. Peterhead 1941-47. Wick 1947-53. Marydale 1953-61. Died Inverness 22 Oct 1961.

LAMONT, JOSEPH: Born Lumphanan 1903. Educated Lumphanan School; Aboyne Higher Grade School; Blairs 1918-23; St Sulpice 1923-28. Ordained Blairs 1928. Aberdeen Cathedral 1928-30. Wick 1930-36. Fetternear 1936-40. Sacred Heart, Aberdeen 1940-54. Keith 1954-73. Died Keith 12 Dec 1973.

LARKIN, RICHARD: Ordained for Passionist Fathers 1950. Served in Kilmarnock. Left Passionists and came to Aberdeen diocese as a secular priest 1957. St Mary's, Inverness 1957-59. Left diocese 1959.

LAWLESS, EDWARD: Ordained 1888. Clova 1912-14. No further entries.

McBAIN, JOHN: Born Huntly 1863. Educated Blairs 1877-81; St Edmund's, Douay 1881-83; Scots College, Rome 1883-89. Ordained Rome 1888. Aberdeen Cathedral 1889-90. St Joseph's, Aberdeen 1890-91. Aboyne 1891-97. Professor, Blairs 1897-1910. Banff 1910-12. Chapeltown 1912-15. Sick leave 1915-18. Aberlour 1918-33. Braemar 1933-38. Stonehaven 1938-40. Retired to Banchory 1940 and died there 14 July 1948.

McCABE, JOHN: Born Mossend 1907. Educated Our Lady's High School, Motherwell; worked as miner; educated for priesthood Campion House, Osterley; St Edmund's College, Ware. Ordained Mossend 1953. Aberdeen Cathedral 1953-55. Chapeltown 1955-61. Sacred Heart, Aberdeen 1961-72. Bulawayo for his health 1972-76. Returned to Scotland but was too ill to work. Became chaplain to the Little Sisters of the Poor, Jersey. Died Jersey 8 Jan 1979.

McCURRACH, GEORGE ALEXANDER: Born Preshome 1915. Educated Blairs 1927-33; St Lo 1933-34; Issy 1934-39. Ordained Blairs 1939. Aberdeen Cathedral 1939-41. Buckie 1941-42. Aberdeen Cathedral 1942-47. Clova 1947-53. RAF chaplain 1953-59. St Ninian's, Inverness 1959-79. Forres 1979-.

MACDONALD, BERNARD GORDON: Born Dufftown 1924. Educated Blairs; St Edmund's College, Ware. Ordained Aberdeen 1948. Aberdeen

Cathedral 1948-55. Holy Family, Aberdeen 1955-61. Dingwall 1961-79. St Ninian's, Inverness 1979-89. Thurso 1989-.

MACDONALD, BRIAN ARCHIEBALD WASON: Born Irvine 1955. Educated Dumfries, Kilwinning, Drygrange. Ordained Aberdeen 1982. Aberdeen Cathedral 1982. St Mary's, Inverness 1982-84. C/o Bishop's House, Aberdeen 1984-89. No further entries.

MACDONALD, CHARLES: Born Auchdregnie Farm, near Tombae 1867. Educated Tombae School; Blairs 1880-84; Douay 1884-86; Issy 1886-88; St Sulpice 1888-91. Ordained Paris 1891. Aberdeen Cathedral 1891-93. Inverurie 1893-94. Huntly 1894-1908. Keith 1908-27. Buckie 1927-45. Retired 1945. Died Portessie 8 July 1949.

MACDONALD, COLIN: Born Roy Bridge 1894. Educated Blairs 1909-15; Valladolid 1915-21, returning home in bad health; Blairs 1921-23. Ordained Blairs 1923. St Mary's, Inverness 1923-24. Aberdeen Cathedral 1924-26. Fetternear 1926-34. Marydale 1934-53. Went to England on sick leave 1953, returning north to go into hospital. Died Aberdeen 9 April 1953.

McDONALD, DAVID: Born Glenmoriston 1858. Educated Blairs 1870-75; St Edmund's, Douay 1875-77; Issy 1877-79; St Sulpice 1879-80; Valladolid 1880-82. Ordained Valladolid 1882. Inverurie 1882-83. Peterhead 1883-86. Dornie 1886-91. Stratherrick 1891-96. Kirkwall 1896-1912. Lerwick 1912-13. Tynet 1913-22. Stonehaven 1922-30. Died Stonehaven 27 Sept 1930.

McDONALD, JOHN: Born Strathglass 1864. Educated Blairs 1878-83; Valladolid 1883-89. Ordained Valladolid 1889. Returned home and died later that year, never having been placed in a parish.

McDONALD, ROBERT ALEXANDER: Born Dufftown 1929. Educated Blairs; St Sulpice. Ordained Dufftown 1952. St Peter's, Aberdeen 1952-56. Kirkwall 1956-58. Dornie 1958-66. Elgin 1966-.

MACDONALD, THOMAS: Born Fanblair, Invernessshire 1867. Educated Blairs 1880-84; Douay 1884-86; Scots College, Rome 1886-88, leaving for health reasons; St Sulpice 1888-91. Ordained Paris 1891. Aberdeen Cathedral 1891. St Joseph's, Aberdeen 1891-92. Banff 1892-94. Marydale 1894-99. St Peter's, Aberdeen 1899-1902. Died Aberdeen 3 Feb 1902.

McGINTY, DESMOND J M: see Glasgow archdiocese

McGREGOR, CHARLES: Born Buckie 1926. Educated Our Lady's High School, Motherwell; Blairs; St Edmund's, Ware. Ordained Baillieston

1954. Aberdeen Cathedral 1954-56. Fetternear 1956-57. Inverurie 1957-62. Our Lady of Aberdeen, Aberdeen 1962-72. Aberdeen Cathedral 1972-82; also administering Our Lady's, Aberdeen 1975-76. Banchory 1982-.

McGREGOR, JAMES: Born Keith 1860. Educated Blairs 1873-77; Scots College, Rome 1877-83. Ordained Rome 1883. Aberdeen Cathedral 1883-91. Dufftown 1891-95. Aberdeen Cathedral 1895-99. Rector, Blairs 1899-1928. Died Blairs 10 Feb 1928.

McHARDY, WALTER: Born Braemar 1888. Educated Blairs 1902-06; Scots College, Rome 1906-13. Ordained Rome 1912. At home in Braemar in bad health 1913-14. Aberdeen Cathedral 1914-15. Inverurie 1915-20. Chapeltown 1920-25. Ballater 1925-28. Died Ballater 10 March 1928.

McINNES, ANGUS: Born Cluny 1876. Educated Blairs, Valladolid. Ordained Valladolid 1899. Lent to Glasgow Archdiocese: St Mary's, Paisley 1899-1900. St Peter's, Aberdeen 1900-01. Stratherrick 1901-07. Went to Glasgow Archdiocese: St Mary's, Glasgow 1907-30. Retired to the north 1930. Died Premnay 8 Feb 1933.

McINTOSH, JOHN: Born Boharm 1856. Educated Blairs 1867-72; Valladolid 1872-79. Ordained Aberdeen 1879. Fochabers 1879-80. Aberdeen Cathedral 1880-86. Peterhead 1886-90. Buckie 1890-1927. Retired to Elgin 1927 and died there 12 May 1928.

MACKAY, DONALD: Born Stronachavie Farm, Tomintoul 1873. Educated Blairs 1887-92; Issy 1892-94; St Sulpice 1894-97. Ordained Paris 1897. Aberdeen Cathedral 1897-98. St Peter's, Aberdeen 1898-99. Wick 1899-1900. Dornie 1900-04. Marydale 1904-18. Preshome 1918-46. Retired 1946. Died near Tomintoul 25 May 1950.

MACKENZIE, COLIN: Born near Turriff 1859. Educated Blairs 1873-77; St Edmund's, Douay 1877-79; Scots College, Rome 1879-85. Ordained Rome 1884. Lent to Archdiocese of St A & E: St Francis Xavier's, Falkirk 1885-86; North Berwick 1886-91. Banff 1891-92. Chapeltown 1892-1912. Braemar 1912-33. Died Braemar 13 June 1933.

MACKENZIE, KENNETH: Born Glasgow 1904. Educated Blairs 1919-24; Scots College, Rome 1924-31. Ordained Rome 1930. Lent to Archdiocese of St A & E: St Columba's, Edinburgh 1931-32. St Mary's, Inverness 1932-34. Fetternear 1934-36. Wick 1936-43. Ballater 1943-49. Tombae 1949-56. Huntly 1956-77. Retired 1977. Died Aberdeen 14 Sept 1990.

MACKENZIE, VALENTINE: Born Glenaladale 1891. Worked in a lawyer's office. Educated Blairs 1906-13; Scots College, Rome 1913-19. Ordained Blairs 1919. Aberdeen Cathedral 1919-22. Fraserburgh 1922-27. Banff

1927-38. St Mary's, Inverness 1938-54. Beauly 1954-62. Retired 1962. Died Inverness 2 March 1970.

MACKIN, EAMON: Ordained 1970. Aberdeen Cathedral 1974. Aviemore 1974-75. No further entries.

MACLAUGHLIN, (James) ANTHONY: Born Inverness 1908. Educated Fransiscan Convent, Inverness; St Mary's School, Lanark; Blairs 1923-29; Valladolid 1929-36. Ordained Valladolid 1936. Aberdeen Cathedral 1936-43. Wick 1943-47. Peterhead 1947-52. Aberlour 1952-60. Fochabers 1960-73. Died Elgin, 11 March 1973.

McLAUGHLIN, THOMAS: Born Cameron Barracks, Inverness, 1891. Educated Roy Bridge School; Inverness High School; Blairs 1905-10; Scots College, Rome 1910-17. Ordained Rome 1917. St Peter's, Aberdeen 1917-23. Banff 1923-27. St Joseph's, Aberdeen 1927-52. Aboyne 1952-62. Banchory 1962-73. Died Aberdeen 28 May 1973.

McLAUGHLIN, WILLIAM: see archdiocese of St Andrews & Edinburgh

McLELLAN, JOSEPH: Born Tomintoul 1871. Educated Blairs 1885-89; Valladolid 1889-92; Issy and St Sulpice 1892-96. Ordained Aberdeen 1896. St Peter's, Aberdeen 1896-98. Aberdeen Cathedral 1898-99. Stonehaven 1899-1907. Inverurie 1907-08. Aboyne 1908-11. Dornie 1911-18. Fetternear 1918-20. Marydale 1920-34. Retired 1934. Died Marydale 4 May 1936.

MACPHERSON, JOHN: Born Aberlour 1887. Educated Blairs 1901-06; St Peter's 1906-08; Issy 1908-10; St Sulpice 1910-13. Ordained Paris 1913. St Peter's, Aberdeen 1913-16. Aboyne 1916-18. Forces chaplain 1918-21. No further entries.

MACQUEEN, DUNCAN: Born Kintail 1853. Educated Blairs 1871-75; Valladolid 1875-82. Ordained Valladolid 1882. Clova 1882-87. St Mary's, Inverness 1887-1918. Died Inverness 10 May 1918.

MACRAE, AENEAS VALENTINE: Born Eskadale 1904. Educated Blairs 1918-23; Coutances 1923-28. Ordained Blairs 1928. Lent to Glasgow archdiocese: Our Holy Redeemer, Clydebank 1928-29. Aberdeen Cathedral 1929-1930. Lent to Dunkeld diocese: St Patrick's, Dundee 1930-37. Fraserburgh 1937-53. Inverurie 1953-55. St Mary's, Inverness 1955-57. Ballater 1957-66. Eskadale 1966-70. Died Eskadale 19 July 1970.

MACWILLIAM, ALEXANDER STUART: Born Buckie 1902. Educated Buckie High School; Blairs 1918-19; Scots College, Rome 1919-26. Ordained Rome 1926. Aberdeen Cathedral 1926-28. Kirkwall 1928-32.

Aboyne 1932-45. Chapeltown 1945-47. St Peter's, Aberdeen 1947-77. Retired 1977. Died Aberdeen 20 March 1988.

McWILLIAM, J LEWIS: Born Buckie 1904. Educated Blairs 1917-22; Valladolid 1922-29. Ordained Valladolid 1929. Aberdeen Cathedral 1929-30. Stonehaven 1930-32. Forres 1932-52. Tomintoul 1952-57. Aberdeen Cathedral 1957-62. Beauly 1962-77. Huntly 1977-.

MALANEY, HUGH: Born Glasgow 1919. Educated Franciscan seminary, Buckingham; Blairs 1942-43; St Peter's 1944-47. Ordained Glasgow 1947. Aberdeen Cathedral 1947-48. St Peter's, Aberdeen 1948-52. St Mary's, Inverness 1952-54. Dornie 1954-57. At Aberdeen Cathedral, serving North Deeside district 1957-58. St Francis', Aberdeen 1958-79. Alness 1979-85. Tain 1985-.

MANDERS, WILLIAM: Born Cardiff 1889. Educated Blairs 1902-06; Scots College, Rome 1906-12. Ordained Rome 1912. Preshome 1912-18. Stratherrick 1918-30. Nairn 1930-38. Banff 1938-40. Stonehaven 1940-53. Retired 1953. Died Edinburgh 2 April 1963.

MANN, ANDREW: Born Keith 1956. Educated Langbank, Blairs, Valladolid. Ordained Keith 1980. Aberdeen Cathedral 1980-83. Peterhead 1983-89. Dornie 1989-.

MANN, CHARLES: Born Turriff 1864. Educated Blairs 1876-81; Issy 1881-83; St Sulpice 1883-86. Ordained Aberdeen 1886. Inverurie 1886-87. Fetternear 1887-93. Aberdeen Cathedral 1893-95. Portsoy 1895-96. Transferred to Glasgow archdiocese. St Mary's, Greenock 1896-1901. Died Greenock 22 April 1901.

MANN, ROBERT: Born Keith 1914. Educated Blairs 1926-32; St Lo 1932-33; Coutances 1933-38. Ordained Blairs 1938. St Mary's, Inverness 1938-42. Buckie 1942-45. Aberdeen Cathedral 1945-47. Aberlour 1947-52. Peterhead 1952-68. Tombae 1968-70. Tomintoul 1970-77. Fochabers 1977-82. Retired 1982. Died Aberdeen 13 Dec 1983.

MARR, JAMES: Born Aberdeen 1891. Educated Blairs 1904-07; Valladolid 1907-17. Ordained Aberdeen 1917. Aberdeen Cathedral 1917-20. Inverurie 1920-22. Tynet 1922-30. Clochan (not serving a parish) 1930-31. Peterhead 1931-41. Aberlour 1941-47. Dufftown 1947-48. Died Dufftown 23 July 1948.

MATHESON, DONALD: Born Tomintoul 1873. Educated Blairs 1889-93; Valladolid 1893-99. Ordained Valladolid 1899. Glengairn 1899-1905. Ballater 1905-08. Huntly 1908-23. Died Huntly 28 March 1923.

MATHESON, JOHN ALEXANDER: Born Tomintoul 1901. Educated Blairs

1916-19; Scots College, Rome 1919-25. Ordained Rome 1925. Aberdeen Cathedral 1925-28. Sacred Heart, Aberdeen 1928-30. Ballater 1930-43. Dufftown 1943-47. Consecrated Bishop of Aberdeen 1947. Died Aberdeen 5 July 1950.

MEANY, JOHN CHARLES: Born Ord near Beauly 1860. Educated Blairs 1875-80; Douay 1880-81; Issy 1881-83; St Sulpice 1883-84; Scots College, Rome 1884-87. Ordained Rome 1887. Aberdeen Cathedral 1887-88. Glengairn 1888-99. Aberdeen Cathedral 1899-1937. Retired 1937. Died Banchory 14 June 1940.

MOORE, JAMES: Ordained 1877. Clova 1907-10. No further entries.

MORAN, PETER ANTONY: see Glasgow archdiocese

MORROW, JAMES: see Paisley diocese

MULLIGAN, WILLIAM: Born Old North, Aberdeenshire 1880. Educated Blairs 1893-97; Propaganda, Rome 1897-1904. Ordained Rome 1904. Lent to Archdiocese of St A & E: St Margaret's, Dunfermline 1904-06; Lochgelly 1906-12. Banff 1912-23. Huntly 1923-56. Retired 1956. Died Musselburgh 3 June 1961.

MURDOCH, ANDREW: Born Blairs 1874. Educated Blairs 1887-92; Issy 1892-93; Scots College, Rome 1893-97. Ordained Blairs 1897. Professor, Blairs 1897-1907. Died Aberdeen 20 Aug 1907.

MURDOCH, WILLIAM: Born Blairs 1901. Educated Blairs 1914-19; St Peter's 1919; Propaganda, Rome 1919-24. Ordained Rome 1924. St Peter's, Aberdeen 1925-27. Fraserburgh 1927-29. Forres 1929-32. Stonehaven 1932-38. Chapeltown 1938-45. Buckie 1945-74. Retired 1974. Died Aberdeen 25 Sept 1987.

MURPHY, EDWARD: see Argyll diocese

MURPHY, MICHAEL (Bruno): Born and educated Ireland. Army trooper in Sudan; joined Trappist Order at Roscrea and was ordained 1907. Forces chaplain 1915-19. Came to Aberdeen diocese 1919. Lerwick 1919-21. Kirkwall 1921-28. Was secularised and affiliated to Aberdeen diocese 1927. Ballater 1928-30. Retired 1930. Died Ireland 27 Jan 1937. (Canning)

NICOL, GEORGE: Born Dufftown 1868. Educated Blairs 1881-85; Douay 1885-87; Scots College, Rome 1887-92. Ordained Rome 1892. Aberdeen Cathedral 1892-93. Fetternear 1893-94. Wick 1894-97. Fraserburgh 1897-99. Tomintoul 1899-1908. Inverurie 1908-11. Sacred Heart, Aberdeen 1911-13. Tombae 1913-24. Died Tombae 4 Feb 1924.

NICOL, WILLIAM: Born Buckie 1909. Educated Blairs 1925-28; St Lo 1928-29; Coutances 1929-34. Ordained Blairs 1934. St Mary's, Inverness 1934. Kingussie Sanitorium 1934-35. Aberdeen Cathedral 1935-36. Retired to the Isle of Wight 1936 and died there 2 April 1939.

O'DONNELL, JAMES BEDE: Born Glasgow 1905. Educated St Mungo's Academy; joined Benedictine Order at Fort Augustus; Roman Catholic University of Washington. Ordained Glasgow 1930. Member of Fort Augustus community 1930-52. Left the Order and offered his services to Aberdeen diocese. Aberdeen Cathedral 1952-53. Marydale 1953. Fraserburgh 1953-59. Sacred Heart, Aberdeen 1959-61. Marydale 1961-78. Died Marydale 5 Oct 1978.

O'RORKE, THOMAS: Born Edinburgh 1904. Educated Blairs 1923-27; Scots College, Rome 1927-34. Ordained Rome 1933. Aberdeen Cathedral 1934-39. Portsoy 1939-48. Australia 1948-49. Dingwall 1949-53. Aberdeen Cathedral 1953-56. Elgin 1956-66. Died Bradford 10 May 1966.

OSEI-BONSU, JOSEPH: According to Anniversary brochure, he was at Aberdeen Cathedral 1979-80. He does not appear in Directories.

PATERSON, DAVID: Born Whitebridge, Invernessshire 1895. Educated Blairs 1909-14; St Peter's 1914-15; Scots College, Rome 1915-21. Ordained Rome 1921. Aberdeen Cathedral 1921-23. Vice-rector, Scots College, Rome 1923-30. Aberdeen Cathedral 1930-53. Banff 1953-59. Retired to Aberdeen 1959 and died there 29 Sept 1965.

PHILLIPS, GEORGE JAMES: Born Corriemulzie, Braemar 1903. Educated Blairs 1918-24; St Lo 1924-25; Coutances 1925-30. Ordained Blairs 1930. Aberdeen Cathedral 1930-31. St Peter's, Aberdeen 1931-33. Clova 1933-47. Chapeltown 1947-55. Dufftown 1955-80. Retired 1980. Died Aboyne 14 March 1986.

RAMSAY, JOHN: see archdiocese of St Andrews & Edinburgh

REDMOND, CHARLES BONNYMAN: Born Port Gordon 1918. Educated Blairs; Issy; Orleans, leaving because of war; St Peter's. Ordained Blairs 1944. On sick leave with tuberculosis 1944-46. St Mary's, Inverness 1946-48. Fetternear 1948-52. Diocesan secretary 1952-53. Stonehaven 1953-66. In Arizona for health 1967 and then with his brother in Liverpool, too ill to work. Died Liverpool 6 Sept 1969.

RITTER, HENRY F: No ordination date given. Aberdeen Cathedral 1916-17. Archdiocese of St A & E: Lochgelly 1917-18. No further entries.

ROBERTSON, JAMES KENNEDY: Born Insch, Aberdeenshire 1899.

Educated Aberdeen University 1918-23. Schoolteacher 1923-30. Became a Catholic 1931. Educated for priesthood Scots College, Rome 1931-38. Ordained Rome 1937. St Mary's, Inverness 1938-46. Preshome 1946-71. Retired 1971. Died Elgin 22 Feb 1973.

ROBSON, JAMES GORDON: Born Aberdeen 1926. Educated Blairs, leaving to serve in the navy during the war; St Edmund's, Ware. Ordained Aberdeen 1953. St Mary's, Inverness 1953-55. Aberdeen Cathedral 1955-56. Tombae 1956-62. Aberdeen Cathedral 1962-72. Sacred Heart, Aberdeen 1972-75. Died Aberdeen 15 Dec 1975.

ROGER, JOHN: Born near Banff 1878. Educated Blairs 1892-96; St Peter's 1896-98; Scots College, Rome 1898-1903. Ordained Rome 1903. Aberdeen Cathedral 1903-11. Inverurie 1911-12. Nairn 1912-20. Died Huntly 23 June 1920.

ROSS, WILLIAM: Ordained 1913. Aberdeen Cathedral 1924-28. No further entries.

SHAW, GEORGE PAUL: Born Aberdeen 1876. Educated Blairs 1889-93; Valladolid 1893-99. Ordained Valladolid 1899. Lent to Glasgow archdiocese: Shieldmuir 1899. Aberdeen Cathedral 1899-1905. Dufftown 1905-30. Tomintoul 1930-34. St Mary's, Inverness 1934-38. Died Blairs 1 April 1938.

SHAW, WILLIAM (1882): Born Aberdeen 1858. Educated Blairs 1871-75; Valladolid 1875-82. Ordained 1882. Professor, Blairs 1882-91. Vice-rector, Blairs 1891-97. Lent to Glasgow archdiocese: St John's, Port Glasgow 1897-98; Linwood 1898-1908. Aberdeen Cathedral 1908-10. Fochabers 1910-37. Died Fochabers 21 May 1937.

SHAW, WILLIAM (1911): Born Blairs 1887. Educated Blairs 1900-03; Valladolid 1903-11. Ordained Valladolid 1911. Aberdeen Cathedral 1911-14. Portsoy 1914-25. Chapeltown 1925-38. Braemar 1938-39. Died Bridge of Earn 6 June 1939.

SHERIDAN, HUGH: Born and educated Ireland. Joined Camillians. Ordained for the Order 1943. In Dublin and USA. Left Order for health reasons. Served in England. Came to Aberdeen diocese 1953. Fetternear 1953-56. St Peter's, Aberdeen 1956-59. Stratherrick 1959-62. Tombae 1962-65. Died Ireland 16 May 1965. (Canning)

SIMPSON, JOHN: Born Aberdeen 1876. Educated Franciscan Convent, Aberdeen; Robert Gordon's College, Aberdeen; Blairs 1890-94; Notre Dame des Champs, Paris 1894-95; Issy 1895-97; Scots College, Rome 1897-1901. Ordained Rome 1900. Aberdeen Cathedral 1901-04. Fetternear 1904-18. Marydale 1918-20. Died Inverness 6 Sept 1920.

SLORACH, JAMES: Born Huntly 1870. Educated Blairs 1883-87; Valladolid 1887-94. Ordained Aberdeen 1894. Kirkwall 1894-96. Lent to Glasgow archdiocese: Chaplain, Good Shepherd Convent, Dalbeth 1896-97. Aberdeen Cathedral 1897-1900. Portsoy 1900-14. Elgin 1914-43. Died Elgin 12 Sept 1943.

SMITH, ALEXANDER MICHAEL GIBNEY: Born Inverness 1922. Educated Blairs; St Peter's. Ordained 1947. Aberdeen Cathedral 1947-52. Kirkwall 1952-56. Aberdeen Cathedral 1956-57. Took certificate in Tropical Medicine and went to Africa 1957-61. Our Lady of Aberdeen, Aberdeen 1961-62. Inverurie 1962-68. Died Aberdeen 14 Oct 1968.

STANLEY, CHARLES: Born Birmingham 1933. Educated Bolton, Drygrange. Ordained Southport 1960. St Mary's, Inverness 1960-62. Aberdeen Cathedral 1962-65. Portsoy 1965-66. Dornie 1966-72. Braemar 1972-80. Dufftown 1980-86. Aberdeen Cathedral 1986-.

STEWART, COLIN: Born Aberdeen 1955. Educated Aberdeen Academy; Scots College, Rome. Ordained Aberdeen 1982. Completing studies, Rome 1982-83. Our Lady of Aberdeen, Aberdeen 1983-90 (part time 1983-86 while taking Dip Ed). Tomintoul 1990-.

STONE, DUNCAN: Born Beauly 1917. Educated Blairs 1931-37; St Sulpice 1937-40; St Peter's 1940-42. Ordained Blairs 1942. St Mary's, Inverness 1942-43. Aberdeen Cathedral 1943-48. Portsoy 1948-51. Spiritual Director, Blairs 1951-54. Nairn 1954-61. Holy Family, Aberdeen 1961-77. St Mary's, Inverness 1977-.

STUART, DOUGLAS GORDON: Born Aberdeen 1900. Educated Gordon's College; became Catholic 1919; Aberdeen University 1920-24; Scots College, Rome 1924-30. Ordained Rome 1929. Aberdeen Cathedral 1930-34. Dingwall 1934-49. Sick leave-coronary thrombosis-1949-51. Dufftown 1951-55. Retired to Aviemore 1955. Died Rothesay 16 Sept 1958.

STUART, ROBERT: Born Calcutta 1903. Educated Radley College, Abingdon; Corpus Christi. Became barrister; trained as singer at Milan; practised law in China, etc; was interned by Japanese at Shanghai. Became Catholic. Educated for priesthood at Beda, Rome; St Sulpice. Ordained Blairs 1953. Aberdeen Cathedral 1953-54. Lent to Archdiocese of St A & E: Immaculate Conception, Bathgate 1954-56. Lumsden 1956-62. Fraserburgh 1962-78. Died on his way to Oxford 14 Nov 1978.

STUART, WILLIAM: Born Tomnavoulin, Glenlivet 1856. Educated Blairs 1869-74; Scots College, Rome 1874-81. Ordained Rome 1879. Braemar 1881-82. Aboyne 1882-91. Tombae 1891-1913. Beauly 1913-30. Retired to Elgin 1930 and died there 26 Nov 1930.

SULLIVAN, ALEXANDER D: Born Buckie 1904. Educated Blairs 1916-22; Valladolid 1922-29. Ordained Valladolid 1929. St Mary's, Inverness 1929-32. Kirkwall 1932-38. Nairn 1938-54. St Mary's, Inverness 1954-77. Nairn 1977-86. Died Nairn 7 Jan 1986.

SYMON, JOHN: Born Aberdeen 1930. Educated Robert Gordon's College, Aberdeen; Blairs; Scots College, Rome. Ordained Rome 1953. Aberdeen Cathedral and continuing studies at Aberdeen University 1953-55. Inverurie 1955-57. Professor, Blairs 1957-61. Professor, Drygrange 1961-72. Our Lady of Aberdeen, Aberdeen 1972-74. C/o King's Gate, Aberdeen 1974-75. Lent to Archdiocese of St A & E: Holyrood High School, Edinburgh 1975-77. Thurso 1977-82. Aberdeen Cathedral 1982-.

TEMPLETON, IAIN McALLISTER: Born Halifax 1957. Educated Heath School, Halifax; Drygrange. Ordained Renton 1986. Aberdeen Cathedral 1986-89. Sacred Heart, Aberdeen 1989-90. Fochabers 1990. Dingwall 1990-.

THAIN, CHARLES: Born Huntly 1902. Educated Blairs 1916-21; Scots College, Rome 1921-28. Ordained Rome 1927. Aberdeen Cathedral 1928-30. Elgin 1930. Stratherrick 1930-56. Died Stratherrick 11 Aug 1956.

THOMSON, ALEXANDER HAY: Born Aberdeen 1876. Educated Blairs 1889-93; Issy; St Sulpice. Ordained Paris 1899. Lent to Glasgow archdiocese: St Aloysius', Glasgow 1899-1900. Wick 1900-02. Dingwall 1902-07. Stonehaven 1907-22. Inverurie 1922-53. Retired to Banchory 1953 and died there 22 Feb 1956.

THOMSON, ANDREW FLEMING: Born Aberdeen 1855. Educated Blairs 1868-72; Valladolid 1872-79. Ordained Aberdeen 1879. Lent to Dunkeld diocese: Arbroath 1879-80; St Joseph's, Dundee 1880-81. Strichen 1881-90. Peterhead 1890-1930. Retired 1930. Died Buffalo, New York 13 Jan 1931.

THOMSON, JOSEPH: Born Fochabers 11 Sept 1872. Educated Blairs 1886-88; Scots College, Rome 1888-96. Ordained Rome 1895. Aberdeen Cathedral 1896-97. Aboyne 1897-1908. Tomintoul 1908-25. From 1925 at Kingussie as chaplain of sanatorium and in bad health; then on sick leave at Inverurie, etc. Died St Mary's Hospital, Lanark 12 Dec 1963.

TOMAN, SIDNEY: Born Aberdeen 1899. Educated Blairs 1912-16; Scots College, Rome 1916-23. Ordained Rome 1922. St Peter's, Aberdeen 1923-25. Wick 1925-30. Peterhead 1930; died there of pneumonia 27 Nov 1930.

TRAYNOR, EDWARD PATRICK ANTHONY: Born Glasgow 1952. Educated Royal Grammar School, High Wycombe; Banbury Grammar School; St

Illtyd's College, Cardiff; St Michael's Academy, Kilwinning; Strathclyde University; North London Polytechnic; Scots College, Rome. Ordained Rome 1985. Completing studies, Rome 1985-87. St Mary's, Inverness 1987-88. Buckie 1988-.

URQUHART, JAMES: Born Inverness 1873. Educated Blairs 1885-89; Petite Communaute, Paris 1889-91; Issy 1891-93; St Sulpice 1893-96. Ordained Aberdeen 1896. Lent to Glasgow archdiocese: St Patrick's, Coatbridge 1896-97. Fetternear 1897-99. Clova 1899-1900. Left diocese and went to South Africa 1901. Died South Africa 26 July 1937.

WALECZEK, ALOYSIUS: Ordained 1939. St Mary's, Inverness 1949-50. No further entries.

WALLS, RONALD JAMES: Born Edinburgh 1920. Educated George Herriot's School, Edinburgh; Edinburgh University. Became a Catholic and studied for the priesthood at Beda, Rome. Ordained Edinburgh 1977. Attached to St Francis', Aberdeen, but staying at Banchory and with care of Banchory and Aboyne 1977-82. Thurso 1982-89. St Joseph's, Aberdeen 1989-.

WALSH, FRANK R: Born Cirencester 1901. Educated Blairs 1915-19; Scots College, Rome 1919-25. Ordained Rome 1925. St Mary's, Inverness 1925-29. Joined White Fathers 1929 and served in England and Scotland. Consecrated Bishop of Aberdeen 1951. Fetternear 1952-56. Resigned as Bishop 1963 and left the diocese. Died Grantham 27 Oct 1974.

WARD, JOHN: see archdiocese of St Andrews & Edinburgh

WATSON, WILLIAM S: Born Aberdeen 1893. Educated Blairs 1908-11; Scots College, Rome 1911-18. Ordained Rome 1918. Professor, Blairs 1918-31. Was in a bad motor cycle accident 1930, and never fully recovered. Tynet 1931-48. Dufftown, in bad health, 1948-51. Died Dufftown 17 Oct 1951.

WISEMAN, GEORGE: Born Deskie, Glenlivet 1867. Educated Blairs 1883-86; Petite Communaute, Paris 1886-89; Propaganda, Rome 1889-95. Ordained Rome 1895. Aberdeen Cathedral 1895-96. Portsoy 1896-99. Fraserburgh 1899-1915. Chapeltown 1915-20. St Joseph's, Aberdeen 1920-27. Keith 1927-53. Died Keith 12 March 1953.

Parishes

ABERDEEN – BISHOPS: 1869-89 John MacDonald (ND). 1889 Colin Grant (ND). 1890-98 Hugh MacDonald C.Ss.R. 1899-1918 Aeneas Chisholm

(ND). 1918-46 George Bennett (St A & E). 1947-50 John Matheson (Abdn). 1951-63 Frank Walsh WF (Abdn). 1965-76 Michael Foylan (Dunkeld). 1977- Mario Conti (Abdn).

ABERDEEN – DIOCESAN SECRETARY (no parish): 1952-53 Charles Redmond.

ABERDEEN – ST MARY'S CATHEDRAL
Heads: 1874-94 William Stopani (ND). 1894-95 Donald Chisholm (ND). 1895-99 James McGregor. 1899-1937 John Meany. 1937-53 David Paterson. 1953-56 Thomas O'Rorke. 1956-57 Alexander Smith. 1957-62 Lewis McWilliam. 1962-72 James Robson. 1972-82 Charles McGregor. 1982-John Symon.
Assistants: 1874-94 Donald Chisholm (ND). 1878-80 Alexander Gerry (ND). 1880-86 John McIntosh. 1883-91 James McGregor. 1887-88 John Meany. 1889-90 John McBain. 1891 Thomas MacDonald. 1891-93 Charles MacDonald (1891). 1892-93 James Henderson. 1892-93 George Nicol. 1893-95 Charles Mann. 1895-96 George Wiseman. 1895-97 Andrew Grant. 1896-97 Joseph Thomson. 1897-98 Donald MacKay. 1897-1900 James Slorach. 1898-99 Joseph McLellan. 1899-1902 Andrew Grant. 1899-1905 George Shaw. 1901-03 Donald MacIntosh (1868). 1901-04 John Simpson. 1903-11 John Roger. 1904-11 Francis Cronin. 1905-06 Bernard Auer. 1906-08 Patrick Keenan. 1907-08 Alexander Bennett. 1908-10 William Shaw (1882). 1911-14 William J Shaw (1911). 1912-13 James Bonnyman. 1913-14 James Bonnyman. 1914-15 Walter McHardy. 1914-18 Andrew Cameron. 1914-30 Alexander Ferguson. 1916-17 Henry Ritter. 1917-20 James Marr. 1918-19 William Bowie. 1919-22 Valentine MacKenzie. 1920-24 Alexander Kerr. 1921-23 David Paterson. 1923-24 Donald Campbell (Argyll). 1924-26 Colin MacDonald. 1924-28 William Ross. 1925-28 John Matheson. 1926-28 Alexander MacWilliam. 1928-30 Charles Thain. 1928-30 Joseph Lamont. 1929-30 Aeneas MacRae. 1929-30 Lewis McWilliam. 1930-31 George Phillips. 1930-34 Douglas Stuart. 1930-37 George Butler. 1930-37 David Paterson. 1934-39 Thomas O'Rorke. 1935-36 William Nicol. 1936-43 James MacLaughlin. 1937-45 Charles Fraser. 1939-41 George McCurragh. 1942-47 George McCurragh. 1943-48 Duncan Stone. 1945-47 Robert Mann. 1947-48 Hugh Malaney. 1947-52 Alexander Smith. 1948 David Keith. 1948-51 John Copland. 1948-55 Bernard MacDonald. 1951-53 David Keith. 1952-53 James Bede O'Donnell. 1953-54 Robert Stuart. 1953-55 John Symon. 1953-55 John McCabe. 1954-56 Charles McGregor. 1955-56 James Robson. 1955-59 John Cunningham. 1957-62 John Cassidy. 1959 John Caslin. 1959-62 Mario Conti. 1962-65 Charles Stanley. 1963-65 Michael Fitzpatrick. 1965 James Carruth OSB. 1965-68 Alistair Doyle. 1966-70 Joseph Gration. 1969 Patrick Fallon (St A & E). 1969-72 Peter Barry. 1971-75 Andrew McKillop OSB. 1974 Andrew Hunkin. 1974 Eamon Mackin. 1975 Gordon Forde. 1975 Paul Steinmetz SJ. 1975-76 Thomas Healy. 1976-79 Gordon Forde. 1979-80

Raymond Coyle. 1979-80 Joseph Osei Bonsu. 1980-83 Andrew Mann. 1982 Brian MacDonald. 1983-85 Christopher Brannan. 1986-Charles Stanley. 1986-89 Iain Templeton.

ABERDEEN – HOLY FAMILY
Heads: 1955-61 Bernard MacDonald. 1961-77 Duncan Stone. 1977- John Gowans.
Assistants: 1964-65 Alistair Doyle. 1965-66 Joseph Gration.

ABERDEEN – OUR LADY OF ABERDEEN: 1961-62 Alexander Smith.
1962-72 Charles McGregor. 1972-74 John Symon. 1974-75 served from Sacred Heart, Aberdeen. 1975-76 served from Cathedral. 1976-77 served from Sacred Heart. 1977-83 Peter Barry. 1983-90 Colin Stewart. 1990- James Birrel.

ABERDEEN – SACRED HEART: 1911-13 George Nicol. 1913-28 Patrick
Keenan. 1928-30 John Matheson. 1930-40 Alexander Ferguson. 1940-54 Joseph Lamont. 1954-59 Patrick Grady. 1959-61 James Bede O'Donnell. 1961-72 John McCabe. 1972-75 James Robson. 1975-76 served from St Joseph's, Aberdeen. 1976-77 John Gowans. 1977-89 served by Jesuits. 1989-90 Iain Templeton. 1990- James Hayes SJ.

ABERDEEN – ST FRANCIS' (North Deeside)
1957-79 Hugh Malaney. 1979-85 John Beveridge. 1985- Christopher Brannan.

ABERDEEN – ST JOSEPH'S
1842-80 served from cathedral.
Heads: 1880-90 Alexander Gerry (ND). 1890-91 John McBain. 1891-92 Thomas MacDonald. 1892-97 Charles Tochetti (ND). 1897-1919 Charles Devine (ND). 1919-20 vacant. 1920-27 George Wiseman. 1927-52 Thomas McLaughlin. 1952-66 George Butler. 1966-74 John Copland. 1974-79 Michael Fitzpatrick. 1979-89 served by Jesuits. 1989-Ronald Walls.
Assistant: 1965-66 John Cunningham.

ABERDEEN – ST PETER'S
Closed 1860-95.
Heads: 1895-99 Donald Chisholm (ND). 1899-1902 Thomas MacDonald. 1902-16 Andrew Grant. 1916-19 George Grant. 1919-47 Andrew Grant. 1947-77 Alexander MacWilliam. 1977-89 Patrick Grady. From 1989 served from Sacred Heart, Aberdeen.
Assistants: 1896-98 Joseph McLellan. 1898-99 Donald MacKay. 1900-01 Angus McInnes. 1901-06 George Grant. 1902 Andrew Grant. 1906-13 James Anton. 1913-16 John MacPherson. 1917-23 Thomas McLaughlin. 1923-25 Sidney Toman. 1925-27 William Murdoch. 1927-29 Alistair Kennedy. 1929-31 Stephen Keane. 1931-33 George Phillips. 1933-38 Wilfrid Davis. 1938-46 Charles Collins. 1946-48 John Copland. 1948-52

Hugh Malaney. 1952-56 Robert McDonald. 1956-59 Hugh Sheridan. 1959-60 Denis Garrity (Motherwell). 1960-62 Bernard Ashworth.

ABERDEEN UNIVERSITY – CHAPLAINS: Until 1986 served by Jesuits. 1986-William R T Anderson (St A & E).

ABERDEEN – NAZARETH HOUSE: CHAPLAINS. 1962-73 Bernard Ashworth.

ABERLOUR: 1909-18 served from Dufftown. 1918-33 John McBain. 1933-41 Alexander Kerr. 1941-47 James Marr. 1947-52 Robert Mann. 1952-60 James McLaughlin. From 1960 served from Dufftown.

ABOYNE: 1876-82 James Paul (ND). 1882-91 William Stuart. 1891-97 John McBain. 1897-1908 Joseph Thomson. 1908-11 Joseph McLellan. 1911-16 George Grant. 1916-18 John MacPherson. 1918-19 Andrew Cameron. 1919-25 George Grant. 1925-32 William Bowie. 1932-45 Alexander MacWilliam. 1945-52 George Butler. 1952-62 Thomas McLaughlin. From 1962 served from Banchory.

ALFORD: Served at various times from Clova, Fetternear, Lumsden. 1962-70 Patrick Grady.

ALNESS: 1977 John Beveridge. 1977-79 served from Dingwall. 1979-85 Hugh Malaney. From 1985 served from Tain.

AVIEMORE: 1958-62 Edward Douglas (Glasgow). 1962-74 David Keith. 1974-75 Eamon Mackin. 1975-77 Patrick Grady. 1977-82 Oliver Martin, O Praem. 1982 John Brady (Motherwell). 1982-83 vacant. 1983-88 Peter Barry. 1988- John McQuade SJ.

BALLATER: 1905-08 Donald Matheson. 1908-19 Alexander Gerry (ND). 1919-25 James Bonnyman. 1925-28 Walter McHardy. 1928-30 Michael Murphy. 1930-43 John Matheson. 1943-49 Kenneth MacKenzie. 1949-52 Alexander Ferguson. 1952-57 Charles Collins. 1957-66 Aeneas MacRae. From 1966 served from Braemar.

BANCHORY: 1931-62 served from Aboyne. 1962-73 Thomas McLaughlin. 1973-77 served from St Francis', Aberdeen. 1977-82 Ronald Walls (attached to St Francis' but resident at Banchory). 1982- Charles McGregor.

BANFF: 1872-1890 Aeneas Chisholm (ND). 1890-91 vacant. 1891-92 Colin MacKenzie (1884). 1892-94 Thomas MacDonald. 1894-1910 Alexander Bissett (1876) (ND). 1910-12 John McBain. 1912-23 William Mulligan. 1923-27 Thomas McLaughlin. 1927-38 Valentine MacKenzie. 1938-40 William Manders. 1940-46 William Clapperton. 1946-53 Wilfrid Davis.

1953-59 David Paterson. 1959-81 Charles Collins. 1981-83 vacant. 1983-89 Alistair Doyle. 1989- Laurence Lochrie SJ.

BEAULY: 1867-86 Donald MacKenzie (ND). 1886-1912 John Cameron (ND). 1912-13 Patrick Keenan. 1913-30 William Stuart. 1930-54 George Grant. 1954-62 Valentine MacKenzie. 1962-77 Lewis McWilliam. 1977-88 David Hughes SMA. 1988-Desmond McGinty (Glasgow)

BLAIRS: National Junior Seminary until 1986 (see under 'Colleges'). 1986-Peter Moran (Glasgow).

BRAEMAR: 1862-82 Donald MacRae (ND). 1882-1912 James Paul (ND). 1912-33 Colin MacKenzie (1884). 1933-38 John McBain. 1938-39 William Shaw (1911). 1939-41 James Bonnyman. 1941-62 Alexander Kerr. 1962 Bernard Ashworth. 1962-64 Edward Douglas (Glasgow). 1964-66 John Copland. 1966-72 Charles Fraser. 1972-80 Charles Stanley. 1980-90 James Morrow. 1990- John Leiper SPS.
Assistants: 1879-81 James Stewart (ND). 1881-82 William Stuart.

BRORA: 1957-59 John Caslin. 1959-65 John Cunningham. 1965-68 Michael Fitzpatrick. 1968-74 Alistair Doyle. 1974- James V O'Neill SJ.

BUCKIE: 1857-90 William Clapperton (ND). 1890-1927 John McIntosh. 1927-45 Charles MacDonald (1891). 1945-74 William Murdoch. 1974-84 David Keith. 1984-85 vacant. 1985-88 John Beveridge. 1988- Edward Traynor.
Assistants: 1930-33 Wilfrid Davis. 1934-41 George Kerr. 1941-42 George McCurrach. 1942-45 Robert Mann.

CHAPELTOWN: 1873-92 John MacEachron (ND). 1892-1912 Colin MacKenzie (1884). 1912-15 John McBain. 1915-20 George Wiseman. 1920-25 Walter McHardy. 1925-38 William Shaw (1911). 1938-45 William Murdoch. 1945-47 Alexander MacWilliam. 1947-55 George Phillips. 1955-61 John McCabe. 1961-65 served from Tombae. From 1965 served from Tomintoul.

CLOVA: A domestic chapel, sometimes supplied by one of the priests of the diocese, sometimes by a chaplain brought in by the family, and sometimes without a resident priest. 1881-82 John Daine (Salford). 1882-87 Duncan MacQueen. 1887-95 George Wilson (ND). 1897-98 Henry Bellasis (Oratory, Birmingham). 1899-1900 James Urquhart. 1901-07 William Fraser (1874) (ND). 1907-10 James Moore (diocese unknown). 1912-14 Edward Lawless (diocese unknown). 1919-29 Andrew Cameron. 1929-33 Alexander Kerr. 1933-47 George Phillips. 1947-53 George McCurrach. From 1953 see Lumsden.

DINGWALL
Heads: 1902-07 Alexander Thomson. 1907-14 William Fraser (ND). 1914-34 Bernard Auer. 1934-49 Douglas Stuart. 1949-53 Thomas O'Rorke. 1953-61 Wilfrid Davis. 1961-79 Bernard MacDonald. 1979-82 John Brady (Motherwell). 1982-90 James Birrell. 1990- Iain Templeton.
Assistant: 1978-79 Raymond Coyle.

DORNIE: 1873-86 John Cameron (ND). 1886-91 David McDonald. 1891-99 Archibald Chisholm (ND). 1899-1900 served by Benedictines. 1900-04 Donald MacKay. 1904-06 James Anton. 1906-11 George Grant. 1911-18 Joseph McLellan. 1918-24 Alexander Bennett. 1924-29 Alexander Kerr. 1929-37 Alistair Kennedy. 1937-45 George Butler. 1945-54 Charles Fraser. 1954-57 Hugh Malaney. 1957-58 Robert Catterall (Salford). 1958-66 Robert McDonald. 1966-72 Charles Stanley. 1972-76 Peter Barry. 1976-78 Thomas Healy. 1978-80 Edward Murphy (Argyll). 1980-89 Raymond Coyle. 1989- Andrew Mann.

DUFFTOWN: 1876-91 William Fraser (ND). 1891-95 James McGregor. 1895-99 Alexander Gerry (ND). 1899-1905 Donald Chisholm (ND). 1905-30 George Shaw. 1930-43 James Anton. 1943-47 John Matheson. 1947-48 James Marr. 1948-51 William Watson. 1951-55 Douglas Stuart. 1955-80 George Phillips. 1980-86 Charles Stanley. 1986-88 served from Fochabers. From 1988 served from Keith.

ELGIN
Heads: 1855-86 John Thomson (ND). 1886-95 Charles MacDonald (1852) (ND). 1895-1914 George Wilson (ND). 1914-43 James Slorach. 1943-56 Bernard Auer. 1956-66 Thomas O'Rorke. 1966- Robert McDonald.
Assistant: 1930 Charles Thain.

ESKADALE: 1869-89 Colin Grant (ND). 1889-99 Allan MacRae (ND). 1899-1918 Donald Chisholm (1885). 1918-54 Aeneas Geddes. 1954-66 Charles Fraser. 1966-70 Aeneas MacRae. 1970-75 Patrick Grady. From 1975 served from Marydale; then from Beauly.

FETTERNEAR
Heads: 1863-87 George Wilson (ND). 1887-93 Charles Mann. 1893-94 George Nicol. 1894-97 Charles Devine (ND). 1897-99 James Urquhart. 1899-1904 Allan MacRae (ND). 1904-18 John Simpson. 1918-20 Joseph McLellan. 1920-26 served from Inverurie. 1926-34 Colin MacDonald. 1934-36 Kenneth MacKenzie. 1936-40 Joseph Lamont. 1940-48 Alexander Ferguson. 1948-52 Charles Redmond. 1952-56 Bishop Frank Walsh. 1956-57 Charles McGregor. From 1957 served from Inverurie.
Assistant: 1953-56 Hugh Sheridan.

FOCHABERS
Heads: 1857-1917 Peter J Weir (ND). 1917-37 William Shaw (1882). 1937-

43 Alistair Kennedy. 1943-48 James Anton. 1948-49 Alexander Ferguson. 1949-60 Alexander Bennett. 1960-73 James MacLaughlin. 1973-74 Thomas Cullen CSSp. 1974-77 James Brennan (St A & E). 1977-82 Robert Mann. 1982-83 vacant. 1983-86 Joseph Hanley MSC. 1986-88 Alexander Lynch SMA. 1988-90 served from Buckie. 1990 Iain Templeton. From 1990 served from Buckie.
Assistants: 1875-77 Archibald Chisholm (ND). 1879-80 John McIntosh. 1908-10 Alexander Bennett. 1910-17 William Shaw (1882).

FORRES: 1929-32 William Murdoch. 1932-52 Lewis McWilliam. 1952-75 Alistair Kennedy. 1975-79 served by Jesuits. 1979- George McCurrach.

FORT AUGUSTUS: 1888-89 Alexander Bissett (1864) (ND). From 1889 served from the Abbey by Benedictines.

FRASERBURGH: 1895-97 James Henderson. 1897-99 George Nicol. 1899-1915 George Wiseman. 1915-22 James Anton. 1922-27 Valentine MacKenzie. 1927-29 William Murdoch. 1929-31 Andrew Cameron. 1931-37 Stephen Keane. 1937-53 Aeneas MacRae. 1953-59 James Bede O'Donnell. 1959-62 Patrick Grady. 1962-78 Robert Stuart. 1978-79 James Maher SDB. 1979-89 Laurence Lochrie SJ. 1989- Raymond Coyle.

GLENGAIRN: 1872-85 Donald Kennedy (ND). 1885-88 Donald Chisholm (1885). 1888-99 John Meany. 1899-1905 Donald Matheson. From 1905 served occasionally from Ballater.

HUNTLY: 1874-94 John Sutherland (ND). 1894-1908 Charles MacDonald (1891). 1908-23 Donald Matheson. 1923-56 William Mulligan. 1956-77 Kenneth MacKenzie. 1977- Lewis McWilliam.

INVERNESS – ST MARY'S:
Heads: 1852-87 William Dawson (ND). 1887-1918 Duncan MacQueen. 1918-28 Francis Cronin. 1928-33 Patrick Keenan. 1933-34 Kenneth MacKenzie. 1934-38 George Shaw. 1938-54 Valentine MacKenzie. 1954-77 Alexander Sullivan. 1977- Duncan Stone.
Assistants: 1903-06 Patrick Keenan. 1906-12 Bernard Auer. 1917-18 William Bowie. 1923-24 Colin MacDonald. 1925-29 Frank Walsh. 1929-32 Alexander Sullivan. 1932-33 Kenneth MacKenzie. 1934 William Nicol. 1934-35 William McLaughlin (St A & E). 1935-37 John Ward (St A & E). 1937-38 Hugh Gordon (St A & E). 1938-42 Robert Mann. 1938-46 James K Robertson. 1942-43 Duncan Stone. 1944-48 Patrick Grady. 1946-48 Charles Redmond. 1948-51 David Keith. 1949-50 Aloysius Waleczek. 1950-51 Douglas Stuart. 1952-54 Hugh Malaney. 1953-55 James Robson. 1955-57 Aeneas MacRae. 1957-59 Richard Larkin. 1960-62 Charles Stanley. 1978-80 John Beveridge. 1979-82 James Birrell. 1982-84 Brian MacDonald. 1987-88 Edward Traynor.

INVERNESS – ST NINIAN'S: 1959-79 George McCurrach. 1979-89 Bernard MacDonald. 1989- Alistair Doyle.

INVERURIE: 1873-82 James Glennie (ND). 1882-83 David McDonald. 1883-86 Charles MacDonald (1852) (ND). 1886-87 Charles Mann. 1887-92 William Dawson (1845) (ND). 1892-93 vacant. 1893-94 Charles MacDonald (1891). 1894-95 Alexander Gerry (ND). 1895-1905 Charles MacDonald (1852) (ND). 1905-07 Aeneas Geddes. 1907-08 Joseph McLellan. 1908-11 George Nicol. 1911-12 John Roger. 1912-13 served from Fetternear. 1913-15 James Anton. 1915-20 Walter McHardy. 1920-22 James Marr. 1922-53 Alexander Thomson. 1953-55 Aeneas MacRae. 1955-57 John Symon. 1957-62 Charles McGregor. 1962-68 Alexander Smith. 1968-69 John Caslin. 1969-70 vacant. 1970-79 Charles Moran MHM. 1979- Gordon Forde.

KEITH
Heads: 1853-92 Charles Tochetti (ND). 1892-1907 John Paul (ND). 1907-08 vacant. 1908-27 Charles MacDonald (1891). 1927-53 George Wiseman. 1953-54 vacant. 1954-73 Joseph Lamont. 1973-74 vacant. 1974 Frank O'Donnell CSSp. 1974- John Copland.
Assistant: 1951-54 Patrick Grady (administrator).

KIRKWALL: 1882-89 Alexander Bissett (1876) (ND). 1889-93 served from Aberdeen. 1893-94 James Henderson. 1894-96 James Slorach. 1896-1912 David McDonald. 1912-19 vacant. 1919-21 served from Lerwick. 1921-28 Michael (Bruno) Murphy. 1928-32 Alexander MacWilliam. 1932-38 Alexander Sullivan. 1938-46 Wilfrid Davis. 1946-52 Charles Collins. 1952-56 Alexander Smith. 1956-58 Robert MacDonald. From 1958 served by Jesuits.

LERWICK: 1912-13 David McDonald. 1913 James Bonnyman. 1913-19 vacant. 1919-21 Michael (Bruno) Murphy. 1921-54 served from Kirkwall. 1954-88 served by Jesuits. 1988- Peter Barry.

LUMSDEN: 1956-62 Robert Stuart. 1962-70 served from Alford. From 1970 served from Huntly.

MARYDALE
Heads: 1869-89 Allan MacRae (ND). 1889-94 Alexander Bissett (1876) (ND). 1894-99 Thomas MacDonald. 1899-1903 Archibald Chisholm (ND). 1903-04 James Anton. 1904-18 Donald MacKay. 1918-20 John Simpson. 1920-34 Joseph McLellan. 1934-53 Colin MacDonald. 1953 James Bede O'Donnell. 1953-61 George Kerr. 1961-78 James Bede O'Donnell. 1978-88 served by Benedictines. From 1988 served from Beauly.
Assistant: 1989-90 James Hayes SJ (resident at Marydale).

NAIRN: 1874-81 John Chisholm (ND). 1881-91 Archibald Chisholm (ND). 1891-1912 Alexander Bissett (1864) (ND). 1912-20 John Roger. 1920-22 served by Benedictines. 1922-30 James Anton. 1930-38 William Manders. 1938-54 Alexander Sullivan. 1954-61 Duncan Stone. 1961-73 Wilfrid Davis. 1973-77 John Cunningham. 1977-86 Alexander Sullivan. 1986- Gerald Hassay SJ.

NORTH DEESIDE: see Aberdeen, St Francis'

PETERHEAD: 1875-83 John Paul (ND). 1883-86 David McDonald. 1886-90 John McIntosh. 1890-1930 Andrew Thomson. 1930 Sidney Toman. 1930-31 vacant. 1931-41 James Marr. 1941-47 George Kerr. 1947-52 James MacLaughlin. 1952-68 Robert Mann. 1968-74 Michael Fitzpatrick. 1974-83 Alistair Doyle. 1983-89 Andrew Mann. From 1989 served from Fraserburgh.

PORTSOY: 1873-89 Charles Devine (ND). 1889-95 William Mann (ND). 1895-96 Charles Mann. 1896-99 George Wiseman. 1899-1900 Alexander Gerry (ND). 1900-14 James Slorach. 1914-25 William Shaw (1911). 1925-39 James Bonnyman. 1939-48 Thomas O'Rorke. 1948-51 Duncan Stone. 1951-64 John Copland. 1964-65 vacant. 1965-66 Charles Stanley. 1966-68 John Cassidy. From 1968 served from Banff.

PRESHOME
Heads: 1858-1917 John Kyle (ND). 1917-18 William Manders. 1918-46 Donald MacKay. 1946-71 James K Robertson. From 1971 served from Buckie.
Assistant: 1912-17 William Manders.

STONEHAVEN: 1877-81 Archibald Chisholm (ND). 1881-99 James Stewart (ND). 1899-1907 Joseph McLellan. 1907-22 Alexander Thomson. 1922-30 David McDonald. 1930-32 Lewis McWilliam. 1932-38 William Murdoch. 1938-40 John McBain. 1940-53 William Manders. 1953-66 Charles Redmond. 1966-67 John Cunningham. 1967-68 Charles Redmond. 1968-69 vacant. From 1969 served by Jesuits.

STRATHERRICK: 1869-88 Alexander Bissett (1864) (ND). 1888-90 Donald Chisholm (1885). 1890-91 Alexander Bissett (1864) (ND). 1891-96 David McDonald. 1896-1901 William Fraser (ND). 1901-07 Angus McInnes. 1907-18 Aeneas Geddes. 1918-30 William Manders. 1930-56 Charles Thain. 1956-59 served from Fort Augustus. 1959-62 Hugh Sheridan. 1962-66 John Cassidy. 1966-67 John Sole OSB. 1967-73 John Cunningham. 1973-83 served from Fort Augustus. 1983-90 Joseph Dalton. 1990- served from Fort Augustus.

STRICHEN: 1874-81 William Farquhar (ND). 1881-90 Andrew Thomson. 1890-94 Alexander Gerry (ND). 1894-95 James Henderson. From 1895 served from Fraserburgh.

SUTHERLAND (excluding Brora, Golspie and Helmsdale): 1954-57 John Caslin.

TAIN: 1985-Hugh Malaney.

THURSO: 1960-67 served from Wick. 1967-77 Mario Conti. 1977-82 John Symon. 1982-89 Ronald Walls. 1989- Bernard MacDonald.

TOMBAE: 1861-83 Charles MacDonald (1852) (ND). 1883-91 William Smith (ND). 1891-1913 William Stuart. 1913-24 George Nicol. 1924-49 Alexander Bennett. 1949-56 Kenneth MacKenzie. 1956-62 James Robson. 1962-65 Hugh Sheridan. 1965-68 served from Tomintoul. 1968-70 Robert Mann. From 1970 served from Tomintoul.

TOMINTOUL: 1874-83 William Smith (ND). 1883-92 John Paul (ND). 1892-99 Donald Chisholm (1885). 1899-1908 George Nicol. 1908-25 Joseph Thomson. 1925-30 George Grant. 1930-34 George Shaw. 1934-43 Bernard Auer. 1943-52 Alistair Kennedy. 1952-57 Lewis McWilliam. 1957-59 Charles Collins. 1959-68 John Caslin. 1968-70 served from Tombae. 1970-77 Robert Mann. 1977-78 John Ramsay (St A & E). 1978-79 John Brady (Motherwell). 1979-90 Charles Skelly SJ. 1990- Colin Stewart.

TYNET: 1860-85 William Loggie (ND). 1885-1913 Donald Kennedy. 1913-22 David McDonald. 1922-30 James Marr. 1930-31 served from Buckie. 1931-48 William Watson. 1948-51 Patrick Grady. 1951-71 served from Preshome. From 1971 served from Buckie.

WICK: 1874-89 William Mann (ND). 1889-94 Charles Devine (ND). 1894-97 George Nicol. 1897-99 Andrew Grant. 1899-1900 Donald MacKay. 1900-02 Alexander Thomson. 1902-12 served from Dingwall. 1912-14 Bernard Auer. 1914-19 James Bonnyman. 1919-25 William Bowie. 1925-30 Sidney Toman. 1930-36 Joseph Lamont. 1936-43 Kenneth MacKenzie. 1943-47 James MacLaughlin. 1947-53 George Kerr. 1953-62 David Keith. 1962-67 Mario Conti. From 1967 served from Thurso.

Diocese of Argyll & the Isles

Secular Clergy

ANGLER, JOHN: Born Fort William 1882. Educated Blairs 1898-1903; Issy 1903-05: St Peter's 1905-09. Ordained Glasgow 1909. Taynuilt 1909-15. Laggan 1915-19. Rothesay 1919-20. Lent to Dunkeld diocese: Lochee, Dundee 1920-22. Glenfinnan 1922-25. Chaplain, Carmelite convent, Oban 1925-28. Dunoon 1928-31. Rothesay 1931-33. Glencoe 1933-60. Retired 1960. Died Fort William 27 Sept 1964.

BARRY, JAMES: Born Cardiff 1877. Educated Choir School, Oban 1887-90; Blairs 1890-94; Notre Dame des Champs, Paris 1894-95; Issy 1895-97; St Sulpice 1897-1901. Ordained Oban 1901. Fort William 1901-03. Glencoe 1903-26. Died Glencoe 16 Feb 1926.

BEGLEY, JOHN: Born and educated Ireland. Ordained Maynooth 1888. Lent to Argyll diocese. Rothesay 1888-90. Resumed his vocation in Ireland 1890 and died there 10 June 1941. (Canning)

BEGUE, FREDERICK: Ordained 1895. Oban 1896-98. Glencoe 1898-1900. No further entries.

BRENNAN, TIMOTHY: Born and educated Ireland. Ordained Maynooth 1897. Lent to Argyll diocese. Fort William 1897-98. Campbeltown 1898-1900. Returned to Ireland 1900. (Canning)

BUTLER, ANDREW: Born Cleator, Cumberland 1881. Educated Hoogstraeten, Belgium; Douay; Issy; St Sulpice 1905-08. Ordained 1908. Oban 1908-09. Rothesay 1909-22. Taynuilt 1922-24. Campbeltown 1924-28. Rothesay 1928-41. Retired 1941 but served Lochgilphead 1943-49. Died Ascog 15 Dec 1963.

CAMERON, HUGH: Born Inveroy, Lochaber 1876. Educated Blairs 1890-94; Propaganda, Rome 1894-98, returning home in bad health; St Peter's 1899; St Sulpice 1899-1900. Ordained Oban 1900. Fort William 1900-01. Oban 1901-02. Laggan 1902-03. Benbecula 1903-08. Castlebay

121

1908-16. Forces chaplain 1916-19. Castlebay 1919-21. Rothesay 1921-28. Kingussie 1928-31. Died while on holiday in Rome 8 March 1931.

CAMERON, ROBERT: Born Fort William 1941. Educated Blairs, Drygrange. Ordained Fort William 1966. Dunoon 1966-71. Castlebay 1971-74. Mingarry 1974-76. Glenfinnan 1976-80. Taynuilt 1980-83. No further entries.

CAMPBELL, DONALD A (1920): Born Bohuntin, Braelochaber 1894. Educated Blairs 1908-14; Scots College, Rome 1914-21. Ordained Rome 1920. Lent to Glasgow Archdiocese: Glasgow Cathedral 1921-22. Fort William 1922. Rothesay 1922-23. Lent to Aberdeen diocese: Aberdeen Cathedral 1923-24. On leave 1924-25. Castlebay 1925-35. Daliburgh 1935-39. Consecrated Bishop of Argyll at Oban 1939. Translated to Archbishopric of Glasgow 1945. Died Lourdes 22 July 1963.

CAMPBELL, DONALD EWEN (1972): Born South Boisdale 1947. Educated Blairs, Valladolid. Ordained Oban 1972. Rothesay 1972-75. Oban 1975-76. Dunoon 1976-83. Taynuilt 1983-85. Eriskay 1985-.

CAMPBELL, DONALD MARTIN (1989): Born South Uist 1964. Educated Langbank; Blairs; Scots College, Rome. Ordained Daliburgh 1989. Fort William 1989-.

CAMPBELL, DUNCAN: Born Arisaig 1889. Educated Blairs 1903-08; Issy 1908-10; St Sulpice 1910-13. Ordained Oban 1913. Daliburgh 1913-16. Forces chaplain 1916-18. Kingussie 1918. Arisaig in addresses, but not under parishes, 1918-19. Bornish 1919-28. Eigg 1928-31. Kingussie 1931. Fort William 1931-34. Taynuilt 1934-55. Died Oban 19 Oct 1955.

CAMPBELL, HUGH: Born South Uist 1874. Educated Blairs 1889-93; Petite Seminaire de Notre Dame des Champs, Paris, returning home in bad health; St Peter's. Ordained Oban 1899. Oban 1899-1900. Bunroy 1900. Bornish 1900. Died Oban 28 Dec 1900.

CAMPBELL, JOSEPH: Born Barra 1904. Educated Blairs 1917-23; St Peter's 1923-29. Ordained Glasgow 1929. Rothesay 1929-30. Lent to Archbishopric of St A & E: Immaculate Conception, Bathgate 1930-32. Northbay 1932-33. Lent to Dunkeld diocese: St John's, Perth 1933-34. Eigg 1934-40. Benbecula 1940-51. Mingarry 1951-62. Glenfinnan 1962-67. Died Glenfinnan 9 Oct 1967.

CHISHOLM, JAMES: Born Strathglass 1854. Educated Blairs 1870-75; Valladolid 1875-82. Ordained Valladolid 1882. Moidart 1882. Castlebay 1882-98. Daliburgh 1898-99. Castlebay 1899-1903. Arisaig 1903-25. Retired to Morar 1925 and died there 30 May 1948.

CLEARY, PATRICK: Born Ireland. Ordained Portsmouth 1892. Lent to Argyll diocese. Campbeltown 1895-98. Left the diocese; went to Australia. (Canning)

COLLINS, REGINALD: Born Paris c1851. Educated London. Ordained London 1874. Joined the Oblates, Bayswater. Became an army chaplain, serving in Egypt, Sudan, South Africa. Came to Argyll diocese 1911. Ardrishaig 1911-33. Died Sussex 25 Sept 1933.

COMYN, WALTER: Born Staffordshire. Ordained for Clifton diocese 1906, and served there 1906-33. Came to Argyll diocese 1933. Glenfinnan 1933-34. Ardrishaig 1934-35. Lochgilphead 1935-40. Retired at Lochgilphead with failing eyesight from 1940. Died Glasgow 17 Jan 1952.

CONLON, AMBROSE: No ordination date given. Dunoon 1938-39. No further entries.

CONWAY, PATRICK. Born and educated Ireland. Ordained Derry 1899. Lent to Argyll diocese. Fort William 1899-1900. Rothesay 1900-01. Resumed his vocation in Ireland 1901 and died there 29 May 1949. (Canning)

COYLE, ANDREW: Born Edinburgh 1944. Educated Valladolid. Ordained Oban 1968. Daliburgh 1968-71. C/o Bishop's House, Oban 1971-74. No further entries.

CULLEY, ALEXANDER JOSEPH: Born Fort William 1944. Educated Fort William School. Had a career in commerce. Educated for priesthood Drygrange, Gillis College. Ordained Fort William 1986. Daliburgh 1986-87. Oban 1987-.

CUMMING, DONALD JOHN: see Glasgow archdiocese

DAWSON, JAMES JOSEPH: Born Huntly 1858. Educated Blairs 1869-72; Valladolid 1872-75, returning home after a severe illness; Issy [and St Sulpice] 1877-81. Ordained Paris 1881. Oban 1881. Eigg 1881-82. Lent to Dunkeld diocese: Lochee, Dundee 1882-85. Rothesay 1885-86. Oban 1886. Professor, Valladolid 1886-90. Oban 1890-95. In England, Spain and Rothesay in bad health 1895-1902. Rothesay 1902-03. Died Rothesay 26 June 1903.

DINNEEN, WILLIAM: Born and educated Ireland. Ordained Maynooth 1943. Lent to Argyll diocese. Castlebay 1946-48. Oban 1948-50. Resumed his vocation in Ireland 1950. (Canning)

DUFFY, JAMES: Ordained 1879. Oban 1900-01. No further entries.

FRASER, WILLIAM: Born Gorebridge 1944. Educated Blairs, Drygrange. Ordained Oban 1969. Rothesay 1969-72. Fort William 1972-76. Mingarry 1976-80. On leave 1980-81. Ballachulish 1981-86. Northbay 1986-.

GALBRAITH, JAMES: Born Castlebay 1896. Educated Castlebay School; Blairs 1911-16; Rue Vaugirard, Paris 1916-21. Ordained Paris 1921. Laggan 1921. Lent to Glasgow Archdiocese: St Anthony's, Glasgow 1921-22; St Luke's, Glasgow 1922-23. Laggan 1923-25. Ardkenneth 1925-41. Mingarry 1941-51. Corpach 1951-62. Morar 1962-68. Retired to Cumnock 1968. Died Prestwick 20 Nov 1979.

GALBRAITH, JOHN ANGUS: Born Brevig, Barra 1945. Educated Blairs, Drygrange. Ordained Oban 1971. Daliburgh 1971-76. Knoydart 1976-80. Campbeltown 1980-85. Oban 1985-.

GALBRAITH, RODERICK COLUMBA: Born Brevig, Barra 1943. Educated Blairs, Drygrange. Ordained Castlebay 1967. Dunoon 1967. Fort William 1967-71. C/o Bishop's House, Oban 1971-74. No further entries.

GEMMELL, RODERICK: see archdiocese of St Andrew's and Edinburgh.

GETTINS, WILFRID: Born Maryhill 1868. Educated Fort Augustus; St Edmund's, Douay; Prior Park, Bath; St Peter's. Ordained Rothesay 1896. Rothesay 1896-1900. Glencoe 1900-03. Laggan 1903-06. Inverie 1906-19. Oban 1919-23. Dunoon 1923-24. Taynuilt 1924-34. Retired 1934. Died Connel Ferry 20 July 1947.

GIBBONS, DANIEL: Born Ireland. Educated Ireland, Paris. Ordained Paris 1925. Lent to Argyll diocese. Fort William 1925-30. Rothesay 1930-31. Resumed his vocation in Ireland 1931 and died there 24 May 1954. (Canning)

GILLIES, ALEXANDER J: Born Morar 1886. Educated Blairs 1902-05; St Peter's 1905-08; Issy 1908-12; St Sulpice 1912-13. Ordained Oban 1913. Professor, Blairs 1913-19. Northbay 1919-23. Daliburgh 1923-33. St Raphael's hospital, Edinburgh, in bad health 1933-35. Kingussie 1935-36. St Raphael's 1936. Died Edinburgh 26 Dec 1936.

GILLIES, IAIN (John): Born Bracara, Morar 1923. Educated Blairs; St Peter's. Ordained Glasgow for Archdiocese of Glasgow 1948. Lent to Argyll diocese. Castlebay 1948-52, during which time he was incardinated into Argyll diocese. Knoydart 1952-64. Arisaig 1964-83. Died Royal Infirmary, Edinburgh 13 Aug 1983.

GILLIES, WILLIAM: Born Fort William 1888. Educated Blairs 1901-05; Scots College, Rome 1905-12. Ordained Rome 1911. Mulroy 1912. Oban in addresses, but not under parishes, 1912-14. Maryhill 1914-15. Ardkenneth 1915-25. Eriskay 1925-40. Kingussie 1940-47. Died Kingussie 13 Feb 1947.

GRANT, KENNETH: Born Fort William 1900. Educated Blairs 1916-18; with Seaforth Highlanders 1918-19; Blairs 1919-21; St Peter's 1921-27. Ordained Glasgow 1927. Benbecula 1927-28. Went to Glasgow Archdiocese: St Mary Immaculate, Glasgow 1928-39; Forces Chaplain, later prisoner of war, 1939-45; Clarkston 1945-46. Consecrated Bishop of Argyll Oban 1946. Died Glasgow 7 Sept 1959.

HENDRY, RONALD J. K: Born Oban 1913. Educated Campion House, Osterley; Blairs; St Peter's. Ordained 1947. Dunoon 1947-50. Kingussie 1950-60. Roy Bridge 1960-.

HESLIN, HUGH: see Paisley diocese

IRELAND, JEROME (Walter): Born India 1914. Educated Fort Augustus. Entered Benedictine novitiate, Fort Augustus 1933. Ordained 1940. Left the Order 1952 and became a secular priest for Argyll diocese. Daliburgh 1952-56. Castlebay 1956-60. Fort William 1960-61. Kingussie 1961-62. Mingarry 1962-74. Died Inverness 3 Aug 1974.

IRELAND, WALTER: see Ireland, Jerome

JOHNSTONE, NEIL ANGUS: see Glasgow archdiocese.

KENNEDY, PATRICK: Born Port Glasgow 1918. Educated Campion House, Osterley; Philosophical-Theological Academy, Paderborn, Germany. Ordained Oban 1959. Daliburgh 1959-60. Castlebay 1960-62. Oban 1962-63. Dunoon 1963-66. Fort William 1966-67. Glenfinnan 1967-68. Kingussie 1968-69. Lochgilphead 1969-76. Rothesay 1976-80. Sick leave 1980-86. Oban 1986-88. Glencoe 1988-89. Oban 1989-.

LEA, MICHAEL: Ordained 1944. Dunoon 1955-56. Oban 1956-59. Rothesay 1959-62. Dunoon 1962-63. Kingussie 1963-64. Knoydart 1964-69. Campbeltown 1969-80. Knoydart 1980-86. Kingussie 1986-.

LOY, PATRICK: see Glasgow archdiocese

LYNCH, MATTHEW JOSEPH: Born Ireland. Ordained 1878. Rothesay 1886-87. No further entries. (Canning)

MACAULAY, JOHN PHILIP: Born South Uist 1952. Educated Langbank, Blairs, Valladolid. Ordained Oban 1976. Daliburgh 1976. Dunoon 1976. Rothesay 1976-82. Corpach 1982-85. Northbay 1985-86. Further studies 1986-.

McAULEY, RODERICK MURDO: Born Dunblane 1963. Educated St Henry's College, Durban, South Africa; Drygrange; Gillis College. Ordained Oban 1988. Daliburgh 1988-.

McCLEMENT, FREDERICK: see McClymont, Bernard

McCLYMONT, BERNARD: Born Chatham, Kent 1867. Educated Stonyhurst; Fort Augustus; St Mary's College, Oscott. Ordained Worcester 1890. Rothesay 1890-93. Laggan 1893-95. Not in Catholic Directory 1895-96. Lent to Galloway diocese: St Margaret's, Ayr 1896-98. Oban 1898-99. Kilmaronaig 1899-1900. Not in Directories 1900-03. Taynuilt 1903-09. Eigg 1909-15. Entered Benedictine novitiate, Fort Augustus. Served in the diocese as a professed religious 1925-35. Went to America.

McCLYMONT, FREDERICK: see McClymont, Bernard. Frederick took the religious name of Bernard when he joined the Benedictines.

MACCORMICK, JOHN: Born South Boisdale 1911. Educated Blairs 1927-32; St Peter's 1932-36. Ushaw 1936-39. Ordained Ushaw 1939. Bornish 1939-40. Dunoon 1940-41. Eigg 1941-46. Eriskay 1946-51. Benbecula 1951-56. Castlebay 1956-66. Lochgilphead 1966-69. Fort William 1969-74. Retired following a stroke 1974. Died Glagow 6 June 1980.

McCULLAGH, FRANCIS: Ordained 1881. Oban 1899-1900. No further entries.

McDONALD, ALLAN: Born Fort William 1859. Educated Blairs 1871-76; Valladolid 1876-82. Ordained Glasgow 1882. Oban 1882-84. Daliburgh 1884-94. No address given 1894-95. Eriskay 1895-1905. Died Eriskay 8 Oct 1905.

MACDONALD, ANGUS: Born Fort William 1859. Educated Blairs 1872-77; St Edmund's, Douay 1877-78; Issy 1878; Scots College, Rome 1878-84. Ordained Rome 1883. Oban 1884-88. Castlebay 1888-89. Craigston 1889-93. Rothesay 1893-95. Arisaig 1895-1903. Rothesay 1903-21. Glenfinnan 1921-22. Dunoon 1922-25. Retired to Whitebridge 1925 and died there 19 Feb 1926.

MACDONALD, JAMES: Born Drimnin, Argyll 1888. Educated Blairs 1904-09; Issy 1909-13; St Sulpice 1913-14. Ordained Paris 1914. Mulroy 1914-16. Fort William 1916-19. Laggan 1919-23. Northbay 1923-29. Glencoe 1929-33. From 1933 suffered from a nervous affliction and served as an assistant, when able, in various places. Catholic Directory has him at Dunoon 1933-34. Went to Paris after the war, and then retired to Dublin, where he died 28 Jan 1979.

MACDONALD, JOHN (1945): see Glasgow archdiocese

MACDONALD, JOHN ANGUS (1970): Born Askernish, South Uist 1945. Educated Blairs, Valladolid. Ordained Oban 1970. Rothesay 1970-71. Fort William 1971-72. Blairs in addresses, but not under staff, 1972-75. Professor, Blairs 1975-78. Vice-rector, Blairs 1978-83. Arisaig 1983-85. Bornish 1985-87. Daliburgh 1987-.

MACDONALD, MICHAEL JOSEPH: Born Inverness 1954. Educated Langbank; Blairs; Scots College, Rome. Ordained Fort William 1978. Completing studies, Rome 1978-80. Oban 1980-82. Rothesay 1982-87. Oban 1987-.

MACDONALD, PATRICK: Born Jochdar, South Uist 1888. Educated Blairs 1904-09; Issy 1909-13; St Sulpice 1913-14. Ordained Paris 1914. Castlebay 1914-19. Eigg 1919-24. Benbecula 1924-31. Mingarry 1931-41. Daliburgh 1941-48. Died Daliburgh 12 Jan 1948.

MACDONALD, RODERICK: Born Mallaig 1925. Educated Blairs; Scots College, Rome. Ordained Rome 1949. Oban 1950-56. Daliburgh 1956-58. Glencoe 1958-62. Campbeltown 1962-69. Dunoon 1969-.

MACDONALD, SAMUEL: Born Achnabobane, Lochaber 1866. Educated Blairs 1883-86; Issy and Jesuit College of Vaugirard 1886-89; Grand Seminary of Philosophy, [Paris] 1889-91; St Sulpice 1891-93; St Peter's 1893-94. Ordained Oban 1894. Oban 1894-95. Laggan 1895-97. Daliburgh 1897-98. Fort William 1898-99. Went to Archdiocese of St A & E: St Patrick's, Edinburgh 1899-1901. No further entries.

MACDONALD, WILLIAM: Born Benbecula 1862. Educated Propaganda, Rome 1879-90. Ordained Rome 1889. Oban 1890-94. Inverie 1894-99. Daliburgh 1899-1903. Glenfinnan 1903-19. Portree 1919-24. Dunoon 1924-41. Died Dunoon 26 April 1941.

McDONELL, ARCHIBALD J. J: Ordained 1873. Knoydart 1899-1905. Oban, not serving the parish 1906-07. No further entries.

MACDOUGALL, ALEXANDER: Born Morar 1859. Educated England; Douay; St Peter's 1886-90. Ordained St Peter's College 1890. Eriskay 1890. Benbecula 1890-1903. Daliburgh 1903-20. Glenfinnan 1920-21. Castlebay 1921-25. Inverie 1925-39. Retired to Bracara, Morar 1939 and died there 10 Dec 1944.

MACDOUGALL, DONALD: Born Cleat, Barra 1924. Educated Blairs 1938-45; St Peter's 1945-49. Ordained Glasgow 1949. Lent to Glasgow archdiocese: St Mary's, Glasgow 1949-51. Oban 1951. Daliburgh 1951-52. Morar 1952-54. Castlebay 1954-56. Eriskay 1956-59. Bornish 1959-63. Died Glasgow 27 Oct 1963.

MACELMAIL, JOHN: Born Paisley 1853. Educated St Edmund's, Douay; Fort Augustus; Oscott; Catholic University of Louvain. Ordained Liege 1883. Oban 1883-84. Knoydart 1884-91. Campbeltown 1891-95. Rothesay 1895-1902. Dunoon 1902-22. Retired, Dunoon, 1922 and died there 6 Oct 1927.

MACEWAN, SYDNEY: Born Glasgow 1908. Educated St Aloysius' College, Glasgow; Scots College, Rome; St Peter's. Ordained 1944. Lent to Glasgow archdiocese: Glasgow cathedral 1944-49. Lochgilphead 1949-66. Rothesay 1966-68. No parish 1968-69. Kingussie 1969-76. Retired 1976.

McGILL, STEPHEN: Born Glasgow 1912. Educated Blairs 1927-31; Grand Seminaire, Coutances 1931-36. Ordained Glasgow 1936. Further studies, Paris 1936-39. Professor, Bourdeaux and Aix en Provence 1939-40. Professor, Blairs 1940-41. Spiritual Director, Blairs 1941-51. Rector, Blairs 1951-60. Consecrated Bishop of Argyll 1960. Translated to Paisley diocese 1968.

MACINNES, COLIN: Born Bornish 1945. Educated Blairs, Valladolid. Ordained Oban 1970. Castlebay 1970-71. Oban 1971-74. Ardkenneth 1974-80. Northbay 1980-85. On foreign missions 1985-.

MACINNES, EWEN: Born South Uist 1908. Educated Blairs 1921-27; St Lo 1927-28; Grand Seminaire, Coutances 1928-33. Ordained Glasgow 1933. Professor, Blairs 1933-41. Castlebay 1941-56. Oban 1956-68. Morar 1968-.

MACINTYRE, DONALD: Born Kilpheder, South Uist 1885. Educated Blairs 1902-05; St Peter's 1905-08; Issy 1908-10; St Sulpice 1910-13. Ordained Oban 1913. Castlebay 1913-14. Eigg 1914-19. Craigston 1919-25. Went to Canada. Served in Edmonton, Alberta 1925-44. Died there 30 Oct 1944.

McISAAC, SAMUEL: Born Canna 1888. Educated Blairs 1903-08; Scots College, Rome 1908-16. Ordained Rome 1915. Castlebay 1916-17. Lent to Dunkeld diocese: St Mary's, Dundee 1917-18. Mingarry 1918-19. Daliburgh 1919-20. Eriskay 1920-25. Craigston 1925-29. Transferred to Glasgow archdiocese 1929. Mossend 1929-34. Tarbrax 1934-38. Chaplain, St Charles' Institute, Carstairs 1938-56; thus moving to Motherwell diocese. Retired to Rothesay 1956 and died there 3 Sept 1960.

MACKAY, DONALD JOSEPH: Born Glasgow 1952. Educated Langbank, Blairs, Valladolid. Ordained Oban 1976. Professor, Langbank 1976-77. Oban 1977-79. Daliburgh 1979-80. Fort William 1980-84. Vice-rector, Valladolid 1984-.

McKAY, GERARD: Born Glasgow 1949. Educated Edinburgh University; Scots College, Rome. Ordained Rome 1975, returning to Scotland 1976. Dunoon 1976. Continuing studies, Rome 1976-79. Lent to Glasgow archdiocese: St Leo's, Glasgow 1979-80; Holy Cross, Glasgow 1980-82; Glasgow, no parish, 1982-85. Taynuilt 1985-.

MACKELLAIG, ALEXANDER: Born Mallaig 1913. Educated Blairs 1928-33; Valladolid 1933-37; Ushaw 1937-39. Ordained Ushaw 1939. Rothesay 1939-46. Eigg 1946-48. Bornish 1948-52. Oban, not serving parish, 1952-56. Taynuilt 1956-60. Kingussie 1960-63. Died Bannockburn 1 Sept 1963.

MACKELLAIG, DOMINIC: Born Morar 1904. Educated Fort William School; Fort Augustus 1921-23; Issy 1923-27; St Sulpice 1927-28. Ordained Glasgow 1928. Lent to Glasgow archdiocese: Renton 1928. Chaplain, Carmelite convent, Oban 1928-30. Fort William 1930-31. Craigston 1931-36. Northbay 1936-46. Roy Bridge 1946-60. Died Roy Bridge 2 Sept 1960.

McKELLAIG, NEIL: Born Morar 1907. Educated Blairs 1923-28; St Lo 1928-29; St Sulpice 1929-34. Ordained Glasgow 1934. Chaplain, Carmelite convent, Oban 1934-35. Oban 1935-40. Bornish 1940-48. Daliburgh 1948-80. Retired 1980. Died Edinburgh 9 April 1982.

MACKENZIE, WILLIAM ANGUS: Born Braefindon, Ross-shire 1861. Educated Blairs 1873-79; St Edmund's, Douay 1879-81; Issy 1881-83; St Sulpice 1883-84; Scots College, Rome 1884-87. Ordained Rome 1887. Castlebay 1887-88. Laggan 1888-93. Craigston 1893-1913. Died Glasgow 2 July 1913.

McKINNEY, CHARLES: Born Oban 1909. Educated Blairs 1922-27; Valladolid 1927-34. Ordained Valladolid 1934. Fort William 1934-36. Rothesay 1936-39. Knoydart 1939-42. Lochgilphead 1942-43. Craigston 1943-46. Went to Glasgow archdiocese: St John's, Glasgow 1946-47. No address given 1947-49. No further entries.

MACKINNON, DONALD WILLIAM: Born Inverness 1947. Educated Blairs, St Sulpice. Ordained Oban 1971. Professor, Langbank 1971-76. Professor, Blairs 1976-81. Oban 1981-85. Kingussie 1985-86. Campbeltown 1986-.

MACKINNON, MALCOLM: Born Barra 1889. Educated Blairs 1904-09; Issy 1909-13; St Sulpice 1913-14. Ordained Paris 1914. Lent to Glasgow archdiocese: Our Lady and St Margaret's, Glasgow 1914. Eriskay 1914-19. Benbecula 1919-24. Eigg 1924-28. Arisaig 1928-33. Rothesay 1933-34. In uncertain health from 1933; on leave of absence 1934-35. Eriskay 1935-36. Dunoon 1936-38. No address given 1938-40. Retired to Barra 1940 and died there 20 Nov 1962 (see also p 43).

MACKINTOSH, ALEXANDER (1904): see Glasgow archdiocese

MACKINTOSH, DONALD: Born Glasnacardoch, Invernessshire 1877. Educated Blairs 1890-94; Notre Dame des Champs, Paris 1894-95; Scots College, Rome 1895-1901. Ordained Rome 1900. Vice-rector, Scots College, Rome 1901-13; and Rector there 1913-22. Consecrated Archbishop of Glasgow 1922. Died Bearsden 8 Dec 1943.

MACKINTOSH, JAMES A: Born Laggan 1909. Educated Blairs 1923-28; St Lo 1928-29; Grand Seminaire, Coutances 1929-34. Ordained Blairs 1934. Daliburgh 1934-35. Lent to Dunkeld diocese 1935 and was affiliated to it 1937. St Mary's, Lochee 1935-46. St John's, Perth 1946-47. Strathtay 1947-62. St Mary Magdalene, Perth 1962-64. Our Lady of Lourdes, Perth 1964-74. Died Perth 19 April 1974.

MACKINTOSH, JOHN (1882): Born Lochaber 1859. Educated Blairs 1872-77; St Edmund's, Douay 1877-78; Issy 1878-80, leaving France in bad health; Valladolid 1880-82. Ordained Valladolid 1882. Mingarry 1882-83. Bornish 1883-1900. Campbeltown 1900-03. Died Campbeltown 16 March 1903.

MACKINTOSH, JOHN (1909): Born Morar 1882. Educated Scots College, Rome 1903-10. Ordained Rome 1909. Eigg 1910. Oban 1910-13. Bornish 1913-19. Mingarry 1919-25. Roy Bridge 1925-46. Died Roy Bridge 8 Feb 1946.

MACLEAN, DUNCAN: Born Craigston 1894. Educated Blairs 1909-15; Scots College, Rome 1915-23, with a year out in the army. Ordained Rome 1922. Rothesay 1923-25. Dunoon 1925. Roy Bridge 1925. Laggan 1925-28. Bornish 1928-40. Daliburgh 1940-41. Dunoon 1941-69. Died Glasgow 21 Aug 1969.

MACLEAN, JOHN: Born Castlebay 1919. Educated Blairs 1933-37; Issy 1937-39; Bordeaux 1939-40; St Peter's 1940-42. Ordained Oban 1942. Chaplain, Carmelite convent, Oban 1942-46. Oban 1946-48. Eigg 1948-52. Bornish 1952-59. Morar 1959-62. Ardkenneth 1962-74. Fort William 1974-80. Daliburgh 1980-86. Died Daliburgh 6 Dec 1986.

McLELLAN, DONALD: Born Kilpheder, South Uist 1854. Educated Blairs 1871-75; Valladolid 1875-80, returning home in bad health; St Peter's 1881-82. Ordained St Peter's College 1882. Eigg 1882-88. Morar 1888-1903. Died Morar 26 Jan 1903.

MACLELLAN, MALCOLM JOSEPH: Born 1926. Educated Eriskay School; Blairs; Scots College, Rome. Ordained Rome 1953. Oban 1954-56. Dunoon 1956-62. Daliburgh 1962-63. Bornish 1963-66. Northbay 1966-73. Benbecula 1973-80. Castlebay 1980-.

McLELLAN, WILLIAM: Born Mallaig 1878. Educated Blairs 1891-95; Notre Dame des Champs, Paris 1895-96; Issy 1896-98; Scots College, Rome 1898-1901. Ordained Rome 1901. Oban 1901-03. Bornish 1903-13. Craigston 1913-19. Inverie 1919-25. Mingarry 1925-31. Eigg 1931-34. Glenfinnan 1934-36. Retired 1936. Died Musselburgh 16 July 1952.

MACMASTER, ARCHIBALD: Born Stepps 1911. Educated St Aloysius' College, Glasgow; Blairs 1927-30; St Lo 1930-31; St Sulpice 1931-36. Ordained Glasgow 1936. Daliburgh 1936. Fort William 1936-59. Northbay 1959-66. Benbecula 1966-68. Rothesay 1968-76. Kingussie 1976-85. Died Kingussie 11 March 1985.

MACMASTER, DONALD B: Born Perth 1902. Educated Blairs 1916-21; Scots College, Rome 1921-27; St Peter's 1927-28. Ordained Glasgow 1928. Lent to Glasgow archdiocese: Immaculate Conception, Glasgow 1928-29. Sick leave 1929-30. Chaplain, Carmelite convent, Oban 1930-34. Sick leave 1934-39. Kingussie 1939-40. Forces chaplain 1940-44. No further entries.

MACMASTER, IAIN: Born Acharacle, Argyll 1942. Educated Blairs; St Sulpice. Ordained Mingarry 1965. Fort William 1965-66. Castlebay 1966-69. Knoydart 1969-71. Taynuilt 1971-80. Glenfinnan 1980-81. Benbecula 1981-86. Dunoon 1986-87. Rothesay 1987-.

MACMASTER, WILLIAM J: Born Kinlochmoidart 1870. Educated Blairs 1883-87; Valladolid 1887-94. Ordained Valladolid 1894. Castlebay 1894. Professor, Valladolid 1894-1902. Oban 1902-03. Castlebay 1903-07. Laggan 1907-15. Taynuilt 1915-22. Fort William 1922-58. Died Glasgow 13 Oct 1958.

MACMILLAN, JOHN (1903): Born Craigston 1880. Educated Blairs 1894-99; Issy 1899-1901; St Sulpice 1901-03. Ordained Oban 1903. Oban 1903-05. Eigg 1905-08. Benbecula 1908-19. Glenfinnan 1919-20. Went to Glasgow archdiocese: Our Lady and St Margaret's, Glasgow 1920-21. No address given 1921-23. Canada 1923-25. Craigston in addresses, but not under parishes, 1925-26. Ballachulish 1926-29. Northbay 1929-36. Craigston 1936-43. Retired 1943. Died Barra 1 June 1951.

MACMILLAN, JOHN ARCHIBALD (1971): Born Kildonan, South Uist 1946. Educated Blairs, Valladolid. Ordained Valladolid 1971. Dunoon 1971-74. Spiritual Director, Blairs 1974-75. Rothesay 1975-76. Daliburgh 1976-80. Eriskay 1980-85. C/o Roy Bridge 1985-86. C/o Bishop's House, Oban 1986-87. Left priesthood.

MACNEIL, JAMES: Born Barra 1953. Educated Langbank; Blairs; Scots College, Rome. Ordained Rome 1977. Oban 1977. Completing studies, Rome 1977-78. Oban 1978-80. Dean of Studies, Scots College, Rome

1980-84. Rome, not on College staff, 1984-85. Dunoon 1985-86. Benbecula 1986-.

MACNEIL, JOHN (1918): Born Castlebay 1894. Educated Castlebay School; Blairs 1908-13; Avignon 1913-15; Issy 1915-16; St Sulpice 1916-18. Ordained Paris 1918. Lent to Glasgow archdiocese: St John's, Glasgow 1918-19; Croy 1919. Professor, Blairs 1919-33. Arisaig 1933-64. Died Oban 30 July 1964.

MACNEIL, JOHN A (1957): see Glasgow archdiocese

MACNEIL, RODERICK JOHN: Born Glasgow 1960. Educated Daliburgh Junior Secondary School; Langbank; Blairs; Valladolid; St Peter's. Ordained Oban 1985. Oban 1985-87. Dunoon 1987-.

MACNEILL, CALUM (Malcolm): Ordained for Salesians 1949. Left the Order and joined Argyll diocese as a secular priest 1958. Daliburgh 1958-62. Castlebay 1962-66. Eriskay 1966-73. Northbay 1973-80. Benbecula 1980-81. Glenfinnan 1981-85. Campbeltown 1985-86. Sick leave, Bishop's House, Oban 1986-.

MACNEILL, JOHN (1903): Born Castlebay 1880. Educated Blairs 1893-98; Issy 1898-1900; St Sulpice 1900-03. Ordained Oban 1903. Eigg 1903-05. Eriskay 1905-14. With Cameron Highlanders 1914-19. Eriskay 1919-20. Daliburgh 1920-23. Morar 1923-58. Died Morar 14 May 1958.

MACNEILL, MALCOLM: see MacNeill, Calum

McPHERSON, COLIN: Born Lochboisdale 1917. Educated Blairs 1931-34; Propaganda, Rome 1934-40. Ordained Rome 1940. Chaplain, Carmelite convent, Oban 1940-42. Knoydart 1942-51. Eriskay 1951-56. Benbecula 1956-66. Fort William 1966-68. Consecrated Bishop of Argyll at Oban 1969. Died Oban 23 March 1990.

McPHERSON, DONALD A: Born Glasgow 1853. Educated Blairs 1872-75; Valladolid 1875-82. Ordained Valladolid 1882. Eigg 1882. Arisaig 1882-95. Oban 1895-96. Transferred to Glasgow archdiocese. St Michael's, Glasgow 1896-97. St Patrick's, Glasgow 1897-1901. Our Lady's, Motherwell 1901-07. Chapelhall 1907-32. Died Chapelhall 21 Nov 1932.

MACQUEEN, ANGUS JOHN: Born Eochar, South Uist 1923. Educated Blairs; St Peter's; St Edmund's College, Ware. Ordained Oban 1951. Dunoon 1951-52. Castlebay 1952-54. Morar 1954-59. Eriskay 1959-66. Castlebay 1966-80. Glencoe 1980-81. Rothesay 1981-87. Bornish 1987-.

MACQUEEN, JOHN: Born Borrodale c1896. Educated Blairs 1909-15; Valladolid 1915-22. Ordained Valladolid 1922. Lent to Dunkeld diocese:

St Joseph's, Dundee 1922-23. Rothesay 1923. Oban 1923-35. Castlebay 1935-41. Rothesay 1941-66. Retired 1966. Died Rothesay 17 May 1979.

MACRAE, ANGUS: Born Cruive, Strathglass 1858. Educated Blairs 1872-77; St Edmund's, Douay 1877-79; Issy 1879-81; St Sulpice 1881-86 (home for a time c1885 in bad health). Ordained Meaux 1886. Ardkenneth 1886. Mingarry 1886-87. Ardkenneth 1887-1903. Morar 1903-23. Died Glasgow 2 June 1923.

McSHANE, JOSEPH G: Born Barrhead 1931. Educated Campion House, Osterley; St Sulpice; Drygrange. Ordained Oban 1961. Oban 1961-62. Rothesay 1962-65. Oban 1965-68. Glenfinnan 1968-76. Lochgilphead 1976-80. Mingarry 1980-86. Glencoe 1986-88. C/o Roy Bridge 1988-89. Arran in addresses, but not under parishes, 1989-.

MACSWEEN, ANGUS: Born Arisaig 1908. Educated Blairs 1923-28; St Lo 1928-29; Grand Seminaire, Coutances 1929-34. Ordained Glasgow 1934. Dunoon 1934-36. Glenfinnan 1936-40. Eigg 1940-41. Ardkenneth 1941-46. No further entries.

MAGUIRE, PETER: Born and educated Ireland. Ordained Dublin 1925. Lent to Argyll diocese. Rothesay 1925-26. Resumed his vocation in Ireland 1926. (Canning)

MALLOY, JOHN BERNARD: see Dunkeld diocese

MARTIN, DONALD: Born Ardnamurchan 1873. Educated Valladolid 1899-1905. Ordained Oban 1905. Oban 1905-06. Castlebay 1906-08. Glencoe 1908-09. Oban 1909-19. Consecrated Bishop of Argyll at Oban 1919. Died Oban 6 Dec 1938.

MORRISON, DONALD: Born Boisdale 1873. Educated Blairs 1890-93; Notre Dame des Champs, Paris 1893-95; Issy 1895-97; St Sulpice 1897-1900. Ordained Paris 1900. Bornish 1900-03. Died Bornish 10 May 1903.

MORRISON, JOHN: Born Kilphedar, South Uist 1912. Educated Blairs 1927-32; Scots College, Rome 1932-39. Ordained Rome 1938. Dunoon 1939-40. Oban 1940-46. Ardkenneth 1946-62. Corpach 1962-86. Retired 1986.

MORRISON, MALCOLM: Born West Kilbride, South Uist 1908. Educated Blairs 1923-28; St Lo 1928-29; Grand Seminaire, Coutances 1929-30; St Peter's 1930-35. Ordained 1935. Chaplain, Carmelite convent, Oban 1935-40. Eriskay 1940-46. Northbay 1946-59. Fort William 1959-66. Bornish 1966-85. Died Daliburgh 14 April 1985.

MORRISON, PATRICK (Peter): Born Boisdale 1871. Educated Blairs 1885-89; Valladolid 1889-92, returning home in bad health; St Peter's 1893-95. Ordained Oban 1895. Oban 1895-96. Died Oban 7 Dec 1896.

MURPHY, EDWARD ANGUS: Born Kippin 1931. Educated Campion House, Osterley; Drygrange. Ordained Fort William 1966. Morar 1966-68. Oban 1968-71. Knoydart 1971-73. Eriskay 1973-76. Oban 1976-77. C/o Bishop's House, Oban 1977-78. Lent to Aberdeen diocese: Dornie 1978-80. Lochgilphead 1980-.

O'NEILL, JAMES A: Ordained 1892. Rothesay 1902-06. Kingussie 1906-07. No further entries.

O'REGAN, PATRICK: Born Ireland. Educated Ireland, Scots College, Rome. Ordained Rome for Argyll 1930. Lent to Archdiocese of St A & E: St Columba's, Edinburgh 1930-31. Benbecula 1931-40. Glenfinnan 1940-62. Taynuilt 1962-71. Died Oban 3 May 1971. (Canning)

PARK, WILLIAM: Ordained for Archdiocese of Liverpool 1929 and served there until 1947 when his health became bad. Kingussie 1947-50. Died Dec 1950.

RIGG, GEORGE: Born Coll, Stornoway 1860. Educated Douay; Issy 1886-88; St Sulpice 1888-91. Ordained Paris 1891. Inverie 1891-94. Daliburgh 1894-97. Died of fever, Daliburgh, 13 Aug 1897.

SHAFFREY, PATRICK: Ordained 1881. Oban 1897-98. Laggan 1898-1902. No further entries. (But see p 195)

SHEEHAN, MICHAEL: Born c1855. Ordained [Ireland?] 1879. Oban 1879-81. (Canning)

TERRY, JOSEPH: Born Oban 1926. Educated Blairs; St Peter's; Scots College, Rome; St Edmund's College, Ware. Ordained Glasgow 1949. Rothesay 1949-59. Fort William 1959-60. Taynuilt 1960-62. Glencoe 1962-80. Rothesay 1980-81. C/o Roy Bridge 1981-82. Lent to Galloway diocese: Our Lady Star of the Sea, Saltcoats 1982-83. Dunoon 1983-85. Glenfinnan 1985-88. Mingarry 1988-.

THOMSON, JOSEPH: see Aberdeen diocese

TOAL, JOSEPH: Born Roy Bridge 1956. Educated Langbank, Blairs, Valladolid. Ordained Oban 1980. Daliburgh 1980-83. Professor, Blairs 1983-86. Ardkenneth 1986-.

WALSHE, AUSTIN: Ordained 1899. Rothesay 1934-35. No further entries.

WEBB, JAMES: Born near Bristol 1883. Worked for Great Western Railway Company. Joined Redemptorists 1908 and was ordained for them 1913. On staff of various Redemptorist seminaries 1913-27. Dunoon 1927-28. Eriskay 1928. Left Redemptorists and was incardinated into Argyll diocese as secular priest. Rothesay 1928-29. Craigston 1929-31. Campbeltown 1931-62. Retired at Campbeltown from 1962 and died there 27 Feb 1975.

WHITTY, THOMAS J: Ordained 1884. Rothesay 1906-09. No further entries.

WRIGHT, RODERICK: see Glasgow archdiocese

WYNNE, THOMAS: Born Fort William 1930. Educated Blairs, St Sulpice. Ordained Fort William 1957. Oban 1957-65. Rothesay 1965-66. Kingussie 1966-68. Oban 1968-85. Arisaig 1985-.

Parishes

BISHOPS: (Argyll diocese unless otherwise stated)
1878-92 Angus MacDonald (WD). 1893-1918 George Smith (WD). 1919-38 Donald Martin. 1939-45 Donald A Campbell. 1946-59 Kenneth Grant. 1960-68 Stephen McGill. 1969-90 Colin MacPherson. 1990-Roderick Wright (Glasgow).

ARDKENNETH, SOUTH UIST
Heads: 1877-87 Donald MacColl (WD). 1887-1903 Angus MacRae. 1903-15 Donald Walker (1870) (WD). 1915-25 William Gillies. 1925-41 James Galbraith. 1941-46 Angus MacSween. 1946-62 John Morrison. 1962-74 John MacLean. 1974-80 Colin MacInnes. 1980-86 Roderick Wright (Glasgow). 1986- Joseph Toal.
Assistant: 1886 Angus MacRae.

ARDRISHAIG (never a proper parish; occasionally served): 1883-96 John MacDonald (1847) (WD), semi-retired. 1911-33 Reginald Collins. 1934-35 Walter Comyn.

ARISAIG
Heads: 1878-82 Donald MacKay (1870) (WD). 1882-95 Donald McPherson. 1895-1903 Angus MacDonald. 1903-25 James Chisholm. 1925-28 Bernard McClymont OSB. 1928-33 Malcolm McKinnon. 1933-64 John MacNeil (1918). 1964-83 John Gillies. 1983-85 John A MacDonald (1970). 1985- Thomas Wynne.
Assistant: 1883-85 John Black.

BARRA: see Castlebay, Craigston, Northbay

BENBECULA
Heads: 1877-90 Donald MacIntosh (WD). 1890-1903 Alexander
  MacDougall. 1903-08 Hugh Cameron. 1908-19 John MacMillan (1903).
  1919-24 Malcolm McKinnon. 1924-31 Patrick MacDonald. 1931-40
  Patrick O'Regan. 1940-51 Joseph Campbell. 1951-56 John MacCormick.
  1956-66 Colin McPherson. 1966-68 Archibald MacMaster. 1968-73 John
  A MacNeil (1957). 1973-80 Malcolm MacLellan. 1980-81 Calum
  MacNeill. 1981-86 Iain MacMaster. 1986- James MacNeil.
Assistant: 1927-28 Kenneth Grant.

BORNISH, SOUTH UIST
Heads: 1870-83 Alexander Campbell (1847) (WD). 1883-1900 John
  Mackintosh (1882). 1900 Hugh Campbell. 1900-03 Donald Morrison.
  1903-13 William McLellan. 1913-19 John Mackintosh (1909). 1919-28
  Duncan Campbell. 1928-40 Duncan MacLean. 1940-48 Neil MacKellaig.
  1948-52 Alexander MacKellaig. 1952-59 John MacLean. 1959-63 Donald
  MacDougall. 1963-66 Malcolm MacLellan. 1966-85 Malcolm Morrison.
  1985-87 John A MacDonald (1970). 1987- Angus MacQueen.
Assistant: 1940-41 John MacCormick.

BUNROY: see Roy Bridge

CAMPBELTOWN: 1879-91 Archibald J.J. MacDonnell. 1891-95 John
  MacElmail. 1895-98 Patrick Cleary. 1898-1900 Timothy Brennan. 1900-
  03 John Mackintosh (1882). 1903-24 John MacDonald (1875) (WD).
  1924-28 Andrew Butler. 1928-31 Bernard McClymont OSB. 1931-62
  James Webb. 1962-69 Roderick MacDonald. 1969-80 Michael Lea. 1980-
  85 John Galbraith. 1985-86 Calum MacNeill. 1986- Donald W
  MacKinnon.

CASTLEBAY, BARRA
Heads: 1867-83 John MacDonald (1847) (WD). 1883-98 James Chisholm.
  1898-99 vacant. 1899-1903 James Chisholm. 1903-07 William
  MacMaster. 1907-08 Donald Martin. 1908-16 Hugh Cameron. 1916-19
  Patrick MacDonald. 1919-21 Hugh Cameron. 1921-25 Alexander
  MacDougall. 1925-35 Donald A Campbell (1920). 1935-41 John
  MacQueen. 1941-56 Ewen MacInnes. 1956-66 John MacCormick. 1966-
  80 Angus MacQueen. 1980- Malcolm MacLellan.
Assistants: 1882-83 James Chisholm. 1887-88 William A MacKenzie. 1888-
  89 Angus MacDonald. 1894 William MacMaster.1906-07 Donald Martin.
  1913-14 Donald MacIntyre. 1914-16 Patrick MacDonald. 1916-17
  Samuel McIsaac. 1946-48 William Dinneen. 1948-52 Iain Gillies. 1952-
  54 Angus MacQueen. 1954-56 Donald MacDougall. 1956-60 Walter
  Ireland. 1960-62 Patrick Kennedy. 1962-66 Calum MacNeill. 1966-69
  Iain MacMaster. 1970-71 Colin MacInnes. 1971-74 Robert Cameron.

CORPACH
Until 1951 served from Fort William.
Heads: 1951-62 James Galbraith. 1962-86 John Morrison. 1986-90 Roderick Wright (Glasgow).
Assistant: 1982-85 John MacAulay.

CRAIGSTON, BARRA: 1889-93 Angus MacDonald. 1893-1913 William A MacKenzie. 1913-19 William McLellan. 1919-25 Donald MacIntyre. 1925-29 Samuel McIsaac. 1929-31 James Webb. 1931-36 Dominic MacKellaig. 1936-43 John MacMillan (1903). 1943-46 Charles McKinney. From 1946 served from Castlebay.

DALIBURGH, SOUTH UIST
Heads: 1877-80 Alexander Forbes (WD). 1880-84 Alexander Mackintosh (WD). 1884-94 Allan McDonald. 1894-97 George Rigg. 1897-98 Samuel MacDonald. 1898-99 James Chisholm. 1899-1903 William MacDonald. 1903-20 Alexander MacDougall. 1920-23 John MacNeill (1903). 1923-33 Alexander Gillies. 1933-35 James A Mackintosh. 1935-39 Donald A Campbell (1920). 1939-40 vacant. 1940-41 Duncan MacLean. 1941-48 Patrick MacDonald. 1948-80 Neil MacKellaig. 1980-86 John MacLean. 1986-87 Alexander Culley. 1987- John A MacDonald (1970).
Assistants: 1890-91 Donald MacIntosh (WD). 1913-16 Duncan Campbell. 1919-20 Samuel McIsaac. 1936 Archibald MacMaster. 1951-52 Donald MacDougall. 1952-56 Walter Ireland. 1958-62 Calum MacNeill. 1959-60 Patrick Kennedy. 1962-63 Malcolm MacLellan. 1964-68 John A MacNeil (1957). 1968-71 Andrew Coyle. 1971-76 John Galbraith. 1976 John MacAulay. 1976-80 John A MacMillan (1971). 1979-80 Donald J MacKay. 1980-83 Joseph Toal. 1988- Roderick McAuley.

DRIMNIN: 1871-87 Donald MacKay (1833) (WD). 1887-96 Donald MacColl (WD). From 1896 served from Oban.

DUNOON
Heads: 1882-85 Herman Van Baer (WD). 1885-1902 John MacDonald (1858) (WD). 1902-22 John MacElmail. 1922-25 Angus MacDonald. 1925-41 William MacDonald. 1941-69 Duncan MacLean. 1969- Roderick MacDonald.
Assistants: 1923-24 William Gettins. 1924-25 William MacDonald. 1925 Duncan MacLean. 1927 James Webb. 1928-31 John Angler. 1931-33 Alexander Mackintosh (Glasgow). 1933-34 James MacDonald. 1934-36 Angus MacSween. 1936-38 Malcolm MacKinnon. 1938-39 Ambrose Conlon. 1939-40 John Morrison. 1940-41 John MacCormick. 1947-50 Ronald Hendry. 1951-52 Angus MacQueen. 1955-56 Michael Lea. 1956-62 Malcolm MacLellan. 1962-63 Michael Lea. 1963-66 Patrick Kennedy. 1966-71 Robert Cameron. 1967 Roderick Galbraith. 1971-74 John A MacMillan (1971). 1974-76 Roderick Wright (Glasgow). 1976 Gerald MacKay. 1976 John MacAulay. 1976-83 Donald E Campbell (1972).

1983-85 Joseph Terry. 1985-86 James MacNeil. 1986-87 Iain MacMaster. 1988- Roderick MacNeil.

EIGG
Heads: 1842-80 Alexander Gillis (WD). 1880-81 vacant. 1881-82 James J Dawson. 1882 Donald MacPherson. 1882-88 Donald McLellan. 1888-1903 Donald Walker (WD). 1903-05 John MacNeill (1903). 1905-08 John MacMillan (1903). 1908-09 vacant. 1909-10 Bernard McClymont. 1910 John Mackintosh (1909). 1910-15 Bernard McClymont. 1915-19 Donald MacIntyre. 1919-24 Patrick MacDonald. 1924-28 Malcolm McKinnon. 1928-31 Duncan Campbell. 1931-34 William McLellan. 1934-40 Joseph Campbell. 1940-41 Angus MacSween. 1941-46 John MacCormick. 1946-48 Alexander MacKellaig. 1948-52 John MacLean. 1952-56 William Bradley CSSR. From 1956 served from Knoydart.
Assistant: 1914-15 Donald MacIntyre.

ERISKAY
Until 1890 served from Daliburgh.
Heads: 1890 Alexander MacDougall. 1890-91 served from Daliburgh. 1891-93 Donald Mackintosh (WD). 1893-95 vacant. 1895-1905 Allan McDonald. 1905-14 John MacNeill (1903). 1914-19 Malcolm MacKinnon. 1919-20 John MacNeill (1903). 1920-25 Samuel McIsaac. 1925-40 William Gillies. 1940-46 Malcolm Morrison. 1946-51 John MacCormick. 1951-56 Colin McPherson. 1956-59 Donald MacDougall. 1959-66 Angus MacQueen. 1966-73 Calum MacNeill. 1973-76 Edward Murphy. 1976-80 John A MacNeil (1957). 1980-85 John A MacMillan (1971). 1985- Donald E Campbell (1972).
Assistants: 1928 James Webb. 1935-36 Malcolm McKinnon.

FORT WILLIAM
Heads: 1871-84 John MacDonald (1858) (WD). 1884-1922 Alexander Mackintosh (1877) (WD). 1922-58 William MacMaster. 1958-59 Archibald MacMaster. 1959-66 Malcolm Morrison. 1966-68 Colin MacPherson. 1968-69 vacant. 1969-74 John MacCormick. 1974-80 John MacLean. 1980- John A MacNeil (1957)
Assistants: 1897-98 Timothy Brennan. 1898-99 Samuel MacDonald. 1899-1900 Patrick Conway. 1900-01 Hugh Cameron. 1901-03 James Barry. 1904-05 Patrick Loy (Glasgow). 1916-19 James MacDonald. 1922 Donald A Campbell (1920). 1925-30 Daniel Gibbons. 1930-31 Dominic MacKellaig. 1931-34 Duncan Campbell. 1934-36 Charles McKinney. 1936-58 Archibald MacMaster. 1959-60 Joseph Terry. 1960-61 Jerome Ireland. 1965-66 Iain MacMaster. 1966-67 Patrick Kennedy. 1967-71 Roderick Galbraith. 1971-72 John A MacDonald (1970). 1972-76 William Fraser. 1976-80 Roderick Wright (Glasgow). 1980-84 Donald J MacKay. 1984-85 Donald Cumming (Glasgow). 1989- Donald M Campbell (1989).

GLENCOE
Until 1898 served from Fort William.
Heads: 1898-1900 Frederick Begue. 1900-03 Wilfrid Gettins. 1903-26 James Barry. 1926-29 John MacMillan (1903). 1929-33 James MacDonald. 1933-60 John Angler. 1960-62 Roderick MacDonald. 1962-80 Joseph Terry. 1980-81 Angus MacQueen. 1981-86 William Fraser. 1986-88 Joseph McShane. 1988-89 Patrick Kennedy. 1989- Robert Eccles OP.
Assistants: 1908-09 Donald Martin. 1958-60 Roderick MacDonald.

GLENFINNAN: 1862-95 Donald MacDonald (WD). 1895-97 vacant. 1897-1903 served from Fort William. 1903-19 William MacDonald. 1919-20 John MacMillan (1903). 1920-21 Alexander MacDougall. 1921-22 Angus MacDonald. 1922-25 John Angler. 1925-29 served from Fort William. 1929-33 James Chisholm (officially retired). 1933-34 Walter Comyn. 1934-36 William McLellan. 1936-40 Angus MacSween. 1940-62 Patrick O'Regan. 1962-67 Joseph Campbell. 1967-68 Patrick Kennedy. 1968-76 Joseph McShane. 1976-80 Robert Cameron. 1980-81 Iain MacMaster. 1981-85 Calum MacNeill. 1985-88 Joseph Terry. From 1988 served from Mingarry.

INVERIE: see Knoydart

KILMARONAIG (never a proper parish): 1899-1900 Bernard McClymont. 1903-04 Bernard McClymont.

KINGUSSIE (Laggan)
Note: The mission was centred at Laggan until 1928. In that year the church at Kingussie opened and the priest moved there, serving Laggan from Kingussie. Kingussie was sometimes served by a priest who was in poor health and staying at the sanitorium.
Laggan: 1877-88 John MacDonald (1875) (WD). 1888-93 William A MacKenzie. 1893-1895 Bernard McClymont. 1895-97 Samuel MacDonald. 1897-98 vacant. 1898-1902 Patrick Shaffrey. 1902-03 Hugh Cameron. 1903-06 Wilfrid Gettins. 1906-07 James A O'Neill. 1907-15 William MacMaster. 1915-19 John Angler. 1919-23 James MacDonald. 1923-25 James Galbraith. 1925-28 Duncan MacLean.
Kingussie: 1928-31 Hugh Cameron. 1931 Duncan Campbell. 1931-35 Bernard McClymont OSB. 1935-36 Alexander Gillies. 1936-39 Joseph Thomson (Aberdeen). 1939-40 Donald MacMaster. 1940-47 William Gillies. 1947-50 William Park. 1950-60 Ronald Hendry. 1960-63 Alexander MacKellaig. 1963-64 Michael Lea. 1964-66 served from Roy Bridge. 1966-68 Thomas Wynne. 1968-69 Patrick Kennedy. 1969-76 Sydney MacEwan. 1976-85 Archibald MacMaster. 1985-86 Donald MacKinnon. 1986- Michael Lea.
Assistants: 1918 Duncan Campbell. 1921 James Galbraith. 1961-62 Jerome Ireland.

KNOYDART (Inverie): 1884 separates again from Morar. 1884-91 John MacElmail. 1891-94 George Rigg. 1894-99 William MacDonald. 1899-1905 Archibald J J McDonell. 1905-06 vacant. 1906-19 Wilfrid Gettins. 1919-25 William McLellan. 1925-39 Alexander MacDougall. 1939-42 Charles McKinney. 1942-51 Colin MacPherson. 1951-52 vacant. 1952-64 John Gillies. 1964-69 Michael Lea. 1969-71 Iain MacMaster. 1971-73 Edward Murphy. 1973-76 John A MacNeil (1957). 1976-80 John Galbraith. 1980-86 Michael Lea. From 1986 served from Fort William.

LAGGAN: see Kingussie

LOCHGILPHEAD: Often served by a 'retired' priest. 1935-40 Walter Comyn. 1940-42 William MacLellan (retired). 1942-43 Charles McKinney. 1943-49 Andrew Butler (retired). 1949-66 Sydney MacEwan. 1966-69 John MacCormick. 1969-76 Patrick Kennedy. 1976-80 Joseph McShane. 1980- Edward Murphy.

MINGARRY (Moidart)
Heads: 1863-92 Charles MacDonald (WD). 1892-93 vacant. 1893-1919 Donald MacIntosh (1860) (WD). 1919-25 John Mackintosh (1909). 1925-31 William McLellan. 1931-41 Patrick MacDonald. 1941-51 James Galbraith. 1951-62 Joseph Campbell. 1962-74 Jerome Ireland. 1974-76 Robert Cameron. 1976-80 William Fraser. 1980-86 Joseph McShane. 1986-88 served from Glenfinnan. 1988- Joseph Terry.
Assistants: 1882 James Chisholm. 1882-83 John Mackintosh (1882). 1886-87 Angus MacRae. 1918-19 Samuel McIsaac.

MOIDART: see Mingarry

MORAR
Heads: 1874-88 Donald Walker (1870) (WD). 1888-1903 Donald McLellan. 1903-23 Angus MacRae. 1923-58 John MacNeill (1903). 1958-59 Angus MacQueen. 1959-62 John MacLean. 1962-68 James Galbraith. 1968- Ewen MacInnes.
Assistants: 1952-54 Donald MacDougall. 1954-58 Angus MacQueen. 1966-68 Edward Murphy.

MULROY: see Roy Bridge

NORTHBAY, BARRA
Until 1919 served from Craigston.
Heads: 1919-23 Alexander Gillies. 1923-29 James MacDonald. 1929-36 John MacMillan (1903). 1936-46 Dominic MacKellaig. 1946-59 Malcolm Morrison. 1959-66 Archibald MacMaster. 1966-73 Malcolm MacLellan. 1973-80 Calum MacNeill. 1980-85 Colin MacInnes. 1985-86 John MacAulay. 1986- William Fraser.
Assistant: 1932-33 Joseph Campbell.

OBAN (Cathedral)

Heads: 1878-79 Bishop Angus MacDonald. 1879-81 Michael Sheehan. 1881 James J Dawson. 1881-82 Bishop Angus MacDonald. 1882-84 Allan MacDonald. 1884-88 Angus MacDonald (1883). 1888-90 John MacDonald (1875) (WD). 1890-95 James J Dawson. 1895-96 Donald McPherson. 1896-98 Frederick Begue. 1898-99 Bernard McClymont. 1899-1900 Francis McCullagh. 1900-01 James Duffy. 1901-02 Hugh Cameron. 1902-03 John MacDonald (1875) (WD). 1903-04 Patrick Loy (Glasgow). 1904-05 John MacMillan (1903). 1905-09 Alexander Mackintosh (Glasgow). 1909-19 Donald Martin. 1919-23 Wilfrid Gettins. 1923-35 John MacQueen. 1935-40 Neil MacKellaig. 1940-46 John Morrison. 1946-48 John MacLean. 1948-51 John MacDonald (Glasgow). 1951-56 Roderick MacDonald. 1956-68 Ewen MacInnes. 1968-85 Thomas Wynne. 1985- John Galbraith.

Assistants: 1883-84 John MacElmail. 1886 James J Dawson. 1890-94 William MacDonald. 1894-95 Samuel MacDonald. 1895-96 Patrick Morrison. 1897-98 Patrick Shaffrey. 1899-1900 Hugh Campbell. 1901-03 William McLellan. 1902-03 William MacMaster. 1903-04 John MacMillan (1903). 1905-06 Donald Martin. 1908-09 Andrew Butler. 1910-13 John Mackintosh (1909). 1946-48 John MacDonald (Glasgow). 1948-50 William Dinneen. 1950-51 Roderick MacDonald. 1951 Donald MacDougall. 1954-56 Malcolm MacLellan. 1956-59 Michael Lea. 1957-65 Thomas Wynne. 1961-62 Joseph McShane. 1962-63 Patrick Kennedy. 1963-64 John A MacNeil (1957). 1965-68 Joseph McShane. 1968-71 Edward Murphy. 1971-74 Colin MacInnes. 1975-76 Donald E Campbell (1972). 1976-77 Edward Murphy. 1977 James MacNeill. 1977-79 Donald Mackay. 1978-80 James MacNeil. 1980-82 Michael MacDonald. 1981-85 Donald MacKinnon. 1985-87 Roderick MacNeil. 1986-88 Patrick Kennedy. 1987-Alexander Culley. 1987-Michael MacDonald. 1989- Patrick Kennedy.

OBAN-CARMELITE CONVENT: CHAPLAINS

1925-28 John Angler. 1928-30 Dominic MacKellaig. 1930-34 Donald MacMaster. 1934-35 Neil McKellaig. 1935-40 Malcolm Morrison. 1940-42 Colin MacPherson. 1942-46 John MacLean. From 1946 served from Oban cathedral.

PORTREE: 1919-24 William MacDonald. From 1924 served from Fort William.

ROTHESAY

Heads: 1867-93 George Smith. 1893-95 Angus MacDonald. 1895-1902 John MacElmail. 1902-03 James J Dawson. 1903-21 Angus MacDonald. 1921-28 Hugh Cameron. 1928-41 Andrew Butler. 1941-66 John MacQueen. 1966-68 Sydney MacEwan. 1968-76 Archibald MacMaster. 1976-80 Patrick Kennedy. 1980-81 Joseph Terry. 1981-87 Angus MacQueen. 1987- Iain MacMaster.

Assistants: 1875-86 Charles Reid (WD). 1885-86 James J Dawson. 1886-87 Matthew J Lynch. 1888-90 John Begley. 1890-93 Bernard McClymont. 1896-1900 Wilfrid Gettins. 1900-01 Patrick Conway. 1902-06 James A O'Neill. 1906-09 Thomas J Whitty. 1909-22 Andrew Butler. 1919-20 John Angler. 1922-23 Donald A Campbell (1920). 1923 John MacQueen. 1923-25 Duncan MacLean. 1925-26 Peter Maguire. 1926-28 John Malloy. 1928-29 James Webb. 1929-30 Joseph Campbell. 1930-31 Daniel Gibbons. 1931-33 John Angler. 1933-34 Malcolm MacKinnon. 1934-35 Austin Walshe. 1935-36 James MacDonald. 1936-39 Charles McKinney. 1939-46 Alexander MacKellaig. 1946-49 Roderick Gemmell (St A & E). 1949-59 Joseph Terry. 1959-62 Michael Lea. 1962-65 Joseph McShane. 1965-66 Thomas Wynne. 1969-72 William Fraser. 1970-71 John A MacDonald (1970). 1972-75 Donald Campbell (1972). 1975-76 John A MacMillan (1971). 1976-82 John MacAulay. 1982-87 Michael J MacDonald. 1987- Donald MacLeod WF.

ROTHESAY-CONVENT OF ST JOSEPH OF NEWARK: CHAPLAINS
1957-67 John McNair (Glasgow). 1967-71 Hugh Heslin (Paisley).

ROY BRIDGE (Bunroy) (Mulroy)
Note: The centre for this mission was at Bunroy until 1905 when it moved to Mulroy, later Roy Bridge. Addresses at Mulroy and Roy Bridge both relate to the same church.
Heads: 1870-1925 Donald MacDougall (WD). 1925 Duncan MacLean. 1925-46 John Mackintosh (1909). 1946-60 Dominic MacKellaig. 1960- Ronald Hendry.
Assistants: 1900 Hugh Campbell. 1912 William Gillies. 1914-16 James MacDonald.

SOUTH UIST: see Ardkenneth, Bornish, Daliburgh

TAYNUILT: 1904-09 Bernard McClymont. 1909-15 John Angler. 1915-22 William MacMaster. 1922-24 Andrew Butler. 1924-34 Wilfrid Gettins. 1934-55 Duncan Campbell. 1955-56 served from Oban. 1956-60 Alexander MacKellaig. 1960-62 Joseph Terry. 1962-71 Patrick O'Regan. 1971-80 Iain MacMaster. 1980-83 Robert Cameron. 1983-85 Donald E Campbell (1972). 1985- Gerard MacKay.

Diocese of Dunkeld

Secular Clergy

ADAMSON, CHARLES: Born Tillicoultry 1938. Educated Blairs, Valladolid. Ordained Valladolid 1962. St Clement's, Dundee 1962-72. Our Lady of Good Counsel, Dundee 1972-73. Our Lady of Sorrows, Dundee 1973-81. Dunblane 1981-88. St John's, Perth 1988-.

ANDREW, ERNEST: Born Aberdeen 1921. Educated Blairs, St Peter's. Ordained Blairs 1946. St Andrew's, Dundee 1946-49. Alloa 1949-56. St Clement's, Dundee 1956-60. St John's, Perth 1960-62. Strathtay 1962-65. Tullibody 1965-74. Our Lady of Lourdes, Perth 1974-.

ANGELOSANTO, ALDO: Born Inverness 1949. Educated Lawside Academy, Dundee; Blairs; Scots College, Rome. Ordained Dundee 1973. Completing studies, Rome 1973-74. Immaculate Conception, Dundee 1974-77. St John's, Perth 1977-81. Newport 1981-88. St Columba's, Dundee 1988-.

ANGLER, JOHN: see Argyll diocese

ASHBY, WILLIAM: Ordained 1875. Montrose 1896-99. Ballechin 1899-1902. Crieff 1902-1905. No further entries.

AYLWARD, RICHARD: Born and educated Ireland. Ordained Maynooth 1898. Lent to Dunkeld diocese. St Patrick's, Dundee 1898-1902. St Andrew's, Dundee 1902-04. Resumed his vocation in Ireland 1904 and died there 1 Dec 1954. (Canning)

BARRON, LIAM: Born and educated Ireland. Ordained Kilkenny 1970. Lent to Dunkeld diocese. St Teresa's, Dundee 1970-71. St Joseph's, Dundee 1971-73. Resumed his vocation in Ireland 1973. (Canning)

BARRON, THOMAS: Born Ireland. Entered the Society for African Missions. Ordained Ireland 1933. Nigeria 1933-39. Chaplain, Royal Navy 1939-47. Left Society for African Missions and came to Dunkeld as a

143

secular priest. Alloa 1947-49. Immaculate Conception, Dundee 1949-57. Montrose 1957-63. Arbroath 1963-71. Our Lady of Good Counsel, Dundee 1971-72. Died Broughty Ferry 8 July 1972. (Canning)

BLAKE, MATTHEW: Born Ireland. Ordained Ireland 1914. Lent to Dunkeld diocese. St Patrick's, Dundee 1914. Immaculate Conception, Dundee 1914-15. Died Ireland 2 Oct 1960. (Canning)

BOYLE, ANTHONY M J: Born Cittagong, E Pakistan 1939. Educated St Columb's College, Derry; All Hallows College, Dublin. Ordained All Hallows for Dunkeld 1962. St Joseph's, Dundee 1962-71. Kinross 1971-76. St Ninian's, Dundee 1976-78. Died Dundee 20 July 1978.

BRADY, HUGH: see archdiocese of St Andrew's and Edinburgh

BRADY, PATRICK: Born Ireland. Ordained Ireland 1889. St Mary's, Dundee 1897-98. St John's, Perth 1898-1900. Newport 1900-08. Went to English mission 1908. Died Husband's Bosworth 7 June 1936. (Canning)

BROEDERS, SEVERINUS: Ordained 1906. St Joseph's, Dundee 1915-16. No further entries.

BROPHY, THOMAS: Born and educated Ireland. Ordained Waterford 1884. Came to Dunkeld diocese. St Mary's, Dundee 1884-99. Immaculate Conception, Dundee 1899-1902. St John's, Perth 1902. Ballechin 1902-05. Crieff 1905-10. Retired to Ireland 1910 and died there 16 Aug 1914. (Canning)

BROUGH, JOSEPH: Born Blairgowrie 1885. Educated Blairs 1899-1904; Scots College, Rome 1904-1910. Ordained Rome 1909. Crieff 1910. St Joseph's, Dundee 1910-14. St John's, Perth 1914-20. St Andrew's, Dundee 1920-27. On sick leave at Blairgowrie 1927-31. On retired list 1931-32. Carnoustie 1932-47. Died Carnoustie 23 Nov 1947.

BROWNE, JAMES: Ordained 1882. St Mary's, Dundee 1882-85. No further entries.

BUNYAN, THOMAS: Ordained 1930. St Joseph's, Dundee 1949-52. St Andrew's, Dundee 1952-53. No further entries.

BUTLER, BARTHOLOMEW: Born and educated Ireland. Ordained Cork for Dunkeld 1943. St Patrick's, Dundee 1943-44. Immaculate Conception, Dundee 1944-56. Kinross 1956-62. Crieff 1962-65. Died 22 March 1965. (Canning)

CAHILL, HUGH: see Glasgow archdiocese.

CAMPBELL, HUGH: Born Edinburgh 1927. Educated Blairs, St Peter's, St Sulpice. Ordained Dundee 1949. St Andrew's, Dundee 1949-61. St Patrick's, Dundee 1961-62. Kinross 1962-64. St Patrick's, Dundee 1964-66. Alloa 1966-67. St Mary's, Dundee 1967-75. St Teresa's, Dundee 1975-77. Immaculate Conception, Dundee 1977-80. C/o Bishop's House 1980-82. St Matthew's, Dundee 1982-86. St John's, Perth 1986-88. Newport 1988-.

CAMPBELL, JOSEPH: see Argyll diocese.

CANTWELL, THOMAS. Born Ireland. Educated Ireland, St Peter's. Ordained Dundee 1902. St John's, Perth 1902-03. Sick leave 1903 onwards. (Canning)

CAREY, WILLIAM: Born and educated Ireland. Ordained Waterford 1909. Lent to Dunkeld diocese. St Andrew's, Dundee 1909-13. No further entries. (Canning)

CAROLAN (Francis) WALTER: Born and educated Ireland. Ordained Ireland 1946. Lent to Dunkeld diocese. St Joseph's, Dundee 1946-48. Resumed his vocation in Ireland 1948. (Canning)

CASEY, JOHN: Born and educated Ireland. Ordained Maynooth 1896. Lent to Dunkeld diocese. St Mary's, Dundee 1897-1903. Resumed his vocation in Ireland 1903 and died there 17 June 1924. (Canning)

CASSIDY, JOSEPH: Born Lochee 1894. Educated Blairs 1910-14; Propaganda, Rome 1914-20. Ordained Rome 1920. St John's, Perth 1920-33. No further appointments. Died Largs 4 July 1954.

CASSIDY, MARK JAMES: Born Perth 1962. Educated St Columba's High School, Perth; Heriot Watt University; Scots College, Rome. Ordained Perth 1988. Immaculate Conception, Dundee 1988-89. St Leonard's, Dundee 1989-.

CHANDLER, ALBERT: see Glasgow archdiocese.

COIA, ROMEO: see Glasgow archdiocese.

CONNELLY, THOMAS: Born Dundee 1860. Educated Blairs 1872-77; Scots College, Rome 1877-83. Ordained Rome 1883. Doune 1883. St Mary's, Dundee 1883-84. Immaculate Conception, Dundee 1884-85. Doune 1885-89. Died Dundee 27 Aug 1889.

CONNOLLY, JOHN JOSEPH: Born and educated Ireland. Ordained Kilkenny for Dunkeld 1952. St Andrew's, Dundee 1952-56. St Joseph's, Dundee 1956-60. Our Lady of Lourdes, Perth 1960-62. Newport 1962-

66. St Leonard's, Dundee 1966-81. St Clement's, Dundee 1981-. (Canning)

CONNOLLY, JOSEPH: Born Dundee 1865. Educated Blairs 1880-84; St Edmund's, Douay 1884-86; Issy 1886-88; St Sulpice 1888-91. Ordained Dundee 1891. Died Dundee 9 Oct 1891.

CONWAY, MICHAEL: see Galloway diocese.

COOGAN, JOHN: Born Dundee 1883. Educated Blairs 1897-1902; Scots College, Rome 1902-08. Ordained Rome 1907. St Patrick's, Dundee 1908-15. Arbroath 1915-16. Strathtay 1916-29. Arbroath 1929-33. Spiritual Director, Scots College, Rome 1933-34. St John's, Perth 1934-35. Crieff 1935-40. St John's, Perth 1940-71. Died Perth 27 Feb 1971.

CREEGAN, JOSEPH: Born Dundee 1941. Educated Lawside Academy, Dundee; Blairs; Drygrange. Ordained Dundee 1966. St Mary Magdalene, Perth 1966-72. St Columba's, Dundee 1972-77. Blairgowrie 1977-81. St Joseph's, Dundee 1981-.

CROTTY, PATRICK: Born Ireland. Ordained Ireland 1887. Lent to Dunkeld diocese. St Mary's, Dundee 1889-95. Ireland 1895-98. St Andrew's, Dundee 1898-1902. Returned to Ireland. According to Canning he joined Redemptorists 1899. (Canning)

CUFFE, PHILIP JOSEPH: Born Ireland. Educated Ireland, Spain. Ordained Ireland 1932. Lent to Dunkeld diocese. Saints Peter and Paul, Dundee 1932-35. Resumed his vocation in Ireland 1935 and died there 8 May 1976. (Canning)

CULHANE, GEORGE. Born Ireland. Educated Ireland, Paris. Ordained 1888. Lent to Dunkeld diocese. St John's, Perth 1888-89. Lent to archdiocese of St Andrew's and Edinburgh. St Patrick's, Edinburgh 1889-91. Resumed his vocation in Ireland 1891 and died there 23 March 1934. (Canning)

CULLERTON, PETER: Born Dundee 1912. Educated Blairs, St Lo, Coutances, Issy, St Sulpice. Ordained Dundee 1937. Lent to Galloway diocese: St Joseph's, Kilmarnock 1937-38; St Mary's, Irvine 1938-40. St Andrew's, Dundee 1940-48. Alva 1948-55. St Pius X, Dundee 1955-81. Died Dundee 9 July 1981.

CUSICK, JOHN J (1930): see Glasgow archdiocese.

DALY, CHARLES (1914): see archdiocese of St Andrew's and Edinburgh

DALY, CHARLES ALOYSIUS (1916): Born Sheepshed, Leicestershire

1892. Educated Blairs 1906-11; Seminary of Versailles 1911-14; Institut Catholique, Paris 1914-16. Ordained Paris 1916. St Joseph's, Dundee 1916-17, but it was too much for his health. Went to south of England 1917. Died Whitchurch 24 Feb 1918.

DAWSON, JAMES JOSEPH: see Argyll diocese.

DAWSON, PETER: Ordained 1889. St Andrew's, Dundee 1895-98. No further entries.

DEMPSEY, EDWARD: Born Alloa 1901. Educated Blairs 1918-23; Issy 1923-27; St Sulpice 1927-28. Ordained Dundee 1928. Crieff 1928. Lent to Glasgow archdiocese: St Mary's, Greenock 1928-29. St Patrick's, Dundee 1929-30. St Mary's, Dundee 1930-34. Saints Peter and Paul, Dundee 1934-36. St John's, Perth 1936-43. Alva 1943-48. Immaculate Conception, Dundee 1948-62. Died Glasgow 27 March 1962.

DEVINE, JOHN: Ordained 1925. Immaculate Conception, Dundee 1934-35. No further entries.

DILLON, THOMAS J: Born Ireland. Educated Ireland, St Peter's. Ordained Killarney for Dunkeld 1942. St Mary's, Dundee 1942-49. St Patrick's, Dundee 1949-55. Carnoustie 1955-63. Alva 1963-70. Retired to Lochee in bad health 1970. Died Lourdes 2 Aug 1982. (Canning)

DOHERTY, JOHN: Born Blairgowrie 1857. Educated Blairs 1869-74; Scots College, Rome 1874-77, returning home due to bronchitis; Blairs 1877-78; St Sulpice 1878-80. Ordained Kinnoull 1881. Immaculate Conception, Dundee 1881-82. Professor, Blairs 1882-83. St Mary's, Dundee 1883-84. Montrose 1884-85. Ballechin 1885-91. Professor, Valladolid 1891-94. Lent to Glasgow archdiocese: Glasgow Cathedral 1894-95. Chaplain, St Joseph's Convent, Lawside 1895-1922. Doune 1922-37. Retired to Whitby 1937 and died there 9 June 1940.

DOHERTY, ROBERT: see Glasgow archdiocese.

DONACHIE, BENJAMIN: Born Dundee 1928. Educated St Andrew's University, St Sulpice. Ordained Dundee 1958. Professor, Blairs 1958-74. Rector, Blairs 1974-80. Chaplain, Little Sisters of the Poor, Dundee 1980-81. Kinross 1981-87. St Ninian's, Dundee 1987-.

DONAGHER, PATRICK: Born and educated Ireland. Ordained Waterford for Dunkeld 1920. St Joseph's, Dundee 1920-21. Lent to Glasgow archdiocese: Kilbirnie 1921-22; Renfrew 1922-23. Immaculate Conception, Dundee 1923-33. Strathtay 1933-37. Newport 1937-40. Arbroath 1940-52. Highvalleyfield 1952-61. Our Lady of Lourdes, Perth 1961-63. Died Perth 10 Nov 1963. (Canning)

DONNELLY, PHILIP: Born Ireland c1912. Educated All Hallows, Dublin. Ordained 1938. Served in Archdiocese of Perth, Australia 1938-48. Came to Dunkeld diocese 1948. St Patrick's, Dundee 1948-59. Auchterarder 1959-63. Montrose 1963-82. Retired to Ireland 1982 and died Cork 20 May 1985.

DOWLING, JAMES: Born Dundee c1855. Educated Blairs; St Edmund's, Douay; Issy. A serious accident interrupted his studies and he then decided to serve on the foreign missions. Joined French Society of Missionaries for West Africa and completed training at Lyons. Ordained 1881. Taught in Egypt. Left Society and came to Dunkeld diocese as secular priest 1893. Immaculate Conception, Dundee 1893-99. Monifieth 1899-1900. Crieff 1900-02. Doune 1902-22. Retired 1922. Died Doune 27 Feb 1923.

DRYSDALE, MARTIN: Born Dunfermline 1950. Educated Langbank; Blairs; Scots College, Rome. Ordained Highvalleyfield 1975. Completing studies, Rome 1975-76. St John's, Perth 1976-77. Professor, St Peter's College 1977-82. Alva 1982-86. St Matthew's, Dundee 1986-.

DURAND, RICHARD A: Born and educated Ireland. Ordained Waterford 1919. St Patrick's, Dundee 1919-20. St Joseph's, Dundee 1920-22. No further entries. (Canning)

DURKIN, EDWARD: Born and educated Ireland. Ordained Dublin for Dunkeld 1956. St Mary's, Dundee 1956-57. Immaculate Conception, Dundee 1957-64. Alloa 1964-65. Strathtay 1965-71. Forfar 1971-74. Tullibody 1974-81. St John's, Perth 1981-87. Died Dundee 23 Dec 1987. (Canning)

EGAN, PATRICK GILBERT: Born Ireland. Educated Ireland, Rome. Ordained Rome 1917. Lent to Dunkeld diocese. St Joseph's, Dundee 1917-20. Resumed his vocation in Ireland 1920 and died there 2 Jan 1956. (Canning)

FAHY, JOHN: Born and educated Ireland. Ordained Loughrea 1919. Lent to Dunkeld diocese. St Joseph's, Dundee 1919-20. St Andrew's, Dundee 1920-21. Resumed his vocation in Ireland 1921 and died there 19 July 1969. (Canning)

FAHY, MICHAEL J: Born and educated Ireland. Offered his services to Dunkeld diocese. Ordained Kinnoull 1915. St Patrick's, Dundee 1915-29. Highvalleyfield 1929-46. Died Dunfermline 19 June 1946. (Canning)

FAIRLIE, GILBERT: Born Ayr 1893. Educated Belmont Abbey. Ordained there 1922. Came to Scotland 1923. St John's, Perth 1923-24. Dunkeld 1924-72. Died Edinburgh 15 July 1972.

FITZGERALD, JAMES (1940): see Glasgow archdiocese.

FIVES, MICHAEL: Ordained 1908. Immaculate Conception, Dundee 1909-13. St John's, Perth 1913-14. St Mary's, Dundee 1914-15. No further entries.

FLYNN, MICHAEL: Ordained 1932. St Joseph's, Dundee 1934-35. No further entries.

FLYNN, WILLIAM: Born and educated Ireland. Ordained Waterford 1906. Lent to Dunkeld diocese. St Patrick's, Dundee 1906-08. St Joseph's, Dundee 1908-14. St Mary's, Dundee 1914-15. Resumed his vocation in Ireland 1915 and died there 12 June 1964. (Canning)

FOLEY, JAMES: Ordained for Society of Missions for Africa 1964. Left the Society 1981. Doune 1977-82. Callander 1982-86. Alloa 1986-.

FOYLAN, MICHAEL: Born Shettleston 1907. Educated Blairs 1920-25; St Lo 1925-26; St Sulpice 1926-31. Ordained Kinnoull 1931. St Andrew's, Dundee 1931-37. St Joseph's, Dundee 1937-46. Highvalleyfield 1946-49. St Andrew's, Dundee 1949-64. Consecrated Bishop of Aberdeen 1965. Died Aberdeen 28 May 1976.

FOYLAN, PETER: Born Glasgow 1915. Educated Blairs 1928-33; Valladolid 1933-34; Issy 1934-39. Ordained Dundee 1939. Lent to archdiocese of St A & E: St Patrick's, Edinburgh 1939-40. St Mary's, Dundee 1940-42. Alloa 1942-43. St John's, Perth 1943-47. St Andrew's, Dundee 1947-49. St Joseph's, Dundee 1949-51. Crieff 1951-62. Immaculate Conception, Dundee 1962-71. St Matthew's, Dundee 1971-76. Arbroath 1976-83. Died Arbroath 18 May 1983.

FRIGERIO, THOMAS EDGAR: see Glasgow archdiocese.

FURLONG, THOMAS: Born and educated Ireland. Ordained Waterford 1881. Lent to Dunkeld diocese. St Joseph's, Dundee 1881-87. Resumed his vocation in Ireland 1887 and died there 31 May 1934. (Canning)

GALLAGHER, DANIEL: Born High Blantyre 1932. Educated St Sulpice. Ordained Dundee 1962. St Andrew's, Dundee 1962-66. Alloa 1966-76. Auchterarder 1976-81. St Matthew's, Dundee 1981-86. Died Dundee 21 April 1986.

GALLAGHER, NEIL: Ordained for Franciscans 1971. Left Order and came to Dunkeld as secular priest. St John's, Perth 1985-86. Callander 1986-.

GANNON, THOMAS: Born Perth 1900. Educated Blairs 1913-19; St Peter's 1919-20; Scots College, Rome 1920-26. Ordained Rome 1926. St Mary's,

Dundee 1926. Immaculate Conception, Dundee 1926-32. His health broke down 1932. Lent to Glasgow archdiocese: St Anne's, Glasgow 1932-36. Sick leave 1936-37. Saints Peter and Paul, Dundee 1937-41. Died Dundee 12 July 1941.

GLEESON, JOHN: Born and educated Ireland. Ordained Ireland 1889. Lent to Dunkeld diocese. St Mary's, Dundee 1889-91. St Patrick's, Dundee 1891-97. Resumed his vocation in Ireland 1897 and died there 12 Aug 1948. (Canning)

GRAHAM, EDWARD: No ordination date given. Ballechin 1895-96. No further entries.

GUINAN, JOSEPH: Born and educated Ireland. Ordained Ireland 1904. Lent to Dunkeld diocese. St Mary's, Dundee 1904-12. Resumed his vocation in Ireland 1912 and died there 22 April 1964. (Canning)

HALLINAN, WILLIAM: Born and educated Ireland. Ordained Waterford 1935. Lent to Dunkeld diocese. St Mary's, Dundee 1935-39. Resumed his vocation in Ireland 1939 and died there 13 Jan 1971. (Canning)

HANLON, JOHN BRESLIN: Born Dundee 1930. Educated Campion House, Osterley; Issy; St Sulpice. Ordained Dundee 1957. St Leonard's, Dundee 1957-60. Alloa 1960-64. Immaculate Conception, Dundee 1964-66. Carnoustie 1966-72. St Teresa's, Dundee 1972-76. St Andrew's, Dundee 1976-81. Immaculate Conception, Dundee 1981-89. Retired 1989.

HARKIN, JOHN JOSEPH: see Galloway diocese.

HARTY, JOHN: Born Glasgow 1950. Educated Lawside Academy, Dundee; Langbank; Blairs; Valladolid. Ordained Perth 1975. St Pius X, Dundee 1975-77. St Ninian's, Dundee 1977-78. St Clement's, Dundee 1978-81. St Leonard's, Dundee 1981-82. Montrose 1982-.

HASSETT, EDMOND: Born and educated Ireland. Ordained Waterford 1889. Lent to Dunkeld diocese. St Joseph's, Dundee 1889-94. Resumed his vocation in Ireland 1894 and died there 21 April 1917. (Canning)

HENDRY, CHARLES: Born Dundee 1933. Educated Blairs, St Sulpice. Ordained Dundee 1955. St John's, Perth 1955-64. Kinross 1964-69. Doune 1969-71. Dunblane 1971-76. Highvalleyfield 1976-82. St Ninian's, Dundee 1982-87. Tullibody 1987-.

HIGGINS, JEREMIAH: Ordained 1932. Highvalleyfield 1949-50. No further entries.

HIGH, JAMES HUNTER: Born Dundee 1945. Educated Harris Academy, Dundee; University of St Andrew's; Beda, Rome. Ordained Dundee 1986. St Ninian's, Dundee 1986-88. Alloa 1988-.

HOLTON, MICHAEL: Ordained 1937. Our Lady of Lourdes, Perth 1959-60. No further entries.

HOWARD, JAMES: Born and educated Ireland. Ordained Thurles for Dunkeld 1944. St Andrew's, Dundee 1944-46. Alloa 1946-47. No further entries. (Canning)

HURLEY, PATRICK: Born and educated Ireland. Ordained Maynooth 1898. Lent to Dunkeld diocese. St Mary's, Dundee 1898-1904. Resumed his vocation in Ireland 1904. (Canning)

JOHNSTON, ALEXANDER: see Glasgow archdiocese.

KAYE, PETER: Born Perth 1911. Educated Blairs 1925-30; St Lo 1930-31; Issy 1931-35; St Sulpice 1935-36. Ordained Kinnoull 1936. Saints Peter and Paul, Dundee 1936-48. Dunblane 1948-56. Arbroath 1956-63. St Columba's, Dundee 1963-74. Alva 1974-82. Died Alva 12 Nov 1982.

KEARNEY, PATRICK. Born and educated Ireland. Ordained Waterford 1890. Lent to Dunkeld diocese. St Andrew's, Dundee 1890-98. Resumed his vocation in Ireland 1898 and died there April 1927. (Canning)

KEATING, PATRICK F: see Glasgow archdiocese.

KEEGAN, GERARD: Born and educated Ireland. Ordained Carlow 1941. St Andrew's, Dundee 1941-46. Forfar 1946-55. St Teresa's, Dundee 1955-64. St Mary Magdalene's, Perth 1964-87. Retired to Dundee 1987. (Canning)

KEENAN, JOSEPH: Born Dundee 1877. Educated Blairs 1891-95; Notre Dame des Champs, Paris 1895-96; Issy 1896-98; Scots College, Rome 1898-1902. Ordained Rome 1901. Lent to Archdiocese of St A & E: St Patrick's, Edinburgh 1902-03. St John's, Perth 1903-11. Ballechin 1911-16. Crieff 1916-35. Immaculate Conception, Dundee 1935-61. Died Dundee 27 April 1961.

KELLY, ADRIAN J: Born and educated Ireland. Ordained Dublin for Dunkeld 1926. St Joseph's, Dundee 1926-29. Not in addresses 1929-30. Chaplain, Kilgraston Convent 1930-43. Montrose 1943-47. Sick leave 1947-48. Lent to Glasgow archdiocese: Croy 1948-50. St John's, Perth 1950-56. Dunblane 1956-61. Highvalleyfield 1961-62. Retired to Ireland in bad health 1962 and died there 22 Nov 1967. (Canning)

KELLY, HENRY: Born Dundee 1911. Educated Blairs 1926-31; St Lo and Issy 1931-37. Ordained Edinburgh 1937. Lent to Glasgow archdiocese: Glenboig 1937-40. St John's, Perth 1940-46. Immaculate Conception, Dundee 1946-49. Montrose 1949-57. No further entries.

KELLY, THOMAS A: Born Dundee 1901. Educated Blairs 1915-21; Issy 1921-25; St Sulpice 1925-26. Ordained Dundee 1926. St Mary's, Dundee 1926-36. Saints Peter and Paul, Dundee 1936-37. Lent to archdiocese of St A & E: Immaculate Conception, Bathgate 1937-38. Moved to Glasgow archdiocese: Our Lady Star of the Sea, Saltcoats 1938-39; St Peter's, Glasgow 1939-47. Beith 1947-61; thus moving to Galloway diocese. Annbank 1961-73. Retired to Dundee 1973 and died there 16 July 1978.

KENNEDY, FRANCIS: Born Dundee 1941. Educated University of St Andrew's; Dundee College of Education; St Sulpice. Ordained Dundee 1970. St Columba's, Dundee 1970-72. St Patrick's, Dundee 1972-73. Professor, Blairs 1973-76. Died Blairs 11 April 1976.

KERR, ALEXANDER: Born Dundee 1902. Educated Blairs 1916-20; St Sulpice 1920-26. Ordained Dundee 1926. St John's, Perth 1926-34. St Mary's, Dundee 1934-40. Retired in bad health 1940. Died Glasgow 19 May 1966.

KILCULLEN, JOHN: Born Dundee 1871. Educated Blairs 1885-89; Propaganda, Rome 1889-95. Ordained Rome 1895. St Patrick's, Dundee 1895-96. St Mary's, Dundee 1896-97. Newport 1897-98. Immaculate Conception, Dundee 1898-1900. St John's, Perth 1900-02. Immaculate Conception, Dundee 1902-08. Montrose 1908-13. Lowvalleyfield 1913-20. Immaculate Conception, Dundee 1920-30. Died Dundee 2 May 1930.

KING, KENNETH: Born and educated Ireland. Ordained Kilkenny for Dunkeld 1966. St Andrew's, Dundee 1966-68. Royal Navy chaplain 1968-76. C/o Bishop's House 1976-83. No further entries. (Canning)

KINNANE, LOUIS A: Ordained 1935. St Mary's, Dundee 1953-55. Doune 1955-57. Highvalleyfield 1957-58. No further entries.

KLEIN, AUGUSTINE ADALBERT: Born Schraudenbach, Bavaria 1914. Educated Benedictine School, Muensterschwarzach, Bavaria; St Edmund's College, Ware. Ordained Dundee 1955. St Patrick's, Dundee 1955-60. St Joseph's, Dundee 1960-62. Chaplain, Little Sisters of the Poor, Dundee 1962-64. Forfar 1964-71. St Andrew's, Dundee 1971-74. St Clement's, Dundee 1974-81. St Teresa's, Dundee 1981-86. Retired 1986.

LAVELLE, MICHAEL: Born Ireland. Educated Blairs; St Edmund's, Douay; Issy; St Sulpice; Scots College, Rome. Ordained Rome 1887. St Joseph's,

Dundee 1887-93. Montrose 1893-94. Doune 1894-1902. St John's, Perth 1902-13. St Mary's, Dundee 1913-35. Died Dundee 26 Oct 1935. (Canning)

LEGGATT, MATTHEW: Born Dundee 1955. Educated Lawside Academy, Dundee; Valladolid. Ordained Dundee 1979. St Ninian's, Dundee 1979-82. St Leonard's, Dundee 1982-83. St Andrew's, Dundee 1983-89. Carnoustie 1989-.

LEITCHMAN, GEORGE: Born Dundee 1912. Educated Blairs 1926-32; St Lo 1932-33; Issy 1933-38. Ordained Dundee 1938. St Andrew's, Dundee 1938-41. Saints Peter and Paul, Dundee 1941-48. St John's, Perth 1948-50. Not in Directories 1950-56. Highvalleyfield 1956-57. Alloa 1957-60. St Leonard's, Dundee 1960-62. Immaculate Conception, Dundee 1962-65. St Joseph's, Dundee 1965-77. C/o Bishop's House 1977-81. Died Waterford 11 Oct 1981.

LOUGHLIN, RUPERT: Ordained for Franciscans 1944. Left the Order and joined Dunkeld as a secular priest. Pitlochry 1977-.

LYNCH, OWEN: Born Dundee 1883. Educated Blairs 1897-1902; Issy 1902-04; St Sulpice 1904-06; St Peter's 1906-08. Ordained Glasgow 1908. Immaculate Conception, Dundee 1908-13. St Andrew's, Dundee 1913-20. St Patrick's, Dundee 1920-29. Strathtay 1929-33. Alva 1933-40. Died Alva 30 Jan 1940.

McBRIDE, FELIX: Born Blantyre 1929. Worked as engineer in Blantyre Engineering Co before training for priesthood. Educated Campion House, Osterley 1949-51; St Peter's College, Wexford 1951-57. Ordained Dundee 1957. St Mary's, Dundee 1957-65. Crieff 1965-77. St Joseph's, Dundee 1977-79. Died Boecillo, Spain 7 Aug 1979.

McBRIDE, KENNETH: Born Dundee 1938. Educated Blairs, Valladolid. Ordained Dundee 1962. Further studies, Rome 1962-63. St John's, Perth 1963-76. Newport 1976-81. St Pius X, Dundee 1981-.

McCAFFREY, KENNETH JOHN: Born Glasgow 1947. Educated St Thomas Aquinas' School, Glasgow; University of Manchester; St Peter's; Institute of Religious Education, Dundalk; St Patrick's College, Thurles; St Patrick's College, Maynooth. Ordained Glasgow 1982. Alva 1982. St Ninian's, Dundee 1982-86. Alva 1986-.

MACCARTHY, ANTHONY: Born and educated Ireland. Ordained Dublin for Dunkeld 1958. Highvalleyfield 1958-62. St Patrick's, Dundee 1962-64. St John's, Perth 1964-71. Strathtay 1971-73. Pitlochry 1973-77. Crieff 1977-84. Our Lady of Good Counsel, Dundee 1984-. (Canning)

McCARTHY, EUGENE: Born and educated Ireland. Ordained Maynooth 1889. Lent to Dunkeld diocese. St Andrew's, Dundee 1889-90. St John's, Perth 1890-97. Resumed his vocation in Ireland 1897 and died there 20 Aug 1948. (Canning)

McCORMACK, JAMES: Born Dundee 1875. Educated Blairs 1889-93; Valladolid 1893-99, returning home in bad health. Ordained Dundee 1899. Bad health prevented his serving on mission. Died Dundee 3 Nov 1900.

McCRUDEN, JAMES RODERICK: Born St Andrew's 1945. Educated Madras College, St Andrew's; University of St Andrew's; University of Edinburgh; Beda, Rome. Ordained Dundee 1988. St John's, Perth 1988-.

McCURRACH, WILLIAM: Born Edinburgh 1875. Educated Blairs 1889-93; Valladolid 1893-99. Ordained Valladolid 1899. St Joseph's, Dundee 1899-1910. Crieff 1910-16. Arbroath 1916-29. St Joseph's, Dundee 1929-35. St Mary's, Dundee 1935-45. Died Dundee 29 Oct 1945.

McDANIEL, JOHN: Born Dundee 1873. Educated Blairs; Issy; Scots College, Rome 1893-97. Ordained Rome 1896. St Patrick's, Dundee 1897-1908. Strathtay 1908-09. Arbroath 1909-13. Alloa 1913-20. St John's, Perth 1920-40. Died Perth 18 March 1940.

McDANIEL, PATRICK: Born Dundee 1875. Educated Blairs 1888-92; Valladolid 1892-99. Ordained 1899. Lent to Galloway diocese: St Margaret's, Ayr 1899-1901; Maybole 1901-09. Vice-rector, Valladolid 1909-11. Alloa 1911-12. St Patrick's, Dundee 1912-13. Immaculate Conception, Dundee 1913-14. St Joseph's, Dundee 1914-15. St Mary's, Dundee 1915-16. Lent to archdiocese of St A & E: Edinburgh Cathedral 1916-20. Retired in bad health 1920. Died Manchester 27 April 1941.

McDERMOTT, FRANCIS J: Born Jersey 1912. Worked as journalist. Joined Cistercians at Mount Melleray. Ordained for Order 1943. Monastic life having proved too much for his health he left the Order and came to Dunkeld as a secular priest 1949. Alloa 1949. St Andrew's, Dundee 1949-52. Chaplain, Little Sisters of the Poor, Dundee 1952-56. St John's, Perth 1956-60. St Patrick's, Dundee 1960-61. Dunblane 1961-71. Highvalleyfield 1971-76. Kinross 1976-79. St Joseph's, Dundee 1979-81. Died Jersey 30 Jan 1981.

McDONALD, JAMES VINCENT: Born Dundee 1864. Educated Blairs 1879-81; Valladolid 1881-87. Ordained Valladolid 1887. Immaculate Conception, Dundee 1887-92. Arbroath 1892-1909. St Patrick's, Dundee 1909-17. St Joseph's, Dundee 1917-29. Died Dundee 4 Jan 1929.

McDONALD, JOHN: Born Dundee 1893. Educated Blairs 1907-12; Grand Seminaire, Bourges 1912-14; St Peter's 1914; Grand Seminaire, Angers

1914-16. Ordained Dundee 1916. St Andrew's, Dundee 1916. St Joseph's, Dundee 1916-18. Immaculate Conception, Dundee 1918-23. Lent to Glasgow archdiocese: St Patrick's, Glasgow 1923-26. Went to English mission, serving at Radford, then Cleethorpes. Died Cleethorpes 11 Feb 1939.

McEVOY, MICHAEL: Born and educated Ireland. Ordained Maynooth 1943. Lent to Dunkeld diocese. St John's, Perth 1943-45. Highvalleyfield 1945-46. St John's, Perth in addresses, but not under parishes, 1946-49. No further entries. (Canning)

McGEE, JOSEPH: Born Crieff 1905. Educated Blairs 1917-22; Valladolid 1922-29. Ordained Valladolid 1929. Saints Peter and Paul, Dundee 1929-31. Professor, Blairs 1931-40. Saints Peter and Paul, Dundee 1940-48. St Joseph's, Dundee 1948-52. Consecrated Bishop of Galloway 1952. Retired 1981. Died Prestwick 5 March 1983.

McGHIE, JAMES: Born Blantyre 1929. Educated St Cuthbert's School, Burnbank; St Joseph's School [?]. Worked as barman. Being a late vocation his own diocese would not accept him, but he was accepted for Nottingham and educated Campion House, Osterley 1949-51; St Edmund's College, Ware 1951-57. Ordained Blantyre 1957. Served in Nottingham diocese 1957 until mid-1970s when he retired due to bad health. After a time in Derby he returned to Blantyre. Filled in during vacancies at St Joseph's, Dundee, 1979, and again 1981. Auchterarder 1981-82. Died Auchterarder 7 May 1982.

McGUIRE, JAMES: Born Motherwell 1925. Educated Mellifont Abbey, Co Louth; St Kieran's College, Kilkenny. Ordained Dundee 1968. St Ninian's, Dundee 1968-79. Kinross 1979-81. No further entries.

McINALLY, HUGH FRANCIS: Born Dundee 1933. Educated Lawside Academy, Dundee; Issy. Ordained Dundee 1963. St Columba's, Dundee 1963-68. St Patrick's, Dundee 1968-72. St Fergus's, Dundee 1972-81. St Leonard's, Dundee 1981-.

McINALLY, PATRICK JOSEPH: Born Montrose 1947. Educated Blairs, Valladolid. Ordained Dundee 1972. St Clement's, Dundee 1972-78. St John's, Perth 1978-81. Blairgowrie 1981-88. Further studies 1988-89. Our Lady of Sorrows, Dundee 1989-.

McISAAC, SAMUEL: see Argyll diocese.

MACKAY, JOHN J: Born Aberfeldy 1867. Educated Breadalbane Academy, Aberfeldy; Morrison's Academy, Crieff; Blairs 1882-85; St Edmund's, Douay 1885-87; Scots College, Rome 1887-93. Ordained Rome 1892. Montrose 1893. St Joseph's, Dundee 1893-95. Died Dundee 5 March 1895.

McKEARNEY, PETER JAMES: Born and educated Ireland. Ordained Monaghan for Dunkeld 1944. St Mary's, Dundee 1944-46. St Patrick's, Dundee 1946-47. Sick leave 1947-51. Highvalleyfield 1951-56. Immaculate Conception, Dundee 1956-58. Tullibody 1958-65. St Andrew's, Dundee 1965-71. St Mary's, Dundee 1971-. (Canning)

McKENNA, DENNIS: Born and educated Ireland. Ordained Dublin 1965. St Patrick's, Dundee 1965-68. Highvalleyfield 1968-74. C/o Bishop's House, Dundee 1974-. (Canning)

McKINLEY, ANDREW: Born Dundee 1888. Educated Blairs 1905-09; Scots College, Rome 1909-16. Ordained Rome 1916. St Mary's, Dundee 1916-18. St Joseph's, Dundee 1918-30. Our Lady of Good Counsel, Dundee 1930-48. St Patrick's, Dundee 1948-64. Died Dundee 6 April 1964.

MACKINTOSH, JAMES A: see Argyll diocese.

McLEAN, ANGUS (1929): see Glasgow archdiocese.

McLEAN, BRIAN FRANCIS: Born St Andrew's 1950. Educated Bell Baxter High School, Cupar; St Patrick's College, Belfast; St George's College, Hong Kong; University of Dundee. Worked in Civil Service before training for priesthood at Scots College, Rome. Ordained Cupar 1986. Further studies, Rome 1986-87. St John's, Perth 1987-.

McMAHON, DANIEL: Ordained 1941. St John's, Perth 1956-59. No further entries. (But see p 302)

McMAHON, JOHN: Born Perth 1886. Educated Blairs 1900-03; Valladolid 1903-06; Propaganda, Rome 1906-11, returning home in bad health; St Peter's 1911-12. Ordained Perth 1912. St Mary's, Dundee 1912-29. Alva 1929-33. Not in addresses 1933-34. Stevenston 1934-36. Chaplain, Little Sisters of the Poor, Dundee 1936-52. Died Dundee 24 Jan 1952.

McMANUS, MICHAEL J: Born Dundee 1859. Educated Blairs 1872-77; Douay 1877-78; Issy 1878-80; St Sulpice 1880-81, returning home in bad health; Valladolid 1881-82. Ordained Valladolid 1882. Blairgowrie 1882-86. No further entries.

McMILLAN, ALEXANDER JOSEPH: Born Glasgow. Educated Blairs 1886-90; Petite Communaute, Issy 1890-91; Seminary of Philosophy [Paris] 1891-92; St Kieren's College, Kilkenny 1892-96. Ordained Ireland 1896. St Mary's, Dundee 1896. St Patrick's, Dundee 1896-97. St John's, Perth 1897-98. Newport 1898-1900. Montrose 1900-01. No address given 1901-03. No further entries.

McNAMARA, PATRICK (1886): see archdiocese of St Andrew's and Edinburgh.

McNAMARA, PATRICK (1940): Born Ireland. Joined the Cistercians and was ordained for the Order 1940. Left the Order and came to Dunkeld as secular priest 1953. St Andrew's, Dundee 1953-64. Blairgowrie 1964-69. Kinross 1969-71. C/o Bishop's House, Dundee 1971-72. Carnoustie 1972-76. C/o Bishop's House 1976-83. Died Australia 8 June 1983. (Canning)

McNEIL, HECTOR: Born Perth 1901. Educated Blairs 1914-20; Propaganda, Rome 1920-24; St Peter's 1924-26. Ordained St Peter's College 1926. Lent to Glasgow archdiocese: St Patrick's, Glasgow 1926-29. St Andrew's, Dundee 1929-37. St Patrick's, Dundee 1937-40. Strathtay 1940-47. Montrose 1947-48. Died Brechin 24 Dec 1948.

MACQUEEN, JOHN: see Argyll diocese.

MACRAE, AENEAS: see Aberdeen diocese.

McSORLEY, MALACHY: Born Ireland. Educated Spain. Ordained Spain for Ireland 1918. Lent to Dunkeld diocese. St Joseph's, Dundee 1918-19. Resumed his vocation in Ireland 1919 and died there 28 June 1946. (Canning)

McSORLEY, PATRICK JAMES: see Galloway diocese.

MALANEY, JAMES: Born Glasgow 1917. Educated Blairs, Bordeaux, St Peter's. Ordained 1945. St Joseph's, Dundee 1945-46. St Patrick's, Dundee 1946-49. St Mary's, Dundee 1949-51. St Joseph's, Dundee 1951-60. Cupar 1960-.

MALCOLM, JOHN: Born Perth 1859. Educated Blairs 1872-77; St Edmund's, Douay 1877-79; Issy 1879-81; St Sulpice 1881-84. Ordained Soissons Cathedral 1884. Doune 1884-85. St John's, Perth 1885-88. Montrose 1888-89. Blairgowrie 1889-1917. St Patrick's, Dundee 1917-30. Retired 1930. Died Dundee 17 June 1932.

MALLOY, JOHN BERNARD: Born Dundee 1900. Educated Blairs 1913-19; St Peter's 1919-20; Scots College, Rome 1920-26. Ordained Rome 1926. Rothesay 1926-28. Lent to archdiocese of St A & E: St Patrick's, Edinburgh 1928-29. St Mary's, Dundee 1929-40. Newport 1940-52. St Joseph's, Dundee 1952-77. Died Dundee 28 March 1977.

MATTHEWS, JAMES: Born Partick 1892. Educated Blairs 1904-07; Valladolid 1907-12. Worked as clerk in shipyard, Partick 1912-14. Returned to Valladolid 1914-19. Ordained Valladolid 1919. Immaculate Conception, Dundee 1919-20. St Mary's, Dundee 1920-30. St Joseph's, Dundee 1930-33. Arbroath 1933-40. Alloa 1940-76. Retired 1976. Died Dundee 1 May 1978.

MEAGHER, JEREMIAH: Born and educated Ireland. Ordained 1884. Lent to Dunkeld diocese. St Andrew's, Dundee 1887-89. Resumed his vocation in Ireland 1889 and died there 7 Sept 1893. (Canning)

MELLOY, DARBY: Born Methven 1907. Educated Blairs 1920-25; Propaganda, Rome 1925-30. Ordained Rome 1930. St Joseph's, Dundee 1930-44. Army chaplain 1944-46. Doune 1946-62. Highvalleyfield 1962-71. St John's, Perth 1971-81. Retired 1981. Died Dundee 24 June 1984.

MILTON, MICHAEL JOHN: Born Keith 1958. Educated Keith Grammar School; Campion House, Osterley; Drygrange; Gillis College. Ordained Lochee 1988. Alloa 1988. St Joseph's, Dundee 1988-.

MORRIS, CHARLES: see Motherwell diocese.

MULLEN, IAN: Born Dundee 1954. Educated Langbank, Blairs, Valladolid. Ordained Dundee 1978. St Pius X, Dundee 1978-81. St John's, Perth 1981-86. Carnoustie 1986-89. Forfar 1989-.

MURPHY, JOHN G: Born Dundee 1942. Educated Blairs, Valladolid. Ordained Dundee 1965. St Leonard's, Dundee 1965-72. St Teresa's, Dundee 1972-73. Died Dundee 16 May 1973.

MURRAY, MICHAEL: Born and educated Ireland. Ordained Maynooth 1889. Lent to Dunkeld diocese. St John's, Perth 1889-90. Resumed his vocation in Ireland 1890 and died there 30 March 1936. (Canning)

NALLY, JAMES N: Born and educated Ireland. Ordained Waterford for Dunkeld 1923. St Mary's, Dundee 1923-25. St Andrew's, Dundee 1925-40. Alva 1940-43. Died Ireland 14 May 1945. (Canning)

NOLAN, JOHN: Born Dundee 1912. Educated Lawside Academy, Dundee; Dundee College of Art; Bradley University, Peoria, Illinois, USA. Teaching career until retiral 1974. Then studied for priesthood at Beda, Rome. Ordained Dundee 1978. St Matthew's, Dundee 1978-81. Tullibody 1981-87. Died Alloa 6 June 1987.

NOONAN, JOHN: Born Dundee 1880. Educated Blairs 1894-99; Scots College, Rome 1899-1905. Ordained Rome 1904. Professor, Blairs 1905-16. St Andrew's, Dundee 1916-20. Newport 1920-30. St Patrick's, Dundee 1930-48. Died Dundee 2 Aug 1948.

O'BRIEN, MATTHEW: Born Ireland. Educated Ireland, Paris. Ordained 1878. Lent to Dunkeld diocese. St Andrew's, Dundee 1879-80. Died Dundee, of typhus, 29 Feb 1880. (Canning)

O'CONNELL, ANTHONY: see Galloway diocese.

O'CONNOR, PATRICK: Born and educated Ireland. Ordained Waterford 1881. Lent to Dunkeld diocese. St Mary's, Dundee 1881-86. St Andrew's, Dundee 1886-87. Resumed his vocation in Ireland 1887 and died there 1 March 1919. (Canning)

O'DONNELL, PATRICK: Born and educated Ireland. Ordained Ireland 1890. Lent to Dunkeld diocese. St Mary's, Dundee 1890-92. Immaculate Conception, Dundee 1892-93. St Mary's, Dundee 1893-96. Resumed his vocation in Ireland 1896 and died there Dec 1931. (Canning)

O'DONOGHUE, JEREMIAH: Born and educated Ireland. Ordained Waterford for Dunkeld 1922. St Joseph's, Dundee 1922-27. St Andrew's, Dundee 1927-29. St Patrick's, Dundee 1929-37. Strathtay 1937-40. Crieff 1940-51. Blairgowrie 1951-59. Our Lady of Lourdes, Perth 1959-61. Immaculate Conception, Dundee 1961-66. Died Dundee 26 Feb 1966. (Canning)

O'DONOHOE, PATRICK GERARD: Born and educated Ireland. Ordained Wexford for Dunkeld 1942. St John's, Perth 1942-43. Alloa 1943-46. St Joseph's, Dundee 1946-48. St John's, Perth 1948-55. Forfar 1955-64. St Patrick's, Dundee 1964-. (Canning)

O'DWYER, JEREMIAH: Born and educated Ireland. Ordained Carlow 1882. Lent to Dunkeld diocese. St Joseph's, Dundee 1882-87. St Mary's, Dundee 1887-88. Resumed his vocation in Ireland 1888 and died there 12 July 1941. (Canning)

O'FARRELL, JOHN JOSEPH: Born Ireland. Educated Ireland, Drygrange. Ordained Dublin for Dunkeld 1964. St Mary's, Dundee 1964-77. Carnoustie 1977-81. Our Lady of Sorrows, Dundee 1981-89. Immaculate Conception, Dundee 1989-. (Canning)

OGILVIE, MAXWELL: Born Broughty Ferry 1891. Educated Repton School, Derbyshire 1904-09; Balliol College, Oxford 1909-11. Became a Catholic 1911 and trained for priesthood at Scots College, Rome 1912-19. Ordained Rome 1918. St Joseph's, Dundee 1919-20. Died from pneumonia following influenza 19 April 1920.

O'HEA, JEREMIAH: Born and educated Ireland. Ordained Carlow 1882. Lent to Dunkeld diocese. St Andrew's, Dundee 1882-85. Immaculate Conception, Dundee 1885-86. Resumed his vocation in Ireland 1886 and died there 14 May 1918. (Canning)

O'NEILL, JOHN: Born Blairgowrie 1859. Educated Blairs 1872-77; St Edmund's, Douay 1877-78; Issy 1878-79; Scots College, Rome 1879-84. Ordained Rome 1884. St Mary's, Dundee 1884-87. St Joseph's, Dundee 1887-89. Alloa 1889-1913. Immaculate Conception, Dundee 1913-20. Died Dundee 25 Feb 1920.

O'ROURKE, THOMAS: Born and educated Ireland. Ordained Maynooth 1914. Lent to Dunkeld diocese. St Andrew's, Dundee 1914-15. Resumed his vocation in Ireland 1915 and died there 1 July 1929. (Canning)

O'SHEA, THOMAS E: Born Ireland. Educated Ireland, Rome. Ordained 1918. Lent to Dunkeld diocese. St John's, Perth 1918-20. St Mary's, Dundee 1920-21. St Andrew's, Dundee 1921-25. Resumed his vocation in Ireland 1925 and died there 12 June 1956. (Canning)

O'SULLIVAN, BASIL: Born Fishguard, Wales 1932. Educated St Finbar's College, Cork; All Hallows College, Dublin. Ordained All Hallows for Dunkeld 1956. St Joseph's, Dundee 1956-57. Further studies, Rome 1957-59. St Joseph's, Dundee 1959-64. St Andrew's, Dundee 1964-70. Alva 1970-74. St Columba's, Dundee 1974-88. Dunblane 1988-.

O'SULLIVAN, EUGENE: Born and educated Ireland. Ordained Kilkenny for Dunkeld 1972. St John's, Perth 1972-78. Forfar 1978-89. St Francis', Dundee 1989-. (Canning)

PAGE, JOHN: Born Dundee 1913. Educated Blairs 1928-32; Propaganda, Rome 1932-38. Ordained Rome 1938. St John's, Perth 1938-40. St Mary's, Dundee 1940-44. Army chaplain 1944-47. St Mary's, Dundee 1947-48. St Andrew's, Dundee 1948-49. Highvalleyfield 1949-52. Arbroath 1952-56. St Clement's, Dundee 1956-73. Died Dundee 4 Oct 1973.

PORTER, JOHN: Ordained 1946. St Mary's, Dundee 1951-53. No further entries.

POWER, ALPHONSUS: Born Ireland. Educated Ireland, St Peter's. Ordained for Dunkeld 1920. St Mary's, Dundee 1920-23. Immaculate Conception, Dundee 1923-26. Lent to Galloway diocese: St Margaret's, Ayr 1926-27; St Joseph's, Kilmarnock 1927-28. Went to Archdiocese of Birmingham 1928. Died Stafford 14 June 1969. (Canning)

PURCELL, EDMUND F: Ordained 1937. St Mary's, Dundee 1948-57. Newport 1957-62. Doune 1962-69. Blairgowrie 1969-76. Immaculate Conception, Dundee 1976-81. Carnoustie 1981-86. Retired 1986.

QUINN, JAMES EDWARD: Born Blairgowrie 1892. Educated Blairs 1907-13; Bourges 1913-14; St Peter's 1914-15; Angers 1915-17. Ordained Angers 1917. Immaculate Conception, Dundee 1917-18. Sick leave, Teignmouth 1918-20. Lent to Glasgow archdiocese: St Agnes's, Lambhill 1920-21; Chapelhall 1921-23. St Joseph's, Dundee 1923-30. Newport 1930-37. Doune 1937-45. St Mary's, Dundee 1945-71. Died Glasgow 16 March 1971.

REDDEN, (Gerald) DON: see Galloway diocese.

REILLY, OWEN JOHN: Born Dundee 1954. Educated Lawside Academy, Dundee; University of Dundee; Scots College, Rome. Ordained Dundee 1986. Kinross 1986. Further studies, Rome 1986-87. St Ninian's, Dundee 1987-.

ROBERTSON, JOHN: Born Johnstone 1933. Educated St Mirin's Academy, Paisley; Blairs; St Peter's. Ordained Paisley 1958. Although ordained for Paisley diocese has served only in Dunkeld diocese. St Pius X, Dundee 1958-68. Auchterarder 1968-76. St Matthew's, Dundee 1976-81. Chaplain, Little Sisters of the Poor, Dundee 1981-82. Auchterarder 1982-88. Highvalleyfield 1988-.

ROCHE, ALPHONSUS: Born Lochee 1879. Educated Blairs 1895-1900; Issy 1900-01; Propaganda, Rome 1901-06. Ordained Rome 1906. Chaplain, Little Sisters of the Poor, Dundee 1906-08. St Patrick's, Dundee 1908-12. Alloa 1912-14. Alva 1914-29. Alloa 1929-40. St Joseph's, Dundee 1940-48. Retired 1948. Died Dundee 9 Aug 1949.

ROCHE, JOHN: Born Lochee 1873. Educated Blairs 1888-92; Petite Seminaire de Notre Dame des Champs, Paris, 1892-93; Valladolid 1893-99. Ordained Valladolid 1899. St Mary's, Dundee 1899-1909. Newport 1909-20. Alloa 1920-29. Saints Peter and Paul, Dundee 1929-40. Died Dundee 6 June 1940.

ROCHE, JOSEPH: Born Lochee 1875. Educated Blairs 1888-92, Valladolid 1892-99. Ordained Valladolid 1899. Lent to Galloway diocese: St Andrew's, Dumfries 1899-1900; Newton Stewart 1900-09. Strathtay 1909-11. St Mary's, Dundee 1911-13. Montrose 1913-43. Retired 1943. Died Dundee 23 Sept 1945.

ROCHE, THOMAS: Born and educated Ireland. Ordained Ireland 1888. Lent to Dunkeld diocese. St Andrew's, Dundee 1889-95. Resumed his vocation in Ireland 1895 and died there 3 Jan 1935. (Canning)

ROONEY, ANDREW J: Born Coatbridge 1923. Educated Campion House, Osterley; St Sulpice. Ordained Dundee 1956. St Andrew's, Dundee 1956-62. Nigerian mission 1962-65. Chaplain, Little Sisters of the Poor, Dundee 1965-66. Newport 1966-76. Alloa 1976-86. St Teresa's, Dundee 1986-.

ROSS, JOHN: Born Dundee 1914. Educated Blairs 1929-33; Valladolid 1933-37; St Peter's 1937-39. Ordained Dundee 1939. Lent to Glasgow archdiocese: St Mary's, Greenock 1939-41. St Andrew's, Dundee 1941-47. St John's, Perth 1947-52. Newport 1952-57. Alva 1957-63. St Ninian's, Dundee 1963-76. Dunblane 1976-81. Retired 1981.

RUSSELL, ROBERT G: Born Ballinluig, Perthshire 1878. Educated Blairs 1891-95; Petite Seminaire de Notre Dame des Champs, Paris 1895-96; Issy 1896-98; St Sulpice 1898-1901. Ordained 1901. Immaculate Conception, Dundee 1901-06. Professor, Blairs 1906-13. Our Lady of Good Counsel, Dundee 1913-30. Immaculate Conception, Dundee 1930-35. St Joseph's, Dundee 1935-40. Died Dundee 6 April 1940.

RYAN, JAMES: Born and educated Ireland. Ordained Waterford 1885. Was affiliated to Dunkeld diocese. Immaculate Conception, Dundee 1885-87. St Mary's, Dundee 1887-89. Moved to diocese of Salford 1889, and served in Manchester. (Canning)

RYAN, PETER: Born Ireland. Educated Ireland, Spain. Ordained Spain for diocese of Los Angeles, USA. Los Angeles 1927-30. On vacation 1930-31. Came to Dunkeld diocese 1931. St Joseph's, Dundee 1931-37. St Andrew's, Dundee 1937-40. Lent to Galloway diocese, and was later incardinated into it. St Andrew's, Dumfries 1940-44. Kirkconnel 1944-48. Kilwinning 1948-63. Our Lady of Mount Carmel, Kilmarnock 1963-71. Millport 1971. Retired to Ireland 1971 and died Limerick 7 Sept 1984. (Canning)

SHARKEY, ALPHONSUS: Born Ireland. Educated Ireland, Paris. Ordained Paris 1934. Lent to Dunkeld diocese. Immaculate Conception, Dundee 1934-44. Resumed his vocation in Ireland 1944 and died there 12 Sept 1975. (Canning)

SHEAHAN, MAURICE: Ordained 1871. Ballechin 1896-99. No further entries.

SHEEHY, PATRICK: Born and educated Ireland. Ordained Waterford 1898. Lent to Dunkeld diocese. St Andrew's, Dundee 1898-1902. St Patrick's, Dundee 1902-06. Resumed his vocation in Ireland 1906 and died there 26 Feb 1926. (Canning)

SHIELDS, THOMAS JOSEPH: Born East Kilbride 1964. Educated St Columba's High School, Dunfermline; Scots College, Rome. Ordained Highvalleyfield 1989. St Francis', Dundee 1989-.

SHINE, JAMES: Born and educated Ireland. Ordained Waterford 1908. Lent to English mission 1908-11. Lent to Dunkeld diocese. St John's, Perth 1911-13. Immaculate Conception, Dundee 1913-14. St Joseph's, Dundee 1914-15. Forces chaplain 1915-18. Died of wounds received in the trenches at Military Hospital, Boulogne 21 April 1918. (Canning)

SMYTH, KEVIN ALOYSIUS: Born and educated Ireland. Ordained Carlow for Dunkeld 1944. St Joseph's, Dundee 1944-49. St Andrew's, Dundee 1949-52. St John's, Perth 1952-56. Auchterarder 1956-59. Blairgowrie

1959-64. St Teresa's, Dundee 1964-72. Our Lady of Good Counsel, Dundee 1972-84. St Andrew's, Dundee 1984-. (Canning)

SREENAN, HUGH JOSEPH: Born Dundee 1933. Educated Blairs, Valladolid, Drygrange. Ordained Dundee 1962. St Mary Magdalene, Perth 1962-66. Immaculate Conception, Dundee 1966-74. Forfar 1974-78. St Ninian's, Dundee 1978-82. Highvalleyfield 1982-88. Blairgowrie 1988-.

STRETCH, WALTER R: Born Hamilton 1878. Educated Blairs 1892-96; St Peter's 1896-98; Issy 1898-1900; St Sulpice 1900-03, returning home in bad health. Ordained Dundee 1903. St Mary's, Dundee 1903-14. Immaculate Conception, Dundee 1914-17. Blairgowrie 1917-51. Died Blairgowrie 30 April 1951.

STUART, HAMISH: Born Dundee 1910. Educated Blairs 1923-29; Valladolid 1929-36. Ordained Valladolid 1936. Lent to Galloway diocese: St Andrew's, Dumfries 1936-37; St Margaret's, Ayr 1937. St Joseph's, Dundee 1937-40. St Patrick's, Dundee 1940-48. Carnoustie 1948-55. Alva 1955-57. St Leonard's, Dundee 1957-66. Immaculate Conception, Dundee 1966-76. Blairgowrie 1976. Retired 1976. Died Dundee 5 June 1978.

STUART, JOHN: Born Dundee 1871. Educated Blairs 1887-92; Issy 1892-94; St Sulpice 1894-96. Ordained Dundee 1896. St Joseph's, Dundee 1896-99. Montrose 1899-1900. Monfieth 1900-01. Montrose 1901-08. Chaplain, Little Sisters of the Poor, Dundee 1908-13. Arbroath 1913-15. Forces chaplain 1915-19. Lent to archdiocese of St A & E: St Margaret's, Dunfermline 1919-20. St Joseph's, Dundee 1920-21. Dundee, no parish, 1921-24. Chaplain, Little Sisters of the Poor, Dundee 1924-36. Retired 1936. Died Edinburgh 2 Aug 1942.

SUTTON, WILLIAM: see Glasgow archdiocese.

SWEENEY, ANTONY: Ordained 1894. St Joseph's, Dundee 1894-1908. No address given 1908-09. Lent to archdiocese of St A & E: St Margaret's, Dunfermline 1909-13; Jamestown (Inverkeithing) 1913-17. St Joseph's, Dundee 1917-18. St Mary's, Dundee 1918-20. Lowvalleyfield 1920-29. Sick leave 1929-31. Retired 1931. Died Edinburgh 2 Aug 1939.

THOMSON, ANDREW F: see Aberdeen diocese.

TOLLAN, WILLIAM MICHAEL: Born Glasgow 1928. Educated St Aloysius' College, Glasgow; University of Glasgow. Career as teacher and headmaster till retiral. Studied for the priesthood at Beda, Rome. Ordained Tullibody 1986. St John's, Perth 1986-87. Kinross 1987-.

WALLACE, JAMES: see Glasgow archdiocese.

WARD, DAVID F: Born Dundee 1938. Educated Blairs, Valladolid. Ordained Valladolid 1962. Highvalleyfield 1962-68. St Columba's, Dundee 1968-70. St Andrew's, Dundee 1970-83. Arbroath 1983-87. No further entries.

WARD, JAMES: Born Dundee 1920. Educated St John's School; Lawside Academy, Dundee; Blairs 1934-37; Propaganda, Rome 1937-39; St Peter's; Oscott. Ordained Blairs for diocese of Northampton 1945. Served in Northampton diocese 1945-52 (Bedford, Lowestoft and the Cathedral). Came to Dunkeld diocese 1952. St Joseph's, Dundee 1952-56. Alloa 1956-57. St Pius X, Dundee 1957-58. Immaculate Conception, Dundee 1958-62. St Leonard's, Dundee 1962-63. Auchterarder 1963-68. St Matthews, Dundee 1968-71. Arbroath 1971-76. St Teresa's, Dundee 1976-81. Died Dundee 14 Oct 1981.

WARRAN (Warren), JOHN T: Born and educated Ireland. Ordained Waterford 1904. Lent to Dunkeld diocese. St Andrew's, Dundee 1904-14. Resumed his vocation in Ireland 1914 and died there 25 Oct 1951. (Canning)

WELSH, THOMAS: Born Collace, Perthshire 1870. Educated St John's School, Perth; Blairs 1883-87; Valladolid 1887-92, returning home in bad health. Professor, Blairs 1892-93. Ordained Perth 1893. Professor, Blairs 1893-1905. Ballechin 1905-08. Our Lady of Good Counsel, Dundee 1908-13. St John's, Perth 1913-20. Died Perth 12 March 1920.

WOODFORD, MICHAEL: see Glasgow archdiocese.

Parishes

BISHOPS: 1878-87 George Rigg (ED). 1890-1900 James A Smith (Dunkeld). 1901-12 Angus MacFarlane (Glasgow). 1913-14 Robert Fraser (Aberdeen). 1914-49 John Toner (Glasgow). 1949-55 James Scanlan (Westminster). 1955-81 William Hart (Glasgow). 1981- Vincent Logan (St A & E).
Auxiliaries: 1939-44 James Maguire (St A & E). 1946-49 James Scanlan (Westminster).

ALLOA
Heads: 1878-80 Augustine MacDermott (ED). 1880-89 James MacGinnes (ED). 1889-1913 John O'Neill. 1913-20 John McDaniel. 1920-29 John Roche. 1929-40 Alphonsus Roche. 1940-76 James Matthews. 1976-86 Andrew Rooney. 1986- James Foley.

Assistants: 1911-12 Patrick McDaniel. 1912-14 Alphonsus Roche. 1942-43 Peter Foylan. 1943-46 Patrick O'Donohoe. 1946-47 James Howard. 1947-49 Thomas Barron. 1949 Francis J McDermott. 1949-56 Ernest Andrew. 1956-57 James Ward. 1957-60 George Leitchman. 1960-64 John B Hanlon. 1964-65 Edward Durkin. 1965-67 Michael Conway. 1966-67 Hugh Campbell. 1966-76 Daniel Gallagher. 1988 Michael J Milton. 1988- James High.

ALVA: Until 1914 served from Alloa. 1914-29 Alphonsus Roche. 1929-33 John McMahon. 1933-40 Owen Lynch. 1940-43 James Nally. 1943-48 Edward Dempsey. 1948-55 Peter Cullerton. 1955-57 Hamish Stuart. 1957-63 John Ross. 1963-70 Thomas J Dillon. 1970-74 Basil O'Sullivan. 1974-82 Peter Kaye. 1982 Kenneth McCaffrey. 1982-86 Martin Drysdale. 1986- Kenneth McCaffrey.

ALYTH: 1879-81 John Prendergast (WD). From 1881 served first from Lochee, then from Blairgowrie.

ARBROATH
Heads: 1874-81 Patrick Fay (ED). 1881-85 James Harris (ED). 1885-92 William Geddes (ED). 1892-1909 James V McDonald. 1909-13 John McDaniel. 1913-15 John Stuart. 1915-16 John Coogan. 1916-29 William McCurragh. 1929-33 John Coogan. 1933-40 James Matthews. 1940-52 Patrick Donagher. 1952-56 John Page. 1956-63 Peter Kaye. 1963-71 Thomas Barron. 1971-76 James Ward. 1976-83 Peter Foylan. 1983-87 David Ward. 1987- James Wallace (Glasgow).
Assistants: 1878-79 Patrick Lonergan (WD). 1879-80 Andrew Thomson (Aberdeen). 1884 Andrew Barrett (ED).

AUCHTERARDER: Until 1884 served from Crieff. 1884-87 Andrew Barrett (ED). 1887-1956 served from Crieff. 1956-59 Kevin Smyth. 1959-63 Philip Donnelly. 1963-68 James Ward. 1968-76 John Robertson. 1976-81 Daniel Gallagher. 1981-82 James McGhie. 1982-88 John Robertson. 1988- Charles Morris (Motherwell).

BALLECHIN: see Strathtay

BLAIRGOWRIE
Heads: 1849-82 John Carmont (ED). 1882-89 Thomas Crumly (ED). 1889-1917 John Malcolm. 1917-51 Walter Stretch. 1951-59 Jeremiah O'Donoghue. 1959-64 Kevin Smyth. 1964-69 Patrick J McNamara (1940). 1969-76 Edmund Purcell. 1976 Hamish Stuart. 1976-77 vacant. 1977-81 Joseph Creegan. 1981-88 Patrick McInally. 1988- Hugh Sreenan.
Assistant: 1882-86 Michael J McManus.

BROUGHTY FERRY: see Dundee, Our Lady of Good Counsel

CALLANDER: Until 1975 served from Doune or Dunblane. 1975-77 James Maher SDB. 1977-82 served from Doune. 1982-86 James Foley. 1986- Neil Gallagher.

CARNOUSTIE: Until 1932 served from Arbroath. 1932-47 Joseph Brough. 1947-48 vacant. 1948-55 Hamish Stuart. 1955-63 Thomas J Dillon. 1963-66 Denis Horgan SMA. 1966-72 John B Hanlon. 1972-76 Patrick J McNamara (1940). 1976-77 vacant. 1977-81 John J O'Farrell. 1981-86 Edmund Purcell. 1986-89 Ian Mullen. 1989- Matthew Leggatt.

CRIEFF: 1875-82 Andrew Barrett (ED). 1882-88 Alphonsus van de Rydt (ED). 1888-91 Peter Butti (ED). 1891-1900 Thomas Crumly (ED). 1900-02 James Dowling. 1902-05 William Ashby. 1905-10 Thomas Brophy. 1910 Joseph Brough. 1910-16 William McCurrach. 1916-35 Joseph Keenan. 1935-40 John Coogan. 1940-51 Jeremiah O'Donoghue. 1951-62 Peter Foylan. 1962-65 Bartholomew Butler. 1965-77 Felix McBride. 1977-84 Anthony McCarthy. 1984- James Fitzgerald (Glasgow).
Assistant: 1928 Edward Dempsey.

CUPAR: 1879-85 Bruce Geddes (ED). 1885-1948 served from various missions. 1948-60 served by Augustinians. 1960- James Malaney.

DOUNE
Heads: 1876-83 Paul MacLachlan (ED). 1883 Thomas Connelly. 1883-85 John Turner (ED). 1885-89 Thomas Connelly. 1889-91 Thomas Crumly. 1891-94 Andrew Barrett (ED). 1894-1902 Michael Lavelle. 1902-22 James Dowling. 1922-37 John Doherty. 1937-45 James E Quinn. 1945-46 Angus McLean (Glasgow). 1946-62 Darby Melloy. 1962-69 Edmund Purcell. 1969-71 Charles Hendry. 1971-77 served from Dunblane or Callander. 1977-82 James Foley.
Assistants: 1884-85 John Malcolm. 1955-57 Louis Kinnane. 1972-73 Alexander Johnston.
From 1982 served from Callander.

DUNBLANE: 1885-89 Bruce Geddes (ED). 1889-91 Andrew Barrett (ED). 1891-1948 served from Doune. 1948-56 Peter Kaye. 1956-61 Adrian Kelly. 1961-71 Francis J McDermott. 1971-76 Charles Hendry. 1976-81 John Ross. 1981-88 Charles Adamson. 1988- Basil O'Sullivan.

DUNDEE – ST ANDREW'S CATHEDRAL
Heads: 1870-1902 Robert Clapperton (ED). 1902-38 John Turner (ED). 1938-39 vacant. 1939-44 Bishop James Maguire. 1944-46 vacant. 1946-49 Bishop James Scanlan. 1949-64 Michael Foylan. 1964-65 vacant. 1965-71 Peter J McKearney. 1971-74 Augustine Klein. 1974-76 vacant. 1976-81 John B Hanlon. 1981-83 David Ward. 1983-84 vacant. 1984- Kevin Smyth.

Assistants: 1876-79 Alphonsus van de Rydt (ED). 1877-86 Michael Phelan (ED). 1879-80 Matthew O'Brien. 1880-82 Patrick Cremin (ED). 1882-85 Jeremiah O'Hea. 1885-89 James Harris (ED). 1886-87 Patrick O'Connor. 1887-89 Jeremiah Meagher. 1889-90 Eugene McCarthy. 1889-95 Thomas Roche. 1890-98 Patrick Kearney. 1895-98 Peter Dawson. 1898-1902 Patrick Crotty. 1898-1902 Patrick Sheehy. 1902-04 Richard Aylward. 1904-14 John T Warran. 1909-13 William Carey. 1913-20 Owen Lynch. 1914-15 Thomas O'Rourke. 1916 John McDonald. 1916-20 John Noonan. 1920-21 John Fahy. 1920-27 Joseph Brough. 1921-25 Thomas O'Shea. 1925-40 James N Nally. 1927-29 Jeremiah O'Donoghue. 1929-37 Hector McNeil. 1931-37 Michael Foylan. 1937-40 Peter Ryan. 1938-41 George Leitchman. 1940-48 Peter Cullerton. 1941-46 Gerard Keegan. 1941-47 John Ross. 1944-46 James Howard. 1946-49 Ernest Andrew. 1947-49 Peter Foylan. 1948-49 John Page. 1949-52 Kevin Smyth. 1949-52 Francis J McDermott. 1949-61 Hugh Campbell. 1952-53 Thomas Bunyan. 1952-56 John Connolly. 1953-64 Patrick McNamara (1940). 1956-62 Andrew Rooney. 1962-66 Daniel Gallagher. 1964-70 Basil O'Sullivan. 1966-68 Kenneth King. 1970-81 David Ward. 1983-89 Matthew Leggatt.

DUNDEE – IMMACULATE CONCEPTION (Lochee)

Heads: 1871-80 Francis Beurms (ED). 1880-88 Peter Butti (ED). 1888-1900 Alphonsus van de Rydt (ED). 1900-13 Thomas Crumly (ED). 1913-20 John O'Neill. 1920-30 John Kilcullen. 1930-35 Robert G Russell. 1935-61 Joseph Keenan. 1961-66 Jeremiah O'Donoghue. 1966-76 Hamish Stuart. 1976-81 Edmund Purcell. 1981-89 John B Hanlon. 1989- John O'Farrell.

Assistants: 1875-79 Conrad Helfrich (ED). 1875-81 James Harris (ED). 1878-80 Albert Linder (ED). 1881-82 Albert Linder (ED). 1881-82 John Doherty. 1882-85 James Dawson (Argyll). 1884-85 Thomas Connelly. 1885-86 Jeremiah O'Hea. 1885-87 James Ryan. 1886-87 Patrick McNamara (1886). 1887-92 James V McDonald. 1889-91 Francis Beurms (ED). 1892-93 Patrick O'Donnell. 1893-99 James Dowling. 1898-1900 John Kilcullen. 1899-1902 Thomas Brophy. 1901-06 Robert G Russell. 1902-08 John Kilcullen. 1908-13 Owen Lynch. 1909-13 Michael Fives. 1913-14 Patrick McDaniel. 1913-14 James Shine. 1914-15 Matthew Blake. 1914-17 Walter R Stretch. 1917-18 James Quinn. 1918-23 John McDonald. 1919-20 James Matthews. 1920-22 John Angler (Argyll). 1923-33 Patrick Donagher. 1923-26 Alphonsus Power. 1926-32 Thomas Gannon. 1932-34 John J Cusick (Glasgow). 1934-35 John Devine. 1934-44 Alphonsus Sharkey. 1935-46 James A Mackintosh (Argyll). 1944-56 Bartholomew Butler. 1946-49 Henry Kelly. 1949-57 Thomas Barron. 1956-58 Peter J McKearney. 1957-64 Edward Durkin. 1958-62 James Ward. 1962-65 George Leitchman. 1964-66 John B Hanlon. 1966-74 Hugh Sreenan. 1974-77 Aldo Angelosanto. 1977-80 Hugh Campbell. 1988-89 Mark J Cassidy.

DUNDEE – OUR LADY OF GOOD COUNSEL (Broughty Ferry)
Heads: 1913-30 Robert Russell. 1930-48 Andrew McKinley. 1948-62 Edward Dempsey. 1962-71 Peter Foylan. 1971-72 Thomas Barron. 1972-84 Kevin Smyth. 1984- Anthony McCarthy.
Assistants: 1972-73 Charles Adamson. 1973-78 Alexander Johnston (Glasgow).

DUNDEE – OUR LADY OF SORROWS: 1967-73 served by Servites. 1973-81 Charles Adamson. 1981-89 John O'Farrell. 1989- Patrick J McInally.

DUNDEE – ST CLEMENT'S
Heads: 1956-73 John Page. 1973-74 vacant. 1974-81 Augustine Klein. 1981- John J Connolly.
Assistants: 1956-60 Ernest Andrew. 1960-62 Patrick McSorley (Galloway). 1962-72 Charles Adamson. 1972-78 Patrick McInally. 1978-81 John Harty.

DUNDEE – ST COLUMBA'S
Heads: 1963-74 Peter Kaye. 1974-88 Basil O'Sullivan. 1988- Aldo Angelosanto.
Assistants: 1963-68 Hugh McInally. 1968-70 David Ward. 1970-72 Francis Kennedy. 1972-77 Joseph Creegan.

DUNDEE – ST FERGUS': 1972-81 Hugh McInally. 1981 amalgamates with St Leonard's to form St Leonard and St Fergus.

DUNDEE – ST FRANCIS'
Until 1989 served by Franciscans.
Head: 1989- Eugene O'Sullivan.
Assistant: 1989- Thomas Shields.

DUNDEE – ST JOSEPH'S
Heads: 1878-1917 Joseph Holder (ED). 1917-29 James V McDonald. 1929-35 William McCurrach. 1935-40 Robert Russell. 1940-48 Alphonsus Roche. 1948-52 Joseph McGee. 1952-77 John Malloy. 1977-79 Felix McBride. 1979 James McGhie. 1979-81 Francis J McDermott. 1981 James McGhie. 1981- Joseph Creegan.
Assistants: 1873-80 Peter Butti (ED). 1874-82 Thomas Crumly (ED). 1880-81 Andrew Thomson (Aberdeen). 1881-87 Thomas F Furlong. 1882-87 Jeremiah O'Dwyer. 1887-89 John O'Neill. 1887-1903 Michael Lavelle. 1889-94 Edmond Hassett. 1893-95 John J Mackay. 1894-1908 Antony Sweeney. 1895-96 James Harris (ED). 1896-99 John Stuart. 1899-1910 William McCurrach. 1908-14 William Flynn. 1910-14 Joseph Brough. 1914-15 Patrick McDaniel. 1914-15 James Shine. 1915-16 Severinus Broeders. 1916-17 Charles A Daly (1916). 1916-18 John McDonald. 1917-18 Antony Sweeney. 1917-19 Patrick G Egan. 1918-19 Malachy

McSorley. 1918-30 Andrew McKinley. 1919-20 Maxwell Ogilvie. 1919-20 John Fahy. 1920-21 John Stuart. 1920-21 Patrick Donagher. 1920-22 Richard Durand. 1921-22 Anthony O'Connell (Galloway). 1922-23 John McQueen (Argyll). 1922-27 Jeremiah O'Donoghue. 1923-30 James Quinn. 1926-29 Adrian J Kelly. 1930-31 Patrick F Keating (Glasgow). 1930-33 James Matthews. 1931-37 Peter Ryan. 1931-44 Darby Melloy. 1934-35 Michael Flynn. 1937-40 Hamish Stuart. 1937-46 Michael Foylan. 1944-49 Kevin Smyth. 1945-46 James Malaney. 1946-48 Patrick O'Donohoe. 1946-48 Walter Carolan. 1949-51 Peter Foylan. 1949-52 Thomas Bunyan. 1951-60 James Malaney. 1952-56 James Ward. 1956-57 Basil O'Sullivan. 1956-60 John J Connolly. 1959-64 Basil O'Sullivan. 1960-62 Augustine Klein. 1962-71 Anthony M J Boyle. 1965-77 George Leitchman. 1971-73 Liam Barron. 1988- Michael Milton.

DUNDEE: ST LEONARD'S (ST LEONARD & ST FERGUS from 1981)
Heads: 1957-66 Hamish Stuart. 1966-81 John J Connolly. 1981- Hugh McInally.
Assistants: 1957-60 John Hanlon. 1960-62 George Leitchman. 1962-63 James Ward. 1965-72 John G Murphy. 1981-82 John Harty. 1982-83 Matthew Leggatt. 1989- Mark J Cassidy.

DUNDEE - ST MARY, OUR LADY OF VICTORIES
Heads: 1878-80 James McGinnes (ED). 1880-87 Augustine McDermott (ED). 1887-1909 Michael Phelan (ED). 1909-13 Peter Butti (ED). 1913-35 Michael Lavelle. 1935-45 William McCurrach. 1945-71 James Quinn. 1971- Peter J McKearney.
Assistants: 1876-79 Bruce Geddes (ED). 1878-80 Patrick Cremin (ED). 1878-83 John Turner (ED). 1879-82 Alphonsus van de Rydt (ED). 1880-81 Albert Linder (ED). 1881-86 Patrick O'Connor. 1882-85 James Browne. 1883-84 James Doherty. 1883-84 Thomas Connelly. 1884-87 John O'Neill. 1884-99 Thomas Brophy. 1886-87 Michael Phelan (ED). 1887-88 Jeremiah O'Dwyer. 1887-89 James Ryan. 1888-89 Francis Beurms (ED). 1889-91 John Gleeson. 1889-95 Patrick Crotty. 1890-92 Patrick O'Donnell. 1893-96 Patrick O'Donnell. 1896 Alexander J McMillan. 1896-97 John Kilcullen. 1897-98 Patrick Brady. 1897-1903 John Casey. 1898-1904 Patrick Hurley. 1899-1909 John Roche. 1903-14 Walter R Stretch. 1904-12 Joseph Guinan. 1911-13 Joseph Roche. 1912-29 John McMahon. 1914-15 William Flynn. 1914-15 Michael Fives. 1915-16 Patrick McDaniel. 1916-18 Andrew McKinley. 1917-18 Samuel McIsaac (Argyll). 1918-20 Antony Sweeney. 1918-20 Charles Daly (1914) (St A & E). 1920-21 Thomas O'Shea. 1920-23 Alphonsus Power. 1920-30 James Matthews. 1921 Anthony O'Connell (Galloway). 1923-25 James N Nally. 1926 Thomas Gannon. 1926-36 Thomas Kelly. 1929-40 John B Malloy. 1930-34 Edward Dempsey. 1934-40 Alexander Kerr. 1935-39 William Hallinan. 1939-47 Robert Doherty (Glasgow). 1940-42 Peter Foylan. 1940-44 John Page. 1942-49 Thomas Dillon. 1944-46 Peter McKearney. 1947-48 John Page. 1948-57 Edmund

Purcell. 1949-51 James Malaney. 1949-63 Denis Horgan. 1951-53 John Porter. 1953-55 Louis A Kinnane. 1956-57 Edward Durkin. 1957-65 Felix McBride. 1964-77 John O'Farrell. 1967-75 Hugh Campbell.

DUNDEE – ST MATTHEW'S
Heads: 1968-71 James Ward. 1971-76 Peter Foylan. 1976-81 John Robertson. 1981-86 Daniel Gallagher. 1986- Martin Drysdale.
Assistants: 1975-77 Rupert Loughlin OFM. 1978-81 John Nolan. 1982-86 Hugh Campbell.

DUNDEE – ST NINIAN'S
Heads: 1963-76 John Ross. 1976-78 Anthony Boyle. 1978-82 Hugh Sreenan. 1982-87 Charles Hendry. 1987- Benjamin Donachie.
Assistants: 1968-79 James McGuire. 1977-78 John Harty. 1979-82 Matthew Leggatt. 1982-86 Kenneth McCaffrey. 1986-88 James High. 1987- Owen Reilly.

DUNDEE – ST PATRICK'S
Heads: 1891-1909 Peter Butti (ED). 1909-17 James V McDonald. 1917-30 John Malcolm. 1930-48 John Noonan. 1948-64 Andrew McKinley. 1964- Patrick O'Donohoe.
Assistants: 1891-97 John Gleeson. 1895-96 John Kilcullen. 1897-1908 John McDaniel. 1898-1902 Richard Aylward. 1902-06 Patrick Sheehy. 1906-08 William Flynn. 1908-12 Alphonsus Roche. 1908-15 John Coogan. 1912-13 Patrick McDaniel. 1914 Matthew Blake. 1915-29 Michael Fahy. 1919-20 Richard Durand. 1920-29 Owen Lynch. 1929-30 Edward Dempsey. 1929-37 Jeremiah O'Donoghue. 1930-37 Aeneas MacRae (Aberdeen). 1937-40 Hector McNeil. 1938-45 Angus McLean (Glasgow). 1940-48 Hamish Stuart. 1943-44 Bartholomew Butler. 1946-47 Peter J McKearney. 1946-49 James Malaney. 1948-59 Philip Donnelly. 1949-55 Thomas Dillon. 1955-60 Augustine Klein. 1958-59 John J Harkin (Galloway). 1959-61 Thomas E Frigerio (Glasgow). 1960-61 Francis J McDermott. 1961-62 Hugh Campbell. 1961-65 Michael Conway (Galloway). 1962-64 Anthony McCarthy. 1964-66 Hugh Campbell. 1965-68 Denis McKenna. 1968-72 Hugh McInally. 1972-73 Francis Kennedy.

DUNDEE – ST PETER AND ST PAUL
Heads: 1929-40 John Roche. 1940-48 Joseph McGee.
Assistants: 1929-31 Joseph McGee. 1931-34 Hugh Cahill (Glasgow). 1932-35 Philip J Cuffe. 1934-36 Edward Dempsey. 1935-36 Hugh Brady (St A & E). 1936-37 Thomas A Kelly. 1936-48 Peter Kaye. 1937-41 Thomas Gannon. 1941-48 George Leitchman.
From 1948 served by Augustinians.

DUNDEE – ST PIUS X
Heads: 1955-81 Peter Cullerton. 1981- Kenneth McBride.

Assistants: 1957-58 James Ward. 1958-68 John Robertson. 1968-75 James Maher SDB. 1975-77 John Harty. 1977-78 Michael Woodford (Glasgo**w).** 1978-81 Ian Mullen.

DUNDEE – ST TERESA OF AVILA
Heads: 1955-64 Gerard Keegan. 1964-72 Kevin Smyth. 1972-76 John B Hanlon. 1976-81 James Ward. 1981-86 Augustine Klein. 1986- Andrew Rooney.
Assistants: 1970-71 Liam Barron. 1972-73 John G Murphy. 1975-77 Hugh Campbell.

DUNDEE – LITTLE SISTERS OF THE POOR: CHAPLAINS
1892-1902 Augustine McDermott (ED). 1902-06 Robert Clapperton (ED). 1906-08 Alphonsus Roche. 1908-13 John Stuart. 1913-24 Thomas Crumly (ED). 1924-36 John Stuart. 1936-52 John McMahon. 1952-56 Francis J McDermott. 1962-64 Augustine Klein. 1964-65 James Carruth OSB. 1965-66 Andrew Rooney. 1966-78 Denis Horgan SMA. 1980-81 Benjamin Donachie. 1981-82 John Robertson. 1982- Albert Chandler (Glasgow).

DUNDEE – ST JOSEPH'S CONVENT, LAWSIDE: CHAPLAINS
1895-1922 John Doherty.

DUNKELD: 1924-72 Gilbert Fairlie. 1972-81 served from Perth. 1981-85 Bishop William Hart. From 1985 served from Perth.

FORFAR: Until 1946 served from Dundee. 1946-55 Gerard Keegan. 1955-64 Patrick O'Donohoe. 1964-71 Augustine Klein. 1971-74 Edward Durkin. 1974-78 Hugh Sreenan. 1978-89 Eugene O'Sullivan. 1989- Ian Mullen.

HIGHVALLEYFIELD (Lowvalleyfield)
Appears in Catholic Directories as 'Lowvalleyfield' until 1932 when it becomes 'Highvalleyfield'.
Heads: 1913-20 John Kilcullen. 1920-29 Antony Sweeney. 1929-46 Michael Fahy. 1946-49 Michael Foylan. 1949-52 John Page. 1952-61 Patrick Donagher. 1961-62 Adrian J Kelly. 1962-71 Darby Melloy. 1971-76 Francis J McDermott. 1976-82 Charles Hendry. 1982-88 Hugh Sreenan. 1988-John Robertson.
Assistants: 1945-46 Michael McEvoy. 1946-48 Angus McLean (Glasgow). 1949-50 Jeremiah Higgins. 1951-56 Peter J McKearney. 1956-57 George Leitchman. 1957-58 Louis Kinnane. 1958-62 Anthony McCarthy. 1962-68 David F Ward. 1968-74 Dennis McKenna.

KINROSS
Heads: 1956-62 Bartholomew Butler. 1962-64 Hugh Campbell. 1964-69 Charles Hendry. 1969-71 Patrick J McNamara (1940). 1971-76 Anthony

Boyle. 1976-79 Francis J McDermott. 1979-81 James McGuire. 1981-87 Benjamin Donachie. 1987- William Tollan.
Assistant: 1986 Owen J Reilly.

LOCHEE: see Immaculate Conception, Dundee

LOWVALLEYFIELD: see Highvalleyfield

MONIFIETH: 1899-1900 James Dowling. 1900-01 John Stuart. 1901-78 served from Dundee. 1978- Romeo Coia (Glasgow).

MONTROSE: 1881-83 Francis Beurms (ED). 1883-84 served from Arbroath. 1884-85 John Doherty. 1885-88 John Shaw (1858) (ND). 1888-89 John Malcolm. 1889-93 Bruce Geddes (ED). 1893 John J Mackay. 1893-94 Michael Lavelle. 1894-96 Andrew Barrett (ED). 1896-99 William Ashby. 1899-1900 John Stuart. 1900-01 Alexander J McMillan. 1901-08 John Stuart. 1908-13 John Kilcullen. 1913-43 Joseph Roche. 1943-47 Adrian J Kelly. 1947-48 Hector McNeil. 1948-49 vacant. 1949-57 Henry Kelly. 1957-63 Thomas Barron. 1963-82 Philip Donnelly. 1982- John Harty.

NEWPORT-ON-TAY: Until 1889 served from Dundee. 1889-91 James Harris (ED). 1891-97 William Sutton (Glasgow). 1897-98 John Kilcullen. 1898-1900 Alexander J McMillan. 1900-08 Patrick Brady. 1908-09 vacant. 1909-20 John Roche. 1920-30 John Noonan. 1930-37 James Quinn. 1937-40 Patrick Donagher. 1940-52 John Malloy. 1952-57 John Ross. 1957-62 Edmund Purcell. 1962-66 John J Connolly. 1966-76 Andrew Rooney. 1976-81 Kenneth McBride. 1981-88 Aldo Angelosanto. 1988- Hugh Campbell.

PERTH – OUR LADY OF LOURDES
Heads: 1959-61 Jeremiah O'Donoghue. 1961-63 Patrick Donagher. 1963-64 vacant. 1964-74 James A Mackintosh. 1974- Ernest Andrew.
Assistants: 1959-60 Michael Holton. 1960-62 John J Connolly.

PERTH – ST JOHN'S
Heads: 1878-85 William Geddes (ED). 1885-1902 John Turner (ED). 1902-13 Michael Lavelle. 1913-20 Thomas Welsh. 1920-40 John McDaniel. 1940-71 John Coogan. 1971-81 Darby Melloy. 1981-87 Edward Durkin. 1987-88 vacant. 1988- Charles Adamson.
Assistants: 1885-88 John Malcolm. 1888-89 George Culhane. 1889-90 Michael Murray. 1890-97 Eugene McCarthy. 1897-98 Alexander J McMillan. 1898-1900 Patrick Brady. 1900-02 John Kilcullen. 1902 Thomas Brophy. 1902-03 Thomas Cantwell. 1903-11 Joseph Keenan. 1911-13 James Shine. 1913-14 Michael Fives. 1914-20 Joseph Brough. 1918-20 Thomas O'Shea. 1920-33 Joseph Cassidy. 1923-24 Gilbert Fairlie. 1926-34 Alexander Kerr. 1933-34 Joseph Campbell (Argyll).

1934-35 John Coogan. 1935-39 Robert Doherty (Glasgow). 1936-43 Edward Dempsey. 1938-40 John Page. 1940-46 Henry Kelly. 1942-43 Patrick O'Donohoe. 1943-45 Michael McEvoy. 1943-47 Peter Foylan. 1946-47 James MacKintosh (Argyll). 1947-52 John Ross. 1948-50 George Leitchman. 1948-55 Patrick O'Donohoe. 1950-56 Adrian J Kelly. 1952-56 Kevin Smyth. 1955-64 Charles Hendry. 1956-59 Daniel McMahon. 1956-60 Francis McDermott. 1959-61 Gerard Don Redden (Galloway). 1960-62 Ernest Andrew. 1961-63 Thomas E Frigerio (Glasgow). 1963-76 Kenneth McBride. 1964-71 Anthony McCarthy. 1972-78 Eugene O'Sullivan. 1976-77 Martin Drysdale. 1977-81 Aldo Angelosanto. 1978-81 Patrick McInally. 1981-86 Ian Mullen. 1985-86 Neil Gallagher. 1986-87 William Tollan. 1986-88 Hugh Campbell. 1987- Brian F McLean. 1988- James R McCruden.

PERTH – ST MARY MAGDALENE'S
Heads: 1962-64 James A Mackintosh. 1964-87 Gerard Keegan.
Assistants: 1962-66 Hugh Sreenan. 1966-72 Joseph Creegan.
From 1987 served from St John's, Perth.

PITLOCHRY: Until 1973 served from Strathtay. 1973-77 Anthony McCarthy. 1977- Rupert Loughlin OFM.

STRATHTAY (Ballechin)
Mission known as 'Ballechin' until 1913, thereafter as 'Strathtay'.
1876-85 John Shaw (ND). 1885-91 John Doherty. 1891-95 James Harris (ED). 1895-96 Edward Graham. 1896-99 Maurice Sheahan. 1899-1902 William Ashby. 1902-05 Thomas Brophy. 1905-08 Thomas Welsh. 1908-09 John McDaniel. 1909-11 Joseph Roche. 1911-16 Joseph Keenan. 1916-29 John Coogan. 1929-33 Owen Lynch. 1933-37 Patrick Donagher. 1937-40 Jeremiah O'Donoghue. 1940-47 Hector McNeil. 1947-62 James A Mackintosh (Argyll). 1962-65 Ernest Andrew. 1965-71 Edward Durkin. 1971-73 Anthony McCarthy. From 1973 served from Pitlochry.

TULLIBODY: Until 1958 served from Alloa. 1958-65 Peter J McKearney. 1965-74 Ernest Andrew. 1974-81 Edward Durkin. 1981-87 John Nolan. 1987- Charles Hendry.

APPROVED SCHOOLS – St Ninian's, Gartmore: See Glasgow Archdiocese.

Diocese of Galloway

Secular Clergy

ARNOLD, PETER: Ordained 1966. St Joseph's, Kilmarnock 1989-.

BANNON, JAMES: See Glasgow Archdiocese.

BARRETT, DAVID: Born and educated Ireland. Ordained Ireland 1891. Lent to Galloway diocese. St Joseph's, Kilmarnock 1891-93. Girvan 1893-96. Not in addresses 1896-97. Galston 1897-99. Resumed his vocation in Ireland 1899 and died there 15 April 1935. (Canning)

BOHAN, WILLIAM: Born and educated Ireland. Ordained All Hallows for Galloway 1901. St Margaret's, Ayr 1901-07. Girvan 1907-09. Muirkirk 1909-18. Newton Stewart 1918-27. Stranraer 1927-44. New Abbey 1944-52. Died Dumfries 23 May 1952. (Canning)

BOLAND, JOSEPH: Born Muirkirk 1945. Educated Blairs, Valladolid. Ordained Muirkirk 1969. St Andrew's, Dumfries 1969-70. Professor, Blairs 1970-75. St Michael's, Kilmarnock 1975-80. Kirkconnel 1980-85. St Matthew's, Kilmarnock 1985-.

BOYD, JOSEPH VINCENT: Born Giffnock 1933. Educated Blairs, St Sulpice. Ordained Ayr 1957. St Michael's, Kilmarnock 1957-67. Millport 1967-71. Kirkconnel 1971-73. Stranraer 1973-77. Largs 1977-88. St Paul's, Ayr 1988-.

BOYD, WILLIAM HENRY: Born Kilmarnock 1959. Educated St Joseph's Academy, Kilmarnock; Drygrange. Ordained Kilmarnock 1984. Troon 1984-85. St Andrew's, Dumfries 1985-89. Annan 1989-.

BRADLEY, STEPHEN GERARD: Born Glasgow 1949. Educated Langbank; Blairs; Scots College, Rome. Ordained Ayr 1973. Kilwinning 1973. In Rome completing studies 1973-74. St Mary's, Irvine 1974-80. St Andrew's, Dumfries 1980-85. Muirkirk 1985-89. Our Lady Star of the Sea, Saltcoats 1989-.

BRADY, HUGH: See Archdiocese of St Andrew's & Edinburgh.

BRADY, JOHN: Born Maybole 1869. Educated Blairs 1882-86, Valladolid 1886-93. Ordained in Scotland 1893. St Andrew's, Dumfries 1893-95. Troon 1895-1909. Retired in bad health 1909. Died Edinburgh 1 Nov 1933.

BRADY, PHILIP ALPHONSUS: Born and educated Ireland. Ordained Ireland for Galloway 1943. St Joseph's, Kilmarnock 1943-53. Kirkconnel 1953-56. Retired to Ireland 1956 and died there 18 Jan 1957. (Canning)

BREEN, LAWRENCE: Born 1908. Educated Holy Cross Academy, Edinburgh; Blairs; St Sulpice. Ordained 1933. St Andrew's, Dumfries 1933-36. St Mary's, Irvine 1936-38. Newton Stewart 1938. Prestwick 1938-64. Died Prestwick 27 April 1964.

BRENNAN, DANIEL: See Glasgow Archdiocese.

BROWN, ARCHIBALD SINCLAIR: Born Ayr 1948. Educated St Margaret's High School, Ayr; St Joseph's High School, Kilmarnock; Valladolid. Ordained Ayr 1972. St Teresa's, Dumfries 1972-75. Professor, Langbank 1975-78. Professor, Blairs 1978-83. St Joseph's, Kilmarnock 1983-85. Maybole 1985-.

BROWN, JOHN KEENAN: Born Ayr 1948. Educated St Margaret's High School, Ayr; Blairs; Valladolid. Ordained Ayr 1972. Largs 1972-77. St Andrew's, Dumfries 1977-80. St Mary's, Irvine 1980-81. Vice-rector, Valladolid 1981-84. Left priesthood 1984.

BURKE, CORNELIUS: See Glasgow Archdiocese.

CALLANAN, CORNELIUS: Born and educated Ireland. Ordained Thurles 1899. Lent to Galloway diocese. St Joseph's, Kilmarnock 1899-1901. Archdiocese of Sydney, Australia 1901-10. Resumed his vocation in Ireland 1910 and died there 8 April 1963. (Canning)

CAMERON, JOHN (1887): see Glasgow Archdiocese.

CAMERON, JOHN M A (1894): Born Braemar 1870. Educated Blairs 1883-87; Valladolid 1887-94. Ordained Valladolid 1894. St Andrew's, Dumfries 1894. St Joseph's, Kilmarnock 1894-97. Wigtown 1897-99. Annbank 1899-1947. Died Annbank 14 March 1947.

CAREY, MICHAEL: Born and educated Ireland. Ordained 1901. St Joseph's, Kilmarnock 1901-04. Birnieknowe 1904-06. Annan 1906-15. Maybole 1915-32. Kirkcudbright 1932-38. St Joseph's, Kilmarnock 1938-51. Died Kilmarnock 20 May 1951. (Canning)

CARMONT, ROBERT: Born Dumfries 1868. Educated St Cuthbert's College, Ushaw, 1884-87 returning home in bad health; Scots College, Rome 1887-93. Ordained Rome 1893. St Margaret's, Ayr 1893-95. Waterside 1895-1903. Auchinleck 1903-04. St Joseph's, Kilmarnock 1904-11. Auchinleck 1911-15. St Margaret's, Ayr 1915-19. Annan 1919-31. Dalbeattie 1931-36. Retired 1936. Died Annan 30 Nov 1937.

CASEY, WILLIAM F: Born Roy Bridge 1869. Educated Blairs 1885-89; Valladolid 1889-93, returning home in bad health; Scots College, Rome 1893-94, returning home in bad health; St Peter's College 1894-95. Ordained Kinnoull 1895. St Andrew's, Dumfries 1895-96. St Margaret's, Ayr 1896-97. Craigeach 1897-98. Annan 1898-99. Resigned in bad health 1899. Died Birmingham 17 Aug 1903.

CATTERALL, ROBERT: Ordained 1929. New Abbey 1970-73. No further entries.

CHAMBERS, MARTIN: Born Glasgow 1964. Educated Langbank, Blairs, Valladolid, Salamanca. Ordained Irvine 1989. Stevenston 1989-.

CLARKE, HENRY C: Born Inverness 1875. Educated Blairs 1890-93; Notre Dame des Champs, Paris 1893-94; Scots College, Rome 1894-1901. Ordained Rome 1900. St Joseph's, Kilmarnock 1901-03. Wigtown 1903-46. Retired 1946. Died Wigtown 19 Oct 1950.

COLLINS, DANIEL: Born Lossiemouth 1857. Educated Blairs 1871-75; Valladolid 1875-82. Ordained Valladolid 1882. Girvan 1882. Cumnock 1882-85. Stranraer 1885-95. St Margaret's, Ayr 1895-1915. Died Ayr 4 April 1915.

COLLINS, JOHN ANTHONY (1969): See Glasgow Archdiocese.

CONNOLLY, JAMES: Ordained 1936. St Andrew's, Dumfries 1937-38. St Joseph's, Kilmarnock 1938-39. No further entries.

CONNOLLY, JOHN J: Born and educated Ireland. Ordained for the Redemptorists 1948. Was secularised and came to Galloway diocese 1966. Our Lady of Mount Carmel, Kilmarnock 1966-67. Kilbirnie 1967-70. St Mary's, Irvine 1970-74. Beith 1974-77. West Kilbride 1977-81. St Paul's, Ayr 1981-88. Retired to Ireland 1988. (Canning)

CONWAY, KEVIN: see Conway, Thomas.

CONWAY, MICHAEL: Born and educated Ireland. Ordained Kilkenny for Galloway 1960. Girvan 1960. Stevenston 1960-61. Lent to Dunkeld diocese: St Patrick's, Dundee 1961-65. Alloa 1965-67. No further entries. (Canning)

CONWAY, THOMAS KEVIN: Born and educated Ireland. Ordained Ireland for Galloway 1943. Kirkcudbright 1943-44. St Andrew's, Dumfries 1944-53. Muirkirk 1953-62. St Andrew's, Dumfries 1962-76. Dalbeattie 1976. (Canning)

COYLE, JAMES: Born Ayr 1919. Educated Blairs 1933-36; Le Grand Seminaire, Coutances 1936-39; St Patrick's College, Thurles 1939-42. Ordained Dumfries 1942. Waterside 1942-44. Stranraer 1944-49. Annbank 1949-50. Chaplain, St Joseph's College, Dumfries 1950-58. Stranraer 1958-66. Our Lady, Star of the Sea, Saltcoats 1966-70. Muirkirk 1970-75. Auchinleck 1975-77. Died Ballochmyle 25 Feb 1977.

CROWLEY, FRANCIS D: Born Glasgow 1932. Educated Fort Augustus; Scots College, Rome. Ordained Rome 1956. St Michael's, Kilmarnock 1956-57. Further studies, Rome 1957-59. Auchinleck 1959-62. St Joseph's, Kilmarnock 1962-63. Professor, Langbank 1963-68. Dalry 1968-74. Girvan 1974-82. Died Glasgow 23 March 1982.

CROWLEY, JOHN: Born Glasgow 1928. Educated Fort Augustus; Scots College, Rome. Ordained Dumfries 1955. Not in addresses 1955-56. St Mary's, Saltcoats 1956-60. Troon 1960-64. Prestwick 1964-65. Castle Douglas 1965-72. Troon 1972-81. Kilwinning 1981-88. Largs 1988-.

CULLERTON, PETER: See Dunkeld diocese.

CUMMINS, THOMAS: Born and educated Ireland. Ordained Maynooth 1933. Lent to Galloway diocese. St Joseph's, Kilmarnock 1935-38. St Andrew's, Dumfries 1938-39. Resumed his vocation in Ireland 1939 and died there 1 Oct 1974. (Canning)

CUNNINGHAM, MICHAEL: Ordained 1881. St Margaret's, Ayr 1881-82. No further entries.

DEVANEY, PATRICK: Born and educated Ireland. Ordained Ireland 1889. Lent to Galloway diocese. St Margaret's, Ayr 1889-90. Kilmarnock 1890-91. Resumed his vocation in Ireland 1891 and died Dublin 28 Aug 1940. (Canning)

DICK, BARRINGTON DOUGLAS: Born 1849. Educated Stonyhurst College, Ascott. Ordained Ascott 1892. Came to Archdiocese of St Andrews and Edinburgh 1894: St Patrick's, Edinburgh, 1894-95; not in Directories 1895-96; St Columba's, Edinburgh 1896-98. New Abbey 1898-1939. Died New Abbey 2 Dec 1939.

DOHERTY, DANIEL: Ordained 1983. St Andrew's, Dumfries 1986-87. Mossblown 1987-89. No further entries.

DOLAN, JAMES: See Glasgow Archdiocese.

DONNELLY, JAMES: Born Dumfries 1884. Educated Blairs 1898-1902; Scots College, Rome 1902-10. Ordained Rome 1908. St Joseph's, Kilmarnock 1911-17. Resigned in bad health 1917. Died Waterford 25 Aug 1958.

DONNELLY, JOHN: Born Wishaw 1921. Educated St Joseph's College, Dumfries; Blairs; St Peter's. Ordained Glasgow 1946. St Joseph's. Kilmarnock 1946-49. Girvan 1949-50. Our Lady Star of the Sea, Saltcoats 1950-53. St Mary's, Irvine 1953-54. Galston 1954-56. Kirkcudbright 1956-64. Hurlford 1964-81. Good Shepherd Cathedral, Ayr 1981-.

DONWORTH, ROBERT: Ordained 1889. St Margaret's, Ayr 1893-95. No further entries.

DOUGLAS, ARCHIBALD (LORD): Born 1850. Became Catholic 1861. Educated Oscott; St Thomas's Seminary, Hammersmith. Ordained Hammersmith 1876. St Vincent's Home for Boys, London 1876-86. Came to Scotland. Annan 1886-93. Not in addresses 1893-99. Annan 1899-1906. Absent on leave 1906-07. Troon 1907-08. Galston 1908-09. Girvan 1909-20. Retired 1920. Died London 13 Jan 1938.

DOYLE, MARTIN: Born Port Glasgow 1888. Educated Blairs 1902-06; Scots College, Rome 1906-14. Ordained Rome 1914. St Andrew's, Dumfries 1914-18. Cumnock 1918-20. St Mary's, Irvine 1920-26. Stranraer 1926-27. Newton Stewart 1927-30. Auchinleck 1930-36. Cumnock 1936-38. Castle Douglas 1938-44. Stranraer 1944-49. Dalbeattie 1949-52. Galston 1952-56. Died Galston 23 May 1956.

DUFFY, FRANCIS OWEN: Born Edinburgh 1914. Educated Blairs 1929-32; Scots College, Rome 1932-38. Ordained Rome 1938. St Margaret's, Ayr 1938-41. Professor, Blairs 1941-55. Annbank 1955-58. St Teresa's, Dumfries 1958-72. Good Shepherd Cathedral, Ayr 1972-81. Troon 1981-.

DUFFY, JOHN: Born Dumbarton 1860. Educated St Patrick's School, [Dumbarton]; St Mungo's Academy, Glasgow; Blairs 1875-81; Scots College, Rome 1881-87. Ordained Rome 1886. Served for a time in various unspecified places 1887. Girvan 1887-88. Castle Douglas 1888-1931. Died Castle Douglas 20 Aug 1931.

DUFFY, JOSEPH: See Glasgow Archdiocese.

ENGLISH, PATRICK: Born and educated Ireland. Ordained Thurles 1891. Offered his services to Galloway diocese. Muirkirk 1891. St Joseph's, Kilmarnock 1891-93. Died Kilmarnock 10 Sept 1893. (Canning)

ENGLISH, WILLIAM: Ordained 1883. Girvan 1883-84. Wigtown 1884-86. No further entries.

FARRINGTON, MICHAEL: Ordained 1970. St Andrew's, Dumfries 1973-77. Stevenston 1977-80. St Joseph's, Kilmarnock 1980-82. N.A D.G.H., Kilmarnock 1982-88. Kirkcudbright 1988-.

FINNEGAN, THOMAS: Born Glasgow 1876. Educated Blairs 1892-95; St Peter's 1895-98; Issy 1898-1900; St Sulpice 1900-03. Ordained Paris 1903. St Joseph's, Kilmarnock 1903-08. On sick leave 1908-10. Galston 1910-13. Hurlford 1913-35. Retired 1935. Died Glasgow 19 March 1936.

FISCHER, LAWRENCE WALLS: Born Gateshead on Tyne 1904. Educated Blairs 1918-23; Scots College, Rome 1923-30. Ordained Rome 1930. St James', Renfrew, Glasgow Archdiocese 1930. St Cuthbert's, Edinburgh, Archdiocese of St A & E, 1930-31. St Joseph's, Kilmarnock 1931-37. Maybole 1937-44. Waterside 1944-53. Ardrossan 1953-80. Died Ballochmyle 10 Oct 1980.

FITZPATRICK, PETER: See Glasgow Archdiocese.

FITZSIMMONS, EDWARD: Ordained 1938. St Joseph's, Kilmarnock 1938-40. St Andrew's, Dumfries 1940-41. No address given 1941-42. Not in Catholic Directory 1942-43. Sick leave, Glasgow 1943-44. Kirkcudbright 1944-45. Died Glasgow 28 July 1946.

FLAHIVE, T: Ordained 1941. St Joseph's, Kilmarnock 1941-43. Stranraer 1943-44. No further entries.

FLANNERY, JOHN: Born and educated Ireland. Ordained in Ireland for Galloway 1948. St Andrew's, Dumfries 1948-58. Stevenston 1958-60. Dalbeattie 1960-66. Stranraer 1966-73. Kilbirnie 1973-81. Catrine 1981-. (Canning)

FLYNN, EAMONN: Born and educated Ireland. Ordained Carlow for Galloway 1966. Kilwinning 1966-67. St Margaret's, Ayr 1967-68. Kilwinning 1968-69. Stevenston 1969-77. Dalry 1977-88. St Margaret's, Irvine 1988-. (Canning)

FORTEMPS, LOUIS: Ordained 1890. Newton Stewart 1899-1900. No further entries.

FOUHY, JOHN: Born and educated Ireland. Ordained Ireland 1889. Lent to Galloway diocese. St Joseph's, Kilmarnock 1889-91. Dalmellington 1891-95. Resumed his vocation in Ireland 1895 and died there 14 Sept 1934. (Canning)

FYFE, ALEXANDER: See Glasgow Archdiocese.

GLENDINNING, JOSEPH: Born Wakefield, Yorkshire 1916. Educated St Michael's College, Leeds. Career with L.M.S. and British Railways. R.A.F. 1940-45. Retired 1976; his wife died. Studied for priesthood Beda, Rome. Ordained Kilwinning 1980. Kilwinning 1980-81. Ardrossan 1981-82. St Margaret's, Ayr 1982-83. Newton Stewart 1983-88. Retired 1988.

GREEN, PATRICK: Ordained 1942. Largs 1964-66. No further entries.

GROGAN, JAMES: Born and educated Ireland. Ordained Kilkenny for Galloway 1950. St Andrew's, Dumfries 1950-51. Annan 1951-55. St Margaret's, Ayr 1955-57. Good Shepherd Cathedral, Ayr 1957-59. Kilbirnie 1959-62. Peru, South America 1962-66. Beith 1966-70. Good Shepherd Cathedral, Ayr 1970-72. Laicised 1973. (Canning)

GUNNING, PATRICK J: Born and educated Ireland. Ordained Carlow for Galloway 1939. Stranraer 1939-43. St Mary's, Irvine 1943-46. Moffat 1946-48. Millport 1948-59. Galston 1959-65. St Brendan's, Saltcoats 1965-81. West Kilbride 1981-87. Died West Kilbride 15 Nov 1987. (Canning)

HAINEY, DANIEL BERNARD: Born Saltcoats 1939. Educated Mt Melleray Seminary; Drygrange. Ordained Saltcoats 1968. St Margaret's, Ayr 1968-70. St Michael's, Kilmarnock 1970-73. c/o Bishop's House 1973-74. St Joseph's, Kilmarnock 1974-78. Annan 1978-89. St Beuno's Pastoral Centre, Wales 1989-.

HAMILL, JOHN: See Glasgow Archdiocese.

HANLON, ROBERT: Born Kilmarnock 1958. Educated St Joseph's Academy, Kilmarnock; Valladolid. Ordained Ayr 1983. Our Lady Star of the Sea, Saltcoats 1983-88. St Paul's, Ayr 1988-.

HANNAN, MICHAEL: Born and educated Ireland. Ordained Maynooth 1899. Lent to Galloway diocese. St Andrew's, Dumfries 1899-1901. Wigtown 1901-03. Kirkcudbright 1903-05. Resumed his vocation in Ireland 1905 and died there 1964. (Canning)

HARBISON, STANISLAUS: Born and educated Ireland. Joined Praemonstratensians and was ordained for them 1953. Holy Trinity Abbey, Kilnacrott 1953-59. Came to Galloway diocese 1959. St Joseph's, Kilmarnock 1959. Annan 1959-60. Gretna 1960-71. Our Lady of Mount Carmel, Kilmarnock 1971-74. Having left Praemonstratensians was incardinated into Galloway diocese. St Teresa's, Dumfries 1974-75. Millport 1975-81. Lockerbie 1981-82. Died Dumfries 26 Sept 1982. (Canning)

HARKIN, JOHN JOSEPH: Born Kilbirnie 1930. Educated St Joseph's College, Lochwinnoch; St Joseph's College, Durham; St Joseph's College, Roosendaal, Holland; Valladolid. Ordained Valladolid 1958. Lent to Dunkeld diocese: St Patrick's, Dundee 1958-59. Good Shepherd Cathedral, Ayr 1959-62. St Andrew's, Dumfries 1962-71. Gretna 1971-77. Waterside 1977-80. Castle Douglas 1980-88. Stranraer 1988-.

HAYES, THOMAS A: Born and educated Ireland. Ordained Dublin for Galloway 1901. St Andrew's, Dumfries 1901-03. Waterside 1903-09. Troon 1909-50. Died Troon 4 Jan 1950. (Canning)

HEAPHY, DANIEL: Born and educated Ireland. Ordained Ireland 1887. Lent to Galloway diocese. Annan 1893-95. Resumed his vocation in Ireland 1895 and died there 14 June 1899. (Canning)

HEELAN, EDWARD (Edmund): Born and educated Ireland. Ordained 1873. Lent to Galloway. St Margaret's, Ayr 1882-85. Resumed his vocation in Ireland 1885 and died there 7 Jan 1901. (Canning)

HEFFRON, SAMUEL A: Born near Ayr 1892. Educated Blairs 1906-11; Scots College, Rome 1911-16; Institut Catholique, Paris 1916-18. Ordained Glasgow 1918. St Andrew's, Dumfries 1918-31. Lent to Archdiocese of St A & E: St Francis Xavier's, Falkirk 1931-32. Newton Stewart 1932-36. St Andrew's, Dumfries 1936-37. Went to Nottingham 1938.

HENNESSY, PATRICK: Born Ireland. Educated Ireland, Paris. Ordained Paris 1938. St Joseph's, Kilmarnock 1938-41. No address given 1941-42. Girvan 1942-45. Resumed his vocation in Ireland 1945. (Canning)

HICKEY, MICHAEL P: Born and educated Ireland. Ordained Waterford 1884. Lent to Galloway diocese. St Andrew's, Dumfries 1884-85. St Joseph's, Kilmarnock 1885-86. Wigtown 1886-89. Birnieknowe 1889-93. Resumed his vocation in Ireland 1893 and died there 19 Nov 1916. (Canning)

HICKSON, JOHN A: Ordained 1880. Muirkirk 1893-94. Went to Glasgow Archdiocese. St Mary's, Coatbridge 1894-98. Strathaven 1898-1901. Helensburgh 1901-02. No further entries.

HIGGINS, JOHN: Ordained 1866. Muirkirk 1880-81. No further entries. (Canning)

HOGAN, JOSEPH: Born and educated Ireland. Ordained Thurles 1888. St Margaret's, Ayr 1888-89. Girvan 1889-90. Maybole 1890-99. Galston 1899-1908. Auchinleck 1908-18. Irvine 1918-36. Died Irvine 30 April 1936. (Canning)

HOURIGAN, JOHN: Born and educated Ireland. Ordained Thurles 1883. Lent to Galloway diocese. St Joseph's, Kilmarnock 1883-85. Cumnock

1885-89. Left in bad health to serve in the Channel Isles. Last parish was St Helier, Jersey. Died Golden while on holiday 5 April 1931. (Canning)

HUGHES, JOHN: Born Dundee 1900. Educated Blairs 1913-19; St Peter's 1919-20; Scots College, Rome 1920-26. Ordained Rome 1926. St Mary's, Irvine 1926-27. St Margaret's, Ayr 1927-28. No further entries.

HUTCHISON, DOUGLAS: Born Kilmarnock 1961. Educated St Joseph's Academy, Kilmarnock; Valladolid. Ordained Kilmarnock 1985. St Teresa's, Dumfries 1985-87. Kilwinning 1987-.

JENNINGS, JAMES B: Born and educated Ireland. Ordained Ireland 1898. Lent to Galloway diocese. St Joseph's, Kilmarnock 1898-99. Wigtown 1899-1901. Lent to Glasgow Archdiocese. St Patrick's, Coatbridge 1901-06. Resumed his vocation in Ireland 1906, and died there 28 Aug 1941. (Canning)

JOYCE, THOMAS: Born 1873. Educated Blairs 1887-91; Paris 1891-92; Scots College, Rome 1892-97. Ordained Rome 1897. St Andrew's, Dumfries 1897. St Joseph's, Kilmarnock 1897-98. Craigeach 1898-99. No address given 1899-1900. Lent to Glasgow Archdiocese: St Mary's, Glasgow 1900-07; Kirkintilloch 1907-08. No address given 1908-09. Auchinleck 1909-11. St Mary's, Irvine 1911-18. Muirkirk 1918-40. Died Muirkirk 2 Dec 1940.

KANE, JOHN: Born Stevenston 1921. Educated Glasgow University; Blairs; Scots College, Rome. Ordained Rome 1951, returning to Scotland 1952. St Joseph's, Kilmarnock 1952-57. Professor, Blairs 1957-64. Dalry 1964-67. Maybole 1967-70. Waterside 1970-77. Auchinleck 1977-85. Galston 1985-89. No further entries.

KEEGANS, PATRICK: Born Saltcoats 1946. Educated Blairs, Valladolid. Ordained Saltcoats 1970. Our Lady of Mount Carmel, Kilmarnock 1970-71. St Andrew's, Dumfries 1971-77. St Margaret's, Ayr 1977-82. Whithorn 1982-87. Lockerbie 1987-88. On sick leave 1988-.

KELLY, DECLAN: Born and educated Ireland. Ordained Carlow for Galloway 1969. St Mary's, Irvine 1969-70. St Brendan's, Saltcoats 1970-71. Girvan 1971-74. Ardrossan 1974-80. Muirkirk 1980-85. Left the priesthood 1985. (Canning)

KELLY, THOMAS A (1926): See Dunkeld diocese.

KENNEDY, STEPHEN: Born and educated Ireland. Ordained Thurles for Galloway 1941. Annan 1941-47. Dalbeattie 1947-49. Annan 1949-50. Castle Douglas 1950-54. Stranraer 1954-58. St Michael's, Kilmarnock 1958-65. St Margaret's, Ayr 1965-77. Newton Stewart 1977-83. Maybole 1983-85. Retired, Ayr, 1985-. (Canning)

KEOGH, DANIEL: Born and educated Ireland. Ordained Maynooth 1893. Lent to Galloway diocese. Annan 1895-98. Cumnock 1898-1903. Resumed his vocation in Ireland 1903 and died Dublin 22 Sept 1922. (Canning)

KERR, JOHN: Born Dumbarton 1922. Educated St Sulpice. Ordained Ayr 1964. Our Lady Star of the Sea, Saltcoats 1964-65. Saltcoats, in addresses, but not under parishes, 1965-66. Prestwick 1966-75. Muirkirk 1975-80. Waterside 1980-81. Chaplain, Benedictine Convent, Dumfries 1981-82. Lockerbie 1982-87. West Kilbride 1987-89. Beith 1989-.

KERR, JOSEPH: Born Ireland. Educated Wexford; Scots College, Rome. Ordained Rome 1936. Annan 1937-39. St Andrew's, Dumfries 1939-40. Annan 1940-49. Stranraer 1949-54. Girvan 1954-74. Retired 1974. Died Girvan 25 March 1975. (Canning)

KERRIN, DANIEL: Born and educated Ireland. Ordained 1885. Dalmellington 1888-91. Girvan 1891-92. No further entries. (Canning)

KIERNAN, FRANCIS ALOYSIUS: Born and educated Ireland. Ordained Waterford 1948. Kilbirnie 1948-59. Millport 1959-67. St Paul's, Ayr 1967-81. St Brendan's, Saltcoats 1981-. (Canning)

KINSLER, JOHN: Born Newmilns 1941. Educated St Joseph's High School, Kilmarnock; Drygrange. Ordained Ayr 1965. St Mary's, Irvine 1965-67. St Joseph's, Kilmarnock 1967-69. C/o Bishop's House 1969-70. Waterside 1970-72. Cumnock 1972-76. Kirkconnel 1976-77. St Teresa's, Dumfries 1977-79. Gretna 1979-.

LANGLEY, HENRY: Born Ireland. Educated Ireland, Blairs, Valladolid. Ordained Valladolid 1893. St Joseph's, Kilmarnock 1893-94. Muirkirk 1894-97. Girvan 1897-1903. Cumnock 1903-07. Dalbeattie 1907-31. Retired 1931. Died 1 April 1943. (Canning)

LAVERTY, HENRY STUART: Born Salford 1854. Educated Blairs 1871-75; Valladolid 1875-82. Ordained Valladolid 1882. Birnieknowe 1882-83. Hurlford 1883-88. Galston 1888-89. Cumnock 1889-90. No further entries.

LEE, JOHN: Ordained 1882. St Joseph's, Kilmarnock 1882-83. Dalbeattie 1883-85. St Andrew's, Dumfries 1885-87. No further entries.

LEEN, JOHN: Born and educated Ireland. Ordained Dublin for Galloway 1942. St Andrew's, Dumfries 1942-47. Newton Stewart 1947-53. Hurlford 1953-64. Troon 1964-72. Castle Douglas 1972-80. Galston 1980-85. Retired 1985. (Canning)

LEEN, MICHAEL: Born and educated Ireland. Ordained Maynooth 1947. Lent to Galloway diocese. Annan 1947-50. St Mary's, Irvine 1950-51. Resumed his vocation in Ireland 1951. (Canning)

LEVERAGE, THOMAS: Born Glasgow 1934. Educated St Joseph's High School, Kilmarnock; Drygrange. Ordained Galston 1960. Largs 1960-63. St Andrew's, Dumfries 1963-64. Stevenston 1964-67. St Paul's, Ayr 1967-71. Good Shepherd Cathedral, Ayr 1971-74. West Kilbride 1974-77. Stranraer 1977-88. Hurlford 1988-.

LITTLETON, MATTHEW: See Glasgow Archdiocese.

LUCEY, DANIEL: Ordained 1926. Chaplain, Benedictine Convent, Dumfries 1951-58. Largs 1958-60. Chaplain, St Joseph's Convent, Barrhill 1960-65. No further entries.

LYNCH, MICHAEL: Born and educated Ireland. Ordained Carlow for Galloway 1955. St Margaret's, Ayr 1955-56. Auchinleck 1956-59. Catholic Mission Society, London 1959-60. Our Lady Star of the Sea, Saltcoats 1960-64. Kirkcudbright 1964-80. Ardrossan 1980-. (Canning)

McALISTER, DANIEL: Born Ireland. Educated Ireland, Spain. Ordained Ireland 1887. Lent to Galloway diocese. Maybole 1887-88. Girvan 1888-89. Muirkirk 1889-91. Dalmellington in addresses, but not under parishes, 1891-92. Resumed his vocation in Ireland 1892 and died there 24 June 1949. (Canning)

McBRIDE, WILLIAM: Born Elderslie 1918. Educated St Aloysius' College, Glasgow; Blairs 1935-36; Le Grand Seminaire, Coutances 1936-39; St Patrick's College, Thurles 1939-41. Ordained Dumfries 1941. St Margaret's, Ayr 1941-52. Dalbeattie 1952-53. Went to Diocese of Southwark 1953.

McBURNIE, WILLIAM J: Born Maxwelltown, Dumfries 1893. Educated Blairs 1910-15; Scots College, Rome 1915-22. Ordained Rome 1921. Cumnock 1922-25. St Joseph's, Kilmarnock 1925-27. St Margaret's, Ayr 1927-31. St Joseph's, Kilmarnock 1931-33. Waterside 1933-37. Galston 1937-40. Kirkcudbright 1940-52. Ardrossan 1952-53. Died Dumfries 22 Aug 1953.

McCABE, PATRICK JOSEPH: Born Bray, Co Wicklow 1932. Educated Rockwell College, Tipperary; University College, Dublin; St John's College, Waterford. Ordained Waterford for Galloway 1961. St Margaret's, Ayr 1961-66. Cumnock 1966-70. C/o Bishop's House 1970-74. Kilwinning 1974-77. On sick leave 1977-.

McCAFFERTY, GEORGE: Born Irvine 1906. Educated Blairs 1922-26; St Lo 1926-27; Coutances 1927-32. Ordained St Peter's College 1932. St Margaret's, Ayr 1932-37. Kirkconnel 1937-44. Castle Douglas 1944-50. Cumnock 1950-65. St Michael's, Kilmarnock 1965-73. Annbank 1973-82. Mossblown 1982-86. Retired to Troon 1986.

McCAIG, JOHN: Born Kilmarnock 1957. Educated St Joseph's Academy, Kilmarnock; Heriot Watt University. Valladolid. Ordained Ayr 1983. Ardrossan 1983-86. Troon 1986-87. No further entries.

McCANN, THOMAS: Born Irvine 1927. Educated St Sulpice. Ordained Irvine 1957. St Margaret's, Ayr 1957-58. Kirkconnel 1958-62. St Teresa's, Dumfries 1962-72. Langholm 1972-.

McCARTHY, DENIS: Born Ireland 1910. Educated Blairs: Valladolid: St Patrick's College, Thurles. Ordained Thurles for Galloway 1939. Annan 1939-40. St Joseph's, Kilmarnock 1940-45. Whithorn 1945-52. Kirkcudbright 1952-56. Galston 1956-59. Retired to Ireland 1959 and died there 2 Jan 1961. (Canning)

McCLUSKEY, MARTIN: Born Kilmarnock 1935. Educated St Sulpice. Ordained Kilmarnock 1959. St Margaret's, Ayr 1959-65. Our Lady Star of the Sea, Saltcoats 1965-72. Newton Stewart 1972-77. St Margaret's, Ayr 1977-.

McCLYMONT, FREDERICK: See Argyll diocese.

McDANIEL, PATRICK: See Dunkeld diocese.

McDERMOTT, HENRY J: Ordained 1952. St Andrew's, Dumfries 1953-54. Largs 1954-58. Chaplain, St Joseph's College, Dumfries 1958-76. No further entries.

McDERMOTT, PATRICK J: Born and educated Ireland. Ordained Wexford for Galloway 1918. St Joseph's, Kilmarnock 1918-31. Waterside 1931-33. St Joseph's, Kilmarnock 1933-35. Archdiocese of Perth, Australia 1935-38. Hurlford 1938-40. Newton Stewart 1940-47. Retired 1947. (Canning)

McFADDEN, WILLIAM RAYMOND: Born Glasgow 1961. Educated St Joseph's Academy, Kilmarnock; Scots College, Rome. Ordained Kilmarnock 1985. Completing studies, Rome 1985-86. Stevenston 1986-89. St Andrew's, Dumfries 1989-.

McFARLANE, HENRY JOSEPH: Born Kilwinning 1943. Educated Blairs, Valladolid. Ordained Ardrossan 1967. St Mary's, Irvine 1967-69. C/o Bishop's House 1969-72. Laicised 1972.

McGARRY, ALEXANDER: Ordained for White Fathers 1958. White Fathers, Rutherglen 1970-73. Came to Galloway diocese 1973; later incardinated into it. Troon 1973-74. Good Shepherd Cathedral, Ayr 1974-77. Beith 1977-88. Sick leave 1988-89. Annbank 1989-.

McGEE, JOHN ANTHONY: Born Kilmarnock 1947. Educated Blairs, Valladolid. Ordained Kilmarnock 1970. Cumnock 1970-71. St Paul's, Ayr 1971-74. Vice-rector, Valladolid 1974-81. Rector, Valladolid 1981-87. C/o Valladolid 1987-88. Beith 1988-89. Galston 1989-.

McGHEE, EDWARD: Born Muirkirk 1947. Educated Blairs, Drygrange. Ordained Cumnock 1972. St Joseph's, Kilmarnock 1972. Our Lady Star of the Sea, Saltcoats 1972-80. Ireland 1980-81. St Mary's, Irvine 1981-84. Kilbirnie 1984-85. Waterside 1985-88. St Brendan's, Saltcoats 1988-.

McGILLIGAN, JOHN: Born and educated Ireland. Ordained Maynooth 1915. Lent to Galloway diocese. Cumnock 1915-16. Not in Directories 1916-18. Lent to Archdiocese of St A & E: St Mary's Cathedral, Edinburgh 1918-19; Broxburn 1919-22. Resumed his vocation in Ireland 1922 and died there 10 July 1977. (Canning)

McGINNESS, SAMUEL: See Glasgow Archdiocese.

McGOWAN, CLEMENT: See Glasgow Archdiocese.

McGRATH, CHARLES: Born and educated Ireland. Ordained Ireland 1948. Lent to Galloway diocese. Largs 1948-52. Resumed his vocation in Ireland 1952. (Canning)

McGREAD, THOMAS JOSEPH: Born Glasgow 1929. Educated Blairs; St Sulpice; St Peter's College, Wexford. Ordained Glasgow 1952. St Andrew's, Dumfries 1952-55. St Joseph's, Kilmarnock 1955-62. Kilbirnie 1962-67. Catrine 1967-70. Cumnock 1970-76. Stevenston 1976-88. Dalry 1988-.

McHARDY, JOSEPH: Born Aboyne 1874. Educated Blairs 1888-92; Scots College, Rome 1892-99. Ordained Blairs 1899. Professor, Blairs 1899-1905. Kirkcudbright 1905-32 (chaplain to Forces 1914-18). St Margaret's, Ayr 1932-65. Retired 1965. Died Ayr 10 June 1966.

McHUGH, FRANCIS PATRICK: Born Glasgow 1931. Educated Blairs; St Joseph's College, Upholland. Ordained Kilmarnock 1956. St Margaret's, Ayr 1956-61. Catholic Workers' College, Oxford 1961-63. St Joseph's, Kilmarnock 1963-67. Catholic Workers' College, Oxford 1967-.

McHUGH, JAMES: Born Stevenston 1935. Educated St John's School, Stevenston; St Michael's College, Irvine; Blairs 1947-53; Drygrange

1953-59. Ordained Stevenston 1959. St Teresa's, Dumfries 1959-62. Cumnock 1962-63. Lent to Archdiocese of St A & E: St Columba's, Edinburgh 1963-64; St Catherine's, Edinburgh 1964-65. St Joseph's, Kilmarnock 1965-67. St Mary's, Irvine 1967-71. Lockerbie 1971-76. Dalry 1976-77. Died Irvine 9 March 1977.

McKINLEY, CHARLES: See Glasgow Archdiocese.

McKNIGHT, WILLIAM: Ordained 1938. St Joseph's, Kilmarnock 1939-40. Annan 1940-41. No further entries.

MACLAUGHLAN, KENNETH BERNARD: Born Kilmarnock 1930. Educated St Joseph's School, Kilmarnock; St Mungo's Academy, Glasgow; Scots College, Rome. Ordained Rome 1959, returning to Scotland 1960. Cumnock 1960-62. St Mary's, Irvine 1962-65. Prestwick 1965-66. Largs 1966-67. No further entries.

McLAUGHLIN, CHARLES: Born and educated Ireland. Ordained Dublin 1950. St Andrew's, Dumfries 1950-51. Stevenston 1951-58. St Joseph's, Kilmarnock 1958-63. Whithorn 1963-72. Kilwinning 1972-81. Kilbirnie 1981-85. Retired to Ireland 1985 and died there 7 March 1987. (Canning)

McLEAN, JOHN: Born Paisley 1928. Educated St Mirin's Academy, Paisley; Open University; Lancaster University; Beda College, Rome. Ordained Rome 1987. St Teresa's, Dumfries 1987-89. Muirkirk 1989-.

McMANUS, MATTHEW FRANCIS: Born Rutherglen 1940. Educated Drygrange. Ordained Ayr 1965. St Margaret's, Ayr 1965-77. Kirkconnel 1977-80. Kirkcudbright 1980-88. Kilwinning 1988-.

McNAMARA, JOHN: Ordained 1948. St Margaret's, Ayr 1966-68. Girvan 1968-71. Cumnock 1971-72. No further entries.

McQUILLAN, JOHN: See Glasgow Archdiocese.

McREDMOND, MICHAEL: Born and educated Ireland. Ordained Maynooth 1895. Lent to Galloway diocese. St Margaret's, Ayr 1895-96. No address given 1896-98. Resumed his vocation in Ireland 1898 and died there 13 July 1907. (Canning)

McSORLEY, PATRICK JAMES: Born and educated Ireland. Ordained Dublin for Galloway 1960. Lent to Dunkeld diocese: St Clement's, Dundee 1960-62. St Joseph's, Kilmarnock 1962-74. St Matthew's, Kilmarnock 1974-85. St Teresa's, Dumfries 1985-. (Canning)

McSPARRAN, ARCHIBALD: See Glasgow Archdiocese.

MAGEE, GERARD: Ordained 1985. Annbank 1989-.

MAGEE, PETER: Born Irvine 1958. Educated St Michael's Academy, Kilwinning; Scots College, Rome. Ordained Ardrossan 1981. St Mary's, Irvine 1981. Completing studies, Rome 1981-82. St Teresa's, Dumfries 1982-84. Further studies, Rome 1984-86. Released from diocese to study at Pontificia Academia Ecclesiastica at request of Vatican 1986.

MANCINI, RALPH: Born Ayr 1930. Educated Blairs; Scots College, Rome. Ordained Rome 1954. St Andrew's, Dumfries 1954-60. St Joseph's, Kilmarnock 1960-62. Newton Stewart 1962-72. Dalbeattie 1972-76. St Andrew's, Dumfries 1976-.

MANNING, JAMES: Born and educated Ireland. Ordained Kilkenny for Galloway 1945. St Joseph's, Kilmarnock 1945-46. St Mary's, Irvine 1946-49. Auchinleck 1949-53. Newton Stewart 1953-58. Castle Douglas 1958-65. Galston 1965-80. Died Ballochmyle 15 Oct 1980. (Canning)

MATHEWS, EUGENE: Born Dumfries 1921. Educated Blairs; Scots College, Rome; St Peter's. Ordained Glasgow 1946. Further studies, Rome 1946-49. Our Lady Star of the Sea, Saltcoats 1949-56. Kirkconnel 1956-63. Maybole 1963-67. Kilbirnie 1967-73. St Michael's, Kilmarnock 1973-82. Girvan 1982-.

MATTHEWS, CHARLES: Born and educated Ireland. Ordained Wexford for Galloway 1952. St Joseph's, Kilmarnock 1952-53. Ardrossan 1953-62. Muirkirk 1962-70. Catrine 1970-81. Millport 1981-87. C/o Bishop's House 1987-89. West Kilbride 1989-. (Canning)

MAXWELL, JOSEPH: Born Newton Stewart 1903. Educated Newton Stewart; Blairs; Grand Seminaire, Coutances. Ordained Dundee 1928. Lent to Glasgow Archdiocese: Renton 1928-30; Renton in addresses, but not under parishes,1930-31. St Andrew's, Dumfries 1931-33. Castle Douglas 1933-36. Birnieknowe 1936-50. Annbank 1950-55. Stevenston 1955-76. Died Stevenston 13 March 1976.

MEAGHER, MARTIN: Born Ireland. Educated Ireland, St Peter's. Ordained 1901. St Margaret's, Ayr 1901-03. Girvan 1903-07. Cumnock 1907-36. St Mary's, Irvine 1936-37. Died Kilmarnock 28 Dec 1937. (Canning)

MEANEY, FRANCIS: Born Ireland. Educated Blairs, Avignon, Issy, St Sulpice. Ordained Paris 1917. St Andrew's, Dumfries 1918-20. On sick leave in South Africa 1920-23. Lent to Glasgow Archdiocese: Cambuslang 1923-24. Not in Directories [on sick leave, England] 1924-28. Lent to Glasgow Archdiocese: Cambuslang 1928. St Margaret's, Ayr 1928-35. Hurlford 1935-38. Waterside 1938-44. Maybole 1944-63. Retired to Ireland 1963 and died there 17 May 1969. (Canning)

MIMNAGH, HUGH: Born Johnstone 1892. Educated St Mungo's Academy, Glasgow; St Columba's College, Derry; St Peter's College, Wexford. Ordained Wexford 1920. St Andrew's, Dumfries 1920-21. Cumnock 1921-22. St Margaret's, Ayr 1922-26. Auchinleck 1926-28. St Joseph's, Kilmarnock 1928-31. Annan 1931-39. Cumnock 1939-50. Stevenston 1950-55. Died Stevenston 23 Oct 1955.

MOORE, FRANCIS PAUL GABRIEL: Born and educated Ireland. Ordained Dublin for Galloway 1960. St Andrew's, Dumfries 1960-62. Good Shepherd Cathedral, Ayr 1962-68. Our Lady of Mount Carmel, Kilmarnock 1968-71. St Mary's, Irvine 1971-75. St Margaret's, Irvine 1975-88. Prestwick 1988-. (Canning)

MORIARTY, MYLES PATRICK: Born and educated Ireland. Ordained Thurles for Galloway 1935. St Margaret's, Ayr 1935-41. Muirkirk 1941-53. Waterside 1953-57. Good Shepherd Cathedral, Ayr 1957-70. Maybole 1970-83. St Margaret's, Ayr 1983-89. Died Ayr 3 Sept 1989. (Canning)

MULHOLLAND, PATRICK: Born and educated Ireland. Ordained Maynooth 1915. Lent to Galloway diocese. Annan 1916-18. Chaplain to Association of the Sacred Heart, Gretna and assistant at Annan 1918-19. Annan 1919-21. Lent to Glasgow Archdiocese: Govan 1921-23. Resumed his vocation in Ireland 1923 and died there 29 June 1947. (Canning)

MULLINS, RICHARD F: Born Ireland. Educated Ireland; University of Louvain. Ordained Thurles 1879. Lent to Galloway diocese. St Andrew's, Dumfries 1880-87. Professor, Thurles 1887-95. Got exeat to return to Galloway diocese 1895. Stranraer 1895-97. New Abbey 1897-98. St Andrew's, Dumfries 1898-99. Chaplain, Marist Brothers, Dumfries 1899-1900. St Andrew's, Dumfries 1900-14. Chaplain, Benedictine Convent, Dumfries 1914-18. St Andrew's, Dumfries 1918-20. Girvan 1920-31. Died Girvan 31 July 1931. (Canning)

MULVENNA, HUGH: Ordained 1934. St Mary's, Irvine 1941-43. Forces chaplain 1943-51. No further entries.

MURPHY, JOHN NICHOLAS (1903): Born Dumfries 1878. Educated Blairs 1892-96; St Peter's 1896-98; Scots College, Rome 1898-1903. Ordained Rome 1903. St Andrew's, Dumfries 1903-09. Waterside 1909-28. St Mary's, Irvine 1928-36. Newton Stewart 1936-38. Dalbeattie 1938-47. Annbank 1947-50. St Mary's, Irvine 1950-55. Died Irvine 1 Dec 1955.

MURPHY, JOHN (1908): Born Maxwelltown 1883. Educated Blairs 1898-1902; Propaganda, Rome 1902-08. Ordained Rome 1908. Birnieknowe 1908-09. St Andrew's, Dumfries 1909-17. Forces chaplain 1917-19. St Margaret's, Ayr 1919-22. Galston 1922-37. Died Glasgow 31 March 1937.

MURPHY, JOHN (1954): Born Annbank 1930. Educated St Margaret's School, Ayr; Blairs; Propaganda, Rome. Ordained Dumfries 1954. St Joseph's, Kilmarnock 1954-58. St Andrew's, Dumfries 1958-62. Ardrossan 1962-63. Kirkconnel 1963-71. Annan 1971-78. Died Nithsdale 25 April 1978.

MURPHY, NICHOLAS FRANCIS KIERAN: Born and educated Ireland. Ordained Kilkenny for Galloway 1945. St Andrew's, Dumfries 1945-47. Auchinleck 1947-49. Troon 1949-52. St Margaret's, Ayr 1952-65. Cumnock 1965-70. Our Lady Star of the Sea, Saltcoats 1970-89. Retired 1989. (Canning)

MURPHY, PATRICK: Born and educated Ireland. Ordained Ireland 1880. Lent to Galloway diocese. Girvan 1880-82. Dalbeattie 1882-83. Birnieknowe 1883-89. Resumed his vocation in Ireland 1889 and died there 28 Jan 1924. (Canning)

MURPHY SEAN (John): Born Ireland and entered Salvatorians there. Ordained 1948. Taught in Salvatorian colleges 1948-53. Came to Galloway 1953. Troon 1953. Hurlford 1953. Our Lady Star of the Sea, Saltcoats 1953-58. Newton Stewart 1958-62. Waterside 1962-70. Auchinleck 1970-75. Died Auchinleck 2 Oct 1975. (Canning)
Note: Presumably he had left the Salvatorians when he came to Galloway as he is not given his religious name, Bonaventure, in Catholic Directories.

MURPHY, THOMAS JOSEPH: Born Kilmarnock 1919. Educated St Joseph's Academy, Kilmarnock; St Aloysius' College, Glasgow; Blairs; Paris; Coutances; Orleans; St Peter's. Ordained 1943. St Margaret's, Ayr 1943-53. Dalbeattie 1953-60. Dalry 1960-64. Prestwick 1964-66. St Mary's, Irvine 1966-85. Auchinleck 1985-.

MURRAY, WILLIAM: Born Douglas 1950. Educated St Joseph's Academy, Kilmarnock; Langbank; Blairs; Valladolid. Ordained Muirkirk 1974. St Michael's, Kilmarnock 1974-75. St Teresa's, Dumfries 1975-78. Good Shepherd Cathedral, Ayr 1978-83. Left the priesthood 1983.

O'BRIEN, DANIEL W (1880): Born and educated Ireland. Ordained Thurles 1880. Lent to Galloway diocese. Castle Douglas 1880-88. Resumed his vocation in Ireland 1888 and died there 3 March 1932. (Canning)

O'BRIEN, DANIEL (1888): Born and educated Ireland. Ordained Maynooth 1888. Lent to Galloway diocese. Later got exeat to stay in Scotland. St Andrew's, Dumfries 1888-1936. Retired 1936. Died Dumfries 11 March 1937. (Canning)

O'CARROLL, MICHAEL (1888): Born Ireland. Educated Ireland, Rome. Ordained 1888. Lent to Galloway diocese. St Margaret's, Ayr 1891-93. Resumed his vocation in Ireland 1893 and died 9 Nov 1942. (Canning)

O'CARROLL, MICHAEL (1924): See Glasgow Archdiocese.

O'CONNELL, ANTHONY: Born and educated Ireland. Ordained Thurles for Galloway 1921. Lent to Dunkeld diocese: St Mary's, Dundee 1921; St Joseph's, Dundee 1921-22. Got bronchial trouble so served in England 1922-27. Girvan 1927-54. Decided to pursue his vocation in Florida for the sake of his health and died in Ireland while on his way there 25 Nov 1954. (Canning)

O'CONNOR, MICHAEL (1915): See Glasgow Archdiocese.

O'CONNOR, WILLIAM JOSEPH: Born Ireland. Educated Ireland, St Peter's. Ordained Glasgow 1908. Lent to Glasgow Archdiocese: St Mary's, Greenock 1908-12. Cumnock 1912-14. St Mary's, Greenock 1914-15. St Joseph's, Kilmarnock 1915-22. Kirkconnel 1922-32. Maybole 1932-37. Waterside 1937-38. Kirkcudbright 1938-40. Galston 1940-52. St Joseph's, Kilmarnock 1952-53. Retired 1953. Died Dublin 18 Aug 1959. (Canning)

O'DWYER, WILLIAM: Born and educated Ireland. Ordained Maynooth 1890. Lent to Galloway diocese. St Margaret's, Ayr 1890-91. Resumed his vocation in Ireland 1891 and died there 14 Jan 1945. (Canning)

O'FARRELL, THOMAS: Ordained 1889. Wigtown 1896-97. No further entries.

O'GORMAN, BENEDICT: Born and educated Ireland. Joined Salvatorian Fathers and was ordained 1942. Was secularised 1953 and joined Galloway diocese. St Margaret's, Ayr 1953-55. Incardinated into Galloway diocese 1955. Annan 1955-59. St Joseph's, Kilmarnock 1959-60. Catrine 1960-64. Went to Archdiocese of Birmingham 1964 and was incardinated into it 1989. (Canning)

O'HANLON, JOHN: Born Dumfries 1878. Educated Blairs 1893-96; St Peter's 1896-97; Scots College, Rome 1897-1901; at home in bad health 1901-03; St Peter's 1903-06. Ordained Glasgow 1906. Birnieknowe 1906-07. On sick leave 1907-09. Joined mission on Isle of Wight 1909.

O'MALLEY, CHARLES J: Born Barbados 1862. Came to Scotland 1869. Educated diocesan seminary, Nottingham; Oscott College. Ordained 1889. Vice-rector, Nottingham diocesan seminary 1888-90. As this was too much for his strength he applied for affiliation to Galloway diocese. Cumnock 1890-98. Dalbeattie 1898-1907. St Margaret's, Ayr 1907-17. Died Ayr 9 Nov 1917.

OMMER, FRANCIS GILMOUR: Born Glasgow 1929. Educated St Aloysius' College, Glasgow; Glasgow Veterinary School; Villa Notre Dame,

Montana-Vermala, Valais, Switzerland; Valladolid. Ordained Valladolid 1960. Prestwick 1960-64. Our Lady Star of the Sea, Saltcoats 1964-66. St Margaret's, Ayr 1966-67. Troon 1967-73. Kirkconnel 1973-76. Cumnock 1976-.

O'REILLY, DERMOT: Born and educated Ireland. Ordained Thurles for Galloway 1916. Cumnock 1916-18. St Mary's, Irvine 1918-20. St Margaret's, Ayr 1920-27. St Mary's, Irvine 1927-28. Gretna 1928-32. Kirkconnel 1932-37. Dalbeattie 1937-38. St Mary's, Irvine 1938-50. Kilbirnie 1950-67. Died Dumfries Infirmary 2 July 1967. (Canning)

O'SULLIVAN, JAMES: Born and educated Ireland. Ordained Carlow for Galloway 1949. Ardrossan 1949-53. Went to diocese of Camden, New Jersey 1953 and was excardinated from Galloway diocese 1959. (Canning)

O'SULLIVAN, JOHN: Born and educated Ireland. Ordained Thurles for Galloway 1920. St Joseph's, Kilmarnock 1920. Cumnock 1920-22. St Joseph's, Kilmarnock 1922-25. St Andrew's, Dumfries 1925-62. Died Dumfries 28 June 1962. (Canning)

O'SULLIVAN, LAURENCE: Born Dublin 1908. Ordained for Passionists 1940. Temporarily exclaustrated to Galloway diocese. Girvan 1955-59. No further entries.

OXLEY, JOSEPH GERARD: Born and educated Ireland. Ordained Kilkenny for Galloway 1950. Annan 1950-51. On sick leave, Ireland 1951-52. New Abbey 1952-61. On sick leave again 1961-62. Waterside 1962-64. Catrine 1964-67. Dalry 1967-68. Died Mullingar 27 June 1968. (Canning)

POLAND, MARTIN DOMINIC: Born Carlisle 1955. Educated Austin Friar's School, Carlisle; Valladolid; Drygrange. Ordained Carlisle 1982. St Joseph's, Kilmarnock 1982-83. Good Shepherd Cathedral, Ayr 1983-87. Whithorn 1987-.

POWER, ALPHONSUS: see Dunkeld diocese.

PUISSANT, LEO L J: Born Sulsique, Belgium 1865. Educated Colleges of Renaix and Kain; Seminaries of St Nicholas and Ghent. Ordained Ghent 1889. Professor at Lokeren College 1888-89 and Eccloo College 1889-94. Spiritual director, private school near Slough 1894-96. Bishop Auckland 1896-97. His health gave way; he came to Galloway diocese 1897. New Abbey 1897. Muirkirk 1897-1909. Galston 1909-22. Died Belgium 5 Aug 1922.

QUINLAN, DENIS FRANCIS: Born and educated Ireland. Ordained Dublin for Galloway 1958. St Teresa's, Dumfries 1958-72. Whithorn 1972-77. St Joseph's, Kilmarnock 1977-. (Canning)

QUINN, JOHN J (1945): Educated St Patrick's College, Carlow. Ordained Carlow 1945. Girvan 1946-49. St Mary's, Irvine 1949-50. Military chaplain 1950-53. St Joseph's, Kilmarnock 1953-54. Annan 1954-57. Waterside 1957-62. Left the priesthood 1962.

QUINN, JOHN (1959): Ordained 1959. St Teresa's, Dumfries 1978-79. Our Lady Star of the Sea, Saltcoats 1979-80. No further entries.

REDDEN, DON (Gerald): Born and educated Ireland. Ordained Dublin for Galloway 1959. Lent to Dunkeld diocese: St John's, Perth 1959-61. Stevenston 1961-64. St Andrew's, Dumfries 1964-69. On missions, Latin America 1969-78. C/o Bishop's House 1978-79. St Joseph's, Kilmarnock 1979-81. Excardinated 1981. (Canning)

REID, ROBERT: Ordained 1965. St Brendan's, Saltcoats 1966-67. St Michael's, Kilmarnock 1967-69. C/o Bishop's House 1969-73. No further entries.

ROCHE, JOSEPH: See Dunkeld diocese.

ROCHE, STEPHEN: Ordained 1915. Largs 1952-53. Chaplain, Marist Brothers, Dumfries 1953-54. No further entries.

ROONEY, CHARLES: Born Kirkinner 1905. Educated Blairs 1920-24; Scots College, Rome 1924-31. Ordained Rome 1931. St Margaret's, Ayr 1931-32. Retired through illness 1932 and died Belfast 9 March 1938.

RYAN, EDMUND JOSEPH: Born and educated Ireland. Ordained Dumfries for Cashel 1886. Lent to Galloway diocese. St Joseph's, Kilmarnock 1886-89. Galston 1889-94. Resumed his vocation in Ireland 1894 and died there 6 July 1943. (Canning)

RYAN, PETER: See Dunkeld diocese.

RYNN, MICHAEL: See Glasgow Archdiocese.

SCANLAN, EDWARD: Born Auchinleck 1907. Educated Blairs 1924-27; Valladolid 1927-34; St Patrick's College, Thurles 1934. Ordained Thurles 1934. St Andrew's, Dumfries 1934-35. Annan 1935-37. St Margaret's, Ayr 1937-38. Newton Stewart 1938-40. Hurlford 1940-53. St Michael's, Kilmarnock 1953-58. Died Irvine 19 Feb 1958.

SHAFFREY, PATRICK: Ordained 1881. St Joseph's, Kilmarnock 1893-95. No further entries. (But see p 134)

SHEEHY, JOHN: Born Airdrie 1859. Educated Blairs 1871-77; Douay 1877-78; Issy 1878; Scots College, Rome 1878-84. Ordained Rome 1884. Girvan 1884-85. St Margaret's, Ayr 1885-87. St Andrew's, Dumfries 1887-88. Kirkcudbright 1888-1903. St Joseph's, Kilmarnock 1903-37. Died Kilmarnock 20 Dec 1937.

SMITH (Smythe) JOHN: Ordained 1896. St Andrew's, Dumfries 1896-99. No further entries.

STUART, HAMISH: See Dunkeld diocese.

TERRY, JOSEPH: See Argyll diocese.

THOMPSON, GEORGE: Born Garrochburn 1928. Educated Kirkcudbright Academy; Scots College, Rome. Left without completing studies; worked in Forestry Commission. Continued education Edinburgh University, Moray House. Career in teaching. Educated for priesthood St John's Seminary, Wonersh, Surrey. Ordained Dumfries 1989. St Teresa's, Dumfries 1989-.

TOAL, JAMES A: Ordained 1965. Gretna 1977-79. No further entries.

TOSH, ALISTAIR GRANT: Born Dumfries 1939. Educated St Joseph's College, Dumfries; Blairs; Drygrange. Ordained Dumfries 1963. Our Lady of Mount Carmel, Kilmarnock 1963-68. Ardrossan 1968-74. Dalry 1974-76. Lockerbie 1976-81. Waterside 1981-85. Kilbirnie 1985-.

TRAINOR, WILLIAM J J: Born Dumfries 1880. Educated Blairs 1893-98; Issy 1898-1900; St Sulpice 1900-03. Ordained Glasgow 1903. St Margaret's, Ayr 1903-04. Lent to Glasgow Archdiocese: St Patrick's, Glasgow 1904-07. Birnieknowe 1907-08. Troon 1908-09. St Joseph's, Kilmarnock 1909-15. Annan 1915-19. Died Annan 19 Aug 1919 following a motor cycle accident.

TULLY, EDWARD: Born and educated Ireland. Ordained Maynooth 1941. Lent to Galloway diocese. St Andrew's, Dumfries 1942-48. Resumed his vocation in Ireland 1948. (Canning)

VAUGHAN, KIERAN S: Ordained 1957. St Andrew's, Dumfries 1971-73. No further entries.

VIGNOLES, REGINALD: Born and educated Ireland. Joined Praemonstratensians. Ordained 1886. Served in Ireland, London, Whithorn. Left Praemonstratensians 1896. Continued in Galloway as secular priest. Craigeach 1896-97. Newton Stewart 1897-1900. Craigeach 1900-08. Galston 1908-09. Newton Stewart 1909-18. Auchinleck 1918-30. No address given 1930-31. Newton Stewart 1931-32. Castle Douglas 1932-38. Died Castle Douglas 17 Nov 1938. (Canning)

WALKER, VINCENT: Born Glasgow 1917. Educated Blairs 1930-35; St Peter's 1935-36; Le Grand Seminaire, Coutances 1936-39; St Patrick's College, Thurles 1939-41. Ordained Dumfries 1941. St Margaret's, Ayr 1941-43. Forces chaplain 1943-48. Chaplain, St Joseph's College, Dumfries 1948-50. Annan 1950-54. St Mary's, Irvine 1954-66. Prestwick 1966-88. Retired 1988.

WALLS, JOHN. Born Ayr 1937. Educated Blairs, Valladolid. Ordained Valladolid 1961. Continuing studies, Rome 1961-63. Ardrossan 1963-68. Good Shepherd Cathedral, Ayr 1968-70. Vice-rector, Valladolid 1970-74. Rector, Valladolid 1974-81. Hurlford 1981-88. Stevenston 1988-.

WALSH (Walshe), JOHN: Born and educated Ireland. Ordained Kilkenny for Galloway 1950. St Mary's, Irvine 1950. Prestwick 1950-51. St Mary's, Irvine 1951-62. New Cumnock 1962-66. Dalbeattie 1966-72. St Teresa's, Dumfries 1972-82. St Michael's, Kilmarnock 1982-. (Canning)

WHEELER, WILLIAM: Ordained 1936. St Andrew's, Dumfries 1937-38. St Margaret's, Ayr 1938-39. Forces chaplain 1939-41. In Ireland 1941-45. Lent to Archdiocese of St A & E: Linlithgow 1945; St Margaret Mary's, Edinburgh 1945-47. Went to Canada 1947.

WHITE, ANTHONY: Born and educated Ireland. Ordained Kilkenny for Galloway 1958. St Mary's, Saltcoats 1958-64. Laicised 1965. (Canning)

WILSON, ALAN JOHN: Born Dumfries 1953. Educated Langbank, Blairs, Valladolid. Ordained Dumfries 1977. St Margaret's, Ayr 1977. Good Shepherd Cathedral, Ayr 1977-78. St Joseph's, Kilmarnock 1978-80. Stevenston 1980-86. Mossblown 1986-89. RAF chaplain 1989-.

WOODS, JOHN: Born Dalbeattie 1855. Educated Blairs 1868-72; Valladolid 1872-79. Ordained Dumfries 1879. St Joseph's, Kilmarnock 1879-82. Newton Stewart 1882-88. St Mary's, Irvine 1888-97. St Joseph's, Kilmarnock 1897-1903. Rector, Valladolid 1903-09. Maybole 1909-15. St Margaret's, Ayr 1915-32. Died while on holiday in Ireland 8 Jan 1932.

WRIGHTSON, ARTHUR: Born Ireland. Educated Ireland; Scots College, Rome. Ordained Dublin 1915. Annan 1915-18. St Margaret's, Ayr 1918-20. Cumnock 1920-21. St Andrew's, Dumfries 1921-25. Gretna 1925-28. Waterside 1928-31. Castle Douglas 1931-32. Gretna 1932-35. On "retired" list from 1936. (Canning)

YOUNG, PATRICK: Born and educated Ireland. Ordained Maynooth 1938. Lent to Galloway diocese. St Andrew's, Dumfries 1938-40. St Joseph's, Kilmarnock 1940-52. Resumed his vocation in Ireland 1952. (Canning)

Parishes

BISHOPS: 1878-93 John McLachlan (WD). 1893-1914 William Turner (ED). 1914-43 James McCarthy (Glasgow). 1943-52 William Mellon (St A & E). 1952-81 Joseph McGee (Dunkeld). 1981- Maurice Taylor (Motherwell).
Coadjutor Bishop: 1935-43 William Mellon (St A & E).

ANNAN
Heads: 1880-81 John Dunne (WD). 1881-85 David MacCartney (ED). 1885-86 vacant. 1886-93 Lord Archibald Douglas. 1893-95 Daniel Heaphy. 1895-98 Daniel Keogh. 1898-99 William Casey. 1899-1906 Lord Archibald Douglas. 1906-15 Michael Carey. 1915-19 William J J Trainor. 1919-31 Robert Carmont. 1931-39 Hugh Mimnagh. 1939-40 Thomas Cummins. 1940-49 Joseph Kerr. 1949-50 Stephen Kennedy. 1950-54 Vincent Walker. 1954-57 John Quinn. 1957-59 Benedict O'Gorman. 1959-71 served by Praemonstratensians. 1971-78 John Murphy. 1978-89 Daniel Hainey. 1989- William Boyd.
Assistants: 1915-18 Arthur Wrightson. 1916-21 Patrick Mulholland. 1934-37 Edward Scanlan. 1937-39 Joseph Kerr. 1939-40 Denis McCarthy. 1940-41 William McKnight. 1941-47 Stephen Kennedy. 1947-50 Michael Leen. 1950-51 Joseph Oxley. 1951-55 James Grogan. 1955-57 Benedict O'Gorman.

ANNBANK (Mossblown)
Before 1898 served from Ayr.
Heads: 1898-99 John MacDonald (1875) (WD). 1899-1947 John M A Cameron (1894). 1947-50 John N Murphy (1903). 1950-55 Joseph Maxwell. 1955-58 Francis Duffy. 1958-61 Daniel Brennan. 1961-73 Thomas A Kelly (Dunkeld). 1973-86 George McCafferty. 1986-89 Alan Wilson. 1989- Alexander McGarry.
Assistants: 1949-50 James Coyle. 1987-89 Daniel Doherty. 1989- Gerard Magee.

ARDROSSAN: Glasgow Archdiocese until 1948.
Heads: 1945-50 Archibald McSparran. 1950-51 Peter Fitzpatrick. 1951-52 vacant. 1952-53 William McBurnie. 1953-80 Lawrence Fischer. 1980- Michael Lynch.
Assistants: 1946-50 Matthew Littleton. 1949-53 James O'Sullivan. 1953-62 Charles Matthews. 1962-63 John Murphy (1954). 1963-68 John Walls. 1968-74 Alistair Tosh. 1974-80 Declan Kelly. 1981-82 Joseph Glendinning. 1983-86 John McCaig. 1986-88 Paul O'Brien, O Carm.

AUCHINLECK (Birnieknowe)
Heads: 1880-81 Patrick Wright (1872) (WD). 1881-83 John O'Neil (WD). 1883-89 Patrick Murphy. 1889-93 Michael Hickey. 1893-1908 John O'Neill (WD). 1908-18 Joseph Hogan. 1918-30 Reginald Vignoles. 1930-36 Martin Doyle. 1936-50 Joseph Maxwell. 1950-53 Matthew Littleton. 1953-61 Michael Rynn. 1961-70 Daniel Brennan. 1970-75 Sean Murphy. 1975-77 James Coyle. 1977-85 John Kane. 1985- Thomas J Murphy.
Assistants: 1882-83 Henry Laverty. 1903-04 Robert Carmont. 1904-06 Michael Carey. 1906-07 John O'Hanlon. 1907-08 William J J Trainor. 1908-09 John Murphy (1908). 1909-11 Thomas Joyce. 1911-15 Robert Carmont. 1915-26 Frederick Letters (WD). 1926-28 Hugh Mimnagh. 1947-49 Nicholas Murphy. 1949-53 James Manning. 1953-56 James Bannon. 1956-59 Michael Lynch. 1959-62 Francis Crowley.

AYR – GOOD SHEPHERD CATHEDRAL
Heads: 1957-70 Myles Moriarty. 1970-72 James Grogan. 1972-81 Francis Duffy. 1981- John Donnelly.
Assistants: 1957-59 James Grogan. 1959-62 John Harkin. 1962-68 Francis Moore. 1968-70 John Walls. 1971-74 Thomas Leverage. 1974-77 Alexander McGarry WF. 1977-78 Alan Wilson. 1978-83 William Murray. 1983-87 Martin Poland.

AYR – ST MARGARET'S
Heads: 1871-90 Patrick McLaughlin (WD). 1890-94 William O'Shaughnessy (WD). 1894-95 Robert Donworth. 1895-1915 Daniel Collins. 1915-32 John Woods. 1932-65 Joseph McHardy. 1965-77 Stephen Kennedy. 1977- Martin McCluskey.
Assistants: 1877-80 Frederick Letters (WD). 1880-81 Edward Morris (WD). 1881-82 Michael Cunningham. 1882-85 Edward Heelan. 1885-87 John Sheehy. 1887-88 Thomas Cummins (WD). 1888-89 Joseph Hogan. 1889-90 Patrick Devany. 1890-91 William O'Dwyer. 1891-93 Michael O'Carroll. 1893-94 Robert Donworth. 1893-95 Robert Carmont. 1895-96 Michael McRedmond. 1896-97 Frederick McClymont (Argyll). 1896-97 William Casey. 1897-98 John MacDonald (1875) (WD). 1899-1901 Patrick McDaniel. 1901-03 Martin Meagher. 1901-07 William Bohan. 1903-04 William J Trainor. 1907-17 Charles O'Malley. 1915-19 Robert Carmont. 1918-20 Arthur Wrightson. 1919-22 John Murphy (1908). 1920-27 Dermot O'Reilly. 1922-26 Hugh Mimnagh. 1926-27 Alphonsus Power (Dunkeld). 1927-28 John Hughes. 1928-35 Francis Meaney. 1927-31 William McBurnie. 1931-32 Charles Rooney. 1932-37 George McCafferty. 1935-41 Myles Moriarty. 1937 Hamish Stuart (Dunkeld). 1937-38 Edward Scanlan. 1938-39 William Wheeler. 1938-41 Francis Duffy. 1941-43 Vincent Walker. 1941-52 William McBride. 1943-53 Thomas Murphy. 1952-65 Nicholas Murphy. 1953-55 Benedict O'Gorman. 1955-56 Michael Lynch. 1955-57 James Grogan. 1956-61 Francis McHugh. 1957-58 Thomas McCann. 1959-65 Martin McCluskey.

1961-66 Patrick McCabe. 1965-77 Matthew McManus. 1966-67 Francis Ommer. 1966-68 John McNamara. 1967-68 Eamonn Flynn. 1968-70 Daniel Hainey. 1977 Alan Wilson. 1977-82 Patrick Keegans. 1982-83 Joseph Glendinning. 1983-86 James Bannon. 1983-89 Myles Moriarty. 1989- Paul O'Brien, O Carm.

AYR – ST PAUL'S
Heads: 1967-81 Francis Kiernan. 1981-88 John Connolly. 1988- Joseph V Boyd.
Assistants: 1967-71 Thomas Leverage. 1971-74 John McGee. 1988- Robert Hanlon.

BARRHILL – ST JOSEPH'S CONVENT: CHAPLAINS
1960-65 Daniel Lucey.

BEITH: Glasgow Archdiocese until 1948.
1947-61 Thomas A Kelly (Dunkeld). 1961-66 Michael Rynn. 1966-70 James Grogan. 1970-74 Daniel Brennan. 1974-77 John J Connolly. 1977-88 Alexander McGarry. 1988-89 John McGee. 1989- John Kerr.

BIRNIEKNOWE: see Auchinleck

CASTLE DOUGLAS
Heads: 1871-81 David McCartney (ED). 1881-88 Daniel W O'Brien. 1888-1931 John Duffy. 1931-32 Arthur Wrightson. 1932-38 Reginald Vignoles. 1938-44 Martin Doyle. 1944-50 George McCafferty. 1950-54 Stephen Kennedy. 1954-58 Daniel Brennan. 1958-65 James Manning. 1965-72 John Crowley. 1972-80 John Leen. 1980-88 John Joseph Harkin.
Assistant: 1933-36 Joseph Maxwell.
From 1988 served from Kirkcudbright.

CATRINE: 1960-64 Benedict O'Gorman. 1964-67 Joseph Oxley. 1967-70 Thomas J McGreed. 1970-81 Charles Matthews. 1981- John Flannery.

CRAIGEACH: 1896-97 Reginald Vignoles. 1897-98 William F Casey. 1898-99 Thomas Joyce. 1899-1900 served from Newton Stewart. 1900-08 Reginald Vignoles. No further mention.

CUMNOCK
Heads: 1874-81 Patrick Wright (WD). 1881-82 vacant. 1882-85 Daniel Collins. 1885-89 John Hourigan. 1889-90 Henry Laverty. 1890-98 Charles O'Malley. 1898-1903 Daniel Keogh. 1903-07 Henry Langley. 1907-36 Martin Meagher. 1936-38 Martin Doyle. 1938-39 vacant. 1939-50 Hugh Mimnagh. 1950-65 George McCafferty. 1965-70 Nicholas Murphy. 1970-76 Thomas McGread. 1976- Francis Ommer.
Assistants: 1912-15 William O'Connor. 1915-16 John McGilligan. 1916-18

Dermot O'Reilly. 1918-20 Martin Doyle. 1920-21 Arthur Wrightson. 1920-22 John O'Sullivan. 1921-22 Hugh Mimnagh. 1922-25 William McBurnie. 1960-62 Kenneth McLaughlan. 1962-63 James McHugh. 1966-70 Patrick McCabe. 1970-71 John McGee. 1971-72 John McNamara. 1972-76 John Kinsler.

DALBEATTIE: 1857-80 Alexander Gordon (ED). 1880-82 Patrick Agnew (ED). 1882-83 Patrick Murphy. 1883-85 John Lee. 1885-98 David McCartney (ED). 1898-1907 Charles O'Malley. 1907-31 Henry Langley. 1931-36 Robert Carmont. 1936-37 vacant. 1937-38 Dermot O'Reilly. 1938-47 John N Murphy (1903). 1947-49 Stephen Kennedy. 1949-52 Martin Doyle. 1952-53 William McBride. 1953-60 Thomas J Murphy. 1960-66 John Flannery. 1966-72 John Walsh. 1972-76 Ralph Mancini. 1976- Thomas Conway.

DALMELLINGTON: 1862-79 Hugh Gallagher (WD). 1879-80 William Dawson (1876) (ND). 1880-88 Frederick Letters (WD). 1888-91 Daniel Kerrin. 1891-95 John Fouhy. From 1895 occasionally served from Waterside.

DALRY: Glasgow Archdiocese until 1948.
1947-60 Joseph Duffy. 1960-64 Thomas J Murphy. 1964-67 John Kane. 1967-68 Joseph Oxley. 1968-74 Francis Crowley. 1974-76 Alistair Tosh. 1976-77 James McHugh. 1977-88 Eamonn Flynn. 1988- Thomas McGread.

DUMFRIES – ST ANDREW'S (Cathedral until 1962)
Heads: 1877-93 William Turner (ED). 1893-1936 Daniel O'Brien. 1936-44 Bishop William Mellon. 1944-62 John W O'Sullivan. 1962-76 Thomas Conway. 1976- Ralph Mancini.
Assistants: 1876-80 Patrick Agnew (WD). 1877-79 John Quinn (WD). 1880-87 Richard Mullins. 1884-85 Michael Hickey. 1885-87 John Lee. 1887-88 John Sheehy. 1888-93 Daniel O'Brien. 1893-95 John Brady. 1894 John Cameron (1894). 1895-96 William Casey. 1896-99 John Smith. 1897 Thomas Joyce. 1898-99 Richard Mullins. 1899-1900 Joseph Roche (Dunkeld). 1899-1901 Michael Hannan. 1900-14 Richard Mullins. 1901-03 Thomas Hayes. 1903-09 John N Murphy (1903). 1909-17 John Murphy (1908). 1914-18 Martin Doyle. 1918-20 Richard Mullins. 1918-20 Francis Meaney. 1918-31 Samuel Heffron. 1920-21 Hugh Mimnagh. 1921-25 Arthur Wrightson. 1925-44 John O'Sullivan. 1931-33 Joseph Maxwell. 1933-36 Lawrence Breen. 1934-35 Edward Scanlan. 1936-37 Samuel Heffron. 1936-37 Hamish Stuart (Dunkeld). 1937-38 James Connolly. 1937-38 William Wheeler. 1938-39 Thomas Cummins. 1938-40 Patrick Young. 1939-40 Joseph Kerr. 1940-41 Edward Fitzsimmons. 1940-44 Peter Ryan. 1942-47 John Leen. 1942-48 Edward Tully. 1944-53 Thomas Conway. 1945-47 Nicholas Murphy. 1948-58 John Flannery. 1950-51 James Grogan. 1950-51 Charles McLaughhlin. 1951-52 James

Bannon. 1952-55 Thomas McGread. 1953-54 Henry J McDermott. 1954-60 Ralph Mancini. 1955-63 Charles McKinley (Glasgow). 1958-62 John Murphy (1954). 1960-62 Francis P Moore. 1962-71 John Harkin. 1963-64 Thomas Leverage. 1964-69 Don Redden. 1969-70 Joseph Boland. 1971-73 Kieran S Vaughan. 1971-77 Patrick Keegans. 1973-77 Michael Farrington. 1977-80 John Brown. 1980-85 Stephen Bradley. 1985-89 William Boyd. 1986-87 Daniel Doherty. 1989- William McFadden.

DUMFRIES – ST TERESA'S
Heads: 1958-72 Francis Duffy. 1972-82 John Walsh. 1982-85 Samuel McGinnes (Glasgow). 1985- Patrick McSorley.
Assistants: 1958-72 Denis Quinlan. 1959-62 James McHugh. 1962-72 Thomas McCann. 1972-75 Archibald Brown. 1974-75 Stanislaus Harbison. 1975-78 William Murray. 1977-79 John Kinsler. 1978-79 John Quinn. 1979-80 Michael Reddan SDS. 1982-84 Peter Magee. 1985-87 Douglas Hutchison. 1987-89 John McLean. 1989- George Thompson.

DUMFRIES – MARIST BROTHERS: CHAPLAINS
St Joseph's College: 1899-1900 Richard F Mullins. 1948-50 Vincent Walker. 1950-58 James Coyle. 1958-76 Henry J McDermott. 1979-85 Patrick G Fitzpatrick (Glasgow).
Juniorate: 1953-54 Stephen Roche.

DUMFRIES – BENEDICTINE CONVENT: CHAPLAINS
1914-18 Richard Mullins. 1951-58 Daniel Lucey. 1981-82 John M A Kerr.

GALSTON
Until 1888 served from Hurlford.
Heads: 1888-89 Henry Laverty. 1889-94 Edmund Joseph Ryan. 1894-96 William J O'Shaughnessy (WD). 1896-97 vacant. 1897-99 David Barrett. 1899-1908 Joseph Hogan. 1908-09 Lord Archibald Douglas. 1909-22 Leo Puissant. 1922-37 John Murphy (1908). 1937-40 William J McBurnie. 1940-52 William J O'Connor. 1952-56 Martin Doyle. 1956-59 Denis McCarthy. 1959-65 Patrick Gunning. 1965-80 James Manning. 1980-85 John Leen. 1985-89 John Kane. 1989- John A McGee.
Assistants: 1908-1909 Reginald Vignoles. 1910-13 Thomas Finnegan. 1954-56 John Donnelly.

GIRVAN
Heads: 1872-90 William J O'Shaughnessy (WD). 1890-91 John A O'Neill. 1891-92 Daniel Kerrin. 1892-93 John Cameron (1887) (Glasgow). 1893-96 David Barrett. 1896-97 William J O'Shaughnessy (WD). 1897-1903 Henry Langley. 1903-07 Martin Meagher. 1907-09 William Bohan. 1909-20 Lord Archibald Douglas. 1920-31 Richard Mullins. 1931-54 Anthony O'Connell. 1954-74 Joseph Kerr. 1974-82 Francis Crowley. 1982- Eugene Mathews.
Assistants: 1878-80 John Dunne (WD). 1880-82 Patrick Murphy. 1882

Daniel Collins. 1882-84 Patrick Wright. 1883-84 William English. 1884-85 John Sheehy. 1887-88 John Duffy. 1888-89 Daniel McAlister. 1889-90 Joseph Hogan. 1927-31 Anthony O'Connell. 1942-45 Patrick Hennessy. 1946-49 John J Quinn (1945). 1949-50 John Donnelly. 1950-54 Cornelius Burke. 1955-59 Laurence O'Sullivan. 1960 Michael Conway. 1968-71 John McNamara. 1971-74 Declan Kelly.

GRETNA: 1918-19 Patrick Mulholland, chaplain to Association of Sacred Heart, living in Gretna, serving Annan. 1925-28 Arthur Wrightson. 1928-32 Dermot O'Reilly. 1932-35 Arthur Wrightson. 1935-39 vacant. 1939-60 served from Annan. 1960-71 Stanislaus Harbison. 1971-77 John J Harkin. 1977-79 James A Toal. 1979- John Kinsler.

HURLFORD: 1883-88 Henry Laverty. 1888-1913 served from Galston. 1913-35 Thomas Finnegan. 1935-38 Francis Meaney. 1938-40 Patrick J MacDermott. 1940-53 Edward Scanlan. 1953 Sean Murphy. 1953-64 John Leen. 1964-81 John Donnelly. 1981-88 John Walls. 1988- Thomas Leverage.

IRVINE – ST MARGARET'S: 1975-88 Francis P G Moore. 1988- Eamonn Flynn.

IRVINE – ST MARY'S
Heads: 1870-79 Thomas Keane (WD). 1879-80 Henry Murphy. 1880-88 Ambrose Graham CSSP. 1888-97 John Woods. 1897-1911 Frederick Letters (WD). 1911-18 Thomas Joyce. 1918-36 Joseph Hogan. 1936-37 Martin Meagher. 1937-38 vacant. 1938-50 Dermot O'Reilly. 1950-55 John N Murphy (1903). 1955-66 Vincent Walker. 1966-85 Thomas Murphy. 1985- Samuel McGinness (Glasgow).
Assistants: 1918-20 Dermot O'Reilly. 1920-26 Martin Doyle. 1926-27 John Hughes. 1927-28 Dermot O'Reilly. 1928-36 John N Murphy (1903). 1936-38 Lawrence Breen. 1938-40 Peter Cullerton (Dunkeld). 1940-41 Hugh Brady (St A & E). 1941-43 Hugh Mulvenna. 1943-46 Patrick Gunning. 1946-49 James Manning. 1949-50 John J Quinn (1945). 1950 John Walsh. 1950-51 Michael Leen. 1951-62 John Walsh. 1953-54 John Donnelly. 1954-55 Vincent Walker. 1962-65 Kenneth McLaughlan. 1965-67 John Kinsler. 1967-69 Henry McFarlane. 1967-71 James McHugh. 1969-70 Declan Kelly. 1970-74 John Connolly. 1971-75 Francis Moore. 1974-80 Stephen Bradley. 1980-81 John Brown. 1981 Peter Magee. 1981-84 Edward McGhee.

KILBIRNIE: Glasgow Archdiocese until 1948.
Heads: 1948-50 Peter Fitzpatrick. 1950-67 Dermot O'Reilly. 1967-73 Eugene Mathews. 1973-81 John Flannery. 1981-85 Charles McLaughlin. 1985- Alistair Tosh.
Assistants: 1948-59 Francis Kiernan. 1959-62 James Grogan. 1962-67 Thomas J McGread. 1967-70 John J Connolly. 1970-77 John Bradley WF. 1984-85 Edward McGhee.

KILMARNOCK – OUR LADY OF MOUNT CARMEL: 1963-71 Peter Ryan.
Assistants: 1963-68 Alistair Tosh. 1966-67 John Connolly. 1968-71
Francis P Moore. 1970-71 Patrick Keegans.
From 1971 served by Praemonstratensians.

KILMARNOCK – ST JOSEPH'S
Heads: 1878-97 David Power (WD). 1897-1903 John Woods. 1903-37 John
Sheehy. 1937-38 vacant. 1938-51 Michael Carey. 1951-52 vacant. 1952-
53 William O'Connor. 1953-77 Matthew Littleton. 1977- Denis Quinlan.
Assistants: 1879-82 John Woods. 1882-83 John Lee. 1883-85 John
Hourigan. 1885-86 Michael Hickey. 1886-89 Edmund Ryan. 1889-91
John Fouhy. 1890-91 Patrick Devany. 1891-93 David Barrett. 1891-93
Patrick English. 1893-94 Henry Langley. 1893-95 Patrick Shaffrey.
1894-97 John M A Cameron (1894). 1897-98 Thomas Joyce. 1898-99
James Jennings. 1899-1901 Cornelius Callanan. 1901-03 Henry Clarke.
1901-04 Michael Carey. 1903-08 Thomas Finnegan. 1904-11 Robert
Carmont. 1909-15 William J J Trainor. 1911-17 James Donnelly. 1915-
22 William O'Connor. 1918-31 Patrick J McDermott. 1920 John
O'Sullivan. 1922-25 John O'Sullivan. 1925-27 William McBurnie. 1927-
28 Alphonsus Power (Dunkeld). 1928-31 Hugh Mimnagh. 1931-33
William McBurnie. 1931-37 Lawrence Fischer. 1933-35 Patrick J
McDermott. 1935-38 Thomas Cummins. 1937-38 Peter Cullerton
(Dunkeld). 1938-39 James Connolly. 1938-40 Edward Fitzsimmons.
1938-41 Patrick Hennessy. 1939-40 William McKnight. 1940-45 Denis
McCarthy. 1940-52 Patrick Young. 1941-43 T Flahive. 1943-53 Philip
Brady. 1945-46 James Manning. 1946-49 John Donnolly. 1949-52
Daniel Brennan. 1952-53 Charles Matthews. 1952-57 John Kane. 1953-
54 John Quinn (1945). 1954-58 John Murphy (1954). 1955-62 Thomas
McGread. 1958-59 Malachy Kiernan CRP. 1958-63 Charles McLaughlin.
1959 Stanislaus Harbison. 1959-60 Benedict O'Gorman. 1960-62 Ralph
Mancini. 1962-63 Francis Crowley. 1962-74 Patrick McSorley. 1963-67
Francis McHugh. 1967-69 John Kinsler. 1969-77 Samuel McGinness
(Glasgow). 1972 Edward McGhee. 1974-78 Daniel Hainey. 1978-80 Alan
Wilson. 1979-81 Don Redden. 1980-82 Michael Farrington. 1982-83
Martin Poland. 1983-85 Archibald Brown. 1989- Peter Arnold.

KILMARNOCK – ST MATTHEW'S: 1974-85 Patrick J McSorley. 1985-
Joseph Boland.

KILMARNOCK – ST MICHAEL'S
Heads: 1953-58 Edward Scanlan. 1958-65 Stephen Kennedy. 1965-73
George McCafferty. 1973-82 Eugene Mathews. 1982- John Walsh.
Assistants: 1956-57 Francis Crowley. 1957-67 Joseph Boyd. 1967-69
Robert Reid. 1970-73 Daniel Hainey. 1974-75 William Murray. 1975-80
Joseph Boland.

KILWINNING: Glasgow Archdiocese until 1948.

Heads: 1948-63 Peter Ryan (Dunkeld). 1963-72 Cornelius Burke. 1972-81 Charles McLaughlin. 1981-88 John Crowley. 1988- Matthew McManus.

Assistants: 1966-67 Eamonn Flynn. 1968-69 Eamonn Flynn. 1973 Stephen Bradley. 1974-77 Patrick McCabe. 1980-81 Joseph Glendinning. 1987- Douglas Hutchison.

KIRKCONNEL

Heads: 1922-32 William J O'Connor. 1932-37 Dermot O'Reilly. 1937-44 George McCafferty. 1944-48 Peter Ryan (Dunkeld). 1948-53 Michael Rynn. 1953-56 Philip Brady. 1956-63 Eugene Mathews. 1963-71 John Murphy (1954). 1971-73 Joseph Boyd. 1973-76 Francis Ommer. 1976-77 John Kinsler. 1977-80 Matthew McManus. 1980-85 Joseph Boland. 1985-86 Patrick McSorley.

Assistant: 1958-62 Thomas McCann.

From 1986 served from St Teresa's, Dumfries.

KIRKCUDBRIGHT

Until 1888 served from Castle Douglas.

Heads: 1888-1903 John Sheehy. 1903-05 Michael Hannan. 1905-32 Joseph McHardy. 1932-38 Michael Carey. 1938-40 William J O'Connor. 1940-52 William J McBurnie. 1952-56 Denis McCarthy. 1956-64 John Donnelly. 1964-80 Michael Lynch. 1980-88 Matthew McManus. 1988- Michael Farrington.

Assistants: 1916-17 Joseph Cottet (Marist). 1943-44 Thomas Conway. 1944-45 Edward Fitzsimmons. 1949-50 John Hammill (Glasgow). 1952-53 James Bannon.

LANGHOLM: Until 1960 served from Annan. 1960-72 served by Praemonstratensians. 1972- Thomas McCann.

LARGS: Glasgow Archdiocese until 1948.

Heads: 1944-77 Clement McGowan. 1977-88 Joseph Boyd. 1988- John Crowley.

Assistants: 1948-52 Charles McGrath. 1952-53 Stephen Roche. 1954-58 Henry J McDermott. 1958-60 Daniel Lucey. 1960-63 Thomas Leverage. 1964-66 Patrick Green. 1966-67 Kenneth McLaughlan. 1970-71 Terence Smyth, O Praem. 1971-72 Thomas Brady, O Praem. 1972-77 John Brown.

LOCKERBIE: Until 1960 served from Annan. 1960-71 served by Praemonstratensians. 1971-76 James McHugh. 1976-81 Alistair Tosh. 1981-82 Stanislaus Harbison. 1982-87 John Kerr. 1987- Patrick Keegans.

MAYBOLE: Until 1887 served from Girvan. 1887-88 Daniel McAlister. 1888-90 served from Girvan. 1890-99 Joseph Hogan. 1899-1901 John

MacDonald (1875) (WD). 1901-09 Patrick McDaniel. 1909-15 John Woods. 1915-32 Michael Carey. 1932-37 William J O'Connor. 1937-44 Lawrence Fischer. 1944-63 Francis Meaney. 1963-67 Eugene Mathews. 1967-70 John Kane. 1970-83 Myles Moriarty. 1983-85 Stephen Kennedy. 1985- Archibald Brown.

MILLPORT, ISLE OF CUMBRAE: Glasgow Archdiocese until 1948.
1948-59 Patrick Gunning. 1959-67 Francis Kiernan. 1967-71 Joseph Boyd. 1971 Peter Ryan (Dunkeld). 1971-74 William Colliston SJ. 1974-75 vacant. 1975-81 Stanislaus Harbison. 1981-87 Charles Matthews. 1987- John Collins (Glasgow).

MOFFAT: Until 1945 served from Annan. 1945-46 Pius Campbell CP. 1946-48 Patrick Gunning. 1948-53 Alexander Fyfe. 1953-57 served from Dumfries. 1957-60 served from Annan. From 1960 served from Lockerbie.

MOSSBLOWN: see Annbank

MUIRKIRK: 1875-79 Henry Murphy (WD). 1879-81 John Higgins. 1881-83 vacant. 1883-89 John O'Neill (WD). 1889-91 Daniel McAlister. 1891 Patrick English. 1891-93 John O'Neill (WD). 1893-94 John Hickson. 1894-97 Henry Langley. 1897-1909 Leo Puissant. 1909-18 William Bohan. 1918-40 Thomas Joyce. 1940-41 vacant. 1941-53 Myles Moriarty. 1953-62 Thomas Conway. 1962-70 Charles Matthews. 1970-75 James Coyle. 1975-80 John Kerr. 1980-85 Declan Kelly. 1985-89 Stephen Bradley. 1989- John McLean.

NEW ABBEY: 1864-96 William Downie (ED). 1896-97 vacant. 1897 Leo Puissant. 1897-98 Richard Mullins. 1898-1939 Barrington Douglas Dick. 1939-44 served from Dumfries. 1944-52 William Bohan. 1952-61 Joseph Oxley. 1961-70 served from Dumfries. 1970-73 Robert Catterall. From 1973 served from Dumfries.

NEW CUMNOCK: Until 1962 served from Kirkconnel. 1962-1966 John Walsh. 1966-76 served from Cumnock. 1976-85 served from Kirkconnel. From 1985 served from Cumnock.

NEWTON STEWART
Heads: 1876-81 John O'Neill (WD). 1881-82 Patrick Wright (WD). 1882-88 John Woods. 1888-97 Frederick Letters (WD). 1897-1900 Reginald Vignoles. 1900-09 Joseph Roche (Dunkeld). 1909-18 Reginald Vignoles. 1918-27 William Bohan. 1927-30 Martin Doyle. 1930-31 vacant. 1931-32 Reginald Vignoles. 1932-36 Samuel Heffron. 1936-38 John N Murphy (1903). 1938 Lawrence Breen. 1938-40 Edward Scanlan. 1940-47 Patrick J McDermott. 1947-53 John Leen. 1953-58 James Manning.

1958-62 Sean Murphy. 1962-72 Ralph Mancini. 1972-77 Martin McCluskey. 1977-83 Stephen Kennedy. 1983-88 Joseph Glendinning.
Assistant: 1899-1900 Louis Fortemps.
From 1988 served from Whithorn.

OLD CUMNOCK: see Cumnock

PRESTWICK
Heads: 1938-64 Lawrence Breen. 1964-66 Thomas Murphy. 1966-88 Vincent Walker. 1988- Francis P G Moore.
Assistants: 1950-51 John Walsh. 1960-64 Francis Ommer. 1964-65 John Crowley. 1965-66 Kenneth McLaughlan. 1966-75 John Kerr.

SALTCOATS – OUR LADY STAR OF THE SEA: Glasgow Archdiocese until 1948.
Heads: 1939-66 Michael O'Connor. 1966-70 James Coyle. 1970-89 Nicholas Murphy. 1989- Stephen G Bradley.
Assistants: 1942-49 Daniel Brennan. 1947-50 Cornelius Burke. 1949-56 Eugene Mathews. 1950-53 John Donnelly. 1953-58 Sean Murphy. 1956-60 John Crowley. 1958-64 Anthony White. 1960-64 Michael Lynch. 1964-65 John Kerr. 1964-66 Francis Ommer. 1965-72 Martin McCluskey. 1972-80 Edward McGhee. 1979-80 John Quinn (1959). 1982-83 Joseph Terry (Argyll). 1983-88 Robert Hanlon. 1988-89 Paul O'Brien, O Carm.

SALTCOATS – ST BRENDAN'S
Heads: 1965-81 Patrick Gunning. 1981-88 Francis Kiernan. 1988- Edward McGhee.
Assistants: 1966-67 Robert Reid. 1970-71 Declan Kelly.

STEVENSTON: Glasgow Archdiocese until 1948.
Heads: 1943-50 John McQuillan. 1950-55 Hugh Mimnagh. 1955-76 Joseph Maxwell. 1976-88 Thomas McGread. 1988- John Walls.
Assistants: 1945-51 James Bannon. 1951-58 Charles McLaughlin. 1958-60 John Flannery. 1960-61 Michael Conway. 1961-64 Don Redden. 1964-67 Thomas Leverage. 1967-69 Charles Moran, MHM. 1969-77 Eamonn Flynn. 1977-80 Michael Farrington. 1980-86 Alan Wilson. 1986-89 William McFadden. 1989- Martin Chambers.

STRANRAER: 1868-79 John Canning (WD). 1879-85 Hugh Gallagher (WD). 1885-95 Daniel Collins. 1895-97 Richard Mullins. 1897-1926 David Power (WD). 1926-27 Martin Doyle. 1927-44 William Bohan. 1944-49 Martin Doyle. 1949-54 Joseph Kerr. 1954-58 Stephen Kennedy. 1958-66 James Coyle. 1966-73 John Flannery. 1973-77 Joseph Boyd. 1977-88 Thomas Leverage. 1988- John J Harkin.

TROON
Until 1895 served from Ayr.
Heads: 1895-1909 John Brady. 1909-50 Thomas Hayes. 1950-64 John
   McQuillan. 1964-72 John Leen. 1972-81 John Crowley. 1981- Francis
   Duffy.
Assistants: 1908-09 William J J Trainor. 1949-52 Nicholas Murphy. 1953
   Sean Murphy. 1960-64 John Crowley. 1967-73 Francis Ommer. 1973-74
   Alexander McGarry WF. 1984-85 William Boyd. 1986-87 John McCaig.

WATERSIDE
Heads: 1895-1903 Robert Carmont. 1903-09 Thomas Hayes. 1909-28 John
   N Murphy (1903). 1928-31 Arthur Wrightson. 1931-33 Patrick J
   McDermott. 1933-37 William McBurnie. 1937-38 William J O'Connor.
   1938-44 Francis Meaney. 1944-53 Lawrence Fischer. 1953-57 Myles
   Moriarty. 1957-62 John J Quinn (1945). 1962-70 Sean Murphy. 1970-
   77 John Kane. 1977-80 John J Harkin. 1980-81 John Kerr. 1981-85
   Alistair Tosh. 1985-88 Edward McGhee. 1988- Robert Hanlon.
Assistants: 1942-44 James Coyle. 1962-64 Joseph Oxley. 1970-72 John
   Kinsler.

WEST KILBRIDE: Glasgow Archdiocese until 1948.
1947-74 Michael O'Carroll. 1974-77 Thomas Leverage. 1977-81 John J
   Connolly. 1981-87 Patrick Gunning. 1987-89 John Kerr. 1989- Charles
   Matthews.

WHITHORN: Until 1945 served from Wigtown. 1945-52 Denis McCarthy.
   1952-54 Daniel Brennan. 1954-63 Cornelius Burke. 1963-72 Charles
   McLaughlin. 1972-77 Denis Quinlan. 1977-82 Samuel McGinness
   (Glasgow). 1982-87 Patrick Keegans. 1987- Martin Poland.

WIGTOWN: 1878-80 Alexander MacKintosh (WD). 1880-84 Alexander
   MacDonell (WD). 1884-86 William English. 1886-89 Michael Hickey.
   1889-96 served by Praemonstratensians. 1896-97 Thomas O'Farrell.
   1897-99 John M A Cameron (1894). 1899-1901 James B Jennings.
   1901-03 Michael Hannan. 1903-46 Henry Clarke. From 1946 served
   from Whithorn.

APPROVED SCHOOLS
St Austin's, Kirkconnel: 1954-56 Alexander Fyfe.
St Mungo's, Mauchline: see Glasgow Archdiocese.

Archdiocese of Glasgow

Secular Clergy

By 1948 the Archdiocese of Glasgow had grown to an unmanageable size. From part of it two new dioceses were created: Motherwell and Paisley; while Northern Ayrshire was transferred to Galloway diocese. The Archdiocese was thereby reduced to Greater Glasgow and Dumbartonshire. It became the metropolitan for Motherwell and Paisley. Priests originally ordained for Glasgow, if they were serving in the parishes affected by the 1948 rearrangement, found themselves attached to new dioceses. This is indicated in the following biographies.

AGNEW, THOMAS: Born and educated Ireland. Ordained Maynooth 1903. Lent to Glasgow. St Agnes', Glasgow 1903-05. Returned to Ireland 1905 and died there 16 May 1959. (Canning)

AHEARNE (Aherne), MICHAEL: Born and educated Ireland. Ordained Waterford 1917. Lent to Glasgow. St John the Baptist's, Uddingston 1918-22. Returned to Ireland 1922 and died there 26 Nov 1956. (Canning)

AHERN, JEREMIAH F: Born and educated Ireland. Ordained Maynooth 1925. Lent to Glasgow. St Joseph's, Tollcross 1925-26. Cambuslang 1926-28. Returned to Ireland 1928 and died there 28 May 1975. (Canning)

AHERN, MICHAEL: Born and educated Ireland. Ordained Maynooth 1896. Lent to Glasgow. Chaplain, Franciscan Convent, Bothwell 1896-97. Chaplain, Franciscan Convent, Glasgow 1897-99. Carfin 1899-1900. St Mirin's, Paisley 1900-03. Returned to Ireland 1903 and died there 9 June 1948. (Canning)

AHERN, WILLIAM: Born and educated Ireland. Ordained Killarney 1900. Lent to Glasgow. Immaculate Conception, Glasgow 1900-06. Returned to Ireland 1906 and died there 18 July 1919. (Canning)

AMBROSE, MYLES: Born and educated Ireland. Ordained for Glasgow 1897. St Mary's, Glasgow 1897-1905. Longriggend 1905-15. Died Longriggend 19 Dec 1915. (Canning)

ANGLAND, JOHN: Born 1856. Ordained 1880. St Mary's, Greenock 1881-83. St Patrick's, Glasgow 1883-86. Houston 1886-91. Chaplain, West Thorn Reformatory, Dalbeth 1891-96. Belgium 1896-1919. Chaplain, West Thorn Reformatory and Good Shepherd Convent, Dalbeth 1919-20. Died Glasgow 17 July 1920.

ASHE, JOHN: Born Ryepatch, Nevada, USA 1889. Educated Christian Brothers School, Dingle, Co Kerry; St Brendan's Seminary, Killarney 1906-08; St Peter's 1908-14. Ordained Glasgow 1914. St Patrick's, Glasgow 1914-18. Duntocher 1918-25. Glasgow Cathedral 1925-31. Neilston 1931-38. Christ the King, Glasgow 1938-45. St Joseph's, Blantyre 1945-58, thus moving to Motherwell diocese. Died Tralee 11 June 1958.

ATKINSON, BARTHOLOMEW F: Born Liverpool 1874. Educated Salford Catholic Grammar School; St Edmund's College, Douay; St Peter's 1895-1900. Ordained 1900. St Anne's, Glasgow 1900-12. Busby 1912-21. St Michael's, Glasgow 1921-22. Leave of absence 1922-26. Airdrie 1926-27. Wishaw 1927-28. Renfrew 1928-30. St Patrick's, Shieldmuir 1930-35. Motherwell 1935-46. Died Motherwell 25 Dec 1946.

AUSTIN, JAMES: Born and educated Ireland. Ordained Maynooth 1900. Lent to Glasgow. St John the Baptist's, Port Glasgow 1900-01. Returned to Ireland 1901 and died there 26 August 1948. (Canning)

AYLWARD, GEORGE: Born and educated Ireland. Ordained Kilkenny for Glasgow 1925. Johnstone 1925-45. Dalry 1945-47. St Simon's, Glasgow 1947-50. St Philomena's, Glasgow 1950-73. Retired to Ireland 1973 and died there 20 July 1981. (Canning)

AYLWARD, JAMES: Born and educated Ireland. Ordained 1937. Lent to Glasgow. St Mungo's, Greenock 1937-42. Returned to Ireland 1942. (Canning)

BACON, GERARD MICHAEL: Born Govan 1955. Educated St Thomas Aquinas' School, Glasgow; worked in banking; continued education St Peter's, St Andrew's College of Education. Taught in Paisley schools. Completed education for priesthood Ushaw. Ordained Glasgow 1986. Immaculate Conception, Glasgow 1986-.

BAIRD, NORMAN: Born Dunfermline 1925. Educated Fort Augustus School; St Peter's; Scots College, Rome. Ordained Rome 1953. Holy Cross, Glasgow 1954-65. Died Glasgow 19 March 1965.

BALMER, FRANCIS JOSEPH: Born Glasgow 1958. Educated Langbank, Blairs, St Peter's. Ordained Glasgow 1983. St Patrick's, Dumbarton 1983-85. St Constantine's, Glasgow 1985-.

BANCEWICZ, ANTHONY JOHN: Born Glasgow 1940. Educated St Aloysius' College, Glasgow; Blairs; St Peter's. Ordained Glasgow 1965. St Margaret Mary's, Glasgow 1965-82. Our Lady of Loreto, Dalmuir 1982-86. St Peter's, Glasgow 1986-.

BANNON, JAMES: Born Motherwell 1915. Educated St Aloysius' College, Glasgow; Blairs; St Peter's. Ordained Glasgow 1943. St Mary's, Paisley 1943-45. Stevenston 1945-51; thus moving to Galloway diocese. St Andrew's, Dumfries 1951-52. Kirkcudbright 1952-53. Birnieknowe 1953-56. C/o Bishop's House, Galloway 1956-83. St Margaret's, Ayr 1983-86. Died Ayr 22 Dec 1986.

BARCLAY, RICHARD: see Barclay, Robert Hugh.

BARCLAY, ROBERT HUGH: Born Glasgow 1902. Educated Blairs 1918-21; St Peter's 1921-27. Ordained Glasgow 1927. St Mirin's, Paisley 1927-44. Forces Chaplain 1944-46. St Mary's, Glasgow 1946-47. St Joseph's, Greenock 1947-59; thus moving to Paisley diocese. St Laurence's, Greenock 1959-61. Paisley Cathedral 1961-71. Died Glasgow 7 Dec 1971.

BARNES, GERARD FRANCIS: Born Glasgow 1961. Educated St Aloysius' College, Glasgow; Langbank; Blairs; St Peter's; Chesters. Ordained Glasgow 1986. St Maria Goretti's, Glasgow 1986-88. St Joseph's, Cumbernauld 1988-.

BARRETT, MICHAEL JOHN: Born Glasgow 1960. Educated St Aloysius' College, Glasgow; St Peter's. Ordained Glasgow 1984. St Augustine's, Glasgow 1984. St Roch's, Glasgow 1984-87. No further entries.

BARRETT, PATRICK: Born and educated Ireland. Ordained Ballina 1922. Lent to Glasgow. Holy Family, Kirkintilloch 1922-25. Returned to Ireland 1925. (Canning)

BARRETT, THOMAS: Ordained 1902. St Michael's, Glasgow 1903-04. No further entries.

BARRON, MICHAEL: Born and educated Ireland. Ordained Waterford 1922. Lent to Glasgow. St John the Baptist's, Uddingston 1922-26. Returned to Ireland 1926 and died there 2 Jan 1971. (Canning)

BARRY, DAVID: Born and educated Ireland. Ordained Maynooth 1904. Lent to Glasgow. Glasgow Cathedral 1905-15. Returned to Ireland 1915 and died there 18 March 1952. (Canning)

BARRY, KEVIN: Born and educated Ireland. Ordained Ireland for Glasgow 1946. Christ the King, Glasgow 1946. Johnstone 1946-47. St Charles', Paisley 1947-60; thus moving to Paisley diocese. St Margaret's, Johnstone 1960-69. St Anthony's, Johnstone 1969-72. Houston 1972-79. Died Glasgow 21 Feb 1979. (Canning)

BARRY, (Thomas) NOEL: Born London 1956. Educated North Monastery, Cork; St Finbarr's College, Farranferris; Valladolid; St Peter's. Ordained Cork 1981. Holy Family, Kirkintilloch 1981-82. St Ninian's, Glasgow 1982-86. Milngavie 1986-.

BARRY, THOMAS: Born and educated Ireland. Ordained Wexford for Glasgow 1945. Blantyre 1945-55; thus moving to Motherwell diocese. New Stevenston 1955-60. St Edward's, Airdrie 1960-72. New Stevenston 1972-77. St Bartholomew's, Coatbridge 1977-89. Calderbank 1989-(Canning)

BARTON, PATRICK: Born and educated Ireland. Ordained Maynooth 1882. Lent to Glasgow. St Aloysius', Glasgow 1882-85. Returned to Ireland 1885 and died there 14 Aug 1944. (Canning)

BATTEL, JOHN CHARLES: Born Ireland. Educated Ireland and Paris. Ordained Paris 1926. Lent to Glasgow; later got exeat to remain there. Govan 1926-45. St Constantine's, Glasgow 1945-46. St Bride's, East Kilbride 1946-52; thus moving to Motherwell diocese. St Patrick's, Coatbridge 1952-58. St Joseph's, Blantyre 1958-69. Chapelhall 1969-78. Died Airdrie 13 Oct 1978. (Canning)

BEATTIE, FELIX: Born Dumbarton 1920. Educated Glasgow University; Scots College, Rome. Ordained Rome 1953. St Mary's, Glasgow 1953-54. Professor, Blairs 1954-57. St Bonaventure's, Glasgow 1957-65. St Columba's, Glasgow 1965-69. Glasgow, no parish 1969-70. Notre Dame, not as chaplain, 1970-74. Chaplain, Notre Dame, 1974-76. St Brendan's, Glasgow 1976-77. On mission with Society of St James the Apostle, Boston and Peru, 1977-79. Awaiting posting 1979-80. Old Kilpatrick 1980-82. Retired 1982.

BEATTIE, ROBERT FURNESS: Born 1905. Educated Blairs 1919-23; Scots College, Rome 1923-30. St Laurence's, Greenock 1930-37. St Augustine's, Coatbridge 1937-40. St Mary's, Paisley 1940-46. No further entries.

BECKETT, ANTONY: Born Greenock 1932. Educated Blairs; St Sulpice; Institut Catholique, Paris. Ordained Paisley for Paisley diocese 1955. Lent to Glasgow; later incardinated into it. St Mary's, Glasgow 1955-63. St Teresa's, Glasgow 1963-66. St Michael's, Dumbarton 1966-70. St Aloysius', Glasgow 1970-71. Faifley 1971-73. All Saints, Glasgow 1973-

74. St Bartholomew's, Glasgow 1974-77. Sacred Heart, Cumbernauld 1977-85. Died Glasgow 4 Feb 1985.

BENNETT, JOHN JOSEPH: Born and educated Ireland. Ordained Carlow for Glasgow 1951. St Paul's, Glasgow 1951-75. St Ninian's, Glasgow 1975-. (Canning)

BERGIN, MALACHY: Born and educated Ireland. Ordained Carlow for Glasgow 1949. St Constantine's, Glasgow 1949-67. St Conval's, Glasgow 1967-74. Immaculate Conception, Glasgow 1974-76. St Alphonsus', Glasgow 1976-78. St Roch's, Glasgow 1978-. (Canning)

BERRY, THOMAS FRANCIS: Born Greenock 1920. Educated St Mary's School, Greenock; Blairs; Scots College, Rome; St Peter's. Ordained 1945. Carfin 1945-46. Further studies, Cambridge University 1946-50. Military Chaplain 1950-61. Died Greenock 28 April 1961.

BEYAERT, ARTHUR: Born Bruges 1854. Educated St Louis, Bruges; Seminary of Roulers; St Bernard's Seminary, Olton; St Peter's. Ordained St Peter's College 1879. Motherwell 1879-82. St Mary's, Paisley 1882-85. St Michael's, Glasgow 1885-90. Holy Family, Kirkintilloch 1890-97. St John the Baptist's, Uddingston 1897-1907. Sick leave 1907-09. Retired to Belgium 1909 and died there 18 Jan 1936.

BLACK, JAMES: Born Glasgow 1894. Educated St Aloysius' College, Glasgow; Glasgow University 1912-13; St Peter's 1913-17; military service 1917-19; St Peter's 1919-20. Ordained Glasgow 1920. St Patrick's, Coatbridge 1920-31. St Peter's, Glasgow 1931-38. Holy Cross, Glasgow 1938-39. Blackwood 1939-41. St Charles', Paisley 1941. Chaplain, Notre Dame Training College 1941-48. Consecrated Bishop of Paisley 1948. Died Kilmacolm 29 March 1968.

BOGAN, HUGH: Born Airdrie 1897. Educated Blairs 1911-16; St Peter's 1916-23. Ordained Glasgow 1923. Barrhead 1923-41. Longriggend 1941-45. Newton 1945-46. St Michael's, Dumbarton 1946-50. St Patrick's, Dumbarton 1950-75. Retired 1975. Died Dumbarton 6 March 1981.

BOLAND, PETER: Born Ireland. Educated Ireland, St Peter's. Ordained Glasgow 1914. St Alphonsus', Glasgow 1914-30. St Mary's, Glasgow 1930-32. Blackwood 1932-34. Shotts 1934-39. St Luke's, Glasgow 1939-44. St Patrick's, Glasgow 1944-73. Retired 1973. Died Ireland 2 Nov 1981. (Canning)

BOLES, JOHN: Born Kelso 1922. Educated Blairs, St Sulpice. Ordained Glasgow 1951. St Anthony's, Glasgow 1951-55. St Alphonsus', Glasgow 1955-63. St Anne's, Glasgow 1963-79. Our Lady of Loreto, Dalmuir 1979-83. Retired 1983.

BONNAR, DONALD: Born Glasgow 1908. Educated St Mungo's Academy, Glasgow; Blairs 1923-27; Valladolid 1927-34. Ordained Rome 1934. Duntocher 1934-36. St Anne's, Glasgow 1936-39. Forces Chaplain 1939-45. St Margaret's, Johnstone 1945-59; thus moving to Paisley diocese. Neilston 1959-68. St Patrick's, Greenock 1968-72. Died Greenock 14 Sept 1972.

BONNYMAN, PETER: Born Clochan, Banffshire 1883. Educated Blairs 1900-03; Issy 1903-05; St Sulpice 1905-07; St Peter's 1907-09. Ordained Glasgow 1909. St Patrick's, Glasgow 1909-10. St Michael's, Glasgow 1910-19. Cardowan 1919-27. Houston 1927-33. St Paul's, Glasgow 1933-42. St Mary's, Glasgow 1942-48. Died Glasgow 4 Aug 1948.

BOVILL, JAMES WILLIAM: Born Glasgow 1943. Educated St Mungo's Academy, Glasgow; St Peter's. Ordained St Peter's College 1967. St Stephen's, Dalmuir 1967-68. No further entries.

BOYCE, PHILIP: Born Glasgow 1905. Educated Blairs 1920-24; St Peter's 1924-26; Scots College, Rome 1926-31. Ordained Rome 1931. Immaculate Conception, Glasgow 1931-32. Renton 1932-37. St Mary's, Hamilton 1937-48; thus moving to Motherwell diocese. St Columba's, Viewpark 1948-50. Chaplain, Bellvue House, Rutherglen 1950-59. Harthill 1959-61. Bargeddie 1961-65. St John the Baptist's, Uddingston 1965-81. St Monica's, Coatbridge 1981-83. Died Coatbridge 14 May 1983.

BOYCE, WILLIAM: Born Ireland. Educated Ireland, Rome. Ordained Rome 1923. Lent to Glasgow. Longriggend 1923-24. Returned to Ireland 1924 and died there 31 Aug 1953. (Canning)

BOYLE, HUGH NOONAN: Born Glasgow 1935. Educated St Aloysius' College, Glasgow; Scots College, Rome. Ordained Rome 1962. St Philomena's, Glasgow 1963-66. St Eunan's, Clydebank 1966-76. Diocesan Chancellor: Archbishop's House 1976-77, Diocesan Office 1977-78. St Albert's, Glasgow 1978-83. Glasgow Cathedral 1983-.

BOYLE, JOHN (1909): Born Glasgow 1883. Educated St Aloysius' College, Glasgow; Blairs 1899-1904; Issy 1904-06; St Sulpice 1906-09. Ordained Paris 1909. St Peter's, Glasgow 1909-27. Harthill 1927-30. Cleland 1930-32. Cardowan 1932-36. St Roch's, Glasgow 1936-65. Died Glasgow 5 Dec 1965.

BOYLE, JOHN (1918): Born Cambuslang 1892. Educated Blairs 1907-12; Seminary of Bourges 1912-15; Seminary of Angers 1915-17; St Peter's 1917-18. Ordained Glasgow 1918. St Alphonsus', Glasgow 1918-26. Shotts 1926-28. St Patrick's, Dumbarton 1928-37. Cleland 1937-44. St

Luke's, Glasgow 1944-46. St John's, Glasgow 1944-67. Died Killearn 22 Jan 1967.

BOYLE, JOHN (1930): Born Carntyne 1906. Educated Blairs 1920-23; Scots College, Rome 1923-30. Ordained Rome 1930. Renfrew 1930-32. St Mary's, Paisley 1932-37. St Laurence's, Greenock 1937-47. St Margaret's, Johnstone 1947-56; thus moving to Paisley diocese. Bishopton 1956-61. St Mungo's, Greenock 1961-69. Chaplain, Convent of Our Lady of the Missions, Glasgow 1969-72. Retired 1972.

BOYLE, JOHN WATTERS (1946): Born Larkhall 1922. Educated Blairs, St Peter's. Ordained Glasgow 1946. Carfin 1946-49; thus moving to Motherwell diocese. St Bride's, East Kilbride 1949-52. St Mary's, Hamilton 1952-59. St James's, Coatbridge 1959-61. Bothwell 1961-68. St James's, Coatbridge 1968-77. New Stevenston 1977-85. Newmains 1985-.

BOYLE, JOSEPH: Born Glasgow 1951. Educated Langbank, Blairs, St Peter's. Ordained St Peter's College 1975. St Martin's, Glasgow 1975-77. Professor, Blairs 1977-84. Glasgow Cathedral 1984-89. St Philomena's, Glasgow 1989-.

BOYLE, RICHARD: Ordained 1881. Johnstone 1881-82. No further entries.

BRADBURN, GEORGE CHARLES: Born Milngavie 1941. Educated Blairs; St Aloysius' College, Glasgow; St Peter's. Ordained Glasgow 1965. St Robert's, Glasgow 1965-69. Professor, Langbank 1969-77. St Stephen's, Dalmuir 1977-85. St Constantine's, Glasgow 1985-88. Spiritual Director, Scots College, Rome 1988-.

BRADLEY, (Lawrence) DENIS: Born Cambuslang 1915. Educated Osterley, St Peter's. Ordained Glasgow 1953. St Catherine's, Glasgow 1953-67. St John's, Glasgow 1967-73. Immaculate Conception, Glasgow 1973-79. St Dominic's, Bishopbriggs 1979-82. Died Glasgow 17 Feb 1982.

BRADLEY, EDWARD: Born Whifflet 1892. Educated Blairs 1907-13; St Sulpice 1913-18. Ordained Glasgow 1918. St Peter's, Glasgow 1918-24. Wishaw 1924-27. Airdrie 1927-32. Motherwell 1932-39. Renton 1939-47. Died Glasgow 17 Feb 1947.

BRADLEY, HUGH J (1916): Born and educated Ireland. Ordained 1916. Lent to Glasgow. St John's, Glasgow 1916-24. Returned to Ireland 1924 and died there 18 Oct 1947. (Canning)

BRADLEY, HUGH (1989): Born Glasgow 1961. Educated Our Lady's High School, Cumbernauld; University of Strathclyde; Scots College, Rome. Ordained Glasgow 1989. Glasgow Cathedral 1989. Further studies, Rome 1989-.

BRADLEY, JOHN: Born Glasgow 1919. Educated St Aloysius' College, Glasgow; St Peter's. Ordained 1944. St Patrick's, Dumbarton 1944-46. Further studies, Oxford University 1946-50. St Ninian's, Glasgow 1950-51. No further entries.

BRADLEY, ROBERT: Born Riddrie 1923. Educated Blairs; St Peter's; Scots College, Rome. Ordained Glasgow 1947. Further studies, Rome 1947-50. St Eunan's, Clydebank 1950-60. Professor, St Peter's College 1960-67. Holy Family, Kirkintilloch 1967-70. St Vincent de Paul's, Glasgow 1970-71. St Luke's, Glasgow 1971-72. Good Shepherd, Glasgow 1972-75. St Stephen's, Glasgow 1975-79. Our Lady and St George, Glasgow 1979-.

BRADLEY, WILLIAM (1911): Born Hamilton 1885. Educated Our Lady's High School, Motherwell; Blairs 1901-04; St Peter's 1904-06; Issy 1906-10; St Sulpice 1910-11. Ordained Paris 1911. Govan 1911-14. St John the Baptist's, Uddingston 1914-15. Mossend 1915-18. St Patrick's, Shieldmuir 1918-19. Ireland 1919-21. Chaplain, Kenmure Industrial School, Glasgow 1921-26. Chaplain, St Charles' Institute, Carstairs 1926-28. Longriggend 1928-30. Renfrew in addresses, but not under parishes, 1930-31. Retired 1931. Died Ireland 15 May 1963.

BRADLEY, WILLIAM (1913): Born Glasgow 1890. Educated Blairs 1903-08; Issy 1908-10; St Sulpice 1910-13. Ordained St Peter's College 1913. Our Holy Redeemer, Clydebank 1913-32. Stevenston 1932-43. Died Glasgow 6 Nov 1943.

BRADY, JOSEPH P: Born Ireland. Educated Ireland, St Peter's. Ordained Paisley for Paisley diocese 1956. Lent to Glasgow, later incardinated into it. St Bartholomew's, Glasgow 1956-64. St Nicholas's, Glasgow 1964-70. Sacred Heart, Cumbernauld 1970-71. St Roch's, Glasgow 1971-73. No further entries. (Canning)

BRADY, LAURENCE: Born and educated Ireland. Ordained Waterford for Glasgow 1929. St Patrick's, Glasgow 1929-51. St Nicholas's, Glasgow 1951-59. St Alphonsus', Glasgow 1959-76. Died Glasgow 26 Aug 1976. (Canning)

BRADY, LUKE: Born and educated Ireland. Ordained Dublin for Glasgow 1940. St Ninian's, Glasgow 1940-42. St Mungo's, Greenock 1942-57; thus moving to Paisley diocese. Clarkston 1957-60. St Paul's, Paisley 1960-76. Barrhead 1976-89. Retired to Ireland 1989. (Canning)

BRADY, PATRICK J: Born and educated Ireland. Ordained for Glasgow 1940. Baillieston 1940-43. St Luke's, Glasgow 1943-49. Duntocher 1949-57. St Saviour's, Glasgow 1957-65. St Albert's, Glagow 1965-. (Canning)

BRADY, THOMAS: Born Glasgow 1906. Educated St Mungo's Academy, Glasgow; Blairs 1921-26; St Peter's 1926-32. Ordained 1932. Chapelhall 1932. Coatdyke 1932-47. Immaculate Conception, Glasgow 1947-53. St Augustine's, Glasgow 1953-82. Died Glasgow 7 Jan 1983.

BRANAGAN, JOHN: Born Coatbridge 1911. Educated Blairs 1926-31; St Peter's 1931-38. Ordained Glasgow 1938. Clarkston 1938-44. Carfin 1944-45. St Michael's, Glasgow 1945-47. St Simon's, Glasgow 1947-52. C/o Diocesan Office 1952-53. St Aloysius', Glasgow 1953-61. St Nicholas's, Glasgow 1961-70. Retired 1970. Died Coatbridge 2 March 1980.

BRANNAN, JOHN: Born Glasgow 1915. Educated Salesian College, Cowley; St Peter's. Ordained Glasgow 1952. St Luke's, Glasgow 1952-60. Duntocher 1960-68. St Stephen's, Dalmuir 1968-70. Glasgow Cathedral 1970-77. St Anne's, Glasgow 1977-79. St Bernard's, Glasgow 1979-80. Glasgow Cathedral 1980-83. St Dominic's, Bishopbriggs 1983-84. St Margaret Mary's, Glasgow 1984-86. Retired 1986.

BREDIN, JOHN: Born and educated Ireland. Ordained Carlow for Glasgow 1928. St Mary's, Glasgow 1928-32. Kilbirnie 1932-33. Cadzow 1933-49; thus moving to Motherwell diocese. Carluke 1949-53. Glenboig 1953-60. St Bernadette's, Motherwell 1960-77. Died Motherwell 9 Nov 1977. (Canning)

BREEN, JOSEPH: Born Wishaw 1912. Educated Blairs 1926-31; St Peter's 1931-38. Ordained Glasgow 1938. St Patrick's, Coatbridge 1938-39. St John's, Glasgow 1939-51. Carntyne 1951-60. St Gabriel's, Glasgow 1960-74. St Bonaventure's, Glasgow 1974-88. Retired 1988.

BRENNAN, DANIEL: Born Glasgow 1917. Educated St Aloysius' College, Glasgow 1929-36; St Peter's 1936-42. Ordained Glasgow 1942. Our Lady's, Saltcoats 1942-49; thus moving to Galloway diocese. St Joseph's, Kilmarnock 1949-52. Whithorn 1952-54. Castle Douglas 1954-58. Annbank 1958-61. Birnieknowe 1961-70. Beith 1970-74. Died London 29 Jan 1974.

BRENNAN, MICHAEL: Born Ireland. Educated Ireland, Paris, St Peter's. Ordained Glasgow 1930. St Peter's, Glasgow 1930-38. Joined Benedictine Order 1938. (Canning)

BRENNAN, PATRICK: Born Ireland. Educated St Aloysius' College, Glasgow; St Peter's. Ordained Glasgow 1931. Burnbank 1931-32. St Columba's, Glasgow 1932-36. Cadzow 1936-40. St Augustine's, Coatbridge 1940-52; thus moving to Motherwell diocese. Harthill 1952-55. Larkhall 1955-61. All Saints, Airdrie 1961-65. On sick leave, then retired, 1965-82. Died Folkstone 24 April 1982. (Canning)

BRENNAN, WILLIAM: Born Paisley 1901. Educated Blairs 1918-19; St Peter's 1919-24. Ordained Glasgow 1924. Sacred Heart, Glasgow 1924-28. Mossend 1928-29. Professor, Blairs 1929-33. Died Aberdeen 17 Nov 1933.

BRETT, JOSEPH: Born and educated Ireland. Ordained Wexford for Glasgow 1928. St Charles', Paisley 1928-34. St Patrick's, Glasgow 1934-44. Chaplain, Barlinnie Prison and St Joseph's Home, Glasgow 1944-49. St Thomas's, Glasgow 1949-62. Died Glasgow 27 July 1962. (Canning)

BREW, CORNELIUS: Born and educated Ireland. Ordained 1924. Lent to Glasgow. Rutherglen 1924-27. Returned to Ireland 1927 and died there 13 Feb 1963. (Canning)

BRODERICK, JOHN DESMOND: Born Glasgow 1924. Educated Blairs, St Peter's. Ordained Glasgow 1952. Immaculate Heart of Mary, Glasgow 1952. St Teresa's, Glasgow 1952-71. Glasgow Cathedral 1971-72. Archbishop's secretary 1972-76. Chaplain, Notre Dame 1976-83. St Stephen's, Dalmuir 1983-89. Glasgow Cathedral 1989-.

BROOKS, THOMAS: Born and educated Ireland. Ordained Kilkenny for Glasgow 1927. Mossend 1927-43. St Mary's, Greenock 1943-47. St Bride's, Bothwell 1947-49; thus moving to Motherwell diocese. Whiterigg 1949-52. St Bride's, East Kilbride 1952-55. Shotts 1955-65. St Bartholomew's, Coatbridge 1965-69. Retired 1969. Died Lanark 2 May 1973. (Canning)

BROSNAN, THOMAS: Born and educated Ireland. Ordained Maynooth 1882. Lent to Glasgow. St Michael's, Glasgow 1883-84. No address given 1884-85. Returned to Ireland 1885 and died there 19 June 1893. (Canning)

BROTHERHOOD, JOHN: Born Durham 1874. Educated Blairs 1890-92; St Peter's 1892-98. Ordained St Peter's College 1898. St Mary's, Glasgow 1898-1907. St Stephen's, Dalmuir 1907-36. Died Glasgow 13 Aug 1936.

BROWN, DAVID: Born Dumbarton 1951. Educated Langbank, Blairs, St Peter's. Ordained Duntocher 1975. St Bartholomew's, Glasgow 1975-76. Holy Cross, Glasgow 1976-82. Bearsden 1982-86. St Helen's, Glasgow 1986-.

BROWN, DUNCAN: Born Glasgow 1861. Educated Blairs 1878-81; Valladolid 1881-87. Ordained Valladolid 1887. Glasgow Cathedral 1887-88. Motherwell 1888-93. Neilston 1893-1900. Burnbank 1900-18. Mossend 1918-26. Retired 1926. Died Glasgow 17 Sept 1932.

BROWN, WILLIAM C (1897): Born London. Educated St Edmund's College, Old Hall 1884-92; St Peter's 1893-97. Ordained Glasgow 1897. Rutherglen 1897-99. St Michael's, Glasgow 1899-1900. St Laurence's,

Greenock 1900-04. Dalry 1904-14. Helensburgh 1914-30. Died Glasgow 8 March 1930.

BROWN, WILLIAM (1906): Born Glasgow 1879. Educated Blairs 1893-1900; St Peter's 1900-06. Ordained Glasgow 1906. St Mary's, Paisley 1906. Sick leave 1906-07. St Anthony's, Glasgow 1907-11. No address given 1911-20. No further entries.

BROWN, WILLIAM E (1929): Born Bromley, Kent 1893. Educated Scots College, Rome 1926-30. Ordained Rome 1929. Chaplain, Glasgow University 1930-45. In a nursing home, Torquay 1945-46. Went to South Africa for health reasons 1946 and died Durban 28 Nov 1957.

BROWNE, DANIEL: Born and educated Ireland. Ordained 1883. Lent to Glasgow. No address given 1883-84. St Patrick's, Coatbridge 1884-88. Returned to Ireland 1888 and died there 15 Sept 1913. (Canning)

BROWNE, PATRICK: Born and educated Ireland. Ordained Listowel 1879. Lent to Glasgow. Maryhill 1880-81. St Michael's, Glasgow 1881-83. Returned to Ireland 1883 and died there 27 Dec 1940. (Canning)

BROWNE, WILLIAM: Born and educated Ireland. Ordained Maynooth 1905. Lent to Glasgow. St Mary's, Greenock 1905-10. Returned to Ireland 1910 and died there 22 Nov 1937. (Canning)

BUCKLEY, PATRICK: Born and educated Ireland. Ordained Maynooth 1886. Lent to Glasgow. St Patrick's, Glasgow 1886-89. Returned to Ireland 1889. (Canning)

BUDDS, EDMOND: Born and educated Ireland. Ordained Waterford for Glasgow 1948. St Aloysius', Glasgow 1948-51. Immaculate Heart of Mary, Glasgow 1951-57. St Michael's, Glasgow 1957-66. St Peter's, Glasgow 1966-73. St Mark's, Carntyne 1973-77. Died Ireland 19 June 1977. (Canning)

BUDIS, PAUL: Born Dumfries 1957. Educated Our Lady's High School, Cumbernauld; Valladolid. Ordained Cumbernauld 1982. St Peter's, Glasgow 1982-84. St Catherine's, Glasgow 1984-86. St Columba's, Glasgow 1986-87. No further entries.

BURKE, ANTHONY JOSEPH: Born Glasgow 1932. Educated St Mungo's Academy, Glasgow; Blairs; St Peter's. Ordained Glasgow 1957. St Margaret Mary's, Glasgow 1957-65. With Missionary Society of St James, Boston 1965-66. St Philomena's, Glasgow 1966-.

BURKE, CORNELIUS: Born and educated Ireland. Ordained for Glasgow 1945. Larkhall 1945-47. Our Lady's, Saltcoats 1947-50; thus moving to

Galloway diocese. Girvan 1950-54. Whithorn 1954-63. Kilwinning 1963-72. Died Mauchline 10 Nov 1972. (Canning)

BURKE, DONAL: Born and educated Ireland. Ordained Kilkenny for Glasgow 1948. St Michael's, Dumbarton 1948-67. St Patrick's, Glasgow 1967-73. St Louise's, Glasgow 1973-80. St Robert's, Glasgow 1980-87. Our Lady and St Margaret's, Glasgow 1987-. (Canning)

BURKE, JAMES J: Born Ireland. Educated Paris. Ordained Paris 1885. Lent to Glasgow. St Mary's, Paisley 1885-87. Alexandria 1887-88. St Vincent's, Glasgow 1888-89. Returned to Ireland 1889 and died there 3 June 1931. (Canning)

BURKE, JEREMIAH: Born and educated Ireland. Ordained Maynooth 1890. Lent to Glasgow. St Mary's, Glasgow 1890-94. Returned to Ireland 1894 and died there 10 March 1939. (Canning)

BURKE, MATTHEW: Born and educated Ireland. Ordained Maynooth 1897. Lent to Glasgow. St Patrick's, Glasgow 1897-98. St John the Baptist's, Uddingston 1898-1900. Returned to Ireland in bad health 1900 and died there 8 Sept 1901. (Canning)

BURKE, NOEL JOSEPH (or Joseph Noel): Born Glasgow 1940. Educated St Aloysius' College, Glasgow; St Peter's. Ordained Glasgow 1965. St Mary's, Glasgow 1965-66. Good Shepherd, Glasgow 1966-72. Our Lady and St George, Glasgow 1972-73. Spiritual Director, Valladolid 1973-79. Balloch 1979-89. Christ the King, Glasgow 1989-.

BURKE, WILLIAM: Born Ireland. Educated Paris. Ordained Paris 1938. Lent to Glasgow. St Patrick's, Shieldmuir 1938-42. St Mungo's, Greenock 1942-43. Returned to Ireland 1943. (Canning)

BURNS, ANDREW: Born Glasgow 1924. Educated St Mungo's Academy, Glasgow; St Peter's. Ordained Glasgow 1953. St Joseph's, Woodside, Glasgow 1953-65. Holy Family, Kirkintilloch 1965-68. Joined Servants of the Paraclete 1968.

BURNS, BARTHOLOMEW (1928): Born and educated Ireland. Ordained Waterford for Glasgow 1928. St Aloysuis', Glasgow 1928-36. St Anthony's, Glasgow 1936-48. St Robert's, Glasgow 1948-75. Died Glasgow 29 Aug 1975. (Canning)

BURNS, BARTHOLOMEW (1960): Born and educated Ireland. Ordained Waterford for Glasgow 1960. St Eunan's, Clydebank 1960-66. St Michael's, Glasgow 1966-72. St Teresa's, Glasgow 1972-73. Wanted by police for suspected IRA activities and fled to Ireland 1973. (Canning)

BURNS, CHARLES: Born Glenboig 1903. Educated Blairs 1916-22; Valladolid 1922-29. Ordained Valladolid 1929. St Mary's, Coatbridge 1929-33. Baillieston 1933-41. St Ninian's, Glasgow 1941-50. Renton 1950-51. Retired 1951. Died Musselburgh 12 Jan 1962.

BURNS, FRANCIS: Born Glasgow 1906. Educated Blairs 1921-24; St Peter's 1924-31. Ordained Rome 1931. St Augustine's, Coatbridge 1931-40. Cadzow 1940-45. Sick leave from 1945. Died Ireland 26 May 1976.

BURNS, GEORGE: Born Glasgow 1919. Educated St Aloysius' College, Glasgow; St Peter's 1935-42. Ordained Glasgow 1942. St Thomas's, Glasgow 1942-50. St Bernadette's, Glasgow 1950-51. St Brendan's, Glasgow 1951-67. Good Shepherd, Glasgow 1967-72. Died Glasgow 24 July 1972.

BURNS, JAMES A: Born Clydebank 1929. Educated Dundee Technical College; Campion House, Osterley; St Peter's. Ordained Glasgow 1962. St Saviour's, Glasgow 1962. Sacred Heart, Glasgow 1962-72. St Constantine's, Glasgow 1972-77. St Thomas's, Glasgow 1977-86. St Maria Goretti's, Glasgow 1986-89. St Stephen's, Dalmuir 1989-.

BURNS, JOHN J N: Born Glasgow 1929. Educated St Mungo's Academy, Glasgow; St Peter's. Ordained Glasgow 1954. St Roch's, Glasgow 1954-69. St Vincent de Paul's, Glasgow 1969-78. St Patrick's, Glasgow 1978-79. Our Lady of Perpetual Succour, Glasgow 1979-82. Our Lady of the Assumption, Glasgow 1982-89. St Catherine's, Glasgow 1989-.

BUTLER, JAMES: Born and educated Ireland. Ordained Carlow for Glasgow 1929. Sacred Heart, Glasgow 1929-43. Mossend 1943-49; thus moving to Motherwell diocese. Sacred Heart, Bellshill 1949-58. Died Bellshill 10 Oct 1958. (Canning)

BYRNE, CHARLES: Born and educated Ireland. Ordained Maynooth 1905. Lent to Glasgow. St Patrick's, Dumbarton 1905-08. Returned to Ireland 1908 and died there 16 Oct 1958. (Canning)

BYRNE, JOHN BERNARD: Born Uddingston 1935. Educated St Aloysius' College, Glasgow; Blairs; St Peter's. Ordained Glasgow 1958. St Bartholomew's, Glasgow 1958-67. St Paul's, Glasgow 1967-68. C/o Diocesan Office 1968-69. No further entries.

BYRNE, JOSEPH: see Archdiocese of St Andrew's & Edinburgh

BYRNE, PATRICK JOSEPH: Born Uddingston 1933. Educated Blairs, Valladolid. Ordained Valladolid 1957. St Luke's, Glasgow 1957-70. St Matthew's, Glasgow 1970-74. All Saints, Glasgow 1974-81. Glasgow Cathedral 1981-83. Died Glasgow 28 Sept 1983.

BYRNE, WILLIAM: Born and educated Ireland. Ordained Galway 1899. Lent to Glasgow. St Peter's, Glasgow 1899-1900. Returned to Ireland 1900 and died there 17 July 1949. (Canning)

CAHILL, HUGH: Born Glasgow 1905. Educated St Aloysius' College, Glasgow 1918-21; Blairs 1921-24; St Peter's 1924-26; Scots College, Rome 1926-31. Ordained Rome 1931. Lent to Dunkeld diocese: Saints Peter and Paul, Dundee 1931-34. Professor, St Peter's College 1934-40. Professor, Blairs 1940-46. Professor, St Peter's College 1946-51. St Bridget's, Baillieston 1951-52, having moved to Motherwell diocese. Newmains 1952-57. All Saints, Airdrie 1957-61. New Stevenston 1961-72. St Mary's, Hamilton 1972-83. Retired 1983.

CAHILL, JOHN: Born Ireland. Educated Ireland, Paris. Ordained Paris 1897. Lent to Glasgow. St John's, Glasgow 1897-1900. St Paul's, Shettleston 1900-05. Returned to Ireland 1905 and died there 29 Feb 1944. (Canning)

CAHILL, THOMAS: Born Rutherglen 1910. Educated Blairs 1924-26; Scots College, Rome 1926-33. Ordained Rome 1932. St Patrick's, Coatbridge 1933-34. St Luke's, Glasgow 1934-37. Saltcoats 1937-39. St Teresa's, Glasgow 1939-47. Christ the King, Glasgow 1947-54. St Philip's, Glasgow 1954-68. St Vincent de Paul's, Glasgow 1968-86. Retired 1986.

CAHILL, WILLIAM L: Born and educated Ireland. Ordained Maynooth 1919. Lent to Glasgow. Our Lady and St Margaret's, Glasgow 1919-25. Returned to Ireland 1925 and died there 15 Jan 1968. (Canning)

CAIRNS, JOSEPH ALAN: Born Govan 1941. Educated Blairs, St Peter's. Ordained Glasgow 1964. Our Lady of Perpetual Succour, Glasgow 1964-65. Our Holy Redeemer, Clydebank 1965-68. St Bartholomew's, Glasgow 1968-69. St Benedict's, Glasgow 1969-89. St James', Glasgow 1989-.

CAIRNS, ROBERT: Born Glasgow 1877. Educated St Mungo's Academy, Glasgow; Blairs 1892-95; St Peter's 1895-1904. Ordained Glasgow 1904. St Patrick's, Dumbarton 1904-05. St Michael's, Glasgow 1905-12. Wishaw 1912-21. Strathaven 1921-26. Retired to Ireland 1926 and died there 20 July 1959.

CAMERON, ALLAN PETER: Born Glasgow 1963. Educated Langbank, Blairs, St Peter's, Chesters. Ordained Glasgow 1987. Christ the King, Glasgow 1987-.

CAMERON, JOHN: Born Newfield, Glenlivet 1861. Educated Blairs 1874-79; St Edmund's, Douay 1879-81; Issy 1881-84, with breaks due to ill health; St Peter's 1884-87. Ordained Glasgow 1887. St Mary's, Glasgow 1887. St Michael's, Glasgow 1887-89. St John's, Port Glasgow 1889-90.

Cleland 1890-91. St Patrick's, Coatbridge 1891-92. Lent to Galloway diocese: Girvan 1892-93. St Patrick's, Glasgow 1893-97. Strathaven 1897-98. No address given 1898-1901. Diocese of Antigonish, Nova Scotia 1901-08. Died Boston, USA 29 July 1908.

CAMPBELL, DONALD A: See Argyll diocese.

CAMPBELL, EDWARD: Born Glasgow 1958. Educated Holyrood School, Glasgow; Langbank; Blairs; St Peter's. Ordained St Peter's College 1982. St Matthew's, Glasgow 1982-86. St Thomas's, Glasgow 1986-.

CAMPBELL, JOHN GERARD: Born Dumbarton 1963. Educated St Patrick's High School, Dumbarton; St Peter's; Chesters. Ordained Dumbarton 1987. St Ninian's, Glasgow 1987-.

CANAVAN, BARTHOLOMEW: Born and educated Ireland. Ordained Maynooth 1901. Lent to Glasgow. St Patrick's, Coatbridge 1901-08. Hamilton 1908. Returned to Ireland 1908 and died there 3 March 1940. (Canning)

CANNON, MICHAEL: Born and educated Ireland. Ordained Maynooth 1912. Lent to Glasgow. St Michael's, Glasgow 1912-14. English Mission 1914-18. Returned to Ireland 1918 and died there 28 Dec 1949. (Canning)

CARNEY, MATTHEW: Born and educated Ireland. Ordained Kilkenny for Blois, France 1941. Lent to St Andrews & Edinburgh: Edinburgh Cathedral 1943-46. Got exeat from Blois and was incardinated into Glasgow Archdiocese. St Alphonsus', Glasgow 1946-67. St Bernard's, Glasgow 1967-79. Dorset 1979-89. No further entries. (Canning)

CARROLL, JAMES: Born and educated Ireland. Ordained Maynooth 1890. Lent to Glasgow. St Patrick's, Dumbarton 1890-91. St John's, Port Glasgow 1891-92. St Mary's, Greenock 1892-96. Returned to Ireland 1896 and died there 2 March 1941. (Canning)

CARROLL, JEREMIAH: Born and educated Ireland. Ordained Kilkenny for Glasgow 1951. St Simon's, Glasgow 1951-55. St Anne's, Glasgow 1955-63. St Mary's, Glasgow 1963-65. Holy Cross, Glasgow 1965-78. St Alphonsus', Glasgow 1978-84. St Paul's, Shettleston 1984-. (Canning)

CARROLL, JOHN JOSEPH: Born Glasgow 1963. Educated Langbank, Blairs, Valladolid, Salamanca. Ordained Glasgow 1989. St Joseph's, Tollcross 1989-.

CARROLL, MATTHEW: Born and educated Ireland. Ordained Waterford 1898. Lent to Glasgow. St Laurence's, Greenock 1898-1905. Returned to Ireland 1905 and died there 10 March 1937. (Canning)

CARTER, JOHN: Born Glasgow 1911. Educated St Aloysius' College, Glasgow; Blairs 1927-30; Scots College, Rome 1930-36. Ordained Rome 1936. Further studies, Oxford 1937-39. Motherwell 1939-40. St Charles', Paisley 1940-44. St Charles', Paisley in addresses, but not under parishes, 1944-46. Immaculate Conception, Glasgow 1946-47. St Joseph's, Glasgow 1947-48. St Roch's, Glasgow 1948-49. Renton 1949-53. Our Lady and St Margaret's, Glasgow 1953-57. Helensburgh 1957-65. Died Helensburgh 15 Nov 1965.

CASEY, DOMINICK: Born and educated Ireland. Ordained Ballaghaderreen 1913. Lent to Glasgow. Cleland 1914-15. Burnbank 1915-18. Returned to Ireland 1918. (Canning)

CASEY, JOHN: Born Glasgow 1959. Educated Langbank; Blairs; Lourdes Secondary School, Glasgow; Valladolid. Ordained Glasgow 1984. St Pius X, Glasgow 1984. St Peter's, Glasgow 1984-.

CASEY, PATRICK FRANCIS: Born and educated Ireland. Ordained Kilkenny for Glasgow 1928. St Patrick's, Dumbarton 1928. Longriggend 1928-29. St John's, Port Glasgow 1929-31. St Alphonsus', Glasgow 1931-49. Our Lady and St George, Glasgow 1949-54. Died Glasgow 5 Feb 1954. (Canning)

CASSIDY, HUGH: Born Glasgow 1907. Educated Blairs 1921-26; St Lo 1926-27; Grand Seminaire, Coutances 1927-32. Ordained St Peter's College 1932. St Michael's, Glasgow 1932. Duntocher 1932-51. Holy Cross, Glasgow 1951-54. St Pius X, Glasgow 1954-76. Roseneath 1976-77. St Dominic's, Bishopbriggs 1977-78. Died Glasgow 4 June 1978.

CASSIDY, THOMAS: Born Glasgow 1909. Educated Blairs 1923-27; Valladolid 1927-34. Ordained Valladolid 1934. St Thomas's, Glasgow 1934-53. Died Chapelizod 15 June 1953.

CAWLEY, JOHN PATRICK: Born Airdrie 1909. Educated Blairs 1923-28; St Peter's 1928-34. Ordained Glasgow 1934. St Roch's, Glasgow 1934-50. St Peter's, Glasgow 1950-55. St Bernadette's, Glasgow 1955-65. Our Lady and St George, Glasgow 1965-79. Retired 1979. Died Glasgow 24 Dec 1987.

CENTRA, CARLOW A: Born and educated Ireland. Ordained Carlow for Glasgow 1950. Cardonald 1950-51. St Paul's, Shettleston 1951-74. St Patrick's, Dumbarton 1974-75. St Thomas's, Glasgow 1975-. (Canning)

CHALMERS, BERNARD M: Born Gillingham, Kent 1931. Educated St Aloysius' College, Glasgow; St Peter's. Ordained Glasgow 1956. Glasgow Cathedral 1956-69. St Bartholomew's, Glasgow 1969-74. Chairman, Catholic Marriage Advisory Council, London 1974-76. Sick leave 1976-78. No further entries.

CHALMERS, JOHN JOSEPH: Born Rosyth 1929. Educated St Sulpice. Ordained Glasgow 1952. Further studies, Rome 1952-54. St John's, Glasgow 1954-71. Our Lady and St Margaret's, Glasgow 1971-79. St Charles', Glasgow 1979-.

CHAMBERS, THOMAS JOSEPH: Born and educated Ireland. Ordained Ireland for Glasgow 1967. St Brendan's, Glasgow 1967-69. St Alphonsus', Glasgow 1969-. (Canning)

CHANDLER, ALBERT: Born Glasgow 1908. Educated St Aloysius' College, Glasgow; Blairs 1923-26; Scots College, Rome 1926-33. Ordained Rome 1932. Carfin 1933-34. St Patrick's, Dumbarton 1934-36. St Laurence's, Greenock 1936-37. St Patrick's, Coatbridge 1937-44. Clarkston 1944-45. Cambuslang 1945-47. St James', Renfrew 1947-56; thus moving to Paisley diocese. Chaplain, St Vincent's Home, Langbank 1956-59. Neilston 1959-63. Chaplain, Good Shepherd Convent, Bishopton 1963-69. Elderslie 1969-74. Chaplain, Franciscan Convent, Paisley 1974-78. Retired 1978-82. Chaplain, Little Sisters of the Poor, Dundee 1982-. (Canning)

CHARLESON, JOHN M M: Born Kirkhill, Invernessshire 1862. Educated Scots College, Rome 1901-05. Ordained Rome 1904. Holy Family, Kirkintilloch 1905-07. Croy 1907-29. Retired 1929. Died Essex 30 June 1942.

CHRISTIE, WILLIAM P: Born Glasgow 1902. Educated St Aloysius' College, Glasgow 1914-17; Blairs 1917-19; St Peter's 1919-25. Ordained Glasgow 1925. St Mary's, Greenock 1925-28. St Columba's, Glasgow 1928-29. No further entries.

CLAEYS, OCTAVIUS F: Born Courtrai, Belgium 1875. Educated Episcopal Seminary, Courtrai; St Peter's 1893-96; Grand Seminaire de Bruges 1896-97; St Peter's 1897-99. Ordained 1899. St Agnes's, Glasgow 1899-1903. Croy 1903-06. Chaplain, Franciscan Convent, Glasgow 1906-07. Professor, St Peter's College 1907-17. Forces Chaplain 1917-18. Professor, St Peter's College 1918-23. Chaplain, Notre Dame Training College 1923-25. Leave of absence 1925-26. Baillieston 1926-28. Wishaw 1928. Died Wemyss 17 Nov 1928.

CLANCY, DANIEL: Born and educated Ireland. Ordained Waterford for Glasgow 1945. St Mary Immaculate, Glasgow 1945-48. St Agnes's, Glasgow 1948-70. St Nicholas's, Glasgow 1970-71. St Benedict's, Glasgow 1971-87. Retired to Ireland 1987. (Canning)

CLANCY, JAMES THOMAS: Born Belfast. Educated Blairs; Scots College, Rome. Ordained Rome 1967. Professor, Blairs 1967-79. Bearsden 1979-

81. Rector, Scots College, Rome 1981-86. St Ninian's, Glasgow 1986-88. Faifley 1988-89. Balloch 1989-. (Canning)

CLARK, JOHN FRANCIS: Born Glasgow 1883. Educated Blairs 1898-1903; Issy 1903-05; St Sulpice 1905-08. Ordained Paris 1908. St Mirin's, Paisley 1908-24. Neilston 1924-31. Barrhead 1931-37. St Mirin's, Paisley 1937-47. Died Paisley 16 April 1947.

CLARKE, JAMES: Born Calderbank 1874. Educated Valladolid 1895-1902. Ordained Valladolid 1902. St Patrick's, Shieldmuir 1902-15. Linwood 1915-20. Kilbirnie 1920-29. St Peter's, Glasgow 1929-38. Retired 1938. Died Glasgow 15 Feb 1942.

CLARKE, PATRICK: Born Wishaw 1892. Educated Blairs 1907-12; Valladolid 1912-19. Ordained Valladolid 1919. St Patrick's, Glasgow 1919-29. Holy Cross, Glasgow 1929-38. St Peter's, Glasgow 1938-39. Largs 1939-44. Cleland 1944-69; thus moving to Motherwell diocese. Died Cleland 11 July 1969.

CLARKE, WILLIAM: Born Larkhall 1933. Educated Our Lady's High School, Motherwell; Dorking, Surrey; St Bonifatius, s'Heerenberg, Holland; St Peter's. Ordained Glasgow 1957. Our Lady of Lourdes, Cardonald 1957. Our Lady and St Margaret's, Glasgow 1957-70. St Stephen's, Dalmuir 1970-77. St Laurence's, Glasgow 1977-82. St Peter's, Glasgow 1982-85. St Catherine's, Glasgow 1985-.

CLEARY, JOHN: Born and educated Ireland. Ordained Maynooth 1906. Lent to Glasgow. St Peter's, Glasgow 1906-10. Returned to Ireland 1910 and died there 20 April 1957. (Canning)

CLINTON, PETER: Born Croy 1923. Educated Campion House, Osterley; St Peter's. Ordained Croy 1969. Our Holy Redeemer, Clydebank 1969-72. St Saviour's, Glasgow 1972-82. St James', Glasgow 1982-88. Holy Cross, Glasgow 1988-.

CLOSE, JAMES P: Born and educated Ireland. Ordained Armagh 1922. Lent to Glasgow. St Peter's, Glasgow 1922-28. Returned to Ireland 1928 and died there 12 May 1978. (Canning)

CLUNE, JAMES: Born Ireland. Educated Ireland; Blairs; Scots College, Rome. Ordained Rome 1916. St Patrick's, Glasgow 1917-31. Professor, St Peter's College 1931-34. Gourock 1934-42. Houston 1942-46. Carntyne 1946-48. Alexandria 1948-57. Died Glasgow 30 Aug 1957. (Canning)

COAKLEY, MATTHEW: Born and educated Ireland. Ordained Carlow for Glasgow 1951. Sacred Heart, Glasgow 1951-55. St Roch's, Glasgow

1955-72. St Margaret Mary's, Glasgow 1972-78. Sacred Heart, Glasgow 1978-82. St Pius X, Glasgow 1982-83. St James', Glasgow 1983-. (Canning)

COGHLAN, JAMES: Born and educated Ireland. Ordained 1879. Lent to Glasgow. Glasgow Cathedral 1879-80. St Anthony's, Glasgow 1880-81. St Mirin's, Paisley 1881-82. Returned to Ireland 1882 and died there 19 Feb 1907. (Canning)

COGHLAN, WILLIAM: Born and educated Ireland. Ordained Dublin for Glasgow 1940. St Patrick's, Shieldmuir 1940-41. St Joseph's, Woodside, Glasgow 1941-45. Larkhall 1945-47. St Anne's, Glasgow 1947-49. Our Holy Redeemer, Clydebank 1949-50. St Mary Immaculate, Glasgow 1950-52. C/o Diocesan Office 1952-53. Not in Directories 1953-58. St Maria Goretti's, Glasgow 1958-71. Died Glasgow 29 Nov 1971. (Canning)

COIA, ROMEO: Born Glasgow 1912. Educated St Mungo's Academy, Glasgow; Glasgow University; St Peter's. Ordained Glasgow 1959. Professor, Blairs 1959-63. St Matthew's, Glasgow 1963-70. Chaplain, St Helen's Convent, Glasgow 1970-75. St Albert's, Glasgow 1975-78. Went to Dunkeld diocese: Monifieth 1978-.

COLBERT, WILLIAM: Born and educated Ireland. Ordained Middleton for Glasgow 1944. St Thomas's, Glasgow 1944-47. Renton 1947-48. St Robert's, Glasgow 1948-49. Sick leave; returned to Ireland 1949. (Canning)

COLFORD, NOEL FRANCIS: Born Glasgow 1940. Educated St Mungo's Academy, Glasgow; Scots College, Rome. Ordained Glasgow 1964. St Mary's, Glasgow 1964-65. Further studies, Rome 1965-68. Immaculate Heart of Mary, Glasgow 1968-70. St Flannan's, Kirkintilloch 1970-83. St Anne's, Glasgow 1983-85. Our Lady Queen of Peace, Glasgow 1985-87. St John Ogilvie's, Glasgow 1987-89. St Lucy's, Cumbernauld 1989-.

COLLERAN, JOHN (James): Born and educated Ireland. Ordained Ballaghaderreen 1924. Lent to Glasgow. Coatdyke 1924-25. Returned to Ireland 1925. (Canning)

COLLINS, DANIEL: Born and educated Ireland. Ordained Maynooth 1893. Lent to Glasgow; later got exeat to remain there. Motherwell 1893-1902. Coatdyke 1902-07. St Roch's, Glasgow 1907-18. Govan 1918-28. Chaplain, St Charles' Institute, Carstairs 1928-29. Baillieston 1929-34. Died Baillieston 2 March 1934. (Canning)

COLLINS, JOHN (1902): Born Ireland. Educated Ireland, Paris. Ordained Maynooth 1902. Lent to Glasgow. St Paul's, Shettleston 1903. St

Anthony's, Glasgow 1903-09. Returned to Ireland 1909 and died there 14 March 1956. (Canning)

COLLINS, JOHN ANTHONY (1969): Born Edinburgh 1920. Educated St Mungo's Academy, Glasgow; St Peter's. Ordained St Peter's College 1969. St Columba's, Glasgow 1969-74. St Martin's, Glasgow 1974-80. St Constantine's, Glasgow 1980-85. St Constantine's, Glasgow in addresses, but not under parishes, 1985-86. C/o Glasgow (no parish) 1986-87. Went to Galloway diocese: Millport 1987-.

COLLINS, MICHAEL (1905): Born and educated Ireland. Ordained Maynooth 1905. Lent to Glasgow. Mossend 1905-09. Returned to Ireland 1909; later affiliated to diocese of Texas. Died Ireland 3 Jan 1947. (Canning)

COLLINS, MICHAEL (1921): Born and educated Ireland. Ordained Derry 1921. Lent to Glasgow. Our Lady and St Margaret's, Glasgow 1921-23. Renfrew 1923-27. Returned to Ireland 1927 and died there 6 Feb 1979. (Canning)

COLVIN, DANIEL: Born Lightburn, near Shettleston, 1877. Educated Blairs 1891-94; Valladolid 1894-1902. Ordained Valladolid 1902. Immaculate Conception, Glasgow 1902-06. Cambuslang 1906-08. Burnbank 1908-15. Largs 1915-18. Gourock 1918-21. St Constantine's, Glasgow 1921-26. Coatdyke 1926-31. St Patrick's, Coatbridge 1931-51; thus moving to Motherwell diocese. Died Coatbridge 8 Dec 1951.

CONDON, CHRISTOPHER: Born and educated Ireland. Ordained Waterford 1940. Barrhead 1940-42. Whiterigg 1942-49; thus moving to Motherwell diocese. St Ignatius', Wishaw 1949-53. St Joseph's, Blantyre 1953-56. St Mark's, Rutherglen 1956-71. Caldercruix 1971-. (Canning)

CONLAN, JOHN: Born Stevenston 1917. Educated Blairs, St Peter's. Ordained 1943. St Peter's, Glasgow 1943-54. Immaculate Conception, Glasgow 1954-68. Our Lady of Perpetual Succour, Glasgow 1968-72. St Martin's, Glasgow 1972-73. Died Glasgow 9 Oct 1973.

CONLON, GEORGE: Born Neilston 1894. Educated Blairs 1908-13; Grand Seminaire de Versailles 1913-14; Scots College, Rome 1914-19; St Peter's 1919-23. Ordained Glasgow 1923. St Anthony's, Glasgow 1923-40. Forces Chaplain 1940-45. St Paul's, Shettleston 1945-70. Died Glasgow 28 May 1970.

CONLON, JOHN: Born Neilston 1885. Educated Blairs 1900-04; St Peter's 1904-06; Issy 1906-10; St Sulpice 1910-11. Ordained Paris 1911. St Peter's, Glasgow 1911-29. Stevenston 1929-32. St Teresa's, Glasgow 1932-37. Died Glasgow 21 Nov 1937.

CONNELL, BERNARD: Born Glasgow 1930. Educated St Mungo's Academy, Glasgow; Campion House, Osterley; Valladolid. Ordained Valladolid 1962. Glasgow Cathedral 1962. St Roch's, Glasgow 1962-67. St Martin's, Glasgow 1967-74. St Anne's, Glasgow 1974-77. Our Lady of the Assumption, Glasgow 1977-80. St Ninian's, Glasgow 1980-86. Immaculate Heart of Mary, Glasgow 1986-.

CONNELLY, JOSEPH: Born Dalmuir 1913. Educated Blairs 1927-32; Scots College, Rome 1932-34; St Peter's 1934-39. Ordained Glasgow 1939. Shettleston and Carntyne 1939-45. Carntyne 1945-46. St Paul's, Shettleston 1946-50. Chaplain, St Ninian's School (Kirkconnell, then Gartmore) 1950-56. St Flannan's, Kirkintilloch 1956-62. St Maria Goretti's, Glasgow 1962-77. Died Glasgow 29 Aug 1977.

CONNOLLY, EUGENE: Born Glasgow 1940. Educated St Mungo's Academy, Glasgow; St Peter's. Ordained Glasgow 1964. St Anthony's, Glasgow 1964-67. Our Lady and St George, Glasgow 1967-71. No further entries.

CONNOLLY, MICHAEL J: Born Wishaw 1912. Educated Blairs 1926-29; Scots College, Rome 1929-36. Ordained Rome 1936. Further studies, Rome 1936-39. Saltcoats 1939-41. Professor, Blairs 1941-46. Ripetitore, Scots College, Rome 1946-51. St Joseph's, Glasgow 1951-56. Helensburgh 1956-57. St Ninian's, Glasgow 1957-63. Rector, St Peter's College 1963-72. Clydebank (no parish) 1972-73. St Stephen's, Dalmuir 1973-83. Died Dalmuir 22 May 1983.

CONNOLLY, ROBERT J: Born Paisley 1913. Educated Blairs 1926-31; Scots College, Rome 1931-38. Ordained Rome 1937. Holy Family, Kirkintilloch 1938-43. Holy Family, Kirkintilloch in addresses, but not under parishes, 1943-45. St Mary's, Coatbridge 1945-46. St Patrick's, Glasgow 1946-55. No further entries.

CONNOLLY, STEPHEN: Born Glasgow 1963. Educated Bellarmine Secondary School, Glasgow; St Peter's; Chesters. Ordained Glasgow 1987. St Roch's, Glasgow 1987-.

CONROY, GERARD JOSEPH: Born Broxburn 1958. Educated Langbank; Blairs; Scots College, Rome. Ordained Dumbarton 1982. St Thomas's, Glasgow 1982. Further studies, Rome 1982-85. St Peter's, Glasgow 1985-89. Professor, Chesters 1989-.

CONROY, JOHN: Born Glasgow 1906. Educated Blairs 1920-23; Scots College, Rome 1923-30. Ordained Rome 1929. St Stephen's, Dalmuir 1930-31. St Patrick's, Dumbarton 1931-35. Professor, St Peter's College 1935-47. Vice-rector, St Peter's College 1947-60. Moved to Motherwell diocese. Motherwell Cathedral 1960-81. Retired 1981.

CONROY, MICHAEL: Born Dumbarton 1950. Educated Langbank, Blairs, St Peter's. Ordained St Peter's College 1974. Holy Cross, Glasgow 1974-76. St Margaret's, Clydebank 1976-81. St Philomena's, Glasgow 1981-83. All Saints, Glasgow 1983-88. Spiritual Director, Chesters 1988-.

CONROY, PAUL MICHAEL: Born Broxburn 1956. Educated Langbank; Blairs; Scots College, Rome. Ordained Dumbarton 1980. St Joseph's, Tollcross 1980. Further studies, Rome 1980-83. Professor, St Peter's College 1983-85. Professor, Chesters 1985-.

CONWAY, JOHN P (1914): Born Glasgow 1888. Educated Blairs 1904-08; Issy 1908-11; St Peter's 1911-14. Ordained Glasgow 1914. Hamilton 1914-24. On mission in China 1924-43. Chaplain, Little Sisters of the Poor, Greenock 1943-46. Chinese mission 1946-51. Kilcreggan 1951-68. Retired 1968. Died Glasgow 18 May 1970.

CONWAY, JOHN (1955): Born Glasgow 1931. Educated Blairs, St Sulpice. Ordained Glasgow 1955. Our Lady of the Assumption, Glasgow 1955-63. St Constantine's, Glasgow 1963-68. St Bernard's, Glasgow 1968-73. St Maria Goretti's, Glasgow 1973-81. St Roch's, Glasgow 1981-84. All Saints, Glasgow 1984-.

CONWAY, JOSEPH E: Born and educated Ireland. Ordained Maynooth 1898. Lent to Glasgow. St Alphonsus', Glasgow 1898-1901. Returned to Ireland 1901. (Canning)

CONWAY, PATRICK: Born and educated Ireland. Ordained Kilkenny for Glasgow 1928. St Mary's, Paisley 1928-38. St Mary's, Paisley in addresses, but not under parishes, 1938-39. St John's, Port Glasgow 1939-44. St Mary's, Glasgow 1944-49. St Conval's, Glasgow 1949-52. St Luke's, Glasgow 1952-69. Retired 1969. Died Ireland 28 Dec 1977. (Canning)

COOGAN, PATRICK F: Born and educated Ireland. Ordained St Peter's College 1923. St Mary Immaculate, Glasgow 1923-41. Blackwood 1941-45. Helensburgh 1945-53. St Maria Goretti's, Glasgow 1953-63. Retired to Ireland 1963 and died there 18 Sept 1972. (Canning)

CORLEY, THOMAS: Born Ireland. Educated Ireland, St Peter's. Ordained Glasgow 1902. St Peter's, Glasgow 1902-03. Blantyre 1903-14. St Aloysius', Glasgow 1914-16. Retired to Ireland in bad health 1916 and died there 5 June 1916. (Canning)

CORR, HENRY: Born Ireland. Educated Blairs; Scots College, Rome. Ordained Rome 1908. St Anthony's, Glasgow 1909-26. Carluke 1926-30. Renfrew 1930-31. Coatdyke 1931-36. St Stephen's, Dalmuir 1936-41.

Kilbirnie 1941-45. St John's, Glasgow 1945-46. Blantyre 1946-51; thus moving to Motherwell diocese. Retired 1951. Died Musselburgh 20 July 1954. (Canning)

CORRIGAN, JAMES PATRICK: Born Glasgow 1937. Educated Blairs, St Peter's. Ordained Glasgow 1961. St Luke's, Glasgow 1961. St Columba's, Glasgow 1961-70. St Robert's, Glasgow 1970-74. Bolivian mission 1974-76. Died Santa Cruz 1 Dec 1976.

COSKER, JAMES: Born Glasgow 1936. Educated Douglas Ewart High School, Newton Stewart; St Peter's. Ordained Glasgow 1961. St Brigid's, Glasgow 1961-83. St Bartholomew's, Glasgow 1983-.

COSTELLO, MICHAEL: Born and educated Ireland. Ordained Maynooth 1920. Lent to Glasgow. St Mary's, Greenock 1921-25. Returned to Ireland 1925 and died there 4 June 1967. (Canning)

COSTEUR, JOSEPH: Born Glasgow 1894. Educated St Aloysius' College, Glasgow; Blairs 1909-12; Valladolid 1912-19. Ordained Valladolid 1919. St Mirin's, Paisley 1919-30. St Patrick's, Shieldmuir 1930-38. Neilston 1938-41. St Charles', Paisley 1941-50; thus moving to Paisley diocese. St Mungo's, Greenock 1950-57. St Patrick's, Greenock 1957-66. Died Greenock 1 March 1966.

COTTER, EDMUND: Born and educated Ireland. Ordained Maynooth 1890. Lent to Glasgow. Sacred Heart, Glasgow 1890. Wishaw 1890-93. Returned to Ireland 1893. (Canning)

COURTNEY, FRANCIS: Born Cardonald 1929. Educated Blairs, St Peter's. Ordained Glasgow 1953. St Thomas's, Glasgow 1953-67. St Eunan's, Clydebank 1967-77. St Brendan's, Glasgow 1977-80. St Jude's, Glasgow 1980-81. Alexandria 1981-.

COURTNEY, JOSEPH: Born Calcutta, India 1880. Educated Blairs 1896-1901; Issy 1901-03; St Sulpice 1903-06. Ordained Paris 1906. St Luke's, Glasgow 1906-08. Johnstone 1908-16. Houston 1916-17. St Anne's, Glasgow 1917-23. Blackwood 1923-29. Newmains 1929-30. St Patrick's, Greenock 1930-49; thus moving to Paisley diocese. Died Greenock 14 March 1949.

COURTNEY, TIMOTHY: Born and educated Ireland. Ordained Maynooth 1911. Lent to Glasgow. Holy Cross, Glasgow 1912-18. Returned to Ireland 1918 and died there 15 Dec 1970. (Canning)

COWHEY, JAMES: Born Ireland. Educated Ireland, Paris. Ordained Paris 1901. Lent to Glasgow. Our Lady and St Margaret's, Glasgow 1901-14. Returned to Ireland 1914 and died there 21 Sept 1956. (Canning)

COWLEY, VINCENT JOHN: Born Glasgow 1913. Educated Blairs 1927-32; St Peter's 1932-39. Ordained Glasgow 1939. Bothwell 1939-40. St Columba's, Uddingston 1940-42. St Mirin's, Paisley 1942-48. St Teresa's, Glasgow 1948-53. Chaplain, St Helen's Convent, Glasgow 1953-70. Milngavie 1970-76. Died Glasgow 23 May 1976.

COYLE, FRANCIS: Born Glasgow 1924. Educated Blairs; St Peter's; Scots College, Rome. Ordained Glasgow 1947. Further studies, Rome 1947-49. Glasgow Cathedral 1949-52. St Charles', Glasgow 1952-67. Archbishop's secretary 1967-72. St Joseph's, Woodside, Glasgow 1972-73. St Philomena's, Glasgow 1973-.

COYLE, JOHN: Born and educated Ireland. Ordained Maynooth 1906. Lent to Glasgow. St Aloysius', Glasgow 1906-09. Returned to Ireland 1909 and died there 9 Dec 1939. (Canning)

COYLE, JOSEPH DANIEL: Born Glasgow 1935. Educated St Aloysius' College, Glasgow; St Peter's. Ordained Glasgow 1958. Glasgow Cathedral 1958. Further studies, Rome 1958-62. St Alphonsus', Glasgow 1962-76. Helensburgh 1976-82. Immaculate Heart of Mary, Glasgow 1982-86. St Vincent de Paul's, Glasgow 1986-.

COYNE, JAMES C: Born and educated Ireland. Ordained Maynooth 1906. Lent to Glasgow. St Peter's, Glasgow 1907. St Patrick's, Glasgow 1907-12. Returned to Ireland 1912 and died there 17 Feb 1934. (Canning)

CRAIGEN, CHARLES: Born Glasgow 1903. Educated Blairs 1918-21; St Peter's 1921-27. Ordained St Peter's College 1927. Immaculate Conception, Glasgow 1927-47. Bargeddie 1947-53; thus moving to Motherwell diocese. Whifflet 1953-66. Died Glasgow 29 May 1966.

CRAWLEY, GEORGE: Born Glasgow 1926. Educated Blairs, St Peter's. Ordained Glasgow 1952. St Barnabas', Glasgow 1952-60. Alexandria 1960-67. St Joseph's, Woodside, Glasgow 1967-70. St Helen's, Glasgow 1970-71. Our Lady of Good Counsel, Glasgow 1971-74. St Conval's, Glasgow 1974-77. St Constantine's, Glasgow 1977-80. St Bernard's, Glasgow 1980-87. St Barnabas', Glasgow 1987-.

CREEDON, DANIEL: Ordained 1937. St Mark's, Carntyne 1968-70. No further entries.

CREEDON, PATRICK J: Born and educated Ireland. Ordained Maynooth 1922. Lent to Glasgow. Shettleston and Carntyne 1922-26. Returned to Ireland 1926; died Surrey 11 Feb 1956. (Canning)

CRERAND, JOHN: Born Ireland. Educated Ireland, St Peter's. Ordained Glasgow 1927. Rutherglen 1927-36. Symington 1936. Died Lanark 17 Dec 1936. (Canning)

CRONIN, FRANCIS: Born Alexandria 1869. Educated Blairs 1884-87; Valladolid 1887-94. Ordained Valladolid 1894. St Mary's, Glasgow 1894. Holy Family, Kirkintilloch 1894. Our Lady and St Margaret's, Glasgow 1894-1901. Gourock 1901-05. Saltcoats 1905-07. Mossend 1907-18. Died Mossend 31 Oct 1918.

CRONIN, PATRICK: Born and educated Ireland. Ordained Cobh 1900. Lent to Glasgow. St Mary's, Coatbridge 1900-06. Returned to Ireland 1906 and died there 16 Aug 1940. (Canning)

CRONIN, RICHARD: Born Ireland. Educated Paris. Ordained Paris 1910. Lent to Glasgow. St Aloysius', Glasgow 1910-14. Returned to Ireland 1914 and died there 16 Feb 1962. (Canning)

CROWE, DANIEL F: Born and educated Ireland. Ordained Maynooth 1911. Lent to Glasgow. St Joseph's, Tollcross 1911-14. Returned to Ireland 1914 and died there 27 April 1973. (Canning)

CRUMLEY, JOHN: Born and educated Ireland. Ordained 1905. Lent to Glasgow. St Luke's, Glasgow 1905-09. Returned to Ireland 1909 and died there 19 Aug 1960. (Canning)

CRUMLY, JOSEPH J: Born Govan 1880. Educated Blairs 1894-1900; St Peter's 1900-06. Ordained Glasgow 1906. Cleland 1906-11. St Roch's, Glasgow 1911-20. Chaplain, Barlinnie Prison and St Joseph's Home 1920-23. Renton 1923-29. St Charles', Paisley 1929-41. St Anne's, Glasgow 1941-49. Retired 1949. Died Glasgow 30 Jan 1952.

CULLEN, JAMES L: Born Ireland. Educated Ireland, St Peter's. Ordained 1916. St Saviour's, Glasgow 1916-30. Glasgow, no parish, 1930-31. St Alphonsus', Glasgow 1931-33. Houston 1933-42. Gourock 1942-43. Sick leave 1943-45. Twechar 1945-56. Sick leave 1956-58. Died Ireland 12 Aug 1958. (Canning)

CULLEN, JOHN: Born and educated Ireland. Ordained Maynooth 1936. Lent to Glasgow. St Paul's, Glasgow in addresses, but not under parishes, 1936-37. St Roch's, Glasgow 1937-39. Returned to Ireland 1939. (Canning)

CULLIGAN, CHARLES: Born and educated Ireland. Ordained Maynooth 1898. Lent to Glasgow. St Charles', Paisley 1898. St John's, Port Glasgow 1898-1900. Returned to Ireland 1900 and died there 25 Sept 1955. (Canning)

CULLINAN (Cullinane), PATRICK J: Born and educated Ireland. Ordained Maynooth 1905. Lent to Glasgow. Duntocher 1905-09. Returned to Ireland 1909 and died there 26 Jan 1937. (Canning)

CUMMING, DONALD JOHN: Born Inverness 1958. Educated Langbank; Blairs; Scots College, Rome. Ordained Rome 1982. St Robert's, Glasgow 1982. Further studies, Rome 1982-84. Lent to Argyll diocese: Fort William 1984-85. Our Lady of Lourdes, Glasgow 1985-.

CUMMINGS, JOHN: Born Blantyre 1903. Educated St Aloysius' College, Glasgow; Blairs 1917-21; St Peter's 1921-27. Ordained Glasgow 1927. Professor, Blairs 1927-35. Our Lady of Lourdes, Glasgow 1935-36. Helensburgh 1936-37. Leave of absence 1937-49. No further entries.

CUMMINS, PATRICK: Born Ireland. Educated Ireland, St Peter's. Ordained Glasgow 1925. Motherwell 1925-37. Blantyre 1937-45. Biggar 1945-46. Houston 1946-50; thus moving to Paisley diocese. St Charles', Paisley 1950-58. St John's, Port Glasgow 1958-72. Died Greenock 27 Dec 1972. (Canning)

CUNNINGHAM, BERNARD: Born and educated Ireland. Ordained Maynooth 1903. Lent to Glasgow. St Michael's, Glasgow 1903-05. Johnstone 1905-06. Returned to Ireland 1906 and died there 8 Dec 1961.

CUNNINGHAM, CHARLES A: Born Glasgow 1863. Educated Blairs 1874-79; St Peter's 1879-83; Scots College, Rome 1883-86. Ordained Rome 1885. St Mirin's, Paisley 1886-91. Carfin 1891-96. St Patrick's, Dumbarton 1896-97. St Vincent's, Glasgow 1897-1902. St Mary Immaculate, Glasgow 1902-08. Linwood 1908-10. Died Linwood 11 Jan 1910.

CUNNINGHAM, THOMAS J (1879): Born Glasgow 1853. Educated Blairs 1868-72; Valladolid 1872-76; St Peter's 1876-79. Ordained Glasgow 1879. St Mary's, Greenock 1879-80. St Michael's, Glasgow 1880-81. Immaculate Conception, Glasgow 1881-84. Busby 1884-88. Cambuslang 1888-91. Died Cambuslang 7 April 1891.

CUNNINGHAM, THOMAS (1953): Born Glasgow 1927. Educated St Patrick's College, Cavan; Mungret College; St Peter's. Ordained Glasgow 1953. St Bonaventure's, Glasgow 1953-68. Holy Family, Kirkintilloch 1968-80. St Brendan's, Glasgow 1980-81. Bonhill 1981-86. Duntocher 1986-.

CURLEY, HUGH: Born and educated Ireland. Ordained Maynooth 1917. Lent to Glasgow. St Mirin's, Paisley 1917-19. Returned to Ireland 1919. (Canning)

CURRIE, DAVID: Born Dumbarton 1931. Educated Blairs; Scots College, Rome. Ordained Rome 1956. St Mary's, Glasgow 1956-62. Holy Cross, Glasgow 1962-65. St Saviour's, Glasgow 1965-67. St Teresa's, Glasgow

1967-72. St Anthony's, Glasgow 1972-77. St Paul's, Shettleston 1977-85. Faifley 1985-.

CURRIE, PATRICK GERARD: Born Dumbarton 1949. Educated St Patrick's High School, Dumbarton; St Peter's. Ordained St Peter's College 1973. St Mary Immaculate, Glasgow 1973-74. St Catherine's, Glasgow 1974-81. Christ the King, Glasgow 1981-89. St Conval's, Glasgow 1989-.

CURRIE, THOMAS: Born Glasgow 1862. Educated Blairs 1877-81; St Edmund's, Douay 1881-83; St Peter's 1883-88. Ordained Glasgow 1888. Our Lady and St Margaret's, Glasgow 1888-90. Pollokshaws 1890-94. Newton 1894-1900. St Anne's, Glasgow 1900-17. Motherwell 1917-35. Died Motherwell 30 May 1935.

CURTIN, MICHAEL: Born and educated Ireland. Ordained 1890. Lent to Glasgow. St John's, Glasgow 1890-93. Returned to Ireland 1893 and died there 2 June 1946. (Canning)

CUSH, (Hugh) CHARLES: Born and educated Ireland. Ordained Carlow for Glasgow 1943. St Stephen's, Dalmuir 1943-65. St Mary's, Glasgow 1965-68. St Philip's, Glasgow 1968-81. Retired to Ireland 1981. Died Nazareth 19 Sept 1985. (Canning)

CUSH, PATRICK: Born Glasgow 1875. Educated Blairs 1891-94; Valladolid 1894-1902. Ordained Valladolid 1902. Cambuslang 1902-06. Immaculate Conception, Glasgow 1906-15. Whiterigg 1915-20. St Charles', Glasgow 1920-29. St John's, Glasgow 1929-32. Died Glasgow 3 Aug 1932.

CUSICK, JOHN (1927): Born Paisley 1902. Educated Blairs 1915-21; St Peter's 1921-27. Ordained Glasgow 1927. St Anthony's, Glasgow 1927-36. St Mary's, Greenock 1936-45. St Roch's, Glasgow 1945-48. Old Kilpatrick 1948-51. St Barnabas', Glasgow 1951-55. St Saviour's, Glasgow 1955-75. Retired 1975. Died Glasgow 29 Feb 1976.

CUSICK, JOHN J (1930): Born Motherwell 1900. Educated by White Fathers Bishop's Waltham and Brittany; St Peter's 1924-30. Ordained Glasgow 1930. St Peter's, Glasgow 1930. Barrhead 1930-32. Lent to Dunkeld diocese: Lochee 1932-34. St Laurence's, Greenock 1934-37. St Patrick's, Glasgow 1937-40. Stevenston 1940-45. 'Retired', Glasgow 1945-49. Chaplain, Helpers of Holy Souls Convent, Wishaw 1949-50; thus moving to Motherwell diocese. Chaplain, Franciscan Convent, Bothwell 1950-58. Biggar 1958-65. Died Law 7 Dec 1965.

CZUBERKIS, JOHN: Ordained 1897. Priest for Lithuanian community. Attached to: Mossend 1904-05; Hamilton 1906-07; Mossend 1907-09. No further entries.

DALY, CHARLES: Born and educated Ireland. Ordained Maynooth 1895. Lent to Glasgow. Mossend 1895-1900. Returned to Ireland 1900 and died there 22 July 1933. (Canning)

DALY, PATRICK: Born and educated Ireland. Ordained Maynooth 1885. St John's, Glasgow 1885-89. Went to New York diocese 1889. Died New York 9 March 1950. (Canning)

DALY, THOMAS: Born and educated Ireland. Ordained Maynooth 1919. Lent to Glasgow. St Alphonsus', Glasgow 1919-20. Renfrew 1920-22. Kilbirnie 1922-25. Returned to Ireland 1925. (Canning)

DALY, WILLIAM: Born Johnstone 1877. Educated Blairs 1890-93; Notre Dame des Champs, Paris 1893-95; Issy 1895-97; St Sulpice 1897-1900. Ordained Paris 1900. Our Lady and St Margaret's, Glasgow 1900-11. Milngavie 1911-16. Stevenston 1916-18. St Saviour's, Glasgow 1918-25. Glasgow Cathedral 1925-47. Died Glasgow 11 May 1947.

DANIEL, JOHN D: Born Shotts 1899. Educated Blairs 1914-16; St Peter's 1916-23. Ordained Glasgow 1923. St Patrick's, Dumbarton 1923-28. St Michael's, Glasgow 1928-40. Strathaven 1940-43. Gourock 1943-45. St Laurence's, Greenock 1945-59; thus moving to Paisley diocese. St Mary's, Greenock 1959-72. Died Greenock 28 Jan 1972.

DANIEL, JOSEPH FRANCIS: Born Shotts 1897. Educated Blairs 1913-15; Valladolid 1915-22. Ordained Valladolid 1922. Glasgow Cathedral 1922-24. Professor, St Peter's College 1924-38. St Thomas's, Glasgow 1938-47. Glasgow Cathedral 1947-65. St Mary Immaculate, Glasgow 1965-81. Died Glasgow 31 Jan 1981.

DAVIN, FRANCIS: Born Ireland. Educated Ireland, Rome. Ordained Rome 1922. Lent to Glasgow. St Mirin's, Paisley 1922-27. Returned to Ireland 1927. (Canning)

DAWSON, BERNARD JOSEPH: Born Ireland. Educated Ireland, Blairs, St Peter's. Ordained St Peter's College 1883. Glasgow Cathedral 1883-90. Kilbirnie 1890-92. St Laurence's, Greenock 1892-98. Retired to Continent 1898. Died Aachen 7 May 1920. (Canning)

DEANS, JOHN: Born Glasgow 1896. Educated Scots College, Rome 1928-36. Ordained Rome 1935. St Patrick's, Glasgow 1936-40. Glenboig 1940-42. Barrhead 1942-46. Wishaw 1946-47. Chaplain, St Ninian's School, Kirkconnel 1947-50. St Paul's, Shettleston 1950-56. Twechar 1956-59. Died Glasgow 18 Sept 1959.

DE BACKER, LOUIS: Born Bruges 1857. Educated St Louis' College, Bruges; Seminary of Roulers; St Peter's 1878-79; Scots College, Rome

1879-82. Ordained Rome 1881. St Patrick's, Glasgow 1882-85. St Mary's, Greenock 1885-87. Cadzow 1887-91. Alexandria 1891-97. St Saviour's, Glasgow 1897-1919. (Obituary states he was in Belgium when war broke out and never returned to Scotland.) Retired to Brussels 1919 and died there 13 June 1932.

DEENEY, PATRICK: Born and educated Ireland. Ordained Maynooth 1918. Lent to Glasgow. St Charles', Paisley 1918-19. Wishaw 1919-23. St Patrick's, Coatbridge 1923-24. Returned to Ireland 1924 and died there 27 Nov 1940. (Canning)

DEERY, HUGH ANTHONY: Born Clydebank 1914. Educated Blairs 1928-33; Scots College, Rome 1933-40. Ordained Rome 1939. Saltcoats 1940-46. Holy Cross, Glasgow 1946-57. St Aloysius', Glasgow 1957-62. Our Lady of Good Counsel, Glasgow 1962-75. St Flannan's, Kirkintilloch 1975-78. St Bernadette's, Glasgow 1978-89. Died Glasgow 23 May 1989.

DELAHUNTY, WILLIAM: Born and educated Ireland. Ordained Maynooth 1919. Lent to Glasgow. St Patrick's, Dumbarton 1919-21. Returned to Ireland 1921 and died there 27 May 1967. (Canning)

DELARGEY, HUGH: Born Motherwell 1885. Educated Blairs 1901-05; Valladolid 1905-07; St Peter's 1907-13. Ordained Glasgow 1913. St Luke's, Glasgow 1913-22. Barrhead 1922-30. Longriggend 1930-36. Coatdyke 1936-41. Died Airdrie 8 Jan 1941.

DELBEKE, THEOPHILUS: Born Harelbeke, West Flanders 1862. Educated St Amand's College, Courtrai 1876-83; Seminary of Roulers 1883-84; St Peter's 1884-87. Ordained Glasgow 1887. Airdrie 1887-93. Helensburgh 1893-1901. Holy Family, Kirkintilloch 1901-19. St Patrick's, Shieldmuir 1919-29. Died Shieldmuir 25 Sept 1929.

DE MEULENAERE, LOUIS: Born Lapscheure, Belgium 1856. Educated Bruges, St Peter's. Ordained Glasgow 1882. St Anthony's, Glasgow 1882-88. Busby 1888-1900. Newton 1900-09. Retired to Bruges 1909 and died there 15 June 1929.

DE MONTI, CHARLES A: Born Glasgow 1866. Educated Blairs 1882-84; Douay 1884-85; Scots College, Rome 1885-90. Ordained Rome 1889. St Mary's, Greenock 1890-95. Professor, St Peter's College 1895-1900. Retired in bad health to South Africa 1900. Died Klerksdorp 1 April 1903.

DEMPSEY, EDWARD: see Dunkeld diocese.

DENNEHY, CORNELIUS: Born Ireland. Educated Ireland, St Peter's. Ordained Glasgow 1913. St Mirin's, Paisley 1913-30. Linwood 1930-33.

Christ the King, Glasgow 1933-38. St Joseph's, Tollcross 1938-45. Carntyne 1945-46. St Aloysius', Glasgow 1946-56. Died Ireland 5 May 1956. (Canning)

DENNEHEY, DENIS J: Born and educated Ireland. Ordained Maynooth 1890. Lent to Glasgow. St Peter's, Glasgow 1890-96. Returned to Ireland 1896 and died there 12 Sept 1937. (Canning)

DENNEHY, JEROME: Born Ireland. Educated Ireland, Paris. Ordained Paris 1912. Lent to Glasgow. St Patrick's, Glasgow 1912-13. Cleland 1913-14. St Michael's, Glasgow 1914-17. Cambuslang 1917-23. Returned to Ireland 1923 and died there 18 May 1952. (Canning)

DENNEHY, JOHN: Born and educated Ireland. Ordained Waterford for Glasgow 1943. St Roch's, Glasgow 1943-47. Duntocher 1947-49. St Luke's, Glasgow 1949-67. St Teresa's, Glasgow 1967-68. St Stephen's, Glasgow 1968-75. St Robert's, Glasgow 1975-80. Died Glasgow 17 Dec 1980. (Canning)

DEVINE, BERNARD V: Born and educated Ireland. Ordained Waterford for Glasgow 1951. Our Lady of Fatima, Glasgow 1951-67. St Augustine's, Glasgow 1967-77. Our Lady of Fatima, Glasgow 1977-81. St Catherine's, Glasgow 1981-87. St Margaret Mary's, Glasgow 1987-. (Canning)

DEVINE, JOHN A: Born Glasgow 1879. Educated Blairs 1894-1900; St Peter's 1900-06. Ordained Glasgow 1906. St Columba's, Glasgow 1906-13. St Charles', Glasgow 1913-22. Gourock 1922-28. St Anthony's, Glasgow 1928-44. Died Glasgow 24 Sept 1944.

DEVINE, JOSEPH: Born Kirkintilloch 1937. Educated St Ninian's High School, Kirkintilloch; Blairs; St Peter's. Ordained Glasgow 1960. Further studies, Rome 1960-64. Archbishop's secretary 1964-65. St Robert's, Glasgow 1965-67. Helensburgh 1967-72. Professor, St Peter's College 1972-74. Assistant chaplain, Glasgow University 1974-77. No further entries.

DEVLIN, BERNARD: Born Glasgow 1930. Educated Blairs, St Peter's. Ordained Glasgow 1955. St Philip's, Glasgow 1955-67. Our Lady of Good Counsel, Glasgow 1967-70. No further entries.

DEVLIN, PETER: Born and educated Ireland. Ordained Maynooth 1923. Lent to Glasgow. Croy 1923-26. Cardonald 1926-30. Returned to Ireland 1930 and died there 9 June 1951. (Canning)

DEVITT, ROBERT: Born Glasgow 1888. Educated St Mungo's Academy, Glasgow; Blairs 1905-07; Valladolid 1907-10; St Peter's 1910-16.

Ordained 1916. St Aloysius', Glasgow 1916-24. St Michael's, Glasgow 1924-27. No address given 1927-28. No further entries.

DIAMOND, PATRICK: Born Coatbridge 1875. Educated Blairs 1891-94; Valladolid 1894-1902. Ordained Valladolid 1902. St Vincent's, Glasgow 1902. St Mary's, Glasgow 1902-14. Dalry 1914-21. Cardowan 1921-32. Died Cardowan 6 March 1932.

DILLON, PATRICK: Born and educated Ireland. Ordained Maynooth 1928. Lent to Glasgow. St Patrick's, Greenock 1928. Sacred Heart, Glasgow 1928-33. Returned to Ireland 1933. (Canning)

DINAN, MICHAEL: Born Ireland. Educated Ireland, Paris. Ordained Paris 1894. Lent to Glasgow. St Michael's, Glasgow 1894-95. Returned to Ireland 1895 and died there 17 Aug 1949. (Canning)

DINNEEN, PATRICK: Born and educated Ireland. Ordained Waterford for Glasgow 1937. St John's, Glasgow 1937-58. St Paul's, Shettleston 1958-70. St Margaret Mary's, Glasgow 1970-78. Roseneath 1978-86. Died Ireland 5 Sept 1986. (Canning)

DIVNEY, EUGENE: Born and educated Ireland. Ordained Carlow for Glasgow 1942. Barrhead 1942-50; thus moving to Paisley diocese. St Laurence's, Greenock 1950-66. Newton Mearns 1966-69. Gourock 1969-75. St Mary's, Paisley 1975-76. Died Glasgow 20 Nov 1976. (Canning)

DOCHERTY (Doherty), JOSEPH: Born Glasgow 1879. Educated St Aloysius' College, Glasgow; St Joseph's College, Dumfries; Blairs 1894-1900; St Peter's 1900-06. Ordained Glasgow 1906. Johnstone 1906-08. St Luke's, Glasgow 1908-16. Forces chaplain 1916-19. St Patrick's, Glasgow in addresses, but not under parishes, 1919-20. Croy 1920-23. Largs 1923-33. Saltcoats 1933-39. Glenboig 1939-40. Chaplain, Kenmure Industrial School 1940-64. Died Edinburgh 6 Aug 1964.

DOCHERTY, THOMAS CARMICHAEL: Born Glasgow 1953. Educated St Mungo's Academy, Glasgow; St Peter's. Ordained Glasgow 1978. St Saviour's, Glasgow 1978. Further studies, Rome 1978-80. St Maria Goretti's, Glasgow 1980-82. C/o Diocesan Office 1982-83. St Vincent's Centre, Langbank 1983-84. Christ the King, Glasgow 1984-89. No further entries.

DOHERTY, CHARLES: Ordained 1924. Croy 1928-29. No further entries.

DOHERTY, CONSTANTINE: Born and educated Ireland. Ordained Maynooth 1919. Lent to Glasgow. St John's, Glasgow 1919-23. St Paul's, Glasgow 1923-26. Returned to Ireland 1926 and died there 28 May 1950. (Canning)

DOHERTY, EDWARD: Born Glasgow 1911. Educated Blairs 1926-31; St Peter's 1931-38. Ordained Glasgow 1938. Kilbirnie 1938-41. Motherwell 1941-47. St Augustine's, Coatbridge 1947-50; thus moving to Motherwell diocese. Our Lady and St Anne's, Hamilton 1950-55. Carluke 1955-59. St Clare's, Easterhouse 1959-65. C/o Diocesan Office 1965-66. St Ninian's, Hamilton 1966-69. St Peter's, Hamilton 1969-73. St Edward's, Airdrie 1973-81. C/o Diocesan Centre 1981-82. In hospital in Ireland 1982-84. Retired 1984.

DOHERTY, JAMES H (1911): Born Coatbridge 1885. Educated Blairs 1900-04; St Peter's 1904-06; Issy 1906-10; St Sulpice 1910-11. Ordained Paris 1911. St Mary's, Glasgow 1911-18. Chaplain, Kenmure Industrial School 1918-21. Not in Directories 1921-22. Sick leave 1922-23. Chaplain, Langbank 1923-26. St Joseph's, Tollcross 1926. Leave of absence 1926-27. Retired (Kingussie Sanatorium) 1927-41. Died Kingussie 9 Feb 1941.

DOHERTY, JAMES JOSEPH (1979): Born Glasgow 1953. Educated Holyrood School, Glasgow; St Peter's. Ordained Glasgow 1979. St Peter's, Glasgow 1979-82. St Laurence's, Glasgow 1982-86. Alexandria 1986-.

DOHERTY, JOHN: see Dunkeld diocese.

DOHERTY (O'Doherty), JOSEPH: Born and educated Ireland. Ordained Maynooth 1916. Lent to Glasgow. Motherwell 1916-25. Returned to Ireland 1925 and died there 29 June 1950. (Canning)

DOHERTY, MARTIN: Born Greenock 1907. Educated St Mary's School, Greenock; St Eunan's, Letterkenny 1922-26; St Peter's 1926-32. Ordained 1932. St John's, Glasgow 1932. Saltcoats 1932-37. Renfrew 1937-47. Immaculate Conception, Glasgow 1947-54. St Jude's, Glasgow 1954-82. Retired 1982.

DOHERTY, MATTHEW: Born and educated Ireland. Ordained Maynooth 1923. Lent to Glasgow. Airdrie 1924-26. Died Ireland 1 Sept 1926. (Canning)

DOHERTY, ROBERT: Born Condorrat, Croy 1905. Educated St Aloysius' College, Glasgow; Blairs 1923-25; St Peter's 1925-31. Ordained Glasgow 1931. Holy Cross, Glasgow 1931-33. Abbey of St André, Bruges 1933-35. Went to Dunkeld diocese: St John's, Perth 1935-39; St Mary's, Dundee 1939-47. Retired in bad health 1947. Died Glasgow 3 May 1979.

DOLAN, JAMES: Born Glasgow 1888. Educated St Aloysius' College, Glasgow; Blairs 1903-06; St Peter's 1906-14. Ordained Glasgow 1914. St Augustine's, Coatbridge 1914-32. Cleland 1932-37. Croy 1937-41. Our Holy Redeemer, Clydebank 1941-45. Kilbirnie 1945-48. Died Kilbirnie 8 April 1948.

DOLAN, THOMAS: Born Glasgow 1938. Educated Holyrood School, Glasgow; Blairs; St Peter's. Ordained Glasgow 1961. St Charles', Glasgow 1961-67. Our Lady of Lourdes, Glasgow 1967-68. No further entries.

DONAGHER, PATRICK: see Dunkeld diocese.

DONNACHIE, NEIL: Born Glasgow 1947. Educated Blairs, St Peter's. Ordained Glasgow 1971. St Maria Goretti's, Glasgow 1971-73. St Peter's, Glasgow 1973-76. St Joseph's, Cumbernauld 1976-.

DONNELLY, ANTHONY: Born Glasgow 1924. Educated Blairs, St Peter's. Ordained Glasgow 1949. St Alphonsus', Glasgow 1949-55. St Anthony's, Glasgow 1955-56. Sick leave 1956-57. St Pius X, Glasgow 1957-58. Not in Directories 1958-62. St Margaret Mary's, Glasgow 1962-64. C/o Diocesan Office 1964-66. Lent to Motherwell diocese: Motherwell Cathedral 1966-67. St Constantine's, Glasgow 1967-72. St Stephen's, Glasgow 1972-75. St Robert's, Glasgow 1975-82. Died Glasgow 30 Jan 1982.

DONNELLY, JAMES: Born Bellshill. Educated Holy Family School, Mossend. Joined Marist Brothers; later entered Cistercian monastery in France. Ordained 1938. Left Order and came to Glasgow archdiocese 1947. St John's, Port Glasgow 1947-60; thus moving to Paisley diocese. Bishopton 1960-62. Chaplain, Good Shepherd Convent, Bishopton 1962-63. Died Paisley 20 March 1963.

DONNELLY, JOHN: Born Shettleston 1887. Educated Blairs 1902-05; Valladolid 1905-07; St Peter's 1907-13. Ordained Glasgow 1913. St Saviour's, Glasgow 1913-25. Vice-rector, St Peter's College 1925-35. Died Ballantrae 12 Aug 1935.

DONNELLY, WILLIAM BERNARD: Born Glasgow 1940. Educated St Aloysius' College, Glasgow; St Peter's. Ordained Glasgow 1965. St Gregory's, Glasgow 1965-67. Faifley 1967-71. C/o Diocesan Office 1971-72. Croy 1972-81. Condorrat 1981-.

DONOVAN, DANIEL: Born and educated Ireland. Ordained Maynooth 1926. Lent to Glasgow. St Patrick's, Glasgow 1926-30. Returned to Ireland 1930 and died there 14 May 1973. (Canning)

DOODY, EDWARD: Born and educated Ireland. Ordained 1880. Joined Glasgow Archdiocese. Sacred Heart, Glasgow 1880-86. St Agnes's, Glasgow 1886-87. Was with Salford diocese; also serving as Royal Navy chaplain; 1887-89. St Michael's, Glasgow 1889-93. St Joseph's, Tollcross 1893-94. Wishaw 1894-96. Airdrie 1896-1924. Died Airdrie 13 Jan 1924. (Canning)

DOOGAN, DOMINIC: Born Glasgow 1946. Educated St Aloysius' College, Glasgow; St Peter's. Ordained Glasgow 1971. Sacred Heart, Glasgow 1971-72. Our Holy Redeemer, Clydebank 1972-75. Our Lady of Lourdes, Glasgow 1975-82. Renton 1982-87. St Peter's, Dumbarton 1987-89. St Patrick's, Glasgow 1989-.

DOOLEY, JAMES: Born Greenock 1914. Educated Blairs 1928-33; Valladolid 1933-37; St Peter's 1937-39. Ordained Glasgow 1939. Glasgow Cathedral 1939-44. St Augustine's, Coatbridge 1944-47. Our Lady of Good Aid, Motherwell 1947-51; thus moving to Motherwell diocese. Royal Navy chaplain 1951-69. Bargeddie 1969-84. St Monica's, Coatbridge 1984-86. Retired 1986. Died Glasgow 21 March 1988.

DOOLEY, MICHAEL: Born Ireland. Educated Ireland, St Peter's. Ordained Glasgow 1927. St Patrick's, Coatbridge 1927-48; thus moving to Motherwell diocese. Calderbank 1948-59. St Columba's, Viewpark 1959-73. Retired 1973. Died Law 14 Sept 1974. (Canning)

DOOLEY, THOMAS: Born and educated Ireland. Ordained Maynooth 1898. Lent to Glasgow. Wishaw 1898-1900. Returned to Ireland 1900 and died there 7 Jan 1939. (Canning)

DOUGAN, FRANCIS: Born Glasgow 1876. Educated Blairs 1893-94; Notre Dame des Champs, Paris 1894-96; Issy 1896-98; St Peter's 1898-1902. Ordained 1902. St Patrick's, Shieldmuir 1902-11. Carfin 1911-14. St Laurence's, Greenock 1914-18. Renfrew 1918-26. Barrhead 1926-29. Died Glasgow 16 May 1929.

DOUGAN, JOHN: Born 1857. Educated Blairs 1874-78; St Peter's 1878-83. Ordained Glasgow 1883. Airdrie 1883-86. St Mirin's, Paisley 1886-89. Cardowan 1889-93. Died Dumbarton 2 Aug 1893.

DOUGLAS, EDWARD: Born Glasgow 1901. Educated Blairs 1916-19; St Peter's 1919-24. Ordained Glasgow 1924. St Alphonsus', Glasgow 1924. Professor, Blairs 1924-40. Glenboig 1940-45. St Anthony's, Glasgow 1945-48. Consecrated Bishop of Motherwell 1948. Retired as bishop 1954. In Glasgow, no parish, 1954-58. Went to Aberdeen diocese: Aviemore 1958-62; Braemar 1962-64. Retired to Glasgow 1964 and died there 12 June 1967.

DOUGLAS, ROBERT: Born Glasgow 1905. Educated St Aloysius' College, Glasgow; Blairs 1921-24; Propaganda, Rome 1924-30. Ordained Rome 1929. St Bride's, Cambuslang 1930-49; thus moving to Motherwell diocese. Halfway 1949-69. Mossend 1969-80. Retired 1980. Died Musselburgh 3 Nov 1988.

DOYLE, PATRICK: Born Port Glasgow 1881. Educated Blairs 1894-1900; St Peter's 1900-06. Ordained Glasgow 1906. St Michael's, Glasgow 1906.

Pollokshaws 1906-22. Cardonald 1922-26. Milngavie 1926-61. Died Milngavie 23 Oct 1961.

DOYLE, THOMAS J: Born Port Glasgow 1878. Educated Blairs 1891-95; St Peter's 1895-1904. Ordained 1904. Newton 1904-08. Rutherglen 1908-18. Strathaven 1918-21. Cleland 1921-25. St Saviour's, Glasgow 1925-51. Died Govan 16 April 1951.

DUANE, DANIEL: Born and educated Ireland. Ordained Maynooth 1910. Lent to Glasgow. St Mary's, Glasgow 1910-11. Holy Family, Kirkintilloch 1911-19. Returned to Ireland 1919 and died there 21 Dec 1956. (Canning)

DUDDY, WILLIAM: Born Carluke 1913. Educated Our Lady's High School, Motherwell; Blairs 1926-31; Scots College, Rome 1931-38. Ordained Rome 1937. St Teresa's, Glasgow 1938-39. Baillieston 1939-40. Professor, Blairs 1940-50. Moved to Motherwell diocese. St Bernadette's, Motherwell 1950-55. Harthill 1955-58. Bargeddie 1958-61. St Luke's, Motherwell 1961-62. St Patrick's, Coatbridge 1962-77. St Margaret's, Airdrie 1977-85. Retired 1985. Died Coatbridge 8 Oct 1986.

DUFFIN, CHARLES: Born Glengarnock 1908. Educated St Brigid's School, Kilbirnie; St Mungo's Academy, Glasgow; Scots College, Rome 1930-37. Ordained Rome 1936. Our Holy Redeemer, Clydebank 1937-39. Forces chaplain 1939-46. St Constantine's, Glasgow 1946-50. St Ninian's, Glasgow 1950-53. St Luke's, Glasgow 1953-57. St Laurence's, Glasgow 1957-67. St John's, Glasgow 1967-79. Retired 1979. Died Glasgow 3 July 1989.

DUFFY, JOHN: Born Calderbank 1920. Educated Blairs, St Peter's. Ordained Glasgow 1946. St Philomena's, Glasgow 1946-48. St Mary Immaculate, Glasgow 1948-50. St Ninian's, Glasgow 1950-52. St Michael's, Glasgow 1952-54. Military chaplain 1954-73. Garelochhead 1973-.

DUFFY, JOSEPH: Born Ireland. Educated Ireland, Rome. Ordained Rome for Glasgow 1927. St Columba's, Glasgow 1927-47. Dalry 1947-60; thus moving to Galloway diocese. Retired to Ireland 1960 and died there 28 June 1970. (Canning)

DUFFY, MICHAEL JOSEPH: Born Glasgow 1954. Educated St Mungo's Academy, Glasgow; Campion House, Osterley; St Peter's. Ordained Carntyne 1983. St Robert's, Glasgow 1983-89. St Ninian's, Glasgow 1989-.

DUGGAN, DENIS (1898): Born and educated Ireland. Ordained Maynooth 1898. Lent to Glasgow. Rutherglen 1898-1907. Whiterigg 1907-08. Returned to Ireland 1908 and died there 29 Jan 1927. (Canning)

DUGGAN, DENIS (1899): Born and educated Ireland. Ordained Thurles 1899. Lent to Glasgow. St Mary's, Paisley 1899-1903. Sacred Heart, Glasgow 1903-08. Returned to Ireland 1908 and died there 28 May 1928. (Canning)

DUMPHY (Dunphy), THOMAS: Born and educated Ireland. Ordained Maynooth 1918. St Anthony's, Glasgow 1918-21. Shotts 1921-23. Emigrated to Australia 1923. (Canning)

DUNLEAVY, MICHAEL: Born Ireland. Ordained for Agen diocese, France 1934. Salford diocese 1951-54. St Michael's, Glasgow 1954-55. (Canning)

DUNN, GERARD: Born Glasgow 1910. Educated St Mungo's Academy, Glasgow; Ushaw College; Fribourg University. Ordained Southwark for Glasgow 1938. Croy 1938-39. Holy Family, Kirkintilloch 1939-60. St Bernard's, Glasgow 1960-67. Died Glasgow 13 Feb 1967.

DUNNE, JOHN JOSEPH: Born Kirkcaldy 1942. Educated Blairs; Scots College, Rome; St Peter's. Ordained St Peter's College 1967. Sacred Heart, Glasgow 1967-73. C/o Diocesan Office 1973-76. No further entries.

DUNNE, JOSEPH: Born Ireland. Educated Osterley, Ireland. Ordained Waterford for Glasgow 1975. St James', Glasgow 1975-76. St Laurence's, Glasgow 1976-78. St Bartholomew's, Glasgow 1978-79. St Paul's, Glasgow 1979-87. St Mary Immaculate, Glasgow 1987-88. C/o Diocesan Office 1988-. (Canning)

DUNNE, RICHARD: Born and educated Ireland. Ordained Kilkenny for Glasgow 1945. Sacred Heart, Glasgow 1945-50. St Mary Immaculate, Glasgow 1950-67. St Patrick's, Dumbarton 1967-69. Garelochhead 1969-73. St Martin's, Glasgow 1973-82. St Gabriel's, Glasgow 1982-. (Canning)

DURCAN, PATRICK: Born and educated Ireland. Ordained for Glasgow 1947. St Mary's, Paisley 1947-69; thus moving to Paisley diocese. St Fergus's, Paisley 1969-75. Gourock 1975-. (Canning)

DURKIN, JAMES: Born Hardgate 1879. Educated St Aloysius' College, Glasgow; Blairs 1895-1900; St Peter's 1900-06. Ordained Glasgow 1906. Cadzow 1906-11. St Patrick's, Shieldmuir 1911-21. Carluke 1921-26. Cardonald 1926-33. St Michael's, Glasgow 1933-52. Died Glasgow 27 May 1952.

DURNING, JAMES: Born Clydebank 1950. Educated Langbank, Blairs, St Peter's. Ordained Clydebank 1975. St Teresa's, Glasgow 1975-77. Our

Lady and St George, Glasgow 1977-80. Holy Family, Kirkintilloch 1980-81. St Flannan's, Kirkintilloch 1981-86. Natal, South Africa 1986-.

EARLEY, JOHN: Born and educated Ireland. Ordained Wexford 1940. Hamilton 1940-46. St Mary's, Greenock 1946-51; thus moving to Paisley diocese. St Margaret's, Johnstone 1951-60. St Aidan's, Johnstone 1960-86. Died Johnstone 1 Jan 1987. (Canning)

EDGAR, HENRY: Born Dundee 1866. Educated Blairs 1881-82; in bad health 1882-92; St Peter's 1892-97. Ordained 1897. St Patrick's, Coatbridge 1897. Barrhead 1897-1913. Cardonald 1913-22. Died Cardonald 21 Aug 1922.

EGAN, THOMAS: Born Ireland. Entered Carmelite Order and was ordained 1916. Left Carmelites and came to Glasgow archdiocese as a secular priest 1926. St Laurence's, Greenock 1926-29. Shotts 1929-32. St Mary's, Glasgow 1932-37. Clarkston 1937-38. Harthill 1938-45. St Simon's, Glasgow 1945-47. Biggar 1947-49; thus moving to Motherwell diocese. Bothwell 1949-55. Newton 1955-73. Died Middleton, Ireland 2 July 1973. (Canning)

ELLIOT, JAMES K: Born Ireland. Educated Ireland, St Peter's. Ordained Glasgow 1926. Kilbirnie 1926-32. St Mary's, Glasgow 1932-46. Immaculate Heart of Mary, Glasgow 1946-48. St Philomena's, Glasgow 1948-50. Died Dublin 21 Oct 1950. (Canning)

FAHEY, JOHN: Born and educated Ireland. Ordained 1921. Lent to Glasgow. St Michael's, Glasgow 1921-22. On staff of Irish College, Paris 1922-23. Returned to Ireland 1923 and died there 1965. (Canning)

FAHEY, PATRICK: Born and educated Ireland. Ordained Maynooth 1920. Lent to Glasgow. St Paul's, Shettleston 1920-22. Returned to Ireland 1922 and died there 30 July 1969. (Canning)

FALLON, GERARD JOSEPH: Born Whitehaven, Cumberland 1923. Educated Campion House, Osterley; St Peter's. Ordained Glasgow 1956. St Jude's, Glasgow 1956-65. St Brendan's, Glasgow 1965-67. C/o Diocesan Office 1967-82. No further entries.

FANNING, MATTHEW: Born and educated Ireland. Ordained Maynooth 1895. St Laurence's, Greenock 1896-97. No address given 1897-98. Returned to Ireland 1898 and died there 9 Oct 1934. (Canning)

FARRELL, HENRY: Born Glasgow 1951. Educated St Patrick's High School, Dumbarton; St Columba's School, Glasgow; Barmulloch College; pursued career in commerce; educated for priesthood St Peter's, Chesters. Ordained Glasgow 1987. Bearsden 1987-.

FARRELL, PATRICK: Born and educated Ireland. Ordained Youghal 1896. Cambuslang 1896-99. Died Cambuslang 13 Jan 1899. (Canning)

FARRELLY, HENRY: Born Ireland. Educated Ireland, St Peter's. Ordained Paisley for Paisley diocese 1956. Lent to Glasgow; never served in Paisley. St Ninian's, Glasgow 1956-63. RAF chaplain 1963-85. Eaglesham 1985-88. Coventry 1988-. (Canning)

FARRY, THOMAS: Born Ireland. Educated Ireland, St Peter's. Ordained Glasgow 1903. Glasgow Cathedral 1903-11. Coatdyke 1911. Sacred Heart, Glasgow 1911-14. St John's, Glasgow 1914-16. No address given 1916-17. St Paul's, Shettleston 1917-19. Immaculate Conception, Glasgow 1919-22. Went to USA for health reasons. Died Glasgow 12 July 1928. (Canning)

FEELY, TIMOTHY PATRICK: Born Ireland. Educated Ireland, St Peter's. Ordained Glasgow 1924. Alexandria 1924-30. Our Lady and St Margaret's, Glasgow 1930-41. Glasgow, no parish, 1941-42. St Robert's, Glasgow 1942-48. St Anthony's, Glasgow 1948-50. Died Glasgow 2 Jan 1951. (Canning)

FEENEY, BERNARD: Born and educated Ireland. Ordained Maynooth 1936. Lent to Glasgow. Mossend 1936-38. St Joseph's, Woodside, Glasgow 1938-40. Returned to Ireland 1940. (Canning)

FEGAN, PETER: Born and educated Ireland. Ordained 1881. Lent to Glasgow. St Mary's, Glasgow 1881-86. Cardowan 1886-89. Returned to Ireland 1900 and died there 8 April 1926. (Canning)

FEHILY, THOMAS: Born and educated Ireland. Ordained Kilkenny for Glasgow 1942. Our Lady and St Margaret's, Glasgow 1942-43. Mossend 1943-53; thus moving to Motherwell diocese. Forces chaplain 1953-77. Blackwood 1977-87. Died New Stevenston 16 Sept 1987. (Canning)

FENNESSY, JAMES P: Born Ireland. Educated Ireland, St Peter's. Ordained Glasgow 1917. St Roch's, Glasgow 1917-29. Blantyre 1929-37. Carluke 1937-43. St Agnes's, Glasgow 1943-70. Died Glasgow 24 April 1970. (Canning)

FENNESSY, RICHARD: Born Ireland. Educated Ireland, St Peter's. Ordained Glasgow 1927. St Mary's, Glasgow 1927-32. Chaplain, West Thorn Reformatory and Good Shepherd Convent, Dalbeth 1932-38. St Michael's, Glasgow 1938-39. Cleland 1939-46. Chaplain, Little Sisters of the Poor, Greenock 1946-51; thus moving to Paisley diocese. Neilston 1951-59. St James', Paisley 1959-70. Died Paisley 25 Aug 1970. (Canning)

FINNEGAN, MALACHY: Born and educated Ireland. Ordained Kilkenny for Glasgow 1943. St Roch's, Glasgow 1943-44. Chapelhall 1944-46. Holy Family, Kirkintilloch 1946-48. St Columba's, Glasgow 1948-61. Died Ireland 10 July 1961. (Canning)

FISCHER, LAWRENCE WALLS: see Galloway diocese.

FISHER, JAMES: Born Glasgow 1916. Educated St Aloysius' College, Glasgow 1928-34; St Peter's 1934-41. Ordained Glasgow 1941. St Patrick's, Coatbridge 1941. St Anthony's, Glasgow 1941-45. St Mary's, Greenock 1945-61; thus moving to Paisley diocese. Bishopton 1961-64. Linwood 1964-77. Died Linwood 20 Dec 1977.

FITZGERALD, DANIEL: Ordained 1939. St Benedict's, Glasgow 1974-75. Our Lady and St George, Glasgow 1975-81. No further entries.

FITZGERALD, EDMOND: Born and educated Ireland. Ordained Maynooth 1900. Lent to Glasgow. Helensburgh 1900. St Michael's, Glasgow 1900-05. Barrhead 1905-12. Returned to Ireland 1912 and died there 20 July 1942. (Canning)

FITZGERALD, EDWARD (1894): Born and educated Ireland. Ordained Maynooth 1894. Lent to Glasgow; later got exeat to remain there. St Mary's, Paisley 1894-96. St Mary's, Glasgow 1896-1902. Helensburgh 1902-06. St Columba's, Glasgow 1906-13. St Charles', Glasgow 1913-20. St Mary's, Glasgow 1920-42. Died Glasgow 30 Sept 1942. (Canning)

FITZGERALD, EDWARD (1909): Born and educated Ireland. Ordained Maynooth 1909. Lent to Glasgow. St John the Baptist's, Uddingston 1909-11. Chaplain, West Thorn Reformatory and Good Shepherd Convent, Dalbeth 1911-12. Returned to Ireland 1912 and died there 25 Nov 1968. (Canning)

FITZGERALD, JAMES (1899): Born and educated Ireland. Ordained 1899. Lent to Glasgow. St John's, Glasgow 1899-1910. Returned to Ireland 1910 and died there 18 May 1947. (Canning)

FITZGERALD, JAMES (1940): Born Ireland. Joined Camillian Fathers and was ordained for them 1940. Left Order and joined Glasgow Archdiocese as a secular priest 1959. St Paul's, Shettleston 1959-70. St Gabriel's, Glasgow 1970-71. Chaplain to Marist Brothers, Partick 1971-74. Chaplain, Kings School, Gutersloh, West Germany 1974-84. Lent to Dunkeld diocese: Crieff 1984-. (Canning)

FITZGERALD, J: Ordained 1890. Johnstone 1890-91. No further entries, but see Fitzgerald, William.

FITZGERALD, SEAN MICHAEL: Born Glasgow 1939. Educated St Aloysius' College, Glasgow; Blairs; St Peter's. Ordained Glasgow 1963. Our Lady of Good Counsel, Glasgow 1963-69. St Mary Immaculate, Glasgow 1969-73. St Charles', Glasgow 1973-74. Our Lady of Consolation, Glasgow 1974-80. St Robert's, Glasgow 1980-85. St Pius X, Glasgow 1985-.

FITZGERALD, THOMAS: Born and educated Ireland. Ordained Maynooth 1883. No address given 1883-84. Rutherglen 1884-85. St Patrick's, Dumbarton 1885-86. Went to California 1886. (Canning)

FITZGERALD, WILLIAM: Born and educated Ireland. Ordained Maynooth 1890 (Directories have 1889). Lent to Glasgow. St Paul's, Shettleston 1891-92. Returned to Ireland 1892 and died there 25 Oct 1897. (Canning)
Note: Canning identifies this man with the Catholic Directory's 'Fitzgerald, J', see above.

FITZGIBBON, JAMES: Born and educated Ireland. Ordained Thurles for Glasgow 1928. Holy Cross, Glasgow 1928-29. Immaculate Conception, Glasgow 1929-30. St Patrick's, Glasgow 1930-34. Airdrie 1934-35. Shettleston and Carntyne 1935-39. Forces chaplain 1939-47. St Columba's, Glasgow 1947-48. Immaculate Heart of Mary, Glasgow 1948-57. St Aloysius', Glasgow 1957-67. Died Glasgow 15 April 1967. (Canning)

FITZGIBBON, JOHN (1928): see Fitzgibbon, James

FITZGIBBON, JOHN (1945): Born and educated Ireland. Ordained Kilkenny for Glasgow 1945. St Peter's, Glasgow 1945-57. St Nicholas's, Glasgow 1957-61. St John Ogilvie's, Glasgow 1961-69. All Saints, Glasgow 1969-81. St Eunan's, Clydebank 1981-87. Retired to Ireland 1987 and died there 20 Nov 1988. (Canning)

FITZGIBBON, MAURICE: Born and educated Ireland. Ordained Maynooth 1898. Lent to Glasgow. St Michael's, Glasgow 1898-1902. Returned to Ireland 1902 and died there 9 Jan 1925. (Canning)

FITZPATRICK, GERMAIN FRANCIS: Born Paisley 1944. Educated Blairs, St Peter's. Ordained St Peter's College 1968. St Bonaventure's, Glasgow 1968-70. Professor, Langbank 1970-73. St Philomena's, Glasgow 1973-76. Duntocher 1976-78. No further entries.

FITZPATRICK, MICHAEL: Born and educated Ireland. Ordained Maynooth 1910. Lent to Glasgow. St Mary's, Greenock 1910-20. Returned to Ireland 1920 and died there 3 Dec 1968. (Canning)

FITZPATRICK, PATRICK GERARD: Born Glasgow 1940. Educated St Mungo's Academy, Glasgow; Blairs; Scots College, Rome. Ordained Rome 1964. Sacred Heart, Cumbernauld 1964-65. Further studies, Rome 1965-68. St Brendan's, Glasgow 1968-70. Our Lady of Fatima, Glasgow 1970-72. St Conval's, Glasgow 1972-74. Chaplain, Marist Brothers, Glasgow 1974-76. Duntocher 1976-78. Chaplain, Marist Brothers, Glasgow 1978-79. Chaplain, St Joseph's College, Dumfries 1979-85. St Columba's, Glasgow 1985-.

FITZPATRICK, PETER: Born Ireland. Educated Ireland, St Peter's. Ordained Glasgow 1914. St Joseph's, Tollcross 1914-33. Strathaven 1933-37. Dalry 1937-45. Kilwinning 1945-48; thus moving to Galloway diocese. Kilbirnie 1948-50. Ardrossan 1950-51. Retired 1951. Died Ardrossan 6 Jan 1952. (Canning)

FLANAGAN, WILLIAM: Born Glasgow 1878. Educated Blairs 1893-97; Notre Dame des Champs, Paris 1897-98; St Peter's 1898-1904. Ordained 1904. St Laurence's, Greenock 1904-10. St Aloysius', Glasgow 1910-20. Whiterigg 1920-26. St Agnes's, Glasgow 1926-37. Mossend 1937-52; thus moving to Motherwell diocese. Retired 1952. Died Glasgow 23 Dec 1958.

FLEMING, CHARLES EDWARD: Born Gateshead, England 1869. Educated Grammar School, Newcastle-on-Tyne; Blairs 1883-85, leaving in bad health; Blairs 1886-87; Petit Communaute, Paris 1887-90. Grand Seminaire, Issy 1890; Scots College, Rome 1890-96. Ordained Rome 1895. Chaplain, West Thorn Reformatory, Dalbeth 1896. St Mary's, Greenock 1896-1903. Carluke 1903-05. Renfrew 1905-14. Our Holy Redeemer, Clydebank 1914-38. Retired 1938. Died Ayr 5 Feb 1939.

FLEMING, JOHN J: Born and educated Ireland. Ordained Dublin 1900. Lent to Glasgow; later got exeat to remain there. Blantyre 1900-03. St John's, Glasgow 1903-14. Renton 1914-23. St Anne's, Glasgow 1923-41. Died Glasgow 8 May 1941. (Canning)

FLETCHER, JAMES: Born Kirkfieldbank, Lanark 1889. Educated Blairs 1913-19; St Peter's 1919-24. Ordained Glasgow 1924. St John's, Glasgow 1924-36. Sacred Heart, Glasow 1936-39. Forces chaplain 1939-45. St Constantine's, Glasgow 1945-67. Died Glasgow 12 Jan 1967.

FLOOD, PATRICK JOSEPH: Born Coatbridge 1885. Educated Blairs 1900-04; Scots College, Rome 1904-10. Ordained Rome 1909. Further studies, Biblical Institute, Rome 1910-13. Glenboig 1913-15. Professor, St Peter's College 1915-16. Sacred Heart, Glasgow 1916-29. Chaplain, West Thorn Reformatory and Good Shepherd Convent, Dalbeth 1929-32. Leave of absence from 1932: taught in Fort Augustus School before going to Australia. Died Brisbane 10 March 1965.

FLYNN, BARTHOLOMEW: Born Glasgow 1877. Educated Blairs 1891-94; Valladolid 1894-98, returning home in bad health; St Peter's 1899-1903. Ordained Glasgow 1903. St Mirin's, Paisley 1903-10. Baillieston 1910-15. Houston 1915-16. Alexandria 1916. Forces chaplain 1916-18. Croy 1918-19. St Patrick's, Glasgow 1919. Duntocher 1919-32. Hamilton 1932-49; thus moving to Motherwell diocese. Died Hamilton 25 Feb 1949.

FLYNN, DENIS: Born Ireland. Educated Ireland, St Peter's. Ordained Glasgow 1917. St Patrick's, Shieldmuir 1917-23. Whifflet 1923-33. Linwood 1933-37. St Columba's, Glasgow 1937-47. Our Lady of Good Aid, Motherwell 1947-56; thus moving to Motherwell diocese. St Patrick's, Shieldmuir 1956-59. Died Shieldmuir 21 Nov 1959. (Canning)

FOGARTY, PHILIP: Born and educated Ireland. Ordained Thurles 1915. Lent to Glasgow. St Mary's, Paisley 1915-24. Returned to Ireland 1924 and died there 16 May 1976. (Canning)

FOLEY, BRENDAN THOMAS: Born Glasgow 1946. Educated St Mungo's Academy, Glasgow; Campion House, Osterley; St Peter's. Ordained St Peter's College 1970. St Flannan's, Kirkintilloch 1970. St Constantine's, Glasgow 1970-73. St Philip's, Glasgow 1973-75. St John Ogilvie's, Glasgow 1975-77. Went to Canada: St John's, Newfoundland 1977-78. No further entries.

FOLEY, JOHN (1883): Born Ireland. Educated Ireland, Belgium. Ordained Killarney 1883. St Anthony's, Glasgow 1883-89. Helensburgh 1889-93. Died Helensburgh 14 Aug 1893. (Canning)

FOLEY, JOHN (1885): see Archdiocese of St Andrews & Edinburgh

FORBES, HENRY: Born Tomintoul 1867. Educated Scots College, Rome 1889-95. Ordained Rome 1893. Glasgow Cathedral 1895-99. Vice-rector, St Peter's College 1899-1914. Rector, St Peter's College 1914-45. Died Glasgow 21 April 1945.

FORBES, WILLIAM: Born Glasgow 1907. Educated Blairs 1921-26; Scots College, Rome 1926-33. Ordained Rome 1932. St Luke's, Glasgow 1933-34. St John the Baptist's, Uddingston 1934-43. Sacred Heart, Glasgow 1943-54. St Laurence's, Glasgow 1954-57. Died Glasgow 1 April 1957.

FOUHY, PETER: Born and educated Ireland. Ordained Maynooth 1894. Lent to Glasgow. St Anthony's, Glasgow 1894-99. Returned to Ireland 1899 and died there 26 Nov 1938. (Canning)

FOX, SEAN (John) EDWARD: Born and educated Ireland. Ordained Belfast for Glasgow 1944. St Mirin's, Paisley 1944-51; thus moving to Paisley diocese. St Joseph's, Greenock 1951-53. Got exeat to diocese of Down and Connor 1953. Died Ireland 29 Jan 1962. (Canning)

FRAWLEY, DENIS: Born and educated Ireland. Ordained Maynooth 1887. Lent to Glasgow. St Peter's, Glasgow 1887-90. St Alphonsus', Glasgow 1890-92. Kilbirnie 1892-93. Returned to Ireland 1893 and died there 20 April 1934. (Canning)

FRENCH, STEPHEN JOHN: Born Glasgow 1957. Educated St Ninian's High School, Kirkintilloch; Blairs; Scots College, Rome. Ordained Kirkintilloch 1982. St Peter's, Glasgow 1982. Further studies, Rome 1982-83. St Michael's, Dumbarton 1983-86. Our Lady of Loreto, Dalmuir 1986-.

FRIEL, DANIEL: Born Helensburgh 1926. Educated Blairs; Scots College, Rome. Ordained Rome 1951. St Mary's, Glasgow 1952-55. Professor, Blairs 1955-66. Glasgow Cathedral 1966-71. Spiritual Director, St Peter's College 1971-72. St Thomas's, Glasgow 1972-77. Our Holy Redeemer, Clydebank 1977-78. St Flannan's, Kirkintilloch 1978-.

FRIEL, EAMON VINCENT: Born Clydebank 1938. Educated Blairs; Scots College, Rome. Ordained Rome 1962. St Thomas's, Glasgow 1963-64. Professor, Blairs 1964-67. Our Lady of Good Counsel, Glasgow 1967-72. Professor, Blairs 1972-77. St Augustine's, Glasgow 1977-78. St Roch's, Glasgow 1978-81. Mission in Zambia 1981-84. Our Lady and St George, Glasgow 1984-86. St Brendan's, Glasgow 1986-89. St John Ogilvie's, Glasgow 1989-.

FRIEL, TERENCE M: Born Helensburgh 1935. Educated St Patrick's High School, Dumbarton; Blairs; St Peter's. Ordained Glasgow 1959. Christ the King, Glasgow 1959-75. Sacred Heart, Cumbernauld 1975-79. Faifley 1979-.

FRIGERIO, THOMAS EDGAR: Born Newcastle-on-Tyne 1907. Educated St Patrick's School, Dumbarton; St Mungo's Academy, Glasgow; St Peter's; Scots College, Rome. Ordained 1931. Glasgow Cathedral 1931-32. St Aloysius', Glasgow 1932-35. Our Lady and St Margaret's, Glasgow 1935-46. Belmont Park Hospital, Waterford 1946-59. Lent to Dunkeld diocese: St Patrick's, Dundee 1959-61; St John's, Perth 1961-63. Belmont Park Hospital from 1963, dying there 16 Dec 1987.

FRYER, GEORGE: Born Clydebank 1918. Educated St Patrick's High School, Dumbarton; St Peter's. Ordained 1943. St Bridget's, Baillieston 1943-51; thus moving to Motherwell diocese. Motherwell Cathedral 1951-59. Carluke 1959-65. St Andrew's, Airdrie 1965-82. Glenboig 1982-88. Retired 1988.

FULLER, MICHAEL: Born and educated Ireland. Ordained Maynooth 1886. Lent to Glasgow. St John's, Glasgow 1886-92. Cleland 1892-93. Returned to Ireland 1893 and died there 29 Oct 1936. (Canning)

FYFE, ALEXANDER: Born Glasgow 1880. Educated Kelvinside Academy, Glasgow University, Glasgow United Free Church College. Was minister in the UF Church in Dumfries, England, Rangoon. Became Catholic 1924; educated for priesthood at Beda, Rome. Ordained St Peter's College 1931. St Michael's, Glasgow 1931-39. Millport 1939-48; thus moving to Galloway diocese. Moffat 1948-53. Chaplain, St Ninian's School, Kirkconnel 1953-54. Chaplain, St Austin's School, Kirkconnel 1954-56. C/o Bishop's House 1956-63. Died Glasgow 30 July 1963.

GAHAGAN, PATRICK: Born Glasgow 1931. Educated Campion House, Osterley; Scots College, Rome. Ordained Rome 1956. Glasgow Cathedral 1957. Duntocher 1957-69. Our Lady of Good Counsel, Glasgow 1969-77. St Peter's, Glasgow 1977-82. Croy 1982-84. Corpus Christi, Glasgow 1984-86. St Conval's, Glasgow 1986-.

GALBRAITH, GEORGE J: Born Glasgow 1879. Educated St Aloysius' College, Glasgow; Blairs 1897-1900; Issy 1900-03; St Peter's 1903-07. Ordained Glasgow 1907. Coatdyke 1907-08. Cambuslang 1908-17. Forces chaplain 1917-19. Holy Family, Kirkintilloch 1919-22. Tarbrax 1922-26. Newton 1926-33. Cardonald 1933-60. Died Glasgow 19 June 1960.

GALBRAITH, JAMES: see Argyll diocese.

GALLACHER (Gallagher), JOSEPH: Born Clydebank 1911. Educated Blairs 1924-28; St Peter's 1928-34. Ordained Glasgow 1934. Mossend 1934. St Charles', Paisley 1934-40. St Charles', Paisley in addresses, but not under parishes, 1940-46. Carntyne 1946-48. St Luke's, Glasgow 1948-53. Renton 1953-55. St Barnabas's, Glasgow 1955-58. Sick leave 1958-59. St Teresa's, Glasgow 1959-63. St Joachim's, Glasgow 1963-79. Died Carmyle 3 May 1979.

GALLACHER, PATRICK: Born Dumbarton 1873. Educated Blairs 1889-92; St Peter's 1892-98. Ordained 1898. Our Lady and St Margaret's, Glasgow 1898-1900. Professor, St Peter's College 1900-08. St Luke's, Glasgow 1908-15. Our Lady and St Margaret's, Glasgow 1915-32. Died Glasgow 26 Dec 1932.

GALLACHER, PAUL: Born Glasgow 1965. Educated St Margaret Mary's School, Glasgow; St Peter's; Chesters. Ordained Glasgow 1989. St Matthew's, Glasgow 1989-.

GALLACHER, PETER MICHAEL: Born Dumbarton 1953. Educated St Aloysius' College, Glasgow; Glasgow University; Scots College, Rome.

Ordained Dumbarton 1979. Our Lady and St George, Glasgow 1979. Further studies, Rome 1979-82. Holy Cross, Glasgow 1982-86. Professor, Chesters 1986-.

GALLAGHER, ANTHONY: Born Glasgow 1949. Educated Langbank, Blairs, St Peter's. Ordained Dalmuir 1973. St Mary's, Glasgow 1973-77. St Catherine's, Glasgow 1977-84. St Jude's, Glasgow 1984-87. Our Lady of Fatima, Glasgow 1987-.

GALLAGHER, BERNARD: Born and educated Ireland. Ordained Maynooth 1921. Lent to Glasgow. Cardonald 1921-26. Returned to Ireland 1926 and died there 8 June 1936. (Canning)

GALLAGHER (Gallacher), CHARLES: Born Glasgow 1891. Educated Blairs 1908-13; Scots College, Rome 1913-20. Ordained Rome 1919. St Luke's, Glasgow 1920-22. St Laurence's, Greenock 1922-30. St Agnes's, Glasgow 1930-33. St Roch's, Glasgow 1933-38. Sick leave 1938-42. Chaplain, Good Shepherd Convent, Castle Huntly 1942-46. Chaplain, St Helen's Convent, Glasgow 1946-52. Died Glasgow 15 Sept 1952.

GALLAGHER, DANIEL M: Born Neilston 1922. Educated Blairs, St Peter's. Ordained Glasgow 1946. St Mary's, Paisley 1946-47. St Brendan's, Glasgow 1947-65. St Vincent de Paul's, Glasgow 1965-66. St Roch's, Glasgow 1966-71. St Nicholas's, Glasgow 1971-74. Renton 1974-76. St Gregory's, Glasgow 1976-.

GALLAGHER, EDWARD JOHN: Born Glasgow 1943. Educated St Aloysius' College, Glasgow; Blairs; Scots College, Rome. Ordained Rome 1967. St Margaret Mary's, Glasgow 1968-70. No further entries.

GALLAGHER, FRANCIS PATRICK: Born Glasgow 1944. Educated Blairs, St Peter's. Ordained St Peter's College 1968. St Philomena's, Glasgow 1968-75. St Michael's, Glasgow 1975-80. Our Lady of Consolation, Glasgow 1980-84. St Albert's, Glasgow 1984-86. St Margaret Mary's, Glasgow 1986-.

GALLAGHER, HUGH: Born Clydebank 1920. Educated St Patrick's High School, Dumbarton; Blairs; St Peter's. Ordained 1945. Gourock 1945-56; thus moving to Paisley diocese. Vice-rector, Valladolid 1956-63. Neilston 1963-64. Chaplain, Little Sisters of the Poor, Greenock 1964-69. St Columba's, Renfrew 1969-72. St Mary's, Greenock 1972-.

GALLAGHER, JOHN: Born and educated Ireland. Ordained Maynooth 1926. Lent to Glasgow. St Thomas's, Glasgow 1926-34. Returned to Ireland 1934 and died there 8 May 1948. (Canning)

GALLAGHER, MICHAEL GERARD PATRICK: Born Glasgow 1960. Educated St Margaret Mary's School, Glasgow; St Patrick's College, Buchlyvie; St Peter's; Chesters. Ordained Glasgow 1989. St Mary's, Duntocher 1989-.

GALLAGHER, OWEN: Born Glasgow 1934. Educated St Mungo's Academy, Glasgow; St Peter's. Ordained Glasgow 1958. St Saviour's, Glasgow 1958-59. Holy Cross, Glasgow 1959-84. Sacred Heart, Cumbernauld 1984-85. Our Lady of Good Counsel, Glasgow 1985-.

GALLAUCHER, ALFRED JOSEPH: Born Gourock 1884. Educated Blairs 1899-1904; Issy 1904-06; St Sulpice 1906-09. Ordained Paris 1909. St Augustine's, Coatbridge 1909-11. Saltcoats 1911-24. Chaplain, West Thorn Reformatory and Good Shepherd Convent, Dalbeth 1924-29. Larkhall 1929-31. Renfrew 1931-38. St Augustine's, Coatbridge 1938-40. Newton 1940-45. St Joseph's, Tollcross 1945-70. Died Gourock 11 Aug 1970.

GALVIN, MORTIMER J: Born and educated Ireland. Ordained Maynooth 1907. Lent to Glasgow. St Charles', Glasgow 1908-09. Alexandria 1909-16. Returned to Ireland 1916 and died there 22 March 1952. (Canning)

GANNON, JOHN F: Born Glasgow 1965. Educated St Andrew's School, Carntyne; St Peter's; Chesters. Ordained Glasgow 1989. St Maria Goretti's, Glasgow 1989-.

GANNON, THOMAS: see Dunkeld diocese.

GARLAND, PETER: Born Croftfoot, Glasgow 1935. Educated Blairs, St Peter's. Ordained Glasgow 1959. Faifley 1959-71. No further entries.

GARRITY, DENIS: Born Bellshill 1912. Educated Blairs 1927-33; St Peter's 1933-41. Ordained Glasgow 1941. St Philomena's, Glasgow 1941-44. Houston 1944-46. St Vincent de Paul's, Glasgow 1946-47. St Ignatius's, Wishaw 1947-49; thus moving to Motherwell diocese. Plains 1949-53. St Columbkille's, Rutherglen 1953-58. Harthill 1958-59. Lent to Aberdeen diocese: St Peter's, Aberdeen 1959-60. Muirhead 1960-61. St Bridget's, Baillieston 1961-62. St Luke's, Motherwell 1962-66. St Ninian's, Hamilton 1966-72. St Monica's, Coatbridge 1972-81. Retired 1981.

GARVEY, PATRICK: Born and educated Ireland. Ordained Maynooth 1909. Lent to Glasgow. St Luke's, Glasgow 1909-13. Returned to Ireland 1913 and died there 2 Aug 1963. (Canning)

GAULE, PATRICK: Born and educated Ireland. Ordained Ireland 1880. Joined Glasgow Archdiocese. St Mary's, Greenock 1880-85. Larkhall 1885-93. St Paul's, Shettleston 1893-1902. Retired to Dublin 1902 and died there 24 Dec 1932. (Canning)

GAVAGAN, MICHAEL: Born Barrhead 1918. Educated Blairs, St Peter's. Ordained 1945. St Roch's, Glasgow 1945-54. Milngavie 1954-62. Chaplain, Barlinnie Prison and St Joseph's Home, Glasgow 1962-68. St Teresa's, Glasgow 1968-69. St Margaret's, Clydebank 1969-77. Holy Family, Kirkintilloch 1977-86. Died Kirkintilloch 5 Jan 1987.

GAVAGAN (Gavigan), THOMAS: Born and educated Ireland. Ordained Maynooth 1897. Lent to Glasgow. St Alphonsus', Glasgow 1897-98. Returned to Ireland 1898. (Canning)

GAVIN, WILLIAM JOHN: Born Glasgow 1945. Educated Blairs, St Peter's. Ordained Glasgow 1969. Good Shepherd, Glasgow 1970-72. Not in Directories 1972-77. Assistant chaplain, University of Strathclyde 1977-78. Croy 1978-.

GAYNOR, PATRICK: Born and educated Ireland. Ordained Maynooth 1911. Lent to Glasgow. Wishaw 1911-12. St Alphonsus', Glasgow 1912-14. Returned to Ireland 1914 and died there 8 Dec 1949. (Canning)

GEERTY, JOHN: Born Wishaw 1871. Educated St Aloysius' College, Glasgow; Blairs 1884-86; Valladolid 1886-93. Ordained Valladolid 1893. St Patrick's, Coatbridge 1893-1931. Died Coatbridge 6 April 1931.

GIBBONS, THOMAS: Born and educated Ireland. Ordained Waterford 1900. Lent to Glasgow. St Mary's, Greenock 1900-11. Returned to Ireland 1911 and died there 18 May 1935. (Canning)

GILFEDDER, CHRISTOPHER PATRICK: Born Glasgow 1928. Educated St Mungo's Academy, Glasgow; Salesian College, Shrigley; St Sulpice. Ordained Glasgow 1954. St John's, Glasgow 1954. Our Lady of Lourdes, Glasgow 1954-61. Professor, Blairs 1961-73. Our Lady and St George, Glasgow 1973-75. Economat des Redemptoristes, Paris 1975-77. Glasgow Cathedral 1977-79. Milngavie 1979-81. St Philomena', Glasgow 1981-82. Our Lady of Perpetual Succour, Glasgow 1982-87. St Dominic's, Bishopbriggs 1987-.

GILFEDDER, FRANCIS: Born Glasgow 1930. Educated Blairs, St Peter's. Ordained Glasgow 1953. Our Lady of the Assumption, Glasgow 1953-67. St Catherine's, Glasgow 1967-73. St Pius X, Glasgow 1973-78. St Gabriel's, Glasgow 1978-81. St Anthony's, Glasgow 1981-87. St Benedict's, Glasgow 1987-88. St Bonaventure's, Glasgow 1988-.

GILLEN, JOHN: Born and educated Ireland. Ordained Kilkenny for Glasgow 1939. St Mary's, Paisley 1939-40. St Augustine's, Coatbridge 1940-44. Glenboig 1944-50; thus moving to Motherwell diocese. St Columba's, Viewpark 1950-53. All Saints, Airdrie 1953-56. Newarthill 1956-69. Our Lady of Lourdes, East Kilbride 1969-74. St Columbkille's, Rutherglen 1974-. (Canning)

GILLESPIE, GEORGE FRANCIS: Born Glasgow 1937. Educated Blairs; Scots College, Rome. Ordained Rome 1961. Faifley 1962-67. Croy 1967-72. St Maria Goretti's, Glasgow 1972-77. St Charles', Glasgow 1977-79. St Anne's, Glasgow 1979-84. St Brendan's, Glasgow 1984-86. Aberlour (Aberdeen diocese), not serving parish, 1986-87. Croy 1987-88. St Joseph's, Cumbernauld 1988-89. Cardross 1989-.

GILLESPIE, JOHN: Born Paisley 1912. Educated Blairs 1927-31; St Peter's 1931-38. Ordained Glasgow 1938. Croy 1938-44. St Philomena's, Glasgow 1944-52. St Anthony's, Glasgow 1952-59. Chaplain, Notre Dame 1959-70. St Agnes's, Glasgow 1970-73. Holy Cross, Glasgow 1973-84. Died Glasgow 24 May 1984.

GILLESPIE, WILLIAM: Born and educated Ireland. Ordained Maynooth 1901. Lent to Glasgow. St Peter's, Glasgow 1902-04. Returned to Ireland 1904 and died there 9 Dec 1920. (Canning)

GILLIES, WILLIAM: see Argyll diocese.

GILLON, DANIEL: Born Glasgow 1876. Educated Blairs 1891-94; Notre Dame des Champs, Paris 1894-95; Issy 1895-97; St Sulpice 1897-1900. Ordained Paris 1900. Johnstone 1900-02. St Michael's, Glasgow 1902-03. Professor, St Peter's College 1903-10. Linwood 1910-15. Died Linwood 5 Feb 1915.

GILMARTIN, JOHN: Born Glasgow 1942. Educated Campion House, Osterley; St Peter's. Ordained St Peter's College 1968. Immaculate Conception, Glasgow 1968-73. St Catherine's, Glasgow 1973-77. Milngavie 1977-79. St Luke's, Glasgow 1979-80. St Vincent's Centre, Langbank 1980-88. London 1988-.

GILMARTIN, PATRICK: Born and educated Ireland. Ordained for Glasgow 1926. St Paul's, Shettleston 1926-28. Shettleston and Carntyne 1928-45. Carntyne 1945-46. Old Kilpatrick 1946-48. St Luke's, Glasgow 1948-52. St Bonaventure's, Glasgow 1952-60. Our Lady of Lourdes, Glasgow 1960-76. Retired to Ireland 1976. (Canning)

GILROY, MICHAEL: Born and educated Ireland. Ordained Maynooth 1939. Lent to Glasgow. St Mary Immaculate, Glasgow 1939-44. St Patrick's, Coatbridge 1944-45. Returned to Ireland 1945 and died there 1 Jan 1975. (Canning)

GLEESON, HENRY: Born and educated Ireland. Ordained Maynooth 1901. Offered his services to Glasgow. Motherwell 1901. Got enteric fever after a few weeks. Died Motherwell 11 Nov 1901. (Canning)

GLEN, THOMAS: Born Paisley 1912. Educated Blairs 1926-30; St Peter's 1930-37. Ordained Glasgow 1937. St Paul's, Glasgow 1937-41. Carfin 1941-42. St Charles', Glasgow 1942-57. Faifley 1957-80. Retired 1980.

GLYNN, JOHN: Born and educated Ireland. Ordained Dublin for Glasgow 1952. St Paul's, Shettleston 1952-60. St Margaret Mary's, Glasgow 1960-65. St Conval's, Glasgow 1965-73. Retired 1973. Died Ireland 29 Aug 1974. (Canning)

GODFREY, JOHN: Born and educated Ireland. Ordained Maynooth 1918. Lent to Glasgow. Hamilton 1918-19. Cadzow 1919-20. Returned to Ireland 1920 and died there 13 Aug 1958. (Canning)

GODLEY, JOHN: Born Ireland. Educated Ireland, Paris. Ordained 1885. Lent to Glasgow. Our Lady and St Margaret's, Glasgow 1885-88. Returned to Ireland 1888 and died there 28 Nov 1938. (Canning)

GOGARTY, JOHN: Born Mossend 1911. Educated Blairs 1926-30; Scots College, Rome 1930-36. Ordained Rome 1936. Stevenston 1937-40. St Patrick's, Glasgow 1940-52. Vice-rector, Scots College, Rome 1952-59. Our Lady of Fatima, Glasgow 1959-73. Retired 1973. Died Ireland 30 Oct 1986.

GOODFELLOW, FRANCIS PATRICK: Born Clydebank 1932. Educated Sacred Heart College, Sunningdale; College of Missioni Africane, Venegono Superiore, Italy; St Peter's. Ordained Glasgow 1957. St Brigid's, Glasgow 1957-59. St Joseph's, Tollcross 1959-62. Mission in Nigeria 1962-68. Christ the King, Glasgow 1968-76. St Roch's, Glasgow 1976-79. Died Glasgow 31 Dec 1979.

GORDON, MICHAEL: Born Dumbarton 1883. Educated St Mungo's Academy, Glasgow; Blairs 1897-1901; St Peter's 1901-04; Scots College, Rome 1904-08. Ordained Rome 1907. St Alphonsus', Glasgow 1908-10. Professor, St Peter's College 1910-17. Died France 27 Aug 1917.

GOURLAY, THOMAS P: Born Glasgow 1877. Educated Blairs 1892-95; St Peter's 1895-1904. Ordained Glasgow 1904. Burnbank 1904-08. Holy Family, Kirkintilloch 1908-11. St Mary's, Paisley 1911-15. St Patrick's, Shieldmuir 1915-17. Chaplain, West Thorn Reformatory and Good Shepherd Convent, Dalbeth 1917-25. Leave of absence 1925-26. Carfin 1926-27. Carfin in addresses, but not under parishes, 1927-29. Retired 1929. Died Inverness 12 March 1932.

GOWANS, JOHN: Born Glasgow 1922. Educated St Peter's. Ordained Glasgow 1953. St John's, Glasgow 1953-54. St Patrick's, Dumbarton 1954-74. St Brendan's, Glasgow 1974-76. Went to Aberdeen diocese. Sacred Heart, Aberdeen 1976-77. Holy Family, Aberdeen 1977-.

GRACE, THOMAS: Born Glasgow 1919. Educated St Mungo's Academy, Glasgow; St Peter's. Ordained 1944. Cardowan 1944-47. Barrhead 1947-68; thus moving to Paisley diocese. Gourock 1968-69. St Mungo's, Greenock 1969-74. St Peter's, Paisley 1974-86. St Aidan's, Johnstone 1986-.

GRACE, VINCENT E: Born Glasgow 1907. Educated Blairs 1923-28; St Peter's 1928-34. Ordained Glasgow 1934. St Mary's, Paisley 1934-36. St Mungo's, Greenock 1936-42. Forces chaplain 1942-46. St Columba's, Glasgow 1946-47. St Mary's, Greenock 1947-50; thus moving to Paisley diocese. RAF chaplain 1950-53. St Andrew's, Greenock 1953-59. Howwood 1959-66. St Patrick's, Greenock 1966-68. Neilston 1968-71. Wemyss Bay 1971-75. Retired 1975. Died Greenock 23 May 1978.

GRAHAM, HENRY G: Born Maxton, Roxburghshire 1874. Became Catholic 1903. Educated Scots College, Rome 1903-07. Ordained Rome 1906. Larkhall 1907. Motherwell 1907-15. Longriggend 1915-17. Consecrated Bishop Auxiliary for Archdiocese of St Andrews & Edinburgh 1917. Retired as bishop 1930. Holy Cross, Glasgow 1930-59. Died Glasgow 5 Dec 1959.

GRAHAM, JAMES: Born Motherwell 1902. Educated Blairs 1917-19; St Peter's 1919-22; Scots College, Rome 1922-26. Ordained Rome 1926. St Paul's, Shettleston 1926-29. St Mary's, Paisley 1929-32. Our Holy Redeemer, Clydebank 1932-39. Forces chaplain 1939-45. Further studies, Maynooth 1945-47. C/o Diocesan Office 1947-48. St Flannan's, Kirkintilloch 1948-51. St Anthony's, Glasgow 1951-55. Died Glasgow 4 March 1955.

GRANT, KENNETH: see Argyll diocese.

GRAU, CASPER P: Born Eil, Germany 1865. Educated St Charles' College, Valkenburg; Rollduc, near Aix-la-chapelle; St Peter's 1893-96. Ordained 1896. St Patrick's, Shieldmuir 1896. St Mirin's, Paisley 1896-99. Returned to Germany 1899 and died there 13 Nov 1935.

GREED, JOHN: Born and educated Ireland. Ordained Maynooth 1898. Lent to Glasgow. Motherwell 1898-1901. Returned to Ireland 1901 and died there 17 March 1941. (Canning)

GREEN, PATRICK: see Archdiocese of St Andrews & Edinburgh

GRIFFIN, DENIS: Born and educated Ireland. Ordained Maynooth 1926. Lent to Glasgow. Holy Cross, Glasgow 1926-28. Returned to Ireland 1928 and died there 15 April 1957. (Canning)

GRIFFIN, PATRICK: Born and educated Ireland. Ordained Maynooth 1900. Lent to Glasgow. Mossend 1900-05. St Luke's, Glasgow 1905-06. Returned to Ireland 1906 and died there 5 May 1946. (Canning)

GRIFFIN, THOMAS: Born and educated Ireland. Ordained Maynooth 1925. Lent to Glasgow. St Mary's, Glasgow 1925-26. Returned to Ireland 1926. (Canning)

GRIFFITH, THOMAS R: Born and educated Ireland. Ordained Maynooth 1915. Lent to Glasgow. Holy Family, Kirkintilloch 1916-18. Returned to Ireland 1918 and died there 10 Feb 1963. (Canning)

GUINAN, THOMAS P: Born and educated Ireland. Ordained Ballina 1922. Lent to Glasgow. St Michael's, Glasgow 1922-24. St Luke's, Glasgow 1924-25. Returned to Ireland 1926 and died there 6 March 1944. (Canning)

GUIRY, MICHAEL: Born and educated Ireland. Ordained Waterford 1922. Lent to Glasgow. St Stephen's, Dalmuir 1922-26. Returned to Ireland 1926 and died there 26 May 1971. (Canning)

GULLANE, PATRICK J: Born and educated Ireland. Ordained Maynooth 1937. Cleland 1937-39. St Michael's, Glasgow 1939-40. Returned to Ireland 1940. (Canning)

GUNNING, DESMOND: Born Partick 1917. Educated St Aloysius' College, Glasgow 1925-34; St Peter's 1934-41. Ordained Glasgow 1941. Glasgow Cathedral 1941-56. St Patrick's, Dumbarton 1956-66. St Helen's, Glasgow 1966-69. With Missionary Society of St James the Apostle in Boston, Peru 1969-75. St Saviour's, Glasgow 1975-81. St Mark's, Carntyne 1981-88. Retired 1988.

GUNNING, PATRICK JOSEPH: Born Ireland. Educated Ireland, St Peter's. Ordained Glasgow 1959. St Anthony's, Glasgow 1959-71. St Helen's, Glasgow 1971-73. St Robert's, Glasgow 1973-76. C/o Diocesan Office 1976-78. No further entries. (Canning)

GUNTHER, HUGH: Born near Coblentz 1874. Educated Emperor William's Gymnasium, Montabaur, near Nassau; St Peter's 1892-99. Ordained 1899. Our Lady and St Margaret's, Glasgow 1899-1906. Chaplain, Nazareth House, Glasgow 1906-07. Cardonald 1907-10. Renton 1910-11. Returned to Germany 1911; still there 1920. No further entries.

GUTAUSKAS, JOSEPH: Serving Lithuanian community. Stationed at: Mossend 1934-42; St Columba's, Glasgow 1942-82. Retired 1982.

HACKETT, MICHAEL: Born and educated Ireland. Ordained Maynooth 1911. Lent to Glasgow. St Patrick's, Glasgow 1911-15. Baillieston 1915-19. Returned to Ireland 1919 and died there 7 April 1964. (Canning)

HACKETT, PATRICK (1887): Born Ireland. Educated St Mungo's Academy, Glasgow; Propaganda, Rome. Ordained Rome 1887. St Laurence's, Greenock 1887-89. Immaculate Conception, Glasgow 1889-93. Cleland 1893-1902. Whifflet 1902-37. Died Whifflet 13 May 1937. (Canning)

HACKETT, PATRICK A (1910): Born and educated Ireland. Ordained Kilkenny 1910. Lent to Glasgow. Holy Cross, Glasgow 1910-17. Returned to Ireland [1917]. (Canning)

HACKETT, THOMAS: School teacher in Glasgow before being educated for priesthood in Belgium and Propaganda, Rome. Ordained Rome 1882. St Patrick's, Glasgow 1882-86. Blantyre 1886-1921. Died Blantyre 5 March 1921.

HAEGER, CHARLES: Born c1860. Ordained 1894. St Mary's, Glasgow 1894-1900. Chaplain, Good Shepherd Convent, Dalbeth 1900-02. Glenboig 1902-19. Went to Germany 1919 and died there 5 Feb 1946.

HAGGARTY, J: Ordained 1924. St Patrick's, Coatbridge 1924-25. No further entries.
Note: this may be the same man as 'Hegarty, Simon' in Canning.

HALLEY (Hally), JAMES: Born and educated Ireland. Ordained Waterford 1926. Lent to Glasgow. St Stephen's, Dalmuir 1926-27. Returned to Ireland 1927. (Canning)

HALLINAN, JAMES E: Born and educated Ireland. Ordained Thurles for Glasgow 1940. St Charles', Glasgow 1940. St Philomena's, Glasgow 1940-47. All Saints, Coatdyke 1947-53; thus moving to Motherwell diocese. Shotts 1953-57. St Thomas's, Wishaw 1957-69. Cleland 1969-74. Died Cleland 30 May 1974. (Canning)

HALLINAN, PATRICK: Born and educated Ireland. Ordained Thurles 1912. Lent to Glasgow. Wishaw 1912-19. Returned to Ireland 1919 and died there 2 June 1938. (Canning)

HAMILL (Hammill), JOHN: Born Kilbirnie 1912. Educated St Michael's School, Irvine; St Mungo's Academy, Glasgow; St Peter's. Ordained Glasgow 1938. St Saviour's, Glasgow 1938-41. Barrhead 1941-42. Glenboig 1942-44. Sick leave 1944-49. Lent to Galloway diocese: Kirkcudbright 1949-50. Sick leave from 1950. Went to England, where he acted as convent chaplain when well enough. Died England 13 Jan 1965.

HAMILL, JOSEPH: Born Clydebank 1901. Educated Blairs 1915-20; St Peter's 1920-26. Ordained Glasgow 1926. St Peter's, Glasgow 1926-30. Glenboig 1930. Rutherglen 1930-39. Holy Family, Kirkintilloch 1939-46. Bishopton 1946-56; thus moving to Paisley diocese. Linwood 1956-63. Died Linwood 28 Oct 1963.

HAMILTON, ALEXANDER: Born Glasgow 1887. Educated St Mungo's Academy 1901-03; Blairs 1903-06; St Peter's 1906-14. Ordained Glasgow 1914. Motherwell 1914-16. Professor, St Peter's College 1916-17. Holy Cross, Glasgow 1917-19. Professor, St Peter's College 1919-35. St Patrick's, Shieldmuir 1935-49; thus moving to Motherwell diocese. St Mary's, Hamilton 1949-71. Died Hamilton 22 Oct 1971.

HAMILTON, FRANCIS (1915): Born Glasgow 1889. Educated Blairs 1904-09; Propaganda, Rome 1909-15. Ordained Rome 1915. Sacred Heart, Glasgow 1915-16. St Patrick's, Glasgow 1916-17. No address given 1917-20. No further entries.

HAMILTON, FRANCIS (1926): Born Rutherglen 1893. Educated Campion House, Osterley 1919-20; St Peter's 1920-26. Ordained Glasgow 1926. St Augustine's, Coatbridge 1926-40. St Joseph's, Woodside, Glasgow 1940-41. St Patrick's, Shieldmuir 1941-46. Linwood 1946-49; thus moving to Paisley diocese. St James's, Renfrew 1949-74. Retired 1974. Died Laconia, USA 15 March 1979.

HANNAH, STEPHEN: Born Glasgow 1963. Educated St Augustine's School, Milton; St Peter's; Chesters. Ordained Glasgow 1988. St Stephen's, Dalmuir 1988-.

HANRAHAN, JOHN: Born and educated Ireland. Ordained Dublin for Glasgow 1950. Croy 1950-67. Christ the King, Glasgow 1967-68. Duntocher 1968-74. St Helen's, Glasgow 1974-84. Holy Cross, Glasgow 1984-. (Canning)

HANRAHAN, MICHAEL: Born and educated Ireland. Ordained Maynooth 1918. Lent to Glasgow. Blantyre 1918-20. Returned to Ireland 1920 and died there 28 Sept 1960. (Canning)

HARAN, JOHN: Born Glasgow 1910. Educated Blairs 1924-29; Valladolid 1929-36. Ordained Valladolid 1936. St Thomas's, Glasgow 1936-40. St Mirin's, Paisley 1940-50; thus moving to Paisley diocese. Bishopton 1950-59. Chaplain, St Vincent's Home, Langbank 1959-61. Houston 1961-72. St Patrick's, Greenock 1972-75. Retired to Ireland 1975.

HARKIN, JOHN: Born and educated Ireland. Ordained Derry 1939. Lent to Glasgow. Our Holy Redeemer, Clydebank 1939-41. Returned to Ireland 1941. (Canning)

HARRINGTON (Hartington), MICHAEL: Born and educated Ireland. Ordained Maynooth 1912. Lent to Glasgow. Cleland 1912-13. Barrhead 1913-21. Returned to Ireland 1921 and died there 19 Jan 1948. (Canning)

HART, DANIEL J. C.: Born Warley, Essex 1932. Educated Blairs; Scots College, Rome. Ordained Rome 1956. St Peter's, Glasgow (and studying at Glasgow University) 1956-61. Professor, Blairs 1961-69. Our Lady of Perpetual Succour, Glasgow 1969-72. St Joseph's, Woodside, Glasgow 1972-84. St Helen's, Glasgow 1984-.

HART, GERARD: Born Dumbarton 1910. Educated St Patrick's High School, Dumbarton 1921-27; St Peter's 1927-33. Ordained Glasgow 1933. St Roch's, Glasgow 1933-42. Carfin 1942-44. Forces chaplain 1944-47. Glasgow Cathedral 1947-54. St Catherine's, Glasgow 1954-72. St Paul's, Glasgow 1972-80. Died Glasgow 2 Dec 1980.

HART, HENRY E: Born Dumbarton 1895. Educated Blairs 1912-16; St Peter's 1916-23. Ordained Glasgow 1923. Motherwell 1923-40. Bothwell 1940-45. Gourock 1945-47. St Mary's, Greenock 1947-59; thus moving to Paisley diocese. Died Greenock 26 Oct 1959.

HART, WILLIAM: Born Dumbarton 1904. Educated Blairs 1919-22; Valladolid 1922-29. Ordained Valladolid 1929. St Mary's, Hamilton 1929-33. St John's, Glasgow 1933-39. Forces chaplain 1939-45. St Michael's, Glasgow 1945-48. Vice-rector, Valladolid 1948-49. St Nicholas's, Glasgow 1949-51. St Saviour's, Glasgow 1951-55. Consecrated Bishop of Dunkeld 1955. Retired 1981.

HARTE, PETER: Born and educated Ireland. Ordained Ballaghaderreen 1923. Lent to Glasgow. St Luke's, Glasgow 1924-34. Returned to Ireland 1934 and died there 20 July 1973. (Canning)

HARTMANN, GISBERT JAMES: Born Montabaur, Germany 1864. Educated Montabaur Gymnasium; St Peter's 1886-90. Ordained St Peter's College 1890. St Patrick's, Glasgow 1890-94. Baillieston 1894-97. Largs 1897-1901. Strathaven 1901-06. Carfin 1906-11. Cadzow 1911-14. Chaplain, Kenmure Industrial School 1914-18. Leave of absence 1918-24. Chaplain, Little Sisters of the Poor, Greenock 1924-43. No address given 1943-45. Died Musselburgh 11 Jan 1946.

HARTY, DANIEL: Born Ireland. Educated Ireland, St Peters. Ordained Glasgow 1917. St Paul's, Shettleston 1917-20. Chaplain, West Thorn Reformatory and Good Shepherd Convent, Dalbeth 1920-23. St Anne's, Glasgow 1923-34. Blackwood 1934-39. Shotts 1939-49; thus moving to Motherwell diocese. St Patrick's, Shieldmuir 1949-56. Retired to Ireland 1956 and died there 28 Nov 1967. (Canning)

HARVEY, GERALD A: Born Glasgow 1907. Educated Blairs 1923-26; Scots College, Rome 1926-33. Ordained Rome 1932. St Anne's, Glasgow 1933-44. St Joseph's, Glasgow 1944-52. C/o Diocesan Office 1952-53. St Saviour's, Glasgow 1953-55. Good Shepherd, Glasgow 1955-64. Died Glasgow 21 Oct 1964.

HASTINGS, PHILIP: Born Clydebank 1920. Educated St Mungo's Academy, Glasgow; Stow College; Jordanhill College; Campion House, Osterley; Valladolid. Ordained Glasgow 1967. Our Holy Redeemer, Clydebank 1967-69. St Patrick's, Glasgow 1969-72. Our Lady of Fatima, Glasgow 1972-73. St Barnabas's, Glasgow 1973-75. St Philip's, Glasgow 1975-81. Awaiting appointment 1981-82. St Luke's, Glasgow 1982-.

HAY, JOHN: Born Glasgow 1944. Educated Blairs, St Peter's. Ordained St Peter's College 1969. St Mary's, Glasgow 1969. Our Lady of Lourdes, Glasgow 1969-75. No further entries.

HAYES, WILLIAM J: Born Ireland. Educated Ireland, St Peter's. Ordained Glasgow 1913. St Roch's, Glasgow 1913-21. Cadzow 1921-31. Larkhall 1931-38. St James's, Renfrew 1938-49; thus moving to Paisley diocese. St Mungo's, Greenock 1949-50. Retired to Dublin 1950 and died there 25 June 1952. (Canning)

HEALY, DERMOT JOHN: Born Glasgow 1951. Educated St Aloysius' College, Glasgow; St Peter's. Ordained Glasgow 1974. St Roch's, Glasgow 1974-76. Chaplain, Kenmure Industrial School 1976-77. Blairs in addresses, but not under College staff, 1977-79. St Matthew's, Bishopbriggs 1979-82. Our Lady of Lourdes, Glasgow 1982-84. St James's, Glasgow 1984-87. On mission with Society of St James the Apostle in Bolivia, then Peru, 1987-.

HEALY, JEREMIAH: Born and educated Ireland. Ordained Waterford for Glasgow 1936. Wishaw 1936-44. St Mary Immaculate, Glasgow 1944-57. St John Ogilvie's, Glasgow 1957-60. Died Glasgow 20 Oct 1960. (Canning)

HEALY, JOHN J: Born and educated Ireland. Ordained Galway 1925. Lent to Glasgow. Our Lady and St Margaret's, Glasgow 1927-30. St Augustine's, Coatbridge in addresses, but not under parishes, 1930-31. Returned to Ireland 1931 and died there 29 June 1964. (Canning)

HEALY, THOMAS (1899): Born Glasgow 1875. Educated Blairs 1889-92; St Peter's 1892-99. Ordained 1899. Cambuslang 1899-1901. Holy Family, Kirkintilloch 1901-02. Johnstone 1902-03. Sick leave in South Africa 1903-10. `Retired' 1910-19. Croy 1919-20. Linwood 1920-28. Baillieston 1928-29. Retired 1929. Went to India in 1931 and died there 22 Aug 1942.

HEALY, THOMAS (1939): Born 1913. Educated St Aloysius' College, Glasgow 1923-27; Blairs 1927-32; St Peter's 1932-39. Ordained Glasgow 1939. Our Holy Redeemer, Clydebank 1939-40. Port Glasgow 1940-46. Clarkston 1946-47. Immaculate Conception, Glasgow 1947-52. St Constantine's, Glasgow 1952-55. Good Shepherd, Glasgow 1955-65. Twechar 1965-70. St Barnabas's, Glasgow 1970-75. Went to Aberdeen diocese: Aberdeen Cathedral 1975-76; Dornie 1976-78. Retired 1978. Died Dornie 24 May 1980.

HEANEY, PATRICK JOSEPH: Born Glasgow 1901. Educated Blairs 1918-22; Scots College, Rome 1922-29. Ordained Rome 1928. Baillieston 1929-32. Barrhead 1932-34. St John the Baptist's, Uddingston 1934-49; thus moving to Motherwell diocese. Biggar 1949-50. Blackwood 1950-53. Bargeddie 1953-58. Sacred Heart, Bellshill 1958-67. Died Glasgow 20 May 1967.

HEARTY, THOMAS: Born Coatbridge 1917. Educated Blairs 1931-35; Scots College, Rome 1935-40; St Peter's 1940-42. Ordained Glasgow 1942. Our Holy Redeemer, Clydebank 1942-44. St Charles', Paisley 1944-66; thus moving to Paisley diocese. Clarkston 1966-73. Barrhead 1973-74. St James', Paisley 1974-80. St John Bosco's, Erskine 1980-.

HEGARTY, SIMON: Born and educated Ireland. Ordained Maynooth 1924. Lent to Glasgow. St Mary's, Greenock 1925-26. St Aloysius', Glasgow 1926-28. Returned to Ireland 1928 and died there 23 Sept 1952. (Canning)
Note: Canning identifies this man with 'Haggarty, J' of the Directories, see above.

HEHIR, DENIS: Born and educated Ireland. Ordained Maynooth 1905. Lent to Glasgow. St Alphonsus', Glasgow 1905-08. Returned to Ireland 1908 and died there 4 Nov 1952. (Canning)

HENDRY, THOMAS JOHN: Born Glasgow 1940. Educated St Aloysius' College, Glasgow; St Peter's. Ordained Glasgow 1966. St Gregory's, Glasgow 1966-80. Chaplain, Glasgow University 1980-85. Sacred Heart, Cumbernauld 1985-.

HENNESSY, MATTHEW: Born and educated Ireland. Ordained 1899. Lent to Glasgow. St Joseph's, Tollcross 1899-1908. Returned to Ireland 1908 and died there 28 Jan 1927. (Canning)

HENRETTY, MICHAEL: Born Riddrie 1928. Educated Blairs, St Peter's, St Sulpice. Ordained Glasgow 1951. Croy 1951-67. St Patrick's, Dumbarton 1967-74. St Michael's, Dumbarton 1974-77. St Mark's, Carntyne 1977-82. St Maria Goretti's, Glasgow 1982-.

HENRY, JAMES: Born and educated Ireland. Ordained Maynooth 1926. Lent to Glasgow. Our Lady and St Margaret's, Glasgow 1926-37. Returned to Ireland 1937. (Canning)

HENRY, PATRICK J: Born Glasgow 1926. Educated Blairs, St Peter's. Ordained Glasgow 1951. St Conval's, Glasgow 1951-62. St Pius X, Glasgow 1962-66. St Vincent de Paul's, Glasgow 1966-67. Milngavie 1967-72. Sacred Heart, Glasgow 1972-78. Bearsden 1978-.

HERON, PATRICK: Born and educated Ireland. Ordained Maynooth 1925. St Roch's, Glasgow 1927-29. St John's, Port Glasgow 1929-31. Returned to Ireland 1931 and died there 29 May 1977. (Canning)

HESLIN, HUGH: see Paisley diocese.

HICKEY, JOHN: Born and educated Ireland. Ordained Waterford for Glasgow 1930. St Saviour's, Glasgow 1930-52. Our Lady of the Assumption, Glasgow 1952-67. Our Lady and St Margaret's, Glasgow 1967-82. Retired to Ireland 1982 and died there 5 Feb 1985. (Canning)

HICKSON, JOHN A: see Galloway diocese.

HIGGINS, EDWARD JOHN: Born Glasgow 1926. Educated Holyrood School, Glasgow; Campion House, Osterley; St Peter's. Ordained Glasgow 1959. St John Ogilvie's, Glasgow 1959-61. Our Holy Redeemer, Clydebank 1961-67. St Roch's, Glasgow 1967-74. Duntocher 1974-86. Our Lady of Fatima, Glasgow 1986-87. Sick leave 1987-88. St Saviour's, Glasgow 1988-.

HIGGINS, JOSEPH: Born and educated Ireland. Ordained Maynooth 1914. Lent to Glasgow. St Laurence's, Greenock 1914-20. Went to Los Angeles for his health. (Canning)

HILGERS, PETER: Born Geilenkirchen, Germany 1866. Educated Huenshoven Gymnasium, Rhineland; Paderborn, Westphalia; St Trond's, Belgium 1886-88; St Peters 1889-91. Ordained St Peter's College 1891. St John's, Glasgow 1891-97. Gourock 1897-1901. Shotts 1901-12. Barrhead 1912-26. Died Barrhead 22 May 1926.

HILL, GERARD C: Born Glasgow 1945. Educated St Mungo's Academy, Glasgow; Blairs; Scots College, Rome. Ordained Glasgow 1968. Glasgow Cathedral 1969-70. St Mary Immaculate 1970-73. Professor, St Peter's College 1973-85. Professor, Chesters 1985-87. Vice-rector, Chesters 1987-.

HILL, ROBERT JAMES: Born Glasgow 1954. Educated St Mungo's Academy, Glasgow; St Peter's. Ordained Glasgow 1977. St Anthony's,

Glasgow, and studying at Glasgow University, 1977-78. St Anthony's, Glasgow 1978-81. Bearsden 1981-82. Professor, Blairs 1982-86. St Albert's, Glasgow 1986-.

HILLEE, CHRISTOPHER: Born and educated Ireland. Ordained Maynooth 1906. Lent to Glasgow. St Patrick's, Coatbridge 1906-15. Returned to Ireland 1915 and died there 12 Dec 1922. (Canning)

HOEY, PATRICK: Born Glasgow 1911. Educated St Mungo's Academy, Glasgow; worked as page boy in hotel; Blairs 1927-32; Scots College, Rome 1932-39. Ordained Rome 1938. St Columbkille's, Rutherglen 1939-49; thus moving to Motherwell diocese. St Mary's, Whifflet 1949-54. Burnbank 1954-55. Blackwood 1955-59. Plains 1959-72. Retired 1972. Died Lanark 22 Aug 1974.

HOGAN, JAMES JOSEPH: Born and educated Ireland. Ordained St Peter's College 1923. St Anthony's, Glasgow 1923-41. Neilston 1941-46. Duntocher 1946-68. Died Glasgow 5 March 1968. (Canning)

HOLLAND, STEPHEN DAVID: Born Helensburgh 1954. Educated St Patrick's High School, Dumbarton; St Peter's. Ordained St Peter's College 1981. Immaculate Conception, Glasgow 1981-83. Holy Cross, Glasgow 1983-86. St Ninian's, Glasgow 1986-87. No further entries.

HOLLAND, WILLIAM: see Archdiocese of St Andrews & Edinburgh

HOLLORAN, THOMAS: Born Dumbarton 1930. Educated Blairs, Valladolid. Ordained Valladolid 1957. St Joseph's, Tollcross 1957-59. St Martin's, Glasgow 1959-65. St Mary's, Glasgow 1965-73. Faifley 1973-79. Spiritual Director, Valladolid 1979-83. Our Lady of Lourdes, Glasgow 1983-86. St Mark's, Carntyne 1986-.

HOLLOWAY, MICHAEL: Born and educated Ireland. Ordained Maynooth 1921. Lent to Glasgow. St Peter's, Glasgow 1921-22. Returned to Ireland 1922 and died there 24 Jan 1962. (Canning)

HOLMES, JOHN: Born and educated Ireland. Ordained Maynooth 1924. Lent to Glasgow. Immaculate Conception, Glasgow 1924-25. St Mary's, Paisley 1925. Returned to Ireland 1925. (Canning)

HOPKINS, FRANCIS: Born and educated Ireland. Ordained Maynooth 1946. Lent to Glasgow. St Mirin's, Paisley 1947-51; thus moving to Paisley diocese. Returned to Ireland 1951. (Canning)

HOPWELL, THOMAS: Born Leicester 1859. Educated Leicester Grammar School; St Marie's College, Rugby; Ratcliffe College; Collegio Mellerio di Duomo d'Ossola, Piedmont, returning home after a serious accident; St

Peter's 1887-89. Ordained Glasgow 1889. St John's, Glasgow 1889-91. Hamilton 1891-92. St Augustine's, Coatbridge 1892-94. Kilbirnie 1894-1919. Died Kilbirnie 8 Dec 1919.

HORAN, JAMES: Born and educated Ireland. Ordained 1936. Lent to Glasgow. St Mary's, Glasgow 1936. St Patrick's, Dumbarton 1936-39. Returned to Ireland 1939. (Canning)

HORGAN, DANIEL J (1898): Born Ireland. Educated Ireland, St Peter's. Ordained St Peter's College 1898. St Mary's, Coatbridge 1898-1904. St Mary Immaculate, Glasgow 1904-06. Strathaven 1906-14. Baillieston 1914-26. St Joseph's, Tollcross 1926-29. St Charles', Glasgow 1929-37. Died Ireland 1 March 1937. (Canning)

HORGAN, DANIEL J (1919): Born and educated Ireland. Ordained Maynooth 1919. Lent to Glasgow. Holy Cross, Glasgow 1919-20. St Mary's, Greenock 1920-24. Returned to Ireland 1924 and died there 5 April 1958. (Canning)

HORGAN, DANIEL (1927): Born Ireland. Educated Ireland, St Peter's. Ordained Glasgow 1927. Johnstone 1927-45. St Mary's, Paisley 1945-46. St Mary's, Greenock 1946-47. St Mary's, Paisley 1947-48; thus moving to Paisley diocese. Howwood 1948-50. Houston 1950-57. St Mungo's, Greenock 1957-61. St Laurence's, Greenock 1961-78. Retired 1978. Died Dublin 7 May 1979. (Canning)

HORGAN, WILLIAM: Born and educated Ireland. Ordained Maynooth 1892. Lent to Glasgow; later got exeat to remain there. St Mary's, Paisley 1892-99. Houston 1899-1905. Stevenston 1905-06. St Laurence's, Greenock 1906-45. St Mary's, Greenock 1945-47. Retired to Ireland 1947 and died there 27 June 1948. (Canning)

HOSIE, ANDREW CALDWELL: Born Helensburgh 1948. Educated St Patrick's High School, Dumbarton; St Peter's. Ordained St Peter's College 1977. St Conval's, Glasgow 1977-79. Glasgow Cathedral 1979-82. St Paul's, Glasgow 1982-.

HOULIHAN, MICHAEL: Born and educated Ireland. Ordained Kilkenny for Glasgow 1943. St Michael's, Glasgow 1943-44. Not in Directories 1944-46. St Mary's, Hamilton 1946-52; thus moving to Motherwell diocese. St Bernadette's, Motherwell 1952-54. Sick leave 1954-55. Calderbank 1955-59. Blackwood 1959-68. Bothwell 1968-84. Retired 1984. Died Glasgow 15 Oct 1986. (Canning)

HOULIHAN, PATRICK: Born and educated Ireland. Ordained 1882. St Peter's, Glasgow 1883-87. St Agnes's, Glasgow 1887-1905. St Mary's, Greenock 1905-23. Died Greenock 4 Jan 1923. (Canning)

HOURIGAN, PATRICK R: Born Ireland. Educated Ireland, St Peter's. Ordained Glasgow 1906. Whifflet 1906-23. Bothwell 1923-30. St Alphonsus', Glasgow 1930-43. Died Bothwell 17 June 1943. (Canning)

HUGHES, JAMES: Born Gartsherrie, near Coatbridge 1878. Educated Blairs 1894-97; Notre Dame des Champs, Paris 1897-98; St Peter's 1898-1904. Ordained 1904. Springburn 1904-05. Professor, Blairs 1905-12. St Alphonsus', Glasgow 1912-18. Bothwell 1918-23. Vice-rector, St Peter's College 1923-24. At Kinnoull Monastery 1924-25. No further entries.

HUGHES, JOHN ANTHONY: Born Glasgow 1949. Educated St Mungo's Academy, Glasgow; Glasgow University; became school teacher; educated for priesthood Scots College, Rome. Ordained Glasgow 1984. St Paul's, Glasgow 1984. Further studies, Rome 1984-86. St Matthew's, Bishopbriggs 1986-.

HUGHES, MARTIN: Born Birkenhead 1909. Educated Blairs 1924-29; Valladolid 1929-36. Ordained Valladolid 1936. St Roch's, Glasgow 1936-43. Our Holy Redeemer, Clydebank 1943-57. St Margaret Mary's, Glasgow 1957-70. Died Glasgow 6 July 1970.

HUGHES, MICHAEL: Born Glasgow 1858. Educated Blairs 1870-74; Scots College, Rome 1874-81. Ordained Rome 1881. Glasgow Cathedral 1881-85. Rutherglen 1885-86. Diocesan secretary 1886-89. St Patrick's, Dumbarton 1889-92. Mossend 1892-1904. Sacred Heart, Glasgow 1904-21. Died Glasgow 2 March 1921.

HUMBLE, JAMES: Born Liverpool 1865. Educated Blairs 1878-83; Valladolid 1883-89. Ordained Valladolid 1889. Maryhill 1889-96. Newmains 1896-1903. Vice-rector, Valladolid 1903-09. Rector, Valladolid 1909-40. Retired 1940. Died Valladolid 9 June 1948.

HURLEY, DENIS AUGUSTINE: Born and educated Ireland. Ordained Wexford for Glasgow 1954. St Augustine's, Glasgow 1954-67. St Constantine's, Glasgow 1967-72. Immaculate Heart of Mary, Glasgow 1972-82. St Jude's, Glasgow 1982-86. Holy Family, Kirkintilloch 1986-. (Canning)

HURLEY, THOMAS A: Born and educated Ireland. Ordained Waterford for Glasgow 1960. St Philomena's, Glasgow 1960-73. Chaplain, Gartnaval Hospital 1973-75. Our Lady of Perpetual Succour, Glasgow 1975-80. St Augustine's, Glasgow 1980-86. St Jude's, Glasgow 1986-. (Canning)

IVORY, JOSEPH: Born and educated Ireland. Ordained Maynooth 1922. Lent to Glasgow. Hamilton 1922-24. Returned to Ireland 1924 and died there 28 Dec 1963. (Canning)

JACKSON, JAMES A: Born Mossend 1915. Educated Blairs 1932-34; St Peter's 1934-41. Ordained Glasgow 1941. Renton 1941-45. St Margaret's, Johnstone 1945-51; thus moving to Paisley diocese. Army chaplain 1951-60. Holy Family, Port Glasgow 1960-66. Bishopton 1966-73. Newton Mearns 1973-.

JACONELLI, FRANCIS: Born Johnstone 1915. Educated Blairs 1928-33; Scots College, Rome 1933-39. Ordained Rome 1939. Motherwell 1940-41. Kilbirnie 1941-47. St Peter's, Glasgow 1947-60. Sacred Heart, Cumbernauld 1960-86. Retired 1986.

JAMIESON, LAWRENCE: Born Glasgow 1938. Educated St Aloysius' College, Glasgow; Blairs; Scots College, Rome. Ordained Rome 1962. St Robert's, Glasgow 1962-65. Ripetitore, Scots College, Rome 1965-70. Collegio San Columbano, Rome 1970-71. St Peter's College in addresses, but not under staff list, 1971-72. Helensburgh 1972-74. St Paul's, Shettleston 1974-75. St Ninian's, Glasgow 1975-80. Sick leave 1980-81. St Margaret Mary's, Glasgow 1981-.

JANSEN, MARTIN H: Born Randerath, Germany 1864. Educated Randerath Gymnasium; College of St Trond, Belgium; Liege Seminary; St Peter's. Ordained St Peter's College 1889. St Vincent's, Glasgow 1889-96. Airdrie 1896-97. Milngavie 1897-1900. Renton 1900-08. St Michael's, Glasgow 1908-19. Holy Family, Kirkintilloch 1919-41. Retired 1941. Died Girvan 10 May 1953.

JENNINGS, JAMES B: see Galloway diocese.

JENNINGS, JOHN: Born and educated Ireland. Ordained Maynooth 1936. Lent to Glasgow. Our Lady of Lourdes, Glasgow 1936-39. Returned to Ireland 1939. (Canning)

JOHNSTON, ALEXANDER: Born 1923. Educated Blairs, St Peter's. Ordained 1947. Our Holy Redeemer, Clydebank 1947-49. St Anne's, Glasgow 1949-50. St Nicholas's, Glasgow 1950-57. Our Lady of Lourdes, Glasgow 1957-70. St Augustine's, Glasgow 1970-71. Lent to Dunkeld diocese: Dunblane in addresses, but not under parishes, 1971-72; Dunblane 1972-73; Broughty Ferry 1973-78. St Teresa's, Glasgow 1978-84. C/o Diocesan Office 1984-87. Our Lady of the Assumption, Glasgow 1987-89. St Catherine's, Glasgow 1989-.

JOHNSTONE, NEIL ANGUS: Born Glasgow 1923. Educated Blairs, St Peter's. Ordained Glasgow 1949 for Argyll diocese. Lent to Glasgow. St Eunan's, Clydebank 1949-59. St Brigid's, Glasgow, 1959-61. No further entries.

JORDAN, JOHN FRANCIS: Born Glasgow 1949. Educated Holy Cross High School, Hamilton; St Peter's. Ordained St Peter's College 1972. St Anne's, Glasgow 1972-74. No further entries.

JOYCE, JOHN (1896): see Archdiocese of St Andrews & Edinburgh

JOYCE, THOMAS: see Galloway diocese.

KANE, CHARLES: Born Glasgow 1929. Educated Blairs, St Peter's. Ordained Glasgow 1955. St Saviour's, Glasgow 1955-65. Holy Cross, Glasgow 1965-70. Chaplain, Notre Dame, Glasgow 1970-73. St Roch's, Glasgow 1973-78. Condorrat 1978-81. St Joseph's, Tollcross 1981-85. St Bernadette's, Glasgow 1985-.

KANE, DUNCAN: Born Carfin 1923. Educated Blairs, St Peter's. Ordained Dumbarton 1946. St Robert's, Glasgow 1946-48. Our Lady and St Margaret's, Glasgow 1948-50. St Barnabas's, Glasgow 1950-53. St Flannan's, Kirkintilloch 1953-66. St Anne's, Glasgow 1966-72. St Bartholomew's, Glasgow 1972-87. Immaculate Heart of Mary, Glasgow 1987-.

KAVANAGH, EDWARD C: Born and educated Ireland. Ordained Maynooth 1927. Lent to Glasgow; got exeat to remain there in 1931. St Patrick's, Greenock 1927-32. St Roch's, Glasgow 1932-33. Motherwell 1933-47. Clarkston 1947-58; thus moving to Paisley diocese. St Charles', Paisley 1958-68. St Margaret's, Johnstone 1968-77. Died Glasgow 16 May 1977. (Canning)

KAY, JOHN GERARD: Born Dumbarton 1956. Educated St Aloysius' College, Glasgow; Blairs; Scots College, Rome. Ordained Dumbarton 1981. Christ the King, Glasgow 1981. Further studies, Rome 1981-82. St Joseph's, Cumbernauld 1982-84. Professor, Blairs 1984-86. Bearsden 1986-87. St Paul's, Glasgow 1987-.

KEANE, HUGH J: Born and educated Ireland. Ordained Maynooth 1917. Lent to Glasgow. St Mirin's, Paisley 1918-22. Returned to Ireland 1922 and died there 31 Aug 1945. (Canning)

KEANE, SIMON: Born Ireland. Educated Ireland, St Peter's 1908-14. Ordained Glasgow 1914. Immaculate Conception, Glasgow 1914-23. Glasgow Cathedral 1923-25. Duntocher 1925-32. Tarbrax 1932-34. Helensburgh 1934-37. St John's, Port Glasgow 1937-50; thus moving to Paisley diocese. Died Port Glasgow 19 Jan 1951. (Canning)

KEANE, STEPHEN ALOYSIUS: see Aberdeen diocese.

KEANE, THOMAS: Born Ireland. Educated Ireland, St Peter's. Ordained St Peter's College 1925. Immaculate Conception, Glasgow 1925-26. St

Paul's, Glasgow 1926-44. Clarkston 1944-47. St Columba's, Glasgow 1947-59. St Paul's, Glasgow 1959-72. Died Glasgow 5 May 1972. (Canning)

KEARNEY, JAMES: Born Ireland. Educated Ireland, St Peter's. Ordained 1902. St Patrick's, Dumbarton 1902-04. Shotts 1904-18. Largs 1918-23. St Paul's, Shettleston 1923-28. Shettleston and Carntyne 1928-45. Died Glasgow 2 May 1945. (Canning)

KEARNEY, JOHN: Born Ireland. Educated Ireland, Paris. Ordained 1880. Lent to Glasgow. No address given 1880-81. St Laurence's, Greenock 1881-82. Returned to Ireland 1882 and died there 27 March 1936. (Canning)

KEARNEY, THOMAS (1880): Born and educated Ireland. Ordained 1880. Lent to Glasgow. Larkhall 1880-81. St Patrick's, Coatbridge 1881-84. Returned to Ireland 1884 and died there 11 Jan 1918. (Canning)

KEARNEY, THOMAS (1903): Born Ireland. Educated Ireland, St Peter's. Ordained 1903. Cambuslang 1903-19. Blackwood 1919-23. St Charles', Paisley 1923-29. St Ignatius's, Wishaw 1929-66; thus moving to Motherwell diocese. Died Wishaw 15 Nov 1966. (Canning)

KEARNS, HUGH: Born Clydebank 1925. Educated Osterley, St Peter's. Ordained Glasgow 1955. Sacred Heart, Glasgow 1955-62. St Conval's, Glasgow 1962-65. Army chaplain 1965-80. Chaplain, St Charles' Hospital, Carstairs 1980-83. Awaiting appointment 1983-84. Our Holy Redeemer, Clydebank 1984-.

KEARNS, MICHAEL: Born and educated Ireland. Ordained Ballina 1923. Lent to Glasgow. St Constantine's, Glasgow 1923-26. St Anthony's, Glasgow 1926-27. Went to Chicago. (Canning)

KEATING, MICHAEL F: Born and educated Ireland. Ordained Kilkenny for Glasgow 1954. St Mary's, Glasgow 1954-56. St Augustine's, Glasgow 1956-69. St Mark's, Glasgow 1969-77. St John Ogilvie's, Glasgow 1977-78. Holy Family, Kirkintilloch 1978-82. St Martin's, Glasgow 1982-. (Canning)

KEATING, PATRICK F: Born Ireland. Educated Ireland, St Peter's. Ordained Kinnoull 1912. St Roch's, Glasgow 1912-15. Glasgow Cathedral 1915-23. Cambuslang 1923-24. Motherwell 1924-27. St Mary's, Glasgow 1927-28. Sick leave 1928-30. Lent to Dunkeld diocese: St Joseph's, Dundee 1930-31. Sick leave 1931-41. Whiterigg 1941-49; thus moving to Motherwell diocese. St Columba's, Viewpark 1949-58. Retired to Dublin 1958 and died there 3 Oct 1963. (Canning)

KEATING, WILLIAM: Born and educated Ireland. Ordained Waterford 1880. Lent to Glasgow. St Patrick's, Glasgow 1880-83. Returned to Ireland 1883 and died there 17 Sept 1902. (Canning)

KEENAGHAN, JAMES: see Paisley diocese.

KEENAN, BERNARD: Born and educated Ireland. Ordained Kilkenny for Glasgow 1930. St Joseph's, Blantyre 1930-51; thus moving to Motherwell diocese. Longriggend 1951-54. Caldercruix 1954-59. St John the Baptist's, Uddingston 1959-65. Burnbank 1965-82. Retired to Dublin 1982. (Canning)

KEENAN, PATRICK: see Aberdeen diocese.

KELLEHER, TIMOTHY: Born and educated Ireland. Ordained Maynooth 1906. Our Holy Redeemer, Clydebank 1906-09. Mossend 1909-15. Returned to Ireland 1915 and died there 10 Feb 1960. (Canning)

KELLY, ADRIAN J: see Dunkeld diocese.

KELLY, EDWARD: Born Govan 1931. Educated St Gerard's School, Glasgow; St Peter's. Ordained Glasgow 1955. Our Holy Redeemer, Clydebank 1955. St Simon's, Glasgow 1955-72. St Charles', Glasgow 1972-77. St Michael's, Dumbarton 1977-84. St Alphonsus', Glasgow 1984-.

KELLY, HENRY: see Dunkeld diocese.

KELLY, HUGH J (1889): Born London 1864. Educated St Aloysius' College, Glasgow; Propaganda, Rome. Ordained Rome 1889. St Mary's, Paisley 1889-93. Airdrie 1893-96. Shotts 1896-1901. St Patrick's, Dumbarton 1901-50. Retired 1950. Died Newry 26 Jan 1953.

KELLY, HUGH (1933): Born Bothwell 1908. Educated Blairs 1922-27; St Peter's 1927-33. Ordained Glasgow 1933. St Aloysius' Glasgow 1933-36. Christ the King, Glasgow 1936-46. Our Lady and St Margaret's, Glasgow 1946-55. St Matthew's, Glasgow 1955-84. Died Glasgow 23 July 1984.

KELLY, JAMES: Born Paisley 1879. Educated Blairs 1893-98; Issy 1898-99; Scots College, Rome 1899-1904. Ordained Rome 1903. St Patrick's, Glasgow 1904-17. Longriggend 1917-24. St Patrick's, Greenock 1924-30. St Joseph's, Woodside, Glasgow 1930-43. Our Lady and St Margaret's, Glasgow 1943-48. St Mary Immaculate, Glasgow 1948-64. Retired 1964. Died Saltcoats 5 Nov 1967.

KELLY, JOHN F: Born and educated Ireland. Ordained Maynooth 1901. Lent to Glasgow. St Alphonsus', Glasgow 1901-06. Returned to Ireland 1906 and died there 18 Jan 1950. (Canning)

KELLY, PATRICK (1908): see Reilly, Patrick (misprint in Directories)

KELLY, PATRICK (1924): Born Cambuslang 1897. Educated Blairs 1909-15; St Peter's 1915-17; military service 1917-20; St Peter's 1920-24. Ordained Glasgow 1924. Cambuslang 1924-26. Chaplain, Kenmure Industrial School 1926-31. St Patrick's, Coatbridge 1931-40. St Stephen's, Dalmuir 1940-42. St Columba's, Viewpark 1942-43. Strathaven 1943-48; thus moving to Motherwell diocese. Glenboig 1948-53. Mossend 1953-69. Retired 1969. Died Saltcoats 29 March 1989.

KELLY, PATRICK (1927): Born Ireland. Educated Ireland, Paris. Ordained Paris 1927. Lent to Glasgow. St Luke's, Glasgow 1927-33. Returned to Ireland 1933 and died there 2 Jan 1963. (Canning)

KELLY, PATRICK J (1951): Born and educated Ireland. Ordained Carlow for Glasgow 1951. St Nicholas's, Glasgow 1951-55. Renton 1955-62. St Joseph's, Tollcross 1962-70. St Mary Immaculate, Glasgow 1970-77. Roseneath 1977-78. Holy Name, Glasgow 1978-. (Canning)

KELLY, THOMAS PATRICK (1925), (1): Born and educated Ireland. Ordained Carlow 1925. St Peter's, Glasgow 1925-45. Longriggend 1945-50; thus moving to Motherwell diocese. St Monica's, Coatbridge 1950-69. Died Coatbridge 7 Dec 1969. (Canning)

KELLY, THOMAS (1925), (2): Born Ireland. Educated Blairs 1913-17; military service 1917-19; St Peter's 1919-25. Ordained Glasgow 1925. Airdrie 1925-27. Saltcoats 1927-39. St Michael's, Glasgow 1939-45. Newmains 1945-52; thus moving to Motherwell diocese. Sick leave 1952-54. Went to Archdiocese of St Andrews & Edinburgh: St John's, Portobello 1954-61; Chaplain, St Margaret's Convent, Hawick 1961-63. Died Hawick 18 Oct 1963. (Canning)

KELLY, THOMAS A (1926): see Dunkeld diocese.

KELLY, WALTER: Born Paris 1867. Educated Blairs 1884-86; Issy 1886-89; St Peter's 1889-94. Ordained Glasgow 1894. St Patrick's, Shieldmuir 1894-1902. Busby 1902-12. Went to South Africa for his health 1912. Died Port Elizabeth 15 Aug 1918.

KELLY, WILLIAM M (1918): Born and educated Ireland. Ordained Maynooth 1918. St Anthony's, Glasgow 1918-19. Returned to Ireland 1919; Was on mission to China before moving to USA. (Canning)

KELLY, WILLIAM JOHN (1989): Born Govan 1959. Educated St Pius X School, Glasgow; Glasgow College; Paisley College; St Peter's; Chesters. Ordained Glasgow 1989. St Augustine's, Glasgow 1989-.

KENNEALLY, BENJAMIN: Born and educated Ireland. Ordained Maynooth 1901. Lent to Glasgow. Mossend 1901-13. Returned to Ireland 1913 and died there 7 Sept 1961. (Canning)

KENNEALLY, JOHN P: Born and educated Ireland. Ordained Waterford 1916. Lent to Glasgow. St Anthony's, Glasgow 1916-21. Returned to Ireland 1921 and died there 22 Dec 1967. (Canning)

KENNEDY, DANIEL: Born Mossend 1908. Educated Blairs 1923-28; St Peter's 1928-34. Ordained Glasgow 1934. Our Holy Redeemer, Clydebank 1934-38. Rutherglen 1938-45. St Anthony's, Glasgow 1945-47. St Agnes's, Glasgow 1947-48. St Philomena's, Glasgow 1948-55. St James's, Glasgow 1955-67. Died Lanark 28 May 1967.

KENNEDY, FRANCIS: Born Glasgow 1946. Educated Holyrood School, Glasgow; Scots College, Rome. Ordained Glasgow 1970. St Brendan's, Glasgow 1971-74. Professor, St Peter's College 1974-83. On mission, Argentina 1983-87. Awaiting appointment 1987-88. St Lucy's, Cumbernauld 1988-89. Argentina 1989-.

KENNEDY, IGNATIUS: Born Glasgow 1923. Educated St Peter's. Ordained Glasgow 1963. St Ninian's, Glasgow 1963-78. Our Lady of Loreto, Dalmuir 1978-79. St Bartholomew's, Glasgow 1979-83. St Bernadette's, Glasgow 1983-85. Died Glasgow 3 May 1985.

KENNEDY, JAMES: Born and educated Ireland. Ordained Maynooth 1917. Lent to Glasgow. St Laurence's, Greenock 1918-21. Returned to Ireland 1921 and died there 15 Feb 1953. (Canning)

KENNEDY, JOSEPH: Born Ireland. Educated Ireland, St Peter's. Ordained Glasgow 1913. Alexandria 1913. Mossend 1913-28. Tarbrax 1928-32. Clarkston 1932-37. Helensburgh 1937-40. St Patrick's, Glasgow 1940-43. Died Glasgow 22 Oct 1943. (Canning)

KENNY, JOHN F: Born and educated Ireland. Ordained Maynooth 1908. Lent to Glasgow. St Patrick's, Glasgow 1908-11. Returned to Ireland 1911 and died there 30 Oct 1943. (Canning)

KEOGH, WILLIAM: Born and educated Ireland. Ordained Maynooth 1901. Lent to Glasgow. Saltcoats 1901-11. St Augustine's, Coatbridge 1911-14. Returned to Ireland 1914 and died there 21 July 1942. (Canning)

KERR, JOSEPH: Born Glasgow 1927. Educated Blairs, St Peter's. Ordained Glasgow 1951. St Michael's, Glasgow 1951-52. Holy Family, Kirkintilloch 1952-55. Our Lady and St Margaret's, Glasgow 1955-60. St Paul's, Glasgow 1960-67. Our Lady of Fatima, Glasgow 1967-74. St Mary Immaculate, Glasgow 1974-76. St Nicholas's, Glasgow 1976-79. St

John's, Glasgow 1979-82. St Luke's, Glasgow 1982-84. Died Glasgow 24 July 1984.

KEVANY, PATRICK: Ordained 1928. St Patrick's, Dumbarton 1928-31. No further entries.

KIERNEY, PAUL JOSEPH: Born Glasgow 1947. Educated Langbank; Blairs; Scots College, Rome. Ordained Cardonald 1981. St Helen's, Glasgow 1981. Further studies, Rome 1981-82. Professor, St Peter's College 1982-85. Professor, Chesters 1985-.

KILCOYNE, ANTHONY: Born Ireland. Educated Ireland, St Peter's. Ordained Glasgow 1934. Hamilton 1934-49; thus moving to Motherwell diocese. Mossend 1949-54. Carluke 1954-55. St Bride's, East Kilbride 1955-59. St Patrick's, Shieldmuir 1959-72. Muirhead 1972-83. Retired 1983. (Canning)

KILPATRICK, JAMES: Born 1912. Educated Motherwell Higher Grade School; St Peter's 1929-35. Ordained 1935. Mossend 1935-37. Professor, Blairs 1937-51. Procurator, Blairs 1951-57. Moved to Motherwell diocese. St Augustine's, Coatbridge 1957-58. St Columba's, Viewpark 1958-59. St Bride's, East Kilbride 1959-71. St Mark's, Rutherglen 1971-82. Retired 1982. Died Rutherglen 4 Jan 1989.

KILPATRICK, SAMUEL JOSEPH: Born Motherwell 1904. Educated Blairs 1919-22; Scots College, Rome 1922-29. Ordained Rome 1929. Carfin 1929-30. Our Lady of Lourdes, Glasgow 1930. St Joseph's, Woodside, Glasgow 1930-43. Milngavie 1943-48. Christ the King, Glasgow 1948-77. Retired 1977. Died Dalmuir 3 Oct 1983.

KINANE, EDWARD: Born and educated Ireland. Ordained Maynooth 1919. Lent to Glasgow. St Augustine's, Coatbridge 1919-22. St Mary's, Glasgow 1922-26. Returned to Ireland 1926 and died there 4 May 1958. (Canning)

KING, JOHN PATRICK: Born Ireland. Educated Blairs, St Peter's. Ordained St Peter's College 1970. St Bonaventure's, Glasgow 1970-71. C/o Diocesan Office 1971-72. St Bernard's, Glasgow 1972-78. Swinford Manor, Kent 1978-84. St Vincent's Centre, Langbank 1984-85. Glengowan House (for homeless young men), Glasgow from 1985, acting as Director 1987-88, and 1989-. (Canning)

KINNANE, MICHAEL: Born and educated Ireland. Ordained Dublin 1914. Lent to Glasgow. St Patrick's, Coatbridge 1915. St Peter's, Glasgow 1915-16. Returned to Ireland 1916 and died there 1960. (Canning)

KINSELLA, MATTHEW: Born Wishaw 1913. Educated Blairs 1926-31; Scots College, Rome 1931-38. Ordained Rome 1938. Coatdyke 1938-39. St Peter's, Glasgow 1939-45. St Patrick's, Greenock 1945-57; thus moving to Paisley diocese. Spiritual Director, Scots College, Rome 1957-61. St Andrew's, Greenock 1961-71. St Mirin's, Paisley 1971-88. Retired 1988.

KIRBY, JAMES: Born Mossend 1941. Educated Blairs, St Peter's. Ordained Glasgow 1966. Sacred Heart, Cumbernauld 1966-70. St Paul's, Shettleston 1970-71. All Saints, Glasgow 1971-72. St Michael's, Glasgow 1972-80. Our Lady of the Assumption, Glasgow 1980-82. Sacred Heart, Glasgow 1982-85. St Paul's, Shettleston 1985-.

KIRK, JAMES H: Born Dumbarton 1866. Educated Blairs 1876-81; Douay 1881-83; St Peter's 1883-88. Ordained Glasgow 1888. St Anthony's, Glasgow 1888-94. St Joseph's, Tollcross 1894-1909. Milngavie 1909-11. Leave of absence 1911-12. No further entries.

KNIGHT, LOUIS: Born Whiteinch 1924. Educated St Columba's College, Newton St Boswell's; Rossington Hall; St Peter's. Ordained Glasgow 1949. St Conval's, Glasgow 1949-51. C/o Diocesan Centre 1951-53. California 1953-78. No further entries.

KUHLER, LUDGER (Louis) WILLIAM: Born Werden, Germany 1864. Educated Essen; St Trond; Seminary of Liege; University of Innsbruck; St Peter's 1888-89. Ordained Glasgow 1889. Wishaw 1889-91. St Mary's, Greenock 1891-92. No further entries.

KUPPERS, HENRY: Ordained 1886. Maryhill 1886-87. St Alphonsus', Glasgow 1887-90. Went to Archdiocese of St Andrews & Edinburgh: Bo'ness 1890-92. No further entries.

LAFFERTY, JAMES: Born Coatdyke 1938. Educated Blairs, St Peter's. Ordained Glasgow 1961. St Pius X, Glasgow 1961-71. St Constantine's, Glasgow 1971-80. St Martin's, Glasgow 1980-85. St Philomena's, Glasgow 1985-87. St Bernard's, Glasgow 1987-.

LAFFERTY, THOMAS: Born Glasgow 1931. Educated Blairs, St Peter's. Ordained Glasgow 1956. St Anthony's, Glasgow 1956-63. No further entries.

LAGAN, JAMES: Born and educated Ireland. Ordained Maynooth 1909. Lent to Glasgow. Cambuslang 1909-10. St Mary's, Paisley 1910-11. Returned to Ireland 1911 and died there 7 Sept 1960. (Canning)

LAGAN, JOHN: Born and educated Ireland. Ordained 1902. Cadzow 1903-06. Returned to Ireland 1906 and died there 1 Sept 1962. (Canning)

LALOR, ANDREW: Born and educated Ireland. Ordained Maynooth 1897. Lent to Glasgow. Johnstone 1897-1900. Returned to Ireland 1900 and died there 8 Nov 1920. (Canning)

LANE, JEREMIAH: Born and educated Ireland. Ordained for Glasgow 1943. St Patrick's, Glasgow 1943-44. Helensburgh 1944-52. Alexandria 1952-58. Retired to Ireland 1958 and died there 29 May 1973. (Canning)

LAVELLE, MICHAEL: Born and educated Ireland. Ordained Maynooth 1905. Lent to Glasgow. Our Holy Redeemer, Clydebank 1905-12. Returned to Ireland 1912 and died there 10 Nov 1949. (Canning)

LAVERTY, HENRY: Born Ireland. Educated Ireland, St Peter's. Ordained St Peter's College 1924. St Saviour's, Glasgow 1924-38. Returned to Ireland 1938 and died there 27 Jan 1979. (Canning)

LAVERY, SAMUEL JOSEPH: Born Hamilton 1912. Educated Blairs 1926-32; St Peter's 1932-39. Ordained Glasgow 1939. St Anne's, Glasgow 1939-41. St Paul's, Glasgow 1941-51. Royal Navy chaplain 1951-68. Roseneath 1968-73. St Agnes's, Glasgow 1973-.

LAVETH, FRANCIS JOSEPH: Born 1872. Ordained 1895. Holy Cross, Glasgow 1895-96. Johnstone 1896-98. Holy Family, Kirkintilloch 1898-99. In Western Australia for health 1899-1903. Chaplain, West Thorn Reformatory and Good Shepherd Convent, Dalbeth 1903-06. Chaplain, Kenmure Industrial School 1906-10. Cardonald 1910-13. 'Retired' in Germany 1913-28. Gourock 1928-34. Glenboig 1934-38. Retired 1938. Died Skelmorlie 9 June 1941.

LAWLOR, JAMES MARTIN: Born Lennoxtown 1963. Educated Langbank, Blairs, St Peter's, Oxford University. Ordained Clydebank 1987. Glasgow Cathedral 1987. Completing degree, Oxford University 1987-89. Balloch 1989-.

LAWN, CHARLES: Born and educated Ireland. Ordained Waterford 1937. Lent to Glasgow. Saltcoats 1938. St Mary's, Paisley 1938-39. Returned to Ireland 1939. (Canning)

LAWTON, EDWARD: Born and educated Ireland. Ordained Maynooth 1901. Lent to Glasgow; later got exeat to remain there. St Patrick's, Glasgow 1901-14. Duntocher 1914-18. St Roch's, Glasgow 1918-36. St Mary Immaculate, Glasgow 1936-48. Retired 1948. Died Ireland 14 Nov 1949. (Canning)

LAYDON, PATRICK: Born Ireland. Educated Jarrow; Dumfries; Blairs 1899-1901; Scots College, Rome 1901-07. Ordained Rome 1906. Sacred Heart, Glasgow 1907-21. Dalry 1921-22. St Michael's, Glasgow 1922-33.

Our Lady and St Margaret's, Glasgow 1933-43. Died Glasgow 29 Jan 1943. (Canning)

LENNON, PETER: Born Glasgow 1937. Educated Blairs, Valladolid. Ordained Valladolid 1961. St Catherine's, Glasgow 1961-74. St Jude's, Glasgow 1974-79. St Roch's, Glasgow 1979-85. Spiritual Director, Scots College, Rome 1985-88. St Benedict's, Glasgow 1988-.

LEONARD, HENRY STEPHEN: Born Partick 1911. Educated St Mungo's Academy, Glasgow; Blairs 1925-30; St Peter's 1930-37. Ordained 1937. St Patrick's, Shieldmuir 1937-40. Houston 1940-43. Royal Navy chaplain 1943-64. Moved to Paisley diocese. Bishopton 1964-66. Died Glasgow 19 March 1966.

LEONARD, JAMES: Born and educated Ireland. Ordained Maynooth 1900. Lent to Glasgow. Wishaw 1900-12. Returned to Ireland 1912 and died there 20 Feb 1943. (Canning)

LEYNE (Lyne), JAMES: Born and educated Ireland. Ordained Maynooth 1924. Lent to Glasgow. Hamilton 1924-26. Returned to Ireland 1926. (Canning)

LIGHTBODY, JOHN: Born Glasgow 1931. Educated St Gerard's School, Glasgow; St Peter's. Ordained Glasgow 1955. Balloch 1955. St Agnes's, Glasgow 1955-67. C/o Diocesan Office 1967-70. No further entries.

LILLIS, GEORGE: Born Ireland. Educated Ireland, Paris. Ordained Maynooth 1905. Lent to Glasgow. Wishaw 1905-08. Sick leave 1908-09. St Patrick's, Coatbridge 1909-10. Returned to Ireland 1910 and died there 7 Nov 1924. (Canning)

LILLIS, JAMES MARTIN: Born and educated Ireland. Ordained Kilkenny for Glasgow 1929. Cambuslang 1929-40. St Laurence's, Greenock 1940-50; thus moving to Paisley diocese. Howwood 1950-59. St Fergus's, Paisley 1959-68. St Charles', Paisley 1968-78. Retired 1978. Died Paisley 22 Jan 1979. (Canning)

LILLIS, RICHARD: Born and educated Ireland. Ordained Kilkenny for Glasgow 1946. St Columba's, Viewpark 1946-48; thus moving to Motherwell diocese. Chaplain, St Charles' Institute, Carstairs 1948-49. Bargeddie 1949-50. St Bride's, Cambuslang 1950-55. St Patrick's, Coatbridge 1955-60. St John the Baptist's, Uddingston 1960-61. St Serf's, Airdrie 1961-72. St Patrick's, Shieldmuir 1972-73. Died Shieldmuir 12 Feb 1973. (Canning)

LINDSAY, EDWARD: Born Dumbarton 1921. Educated Campion House, Osterley; St Peter's. Ordained Glasgow 1955. St Patrick's, Glasgow 1955-

68. Chaplain, Barlinnie Prison and St Joseph's Home, Glasgow 1968-82. St Margaret Mary's, Glasgow 1982-84. St Philip's, Glasgow 1984-.

LINK, PETER: Born Liershahn, Germany 1853. Educated Montabaur Gymnasium; Bonn University; St Peter's 1878-80. Ordained St Peter's College 1879. Our Lady and St Margaret's, Glasgow 1880-86. Holy Cross, Glasgow 1886-89. No further entries.

LITTLE, JOHN: Born Clydebank 1903. Educated Blairs 1917-23; St Peter's 1923-29. Ordained Glasgow 1929. Holy Cross, Glasgow 1929-30. St Mirin's, Paisley 1930-37. Shettleston and Carntyne 1937-45. Carntyne 1945-46. St Paul's, Shettleston 1946-51. St Flannan's, Kirkintilloch 1951-58. Died Muirhead 14 Dec 1958.

LITTLE, MICHAEL: Born Dalmuir 1907. Educated St Patrick's High School, Dumbarton; Blairs 1924-28; St Peter's 1928-34. Ordained Glasgow 1934. Glasgow Cathedral 1934. Shotts 1934-48; thus moving to Motherwell diocese. Motherwell Cathedral 1948-54. Blackwood 1954-55. Muirhead 1955-60. Died Muirhead 19 March 1960.

LITTLETON, MATTHEW: Born and educated Ireland. Ordained for Glasgow 1929. St Patrick's, Glasgow 1929. Croy 1929-31. St Joseph's, Woodside, Glasgow 1931-36. Rutherglen 1936-40. St John's, Port Glasgow 1940-46. Ardrossan 1946-50; thus moving to Galloway diocese. Auchinleck 1950-53. St Joseph's, Kilmarnock 1953-77. Died Kilmarnock 9 Aug 1977. (Canning)

LOFTUS, THOMAS: Born and educated Ireland. Ordained Maynooth 1924. Lent to Glasgow. St Aloysius', Glasgow 1924-30. Returned to Ireland 1930. (Canning)

LOGUE, DANIEL: see Archdiocese of St Andrews & Edinburgh

LORD, GERARD: Born Ireland. Educated Ireland, St Peter's. Ordained Glasgow 1929. St Patrick's, Shieldmuir 1929. Sick leave (arm amputated after accident) 1929-35. St Mary's, Glasgow 1935-36. Not in Directories 1936-37. Duntocher 1937-41. Retired to Ireland 1941 and died there 7 June 1973. (Canning)

LOUGHLIN, JOHN: Born Glasgow 1932. Educated St Aloysius' College, Glasgow; St Peter's. Ordained Glasgow 1957. St Alphonsus', Glasgow 1957. St Robert's, Glasgow 1957-62. St Aloysius', Glasgow 1962-70. St Columba's, Glasgow 1970-77. St Constantine's, Glasgow 1977-81. Our Lady Queen of Peace, Glasgow 1981-85. St Roch's, Glasgow 1985-.

LOVE, ALAN: Born Johnstone 1949. Educated John Neilson High School, Paisley; St Peter's. Ordained St Peter's College 1978. St Flannan's,

Kirkintilloch 1978-81. C/o Diocesan Office 1981-82. St Bernard's, Glasgow 1982-85. C/o Diocesan Office 1985-.

LOWERY, WILLIAM: Born Ireland. Educated Ireland, St Peter's. Ordained Glasgow 1929. St Joseph's, Tollcross 1929-50. St Catherine's, Glasgow 1950-54. Died Glasgow 21 Sept 1954. (Canning)

LOWRIE, HUGH ANTHONY: Born Glasgow 1949. Educated Langbank, Blairs, Valladolid. Ordained Glasgow 1974. St Joseph's, Tollcross 1974-76. Professor, Langbank 1976-78. Professor, Blairs 1978-81. Our Lady and St George, Glasgow 1981-83. St Helen's, Glasgow 1983-86. Holy Cross, Glasgow 1986-88. St Stephen's, Dalmuir 1988-89. St Gabriel's, Glasgow 1989-.

LOY, PATRICK: Born Auchinleck 1879. Educated Blairs 1892-96; St Peter's 1896-98; Scots College, Rome 1898-1903. Ordained Rome 1903. Lent to Argyll diocese: Oban 1903-04; Fort William 1904-05. St John's, Glasgow 1905-08. Alexandria 1908-09. St Charles', Glasgow 1909-28. St Patrick's, Dumbarton 1928-29. Leave of absence 1929-30. St Aloysius', Glasgow 1930-32. Burnbank 1932-33. Leave of absence 1933-46; serving at Pembroke Dock during the war. St Mary's, Coatbridge 1946-47. Our Lady and St Margaret's, Glasgow 1947-48. No address given 1948-49. C/o Diocesan Office 1949-51. Disappears from Directories thereafter. Died Port Glasgow 21 Oct 1973.

LUCEY, DENIS: Born and educated Ireland. Ordained Wexford for Glasgow 1936. St Patrick's, Dumbarton 1936-39. St Aloysius', Glasgow 1939-45. Cadzow 1945-48; thus moving to Motherwell diocese. Motherwell Cathedral 1948-54. St Paul's, Hamilton 1954-60. Muirhead 1960-64. St Augustine's, Coatbridge 1964-71. Died Law 7 Nov 1971. (Canning)

LYNAGH, WILLIAM: Ordained 1921. St Agnes's, Glasgow 1921-24. Hamilton 1924-26. No further entries.

LYNCH, ANDREW: Born Glasgow 1870. Educated Blairs 1884-88; Issy 1888-90; St Peter's 1890-95. Ordained Glasgow 1895. Barrhead 1895. St Mary's, Greenock 1895-1900. Professor, St Peter's College 1900-03. St Paul's, Glasgow 1903-05. Sick leave 1905-06. St Patrick's, Glasgow 1906-36. Died Glasgow 30 April 1936.

LYNCH, BERNARD: Born Glasgow 1873. Educated St Aloysius' College, Glasgow; Mount St Mary's, Chesterfield; St Peter's. Ordained 1895. St John's, Port Glasgow 1895-96. Archbishop's chaplain 1896-99. Glasgow Cathedral 1899-1905. Duntocher 1905-14. Saltcoats 1914-23. Immaculate Conception, Glasgow 1923-25. Died Glasgow 3 Dec 1925.

LYNCH, JOHN (1905) Born and educated Ireland. Ordained Maynooth 1905. Lent to Glasgow. St Aloysius', Glasgow 1905-10. Chaplain, West

Thorn Reformatory and Good Shepherd Convent, Dalbeth 1910-11. Returned to Ireland 1911 and died there 8 March 1934. (Canning)

LYNCH, JOHN (1925): Born Ireland. Educated Ireland, Paris. Ordained Paris 1925. Lent to Glasgow. St John's, Glasgow 1925-27. Returned to Ireland 1927 and died there 27 Feb 1938. (Canning)

LYNCH, PATRICK J: Born and educated Ireland. Ordained Maynooth 1937. St Mary's, Coatbridge 1937-42. Returned to Ireland 1942. (Canning)

LYNE, MICHAEL: Born and educated Ireland. Ordained Dublin for Glasgow 1941. Christ the King, Glasgow 1941-42. Shettleston and Carntyne 1942-45. Carntyne 1945-51. St Joseph's, Woodside, Glasgow 1951-67. St Bonaventure's, Glasgow 1967-68. St Martin's, Glasgow 1968-72. St Michael's, Glasgow 1972-. (Canning)

LYNE, THOMAS: Born Ireland. Educated Ireland, Paris. Ordained Killarney 1897. Lent to Glasgow. Our Holy Redeemer, Clydebank 1897-1905. Returned to Ireland 1905 and died there 14 March 1961. (Canning)

LYONS, JOHN A (1907): Born Glasgow 1882. Educated Blairs 1896-1901; St Peter's 1901-05; Scots College, Rome 1905-08. Ordained Rome 1907. St Joseph's, Tollcross 1908-11. Glasgow Cathedral 1911-16. St Aloysius', Glasgow 1916-24. Newmains 1924-29. Alexandria 1929-37. Retired 1937. Died Glasgow 16 May 1955.

LYONS, JOHN (1980): Ordained 1980. Holy Cross, Glasgow 1987-.

LYONS, PATRICK: Born and educated Ireland. Ordained Maynooth 1920. Lent to Glasgow. St Mary's, Paisley 1920-22. Returned to Ireland 1922. (Canning)

McALISTER (McAllister), JOHN (1888): Born and educated Ireland. Ordained Maynooth 1888. Lent to Glasgow. St Patrick's, Coatbridge 1888-91. Returned to Ireland 1891 and died there 22 Nov 1900. (Canning)

McALLISTER, JOHN (1891): Born Ireland. Educated Blairs, Douay, St Peter's. Ordained St Peter's College 1891. Glasgow Cathedral 1891-92. Longriggend 1892-96. St Vincent's, Glasgow 1896-97. Immaculate Conception, Glasgow 1897-98. St Charles', Paisley 1898-1917. Shotts 1917-34. Died Shotts 26 May 1934. (Canning)

McATEER, THOMAS: Born Glasgow 1917. Educated Blairs, St Peter's. Ordained 1943. St Agnes's, Glasgow 1943-47. St Anthony's, Glasgow 1947-50. Military chaplain 1950-73. Roseneath 1973-76. Milngavie 1976-86. Cardross 1986-89. Our Holy Redeemer, Clydebank 1989-.

McAULEY, JOHN GERARD: Born Dumbarton 1946. Educated St Aloysius' College, Glasgow; Blairs; Valladolid. Ordained Dumbarton 1970. Holy Cross, Glasgow 1970-72. St Mary's, Glasgow 1972-73. Professor, Blairs 1973-78. St Augustine's, Glasgow 1978-80. St Gregory's, Glasgow 1980-89. St Brendan's, Glasgow 1989-.

McAULEY, JOSEPH LOUIS: Born Dumbarton 1947. Educated Blairs; St Patrick's High School, Dumbarton; Glasgow University; practised as solicitor; educated for priesthood Scots College, Rome. Ordained Dumbarton 1984. Glasgow Cathedral 1984. Further studies, Rome 1984-85. St Eunan's, Clydebank 1985-86. St Monica's, Glasgow 1986-88. Sacred Heart, Cumbernauld 1988-.

McAVEETY, JOHN PATRICK: Born Glasgow 1930. Educated Blairs; Scots College, Rome. Ordained Rome 1956. St Paul's, Glasgow 1957-58. St Constantine's, Glasgow 1958-63. Our Lady of the Assumption, Glasgow 1963-65. Sick leave 1965-67. Our Lady of Consolation, Glasgow 1967-73. St Michael's, Dumbarton 1973-77. Died Dumbarton 22 March 1977.

McAVOY, WILLIAM: Born Glasgow 1862. Educated Blairs 1877-82; Douay 1882-83; St Peter's 1883-88. Ordained Glasgow 1888. St John's, Glasgow 1888-90. St Patrick's, Dumbarton 1890-95. Cadzow 1895-1903. Hamilton 1903-32. Died Hamilton 13 Aug 1932.

McBREARTY, DENIS: Born Dumbarton 1872. Educated Blairs 1886-89; Issy 1889-91; St Peter's 1891-96. Ordained 1896. St Peter's, Glasgow 1896-1900. Shotts 1900-04. Cardowan 1904-08. Carfin 1908-15. St Aloysius', Glasgow 1915-46. Died Littlehampton 8 Sept 1946.

McBRIDE, ALEXANDER: Born Glasgow 1886. Educated St Aloysius' College, Glasgow; Blairs 1902-06; St Peter's 1906-14. Ordained Glasgow 1914. St Anthony's, Glasgow 1914-18. Rutherglen 1918-30. St Laurence's, Greenock 1930-36. Longriggend 1936-41. Coatdyke 1941-51; thus moving to Motherwell diocese. St Bridget's, Baillieston 1951-55. Died Baillieston 10 March 1955.

McBRIDE, JAMES: Born Ireland. Educated Ireland, Paris. Ordained Paris 1909. Lent to Glasgow. St Peter's, Glasgow 1909-15. Returned to Ireland 1915 and died there 15 March 1946. (Canning)

McBRIDE, PETER JOSEPH: Born Renton 1957. Educated Langbank, Blairs, St Peter's. Ordained Renton 1981. St Margaret's, Clydebank 1981-85. St Bartholomew's, Glasgow 1985-88. St Vincent de Paul's, Glasgow 1988-.

McCABE, JOHN J: Born Glasgow 1931. Educated Blairs, Valladolid. Ordained Valladolid 1957. Our Holy Redeemer, Clydebank 1957.

Immaculate Conception, Glasgow 1957-74. Helensburgh 1974-76. Christ the King, Glasgow 1976-81. St Maria Goretti's, Glasgow 1981-83. Our Lady and St Margaret's, Glasgow 1983-85. St Joseph's, Cumbernauld 1985-88. Our Lady of Lourdes, Glasgow 1988-.

McCABE, MICHAEL (1889): Born Crieff 1866. Educated Blairs 1879-83; Valladolid 1883-89. Ordained Valladolid 1889. St Patrick's, Glasgow 1889-96. Dalry 1896-1904. Alexandria 1904-23. Johnstone 1923-24. Died Johnstone 19 Sept 1924.

McCABE, MICHAEL D (1957): Born Glasgow 1932. Educated St Joseph's College, Dumfries; St Peter's. Ordained Glasgow 1957. St Patrick's, Glasgow 1957. Helensburgh 1957-60. Good Shepherd, Glasgow 1960-67. Croy 1967-74. St Bernard's, Glasgow 1974-81. St Matthew's, Bishopbriggs 1981-85. Our Lady of Fatima, Glasgow 1985-86. Milngavie 1986-.

McCABE, THOMAS P: Born and educated Ireland. Ordained Carlow for Glasgow 1938. Duntocher 1938-47. St Roch's, Glasgow 1947-50. Leave of absence 1950-51. St Luke's, Glasgow 1951-52. No further entries. (Canning)

McCAFFERTY, PETER: Born Motherwell 1932. Educated Our Lady's High School, Motherwell; Campion House, Osterley; St Peter's. Ordained Glasgow 1960. St Pius X, Glasgow 1960. St Nicholas's, Glasgow 1960-64. St Bartholomew's, Glasgow 1964-78. St Ninian's, Glasgow 1978-82. St Saviour's, Glasgow 1982-87. St Teresa's, Glasgow 1987-.

McCALLION, GERALD PATRICK: Born Dumbarton 1925. Educated Blairs, St Peter's, St Sulpice. Ordained Glasgow 1949. St Michael's, Glasgow 1949. St Vincent de Paul's, Glasgow 1949-57. St Charles', Glasgow 1957-68. Our Holy Redeemer, Clydebank 1968-72. St John's, Glasgow 1972-75. Our Lady of Loreto, Dalmuir 1975-78. Died Glasgow 27 Jan 1979.

McCANN, FRANCIS A: Born Glasgow. Taught at St David's, Cardiff. Educated for priesthood St Mary's College, Hammersmith; St Peter's; Issy 1889-91; St Sulpice 1891-94. Ordained Paris 1894. Shotts 1894. Pollokshaws 1894-97. St Michael's, Glasgow 1897-99. St Peter's, Glasgow 1899-1902. Croy 1902-07. Coatdyke 1907-26. St Columba's, Glasgow 1926-29. Retired 1929. Died Largs 7 May 1938.

McCANN, PETER (1940): Born Glasgow 1915. Educated Blairs 1929-33; St Peter's 1933-40. Ordained Glasgow 1940. St Luke's, Glasgow 1940-43. St John the Baptist's, Uddingston 1943-56; thus moving to Motherwell diocese. St James's, Coatbridge 1956-68. Strathaven 1968-77. St Patrick's, Coatbridge 1977-83. St John Ogilvie's, Blantyre 1983-.

McCANN, PETER (1949): Born Dumbarton 1922. Educated Blairs, St Peter's. Ordained Glasgow 1949. St Robert's, Glasgow 1949-67. St Thomas's, Glasgow 1967-74. Our Holy Redeemer, Clydebank 1974-82. Died France 1 May 1982.

McCANN, ROBERT GERARD: Born Glasgow 1956. Educated Our Lady's School, Cardonald; St Peter's. Ordained St Peter's College 1980. St Conval's, Glasgow 1980-.

McCANN, THOMAS: Born Hamilton 1890. Educated St Aloysius' College, Glasgow; Blairs 1906-11; St Sulpice 1911-16. Ordained 1916. St Patrick's, Glasgow 1916-26. St Mirin's, Paisley 1926-29. St Roch's, Glasgow 1929-33. Bothwell 1933-40. St Columba's, Viewpark 1940-49; thus moving to Motherwell diocese. St Margaret's, Airdrie 1949-67. Retired 1967. Died East Kilbride 5 Sept 1972.

McCARNEY, FELIX: see Paisley diocese.

McCARTHY, FLORENCE: Born and educated Ireland. Ordained Maynooth 1897. Lent to Glasgow. Glasgow Cathedral 1897-1905. Returned to Ireland 1905 and died there 13 Oct 1963. (Canning)

McCARTHY, JAMES: Born Newcastle-on-Tyne 1853. Educated Blairs 1869-72; Valladolid 1872-76; St Peter's 1876-79. Ordained Glasgow 1879. Our Lady and St Margaret's, Glasgow 1879-84. St John's, Port Glasgow 1884-99. St Mary Immaculate, Glasgow 1899-1900. Glasgow Cathedral 1900-14. Consecrated Bishop of Galloway 1914. Died Dumfries 24 Dec 1943.

McCARTHY, JOHN: Born Glasgow 1932. Educated Blairs, St Sulpice, St Peter's. Ordained Glasgow 1956. St Laurence's, Glasgow 1956-64. No further entries.

McCARTHY, MICHAEL (1882): Ordained 1882. St Mary's, Glasgow 1883-85. No further entries.

McCARTHY, MICHAEL (1909): Born Ireland. Educated Ireland, St Peter's. Ordained Glasgow 1909. Our Lady and St Margaret's, Glasgow 1909-26. Larkhall 1926-29. St Joseph's, Tollcross 1929-38. St Teresa's, Glasgow 1938-48. Our Lady and St Margaret's, Glasgow 1948-67. Died Glasgow 7 Oct 1967. (Canning)

McCARTHY, PATRICK A: Born Ireland. Educated Ireland; Le Mans, France; Oscott; St Peter's. Ordained Glasgow 1897. St Augustine's, Coatbridge 1897-1900. Immaculate Conception, Glasgow 1900-02. Motherwell 1902-06. Largs 1906-08. Gourock 1908-18. Stevenston 1918-29. Cleland 1929-30. St John the Baptist's, Uddingston 1930-59;

thus moving to Motherwell diocese. Died Uddingston 15 March 1959. (Canning)

McCAULAY, RODGER (Roger): Born and educated Ireland. Ordained for Glasgow 1928. St Peter's, Glasgow 1928-39. Saltcoats 1939-40. Leave of absence (in Ireland for health) 1940-69. Died Dublin 3 April 1969. (Canning)

McCHRYSTAL, JAMES J: Born Mossend 1891. Educated Blairs 1906-11; Scots College, Rome 1911-18. Ordained Rome 1917. Sacred Heart, Glasgow 1918-23. Professor, Blairs 1923-29. Our Lady and St Margaret's, Glasgow 1929-30. St John's, Port Glasgow 1930-35. Died Port Glasgow 18 May 1935.

McCLUSKEY, ROBERT JAMES: Born Glasgow 1854. Educated St Aloysius' College, Glasgow; Rockwell 1871-76; Issy 1876-77; Propaganda, Rome 1877-82. Ordained Rome 1882. St Peter's, Glasgow 1882-86. Duntocher 1886-98. Sick leave 1898-99. Renfrew 1899-1905. Carluke 1905-21. Gourock 1921-22. Died Gourock 2 Aug 1922.

McCOLL, PHILIP: Born Glasgow 1862. Educated Blairs 1878-81; St Peter's 1881-86. Ordained Glasgow 1886. St Mary's, Glasgow 1886-93. Saltcoats 1893-99. St John's, Port Glasgow 1899-1930. Retired 1930. Died Glasgow 23 Oct 1939.

McCONNACHIE, PETER: Born Banff 1869. Educated Blairs 1881-86; Valladolid 1886-93. Ordained Valladolid 1893. St Mirin's, Paisley 1893-1900. Carluke 1900-03. Cadzow 1903-13. Died Lanark 8 Dec 1913.

McCONNELL, MICHAEL: Ordained 1924. St Mary's, Glasgow 1924-25. No further entries.
Note: this is almost certainly the same person as 'O'Carroll, Michael' (see below), but wrongly entered in the Directory for 1925.

McCORMACK, MICHAEL: Born and educated Ireland. Ordained Maynooth 1898. Lent to Glasgow. Mossend 1898-1901. Returned to Ireland 1901 and died there 26 March 1918. (Canning)

McCORMICK, ALEXANDER (1895): Born Port Glasgow 1871. Educated Blairs 1884-89; Petit Communaute, Paris 1889-90; St Peter's 1890-95. Ordained 1895. St Mary's, Glasgow 1895-96. St Patrick's, Shieldmuir 1896-99. St Charles', Glasgow 1899-1900. Chaplain, West Thorn Reformatory, Dalbeth 1900-03. Carluke 1903. Retired to Rothesay with consumption and died there 26 Dec 1903.

McCORMICK, ALEXANDER (1918): Born Port Glasgow 1892. Educated Blairs 1908-13; St Sulpice 1913-17; St Peter's 1917-18. Ordained

Glasgow 1918. Holy Cross, Glasgow 1918-22. No address given 1922-23. No further entries.

McCRANOR, HUGH: Born Paisley 1912. Educated Blairs 1926-30; St Peter's 1930-37. Ordained St Peter's College 1937. St Mary's, Glasgow 1937. St Laurence's, Greenock 1937-39. Houston 1939-40. Christ the King, Glasgow 1940-59. Balloch 1959-60. Died Balloch 25 Aug 1960.

McCREADY, JOHN (1897): Born and educated Ireland. Ordained Maynooth 1897. Lent to Glasgow. St Peter's, Glasgow 1897-98. Blantyre 1898-1900. Returned to Ireland 1900 and died there 20 Jan 1933. (Canning)

McCREADY, JOHN (1935): Born Coatbridge 1910. Educated Motherwell Higher Grade School; Blairs 1926-29; Scots College, Rome 1929-35. Ordained Rome 1935. St Mary Immaculate, Glasgow 1936-37. Rutherglen 1937. Holy Family, Kirkintilloch 1937-39. St Patrick's, Dumbarton 1939-56. St Mark's, Carntyne 1956-67. St Columba's, Glasgow 1967-84. Retired 1984. Died Glasgow 20 March 1987.

McCRORY, JOHN: Born Partick 1899. Educated St Peter's School, Partick; St Mungo's Academy, Glasgow; Blairs 1913-14; military service, Irish Guards 1914-19; St Peter's 1919-24. Ordained Glasgow 1924. Glasgow Cathedral 1924-31. Whiterigg 1931-32. Chaplain, Kenmure Industrial School 1932-34. Shettleston and Carntyne 1934-35. Professor, Blairs 1935-41. Baillieston 1941-42. Sick leave 1942-45. Bothwell 1945-47. Brighton 1947-49. Moved to Motherwell diocese. Chaplain, Bellevue House, Rutherglen 1949-50. Longriggend 1950-51. All Saints, Airdrie 1951-52. Chapelhall 1952-62. St Bridget's, Baillieston 1962-68. Retired to Brighton 1968 and died there 13 July 1972.

McCULLA, THOMAS: Born Ireland. Educated Spain. Ordained 1887. Lent to Glasgow. Sacred Heart, Glasgow 1887-90. Returned to Ireland 1890 and died there 2 Nov 1946. (Canning)

McDADE, GERALD S: Born Paisley 1899. Educated Blairs 1913-20; St Peter's 1920-26. Ordained Glasgow 1926. St Joseph's, Tollcross 1926-29. St Mary's, Greenock 1929-31. St John's, Port Glasgow 1931-33. St Mary's, Greenock 1933-36. St Aloysius', Glasgow 1936-39. Holy Cross, Glasgow 1939-46. Neilston 1946-47. St Stephen's, Dalmuir 1947-55. Died Dalmuir 22 July 1955.

MACDAID, DENIS F: Born Ireland. Educated Ireland, Rome. Ordained 1924. Lent to Glasgow. Mossend 1924-27. Returned to Ireland 1927. (Canning)

McDAID, JAMES: Born and educated Ireland. Ordained Maynooth 1903. Lent to Glasgow. St Mary's, Greenock 1903-08. Returned to Ireland 1908 and died there 18 June 1943. (Canning)

McDAID, NEIL FRANCIS: Born Glasgow 1920. Educated St Mungo's Academy, Glasgow; Royal Technical College, Glasgow; St Peter's. Ordained Glasgow 1963. St Maria Goretti's, Glasgow 1963-71. St Brendan's, Glasgow 1971-74. Our Lady of Good Counsel, Glasgow 1974-78. St Brigid's, Glasgow 1978-87. Retired 1987.

McDERMOTT, JOHN B (1927): Born Ireland. Educated Ireland, Spain. Ordained Salamanca 1927. Lent to Glasgow. Burnbank 1927-32. Cadzow 1932-33. Sacred Heart, Glasgow 1933-37. Returned to Ireland 1937 and died there 3 March 1949. (Canning)

McDERMOTT, JOHN PATRICK (1964): Born Glasgow 1911. Educated St Mungo's Academy, Glasgow; Glasgow University; St Peter's. Ordained Glasgow 1964. St Gabriel's, Glasgow 1964-70. St Brendan's, Glasgow 1970-71. Died Glasgow 12 July 1971.

MACDONALD, ALEXANDER: Born Bohuntine, Lochaber 1869. Educated Blairs 1885-89; Valladolid 1889-95. Ordained Valladolid 1895. St Michael's, Glasgow 1895-96. Chaplain, West Thorn Reformatory, Dalbeth 1896-99. St Patrick's, Glasgow 1899-1905. Died Glasgow 28 April 1905.

MACDONALD, ANGUS JOSEPH: Born Glasgow 1945. Educated Blairs, St Peter's. Ordained St Peter's College 1970. St Helen's, Glasgow 1970. St Stephen's, Dalmuir 1970-88. Diocesan Pastoral Centre 1988-.

MACDONALD, EDMUND: Born Greenock 1887. Educated Blairs 1903-08; Issy 1908-12; St Sulpice 1912-13. Ordained Paris 1913. St Charles', Glasgow 1913-26. St Columba's, Glasgow 1926-28. St Charles', Glasgow 1928-30. Strathaven 1930-33. Newton 1933-40. St Augustine's, Coatbridge 1940-63; thus moving to Motherwell diocese. Died Coatbridge 16 Oct 1963.

MACDONALD, HUGH (1906): Born Greenock 1880. Educated Blairs 1894-1900; St Peter's 1900-06. Ordained Glasgow 1906. Carntyne 1906-12. St Paul's, Shettleston 1912-17. Blantyre 1917-21. Newmains 1921-24. St Bride's, Cambuslang 1924-50; thus moving to Motherwell diocese. Died Glasgow 28 Dec 1950.

MACDONALD, JAMES: Born Glasgow 1872. Educated Blairs 1885-89; Issy 1889-91; St Peter's 1891-96. Ordained 1896. Maryhill 1896-1900. St Patrick's, Dumbarton 1900-03. Johnstone 1903-05. Houston 1905-27. Retired 1927. Died Dublin 4 Jan 1929.

McDONALD, JOHN (1916): see Dunkeld diocese.

MACDONALD, JOHN (1945): Born Arisaig 1918. Educated Blairs, St Peter's. Ordained 1945. Our Lady and St Margaret's, Glasgow 1945-46. Lent to Argyll diocese: Oban 1946-51. St Mary's, Glasgow 1951-65. St Stephen's, Dalmuir 1965-70. Balloch 1970-74. St Anne's, Glasgow 1974-84. Retired 1984.

McDONALD, WILLIAM: Born Dalmuir 1915. Educated Blairs 1930-34; St Peter's 1934-41. Ordained Glasgow 1941. Our Lady of Lourdes, Glasgow 1941. Helensburgh 1941-47. St Teresa's, Glasgow 1947-52. St Conval's, Glasgow 1952-59. Balloch 1959-63. St Michael's, Glasgow 1963-64. Chaplain, Carmelite Convent, Glasgow 1964-69. Retired 1969. Died Glasgow 5 May 1970.

McDONNELL, GEORGE: Ordained 1885. Motherwell 1885-88. No further entries.

McDONNELL, JAMES: Born Ireland. Educated Rome. Ordained Rome 1895. Lent to Glasgow. Blantyre 1895-98. Returned to Ireland 1898 and died there 18 Aug 1940. (Canning)

MACDONNELL, MICHAEL: Born and educated Ireland. Ordained Maynooth 1904. Lent to Glasgow. St Laurence's, Greenock 1905-14. Returned to Ireland 1914 and died there 11 Dec 1963. (Canning)

MACDOUGALL, DONALD: see Argyll diocese.

McEACHEN, ANGUS: Born Arisaig 1867. Educated Blairs 1881-84; Douay 1884-87; St Peter's 1887-91. Ordained Glasgow 1891. St Alphonsus', Glasgow 1891-97. Greengairs 1897-1900. Whiterigg 1900-03. Rutherglen 1903-09. Newton 1909-15. St Peter's, Glasgow 1915-20. Retired to London 1920 and died there 23 July 1939.

McELENEY, MICHAEL J; Born and educated Ireland. Ordained Carlow for Glasgow 1934. Shettleston and Carntyne 1934-42. Forces chaplain 1942-59. St Nicholas's, Glasgow 1959-61. Milngavie 1961-70. Retired 1970. Died Ireland 9 Aug 1976. (Canning)

McELHOLM, JOSEPH: Born and educated Ireland. Ordained Kilkenny for Glasgow 1948. St Anthony's, Glasgow 1948-73. Our Lady of Fatima, Glasgow 1973-77. Christ the King, Glasgow 1977-87. Died Glasgow 24 June 1987. (Canning)

McELLIN, EDWARD: Born and educated Ireland. Ordained Maynooth 1936. Lent to Glasgow. St Aloysius', Glasgow 1936-39. Returned to Ireland 1939. (Canning)

McELMAIL, FRANCIS: Ordained 1894. Sacred Heart, Glasgow 1898-1902. No further entries.

McELROY, CHRISTOPHER JOSEPH: Born Glasgow 1955. Educated Langbank; Blairs; Scots College, Rome. Ordained Glasgow 1980. St Helen's, Glasgow 1980. Further studies, Rome 1980-81. St Mary Immaculate, Glasgow 1981-87. St Teresa's, Glasgow 1987-.

McELROY, JOHN: see Paisley diocese.

McELWEE, CHARLES JAMES: Born Clydebank 1950. Educated St Columba's High School, Clydebank; St Peter's. Ordained Clydebank 1984. St Helen's, Glasgow 1984. St Gregory's, Glasgow 1984-.

McELWEE, PATRICK J: Ordained 1923. St Patrick's, Coatbridge 1924-28. No further entries.

McERLAIN, JOSEPH: Born and educated Ireland. Ordained Wexford for Glasgow 1926. St Alphonsus', Glasgow 1926-46. Biggar 1946-47. St Vincent de Paul's, Glasgow 1947-54. Retired to Ireland 1954 and died there 18 Oct 1960. (Canning)

MACEVOY, THOMAS: Born Ireland. Educated Ireland, France. Ordained Newry 1883. Johnstone 1883-84. St Patrick's, Coatbridge 1884-89. Chaplain, West Thorn Reformatory, Dalbeth 1889-91. Renfrew 1891-99. Died Rothesay 30 June 1899. (Canning)

McEWAN, DANIEL: Born Glasgow 1930. Educated St Peter's; Scots College, Rome. Ordained Rome 1955. St Maria Goretti's, Glasgow 1955-61. St Eunan's, Clydebank 1961-67. Our Lady of the Assumption, Glasgow 1967-76. Balloch 1976-79. Our Lady of Loreto, Dalmuir 1979-82. No further entries.

McEWAN, HUGH G (1948): Born Glasgow 1925. Educated Blairs; St Peter's; Scots College, Rome. Ordained Rome 1948. Further studies, Rome 1948-51. Ripetitore, Scots College, Rome 1951-59. Vice-rector, Rome 1959-65. Archbishop's secretary 1965-67. Our Lady and St Margaret's, Glasgow 1967-73. St Michael's, Dumbarton 1973-88. Retired 1988. Died Glasgow 23 Sept 1989.

McEWAN, HUGH J (1960): Born Glasgow 1936. Educated St Aloysius' College, Glasgow; Blairs; Scots College, Rome. Ordained Rome 1960. St Benedict's, Glasgow 1961-69. St Michael's, Dumbarton 1969-73. Vice-rector, Scots College, Rome 1973-75. Our Holy Redeemer, Clydebank 1975-77. St Mark's, Glasgow 1977-78. Our Lady and St Margaret's, Glasgow 1978-83. Diocesan Pastoral Centre 1983-88. St Peter's Pastoral

Centre in addresses, but not under Centre, 1988-89. St Joachim's, Glasgow 1989-.

McEWAN, JAMES: Born Glasgow 1911. Educated St Charles' College Seminary, Ohio, USA 1924-28; Scots College, Rome 1928-35. Ordained Rome 1934. St John's, Port Glasgow 1935-39. St Mary's, Paisley 1939-48. No further entries.

MACEWAN, SYDNEY: see Argyll diocese.

McEWAN, THOMAS: Born Glasgow 1881. Educated St Aloysius' College, Glasgow 1895-99; Blairs 1899-1901; Scots College, Rome 1901-07. Ordained Rome 1906. St Mary's, Glasgow 1907-24. St Thomas's, Glasgow 1924-38. Our Holy Redeemer, Clydebank 1938-41. Died Glasgow 30 March 1941.

McFADDEN, CHARLES (1926): Born and educated Ireland. Ordained Maynooth 1926. Lent to Glasgow. St Aloysius', Glasgow 1926-33. Returned to Ireland 1933 and died there 11 Nov 1977. (Canning)

McFADDEN, CHARLES (1950): Born Govan 1926. Educated Blairs; Scots College, Rome. Ordained Rome 1950. St Alphonsus', Glasgow 1950-52. St Simon's, Glasgow 1952-65. St Bonaventure's, Glasgow 1965-70. St Jude's, Glasgow 1970-74. Economat des Redemptoristes, Paris 1974-76. St Joseph's, Woodside, Glasgow 1976-84. St Stephen's, Glasgow 1984-.

McFADDEN, FRANCIS: Born and educated Ireland. Ordained Maynooth 1936. Lent to Glasgow. St Mary's, Paisley 1936-38. Returned to Ireland 1938 and died there 18 June 1973. (Canning)

McFADYEN, WILLIAM: Ordained 1927. St Stephen's, Dalmuir 1927-30. St Saviour's, Glasgow 1930-35. No further entries.

McFARLANE, FRANCIS J: see Archdiocese of St Andrews & Edinburgh

MACFARLANE, PETER: Born Fort William 1884. Educated Blairs 1899-1903; Scots College, Rome 1903-09. Ordained Rome 1908. St Stephen's, Dalmuir 1909-17. St Mary's, Greenock 1917-19. Burnbank 1919-20. St Paul's, Shettleston 1920-26. Whiterigg 1926-31. Died Whiterigg 26 Oct 1931.

McFAUL, HENRY: Born and educated Ireland. Ordained Maynooth 1927. Lent to Glasgow. St Roch's, Glasgow 1927-32. Returned to Ireland 1932 and died there 23 Dec 1973. (Canning)

McFAUL, JOHN: Born Glasgow 1915. Educated Blairs 1929-34; St Peter's 1934-41. Ordained Glasgow 1941. Saltcoats 1941-47. St Teresa's,

Glasgow 1947-60. Spiritual Director, Valladolid 1960-63. St Conval's, Glasgow 1963-67. St Leo's, Glasgow 1967-69. St Luke's, Glasgow 1969-81. Died Glasgow 4 March 1981.

McGARRIGLE, GEORGE: Born Glasgow 1929. Educated St Mungo's Academy, Glasgow; Beda, Rome. Ordained Glasgow 1978. St Margaret's, Clydebank 1978-81. St Bernadette's, Glasgow 1981-83. St Pius X, Glasgow 1983-84. Our Lady of Perpetual Succour, Glasgow 1984-89. St Eunan's, Clydebank 1989-.

McGARRITY, NEIL ANTHONY MICHAEL: Born Clydebank 1964. Educated St Columba's High School, Clydebank; St Peter's; Chesters. Ordained Glasgow 1989. St Teresa's, Glasgow 1989-.

McGARRY, JOHN: Born Ireland. Educated Ireland, Rome. Ordained Rome 1934. Lent to Glasgow. Houston 1934-35. Airdrie 1935-44. Returned to Ireland 1944. (Canning)

McGEE, EUGENE: Born and educated Ireland. Ordained Dublin for Glasgow 1952. St Saviour's, Glasgow 1952-60. Holy Family, Kirkintilloch 1960-67. Alexandria 1967-79. St Stephen's, Glasgow 1979-84. St Matthews, Bishopbriggs 1984-. (Canning)

McGENNIS, EDWARD: Born and educated Ireland. Ordained 1919. Lent to Glasgow. Cambuslang 1919-23. St Anne's, Glasgow 1923-24. Returned to Ireland 1924. (Canning)

McGHEE, CHARLES: Born Sale, Gippsland, Australia 1861. Educated Blairs 1876-81; St Peter's 1881-86. Ordained Glasgow 1886. St Patrick's, Glasgow 1886-91. Houston 1891-99. St Anne's, Glasgow 1899-1900. No address given 1900-01. Lent to Archdiocese of St Andrews & Edinburgh: Edinburgh Cathedral 1901-02; no address given 1902-03; Lennoxtown 1903-06. Not in Directories 1906-07. No address given 1907-11. Cleland 1911-12. No address given 1912-13. St Mary Immaculate, Glasgow 1913. Died Pollokshaws 6 March 1913.

McGHEE, JAMES: Born Clydebank 1937. Educated Blairs; Scots College, Rome. Ordained Rome 1961. Professor, Langbank 1961-70. Further studies, Rome 1970-74. No further entries.

McGHEE, WILLIAM: Born Glasgow 1899. Educated Blairs 1915-18; military service 1918-19; St Peter's 1919-24. Ordained Glasgow 1924. Glasgow Cathedral 1924-41. Newmains 1941-45. Christ the King, Glasgow 1945-48. St Mark's, Carntyne 1948-55. Holy Family, Kirkintilloch 1955-77. Retired 1977. Died Glasgow 4 Sept 1978.

McGHIE, THOMAS: Born Hamilton 1904. Educated St Mungo's Academy, Glasgow 1917-18; Blairs 1918-24; St Peter's 1924-30. Ordained Glasgow

1930. Renton 1930-32. Immaculate Conception, Glasgow 1932-42. St Columbkille's, Rutherglen 1942-50; thus moving to Motherwell diocese. St Bartholomew's, Coatbridge 1950-65. Died Coatbridge 13 Jan 1965.

McGILL, JAMES: Born Whifflet 1915. Educated Blairs 1929-34; St Peter's 1934-41. Ordained Glasgow 1941. St Mary's, Glasgow 1941-44. Immaculate Conception, Glasgow 1944-47. Larkhall 1947-49; thus moving to Motherwell diocese. Cleland 1949-59. Strathaven 1959-64. St Peter's, Hamilton 1964-69. Calderbank 1969-82. Retired 1982. Died Cleland 12 March 1986.

McGINLAY, HUGH (1964): Born Ayr 1940. Educated St Patrick's High School, Dumbarton; St Peter's. Ordained Glasgow 1964. Further studies, Rome 1964-68. St Constantine's, Glasgow 1968-69. C/o Diocesan Office 1969-70. St Joseph's, Woodside, Glasgow 1970-71. St Joseph's, Woodside, Glasgow in addresses, but not under parishes, 1971-72. St Joseph's, Woodside, Glasgow 1972-77. Mount Oliver, Ireland 1977-78. No further entries.

McGINLAY, HUGH JAMES (1977): Born Dumbarton 1949. Educated St Patrick's High School, Dumbarton; Scots College, Rome. Ordained Dumbarton 1977. St Teresa's, Glasgow 1977-80/1. St Bartholomew's, Glasgow 1980/1-83. St Margaret Mary's, Glasgow 1983-85. C/o Diocesan Office 1985-89. No further entries.

McGINLAY, JOHN JOSEPH (1940): Born Glasgow 1916. Educated St Charles' School, Glasgow; St Aloysius' College, Glasgow; St Peter's 1933-40. Ordained Glasgow 1940. Rutherglen 1940-42. St Joseph's, Tollcross 1942-43. Holy Family, Kirkintilloch 1943-65. St Bernadette's, Glasgow 1965-78. Our Lady of the Assumption, Glasgow 1978-82. St Mark's, Carntyne 1982-86. Died Glasgow 19 Feb 1986.

McGINLEY, JAMES: Born Glasgow 1921. Educated Blairs; Scots College, Rome; St Peter's. Ordained Glasgow 1946. St Patrick's, Dumbarton 1946. Professor, Blairs 1946-56. Immaculate Conception, Glasgow 1956-60. Sick leave from 1960. Died Leeds 12 Oct 1962.

McGINLEY, JOHN DAMIEN (1968): Born Bridge of Allan 1944. Educated Blairs, St Peter's. Ordained St Peter's College 1968. St Mary's, Glasgow 1968-71. St Augustine's, Glasgow 1971-72. St Laurence's, Glasgow 1972-76. St Paul's, Glasgow 1976-77. St Stephen's, Glasgow 1977-87. No further entries.

McGINLEY, JOHN GERARD (1985): Born Clydebank 1961. Educated St Andrews High School, Clydebank; St Peter's; Chesters. Ordained Dalmuir 1985. St Martin's, Glasgow 1985-88. All Saints, Glasgow 1988-.

McGINLEY, TEAGUE: Born and educated Ireland. Ordained Maynooth 1921. Lent to Glasgow. St Laurence's, Greenock 1921-26. Returned to Ireland 1926 and died there 14 March 1949. (Canning)

McGINLEY, WILLIAM: Born Glasgow 1938. Educated Holyrood School, Glasgow; Blairs; St Peter's. Ordained Glasgow 1962. St Bernard's, Glasgow 1962-68. St Charles', Glasgow 1968-73. Our Lady of Consolation, Glasgow 1973-74. St Pius X, Glasgow 1974-75. St Paul's, Shettleston 1975-76. St Stephen's, Glasgow 1976-77. St Mary Immaculate, Glasgow 1977-81. St Brendan's, Glasgow 1981-86. Duntocher 1986-.

McGINN, HENRY: Born Partick 1922. Educated Blairs, St Peter's. Ordained Glasgow 1947. Our Lady of Good Aid, Motherwell 1947-48; thus moving to Motherwell diocese. St Columbkille's, Rutherglen 1948-54. St Columba's, Viewpark 1954-62. St Benedict's, Easterhouse 1962-68. Larkhall 1968-.

McGINNESS, SAMUEL: Born Heathfield, Lanarkshire 1932. Educated St Aloysius' College, Glasgow; Scots College, Rome. Ordained Rome 1956. St Constantine's, Glasgow 1957-67. C/o Diocesan Office 1967-69. Went to Galloway diocese. St Joseph's, Kilmarnock 1969-77. Whithorn 1977-82. St Teresa's, Dumfries 1982-85. St Mary's, Irvine 1985-.

McGINTY, DESMOND JOSEPH MARTIN: Born Glasgow 1944. Educated Blairs, St Peter's. Ordained St Peter's College 1968. St James's, Glasgow 1968-69. St Robert's, Glasgow 1969-72. All Saints, Glasgow 1972-73. St Ninian's, Glasgow 1973-75. St Aloysius', Glasgow 1975-78. RAF chaplain 1978-82. Our Lady of Lourdes, Glasgow 1982-85. RAF chaplain 1985-88. Went to Aberdeen diocese. Beauly 1988-.

McGIVNEY, BERNARD: Ordained 1882. St John's, Glasgow 1883-86. No further entries.

McGLADRIGAN, JAMES: Born Glasgow 1935. Educated Blairs, St Peter's. Ordained Glasgow 1960. St John's, Glasgow 1960-61. St Peter's, Glasgow 1961-66. No further entries.

McGLINCHEY, CHARLES: Born Ireland. Educated Ireland, Paris. Ordained Paris 1914. Lent to Glasgow. Croy 1914-17. St John the Baptist's, Uddingston 1917-18. Returned to Ireland 1918 and died there 23 Sept 1958. (Canning)

McGLINCHEY, DANIEL (1927): Born Rutherglen 1903. Educated Blairs 1918-20; Propaganda, Rome 1920-24; St Peter's 1924-27. Ordained Glasgow 1927. St Mary's, Greenock 1927-29. St Patrick's, Dumbarton 1929-34. St Charles', Paisley 1934-47. Neilston 1947-51; thus moving to

Paisley diocese. Gourock 1951-69. Retired 1969. Died Greenock 28 Aug 1973.

McGLINCHEY, DANIEL (1932): Born Glasgow 1908. Educated St Mungo's Academy, Glasgow; Blairs 1923-26; Scots College, Rome 1926-33. Ordained Rome 1932. St Mary Immaculate, Glasgow 1933. St Margaret's, Airdrie 1933-49; thus moving to Motherwell diocese. St John the Baptist's, Uddingston 1949-53. St Peter's, Hamilton 1953-64. Muirhead 1964-72. Died Muirhead 22 Jan 1972.

McGLYNN, DOMINIC: Born Glasgow 1901. Educated Blairs 1914-20; St Peter's 1920-26. Ordained Glasgow 1926. Hamilton 1926-37. St Mary's, Paisley 1937-43. Forces chaplain 1943-46. New Stevenston 1946-61; thus moving to Motherwell diocese. Retired 1961. Died Edinburgh 22 Sept 1972.

McGLYNN, TIMOTHY: Born Glasgow 1943. Educated St Gerard's School, Glasgow; Campion House, Osterley; St Peter's. Ordained St Peter's 1970. St Margaret's, Clydebank 1970-75. St Philomena's, Glasgow 1975-78. St Alphonsus', Glasgow 1978-81. Royal Navy chaplain 1981-85. Died Plymouth 3 June 1985.

McGOLDRICK, COLUMBA: Born and educated Ireland. Ordained Maynooth 1925. Lent to Glasgow. St Patrick's, Shieldmuir 1925-30. St Charles', Glasgow 1930-31. Returned to Ireland 1931 and died there 25 May 1968. (Canning)

McGOLDRICK, WILLIAM: Born Glasgow 1892. Educated Blairs 1907-12; Valladolid 1912-19. Ordained Valladolid 1919. St Patrick's, Dumbarton 1919-20. St Charles', Paisley 1920-28. St Luke's, Glasgow 1928-37. Strathaven 1937-40. St Philomena's, Glasgow 1940-48. Our Holy Redeemer, Clydebank 1948-68. Retired 1968. Died Clydebank 10 May 1970.

McGONAGLE, PATRICK: Born Rutherglen 1882. Educated Blairs 1896-1900; Issy 1900-02; St Sulpice 1902-06. Ordained Paris 1906. St Alphonsus', Glasgow 1906-12. Professor, Blairs 1912-34. Prefect of Studies, Blairs 1934-39. Rector, Blairs 1939-47. Our Lady and St Anne's, Hamilton 1947-70; thus moving to Motherwell diocese. Died Hamilton 20 Jan 1970.

McGOVERN, PATRICK B (1947), (1): Born Rutherglen 1924. Educated Blairs, St Peter's. Ordained Glasgow 1947. New Stevenston 1947-53; thus moving to Motherwell diocese. St Monica's, Coatbridge 1953-62. Calderbank 1962-69. St Bartholomew's, Coatbridge 1969-77. Moodiesburn 1977-83. St Ignatius's, Wishaw 1983-.

McGOVERN, PATRICK J (1947), (2): Born and educated Ireland. Ordained Carlow for Glasgow 1947. St Aloysius', Glasgow 1947-49. Immaculate Heart of Mary, Glasgow 1949-51. St Roch's, Glasgow 1951-57. St Peter's, Glasgow 1957-73. Twechar 1973-78. St Aloysius', Glasgow 1978-81. Retired 1981. Died Glasgow 18 March 1983. (Canning)

McGOWAN, CLEMENT: Born Glasgow 1901. Educated Blairs 1916-19; St Peter's 1919-25. Ordained Glasgow 1925. Kilbirnie 1925-27. Chapelhall 1927-44. Largs 1944-77; thus moving to Galloway diocese. Retired 1977. Died Glasgow 25 Aug 1981.

McGRATH, COLMAN: Born Glasgow 1939. Educated St Aloysius' College, Glasgow; Blairs; Scots College, Rome; St Peter's. Ordained Glasgow 1962. St Thomas's, Glasgow 1962-63. Professor, Blairs 1963-78. Faifley 1978-79. St Helen's, Glasgow 1979-83. Spiritual Director, St Peter's College 1983-85. Spiritual Director, Chesters 1985-88. St Ninian's, Glasgow 1988-89. St Bernadette's, Glasgow 1989-.

McGRATH, DENIS MICHAEL (1927): Born Ireland. Educated Ireland, St Peter's. Ordained Glasgow 1927. St Patrick's, Dumbarton 1927. St Michael's, Glasgow 1927-31. Cadzow 1931-36. St Aloysius', Glasgow 1936-39. Sick leave 1939-48. Moved to Paisley diocese. St Fergus's, Paisley 1948-51. Chaplain, St Vincent's Home, Langbank 1951-52. Retired 1952. Died Ireland 4 Jan 1968. (Canning)

McGRATH, DENIS (1928): Born and educated Ireland. Ordained Waterford 1928. Lent to Glasgow. St Saviour's, Glasgow 1928-30. Returned to Ireland 1930 and died there May 1978. (Canning)

McGRATH, JEREMIAH: Born and educated Ireland. Ordained Maynooth 1910. Lent to Glasgow. St Roch's, Glasgow 1911-12. Chaplain, West Thorn Reformatory and Good Shepherd Convent, Dalbeth 1912-16. Returned to Ireland 1916 and died there 19 Nov 1966. (Canning)

McGRATH, MARK: Born and educated Ireland. Ordained Maynooth 1901. Lent to Glasgow. St Anne's, Glasgow 1901-04. Returned to Ireland 1904 and died there 30 Nov 1928. (Canning)

McGRATH, THOMAS: Born and educated Ireland. Ordained 1886. Lent to Glasgow. St Patrick's, Dumbarton in addresses, but not under parishes, 1886-87. St Patrick's, Dumbarton 1887-88. Returned to Ireland and died there 10 March 1941. (Canning)

McGREGOR, THOMAS P: see Archdiocese of St Andrews & Edinburgh

McGRORRY, JOHN JOSEPH: Born Dumbarton 1959. Educated St Patrick's High School, Dumbarton; Scots College, Rome. Ordained

Dumbarton 1982. Christ the King, Glasgow 1982. Further studies, Rome 1982-84. St Joseph's, Cumbernauld 1984-88. New York 1988-89. Dumbarton in addresses, but not under parishes, 1989-.

McGRORY, JAMES J: Born Shettleston 1887. Educated Blairs 1902-06; St Peter's 1906-14. Ordained Glasgow 1914. Cadzow 1914-17. Our Lady and St Margaret's, Glasgow 1917-20. St Laurence's, Greenock 1920-22. St Luke's, Glasgow 1922-28. St John the Baptist's, Uddingston 1928-30. Holy Cross, Glasgow 1930-40. Died Glasgow 13 May 1940.

McGRORY, JOHN: see McCrory, John

McGRORY, THOMAS: Born Shettleston 1889. Educated Blairs 1903-08; Issy 1908-13. Ordained Paris 1913. St Patrick's, Dumbarton 1913-28. Leave of absence 1928-32. St Teresa's, Glasgow 1932-46. Chaplain, St Mungo's Approved School, Mauchline 1946-56. Chaplain, St Ninian's School, Perthshire 1956-65. Retired 1965. Died Musselburgh 18 April 1975.

McGUCKIN, JOHN: Born Bellshill 1912. Educated Blairs 1926-30; St Peter's 1930-37. Ordained Glasgow 1937. Our Lady and St Margaret's, Glasgow 1937-44. St Paul's, Glasgow 1944-59. St Columba's, Glasgow 1959-67. Glasgow Cathedral 1967-80. Retired 1980. Died New Bedford, USA 10 Aug 1982.

McGUIRE, JOHN: Born Glasgow 1943. Educated Blairs, Valladolid. Ordained Glasgow 1968. St Joseph's, Cumbernauld 1968-76. On mission, Brazil 1976-.

McGUIRE, THOMAS: see Maguire, Thomas

McGURK, ALOYSIUS: Born and educated Ireland. Ordained Wexford for Glasgow 1925. St Mary's, Greenock 1925-34. Mossend 1934-36. Duntocher 1936-37. Retired to Ireland in bad health 1937 and died there 11 Jan 1953. (Canning)

McGURK, ANTHONY: Born and educated Ireland. Ordained Carlow for Glasgow 1940. Burnbank 1941-48; thus moving to Motherwell diocese. St Patrick's, Coatbridge 1948-58. Our Lady of Lourdes, East Kilbride 1958-69. St Joseph's, Blantyre 1969-82. Calderbank 1982-89. Retired 1989. (Canning)

McGURK, HUGH: Born New Stevenston 1919. Educated Blairs; Scots College, Rome; Blairs; St Peter's. Ordained 1945. St John's, Port Glasgow 1945-46. Professor, Blairs 1946-59. Moved to Motherwell diocese. Motherwell Cathedral 1959-61. Harthill 1961-65. All Saints, Airdrie 1965-72. Shotts 1972-79. Died Shotts 15 Aug 1979.

McGURK, THOMAS: Born New Stevenston 1919. Educated Blairs; Scots College, Rome; St Peter's. Ordained 1945. St Saviour's, Glasgow 1945-46. Further studies, Cambridge 1946-50. Moved to Motherwell diocese. Professor, Blairs 1950-64. St Joseph's, Blantyre 1964-65. Bargeddie 1965-69. Director, Religious Education Centre, Motherwell 1969-78. Sacred Heart, Bellshill 1978-83. Holytown 1983-.

McHUGH, MICHAEL: Born and educated Ireland. Ordained Maynooth 1903. Lent to Glasgow. St Peter's, Glasgow 1903-04. Returned to Ireland 1904 and died there 28 April 1959. (Canning)

McHUGH, PATRICK: Born Greenock 1906. Educated St Mary's School, Greenock; Blairs 1920-24; St Peter's 1924-30. Ordained Glasgow 1930. Motherwell 1930-32. Langloan 1932-35. Holy Family, Kirkintilloch 1935-39. Forces chaplain 1939-45. Renton 1945-47. St Patrick's, Coatbridge 1947-50; thus moving to Motherwell diocese. St Andrew's, Airdrie 1950-58. Died Glasgow 1 May 1958.

McHUGO, ANTHONY: Born and educated Ireland. Ordained Glasgow 1948. Renton 1948-49. St Roch's, Glasgow 1949-66. St Pius X, Glasgow 1966-73. St Lucy's, Cumbernauld 1973-78. Bonhill 1978-81. St Brendan's, Glasgow 1981-89. Retired 1989. (Canning)

McILVAINE, JOHN: Born Dumbarton 1877. Educated Blairs 1893-97; Notre Dame des Champs, Paris 1897-98; St Peter's 1898-1904. Ordained 1904. St Patrick's, Dumbarton 1904-05. Glasgow Cathedral 1905-16. Forces chaplain 1916-18. Died at sea 26 Feb 1918.

McINNES, ANGUS: see Aberdeen diocese.

McINTYRE, FRANCIS: Born and educated Ireland. Ordained Maynooth 1918. Lent to Glasgow. St Peter's, Glasgow 1918-24. Returned to Ireland 1924 and died there 9 Feb 1974. (Canning)

McINTYRE, JOHN (1905): Born and educated Ireland. Ordained Maynooth 1905. Lent to Glasgow. Johnstone 1905-09. Returned to Ireland 1909 and died there 30 Jan 1952. (Canning)

McINTYRE, JOHN (1920): Born Glasgow 1895. Moved to Ireland. Educated Letterkenny Seminary, Maynooth. Ordained for Raphoe diocese 1920. Lent to Glasgow; later got exeat to remain there. Barrhead 1920-21. St Patrick's, Shieldmuir 1921. St Michael's, Glasgow 1921-33. St John's, Port Glasgow 1933-40. Newmains 1940-41. Croy 1941-45. St Alphonsus', Glasgow 1945-47. St Mirin's, Paisley 1947-61; thus moving to Paisley diocese. Died Paisley 29 April 1961.

MACISAAC, SAMUEL: see Argyll diocese.

McKAY, EDWARD: see Archdiocese of St Andrews & Edinburgh

McKAY, GERARD: see Argyll diocese.

McKAY, HENRY (Harry) JAMES: Born Dumbarton 1942. Educated St Patrick's High School, Dumbarton; Scots College, Rome. Ordained Dumbarton 1966. Further studies, Rome 1966-67. St Martin's, Glasgow 1967-75. Christ the King, Glasgow 1975-83. St Flannan's, Kirkintilloch 1983-.

MACKAY, JOHN: Born New Kilpatrick 1915. Educated St Peter's 1933-36; Scots College, Rome 1936-40; St Peter's 1940-42. Ordained Glasgow 1942. Johnstone 1942-45. Professor, St Peter's College 1945-72. Chaplain, St Charles' Hospital, Carstairs 1972-80. Retired 1980.

McKEAGUE, HUGH: Born and educated Ireland. Ordained Maynooth 1936. Lent to Glasgow. St Mary's, Glasgow 1936-41. Returned to Ireland 1941. (Canning)

McKEE, JOHN J: Born Kirkcaldy 1926. Educated St Columba's College, Derry; St Patrick's College, Carlow. Ordained Carlow for Glasgow 1952. Immaculate Conception, Glasgow 1952-57. St Vincent de Paul's, Glasgow 1957-69. St John Ogilvie's, Glasgow 1969-75. St Bernadette's, Glasgow 1975-80. St Louise's, Glasgow 1980-.

MACKELLAIG, ANGUS: Born Morar 1914. Educated Blairs 1930-34; St Peter's 1934-41. Ordained Glasgow 1941. St Ninian's, Glasgow 1941-42. Clarkston, no parish 1942-43. Houston 1943-44. Professor, Blairs 1944-46. Chaplain, St Ninian's School, Kirkconnel 1946-47. Carstairs House in addresses, but not under Institute, 1947-48. Burnbank 1948-54; thus moving to Motherwell diocese. St Bartholomew's, Coatbridge 1954-58. St Benedict's, Easterhouse 1958-62. C/o Diocesan Office 1962-64. St Bride's, Cambuslang 1964-67. Newmains 1967-76. Retired 1976.

MACKELLAIG, DOMINIC: see Argyll diocese.

McKELVIE, JOHN ALOYSIUS: Born Bridge of Allan 1943. Educated St Aloysius' College, Glasgow; Blairs; St Peter's. Ordained Glasgow 1966. St Mary's, Glasgow 1966-72. Further studies, Catechetical Centre, Dundalk 1972-73. St Helen's, Glasgow 1973-75. Further studies, L'Institut Catholique, Paris 1975-76. St Joseph's, Woodside, Glasgow 1976-78. St Margaret Mary's, Glasgow 1978-83. Chaplain, St Andrew's College of Education 1983-84. Died Bearsden 27 Nov 1984.

McKELVIE, PETER CLAVER: Born Glasgow 1939. Educated St Aloysius' College, Glasgow; St Peter's. Ordained Glasgow 1963. St Martin's, Glasgow 1963-67. St Philip's, Glasgow 1967-73. St Constantine's,

Glasgow 1973-76. St Saviour's, Glasgow 1976-88. St James's, Glasgow 1988-.

McKENNA, CHARLES: Born and educated Ireland. Ordained Maynooth 1917. Lent to Melbourne, Australia 1917-26. Lent to Glasgow. St Columba's, Glasgow 1926-27. St John's, Glasgow 1927-29. Returned to Ireland 1929. (Canning)
Note: Directories have wrongly ascribed an ordination date of 1926 to this man.

McKENNA, JAMES: Born Ireland. Educated Ireland, St Peter's. Ordained 1902. St John the Baptist's, Uddingston 1902-06. Chaplain, West Thorn Reformatory and Good Shepherd Convent, Dalbeth 1906-10. St Aloysius', Glasgow 1910-16. Milngavie 1916-26. Renfrew 1926-28. Renfrew in addresses, but not under parishes, 1928-29. St Columba's, Glasgow 1929-37. St Margaret's, Airdrie 1937-49; thus moving to Motherwell diocese. Died Airdrie 30 Jan 1949. (Canning)

McKENNA, JOHN: Born Coatbridge 1897. Educated Blairs 1912-16; St Peter's 1916-23. Ordained Glasgow 1923. Glasgow Cathedral 1923-24. Saltcoats 1924-27. Burnbank 1927-36. Died Burnbank 26 Feb 1936.

McKENNA, MICHAEL: Born and educated Ireland. Ordained Maynooth 1911. St Patrick's, Coatbridge 1911-13. Not in Directories 1913-14. Forces chaplain 1914-18. Cardowan 1918-19. Returned to Ireland 1919 and died there 20 Feb 1960. (Canning)

McKENNA, PAUL: Born and educated Ireland. Ordained Maynooth 1908. Lent to Glasgow. Immaculate Conception, Glasgow 1908-12. Returned to Ireland 1912 and died there 12 Dec 1943. (Canning)

McKENZIE, ALFRED: Born Glasgow 1955. Educated Langbank; Blairs; Scots College, Rome. Ordained Glasgow 1979. St Helen's, Glasgow 1979. Further studies, Rome 1979-80. Our Lady and St George, Glasgow 1980-.

McKENZIE, ANDREW: Born Glasgow 1964. Educated Lourdes School, Cardonald; St Peter's; Chesters. Ordained Cardonald 1988. St Michael's, Dumbarton 1988-.

McKEOWN, THOMAS: Born Glasgow 1915. Educated St Aloysius' College, Glasgow; Blairs; St Peter's. Ordained Glasgow 1942. St Mary Immaculate, Glasgow 1942-43. St Mary's, Greenock 1943-47. St Philomena's, Glasgow 1947-56. Sacred Heart, Glasgow 1956-67. St Brendan's, Glasgow 1967-81. Died Glasgow 23 March 1981.

McKINLEY, CHARLES: Born Dundee 1906. Educated St Joseph's School, Dundee; Lawside Academy, Dundee; Blairs 1921-24; St Paul's College, Cherbourg 1924-25; Grand Seminaire, Coutances 1925-30. Ordained Dundee 1930. St Ninian's, Glasgow 1930-37. Professor, Blairs 1937-47. Whifflet 1947-49; thus moving to Motherwell diocese. Cadzow 1949-50. Sick leave 1950-51. St Margaret's, Airdrie 1951-54. Went to Galloway diocese: St Andrew's, Dumfries 1954-63. Died Dublin 25 July 1963.

McKINNEY, CHARLES: see Argyll diocese

McKINNON, DONALD: Born Eoligarry 1920. Educated Blairs, St Peter's. Ordained Glasgow 1946. St Teresa's, Glasgow 1946-67. St Vincent de Paul's, Glasgow 1967-70. St Mark's, Glasgow 1970-73. St Teresa's, Glasgow 1973-84. St Joseph's, Tollcross 1984-87. Died Blackburn, Lancashire 15 Aug 1987.

MACKINNON, MALCOLM: see Argyll diocese

MACKINTOSH, ALEXANDER: Born Bunroy, Lochaber 1878. Educated Blairs; Notre Dame des Champs, Paris; Scots College, Rome. Ordained Rome 1904. St John's, Glasgow 1905. Lent to Argyll diocese: Oban 1905-09. Duntocher 1909-10. St John's, Glasgow 1910-18. Glenboig 1918-30. Glenboig in addresses, but not under parishes, 1930-31. Lent to Argyll diocese: Dunoon 1931-33. Wishaw 1933-36. Retired 1936. Died Roy Bridge 10 Dec 1954.

MACKINTOSH, ANGUS: Born Kinchillie, Lochaber 1873. Educated Blairs 1887-92; St Peter's 1892-98. Ordained 1898. St Patrick's, Glasgow 1898-99. Archbishop's secretary 1899-1901. St Patrick's, Glasgow 1901-06. Helensburgh 1906-14. St Paul's, Glasgow 1914-33. Rutherglen 1933-39. Died Glasgow 30 April 1939.

MACKLE, JOSEPH MICHAEL: Born Lanark 1965. Educated Turnbull High School, Glasgow; Valladolid; St Peter's; Chesters. Ordained 1989. St Peter's, Glasgow 1989-.

McKNIGHT, NEIL: Born Greenock 1899. Educated St Mungo's Academy, Glasgow; Training College, Glasgow; St Peter's 1923-29. Ordained Glasgow 1929. St Columba's, Glasgow 1929-32. Carfin 1932-33. St Joseph's, Tollcross 1933-42. Chaplain, St Charles' Institute, Carstairs 1942-43. St Joseph's, Tollcross 1943-50. Died Glasgow 22 Jan 1950.

McLACHLAN, DAVID: Born Glasgow 1932. Educated Blairs, St Peter's. Ordained Glasgow 1958. St Patrick's, Dumbarton 1958-59. Our Lady and St George, Glasgow 1959-62. Helensburgh 1962-65. On mission with Society of St James the Apostle, Boston, then Bolivia 1965-86. St Laurence's, Glasgow 1986-.

McLACHLAN, JAMES: Born Coatbridge 1856. Educated St Cuthbert's College, Ushaw 1870-73; Douay 1873-76; Ushaw 1876-82. Ordained Glasgow 1882. Johnstone 1882-83. Diocesan secretary 1883-86. No further entries.

McLACHLAN, PETER: Born Birkenhead 1895. Educated Blairs 1910-15; Valladolid 1915-22. Ordained Valladolid 1922. Immaculate Conception, Glasgow 1922-23. St Mary's, Paisley 1923-26. Went to south of England in bad health 1926. Died Torquay 26 May 1937.

McLACHLAN, WILLIAM: Born Glasgow 1864. Educated Blairs 1878-81; St Peter's 1881-86. Ordained Glasgow 1886. Glasgow Cathedral 1886-87. Died Glasgow 21 Jan 1887.

McLAREN, ANTHONY: Born Glasgow 1959. Educated Langbank, Blairs, St Peter's. Ordained St Peter's College 1983. St Teresa's, Glasgow 1983. Christ the King, Glasgow 1983-87. St Roch's, Glasgow 1987-.

McLAREN, JOHN: Born Croy 1930. Educated Blairs, St Peter's. Ordained Glasgow 1954. Our Lady of Fatima, Glasgow 1954-70. St Michael's, Dumbarton 1970-76. St James's, Glasgow 1976-82. All Saints, Glasgow 1982-84. St Teresa's, Glasgow 1984-87. St Catherine's, Glasgow 1987-88. Died Glasgow 1 Feb 1989.

McLAUGHLIN, DANIEL L: Born and educated Ireland. Ordained Maynooth 1916. Lent to Glasgow. Chaplain, West Thorn Reformatory and Good Shepherd Convent, Dalbeth 1916-17. St Patrick's, Shieldmuir 1917-18. Mossend 1918-24. Returned to Ireland 1924 and died there 25 Oct 1964. (Canning)

McLAUGHLIN, IAN: Born Glasgow 1911. Educated Blairs 1927-30; Scots College, Rome 1930-36. Ordained Rome 1936. St Anne's, Glasgow 1937-39. Our Lady of Good Aid, Motherwell 1939-48; thus moving to Motherwell diocese. Shotts 1948-55. St Ninian's, Hamilton 1955-66. St Mary's, Coatbridge 1966-77. Retired 1977. Died Glasgow 3 Dec 1981.

McLAUGHLIN, JAMES (1923): Born and educated Ireland. Ordained Maynooth 1923. Lent to Glasgow. St Paul's, Shettleston 1923-29. Returned to Ireland 1929 and died there 26 Oct 1963. (Canning)

McLAUGHLIN, JAMES (1973): Ordained 1973. Our Lady of Lourdes, Glasgow 1975-80. Sick leave 1980-81. St Constantine's, Glasgow 1981-84. C/o Diocesan Office 1984-89. No further entries.

McLAUGHLIN, JOHN: Born Glasgow 1903. Educated Blairs 1917-22; Valladolid 1922-29. Ordained Valladolid 1929. Baillieston 1929. St Mary's, Greenock 1929-43. St Columba's, Viewpark 1943-50; thus moving to Motherwell diocese. Harthill 1950-51. Died Glasgow 3 Dec 1951.

McLAUGHLIN, WILLIAM J: Born Glasgow 1874. Educated Blairs 1889-92; Notre Dame des Champs, Paris 1892-93; Propaganda, Rome 1893-99. Ordained Rome 1899. St Mirin's, Paisley 1899-1908. Whiterigg 1908-15. St Luke's, Glasgow 1915-18. St Patrick's, Glasgow 1918-40. Died Glasgow 18 March 1940.

McLEAN, ANGUS (1929): Born Glasgow 1903. Educated St Mungo's Academy, Glasgow; Blairs; Valladolid 1922-29. Ordained Valladolid 1929. Further studies, Valladolid 1929-30. Alexandria 1930-33. Professor, Blairs 1933-37. Leave of absence 1937-38. Went to Dunkeld diocese. St Patrick's, Dundee 1938-45. Doune 1945-46. Highvalleyfield 1946-48. Died Glasgow 22 Dec 1948.

MACLEAN, ANGUS EWAN (1969): Born Glasgow 1944. Educated St Aloysius' College, Glasgow; Valladolid; St Peter's. Ordained St Peter's College 1969. Immaculate Heart of Mary, Glasgow 1969. St Constantine's, Glasgow 1969-70. Holy Family, Kirkintilloch 1970-78. Immaculate Conception, Glasgow 1978-79. Spiritual Director, Blairs 1979-86. Director, National Vocations Office 1986-.

MACLELLAN, ALISTAIR: Born Glasgow 1937. Educated Blairs, St Peter's. Ordained Glasow 1962. St Alphonsus', Glasgow 1962. Milngavie 1962-67. Our Holy Redeemer, Clydebank 1967-71. St Gabriel's, Glasgow 1971-78. St Philomena's, Glasgow 1978-81. Faifley 1981-85. St Margaret Mary's, Glasgow 1985-86. St Joseph's, Tollcross 1986-88. Victoria, Australia 1988-.

McLELLAN, WILLIAM: Born Glasgow 1929. Educated Campion House, Osterley; St Peter's. Ordained Glasgow 1962. Our Lady of Good Counsel, Glasgow 1962-67. St Agnes's, Glasgow 1967-74. St Charles', Glasgow 1974-77. Croy 1977-79. St Conval's, Glasgow 1979-82. Our Lady of the Assumption, Glasgow 1982-87. St Anthony's, Glasgow 1987-.

McLEOD, FRANCIS: Born Glasgow 1911. Educated Blairs 1927-31; Scots College, Rome 1931-38. Ordained Rome 1937. Carfin 1938-41. Gourock 1941-42. St Mary's, Greenock 1942-46. Chapelhall 1946-47. St Paul's, Shettleston 1947-52. C/o Diocesan Office 1952-53. St Teresa's, Glasgow 1953-59. Went to Shrewsbury diocese. Died Birkenhead 20 June 1977.

McLOUGHLIN, (Bernard) THOMAS: Born and educated Ireland. Ordained Maynooth 1926. Lent to Glasgow. St Mary's, Glasgow 1926-32. Shotts 1932-33. Glenboig 1933-34. Returned to Ireland 1934. (Canning)

McMAHON, DANIEL: Born Paisley 1915. Educated Blairs 1930-34; St

Peter's 1934-41. Ordained Glasgow 1941. St Anne's, Glasgow 1941-49. St Stephen's, Dalmuir 1949-50. Our Lady and St Margaret's, Glasgow 1950-52. An alcoholic, he found his vocation working with alcoholics in New Jersey, USA. Died Ireland 7 June 1978. (see p 156)

McMAHON, JAMES: Born Paisley 1921. Educated Blairs; Scots College, Rome; St Peter's. Ordained Glasgow 1946. St Saviour's, Glasgow 1946-57. Spiritual Director, St Peter's College 1957-69. Glasgow Cathedral 1969-70. Twechar 1970-72. Rector, St Peter's College 1972-80. St Paul's, Glasgow 1980-87. Christ the King, Glasgow 1987-.

McMAHON, JOHN: see Dunkeld diocese

McMAHON, LAWRENCE: Born Glasgow 1936. Educated St Mungo's Academy, Glasgow; Blairs; Scots College, Rome. Ordained Rome 1960. St Peter's, Glasgow 1961-72. St Augustine's, Glasgow 1972-87. St Robert's, Glasgow 1987-.

McMANAMON, FRANCIS: Ordained 1938. St Peter's, Glasgow 1975-77. No further entries.

MACMASTER, DONALD B: see Argyll diocese

McMENAMIN, DONAL IGNATIUS: Born and educated Ireland. Ordained Kilkenny for Glasgow 1948. St Ninian's, Glasgow 1948-51. Cardonald 1951-74. St Nicholas's, Glasgow 1974-76. Renton 1976-81. Died Glasgow 25 Nov 1981. (Canning)

McMENEMY, JOHN: Born Glasgow 1875. Educated St Mungo's Academy, Glasgow; Blairs 1891-92; Notre Dame des Champs, Paris 1892-93; Valladolid 1893-99. Ordained Valladolid 1899. St Patrick's, Glasgow 1899-1908. Largs 1908-15. Stevenston 1915-16. St Agnes's, Glasgow 1916-26. Mossend 1926-36. Died Mossend 13 Dec 1936.

McMILLAN, JOHN (1898): Born Glasgow 1875. Educated Blairs 1889-92; Notre Dame des Champs, Paris 1892-93; Scots College, Rome 1893-99. Ordained Rome 1898. St Anthony's, Glasgow 1899-1903. St Paul's, Shettleston 1903-04. Sacred Heart, Glasgow 1904-07. Chaplain, Barlinnie Prison and St Joseph's Home, Glasgow 1907-11. Bothwell 1911-18. St Luke's, Glasgow 1918-23. St Mary's, Greenock 1923-45. Died Greenock 26 April 1945.

MACMILLAN, JOHN (1903): see Argyll diocese

McMULLAN, ALPHONSUS: Born and educated Ireland. Ordained Waterford for Glasgow 1941. Blantyre 1941-42. No further entries. (Canning)

McMULLAN, DERMOT: Born Ireland. Educated St Patrick's High School, Dumbarton; Blairs; St Peter's. Ordained Glasgow 1946. St Aloysius', Glasgow 1946. Cleland 1946-49, thus moving to Motherwell diocese. St Columbkille's, Rutherglen 1949-56. All Saints, Airdrie 1956-60. Died Glasgow 1 Feb 1960. (Canning)

McMULLAN, WILLIAM: Born and educated Ireland. Ordained Maynooth 1918. Lent to Glasgow. Immaculate Conception, Glasgow 1918-19. St Paul's, Shettleston 1919-20. Baillieston 1920-25. In USA 1925-30. Returned to Ireland 1930 and died there 1 June 1941. (Canning)

McMULLEN, PATRICK B: Born Ireland. Entered the Franciscan Order and was ordained 1886. Left Order and came to Glasgow as a secular priest 1900. Chaplain, Barlinnie Prison and St Joseph's Home, Glasgow 1900-07. Chaplain, Franciscan Convent, Glasgow 1907-12; Chaplain, Franciscan Convent, Bothwell 1912-45. Died Ireland 31 Jan 1946. (Canning)

McNAIR, JOHN: Born Glasgow 1901. Educated Blairs 1917-20; St Peter's 1920-26. Ordained Glasgow 1926. Blantyre 1926-29. St Mirin's, Paisley 1929-38; St Joseph's, Woodside, Glasgow 1938-40. St Augustine's, Coatbridge 1940-42. Sick leave 1942-44. Chaplain, Good Shepherd Convent, Dalbeth 1944-49. Chaplain, Kingussie Sanatorium 1949-52. In hospital in England 1952-54. Kingussie Sanatorium 1954-59. Chaplain, Sisters of Joseph, Rothesay 1959-67. Died Rothesay 21 Nov 1967.

McNAIRNEY, MICHAEL: Born Airdrie 1861. Educated Blairs 1876-81; St Peter's 1881-86. Ordained Glasgow 1886. St Peter's, Glasgow 1886-91. Milngavie 1891-92. St Patrick's, Dumbarton 1892-93. Milngavie 1893-97. St Michael's, Glasgow 1897-99. St Peter's, Glasgow 1899-1929. Died Glasgow 29 April 1929.

McNALLY, JAMES: Born and educated Ireland. Ordained Maynooth 1920. Lent to Glasgow. St Aloysius', Glasgow 1920-26. Returned to Ireland 1926 and died there 4 Oct 1944. (Canning)

McNAMARA, JOHN: Born Barrhead 1938. Educated St John's School, Barrhead; St Patrick's College, Buchlyvie; St Peter's. Ordained St Peter's College 1978. St Michael's, Dumbarton 1978-83. St Teresa's, Glasgow 1983-89. C/o Diocesan Office 1989-.

McNAUGHT, EDWARD: Born Glasgow 1949. Educated Langbank, Blairs, Valladolid. Ordained Glasgow 1973. St Paul's, Glasgow 1973. St Teresa's, Glasgow 1973-76. St Joseph's, Tollcross 1976-78. Our Lady of Good Counsel, Glasgow 1978-79. Professor, Blairs 1979-86. St Patrick's, Dumbarton 1986-.

McNEIL, HECTOR: see Dunkeld diocese

MACNEIL, JOHN (1918): see Argyll diocese

MACNEIL, JOHN (1957): Born Barra 1933. Educated Blairs, St Peter's. Ordained 1957. St Martin's, Glasgow 1957-59. St Conval's, Glasgow 1959-63. Went to Argyll diocese. Oban 1963-64. Daliburgh 1964-68. Benbecula 1968-73. Knoydart 1973-76. Eriskay 1976-80. Fort William 1980-.

McNICHOLAS, MICHAEL: Born and educated Ireland. Ordained Wexford for Glasgow 1927. Holy Cross, Glasgow 1927-31. St Mary's, Greenock 1931-33. St Michael's, Glasgow 1933-41. Carfin 1941-42. St Teresa's, Glasgow 1942-48. St James's, Paisley 1948-59; thus moving to Paisley diocese. Died Dublin 31 Aug 1959. (Canning)

McNULTY, JOSEPH: Born Glasgow 1963. Educated Langbank, Blairs, St Peter's, Chesters. Ordained Glasgow 1988. Our Lady of Lourdes, Glasgow 1988-.

McPARTLIN, FRANCIS J MARTIN: Born Glasgow 1928. Educated St Mungo's Academy, Glasgow; Campion House, Osterley; St Peter's. Ordained Glasgow 1958. Our Lady of Lourdes, Glasgow 1958-60. Immaculate Conception, Glasgow 1960-71. St Teresa's, Glasgow 1971-75. St Helen's, Glasgow 1975-79. Alexandria 1979-86. Roseneath 1986-.

McPHAIL, EWEN JOSEPH: Born Glasgow 1950. Educated St Aloysius' College, Glasgow; St Peter's. Ordained St Peter's 1974. St Conval's, Glasgow 1974-76. St Paul's, Shettleston 1976-81. St Jude's, Glasgow 1981-84. St Ninian's, Glasgow 1984-.

McPHERSON, DONALD A: see Argyll diocese

McPOLIN, OWEN: Born and educated Ireland. Ordained Maynooth 1886. Lent to Glasgow. Rutherglen 1886-87. Pollokshaws 1887-88. St Patrick's, Glasgow 1888-89. Returned to Ireland 1889 and died there 5 Jan 1941. (Canning)

McQUILLAN, JOHN: Born Mossend 1889. Educated Blairs 1904-08; Scots College, Rome 1908-16. Ordained Rome 1915. Glasgow Cathedral 1916-23. Professor, St Peter's College 1923-31. Symington (Catholic Land Colony Scheme) 1931-36. Teaching, Fort Augustus, 1936-38. Professor, St Peter's College 1938-43. Stevenston 1943-50; thus moving to Galloway diocese. Troon 1950-64. Retired 1964. Died Kingussie 31 July 1970.

MACRAE, AENEAS: see Aberdeen diocese

McROBERTS, DAVID: Born Wishaw 1912. Educated Our Lady's High School, Motherwell 1923-27; Blairs 1927-31; Scots College, Rome 1931-38. Ordained Rome 1937. St Peter's, Glasgow 1938-43. Professor, St Peter's College 1943-63. Moved to Motherwell diocese. Chaplain, St Charles' Institute, Carstairs 1963-72. Keeper, Scottish Catholic Archives, Edinburgh 1972-78. Died Edinburgh 25 Nov 1978.

McRORY, JAMES: Born and educated Ireland. Ordained 1909. Lent to Glasgow. Croy 1909-13. St Anne's, Glasgow 1913-14. Returned to Ireland 1914 and died there 6 Aug 1952. (Canning)

McRORY, PATRICK: Born and educated Ireland. Ordained Maynooth 1919. Lent to Glasgow. St Mary's, Glasgow 1919-24. Died Ireland 11 April 1924. (Canning)

McSHANE, JAMES: Born Barrhead 1924. Educated Blairs; St Peter's; Scots College, Rome. Ordained Glasgow 1947. Further studies, Rome 1947-50. St Brendan's, Glasgow 1950-51. Carntyne 1951-55. Professor, St Peter's College 1955-67. Further studies, Notre Dame College of Education, Glasgow 1967-68. St Helen's, Glasgow 1968-69. Crow Street, Glasgow, no parish, 1969-77. St Margaret's, Clydebank 1977-.

McSPARRAN, ARCHIBALD: Born Ardrossan 1882. Educated St Mungo's Academy, Glasgow; Blairs 1897-1901; St Peter's 1901-08. Ordained Glasgow 1908. St Patrick's, Dumbarton 1908-26. Strathaven 1926-29. Croy 1929-32. St John's, Glasgow 1932-45. Ardrossan 1945-50; thus moving to Galloway diocese. Died Ardrossan 10 March 1950.

McVANN, JAMES: Born and educated Ireland. Ordained Maynooth 1924. Lent to Glasgow. St Mirin's, Paisley 1924-26. St Mary's, Paisley 1926-34. Returned to Ireland 1934 and died there 18 Aug 1942. (Canning)

McVANN, THOMAS: Born Ireland. Educated Ireland, Paris. Ordained Paris 1928. Lent to Glasgow. Johnstone 1928-42. Returned to Ireland 1942. (Canning)

McWILLIAMS, HENRY: Born and educated Ireland. Ordained Maynooth 1937. Lent to Glasgow. St Teresa's, Glasgow 1937-38. St Roch's, Glasgow 1938-43. Returned to Ireland 1943 and died there 17 Feb 1976. (Canning)

MAGAURAN, BERNARD: Born Glasgow 1906. Educated St Aloysius' College, Glasgow; Mount Melleray; St Peter's. Ordained Glasgow 1930. Blantyre 1930 (-31?). St Joseph's, Woodside, Glasgow 1930/1-32. St Teresa's, Glasgow 1932-39. St Patrick's, Dumbarton 1939-44. Forces chaplain 1944-46. Alexandria 1946-51. Balloch 1951-59. St Michael's, Dumbarton 1959-73. Retired 1973. Died Alexandria 11 Aug 1981.

MAGAURAN, FRANCIS BERNARD: Born Newcastle-on-Tyne 1901. Educated Blairs 1917-19; St Peter's 1919-20; Scots College, Rome 1920-25. Ordained Rome 1925. Our Lady and St Margaret's, Glasgow 1925-26. Croy 1926-28. Cambuslang 1928-30. Vice-rector, Scots College, Rome 1930-33. St Mary's, Greenock 1933-43. Carluke 1943-47. Gourock 1947-51; thus moving to Paisley diocese. St John's, Port Glasgow 1951-58. St Mary's, Paisley 1958-74. Died Paisley 12 Jan 1975.

MAGEE, BRIAN: Born Glasgow 1954. Educated St Thomas Aquinas' School, Glasgow; Langbank; Blairs; St Peter's. Ordained St Peter's College 1979. St Thomas's, Glasgow 1979-81. St Gregory's, Glasgow 1981-84. St Dominic's, Bishopbriggs 1984-85. Chaplain, Glasgow University 1985-.

MAGUIRE, DESMOND BRIAN: Born Kirkintilloch 1931. Educated Blairs, St Sulpice. Ordained Glasgow 1954. Christ the King, Glasgow 1954-67. St Gregory's, Glasgow 1967-77. Our Lady of Good Counsel, Glasgow 1977-83. St Augustine's, Glasgow 1983-.

MAGUIRE, THOMAS: Born Glasgow 1913. Educated Blairs 1926-31; St Peter's 1931-38. Ordained Glasgow 1938. Saltcoats 1938-40. St Agnes's, Glasgow 1940-53. Our Lady and St George, Glasgow 1953-59. Twechar 1959-65. Good Shepherd, Glasgow 1965-67. Our Lady of the Assumption, Glasgow 1967-75. Alexandria 1975-81. Retired 1981.

MAHER, GERALD: Born Bellshill 1921. Educated Blairs; Scots College, Rome; St Peter's. Ordained 1945. Johnstone 1945-46. Further studies, Cambridge 1946-49. Moved to Motherwell diocese. Professor, Blairs 1949-65. Our Lady and St Anne's, Hamilton 1965-66. St Paul's, Hamilton 1966-71. St Bride's, East Kilbride 1971-80. Mossend 1980-.

MAHER, JEREMIAH: Born and educated Ireland. Ordained Maynooth 1892. Lent to Glasgow. St Alphonus', Glasgow 1892-94. Returned to Ireland 1894 and died there April 1922. (Canning)

MAHON, HUGH C: Born and educated Ireland. Ordained Thurles for Glasgow 1944. St Mary Immaculate, Glasgow 1944-45. Dalry 1945-46. St Mark's, Glasgow 1946-47. St Augustine's, Coatbridge 1947-58; thus moving to Motherwell diocese. Mossend 1958-60. Moodiesburn 1960-71. Died Glasgow 5 March 1971. (Canning)

MAHON, JOSEPH: Born Ireland. Educated Ireland, Rome. Ordained Rome 1935. Lent to Glasgow. St Saviour's, Glasgow 1935-52. Not in Directories 1952-53. Sacred Heart, Glasgow 1953-56. St Philomena's, Glasgow 1956-59. No further entries. (Canning)

MAHON, MICHAEL: see Mahon, William

MAHON, WILLIAM (Michael): Born Ireland. Educated Ireland, Spain. Ordained Carlow 1926. Lent to Glasgow. St Mary's, Paisley 1926-28. Returned to Ireland 1928. (Canning)

MALLON, FRANCIS JOSEPH: Born Govan 1923. Educated St Boswell's; Bishop's Waltham; Osterley; St Peter's. Ordained Glasgow 1954. St Philomena's, Glasgow 1954-58. St Mary Immaculate, Glasgow 1958-69. Glasgow, no parish, 1969-70. Stella Maris Club, Glasgow 1970-78. St Vincent de Paul's, Glasgow 1978-83. Immaculate Heart of Mary, Glasgow 1983-87. St Bartholomew's, Glasgow 1987-.

MALLON, WILLIAM: Born Glenboig 1904. Educated Blairs 1917-22; Valladolid 1922-30. Ordained Valladolid 1929. St Patrick's, Greenock 1930. St Mary's, Greenock 1930-33. St Alphonsus', Glasgow 1933-50. St Bernadette's, Glasgow 1950-55. St Stephen's, Dalmuir 1955-72. Died Dalmuir 2 Jan 1973.

MANGAN, FRANCIS G: Born and educated Ireland. Ordained Maynooth 1918. Baillieston 1919-20. Saltcoats 1920-24. St Aloysius', Glasgow 1924. Returned to Ireland 1924 and died there 1974. (Canning)

MANGAN, WILLIAM: Born and educated Ireland. Ordained Maynooth 1904. Lent to Glasgow. Holy Cross, Glasgow 1904-12. Returned to Ireland 1912 and died there 1 Nov 1931. (Canning)

MANN, CHARLES: see Aberdeen diocese

MANNING, JOHN: Born and educated Ireland. Ordained Waterford for Glasgow 1951. St Roch's, Glasgow 1951-55. St Michael's, Dumbarton 1955-66. St James's, Glasgow 1966-75. St Margaret's, Clydebank 1975-77. St Anthony's, Glasgow 1977-81. St Philip's, Glasgow 1981-84. Our Lady of Loreto, Dalmuir 1984-. (Canning)

MANNION, THOMAS GILLEN (1945): Born Glasgow 1919. Educated Blairs, St Peter's. Ordained 1945. St Patrick's, Shieldmuir 1945-47. Professor, Blairs 1947-70. St Eunan's, Clydebank 1970-81. St Joseph's, Cumbernauld 1981-84. Retired 1984.

MANNION, THOMAS (1946): Born Glasgow 1920. Educated Blairs, St Peter's. Ordained Glasgow 1946. St Brendan's, Glasgow 1946-47. St Mary's, Paisley 1947-68; thus moving to Paisley diocese. Holy Family, Port Glasgow 1968-69. St Francis's, Port Glasgow 1969-77. St Mary's, Paisley 1977-.

MARNANE, TIMOTHY: Born Salt Lake City, USA. Educated Ireland, Paris. Ordained Paris 1926. Lent to Glasgow. Hamilton 1926-28. Returned to Ireland 1928. (Canning)

MARR, PETER: Born Clydebank 1939. Educated St Patrick's High School, Dumbarton; Blairs; St Peter's. Ordained Glasgow 1963. Immaculate Heart of Mary, Glasgow 1963-68. St Patrick's, Glasgow 1968-69. St James's, Glasgow 1969-82. St Agnes's, Glasgow 1982-.

MARTIN, AIDAN: Born Glasgow 1958. Educated Langbank; Blairs; Scots College, Rome. Ordained Glasgow 1982. St Helen's, Glasgow 1982. Further studies, Rome 1982-84. Duntocher 1984-.

MARTIN, JAMES: Born and educated Ireland. Ordained Carlow for Glasgow 1952. Our Holy Redeemer, Clydebank 1952-65. St Margaret Mary's, Glasgow 1965-72. St Peter's, Glasgow 1972-79. St James's, Glasgow 1979-83. St Saviour's, Glasgow 1983-. (Cannning)

MARTIN, JOHN J: Born and educated Ireland. Ordained Kilkenny for Glasgow 1929. St Patrick's, Glasgow 1929-49. St James's, Glasgow 1949-55. St Joseph's, Woodside, Glasgow 1955-62. St Teresa's, Glasgow 1962-73. St Patrick's, Glasgow 1973-79. Died Glasgow 20 March 1979. (Canning)

MAUGARUAN, BERNARD (1918): see Magauran, Bernard (1930); (totally incorrect entry in Directory).

MAXWELL, JOSEPH: see Galloway diocese

MEACHER, GERARD IGNATIUS: Born Glasgow 1951. Educated St Thomas Aquinas' School, Glasgow; St Peter's. Ordained Glasgow 1977. St Roch's, Glasgow 1977. St Robert's, Glasgow 1977-79. No further entries.

MEADE, JOHN: Born and educated Ireland. Ordained Maynooth 1903. Lent to Glasgow. Immaculate Conception, Glasgow 1903-08. Returned to Ireland 1908 and died there 6 March 1959. (Canning)

MEAGHER, FRANCIS: Born Glasgow 1933. Educated St Mungo's Academy, Glasgow; Campion House, Osterley; St Peter's. Ordained Glasgow 1960. St Patrick's, Dumbarton 1960-67. St Luke's, Glasgow 1967-71. St Vincent de Paul's, Glasgow 1971-73. Our Lady and St George, Glasgow 1973-77. St Teresa's, Glasgow 1977-78. St Ninian's, Glasgow 1978-84. Holy Cross, Glasgow 1984-87. St Eunan's, Clydebank 1987-89. St Joseph's, Cumbernauld 1989-.

MEANEY, FRANCIS: see Galloway diocese

MEECHAN, DENIS: Born Duntocher 1905. Educated Blairs 1919-24; Scots College, Rome 1924-31. Ordained Rome 1931. Glasgow Cathedral 1931-47. Spiritual Director, Scots College, Rome 1947-54. Our Lady and St

George, Glasgow 1954-65. Glasgow Cathedral 1965-67. Sacred Heart, Glasgow 1967-74. Balloch 1974-89. Died Glasgow 19 March 1989.

MEECHAN, JAMES: Born Clydebank 1918. Educated Scots College, Rome 1935-40; St Peter's 1940-42. Ordained Glasgow 1942. St Mary's, Coatbridge 1942-45. Further studies, Maynooth 1945-48. Professor, St Peter's College 1948-67. St Michael's, Glasgow 1967-72. Our Lady of Perpetual Succour, Glasgow 1972-82. Corpus Christi, Glasgow 1982-84. Died Glasgow 8 Aug 1984.

MEECHAN, MICHAEL: Born Clydebank 1916. Educated St Patrick's High School, Dumbarton; Scots College, Rome 1932-40. Ordained Rome 1939. St Anthony's, Glasgow 1940-52. Spiritual Director, Valladolid 1952-60. St Bonaventure's, Glasgow 1960-67. St Constantine's, Glasgow 1967-78. St Barnabas's, Glasgow 1978-87. St Joseph's, Tollcross 1987-.

MEEHAN (Meechan), JAMES: Born and educated Ireland. Ordained Kilkenny for Glasgow 1929. Longriggend 1929-30. Our Holy Redeemer, Clydebank 1930-33. St John's, Glasgow 1933-50. Our Lady of Fatima, Glasgow 1950-59. St Flannan's, Kirkintilloch 1959-66. Helensburgh 1966-87. Retired 1987. (Canning)

MEEHAN, THOMAS: Born and educated Ireland. Ordained Maynooth 1897. Lent to Glasgow. St Laurence's, Greenock 1897-1900. Returned to Ireland 1900 and died there 11 Sept 1940. (Canning)

MEIKLEHAM, THOMAS: Born Plymouth 1908. Educated Blairs 1924-28; St Peter's 1928-34. Ordained Glasgow 1934. Dalry 1934-45. St Mary Immaculate, Glasgow 1945-50. Chaplain, Notre Dame 1950-59. St Brendan's, Glasgow 1959-67. St Aloysius', Glasgow 1967-78. Twechar 1978-.

MENTON, JAMES: Born and educated Ireland. Ordained Maynooth 1924. Lent to Glasgow. St Augustine's, Coatbridge 1924-25. Airdrie 1925. Returned to Ireland 1925 and died there 2 Feb 1936. (Canning)

MESKELL, RICHARD: Born and educated Ireland. Ordained Waterford 1894. Lent to Glasgow. St Augustine's, Coatbridge 1894-97. St Mary Immaculate, Glasgow 1897-1902. Returned to Ireland 1902 and died there 20 Nov 1934. (Canning)

MILLIGAN, HUGH: see Archdiocese of St Andrews & Edinburgh

MILLS, JOSEPH PHILIP: Born Glasgow 1941. Educated St Mungo's Academy, Glasgow; Campion House, Osterley; St Peter's. Ordained St Peter's College 1967. St Alphonsus', Glasgow 1967-69. Holy Cross, Glasgow 1969-75. St Robert's, Glasgow 1975-76. St Michael's,

Dumbarton 1976-85. St Patrick's, Dumbarton 1985-86. St Laurence's, Glasgow 1986-89. St Brendan's, Glasgow 1989-.

MISSET, FRANCIS THOMAS: Born Glasgow 1903. Educated Blairs 1918-23; St Peter's 1923-29. Ordained Glasgow 1929. Alexandria 1929-30. Carfin 1930. St Joseph's, Woodside, Glasgow 1930-38. Burnbank 1938-41. St Patrick's, Coatbridge 1941-48; thus moving to Motherwell diocese. Cadzow 1948-49. St Patrick's, Shieldmuir 1949-51. Sick leave from 1951. Died Waterford 11 Oct 1956.

MOLLOY, DANIEL: Born Ireland. Educated Ireland, Rome. Ordained Rome 1925. On English mission 1925-26. Lent to Glasgow. St Charles', Glasgow 1927-28. St Charles', Glasgow in addresses, but not under parishes, 1928-29. St Charles', Glasgow 1929-31. Returned to Ireland 1931. (Canning)

MOLLOY, FRANCIS: Born and educated Ireland. Ordained Wexford for Paisley 1956. Lent to Glasgow. St Patrick's, Glasgow 1956-57. St John's, Glasgow 1957-60. Got exeat from Paisley. Went to Ireland 1960. (Canning)

MOLLOY, PATRICK J: Born and educated Ireland. Ordained Maynooth 1923. Lent to Glasgow. Cardonald 1924-25. St Patrick's, Greenock 1925-27. Returned to Ireland 1927. (Canning)

MOLLOY, WILLIAM J: Born Maleaporam, Madras Presidency 1877. Educated Blairs 1893-96; Notre Dame des Champs, Paris 1896-97; St Peter's 1897-1904. Ordained Glasgow 1904. Coatdyke 1904-07. St Roch's, Glasgow 1907-11. Chaplain, Barlinnie Prison and St Joseph's Home, Glasgow 1911-20. St Roch's, Glasgow 1920-21. Clarkston 1921-28. Linwood 1928-30. Helensburgh 1930-34. Barrhead 1934-41. No address given 1941-42. No further entries.

MOLLUMBY, EDMOND: Ordained 1930. Directory for 1931 is full of errors as far as Glasgow is concerned. This man is down as being both at St Joseph's, Woodside, Glasgow and at Motherwell, 1930-31. (No further entries). He may even be identified with 'Molumby, Edward (1930)'; see below.

MOLLUMBY, EDWARD: Born and educated Ireland. Ordained Thurles 1896. Lent to Glasgow. St John the Baptist's, Uddingston 1900-01. Returned to Ireland 1901 and died there 10 June 1926. (Canning)

MOLONEY, JAMES: Born and educated Ireland. Ordained Maynooth 1907. Lent to Glasgow. St Patrick's, Coatbridge 1908-09. Returned to Ireland 1909 and died there 5 Oct 1957. (Canning)

MOLUMBY, EDWARD: Born and educated Ireland. Ordained Thurles for Glasgow 1930. Cardonald 1930-37. Biggar 1937-40. Imprisoned; then deported to Ireland as an enemy of the state; 1940-45. St Simon's, Glasgow 1945-47. St Michael's, Glasgow 1947-51. Immaculate Heart of Mary, Glasgow 1951-52. St Conval's, Glasgow 1952-60. St Anthony's, Glasgow 1960-77. Retired 1977. Died Ireland 20 March 1982. (Canning)

MONAGHAN, WILLIAM: Born Glasgow 1947. Educated St Roch's School, Glasgow; Campion House, Osterley; St Peter's. Ordained St Peter's College 1974. St Margaret's, Clydebank 1974-76. St Bartholomew's, Glasgow 1976-80. Our Lady of Fatima, Glasgow 1980-.

MONE, JOHN ALOYSIUS: Born Glasgow 1929. Educated St Sulpice; Institut Catholique, Paris. Ordained Glasgow 1952. St Ninian's, Glasgow 1952-75. Our Lady and St George, Glasgow 1975-79. St Joseph's, Tollcross 1979-84. Consecrated Bishop Auxiliary for Glasgow 1984. Became Bishop of Paisley 1988.

MONE, WILLIAM: Born Glasgow 1931. Educated Blairs, St Peter's. Ordained Glasgow 1955. Glasgow Cathedral 1955. St Peter's, Glasgow 1955-75. St Teresa's, Glasgow 1975-83. Immaculate Conception, Glasgow 1983-.

MONTGOMERY, JAMES: Born Airdrie 1881. Educated St Augustine's School, Coatbridge; Blairs 1896-1901; St Peter's 1901-10. Ordained Kinnoull 1910. Saltcoats 1910-14. St Paul's, Shettleston 1914-23. Chaplain, Barlinnie Prison and St Joseph's Home, Glasgow 1923-26. Tarbrax 1926-28. Helensburgh 1928-29. Strathaven 1929-30. Bothwell 1930-33. Burnbank 1933-44. Retired 1944. Died Girvan 20 June 1947.

MONTGOMERY, JOHN: Born Airdrie 1860. Educated Blairs 1872-78; St Peter's 1878-83. Ordained Glasgow 1883. St Mirin's, Paisley 1883-86. St Alphonsus', Glasgow 1886-90. Our Holy Redeemer, Clydebank 1890-1914. Rutherglen 1914-33. Died Rutherglen 10 Feb 1933.

MOONEY, HENRY: see Paisley diocese

MOONEY, MICHAEL: Born Port Glasgow 1919. Educated St Mungo's Academy, Glasgow; St Columba's School, Greenock; St Peter's. Ordained 1944. St Michael's, Glasgow 1944-57. Holy Cross, Glasgow 1957-69. Corpus Christi, Glasgow 1969-78. St Margaret Mary's, Glasgow 1978-87. Our Lady of Perpetual Succour, Glasgow 1987-.

MOORE, DANIEL: Born and educated Ireland. Ordained Carlow for Glasgow 1942. Sacred Heart, Glasgow 1942-54. Sick leave 1954-55. Duntocher 1955-60. St Barnabas's, Glasgow 1960-68. St Bonaventure's,

Glasgow 1968-74. Sacred Heart, Glasgow 1974-77. Retired 1977. Died Ireland 19 June 1982. (Canning)

MOORE, PETER J: Born and educated Ireland. Ordained 1932. Lent to Glasgow. Shotts 1933-34. Returned to Ireland 1934. (Canning)

MOORE, THOMAS J: see Archdiocese of St Andrews & Edinburgh

MORAN, PETER ANTONY: Born Glasgow 1935. Educated St Aloysius' College, Glasgow; Scots College, Rome. Ordained Rome 1959. St Paul's, Glasgow , and studying at Glasgow University, 1959-62. St Peter's, Glasgow 1962-64. Professor, Blairs 1964-85. Vice-rector, Blairs 1985-86. Blairs parish 1986-.

MORGAN, GEORGE: Born Blantyre 1941. Educated St Mungo's School, Alloa; Mount Melleray Seminary; St John's College, Waterford; St Peter's. Ordained St Peter's College 1975. St Benedict's, Glasgow 1975-81. Milngavie 1981-84. St Martin's, Glasgow 1984-.

MORGAN, WILLIAM: Born Longriggend 1913. Educated Blairs 1928-33; Scots College, Rome 1933-40. Ordained Rome 1939. Our Holy Redeemer, Clydebank 1940-54. Glasgow Cathedral 1954-62. St Thomas's, Glasgow 1962-75. Immaculate Heart of Mary 1975-83. Retired 1983.

MORIARTY, (James) BRENDAN: Born and educated Ireland. Ordained Waterford for Glasgow 1937. St Roch's, Glasgow 1937-41. RAF chaplain 1941-59. St Paul's, Glasgow 1959-60. St Benedict's, Glasgow 1960-71. Retired 1971. Died Reading 16 July 1976. (Canning)

MORREN, BRIAN: Born Dunoon 1941. Educated Blairs, St Peter's. Ordained Glasgow 1965. Sacred Heart, Cumbernauld 1965-66. Professor, Langbank 1966-75. St Matthew's, Bishopbriggs 1975-81. St Gabriel's, Glasgow 1981-89. On sabbatical leave 1989-.

MORRIS, DAVID: Born St Asaph, North Wales 1865. Educated Blairs 1878-83; Valladolid 1883-89. Ordained Valladolid 1889. St Anthony's, Glasgow 1889. St Aloysius', Glasgow 1889-92. St Mary's, Greenock 1892-96. Gourock 1896-97. No address given 1897-1905. St Paul's, Shettleston 1905-09. Johnstone 1909-25. Retired 1925. Died Glasgow 29 Dec 1943.

MORRIS, GERARD: Ordained 1924. St Peter's, Glasgow 1924-26. No further entries.

MORRIS, MICHAEL: Born and educated Ireland. Ordained Maynooth 1906. Lent to Glasgow. St Peter's, Glasgow 1907-09. Melbourne 1909-16. Returned to Ireland 1916 and died there 25 July 1944. (Canning)

MORRISON, JAMES F: Born Glasgow 1860. Educated Blairs 1874-79; St Peter's 1879-84. Ordained Glasgow 1884. Maryhill 1884-87. St Mary's, Greenock 1887-91. Cambuslang 1891-1900. St Mary Immaculate, Glasgow 1900-16. Died Torquay 15 June 1916.

MORRISON, PETER: Born Glasgow 1894. Educated Blairs 1910-15; Valladolid 1915-22. Ordained Valladolid 1922. St Mirin's, Paisley 1922-33. Chaplain, Barlinnie Prison and St Joseph's Home, Glasgow 1933-44. Burnbank 1944-46. St Luke's, Glasgow 1946-48. St Joseph's, Woodside, Glasgow 1948-55. Sacred Heart, Glasgow 1955-67. Died Glasgow 23 July 1967.

MORRISSEY, MICHAEL B: Born and educated Ireland. Ordained Waterford 1909. Lent to Glasgow. St Paul's, Shettleston 1909-17. Returned to Ireland 1917 and died there 30 Aug 1952. (Canning)

MORTIMER, RONALD: Born Glasgow 1860. Educated Blairs 1874-79; St Peter's 1879-84. Ordained Glasgow 1884. Motherwell 1884-86. St Aloysius', Glasgow 1886-88; St Patrick's, Dumbarton 1888-90. St John the Baptist's, Uddingston 1890-97. No further entries.

MOSS, JOHN: Born and educated Ireland. Ordained Kilkenny for Glasgow 1943. St Bridget's, Baillieston 1943-58; thus moving to Motherwell diocese. St Patrick's, Shieldmuir 1958-60. St Paul's, Hamilton 1960-66. St Clare's, Easterhouse 1966-72. St Augustine's, Coatbridge 1972-85. Retired 1985. (Canning)

MULDOON, JOHN: Born Glasgow 1929. Educated St Mungo's Academy, Glasgow; Campion House, Osterley; St Peter's. Ordained Glasgow 1959. Glasgow Cathedral 1959-67. St Charles', Glasgow 1967-69. Spiritual Director, St Peter's 1969-71. St Saviour's, Glasgow 1971-72. Our Holy Redeemer, Clydebank 1972-74. St Peter's, Dumbarton 1974-87. St Leo's, Glasgow 1987-.

MULHALL, JOSEPH: Born and educated Ireland. Ordained Carlow for Glasgow 1949. St Aloysius', Glasgow 1949-74. Condorrat 1974-. (Canning)

MULHOLLAND, PATRICK: see Galloway diocese

MULLEN, ALPHONSUS: Born and educated Ireland. Ordained Maynooth 1919. Lent to Glasgow. Shotts 1919-21. Burnbank 1921-22. Returned to Ireland 1922 and died there 20 Jan 1962. (Canning)

MULLEN, GEORGE: Born Wishaw 1911. Educated Blairs 1926-30; St Peter's 1930-37. Ordained Glasgow 1937. Sacred Heart, Glasgow 1937-42. Immaculate Conception, Glasgow 1942-44. Forces chaplain 1944-47.

St Mary's, Coatbridge 1947-53; thus moving to Motherwell diocese. New Stevenston 1953-55. Bothwell 1955-58. St Andrew's, Airdrie 1958-65. Carfin 1965-85. Retired 1985.

MULLEN, JAMES: Born Gourock 1865. Educated Blairs 1880-83; Douay 1883-86; St Peter's 1886-91. Ordained St Peter's College 1891. St Peter's, Glasgow 1891-98. Duntocher 1898-1905. St Agnes's, Glasgow 1905-16. St Mary Immaculate, Glasgow 1916-18. Died Pollokshaws 23 Jan 1918.

MULLEN, WILLIAM: Born Glasgow 1876. Educated St Edmund's, Douay; Notre Dame des Champs, Paris; St Peter's 1895-1901. Ordained 1901. Archbishop's chaplain 1901-02. Johnstone 1902-05. Went to South Africa for health 1905. Died Kimberley 23 May 1911.

MULLER, PETER: Born Leubsdorf, Germany 1859. Educated Linz; St Peter's 1879-84. Ordained Glasgow 1884. Johnstone 1884-90. Shotts 1890-93. Burnbank 1893-1900. St Augustine's, Coatbridge 1900-29. Retired 1929. Died Largs 1 May 1931.

MULLIN, JAMES: Born Glasgow 1867. Educated St Aloysius' College, Glasgow; Blairs 1880-84; Douay 1884-85; Scots College, Rome 1885-91. Ordained Rome 1890. St Mirin's, Paisley 1891-97. Holy Family, Kirkintilloch 1897-1901. St Patrick's, Glasgow 1901-18. Immaculate Conception, Glasgow 1918-23. Glasgow Cathedral 1923-25. Cleland 1925-29. St Augustine's, Coatbridge 1929-38. St Peter's, Glasgow 1938-48. Died Partick 18 March 1948.

MULLINS, ANTHONY: Born and educated Ireland. Ordained 1901. Lent to Glasgow; affiliated to it 1910. St John's, Port Glasgow 1901-13. Blackwood 1913-19. St Michael's, Glasgow 1919-21. Sacred Heart, Glasgow 1921-55. Died Mallow 3 Oct 1955. (Canning)

MULVENNA, JAMES A: Born Dumbarton 1883. Educated Blairs 1897-1901; St Peter's 1901-03; Issy 1903-05; St Sulpice 1905-07. Ordained Paris 1907. Rutherglen 1907-08. Newton 1908-09. St Anthony's, Glasgow 1909-15. Died Govan 9 March 1915.

MULVEY, MICHAEL: Born Shotts 1881. Educated Blairs, St Peter's. Ordained Glasgow 1908. St Patrick's, Dumbarton 1908-09. Coatdyke 1909-11. St Joseph's, Tollcross 1911-13. St Laurence's, Greenock 1913-14. Blantyre 1914-15. Retired 1915. Died Carnwath 15 April 1953. (see p 50)

MULVIHILL, THOMAS: Born and educated Ireland. Ordained Maynooth 1920. Lent to Glasgow. St Anne's, Glasgow 1920-23. Chapelhall 1923-27. Returned to Ireland 1927 and died there 2 Dec 1969. (Canning)

MUNNELLY, MICHAEL: Born and educated Ireland. Ordained Maynooth 1921. Lent to Glasgow. St Constantine's, Glasgow 1921-23. Returned to Ireland 1923 and died there 21 Jan 1961. (Canning)

MURIE, DAVID: Born Airdrie 1864. Educated Airdrie Academy; St Aloysius' College, Glasgow; Blairs 1878-83; Valladolid 1883-86, returning home in bad health; St Peter's 1887-89. Ordained Glasgow 1889. St Patrick's, Glasgow 1889-90. St Mary's, Glasgow 1890-95. Johnstone 1895-97. Alexandria 1897-99. Renton 1899-1900. Died Airdrie 7 June 1900.

MURIE, PETER ALOYSIUS: Born Airdrie 1893. Educated Blairs 1907-13; Propaganda, Rome 1913-14; St Peter's 1914-19. Ordained Glasgow 1919. St Michael's, Glasgow 1919-28. Longriggend 1928-30. Barrhead 1930-34. In south of England in bad health 1934-39. St Ninian's, Glasgow 1939-41. Chapelhall 1941-52; thus moving to Motherwell diocese. Mossend 1952-53. Carluke 1953-54. Sick leave in Aviemore 1954-55 and Paisley 1955-58. Chaplain, Providence House, Worcester, Massachusetts, USA 1958-64. Died Worcester, USA 11 Jan 1964.

MURPHY, BRENDAN: Born and educated Ireland. Ordained Wexford for Glasgow 1940. Clarkston 1940-47. St Columba's, Glasgow 1947-65. St Gregory's, Glasgow 1965-76. Our Lady of Lourdes, Glasgow 1976-88. Died Troon 4 July 1988. (Canning)

MURPHY, FRANCIS: Born and educated Ireland. Ordained for Glasgow 1941. Our Lady of Lourdes, Glasgow 1941-57. Immaculate Heart of Mary 1957-67. Bearsden 1967-78. Corpus Christi, Glasgow 1978-82. Retired to Ireland 1982. (Canning)

MURPHY, JAMES (1935): Born and educated Ireland. Ordained Maynooth 1935. Lent to Glasgow. St Roch's, Glasgow 1935-36. Returned to Ireland 1936 and died there 12 Feb 1952. (Canning)

MURPHY, JAMES (1943): Born Gartcosh 1917. Educated Blairs, St Peter's. Ordained 1943. St Mungo's, Greenock 1943-64; thus moving to Paisley diocese. Neilston 1964-68. Howwood 1968-73. Bishopton 1973-78. St Laurence's, Greenock 1978-80. Neilston 1980-.

MURPHY, JAMES (1947): Born and educated Ireland. Ordained Thurles 1947. St John's, Port Glasgow 1947-51; thus moving to Paisley diocese. Paisley Cathedral 1951-68. St Laurence's, Greenock 1968-69. Newton Mearns 1969-73. St John's, Port Glasgow 1973-89. Retired to Ireland 1989. (Canning)

MURPHY, JOHN L (1881): Born and educated Ireland. Ordained 1881. St John's, Glasgow 1881-86. St John the Baptist's, Uddingston 1886-90. St Laurence's, Greenock 1890-96. St Aloysius', Glasgow 1896-1908. Retired 1908. Died Ireland 26 April 1913. (Canning)

MURPHY, JOHN J (1901): Born and educated Ireland. Ordained Maynooth 1901. Lent to Glasgow. Cadzow 1901-03. Hamilton 1903-14. Returned to Ireland 1914 and died there 8 Aug 1934. (Canning)

MURPHY, JOHN J (1914): Born Kendal, Westmoreland 1887. Educated St Mungo's Academy, Glasgow; St Aloysius' College, Glasgow; Blairs 1903-06; St Peter's 1906-14. Ordained Glasgow 1914. Carfin 1914-32. Whiterigg 1932-37. Alexandria 1937-48. St Teresa's, Glasgow 1948-61. Died Glasgow 28 Nov 1961.

MURPHY, JOHN J (1923): Born Ireland. Educated Ireland, St Peter's. Ordained Glasgow 1923. Cambuslang 1923. Immaculate Conception, Glasgow 1923-30. Died Glasgow 14 Jan 1930. (Canning)

MURPHY, JOSEPH: Born and educated Ireland. Ordained Wexford for Glasgow 1954. St Nicholas's, Glasgow 1954-60. St Teresa's, Glasgow 1960-67. St Saviour's, Glasgow 1967-70. St Agnes's, Glasgow 1970-77. St Louise's, Glasgow 1977-82. Sacred Heart, Glasgow 1982-. (Canning)

MURPHY, MARTIN: Born and educated Ireland. Ordained Maynooth 1912. Lent to Glasgow. Immaculate Conception, Glasgow 1912-14. Returned to Ireland 1914 and died there 7 April 1953. (Canning)

MURPHY, MICHAEL J: Born and educated Ireland. Ordained Maynooth 1922. Lent to Glasgow. St Charles', Glasgow 1922-25. Returned to Ireland 1925. (Canning)

MURPHY, PATRICK: Born and educated Ireland. Ordained Maynooth 1905. Lent to Glasgow. St John's, Port Glasgow 1905-09. Returned to Ireland 1909 and died there 30 April 1945. (Canning)

MURPHY, PETER JOSEPH (1943): Born Glasgow 1917. Educated St Aloysius' College, Glasgow; Blairs; St Peter's. Ordained 1943. St Margaret's, Airdrie 1943-53; thus moving to Motherwell diocese. Carfin 1953-59. Blackwood 1959. Calderbank 1959-62. Director, Catholic Child Care Office, Glasgow 1962-69. Died Carlisle 31 Oct 1969.

MURPHY, PETER (1969): Ordained 1969. Glasgow Cathedral 1969-82. St Philomena's, Glasgow 1982-85. St Dominic's, Bishopbriggs 1985-.

MURPHY, THOMAS A (1915): Born and educated Ireland. Ordained Maynooth 1915. Lent to Glasgow. St Peter's, Glasgow 1916-21. Returned to Ireland 1921 and died there 22 June 1962. (Canning)

MURPHY, THOMAS P (1932): Born Dalry 1906. Educated St Mungo's Academy, Glasgow; Blairs 1920-26; St Peter's 1926-32. Ordained 1932. St Joseph's, Woodside, Glasgow 1932. St Teresa's, Glasgow 1932-46. Largs 1946-48. Died Wemyss Bay 20 March 1948.

MURPHY, THOMAS (1948): Born and educated Ireland. Ordained Kilkenny for Glasgow 1948. St Robert's, Glasgow 1948-52. St Ninian's, Glasgow 1952-73. St Mary's, Glasgow 1973-75. Our Lady of the Assumption, Glasgow 1975-78. St Conval's, Glasgow 1978-86. Corpus Christi, Glasgow 1986-. (Canning)

MURPHY, WILLIAM (1907): Born and educated Ireland. Ordained Maynooth 1907. Lent to Glasgow. St Roch's, Glasgow 1907-10. Returned to Ireland 1910 and died there 3 Nov 1947. (Canning)

MURPHY, WILLIAM (1952): Born and educated Ireland. Ordained Dublin for Glasgow 1952. St Alphonsus', Glasgow 1952-62. Renton 1962-74. Our Lady of Lourdes, Glasgow 1974-75. St Paul's, Glasgow 1975-79. St Joachim's, Glasgow 1979-89. Died Ireland 26 July 1989. (Canning)

MURRAY, EUGENE: Born Govan 1885. Educated Blairs 1900-04; Issy 1904-06; St Sulpice 1906-09. Ordained Paris 1909. St Charles', Glasgow 1909-28. Clarkston 1928-32. Croy 1932-37. St Mary's, Coatbridge 1937-53; thus moving to Motherwell diocese. Died Glasgow 26 June 1953.

MURRAY, JOHN (1893): Born and educated Ireland. Ordained 1893. Lent to Glasgow. St Alphonsus', Glasgow 1893-98. Returned to Ireland 1898 and died there 12 April 1918. (Canning)

MURRAY, JOHN VINCENT (1934): Born Glasgow 1909. Educated St Aloysius' College, Glasgow; Blairs 1924-28; St Peter's 1928-34. Ordained Glasgow 1934. Barrhead 1934-42. Alexandria 1942-45. St Patrick's, Coatbridge 1945-48; thus moving to Motherwell diocese. St Mary's, Hamilton 1948-54. Garthamlock 1954-59. St Bernadette's, Motherwell 1959-60. Glenboig 1960-69. Newarthill 1969-72. Died Troon 27 June 1972.

MURRAY, JOSEPH: Born Coatbridge 1879. Educated Blairs 1894-1900; St Peter's 1900-06. Ordained Glasgow 1906. St Paul's, Glasgow 1906-23. Newton 1923-25. Died Glasgow 7 July 1925.

MURRAY, MICHAEL J: Born and educated Ireland. Ordained Thurles 1911. Lent to Glasgow. St Mary's, Paisley 1911-18. Returned to Ireland 1918 and died there 21 April 1957. (Canning)

MURRAY, NOEL: Born Ireland. Educated Ireland, St Peter's. Ordained Paisley for that diocese 1954. Lent to Glasgow. St Peter's, Glasgow 1954-61. Was incardinated into Glasgow Archdiocese. Forces chaplain 1961-66. C/o Diocesan Office 1966-68. St Brendan's, Glasgow 1968-71. St Bonaventure's, Glasgow 1971-74. St Aloysius', Glasgow 1974-. (Canning)

MURRAY, PAUL GRAHAM: Born Glasgow 1961. Educated Holyrood School, Glasgow; Glasgow University; Scots College, Rome. Ordained

Glasgow 1988. Glasgow Cathedral 1988. Chaplain, Stobhill Hospital 1988. St Mary's, Glasgow 1988-.

MURRAY, PETER: Born Glasgow 1869. Educated Blairs 1883-87; Valladolid 1887-94. Ordained Valladolid 1894. St Michael's, Glasgow 1894. St John's, Glasgow 1894-1901. Largs 1901-06. Cleland 1906-21. Blantyre 1921-23. Alexandria 1923-29. Barrhead 1929-31. Died Barrhead 6 July 1931.

MURRAY, THOMAS J (1916): Born Glasgow 1891. Educated Blairs 1906-11; Issy, St Sulpice 1911-16. Ordained Glasgow 1916. Hamilton 1916-17. Alexandria 1917-21. Wishaw 1921-33. Spiritual Director, St Peter's College 1933-46. Newton 1946-52; thus moving to Motherwell diocese. All Saints, Coatdyke 1952-57. St Bride's, Cambuslang 1957-73. Retired 1973. Died Greenock 2 July 1975.

MURRAY, THOMAS (1936): Born Wishaw 1913. Educated Blairs 1926-30; Scots College, Rome 1930-37. Ordained Rome 1936. St Luke's, Glasgow 1937-39. Carfin 1939-42. St Roch's, Glasgow 1942-54. Spiritual Director, Scots College, Rome 1954-57. Immaculate Heart of Mary, Glasgow 1957-75. St Patrick's, Dumbarton 1975-.

MURRIN, DENIS: Born and educated Ireland. Ordained Letterkenny 1907. Lent to Glasgow. St Mary Immaculate, Glasgow 1908-13. Returned to Ireland 1913 and died there 5 Dec 1939. (Canning)

MURTAGH, BRENDAN JOHN: Born Dundalk, Ireland 1951. Educated St Gerard's School and Holyrood School, Glasgow; worked as hospital laboratory technichian; Paisley College of Technology; St Peter's; Chesters. Ordained Dumbreck 1985. St Michael's, Dumbarton 1985-.

NAGLE, JOHN: Born and educated Ireland. Ordained Maynooth 1892. Lent to Glasgow. St Aloysius', Glasgow 1892-98. Returned to Ireland 1898 and died there 16 Oct 1919. (Canning)

NEE, JOSEPH: Born Burnbank 1917. Educated Blairs, St Peter's. Ordained 1945. Alexandria 1945-46. St Michael's, Dumbarton 1946-55. St Philomena's, Glasgow 1955-56. St Catherine's, Glasgow 1956-60. St Mark's, Glasgow 1960-69. St Leo's, Glasgow 1969-87. Died Glasgow 21 April 1987.

NEVIN, JAMES E A: Born and educated Ireland. Ordained Carlow for Glasgow 1929. Shettleston and Carntyne 1929-37. St Mirin's. Paisley 1937-54; thus moving to Paisley diocese. St Peter's, Paisley 1954-61. Died Paisley 16 April 1961. (Canning)

NEWMAN, JOHN: Born Glasgow 1940. Educated Blairs, St Peter's. Ordained Glasgow 1964. St Michael's, Glasgow 1964-72. Forces chaplain, serving in Germany 1972. Died Neunstadt 4 Dec 1972.

NOLAN, JAMES (1885): Born and educated Ireland. Ordained 1885. Lent to Glasgow. St Mary's, Glasgow 1885-90. Returned to Ireland 1890 and died there 7 June 1927. (Canning)

NOLAN, JAMES (1902): Born and educated Ireland. Ordained Maynooth 1902. Lent to Glasgow; was affiliated to it 1910. Sacred Heart, Glasgow 1902-15. Newton 1915-23. St Luke's, Glasgow 1923-38. Died Glasgow 11 Oct 1938. (Canning)

NOLAN, JOHN: Born and educated Ireland. Ordained Maynooth 1902. Lent to Glasgow. Holy Family, Kirkintilloch 1902-10. Returned to Ireland 1910 and died there 3 April 1951. (Canning)

NOON, JOHN: Born Glasgow 1907. Educated St Mungo's Academy, Glasgow; Blairs 1923-26; St Peter's 1926-32. Ordained 1932. St Mary's, Glasgow 1932-48. Milngavie 1948-54. St Joachim's, Glasgow 1954-63. St Ninian's, Glasgow 1963-75. Retired 1975. Died Glasgow 1 Nov 1976.

NORBUT, JOSEPH: Ordained 1909. Mossend 1912-20; probably serving Lithuanian Community. No further entries.

NUGENT, GERARD JOSEPH: Born Ireland. Educated Blairs, St Peter's. Ordained St Peter's College 1967. St Peter's, Dumbarton 1967-74. St Thomas's, Glasgow 1974-78. St Robert's, Glasgow 1978-83. St Teresa's, Glasgow 1983-87. St Philomena's, Glasgow 1987-89. Our Lady of the Assumption, Glasgow 1989-. (Canning)

NYHAN, DANIEL: Born and educated Ireland. Ordained Maynooth 1903. Lent to Glasgow. St Mary's, Paisley 1903-07. Retired 1907. (Canning)

NYHAN, JOHN: Born Ireland. Educated Paris. Ordained Paris 1890. Lent to Glasgow; later got exeat to remain there. Longriggend 1890-92. St Patrick's, Coatbridge 1892-96. Longriggend 1896-1903. Johnstone 1903-17. Died Johnstone 15 Dec 1917. (Canning)

O'BOYLE, MICHAEL: Born and educated Ireland. Ordained Maynooth 1906. Lent to Glasgow. St John the Baptist's, Uddingston 1907-08. In San Francisco and New Zealand 1908-21. Returned to Ireland 1921 and died there 3 July 1928. (Canning)

O'BRIEN, ANDREW JOSEPH: Born Glasgow 1869. Educated Blairs 1883-86; Valladolid 1886-93. Ordained Valladolid 1893. Immaculate Conception, Glasgow 1893-97. Chaplain, Good Shepherd Convent,

Dalbeth 1897-1900. Milngavie 1900-04. St Paul's, Shettleston 1904-12. Shettleston and Carntyne 1912-23. Leave of absence from 1923. Died Rothesay 3 April 1947.

O'BRIEN, DANIEL: Born Mossend 1901. Educated Blairs 1918-20; St Peter's 1920-26. Ordained Glasgow 1926. St John the Baptist's, Uddingston 1926-34. St Luke's, Glasgow 1934-35. Sick leave 1935-36. Died Aberdeen 19 Nov 1936.

O'BRIEN, HUGH: Born Glasgow 1890. Educated Blairs 1908-12; Valladolid 1912-19. Ordained Valladolid 1919. Cleland 1919-30. St John's, Port Glasgow 1930-31. Croy 1931-38. Larkhall 1938-45. Glenboig 1945-48. No further entries.

O'BRIEN, JOHN JOSEPH: Born and educated Ireland. Ordained Wexford for Glasgow 1950. St Joseph's, Tollcross 1950-67. Immaculate Heart of Mary, Glasgow 1967-72. St Luke's, Glasgow 1972-75. St Mary's, Glasgow 1975-78. Our Lady of Consolation, Glasgow 1978-. (Canning)

O'BRIEN, MICHAEL: Born Ireland. Educated Ireland, St Peter's. Ordained Glasgow 1914. St Mary's, Glasgow 1914-22. Burnbank 1922-24. St Mary's, Paisley 1924-26. Chaplain, Barlinnie Prison and St Joseph's Home, Glasgow 1926-33. Harthill 1933-38. Larkhall 1938-55; thus moving to Motherwell diocese. Died Stonehouse 11 June 1955. (Canning)

O'BRIEN, PATRICK (1918): Born and educated Ireland. Ordained Maynooth 1918. Lent to Glasgow. Chaplain, West Thorn Reformatory and Good Shepherd Convent, Dalbeth 1918-19. Holy Cross, Glasgow 1919-26. Returned to Ireland 1926 and died there 1972. (Canning)

O'BRIEN, PATRICK GERALD (1984): Born Glasgow 1960. Educated Langbank; Blairs; Scots College, Rome. Ordained Glasgow 1984. Further studies, Rome 1984-85. St Stephen's, Dalmuir 1985-88. No further entries.

O'BRIEN, WILLIAM P: Born Glasgow 1860. Educated Blairs 1872-77; Scots College, Rome 1877-83. Ordained Rome 1883. St Mary's, Greenock 1883-88. Glasgow Cathedral 1888-89. Holy Cross, Glasgow 1889-1930. Retired 1930. Died Rothesay 4 Jan 1937.

O'CALLAGHAN, GERALD: Born Glasgow 1915. Educated North Monastery School, Cork; Blairs; St Peter's. Ordained 1939. St Mary's, Glasgow 1939-46. Newton 1946-53; thus moving to Motherwell diocese. St Columba's, Viewpark 1953-54. RAF chaplain 1954-57. C/o Diocesan Office 1957-58. Stepps 1958-65. C/o Diocesan Office 1965-66. Biggar 1966-71. Retired to Ireland 1971.

O'CALLAGHAN, HUMPHRY: Born and educated Ireland. Ordained 1880. Gave his services to Glasgow. St Mary's, Greenock 1880-81. St Patrick's, Glasgow 1881-82. No further entries. (Canning)

O'CALLAGHAN, JOHN (1886): Born Ireland. Educated Paris, Ireland. Ordained Maynooth 1886. Lent to Glasgow. Sacred Heart, Glasgow 1886-87. Rutherglen 1887-88. On American mission 1889-1900. Returned to Ireland 1900 and died there 27 Jan 1934. (Canning)

O'CALLAGHAN, JOHN J (1900): Born and educated Ireland. Ordained Maynooth 1900. Lent to Glasgow. St Charles', Glasgow 1900-03. St Aloysius', Glasgow 1903-10. St Laurence's, Greenock 1910-13. Returned to Ireland 1913 and died there 2 Dec 1938. (Canning)

O'CALLAGHAN, JOHN (1917): Born Ireland. Educated Blairs, Scots College, Rome. Ordained Rome 1917. St Mary's, Glasgow 1918-19. Professor, Blairs 1919-34. Longriggend 1934-35. St Luke's, Glasgow 1935-36. Cardowan 1936-49; thus moving to Motherwell diocese. Shotts 1949-55. Died Shotts 15 April 1955. (Canning)

O'CALLAGHAN, RICHARD: Born Glasgow 1913. Educated Blairs 1928-33; St Lo 1933-34; Grand Seminaire, Coutances 1934-39. Ordained 1939. St Patrick's, Dumbarton 1939-54. Military chaplain 1954-56. St Paul's, Shettleston 1956-57. C/o Diocesan Office 1957-58. St Pius X, Glasgow 1958-62. St Leo's, Glasgow 1962-67. St Laurence's, Glasgow 1967-70. C/o Diocesan Office 1970-72. Retired to Ireland 1972.

O'CARROLL, MICHAEL: Born and educated Ireland. Ordained 1924. St Mary's, Glasgow 1924-27. Johnstone 1927-28. St Mary's, Paisley 1928-29. Shettleston and Carntyne 1929-34. Chaplain, Kenmure Industrial School 1934-40. Whiterigg 1940-42. Barrhead 1942-47. West Kilbride 1947-74; thus moving to Galloway diocese. Retired to Ireland 1974 and died there 21 July 1978. (Canning)

O'CARROLL, WILLIAM: Born Ireland. Educated Ireland, St Peter's. Ordained Glasgow 1902. St Anthony's, Glasgow 1902-16. Newmains 1916-21. Died Lanark 26 Sept 1921. (Canning)

O'CONNELL, DANIEL: Born and educated Ireland. Ordained Maynooth 1910. Lent to Glasgow. St Peter's, Glasgow 1910-11. Returned to Ireland 1911. (Canning)

O'CONNELL, DAVID: Born and educated Ireland. Ordained Maynooth 1894. Lent to Glasgow. St Laurence's, Greenock 1895-96. Returned to Ireland 1896 and died there 17 Feb 1951. (Canning)

O'CONNELL, GERALD: Born Aberdare, South Wales 1861. Educated Aberdare Grammar School 1876-80; St Joseph's College, Kelvedon,

Essex 1880-83; St Joseph's College, Mill Hill 1883-86, but ill health made him abandon the idea of foreign mission work; St Peter's 1886-88. Ordained Glasgow 1888. Sacred Heart, Glasgow 1888-93. Died Glasgow 10 June 1893.

O'CONNELL, MICHAEL J: Born and educated Ireland. Ordained Kilkenny for Glasgow 1940. St Joseph's, Woodside, Glasgow 1940-47. St Vincent de Paul's, Glasgow 1947-49. St Michael's, Glasgow 1949-66. Holy Family, Kirkintilloch 1966-75. St Laurence's, Glasgow 1975-86. Retired 1986. (Canning)

O'CONNELL, WILLIAM JOSEPH: Born Glasgow 1946. Educated St Peter's; College of St Robert Bellarmine, Heythrop, Oxfordshire. Ordained Glasgow 1970. Immaculate Heart of Mary 1970-72. No further entries.

O'CONNOR, EUGENE: Born and educated Ireland. Ordained 1902. Lent to Glasgow. Baillieston 1903-10. Returned to Ireland 1910 and died there 7 Oct 1935. (Canning)

O'CONNOR, JAMES (1911): Born and educated Ireland. Ordained Maynooth 1911. Lent to Glasgow. Holy Family, Kirkintilloch 1911-16. Forces chaplain 1916-18. Returned to Ireland 1918 and died there 27 April 1972. (Canning)

O'CONNOR, JAMES (1923): Born and educated Ireland. Ordained Ballina 1923. Lent to Glasgow. St Paul's, Shettleston 1924-25. St Patrick's, Coatbridge 1925-27. Returned to Ireland 1927 and died there 19 June 1968. (Canning)

O'CONNOR, JEREMIAH: Born and educated Ireland. Ordained Kilkenny for Glasgow 1945. St Mary's, Glasgow 1945-65. Chaplain, St Ninian's School, Gartmore 1965-68. Retired 1968. Died Cardiff 21 May 1971. (Canning)

O'CONNOR, MAURICE: Born and educated Ireland. Ordained Maynooth 1915. Lent to Glasgow. St Mary's, Greenock 1915-21. Returned to Ireland 1921 and died there 22 May 1952. (Canning)

O'CONNOR, MICHAEL P (1895): Born and educated Ireland. Ordained Maynooth 1895. Lent to Glasgow. St Patrick's, Dumbarton 1895-96. No address given 1896-98. Returned to Ireland 1898 and died there 22 March 1944. (Canning)

O'CONNOR, MICHAEL (1915): Born Ireland. Educated Ireland, St Peter's. Ordained 1915. Immaculate Conception, Glasgow 1915-27. Motherwell 1927-33. Largs 1933-39. Our Lady, Saltcoats 1939-66; thus moving to Galloway diocese. Died Ballochmyle 25 Feb 1966. (Canning)

O'CONNOR, MICHAEL (1927): Born and educated Ireland. Ordained Kilkenny for Glasgow 1927. Cardowan 1927-44. St Anne's, Glasgow 1944-47. Muirhead 1947-55; thus moving to Motherwell diocese. Died Muirhead 28 Nov 1955. (Canning)

O'CONNOR, PETER: Born Kilwinning. Educated St John's College, Waterford; Clonliffe College, Dublin; [Scots College] Rome. Ordained Rome 1892. St Mary's, Glasgow 1893-98. Immaculate Conception, Glasgow 1898-1900. Busby 1900-02. St Paul's, Shettleston 1902-04. Sick leave 1904-10. 'Retired' 1910-18. Burnbank 1918-26. Immaculate Conception, Glasgow 1926-41. Died Maryhill 24 July 1941.

O'CONNOR, THOMAS: Born and educated Ireland. Ordained Maynooth 1914. Lent to Glasgow. Our Lady and St Margaret's, Glasgow 1914-16. Glasgow Cathedral 1916-21. Motherwell 1921-23. Returned to Ireland 1923 and died there 18 June 1952. (Canning)

O'CONNOR, WILLIAM JOSEPH: see Galloway diocese

O'DEA, DANIEL: Born and educated Ireland. Ordained Ennis 1910. Lent to Glasgow. St Patrick's, Coatbridge 1910-11. Returned to Ireland 1911 and died there 27 April 1967. (Canning)

O'DEA, JOHN: Born and educated Ireland. Ordained Maynooth 1901. Lent to Glasgow. Carfin 1901-04. Returned to Ireland 1904 and died there 2 Jan 1934. (Canning)

O'DOHERTY, DANIEL: Born Greenock 1914. Educated St Patrick's College, Thurles; St Peter's 1935-41. Ordained Buncrana, Co Donegal 1941. St Mary Immaculate, Glasgow 1941-44. St Ignatius, Wishaw 1944-58; thus moving to Motherwell diocese. Bothwell 1958-61. Caldercruix 1961-71. C/o Diocesan Office 1971-75. Biggar 1975-76. Halfway 1976-85. Retired 1985.

O'DOHERTY, FRANCIS: Born and educated Ireland. Ordained Maynooth 1921. Lent to Glasgow. St Roch's, Glasgow 1921-27. Returned to Ireland 1927. (Canning)

O'DOHERTY, THOMAS: Born and educated Ireland. Ordained Maynooth 1927. Lent to Glasgow. St Mirin's, Paisley 1927-28. Shotts 1928-29. St Laurence's, Greenock 1929-34. Returned to Ireland 1934. (Canning)

O'DONNELL, HUGH: Born Glasgow 1924. Educated Osterley, St Peter's. Ordained Glasgow 1953. St Robert's, Glasgow 1953-70. St Nicholas's, Glasgow 1970-72. Our Lady of Perpetual Succour, Glasgow 1972-79. Croy 1979-81. St Mary Immaculate, Glasgow 1981-.

O'DONNELL, JOHN F (1918): Born Dundee 1891. Educated Blairs; St Sulpice 1913-14; St Peter's 1914; Paris 1914-18. Ordained Glasgow 1918. St John's, Glasgow 1918-33. Shotts 1933-34. St Mary's, Coatbridge 1934-37. Newmains 1937-40. Helensburgh 1940-45. St Margaret's, Johnstone 1945-68; thus moving to Paisley diocese. Died Clydebank 3 March 1968.

O'DONNELL, JOHN (1944): Born Dumbarton 1918. Educated St Patrick's High School, Dumbarton; St Peter's. Ordained 1944. St Roch's, Glasgow 1944-45. Rutherglen 1945-48; thus moving to Motherwell diocese. Motherwell Cathedral 1948-56. Cathedral House in addresses, but not under parishes, 1956-57. Newmains 1957-67. St Ignatius's, Wishaw 1967-83. Retired 1983. Died Wishaw 3 March 1989.

O'DONOGHUE, JEREMIAH (Jerome): Born and educated Ireland. Ordained Maynooth 1905. Lent to Glasgow. Immaculate Conception, Glasgow 1906-14. Returned to Ireland 1914 and died there 19 June 1932. (Canning)

O'DONOGHUE, JOHN: Born Ireland. Educated Ireland, St Peter's. Ordained Glasgow 1924. St Mary's, Glasgow 1924-27. Died Glasgow 6 May 1927. (Canning)

O'DONOGHUE, MICHAEL: Born Ireland. Educated Ireland, Paris. Ordained 1905. Lent to Glasgow. St Mary's, Greenock 1905-16. Returned to Ireland 1916 and died there 28 March 1970. (Canning)

O'DONOVAN, JOHN: Ordained 1879. Maryhill 1879-80. No further entries.

O'DRISCOLL, FLORENCE: Born and educated Ireland. Ordained Maynooth 1900. Lent to Glasgow. St Aloysius', Glasgow 1900-04. Returned to Ireland 1904. (Canning)

O'DRISCOLL, JEREMIAH: Born Ireland. Educated Paris. Ordained Paris 1894. Lent to Glasgow. St Patrick's, Glasgow 1894-1901. Cambuslang 1901-03. Longriggend 1903-05. Returned to Ireland 1905 and died there 17 April 1949. (Canning)

O'FARRELL, PETER: Born and educated Ireland. Ordained Waterford for Glasgow 1962. St Aloysius', Glasgow 1962-75. St Joseph's, Cumbernauld 1975-81. St Laurence's, Glasgow 1981-82. St Louise's, Glasgow 1982-. (Canning)

O'FLAHERTY, PATRICK: Born Jedburgh 1903. Educated Holy Cross Academy, Edinburgh; Redemptorist College, Bishop Eton; St Peter's 1923-29. Ordained Glasgow 1929. Our Holy Redeemer, Clydebank 1929-32. Died Edinburgh 13 Aug 1932.

O'FLYNN, DANIEL: Born and educated Ireland. Ordained Maynooth 1945. Lent to Glasgow. Duntocher 1945-46. St John's, Port Glasgow 1946-48. Returned to Ireland 1948. (Canning)

O'FLYNN, FLORENCE: Born Ireland. Educated Paris. Ordained Paris 1939. Lent to Glasgow. St Laurence's, Greenock 1939-47. Returned to Ireland 1947. (Canning)

O'FLYNN, JEREMIAH: Born Ireland. Educated Blairs; Scots College, Rome. Ordained Rome 1936. St Ninian's, Glasgow 1937-50. St Joseph's, Tollcross 1950-57. St Martin's, Glasgow 1957-68. Duntocher 1968-86. Retired to Ireland 1986. (Canning)

O'FREIL, THOMAS: Born and educated Ireland. Ordained Maynooth 1939. Lent to Glasgow. St Aloysius', Glasgow 1939-52. Returned to Ireland 1952. (Canning)

O'GRADY, JOHN: Born and educated Ireland. Ordained Maynooth 1906. Lent to Glasgow. Blantyre 1907-12. Returned to Ireland 1912 and died there 22 June 1947. (Canning)

O'GRADY, MICHAEL DAVITT: Born Glasgow 1912. Educated St Aloysius' College, Glasgow; Glasgow University; taught mathematics and science; educated for priesthood St Peter's. Ordained Glasgow 1966. St Brigid's, Glasgow 1966-78. Retired 1978. Died Glasgow 25 Jan 1987.

O'HAGAN, JOHN: Born Clydebank 1929. Educated Campion House, Osterley; St Peter's. Ordained Glasgow 1955. St Mark's, Carntyne 1955-68. Our Lady of Lourdes, Glasgow 1968-74. Our Lady of Fatima, Glasgow 1974-79. Immaculate Conception, Glasgow 1979-83. St Brigid's, Glasgow 1983-.

O'HAGAN, JOSEPH: Born Ireland. Educated Ireland, Rome. Ordained Rome 1936. Lent to Glasgow. Newmains 1936-37. St Mary's, Glasgow 1937-39. Returned to Ireland 1939. (Canning)

O'HALLORAN, JOHN: Ordained 1962. St Anthony's, Glasgow 1967-72. No further entries.

O'HALLORAN, PATRICK: Born and educated Ireland. Ordained Maynooth 1898. Lent to Glasgow. Hamilton 1898-1903. Returned to Ireland 1903 and died there 24 Nov 1947. (Canning)

O'HALLORAN, THOMAS: Born Newcastle-on-Tyne 1891. Educated Blairs 1908-13; Seminary of Versailles 1913-14; St Peter's 1914; Institut Catholique, Paris 1914-18. Ordained Glasgow 1918. St Mary's, Paisley 1918-21. Blantyre 1921-30. Died Glasgow 30 Sept 1930.

O'HANLON, EDMUND: Born Ireland. Educated Ireland, St Peter's. Ordained Glasow 1913. Blantyre 1913. St Agnes's, Glasgow 1913-20. Joined Vincentian Order 1920. Died Ireland 20 Nov 1959. (Canning)

O'HANLON, JOHN: Born and educated Ireland. Ordained Maynooth 1912. Lent to Glasgow. Our Holy Redeemer, Clydebank 1912-22. Returned to Ireland 1922 and died there 27 Jan 1946. (Canning)

O'HANLON, THOMAS: Born and educated Ireland. Ordained Maynooth 1912. Lent to Glasgow. Blantyre 1912-17. St John's, Glasgow 1917-18. Shotts 1918-19. St Stephen's, Dalmuir 1919-22. Returned to Ireland 1922 and died there 15 July 1955. (Canning)

O'HARA, EDWARD: Born and educated Ireland. Ordained Carlow for Glasgow 1942. St Augustine's, Coatbridge 1942-47. St Mark's, Carntyne 1947-48. Good Shepherd, Glasgow 1948-55. Holy Family, Kirkintilloch 1955-67. St Mark's, Carntyne 1967-70. St Joseph's, Tollcross 1970-79. Retired to Ireland 1979 and died there 23 April 1988. (Canning)

O'HARA, JOHN G: Born Shettleston 1927. Educated Blairs, St Sulpice. Ordained Glasgow 1951. St John's, Glasgow 1951. St Bernadette's, Glasgow 1951-52. Our Lady and St Margaret's, Glasgow 1952-53. St Agnes's, Glasgow 1953-55. Balloch 1955-59. St Patrick's, Glasgow 1959-78. Our Lady Queen of Peace, Glasgow 1978-81. St Luke's, Glasgow 1981-82. Died Glasgow 12 June 1982.

O'HARE, JAMES MARIE: Born Renton 1942. Educated Blairs, Valladolid. Ordained Glasgow 1967. St Laurence's, Glasgow 1967-72. St Roch's, Glasgow 1972-79. No further entries.

O'HEA, TIMOTHY: Born and educated Ireland. Ordained Maynooth 1884. Lent to Glasgow. St Alphonsus', Glasgow 1884-86. Airdrie 1886-87. Returned to Ireland 1887 and died there 20 April 1929. (Canning)

O'HERLIHY (Herlihy), DANIEL J: Born and educated Ireland. Ordained Maynooth 1904. Lent to Glasgow. St Augustine's, Coatbridge 1904-11. Returned to Ireland 1911 and died there 6 July 1945. (Canning)

O'KANE, HENRY: Born Ireland. Educated Ireland, Rome. Ordained Rome 1938. Lent to Glasgow. Our Holy Redeemer, Clydebank 1940-41. Returned to Ireland 1941. (Canning)

O'KANE, JEREMIAH: Born Glasgow 1913. Educated St Peter's 1930-37. Ordained Glasgow 1937. Holy Cross, Glasgow 1937-51. C/o Diocesan Office 1951-53. No further entries. Died Ireland 8 March 1987.

O'KANE, ROBERT: Born and educated Ireland. Ordained Derry for Glasgow 1942. St Anne's, Glasgow 1942-49. St Luke's, Glasgow 1949-

51. St Conval's, Glasgow 1951-52. Our Lady and St Margaret's, Glasgow 1952-67. St Joseph's, Woodside, Glasgow 1967-72. Immaculate Conception, Glasgow 1972-83. Died Glasgow 5 May 1983. (Canning)

O'KANE, THOMAS J: Born Ireland. Educated Blairs, St Peter's. Ordained Glasgow 1927. Wishaw 1927-46. St Matthew's, Glasgow 1946-52. St Michael's, Glasgow 1952-67. Retired to Ireland 1967 and died there 25 Feb 1969. (Canning)

O'KEEFE, ANDREW J: Born Ireland. Educated Ireland, Paris. Ordained Paris 1912. Lent to Glasgow. St Anne's, Glasgow 1912-17. Barrhead 1917-23. Returned to Ireland 1923 and died there 10 May 1965. (Canning)

O'KEEFE, DANIEL: Born Ireland. Educated Ireland, St Peter's. Ordained St Peter's College 1924. St Alphonsus', Glasgow 1925-31. St Charles', Glasgow 1931-42. St Vincent de Paul's, Glasgow 1942-47. St Alphonsus', Glasgow 1947-59. Died Glasgow 27 Jan 1959. (Canning)

O'KEEFFE, MICHAEL (1882): Born and educated Ireland. Ordained 1882. Lent to Glasgow. St Mirin's, Paisley 1882-85. Returned to Ireland 1885 and died there 18 Jan 1937. (Canning)

O'KEEFFE, MICHAEL (1948): Born and educated Ireland. Ordained Kilkenny for Glasgow 1948. Holy Cross, Glasgow 1948-60. Helensburgh 1960-62. Our Lady and St George, Glasgow 1962-73. St Dominic's, Glasgow 1973-87. St Eunan's, Clydebank 1987-. (Canning)

O'KELLEHER, TIMOTHY: Born and educated Ireland. Ordained Maynooth 1907. Lent to Glasgow. St Roch's, Glasgow 1907-12. Cardowan 1912-18. Returned to Ireland 1918 and died there 10 March 1964. (Canning)

O'KENNEDY, MICHAEL: Born and educated Ireland. Ordained Maynooth 1907. Lent to Glasgow. Sacred Heart, Glasgow 1908-18. Returned to Ireland 1918 and died there 3 Feb 1965. (Canning)

O'LEARY, CORNELIUS: Born Ireland. Educated Ireland, Rome. Ordained Kilkenny for Glasgow 1926. Sacred Heart, Glasgow 1926-36. St John's, Glasgow 1936-46. St Brendan's, Glasgow 1946-59. St Peter's, Glasgow 1959-74. Died Glasgow 11 Sept 1974. (Canning)

O'LEARY, DANIEL: Born and educated Ireland. Ordained Dublin for Glasgow 1940. Our Lady of Lourdes, Glasgow 1940-41. St Joseph's, Woodside, Glasgow 1941-51. St Constantine's, Glasgow 1951-52. Immaculate Heart of Mary, Glasgow 1952-56. St James's, Glasgow 1956-66. Alexandria 1966-70. St Paul's, Shettleston 1970-84. St Anne's, Glasgow 1984-. (Canning)

O'LEARY, JEREMIAH: Born and educated Ireland. Ordained Dublin for Glasgow 1927. Immaculate Conception, Glasgow 1927-28. Hamilton 1928-34. Alexandria 1934-47. Renton 1947-50. St Michael's, Dumbarton 1950-59. Died Renton 19 March 1959. (Canning)

O'LEARY, JOSEPH: Born Ireland. Educated Ushaw, Douay, St Peter's. Ordained 1901. St Mary's, Greenock 1901-05. Motherwell 1905-14. Strathaven 1914-18. Duntocher 1918-19. Sick leave 1919-20. Airdrie 1920-23. Chaplain, West Thorn Reformatory and Good Shepherd Convent, Dalbeth 1923-24. St Joseph's, Tollcross 1924-26. Chaplain, St Vincent's Home, Langbank 1926-41. St Patrick's, Greenock 1941-46. Chaplain, Langbank 1946-51; thus moving to Paisley diocese. Died Glasgow 31 Jan 1951. (Canning)

O'LEARY, NORBERT: Born and educated Ireland. Ordained Maynooth 1920. Lent to Glasgow. St Patrick's, Dumbarton 1921-23. Returned to Ireland 1923. (Canning)

O'LOUGHLIN, PATRICK: Born and educated Ireland. Ordained Maynooth 1923. Lent to Glasgow. Shotts 1923-26. Our Lady and St Margaret's, Glasgow 1926-29. Returned to Ireland 1929 and died there 6 Feb 1969. (Canning)

O'MAHONY, JOHN (1910): Born and educated Ireland. Ordained Maynooth 1910. Lent to Glasgow. St Mirin's, Paisley 1910-18. Returned to Ireland 1918 and died there 8 March 1951. (Canning)

O'MAHONY, JOHN (1915): Born and educated Ireland. Ordained Maynooth 1915. Lent to Glasgow. St Roch's, Glasgow 1916-17. Returned to Ireland 1917 and died there 26 July 1957. (Canning)

O'MAHONY, PATRICK: Born and educated Ireland. Ordained Carlow 1922. Lent to Glasgow. Holy Cross, Glasgow 1922-27. Returned to Ireland 1927 and died there 22 Aug 1964. (Canning)

O'MAHONY, TIMOTHY: Born and educated Ireland. Ordained Maynooth 1922. Lent to Glasgow. St Anthony's, Glasgow 1922-23. Returned to Ireland 1923. (Canning)

O'MEARA, GERARD J: Born and educated Ireland. Ordained Carlow for Glasgow 1956. Immaculate Heart of Mary, Glasgow 1956-63. No further entries. (Canning)

O'NEIL, WILLIAM JOHN: Born Knockando 1950. Educated Langbank, Blairs, St Peter's. Ordained Kirkintilloch 1974. Our Lady of Consolation, Glasgow 1974-76. St Gregory's, Glasgow 1976-79. No further entries.

O'NEILL, ANTHONY: Born and educated Ireland. Ordained Maynooth 1898. Lent to Glasgow. St Patrick's, Coatbridge 1898-99. Returned to Ireland 1899 and died there 1 May 1930. (Canning)

O'NEILL, JAMES (1887): Born Ireland. Educated Rome. Joined Franciscan Order. Ordained 1887. Came to Scotland as secular priest 1899. Chaplain, Franciscan Convent, Bothwell 1899-1906. Stevenston 1906-15. Died Dublin 8 Jan 1915. (Canning)

O'NEILL, JAMES A (1929): Born Paisley 1905. Educated Blairs 1920-23; St Peter's 1923-29. Ordained Glasgow 1929. St Thomas's, Glasgow 1929-44. Forces chaplain 1944-46. Barrhead 1946-51; thus moving to Paisley diocese. St Andrew's, Greenock 1951-61. Died Greenock 29 Jan 1961.

O'NEILL, JOHN: Born Glasgow 1963. Educated Langbank, Blairs, St Peter's, Chesters. Ordained Glasgow 1988. St Constantine's, Glasgow 1988-.

O'NEILL, SEAN V: Born and educated Ireland, Ordained Wexford for Glasgow 1951. St Patrick's, Glasgow 1951-65. St Saviour's, Glasgow 1965-74. St Paul's, Shettleston 1974-77. St Maria Goretti's, Glasgow 1977-82. Old Kilpatrick 1982-. (Canning)

O'NEILL, THOMAS J: Born Motherwell 1906. Educated St Aloysius' College, Glasgow; Blairs; St Peter's. Ordained Glasgow 1931. St Charles', Glasgow 1931-42. Forces chaplain 1942-46. St Patrick's, Shieldmuir 1946-52; thus moving to Motherwell diocese. Plains 1952-59. Garthamlock 1959-69. Halfway 1969-75. Died Glasgow 19 Dec 1975.

OOGHE, ALPHONSUS: Born Woumen, Belgium 1869. Accepted for Glasgow Archdiocese. Ordained 1895. St Patrick's, Dumbarton 1895-1902. Barrhead 1902-05. St Paul's, Glasgow 1905-14. St Mirin's, Paisley 1914-23. Died Paisley 22 Feb 1923.

O'REILLY, JAMES: Born and educated Ireland. Ordained Dublin for Glasgow 1950. St Constantine's, Glasgow 1950-57. St Laurence's, Glasgow 1957-60. Our Lady and St Margaret's, Glasgow 1960-65. St Jude's, Glasgow 1965-66. St Teresa's, Glasgow 1966-75. Holy Name, Glasgow 1975-78. Cardross 1978-86. Bonhill 1986-. (Canning)

O'REILLY, PHILIP: Born and educated Ireland. Ordained Carlow for Glasgow 1941. Our Holy Redeemer, Clydebank 1942-48. St Anthony's, Glasgow 1948-58. Sick leave 1958-63. St Alphonsus', Glasgow 1963-83. Died Glasgow 18 April 1983. (Canning)

O'RIORDAN, CHARLES: Born and educated Ireland. Ordained Maynooth 1920. Lent to Glasgow. Cadzow 1920-21. St Roch's, Glasgow 1921-27. Returned to Ireland 1927 and died there 1 May 1945. (Canning)

O'RIORDAN, JOHN: Born and educated Ireland. Ordained Kilkenny 1929. Paisley in addresses, but not under any parish, 1929-30. St Charles', Paisley 1930-34. St Mary's, Greenock 1934-38. St Agnes's, Glasgow 1938-40. Our Lady of Lourdes, Glasgow 1940-50. St Barnabas's, Glasgow 1950-51. Old Kilpatrick 1951-75. Died Cork 25 April 1975. (Canning)

O'RIORDAN, MICHAEL L: Born Ireland. Educated Ireland, St Peter's. Ordained Glasgow 1925. St Mary's, Paisley 1925-28. Went to Plymouth diocese; later to Portsmouth diocese. Died Isle of Wight 26 April 1965. (Canning)

O'ROURKE, (John) FRANCIS: Born Clydebank 1928. Educated Campion House, Osterley; St Peter's. Ordained Glasgow 1955. St Michael's, Glasgow 1955-63. Balloch 1963-76. St Mary Immaculate, Glasgow 1976-81. St Constantine's, Glasgow 1981-84. St Luke's, Glasgow 1984-.

O'ROURKE, THOMAS: Born Glasgow 1937. Educated St Michael's College, Irvine; St Joseph's High School, Kilmarnock; Valladolid. Ordained Valladolid 1961. St Philomena's, Glasgow 1961-68. Professor, Langbank 1968-76. Diocesan Centre 1976-82. Holy Family, Kirkintilloch 1982-87. St Peter's, Dumbarton 1987-.

ORR, WILLIAM: Ordained 1896. St Patrick's, Glasgow 1896-97. Baillieston 1897-1903. St Patrick's, Dumbarton 1903-04. Carfin 1904-06. Motherwell 1906-18. Leave of absence from 1918. Died Germany 17 Jan 1941.

OSBORNE, PATRICK: Born and educated Ireland. Ordained Waterford for Glasgow 1959. St Joseph's, Woodside, Glasgow 1959-67. St Thomas's, Glasgow 1967-72. Corpus Christi, Glasgow 1972-79. Spiritual Director, St Peter's College 1979-83. Our Lady and St George, Glasgow 1983-84. St Joseph's, Woodside, Glasgow, winding up parish, 1984-85. Diocesan Pastoral Centre, Glasgow 1985-86. Sacred Heart, Cumbernauld 1986-. (Canning)

O'SHEA, JOHN: Born and educated Ireland. Ordained Waterford 1899. Lent to Glasgow. St Peter's, Glasgow 1900-07. Returned to Ireland 1907 and died there 1944. (Canning)

O'SHEA, TIMOTHY: Born Ireland. Educated Ireland, Paris. Ordained Killarney 1897. Lent to Glasgow. St John's, Port Glasgow 1897-1905. Returned to Ireland 1905 and died there 12 July 1943. (Canning)

O'SULLIVAN, DANIEL (1895): Born and educated Ireland. Ordained Maynooth 1895. Lent to Glasgow; later got exeat to remain there. Sacred Heart, Glasgow 1895-1904. Milngavie 1904-09. St Joseph's, Tollcross 1909-26. Burnbank 1926-32. Died Glasgow 26 Oct 1932. (Canning)

O'SULLIVAN, DANIEL (1929): Born and educated Ireland. Ordained Kilkenny for Glasgow 1929. St Patrick's, Coatbridge 1929-33. St Roch's, Glasgow 1933-36. Sick leave 1936-37. Helensburgh 1937-44. Went to American mission. Was excardinated for Tucson diocese 1961. (Canning)

O'SULLIVAN, JEREMIAH: Born Ireland. Educated Ireland, St Peter's. Ordained Glasgow 1927. Saltcoats 1927. Airdrie 1927-31. St John's, Port Glasgow 1931-48. St Fergus's, Paisley 1948-59; thus moving to Paisley diocese. Died Glasgow 2 March 1959. (Canning)

O'SULLIVAN, JOHN M (1946): Born and educated Ireland. Ordained Wexford for Glasgow 1946. St Anthony's, Glasgow 1946-48. Our Holy Redeemer, Clydebank 1948-52. St Bernadette's, Glasgow 1952-53. Went to American mission 1953. (Canning)
Note: see 'O'Sullivan, Sean' below

O'SULLIVAN, JOHN (1954): Born Dumbarton 1920. Educated Osterley, St Peter's. Ordained Glasgow 1954. Sacred Heart, Glasgow 1954-57. St Vincent de Paul's, Glasgow 1957-66. St Flannan's, Kirkintilloch 1966-76. Our Lady of Consolation, Glasgow 1976-77. St Agnes's, Glasgow 1977-82. St Monica's, Glasgow 1982-.

O'SULLIVAN, MICHAEL J: Born and educated Ireland. Ordained Kilkenny for Glasgow 1929. Newton 1929-46. St Constantine's, Glasgow 1946-51. Renton 1951-74. Retired 1974. Died Ireland 10 Sept 1977. (Canning)

O'SULLIVAN, PATRICK J (1918): Born and educated Ireland. Ordained Maynooth 1918. Lent to Glasgow. Either St Alphonsus', Glasgow or Burnbank 1918-19: Directories have him in both places; Canning has him in Glasgow. Returned to Ireland 1919 and died there 14 Dec 1966. (Canning)

O'SULLIVAN, PATRICK J (1937): Born and educated Ireland. Ordained Maynooth 1937. Lent to Glasgow. Hamilton 1937-40. Returned to Ireland 1940 and died there 9 Feb 1962. (Canning)

O'SULLIVAN, PETER: Born Ireland. Educated Ireland, Paris. Ordained Maynooth 1918. Lent to Glasgow. St Patrick's, Coatbridge 1918-23. Returned to Ireland 1923 and died there 4 Nov 1978. (Canning)

O'SULLIVAN, SEAN: Ordained 1946. St Bernadette's, Glasgow 1953-59. No further entries.
Note: This may be the same man as 'O'Sullivan, John M (1946)', see above.

O'SULLIVAN, TIMOTHY (1893): Born and educated Ireland. Ordained Maynooth 1893. Lent to Glasgow. Rutherglen 1893-97. Returned to Ireland 1897 and died there 3 Nov 1945. (Canning)

O'SULLIVAN, TIMOTHY (1899): Born and educated Ireland. Ordained Maynooth 1899. Lent to Glasgow. St Michael's, Glasgow 1916-21. No further entries. (Canning)

O'SULLIVAN, VINCENT T: Born and educated Ireland. Ordained 1928. Sacred Heart, Glasgow 1928-48. Good Shepherd, Glasgow 1948-55. St Charles', Glasgow 1955-79. Died Glasgow 3 Nov 1979. (Canning)

PARKINSON, HENRY: Born Ireland. Ordained for Kiltegan Fathers 1957 and served in Kenya. Came to Scotland 1967; joined Glasgow Archdiocese as a secular priest. Bearsden 1968-79. St Peter's, Glasgow 1979-86. St Michael's, Dumbarton 1986-. (Canning)

PATERSON, ROBERT: Ordained 1894. St Anthony's, Glasgow 1894-1902. Cleland 1902-06. St Mark's, Carntyne 1906-12. Shotts 1912-17. St Anne's, Glasgow 1917-23. Blantyre 1923-45. Died Glasgow 15 Sept 1945.

PETRANSKIS, JOSEPH: Ordained 1916. Almost certainly serving Lithuanian community: stationed at Mossend 1920-34. No further entries.

PHELAN, JAMES: Born and educated Ireland. Ordained Waterford 1924. Lent to Glasgow. St Aloysius', Glasgow 1924-26. St Mary's, Greenock 1926-27. Returned to Ireland 1927. (Canning)

PIRRIE, FREDERICK R: Born Coatbridge 1877. Educated St Aloysius' College, Glasgow; Blairs 1892-95; St Peter's 1895-1904. Ordained 1904. St Alphonsus', Glasgow 1904-05. Professor, Blairs 1905-14. Vice-rector, Blairs 1914-15. Glenboig 1915-18. Vice-rector, Blairs 1918-19. St Charles', Paisley 1919-23. St Mary's, Paisley 1923-57; thus moving to Paisley diocese. Died Jersey 1 Sept 1957.

PLUNKETT, BERNARD: Born and educated Ireland. Ordained Maynooth 1924. Lent to Glasgow. St Anne's, Glasgow 1924-25. Returned to Ireland 1925 and died there 7 March 1970. (Canning)

PLUNKETT, PATRICK: Born Wishaw 1880. Educated Blairs 1901-03; Valladolid 1903-11. Ordained Valladolid 1911. Our Lady and St Margaret's, Glasgow 1911-29. Kilbirnie 1929-36. Cadzow 1936-39. St Columbkille's, Rutherglen 1939-57; thus moving to Motherwell diocese. Retired 1957. Died Wishaw 23 Jan 1963.

POWER, DAVID (1910): Born and educated Ireland. Ordained Maynooth 1910. Lent to Glasgow. St Peter's, Glasgow 1910-18. Returned to Ireland 1918 and died there 23 April 1971. (Canning)

POWER, DAVID (1920): Born and educated Ireland. Ordained Waterford 1920. Lent to Glasgow. St Patrick's, Glasgow 1920-21. St Laurence's, Greenock 1921. St Patrick's, Shieldmuir 1921-25. Returned to Ireland 1925 and died there 24 Feb 1976. (Canning)

POWER, DAVID LEO (1928): Born Ireland. Educated Ireland, St Peter's. Ordained 1928. St Mary's, Glasgow 1928-32. Holy Family, Kirkintilloch 1932-35. Renfrew 1935-37. Mossend 1937-42. Went to Portsmouth diocese. (Canning)

POWER, DENIS: Born Ireland. Educated Ireland, Spain. Ordained 1919. Lent to Glasgow. Our Holy Redeemer, Clydebank 1919-25. Returned to Ireland 1925 and died there 6 Feb 1968. (Canning)

POWER, JOHN J: Born Ireland. Educated Ireland, St Peter's. Ordained Glasgow 1913. St Paul's, Shettleston 1913-14. Saltcoats 1914-20. St Anne's, Glasgow 1920-24. Jersey 1924-25. Newton 1925-26. St Patrick's, Dumbarton 1926-28. Went to Birmingham archdiocese 1928. Died Dublin 15 July 1969. (Canning)

POWER, JOSEPH: Born and educated Ireland. Ordained Thurles 1940. Glasgow Cathedral 1940. Holy Cross, Glasgow 1940-41. St Michael's, Glasgow 1941-52. St Robert's, Glasgow 1952-65. Died Glasgow 13 April 1965. (Canning)

POWER, MICHAEL: Born and educated Ireland. Ordained Waterford 1920. Lent to Glasgow. Sacred Heart, Glasgow 1920-25. Returned to Ireland 1925 and died there 11 Feb 1955. (Canning)

POWER, NICHOLAS (1879): Ordained 1879. St Mirin's, Paisley 1879-81. St Anthony's, Glasgow 1881-82. No further entries.

POWER, NICHOLAS (1914): Born Ireland. Educated Ireland, Rome. Ordained Rome 1914. Lent to Glasgow. St Patrick's, Glasgow 1915-19. Returned to Ireland 1919 and died there 23 Jan 1966. (Canning)

POWER, RICHARD: Born and educated Ireland. Ordained Maynooth 1925. Lent to Glasgow. Sacred Heart, Glasgow 1925-29. Returned to Ireland 1929 and died there 1 March 1970. (Canning)

PRENDERGAST, JAMES F (1903): Born and educated Ireland. Ordained Maynooth 1903. Lent to Glasgow. St Patrick's, Glasgow 1903-09. Returned to Ireland 1909 and died there 8 Nov 1950. (Canning)

PRENDERGAST, JAMES P (1904): Born and educated Ireland. Ordained Maynooth 1904. Lent to Glasgow. St Anthony's, Glasgow 1905. St Mary's, Glasgow 1905-11. Returned to Ireland 1911 and died there 3 Oct 1937. (Canning)

PRENDIVILLE, EDWARD: Born and educated Ireland. Ordained Maynooth 1904. Lent to Glasgow. St Peter's, Glasgow 1904-11. Returned to Ireland 1911 and died there 15 Oct 1951. (Canning)

PURCELL, LEONARD ANTHONY: Born Glasgow 1958. Educated St Mungo's Academy, Glasgow; joined Strathclyde Police; educated for priesthood St Peter's, Chesters. Ordained Rome 1985. St Robert's, Glasgow 1985-.

QUIGLEY, DAVID: Born Glasgow 1887. Educated Blairs 1904-08; Valladolid 1908-17. Ordained Valladolid 1917. Longriggend 1917. St Patrick's, Glasgow 1917-26. Holy Family, Kirkintilloch 1926-37. Linwood 1937-42. St Paul's, Glasgow 1942-59. Died Whiteinch 3 June 1959.

QUILLINAN, MATTHEW P: Born Ireland. Educated Ireland, St Peter's. Ordained Glasgow 1913. St Joseph's, Tollcross 1913-24. St Agnes's, Glasgow 1924-30. Carluke 1930-37. Renton 1937-39. Cadzow 1939-47. Died Glasgow 20 Jan 1948. (Canning)

QUINLAN, MARTIN (1899): Born and educated Ireland. Ordained Maynooth 1899. Lent to Glasgow. St Anthony's, Glasgow 1899-1907. Returned to Ireland 1907 and died there 30 Nov 1953. (Canning)

QUINLAN, MARTIN (1942): Born and educated Ireland. Ordained Dublin for Glasgow 1942. St Charles', Glasgow 1942-57. Our Holy Redeemer, Clydebank 1957-67. St James's, Glasgow 1967-76. St Pius X, Glasgow 1976-. (Canning)

QUINLAN, MICHAEL: Born and educated Ireland. Ordained Maynooth 1920. Lent to Glasgow. Burnbank 1920-21. Alexandria 1921-25. St Mirin's, Paisley 1925-27. Returned to Ireland 1927 and died there 31 July 1971. (Canning)

QUINN, JAMES EDWARD (1917): see Dunkeld diocese

QUINN, JAMES (1942): Born Clydebank 1915. Educated Blairs 1931-35; St Peter's 1935-42. Ordained Glasgow 1942. Blantyre 1942-46. St Michael's, Dumbarton 1946-60. St Vincent de Paul's, Glasgow 1960-65. St Martin's, Glasgow 1965-67. St Joseph's, Cumbernauld 1967-74. St Gabriel's, Glasgow 1974-82. Retired 1982.

QUINN, JOHN GERARD (1931): Born Motherwell 1900. Educated St Aloysius' College, Glasgow 1914-25; St Peter's 1925-31. Ordained

Glasgow 1931. Glasgow Cathedral 1931-39. Forces chaplain 1939-45. Our Lady and St Margaret's, Glasgow 1945-52. St Matthew's, Glasgow 1952-55. Died Glasgow 25 July 1955.

QUINN, JOHN PATRICK (1983): Born Clydebank 1959. Educated Langbank; Blairs; Scots College, Rome. Ordained Clydebank 1983. Our Holy Redeemer, Clydebank 1983. St Peter's, Glasgow 1983. St Barnabas's, Glasgow 1983. Further studies, Rome 1983-84. St Joseph's, Cumbernauld 1984-88. St Margaret Mary's, Glasgow 1988-.

QUINN, JOSEPH: see Paisley diocese

QUINN, THOMAS: Ordained 1958. St Aloysius', Glasgow 1971-74. No further entries.

QUINN, VINCENT: Born Thornliebank 1944. Educated Blairs, St Peter's. Ordained St Peter's College 1968. St Barnabas's, Glasgow 1968-71. Sacred Heart, Cumbernauld 1971-82. No further entries.

RACEWICZ, ANTONY: Ordained 1898. Served Lithuanian community: stationed at Mossend 1905-06. No further entry.

RAE, JOHN: Born Carfin 1921. Educated St Mary's School, Whifflet; Our Lady's High School, Motherwell; Scots College, Rome 1937-40; St Peter's 1940-44. Ordained St Peter's College 1944. Sacred Heart, Glasgow 1944. Further studies, Oxford University 1944-48. Professor, St Peter's College 1948-59. Died Cardross 11 June 1959.

RAWLINGS, FREDERICK: Born and educated Ireland. Ordained Carlow 1941. Our Lady and St Margaret's, Glasgow 1941-66. Our Lady of Consolation, Glasgow 1966-78. Retired to Ireland 1978. (Canning)

REGAN, JOSEPH: Born and educated Ireland. Ordained Maynooth 1936. Lent to Glasgow. St Luke's, Glasgow 1936-40. Returned to Ireland 1940. (Canning)

REIFENRATH, ALOYSIUS: Born Herdorf, Germany 1864. Educated Montabaur Gymnasium 1883-87; St Peter's 1887-91. Ordained St Peter's College 1891. Johnstone 1891-95. St Mary's, Glasgow 1895-98. Chaplain, Barlinnie Prison and St Joseph's Home, Glasgow 1898-1900. Neilston 1900-24. Johnstone 1924-45. Died Glasgow 11 Sept 1945.

REILLY, BRIAN CHARLES: Born Glasgow 1950. Educated St Aloysius' College, Glasgow; Glasgow University; Scots College, Rome. Ordained Glasgow 1977. Our Holy Redeemer, Clydebank 1977. Further studies, Rome 1977-79. Holy Cross, Glasgow 1979-82. Professor, St Peter's College 1982-85. St Margaret's, Clydebank 1985-.

REILLY, JAMES VINCENT: Born Paisley 1919. Educated St Mirin's Academy, Paisley; Blairs; St Peter's. Ordained 1945. St Stephen's, Dalmuir 1945-49. St Anne's, Glasgow 1949-60. St Laurence's, Glasgow 1960-67. St Mary Immaculate, Glasgow 1967-70. Alexandria 1970-75. St Barnabas's, Glasgow 1975-78. St Lucy's, Cumbernauld 1978-84. Retired 1984.

REILLY, PATRICK: Born Stevenston 1884. Educated Blairs 1898-1903; Issy 1903-05; St Sulpice 1905-08. Ordained Paris 1908. St John the Baptist's, Uddingston 1908-17. Croy 1917-18. Coatdyke 1918-24. Harthill 1924-27. St Ninian's, Glasgow 1927-41. Died Glasgow 10 March 1941.

REILLY, THOMAS: Born Glasgow 1911. Educated St Aloysius' College, Glasgow 1923-28; Blairs 1928-30; St Peter's 1930-36. Ordained Glasgow 1936. St Augustine's, Coatbridge 1936-37. St Mary's, Glasgow 1937-44. Croy 1944-51. Duntocher 1951-55. St Constantine's, Glasgow 1955-58. Sacred Heart, Cumbernauld 1958-60. St John Ogilvie's, Glasgow 1960-78. St Monica's, Glasgow 1978-82. Died Glasgow 7 March 1982.

RENFREW, CHARLES: Born Glasgow 1929. Educated St Aloysius' College, Glasgow; Scots College, Rome. Ordained Rome 1953. Immaculate Conception, Glasgow 1953-56. Professor, Blairs 1956-57. Procurator, Blairs 1957-61. Rector, Langbank 1961-74. Made Vicar General 1974. No parish 1974-75. Chaplain, Bon Secours Convent, Glasgow 1975-89. Consecrated Bishop Auxiliary for Glasgow 1977.

RENUCCI, BRUNO: Born Glasgow 1921. Educated St Mungo's Academy, Glasgow; Campion House, Osterley; Propaganda, Rome. Ordained Rome 1954. St Mary Immaculate, Glasgow 1955-70. Our Lady and St Margaret's, Glasgow 1970-78. Our Holy Redeemer, Clydebank 1978-89. Chaplain, Bon Secours Convent, Glasgow 1989-.

RICE, PATRICK: Born Rutherglen 1913. Educated St Columbkille's School, Rutherglen; Sacred Heart Juniorate, Dumfries; Blairs 1928-31; St Peter's 1931-38. Ordained Glasgow 1938. Dalry 1938-39. Christ the King, Glasgow 1939-40. St Patrick's, Glasgow 1940-46. Holy Family, Port Glasgow 1946-51; thus moving to Paisley diocese. Chaplain, Royal Navy 1951-59. Houston 1959-61. Clarkston 1961-66. Holy Family, Port Glasgow 1966-71. C/o Diocesan Office 1971-72. St Anthony's, Johnstone 1972-75. Retired 1975. Died Spain 3 Oct 1983.

RICHEN, LAURENCE: Ordained 1879. Glasgow Cathedral 1881-82. Motherwell 1882-84. Professor, St Peter's College 1884-87. No further entries.

RIORDAN, CHARLES: Born and educated Ireland. Ordained Maynooth 1920. Lent to Glasgow. St Roch's, Glasgow 1921-27. Returned to Ireland 1927 and died there 1 May 1945. (Canning)

RITCHIE, GEORGE: Born Huntly 1859. Educated Blairs 1871-76; Valladolid 1876-82. Ordained Glasgow 1882. St John's, Port Glasgow 1882-89. Milngavie 1889-91. St Patrick's, Shieldmuir 1891-1914. Glasgow Cathedral 1914-23. Died Glasgow 16 Aug 1923.

RITCHIE, JOHN: Born Huntly 1857. Educated Blairs 1869-74; Scots College, Rome 1874-81. Ordained Rome 1880. Professor, St Peter's College 1881-99. St Michael's, Glasgow 1899-1900. Diocesan secretary 1900-29. Retired 1929. Died Glasgow 7 May 1938.

ROBERTS, JOHN: Born Glasgow 1928. Educated Blairs, St Peter's. Ordained Glasgow 1953. St Patrick's, Glasgow 1953-59. St Eunan's, Clydebank 1959-61. Our Lady of Lourdes, Glasgow 1961-67. St Laurence's, Glasgow 1967-81. Our Lady of Fatima, Glasgow 1981-84. St Columba's, Glasgow 1984-.

ROBERTSON, DONALD: Born Glasgow 1903. Educated St Aloysius' College, Glasgow; Blairs; St Peter's 1923-29. Ordained Glasgow 1929. St Peter's, Glasgow 1929-50. St Simon's, Glasgow 1950-72. Retired 1972. Died Baillieston 15 Sept 1973.

ROCHE, JOHN (1903): Born and educated Ireland. Ordained Maynooth 1903. Lent to Glasgow. St Charles', Glasgow 1903-08. Returned to Ireland 1908 and died there 29 July 1949. (Canning)

ROCHE, JOHN (1910): Born and educated Ireland. Ordained Maynooth 1910. Lent to Glasgow. St Anne's, Glasgow 1910-20. Returned to Ireland 1920 and died there 29 Dec 1960. (Canning)

ROCHE, MICHAEL: Born and educated Ireland. Ordained Maynooth 1915. Lent to Glasgow. St Mary's, Greenock 1916-17. Returned to Ireland 1917 and died there 25 June 1964. (Canning)

ROCHEAD, JAMES: Born Leith 1857. Educated Blairs 1871-75; Valladolid 1875-82. Ordained Palencia 1882. Maryhill 1882-86. Johnstone 1886-89. Rutherglen 1889-90. Rutherglen in addresses, but not under parishes, 1890-91. In Salford diocese and USA 1891-94. St Peter's, Glasgow 1894-99. Rutherglen 1899-1903. Died Glasgow 13 May 1903.

ROGAN, ELLIS P: Born Glasgow 1863. Educated Blairs 1876-81; Douay 1881-82; Scots College, Rome 1882-88. Ordained Rome 1887. St Mary's, Greenock 1888-90. Professor, St Peter's College 1890-1900. St Michael's, Glasgow 1900-08. St Mirin's, Paisley 1908-14. St Patrick's, Shieldmuir 1914-19. Died Shieldmuir 22 April 1919.

ROGAN, JOHN: Born Tollcross, Glasgow 1901. Educated Blairs 1914-21; St Peter's 1921-27. Ordained St Peter's College 1927. St Peter's, Glasgow

1927-31. Chaplain, Kenmure Industrial School 1931-32. Leave of absence 1932-33. Alexandria 1933-34. Hamilton 1934-37. Leave of absence 1937-40. St Patrick's, Coatbridge 1940. Died Coatbridge 30 Dec 1940.

ROGER, JOHN: Born Maryhill 1901. Educated Blairs 1914-20; Valladolid 1920-27. Ordained Valladolid 1927. St Mirin's, Paisley 1927-37. St Mary's, Coatbridge 1937-47. Carluke 1947-49; thus moving to Motherwell diocese. Cardowan 1949-58. Died Cardowan 9 March 1958.

ROGERS, GERARD: Born Glasgow 1908. Educated St Mungo's Academy, Glasgow; St Peter's; Scots College, Rome. Ordained Rome 1931. St John's, Glasgow 1931-32. Further studies, Rome 1932-35. St Patrick's, Dumbarton 1935-36. Further studies, Rome 1936-37. St Patrick's, Dumbarton 1937-39. At Chaplaincy, Glasgow University (not acting as chaplain) 1939-40. St Thomas's, Glasgow 1940-42. C/o St Peter's College 1942-45. Chaplain, Franciscan Convent, Bothwell 1945-49; thus moving to Motherwell diocese. Vicar General, Diocesan Office, 1949-56. Motherwell Cathedral 1956-60. Judge Prelate of Sacred Roman Rota 1960-74. Died Rome 10 Aug 1975.

ROGERS, HERBERT G: Born Glasgow 1903. Educated St Mungo's Academy, Glasgow; Blairs 1921-23; Scots College, Rome 1923-31. Ordained Rome 1930. St Agnes's, Glasgow 1931-38. St Mary's, Greenock 1938-40. Saltcoats 1940-42. Chaplain, St Mungo's School, Mauchline 1942-46. Chaplain, Convent of Mercy, Baillieston 1946-49; thus moving to Motherwell diocese. To California for health 1949. Died California 25 Aug 1973.

ROGERS, PATRICK: Born Glasgow 1903. Educated Blairs 1918-23; Scots College, Rome 1923-30. Ordained Rome 1929. Immaculate Conception, Glasgow 1930-46. Spiritual Director, Blairs College 1946-55. St Aloysius', Glasgow 1955-57. Died Dundee 20 Feb 1957.

RONAN, JAMES: Born and educated Ireland. Ordained Maynooth 1919. Lent to Glasgow. St Mary's, Greenock 1919-25. Returned to Ireland 1925. (Canning)

RONAYNE, MAURICE: Born and educated Ireland. Ordained Maynooth 1900. Lent to Glasgow. St Peter's, Glasgow 1900-09. Returned to Ireland 1909 and died there 20 Aug 1938. (Canning)

ROONEY, JOHN A: Born Glasgow 1898. Educated St Mungo's Academy, Glasgow; Blairs 1914-19; St Peter's 1919-24. Ordained Glasgow 1924. Saltcoats 1924-32. Airdrie 1932-34. Glenboig 1934-38. St Mirin's, Paisley 1938-42. St Bridget's, Baillieston 1942-50; thus moving to Motherwell diocese. St Bride's, Cambuslang 1950-57. St Columbkille's, Rutherglen 1957-74. Died London 9 June 1974.

ROSS, JOHN: see Dunkeld diocese

ROSSI, GAETANO: Born Palestrina, Rome 1916. Educated at Diocesan Seminary, Palestrina 1927-32; Diocesan Seminary, Veroli 1932-33; Collegio Leonismo 1933-37; St Peter's 1937-39. Ordained Glasgow 1939. St John's, Port Glasgow 1939-40. Glasgow, no parish, 1940-41. Holy Cross, Glasgow 1941-62. St Joseph's, Woodside, Glasgow 1962-67. St Anne's, Glasgow 1967-74. St Peter's, Glasgow 1974-.

ROTA, FRANCIS: Ordained 1913. Our Holy Redeemer, Clydebank 1932-40. Motherwell 1940-47. Died Italy 7 Dec 1947.

ROURKE, THOMAS B: Born Lanark 1887. Educated Blairs 1902-05; Valladolid 1905-07; St Peter's 1907-13. Ordained Glasgow 1913. Partick 1913-15. St Anthony's, Glasgow 1915-20. Chaplain, St Vincent's Home, Langbank 1920-23. St Patrick's, Shieldmuir 1923-30. Harthill 1930-32. Chapelhall 1932-41. St Ninian's, Glasgow 1941-57. Retired 1957. Died Lanark 2 Nov 1964.

ROWAN, NICHOLAS: Born and educated Ireland. Ordained Kilkenny for Glasgow 1947. St John's, Glasgow 1947-67. St Charles', Glasgow 1967-72. Twechar 1972-73. St Peter's, Dumbarton 1973-87. St Brigid's, Glasgow 1987-. (Canning)

RUANE, AUSTIN: Born and educated Ireland. Ordained Wexford for Glasgow 1949. Helensburgh 1949-57. Sacred Heart, Glasgow 1957-72. Holy Family, Kirkintilloch 1972-73. Retired 1973. Died Ireland 20 Dec 1981. (Canning)

RYAN, CHRISTOPHER JOHN: Born Clydebank 1943. Educated Blairs; Scots College, Rome. Ordained Clydebank 1968. Our Lady and St George, Glasgow 1969-72. Further studies, Cambridge University 1972-80. Pontifical Institute of Medieval Studies, Toronto 1980-86. No further entries.

RYAN, EDMUND: Born and educated Ireland. Ordained Maynooth 1925. Lent to Glasgow. St John's, Glasgow 1925. St Charles', Glasgow 1925-26. Govan 1926-27. Returned to Ireland 1927. (Canning)

RYAN, EDWARD: Born and educated Ireland. Ordained Waterford 1921. Lent to Glasgow. Sacred Heart, Glasgow 1921-26. Returned to Ireland 1926. (Canning)

RYAN, GEORGE J: Born and educated Ireland. Ordained Derry 1901. Lent to Glasgow. St Mary Immaculate, Glasgow 1902-04. St Alphonsus', Glasgow 1904-05. Returned to Ireland 1905 and died there 5 Jan 1941. (Canning)

RYAN, JAMES: Born Clydebank 1937. Educated St Patrick's High School, Dumbarton; St Peter's. Ordained St Peter's College 1967. Our Lady of Consolation, Glasgow 1967-74. St Patrick's, Dumbarton 1974-83. Spiritual Director, Valladolid 1983-.

RYAN, JOHN (1913): Born Ireland. Educated Ireland, St Peter's. Ordained Glasgow 1913. St John's, Port Glasgow 1913-30. Carluke 1930. Glenboig 1930-34. St Mungo's, Greenock 1934-44. St Alphonsus', Glasgow 1944-45. Croy 1945-54. Died Glasow 22 Oct 1954. (Canning)

RYAN, JOHN (1950): Born and educated Ireland. Ordained Kilkenny for Glasgow 1950. St John's, Glasgow 1950-57. St Paul's, Shettleston 1957-59. St Philomena's, Glasgow 1959-60. To California 1960. Excardinated from Glasgow 1963. (Canning)

RYAN, PATRICK: Born and educated Ireland. Ordained 1892. Lent to Glasgow; later got exeat to remain there. St John's, Glasgow 1892-99. Saltcoats 1899-1905. St Luke's, Glasgow 1905-08. St Aloysius', Glasgow 1908-15. St John's, Glasgow 1915-29. Died Glasgow 10 April 1929. (Canning)

RYAN, ROBERT: Born and educated Ireland. Ordained Waterford for Glasgow 1949. Good Shepherd, Glasgow 1949-55. Spiritual Director, St Peter's College 1955-57. Died Waterford 11 Sept 1957. (Canning)

RYAN, WILLIAM: Born and educated Ireland. Ordained Thurles 1912. Lent to Glasgow. St Mary's, Greenock 1912-15. Became Forces chaplain 1916. (Canning)

RYNN, MICHAEL: Born and educated Ireland. Ordained for Glasgow 1928. St Mary's, Paisley 1928-29. St Roch's, Glasgow 1929-33. Kilbirnie 1933-48; thus moving to Galloway diocese. Kirkconnell 1948-53. Birnieknowe 1953-61. Beith 1961-66. Retired to Clonakilty 1966 and died there 22 Feb 1978. (Canning)

RYNN, SEAN: Ordained 1965. Good Shepherd, Glasgow 1968-70. No further entries.

SAVAGE, MICHAEL COLIN: Born Glasgow 1959. Educated St Aloysius' College, Glasgow; St Peter's. Ordained Glasgow 1983. Holy Family, Kirkintilloch 1983-88. St Flannan's, Kirkintilloch 1988-.

SCANLAN, WILLIAM: Born and educated Ireland. Ordained Maynooth 1899. Lent to Glasgow. St Patrick's, Shieldmuir 1899-1902. Lent to Portsmouth diocese 1902-05. Returned to Ireland 1905 and died there 30 March 1951. (Canning)

SCANLON (Scanlan), JAMES J: Born and educated Ireland. Ordained 1918. Lent to Glasgow. St Patrick's, Glasgow 1918-23. Airdrie 1923-25. Returned to Ireland 1925 and died there 24 Dec 1950. (Canning)

SCANLON, JOHN J: Born Ireland. Educated Ireland, St Peter's. Ordained Glasgow 1919. St Mary's, Greenock 1919-30. St Joseph's, Woodside, Glasgow 1930-38. Clarkston 1938-44. St Mungo's, Greenock 1944-49; thus moving to Paisley diocese. St Patrick's, Greenock 1949-57. Chaplain, Little Sisters of the Poor, Greenock 1957-64. Died Greenock 29 Jan 1964. (Canning)

SCANNELL, DANIEL: Born and educated Ireland. Ordained Cobh 1900. Lent to Glasgow. St Alphonsus', Glasgow 1900-12. Returned to Ireland 1912 and died there 17 Nov 1931. (Canning)

SCANNELL, DENIS: Born Ireland. Educated Ireland, Blairs, Valladolid. Ordained Valladolid 1902. Our Holy Redeemer, Clydebank 1902-14. No address given in Directories; Canning has Croy; 1914-15. St Patrick's, Coatbridge 1915-23. Cadzow 1923-36. Kilbirnie 1936-41. Died Kilbirnie 29 May 1941. (Canning)

SCANNELL, JOHN: Born Ireland. Educated Ireland, Douay. Ordained 1890. Offered his services to Glasgow. St John's, Port Glasgow 1890-92; caught typhus, which permanently affected his health. Glasgow Cathedral 1892-97. Larkhall 1897-1904. Mossend 1904-07. Died Mossend 4 July 1907. (Canning)

SCULLION, DANIEL: Born Dumbarton 1905. Educated Blairs 1921-24; St Peter's 1924-26; Scots College, Rome 1926-31. Ordained Rome 1931. St Patrick's, Glasgow 1931-53. Helensburgh 1953-56. Died Glasgow 15 May 1956.

SEWARDS, RICHARD HEWITT: Born Isle of Wight 1920. RAF gunner in war. Educated St Peter's. Ordained Glasgow 1960. St Saviour's, Glasgow 1960-61. Holy Cross, Glasgow 1961-64. On mission, mainly in New Guinea, from 1964. Died New Guinea 18 April 1982.

SEXTON, PETER: Born and educated Ireland. Ordained Kilkenny for Glasgow 1925. St Anne's, Glasgow 1925-32. St Patrick's, Greenock 1932-45. St Catherine's, Harthill 1945-50; thus moving to Motherwell diocese. St Bernadette's, Motherwell 1950-59. St Patrick's, Coatbridge 1959-62. Died Ireland 10 Aug 1962. (Canning)

SHARKEY, MICHAEL: Born Glasgow 1959. Educated Langbank, Blairs, St Peter's. Ordained Glasgow 1983. St Vincent de Paul's, Glasgow 1983. St Joseph's, Tollcross 1983-.

SHARKEY, THOMAS: Born Glasgow 1910. Educated Blairs 1926-28; Scots College, Rome 1928-36. Ordained Rome 1935. Carfin 1936-41. St Saviour's, Glasgow 1941-44. Forces chaplain 1944-47. St Mary's, Glasgow 1947-53. St Ninian's, Glasgow 1953-55. Died Glasgow 26 Nov 1955.

SHAW, GEORGE PAUL: see Aberdeen diocese

SHAW, WILLIAM: see Aberdeen diocese

SHEARY, JOHN JOSEPH (1965): Born and educated Ireland. Ordained Wexford for Glasgow 1965. Good Shepherd, Glasgow 1965-66. Our Lady and St Margaret's, Glasgow 1966-71. Faifley 1971-78. Spiritual Director, St Peter's College 1978-79. Died Ireland 29 Jan 1979. (Canning)

SHEAREY, JOHN (1969): Born Ireland. Educated Ireland, Rome. Ordained Nenagh for Glasgow 1969. St Matthew's, Glasgow 1969-75. Vice-rector, Scots College, Rome 1975-78. St Pius X, Glasgow 1978-82. Helensburgh 1982-87. Immaculate Conception, Glasgow 1987-. (Canning)

SHEARY, JOSEPH: Born and educated Ireland. Ordained Wexford for Glasgow 1942. St Thomas's, Glasgow 1942. St Luke's, Glasgow 1942-47. St Laurence's, Greenock 1947-50; thus moving to Paisley diocese. Barrhead 1950-66. Howwood 1966-68. St Fergus's, Paisley 1968-69. Died 30 Oct 1969. (Canning)

SHEARY, PATRICK J: Born and educated Ireland. Ordained Wexford for Glasgow 1935. St Stephen's, Dalmuir 1935-41. Croy 1941-48. St Mary's, Glasgow 1948-55. St Brigid's, Glasgow 1955-83. Died Glasgow 1 July 1983. (Canning)

SHEEHAN, DANIEL V: Born and educated Ireland. Ordained 1920. Lent to Glasgow. Johnstone 1920-27. Returned to Ireland 1927 and died there 17 Jan 1938. (Canning)

SHEEHAN, DENIS M (1915): Born and educated Ireland. Ordained Maynooth 1915. Lent to Glasgow. Motherwell 1916-21. Returned to Ireland 1921 and died there 22 Nov 1941. (Canning)

SHEEHAN, DENIS (1918): Born and educated Ireland. Ordained Maynooth 1918. Lent to Glasgow. St Anthony's, Glasgow 1918. St John's, Glasgow 1918-25. Returned to Ireland 1925 and died there 6 Oct 1976. (Canning)

SHEEHAN, JAMES: Born and educated Ireland. Ordained Carlow for Glasgow 1947. St Laurence's, Greenock 1947-57; thus moving to Paisley diocese. St Charles', Paisley 1957-71. Neilston 1971-80. St Patrick's, Greenock 1980-. (Canning)

344 *Scottish Secular Clergy, 1879-1989*

SHEEHAN, MICHAEL: Born and educated Ireland. Ordained Maynooth 1920. Lent to Glasgow. Blantyre 1920-26. Returned to Ireland 1926 and died there 24 Nov 1944. (Canning)

SHEEHAN, PATRICK: Born and educated Ireland. Ordained Maynooth 1906. Lent to Glasgow. Our Lady and St Margaret's, Glasgow 1906-17. Cadzow 1917-18. Returned to Ireland 1918 and died there 13 March 1967. (Canning)

SHEEHY, JOHN J: Born and educated Ireland. Ordained Maynooth 1890. Lent to Glasgow. Our Lady and St Margaret's, Glasgow 1890-96. Our Lady and St Margaret's, Glasgow in addresses, but not under parishes, 1896-97. Returned to Ireland 1897 and died there 18 Nov 1913. (Canning)

SHERIDAN, CHARLES: Born Glasgow 1909. Educated St Aloysius' College, Glasgow; Blairs 1923-27; St Peter's 1927-33. Ordained Glasgow 1933. St Patrick's, Shieldmuir 1933-37. Our Lady of Lourdes, Glasgow 1937-54. Croy 1954-81. Died Glasgow 4 Jan 1982.

SHERIDAN, JOHN A (1931): Born Manchester 1906. Educated Eccles Secondary School; Blairs 1922-25; Scots College, Rome 1925-31. Ordained Rome 1931. Further studies, Rome 1931-33. Vice-rector, Scots College, Rome 1933-38. Further studies, Cambridge University 1938-41. Professor, Blairs 1941-46. Headmaster, Blairs 1946-49. Moved to Motherwell diocese. Airdrie 1949-50. St Joseph's, Blantyre 1950-52. Newton 1952-55. St Bridget's, Baillieston 1955-61. Alberta, Canada 1961-67. St Margaret's, Airdrie 1967-77. Retired 1977.

SHERIDAN, JOHN (1956): Born Clydebank 1929. Educated Campion House, Osterley; Valladolid. Ordained Valladolid 1956. St Philomena's, Glasgow 1956-63. Spiritual Director, Valladolid 1963-69. St Charles', Glasgow 1969-72. Good Shepherd, Glasgow 1972-75. St Pius X, Glasgow 1975-81. All Saints, Glasgow 1981-83. St Leo's, Glasgow 1983-85. Our Lady and St Margaret's, Glasgow 1985-87. St Paul's, Glasgow 1987-.

SHERIDAN, PATRICK (1903): Born and educated Ireland. Ordained Maynooth 1903. Lent to Glasgow. St Charles', Glasgow 1903-09. Returned to Ireland 1909 and died there 3 Sept 1933. (Canning)

SHERIDAN, PATRICK ALOYSIUS (1928): Born and educated Ireland. Ordained Kilkenny for Glasgow 1928. Holy Cross, Glasgow 1928-48. St Eunan's, Clydebank 1948-70. Died Clydebank 11 June 1970. (Canning)

SHERIDAN, WILLIAM J: Born and educated Ireland. Ordained Maynooth 1907. Lent to Glasgow. Glasgow Cathedral 1907-08. Coatdyke 1908-09.

St Patrick's, Dumbarton 1909-15. Returned to Ireland 1915 and died there 9 Dec 1957. (Canning)

SHIELS, MATTHEW: Born Ireland. Educated Ireland, Paris. Ordained Paris 1928. Lent to Glasgow. St Stephen's, Dalmuir 1928-29. St John's, Glasgow 1929-33. Returned to Ireland 1933 and died there 9 Feb 1952. (Canning)

SHINNICK, JOSEPH: Born and educated Ireland. Ordained Maynooth 1901. Lent to Glasgow. St Agnes's, Glasgow 1901-13. Returned to Ireland 1913 and died there 16 Feb 1935. (Canning)

SHVAEISTRIS, ANTONY: Ordained 1906. St Luke's, Glasgow 1914-20; probably serving Lithuanian community. No further entries.

SIEGER, JOSEPH: Born Greenock 1879. Educated Blairs 1894-1900; St Peter's 1900-06. Ordained Glasgow 1906. Hamilton 1906-18. Cadzow 1918-19. Hamilton 1919-22. Dalry 1922-28. Died Glasgow 8 Feb 1928.

SIMCOX, JAMES: Born and educated Ireland. Ordained Dublin for Glasgow 1953. Good Shepherd, Glasgow 1953-60. St Patrick's, Dumbarton 1960-74. St Paul's, Glasgow 1974-81. Renton 1981-. (Canning)

SLATTERY, JAMES: Born Ireland. Educated Ireland, Paris. Ordained Paris 1912. Lent to Glasgow. St Patrick's, Coatbridge 1913-18. Returned to Ireland 1918 and died there 13 Nov 1955. (Canning)

SLAVIN, WILLIAM JOHN: Born Bristol 1940. Educated Blairs; Scots College, Rome. Ordained Rome 1964. St Brigid's, Glasgow 1964-65. Our Lady of Perpetual Succour, Glasgow 1965-69. St Michael's, Glasgow 1969-75. Bangladesh 1975-80. St John's, Glasgow 1980-81. Glasgow, no parish, 1981-89. Our Lady of the Assumption, Glasgow 1989-.

SLORACH, JAMES: see Aberdeen diocese

SMITH, DONALD A: Ordained 1943. St Bonaventure's, Glasgow 1953-57. No further entries.

SMITH, PATRICK: Born Ireland. Educated Ireland, St Peter's. Ordained Glasgow 1939. St Aloysius', Glasgow 1939-57. Chaplain, Barlinnie Prison and St Joseph's Home, Glasgow 1957-62. Our Lady of Perpetual Succour, Glasgow 1962-68. Our Holy Redeemer, Clydebank 1968-71. Died Clydebank 8 Dec 1971. (Canning)

SMITH, PETER: Born Glasgow 1958. Educated Our Lady's High School, Cumbernauld; Glasgow University; Jordanhill College of Education; St

Peter's. Ordained Cumbernauld 1984. St Brendan's, Glasgow 1984. St Anne's, Glasgow 1984-85. Virginia, USA 1985-87. St Augustine's, Glasgow 1987-.

SMITH, THOMAS: Born Dumfries 1862. Educated Blairs 1876-81; St Peter's 1881-86. Ordained Glasgow 1886. Our Lady and St Margaret's, Glasgow 1886-91. Dalry 1891-96. Carfin 1896-1900. Died Carfin 20 June 1900.

SMITH, WILLIAM J: Born Perth 1902. Educated St John's School, Perth; career in chemistry; educated for priesthood Fort Augustus 1924-26; St Peter's 1926-32. Ordained 1932. Carfin 1932-39. Forces chaplain 1939-45. Carfin 1945-53; thus moving to Motherwell diocese. Blackwood 1953-54. Sick leave 1954. St Bride's, East Kilbride 1954-57. Shotts 1957-58. Chapelhall 1958-59. Cleland 1959-60. Bargeddie 1960. In hospital from 1960. Died Glasgow 16 Jan 1961.

SMYTH, JAMES: Born and educated Ireland. Ordained Maynooth 1902. Lent to Glasgow. Blantyre 1903-07. Returned to Ireland 1907 and died there 29 Oct 1951. (Canning)

SMYTH, PATRICK: Born and educated Ireland. Ordained Maynooth 1899. Lent to Glasgow. St Patrick's, Coatbridge 1899-1903. Returned to Ireland 1903 and died there 22 Nov 1936. (Canning)

SREENAN, PATRICK: Born and educated Ireland. Ordained Maynooth 1906. Lent to Glasgow. St Mary's, Paisley 1907-09. Returned to Ireland 1909 and died there 6 Jan 1949. (Canning)

STACK, GERALD: Born Glasgow 1862. Educated Blairs 1876-81; Scots College, Rome 1881-87. Ordained Rome 1887. Maryhill 1887-89. St Laurence's, Greenock 1889-92. Professor, St Peter's College 1892-1900. Cambuslang 1900-29. Died Glasgow 5 May 1929.

STEVEN, FRANCIS A R: Born Glasgow 1870. Educated Blairs 1883-87; Valladolid 1887-94. Ordained Valladolid 1894. Professor, Valladolid 1894-1903. Leave of absence 1903-04. Larkhall 1904-26. Saltcoats 1926-32. Died Saltcoats 19 Dec 1932.

STEWART, DANIEL: Born Glasgow 1866. Educated Blairs 1881-84; Douay 1884-87; St Peter's 1887-91. Ordained St Peter's College 1891. Glasgow Cathedral 1891-95. Archbishop's chaplain 1895-96. Our Lady and St Margaret's, Glasgow 1896-99. St Charles', Glasgow 1899-1913. Immaculate Conception, Glasgow 1913-17. Died Glasgow 24 Dec 1917.

STOPANI, WILLIAM: Born Lerwick 1883. Educated Blairs 1900-03; Valladolid 1903-11. Ordained Valladolid 1911. St Augustine's, Coatbridge 1911-30. Newmains 1930-37. Died Lanark 20 March 1937.

STRAIN, DESMOND: Born Glasgow 1923. Educated St Peter's. Ordained Glasgow 1949. Further studies, Oxford University 1949-52. St Bonaventure's, Glasgow 1952-53. Professor, Blairs 1953-59. Professor, St Peter's College 1959-67. Glasgow Cathedral 1967-69. Duntocher 1969-74. St Joseph's, Cumbernauld 1974-81. St Saviour's, Glasgow 1981-83. Retired 1983. Died Kilsyth 21 Nov 1986.

STRICKLAND, WILLIAM J: Born Paisley 1919. Educated St Mirin's Academy, Paisley; Blairs; Scots College, Rome; St Peter's. Ordained 1945. Our Holy Redeemer, Clydebank 1945-47. Alexandria 1947-60. St Anne's, Glasgow 1960-66. St Michael's, Glasgow 1966-69. St Monica's, Glasgow 1969-76. Retired 1976.

STUART, GEORGE: Born Glasgow 1884. Educated Blairs 1899-1903; Scots College, Rome 1903-09. Ordained Rome 1908. St John's, Port Glasgow 1909-29. Renton 1929-37. St Agnes's, Glasgow 1937-43. St Joseph's, Woodside, Glasgow 1943-48. St Peter's, Glasgow 1948-59. Died Largs 28 Aug 1959.

STUART, JOHN: Born Glasgow 1885. Educated St Aloysius' College, Glasgow; Blairs 1901-05; St Peter's 1905-06; Issy 1906-07; St Peter's 1907-13. Ordained Glasgow 1913. St Mary Immaculate, Glasgow 1913-28. Holy Cross, Glasgow 1928-29. Blackwood 1929-32. Duntocher 1932-46. Retired 1946. Died Glasgow 4 Aug 1964.

SULLIVAN, JOSEPH EDWARD: Born Glasgow 1961. Educated St Andrew's, School, Carntyne; Glasgow University; Scots College, Rome. Ordained Shettleston 1986. Immaculate Conception, Glasgow 1986. Holy Cross, Glasgow 1986. St Flannan's, Kirkintilloch 1986-88. Holy Family, Kirkintilloch 1988-.

SUTTON, WILLIAM: Born and educated Ireland. Ordained Maynooth 1890. Lent to Glasgow. Glasgow Cathedral 1890-91. Newport 1891-97. Returned to Ireland 1897 and died there 13 Nov 1910. (Canning)

SWEENEY, ANTHONY AIDAN: Born Glasgow 1947. Educated St Aloysius' College, Glasgow; Lourdes School, Glasgow; St Peter's. Ordained St Peter's College 1974. St Gregory's, Glasgow 1974-76. St Peter's, Glasgow 1976-79. Faifley 1979-81. Duntocher 1981-84. St Pius X, Glasgow 1984-85. St Brigid's, Glasgow 1985-.

SWEENEY, BERNARD J: Born and educated Ireland. Ordained Maynooth 1903. Lent to Glasgow. Cardowan 1903-04. Lent to Salford diocese 1904-09. Returned to Ireland 1909. (Canning)

SWEENEY, JAMES: Bon Glasgow 1894. Educated St Peter's 1924-30. Ordained 1930. Our Lady and St Margaret's, Glasgow 1930-45. St

Aloysius', Glasgow 1945-47. St Anne's, Glasgow 1947-49. Chaplain, Barlinnie Prison and St Joseph's Home, Glasgow 1949-54. St Vincent de Paul's, Glasgow 1954-68. Retired to Ireland 1968, and died there 3 March 1976.

SWEENEY, JOSEPH P (1903): Born and educated Ireland. Ordained Maynooth 1903. Lent to Glasgow. St Augustine's, Coatbridge 1904-09. Returned to Ireland 1909 and died there 13 Feb 1967. (Canning)

SWEENEY, JOSEPH (1927): Born and educated Ireland. Ordained Kilkenny for Glasgow 1927. St Anthony's, Glasgow 1927-46. Holy Family, Port Glasgow 1946-66; thus moving to Paisley diocese. Died Greenock 8 July 1966. (Canning)

SWEENEY, MICHAEL J: Born Ireland. Educated Ireland, St Peter's. Ordained Glasgow 1925. Baillieston 1925-33. Whifflet 1933-37. St Laurence's, Greenock 1937-40. Cambuslang 1940-45. Blackwood 1945-50; thus moving to Motherwell diocese. Retired to Ireland 1950 and died there 3 Sept 1959. (Canning)

SWEENEY, PETER: Born Glasgow 1951. Educated Langbank; Blairs; Scots College, Rome. Ordained Glasgow 1975. St Robert's, Glasgow 1975. Further studies, Rome 1975-76. St Eunan's, Clydebank 1976-85. St Anne's, Glasgow 1985-.

SYNNOTT, HENRY: Born and educated Ireland. Ordained Maynooth 1912. Lent to Glasgow. Barrhead 1912-17. St Stephen's, Dalmuir 1917-19. Returned to Ireland 1919 and died there 15 Jan 1962. (Canning)

TAGGART, FRANCIS P: Born Coatbridge 1888. Educated St Aloysius' College, Glasgow; Blairs 1903-05; Valladolid 1905-07; St Peter's 1907-13. Ordained Glasgow 1913. St Patrick's, Glasgow 1913-16. St Luke's, Glasgow 1916-24. Leave of absence 1924-25. Coatdyke 1925-32. Harthill 1932-33. Sick leave 1933-51. Chaplain, Carmelite Convent, Glasgow 1951-64. Died Glasgow 20 March 1964.

TANGNEY, NICHOLAS: Born and educated Ireland. Ordained Maynooth 1918. Lent to Glasgow. Motherwell 1918-23. Returned to Ireland 1923 and died there 15 Jan 1973. (Canning)

TANSEY, ANTHONY: Born and educated Ireland. Ordained Carlow for Glasgow 1953. St Philomena's, Glasgow 1953-81. Croy 1981-86. Retired 1986. (Canning)

TARTAGLIA, GERARD: Born Glasgow 1961. Educated St Mungo's Academy, Glasgow; Langbank; Blairs; Scots College, Rome. Ordained

Glasgow 1985. Glasgow Cathedral 1985. Further studies, Rome 1985-86. Holy Cross, Glasgow 1986-.

TARTAGLIA, PHILIP: Born Glasgow 1951. Educated St Mungo's Academy, Glasgow; Langbank; Blairs; Scots College, Rome. Ordained Glasgow 1975. St Matthew's, Glasgow 1975. Further studies, Rome 1975-76. St Matthew's, Glasgow 1976. Post-graduate studies, Rome 1976-78. Vice-rector, Scots College, Rome 1978-79. Professor, St Peter's College 1979-80. Our Lady of Lourdes, Glasgow 1980-81. Professor, St Peter's College, 1981-85. Vice-rector, Chesters 1985-87. Rector, Chesters 1987-.

TAYLOR, ALEXANDER (1903): Born Greenock 1876. Educated Blairs 1892-95; St Peter's 1895-1900; Scots College, Rome 1900-04. Ordained Rome 1903. St Anthony's, Glasgow 1904-05. Died Govan 29 May 1905.

TAYLOR, JOHN: Born Enzie, Banffshire 1854. Educated Blairs 1868-72; Valladolid 1872-79. Ordained Dumfries 1879. Johnstone 1879. St Patrick's, Glasgow 1879-81. St Patrick's, Dumbarton 1881-85. Cambuslang 1885-88. Motherwell 1888-1917. Died Motherwell 8 Oct 1917.

TAYLOR, THOMAS N (1897): Born Greenock 1873. Educated St Aloysius' College, Glasgow; Blairs; Issy; St Sulpice; Catholic Institute, Paris. Ordained Paris 1897. St Patrick's, Dumbarton 1897-1900. Professor, St Peter's College 1900-15. Carfin 1915-63; thus moving to Motherwell diocese. Died Carfin 1 Dec 1963.

TAYLOR, THOMAS J (1934): Born Kilmarnock 1908. Educated Blairs 1923-27; Valladolid 1927-34. Ordained Valladolid 1934. St Mary Immaculate, Glasgow 1934-45. St Patrick's, Glasgow 1945-55. St Mark's, Glasgow 1955-56. Died Glasgow 4 March 1956.

TEDESCHI, SABATINO: Born Clydebank 1934. Educated St Patrick's High School, Dumbarton; Blairs; St Peter's. Ordained Glasgow 1959. St Saviour's, Glasgow 1959. St Constantine's, Glasgow 1959-71. St Pius X, Glasgow 1971-74. St Saviour's, Glasgow 1974-76. St Margaret Mary's, Glasgow 1976-81. St Margaret's, Clydebank 1981-83. St Maria Goretti's, Glasgow 1983-86. Croy 1986-.

TEEHAN, MICHAEL: Born and educated Ireland. Ordained Kilkenny for Glasgow 1928. Hamilton 1928-29. Helensburgh 1929-30. St Mirin's, Paisley 1930-49; thus moving to Paisley diocese. Linwood 1949-56. Barrhead 1956-76. Retired to Ireland 1976 and died there 4 Dec 1982. (Canning)

TENNANT, JOHN R: Born Glasgow 1887. Educated St Mungo's Academy, Glasgow; Blairs 1903-06; St Peter's 1906-07; Scots College, Rome 1907-

15. Ordained Rome 1914. St Patrick's, Shieldmuir 1915. Professor, Blairs 1915-33. St Mary Immaculate, Glasgow 1933-34. Baillieston 1934-41. Holy Family, Kirkintilloch 1941-55. Died Glasgow 5 Sept 1955.

THOMPSON, FREDERICK: Born Glasgow 1928. Educated Blairs, St Peter's. Ordained Glasgow 1952. Glasgow Cathedral 1952-59. Nigerian mission 1959-61. St Saviour's, Glasgow 1961-71. St Joseph's, Tollcross 1971-83. St Maria Goretti's, Glasgow 1983-86. Retired 1986. Died Paisley 21 Sept 1987.

THOMSON, ALEXANDER: see Aberdeen diocese

THORNTON, STEPHEN A: Born Glasgow 1871. Educated Blairs; France 1889-91; Scots College, Rome 1891-97. Ordained Rome 1896. Professor, St Peter's College 1897-98. St Aloysius', Glasgow 1898-99. Sick leave 1899-1900. St John's, Glasgow 1900-05. Gourock 1905-08. Renton 1908-14. Cadzow 1914-23. Saltcoats 1923-26. Airdrie 1926-36. Died Glasgow 18 Nov 1936.

TIERNEY, PATRICK: Born Partick 1923. Educated St Peter's School, Partick; Blairs; St Peter's. Ordained 1947. Further studies, Rome 1947-49. St Thomas's, Glasgow 1949-63. Professor, St Peter's College 1963-67. St Joseph's, Woodside, Glasgow 1967-69. St Teresa's, Glasgow 1969-72. St Simon's, Glasgow 1972-.

TIERNEY, THOMAS: Born Milngavie 1915. Educated Campion House, Osterley; St Peter's. Ordained Glasgow 1952. St Patrick's, Glasgow 1952-59. St Bernadette's, Glasgow 1959-75. Our Lady of Lourdes, Glasgow 1975-82. Retired 1982.

TOBIN, JOHN: Born and educated Ireland. Ordained Waterford for Glasgow 1950. Our Lady and St George, Glasgow 1950-67. St Bartholomew's, Glasgow 1967-68. St Benedict's, Glasgow 1968-73. St Robert's, Glasgow 1973-75. Old Kilpatrick 1975-80. Faifley 1980-84. Died Faifley 12 Dec 1984. (Canning)

TOBIN, PATRICK: Born and educated Ireland. Ordained Kilkenny for Glasgow 1948. St Flannan's, Kirkintilloch 1948-53. St Barnabas's, Glasgow 1953-73. Bonhill 1973-78. St John Ogilvie's, Glasgow 1978-89. Retired 1989. (Canning)

TOBIN, WILLIAM: Born and educated Ireland. Ordained Waterford for Glasgow 1949. St Joseph's, Woodside, Glasgow 1949-50. St Stephen's, Dalmuir 1950-67. St Joseph's, Tollcross 1967-74. St Monica's, Glasgow 1974-78. St Constantine's, Glasgow 1978-. (Canning)

TOHER, PATRICK: Ordained 1951. St Flannan's, Kirkintilloch 1969-70. No further entries.

TOLAN, ANDREW: Born Glasgow 1932. Educated Holyrood School, Glasgow; St Peter's. Ordained Glasgow 1956. St Pius X, Glasgow 1956-60. St Paul's, Shettleston 1960-74. St Brendan's, Glasgow 1974-84. St Lucy's, Cumbernauld 1984-.

TONCHER (Toncker), GUIDO: Ordained 1909. St John's, Glasgow 1926-37. No further entries.

TONER, JOHN: Born Glasgow 1857. Educated Blairs 1871-75; Valladolid 1875-82. Ordained Valladolid 1882. St Laurence's, Greenock 1882-87. Professor, St Peter's College 1887-90. St Michael's, Glasgow 1890-97. St Patrick's, Glasgow 1897-1901. Rutherglen 1901-14. No further entries.

TORLEY, PATRICK: Born Dalmuir 1894. Educated St Aloysius' College, Glasgow; Blairs; St Sulpice. Ordained Glasgow 1918. Holy Family, Kirkintilloch 1918-32. St Mary's, Glasgow 1932-37. Whiterigg 1937-41. Immaculate Conception, Glasgow 1941-72. Retired 1972. Died Glasgow 5 Sept 1974.

TOWIE, JAMES: Born Ireland. Educated Blairs, St Peter's. Ordained Glasgow 1895. Glasgow Cathedral 1895-1903. Whiterigg 1903-07. St John the Baptist's, Uddingston 1907-30. St John's, Port Glasgow 1930-37. Died Port Glasgow 28 Sept 1937. (Canning)

TOY, DANIEL: Born Greenock 1908. Educated Blairs 1925-28; St Peter's 1928-34. Ordained Glasgow 1934. St Patrick's, Glasgow 1934-37. St Luke's, Glasgow 1937-49. St Anne's, Glasgow 1949-55. St Bartholomew's, Glasgow 1955-72. St Catherine's, Glasgow 1972-81. St Lucy's, Cumbernauld 1981-84. Our Lady of Good Counsel, Glasgow 1984-85. Our Lady and St Margaret's, Glasgow 1985-87. Sacred Heart, Glasgow 1987-.

TRACEY, DAVID: Born Kirkintilloch 1938. Educated Blairs, St Peter's. Ordained Glasgow 1962. St John's, Glasgow 1962-65. Our Lady of the Assumption, Glasgow 1965-77. St Martin's, Glasgow 1977-84. St Conval's, Glasgow 1984-89. Our Lady of Perpetual Succour, Glasgow 1989-.

TRACY, PETER: Born and educated Ireland. Ordained Maynooth 1897. Lent to Glasgow. St Mary's, Paisley 1897-99. Returned to Ireland 1899 and died there 23 Sept 1944. (Canning)

TRAINER, DAVID: Born Glasgow 1943. Educated Blairs, St Peter's. Ordained St Peter's College 1968. St Paul's, Glasgow 1968-73. Professor, Langbank 1973-78. Professor, Blairs 1978-83. Immaculate Conception, Glasgow 1983-87. Holy Family, Kirkintilloch 1987-.

TRAINOR, WILLIAM J J: see Galloway diocese

TRAVERS, PETER: Born and educated Ireland. Ordained Kilkenny for Glasgow 1928. St Roch's, Glasgow 1928-29. Sick leave from 1929. Died Ireland 24 Aug 1974. (Canning)

TRAYNOR, JAMES G: Born Motherwell 1910. Educated Blairs 1924-28; St Peter's 1928-34. Ordained Glasgow 1934. St Thomas's, Glasgow 1934-49. Carntyne 1949-51. Military chaplain 1951-54. Chaplain, Barlinnie Prison and St Joseph's Home, Glasgow 1954-57. Alexandria 1957-66. St Roch's, Glasgow 1966-78. Retired to Southampton 1978.

TRAYNOR, OWEN: Born Coatbridge 1907. Educated Blairs 1923-28; Scots College, Rome 1928-35. Ordained Rome 1934. St Mungo's, Greenock 1935-36. St Joseph's, Woodside, Glasgow 1936-41. St Anne's, Glasgow 1941-47. Clarkston 1947-54; thus moving to Paisley diocese. Sick leave 1954-57. St John's, Port Glasgow 1957-58. Died Port Glasgow 23 Aug 1958.

TREANOR, CHARLES J: Born Glasgow 1888. Educated Blairs 1904-06; St Peter's 1906-07; Scots College, Rome 1907-15. Ordained Rome 1914. St Patrick's, Dumbarton 1915-19. Professor, St Peter's College 1919-45. Rector, St Peter's College 1945-63. Died Glasgow 24 Jan 1963.

TRITSCHLER, FERDINAND C: Born Glasgow 1904. Educated Blairs 1918-23; St Peter's 1923-29. Ordained Glasgow 1929. St Stephen's, Dalmuir 1929-40. St Michael's, Glasgow 1940-43. Forces chaplain 1943-46. St Aloysius', Glasgow 1946. St Mary's, Paisley 1946-47. St Joseph's, Greenock 1947-51; thus moving to Paisley diocese. Chaplain, Little Sisters of the Poor, Greenock 1951-57. Houston 1957-59. St Joseph's, Greenock 1959-75. Retired 1975. Died Greenock 26 May 1979.

TROY, JAMES: Born Ireland. Educated Blairs, Issy, St Sulpice, St Peter's. Ordained Glasgow 1907. Parkhead 1907-09. Rutherglen 1909-24. Longriggend 1924-28. Dalry 1928-37. Barrhead 1937-56; thus moving to Paisley diocese. Died Barrhead 30 June 1956. (Canning)

URQUHART, JAMES: see Aberdeen diocese

VACCARO, GUIDO ANTONIO: Born and educated Ireland. Ordained Carlow for Glasgow 1948. St Charles', Glasgow 1948-52. St Philomena's, Glasgow 1952-53. Went to Nottingham diocese 1953. Died Ireland 25 Feb 1977. (Canning)

VALLELY, CHARLES: Born Cleland 1916. Educated St Peter's 1934-41. Ordained Glasgow 1941. St Charles', Glasgow 1941-42. Carfin 1942-45. St Joseph's, Woodside, Glasgow 1945-54. St Roch's, Glasgow 1954-62.

Glasgow Cathedral 1962-66. St Peter's, Dumbarton 1966-73. Died Dumbarton 16 April 1973.

VAN DER HEYDE, ADRIAN: Born 1861. Educated St Joseph's College, Pannerden; Megen Gymnasium, North Brabant; Roulers Seminary; St Peter's 1881-84. Ordained Glasgow 1884. St Mary's, Glasgow 1884-89. No further entries.

VAN HECKE, JOSEPH: Born Bruges 1854. Educated St Louis College, Bruges; Roulers Seminary; St Peter's. Ordained 1879. St John's, Glasgow 1879-85. St Paul's, Shettleston 1885-93. Wishaw 1893-1927. Died Wishaw 20 Dec 1927.

VAN WYK, WILLIAM: Ordained 1881. St Patrick's, Glasgow 1885-86. No further entries.

VASILIAUSKAS, FRANCIS: Ordained 1893. Mossend 1910-12. St Luke's, Glasgow 1912-13. Probably serving Lithuanian community. No further entries.

VAUGHAN, EDWARD: Born and educated Ireland. Ordained Maynooth 1904. Lent to Glasgow. St Michael's, Glasgow 1904-10. Returned to Ireland 1910 and died there 10 March 1957. (Canning)

VESEY, EDWARD: Ordained 1962. St Conval's, Glasgow 1976-80. St Benedict's, Glasgow 1980-86. Our Lady of Lourdes, Glasgow 1986-88. With Society of St James the Apostle, Boston and Ecuador, from 1988.

WALDRON, JOHN A: Born and educated Ireland. Ordained Maynooth 1903. Lent to Glasgow. St Anne's, Glasgow 1904-10. Returned to Ireland 1910 and died there 2 Feb 1961. (Canning)

WALDRON, PATRICK: Born and educated Ireland. Ordained Maynooth 1905. Lent to Glasgow. St Anthony's, Glasgow 1905-09. Returned to Ireland 1909 and died there 14 Oct 1958. (Canning)

WALL, JOHN: Born and educated Ireland. Ordained Maynooth 1916. Lent to Glasgow. St Mary's, Greenock 1916-25. Returned to Ireland 1925 and died there 21 Feb 1928. (Canning)

WALL, THOMAS: Born and educated Ireland. Ordained Thurles 1911. Lent to Glasgow. St Mary's, Greenock 1911-19. Returned to Ireland 1919 and died there 3 Oct 1935. (Canning)

WALLACE, JAMES: Ordained 1957. St Maria Goretti's, Glasgow 1978-79. Not in Directories 1979-80. St Roch's, Glasgow 1980-87. Went to Dunkeld diocese: Arbroath 1987-.

WALSH, JAMES (1924): Born and educated Ireland. Ordained Maynooth 1924. Lent to Glasgow. St Anne's, Glasgow 1924-37. St Luke's, Glasgow 1937-42. Got exeat to remain in Glasgow. Linwood 1942-46. Burnbank 1946-64; thus moving to Motherwell diocese. Retired 1964. Died Ireland 5 March 1965. (Canning)

WALSH, JAMES B (1925): Born and educated Ireland. Ordained Maynooth 1925. Lent to Glasgow. Holy Family, Kirkintilloch 1925-26. St Patrick's, Glasgow 1926-34. Returned to Ireland 1934 and died there 18 Dec 1970. (Canning)

WALSH, JAMES LEO (1960): Born Kirkintilloch 1937. Educated St Ninian's High School, Kirkintilloch; Blairs; St Peter's. Ordained Glasgow 1960. Further studies, Rome 1960-65. Helensburgh 1965-67. St Robert's, Glasgow 1967-75. St Basil's College, Toronto 1975-88. Director, Glengowan House, Glasgow 1988-89. No further entry.

WALSH, JAMES F (1962): Born Glasgow 1937. Educated Blairs, St Peter's. Ordained Glasgow 1962. Further studies, Rome 1962-64. St Thomas's, Glasgow 1964-67. Professor, St Peter's College 1967-77. Died Glasgow 28 Aug 1977.

WALSH, JOHN: Born and educated Ireland. Ordained Maynooth 1901. Lent to Glasgow. St John the Baptist's, Uddingston 1901-08. Coatdyke 1908-09. St Peter's, Glasgow 1909. Returned to Ireland 1909 and died there 24 Jan 1959. (Canning)

WALSH, JOSEPH: Born Kirkintilloch 1954. Educated St Ninian's High School, Kirkintilloch; St Peter's. Ordained Kirkintilloch 1978. St Teresa's, Glasgow 1978. Further studies, Rome 1978-81. Our Lady of Lourdes, Glasgow 1981-.

WALSH, MICHAEL JOSEPH: Born Kirkintilloch 1913. Educated Scots College, Rome 1933-39. Ordained Rome 1938. Coatdyke 1939-41. St Michael's, Glasgow 1941-44. Forces chaplain 1944-47. St Luke's, Glasgow 1947-48. Carntyne 1948-49. Professor, Blairs 1949-60. Balloch 1960-70. St Laurence's, Glasgow 1970-75. Our Lady of Good Counsel, Glasgow 1975-85. Died Glasgow 2 May 1985.

WALSH, NICHOLAS: Born and educated Ireland. Ordained Waterford 1919. Lent to Glasgow. St Mirin's, Paisley 1919-25. Returned to Ireland 1925 and died there 1941. (Canning)

WALSH, WILLIAM: Born and educated Ireland. Ordained Maynooth 1900. Lent to Glasgow. St Mary's, Paisley 1900-11. Returned to Ireland 1911 and died there 10 Dec 1945. (Canning)

WALSHE (Walsh), JAMES: Born and educated Ireland. Ordained Waterford 1937. Lent to Glasgow. Motherwell 1937-39. St Anne's, Glasgow 1939-42. Returned to Ireland 1942. (Canning)

WALSHE, PETER F: Born and educated Ireland. Ordained Waterford 1914. Lent to Glasgow. St John's, Glasgow 1914-16. Alexandria 1916-17. Military chaplain 1917-19. Returned to Ireland 1919 and died there 19 May 1972. (Canning)

WARD, ALPHONSUS: Born and educated Ireland. Ordained Maynooth 1898. Lent to Glasgow. St Peter's, Glasgow 1898-1902. Returned to Ireland 1902 and died there 22 March 1963. (Canning)

WARD, JAMES CUTHBERT (1928): Born Edinburgh 1904. Educated Blairs 1919-22; St Kieran's College, Kilkenny 1922-23; St Peter's 1923-28. Ordained St Peter's College 1928. Immaculate Conception, Glasgow 1928. St Charles', Glasgow 1928-29. Our Lady and St Margaret's, Glasgow 1929-30. St Patrick's, Shieldmuir 1930-48; thus moving to Motherwell diocese. Strathaven 1948-55. Died Edinburgh 14 May 1955.

WARD, JAMES (1929): Born Dumbarton 1905. Educated St Peter's 1923-29. Ordained Glasgow 1929. St Charles', Glasgow 1929-48. Chaplain, Notre Dame 1948-50. Vicar General, Diocesan Office 1950-60. Consecrated Auxiliary Bishop of Glasgow 1960. At Diocesan Office 1960-65. Holy Cross, Glasgow 1965-73. Died Glasgow 21 Oct 1973.

WARD, JOHN FLYNN: Born Alexandria 1938. Educated St Patrick's High School, Dumbarton; St Peter's. Ordained St Peter's College 1969. St Jude's, Glasgow 1969-70. St Margaret Mary's, Glasgow 1970-76. Army chaplain 1976-.

WARD, MAURICE: Born Glasgow 1936. Educated St Aloysius' College, Glasgow; Scots College, Rome. Ordained Rome 1960. St Martin's, Glasgow 1961-63. Professor, Langbank 1963-73. St Bernard's, Glasgow 1973-74. Rector, Langbank 1974-78. Chaplain, St Vincent's Centre, Langbank 1978-80. Rector, St Peter's College 1980-85. Rector, Chesters 1985-87. Helensburgh 1987-.

WARD, MICHAEL: Born Ireland. Educated Ireland, St Peter's. Ordained Glasgow 1924. Our Holy Redeemer, Clydebank 1924-38. St Anne's, Glasgow 1938-41. Biggar 1941-45. Our Holy Redeemer, Clydebank 1945-48. St Mary's, Glasgow 1948-73. Retired 1973. Died Govan 22 May 1977. (Canning)

WARNAGIRIS, VINCENT: Ordained 1886. St John's, Glasgow 1898-1900. No further entries.

WATT, ARCHIBALD: Born Glasgow 1900. Educated Blairs 1913-19; St Peter's 1919-24. Ordained Glasgow 1924. Burnbank 1924-27. St John the Baptist's, Uddingston 1927-28. St Peter's, Glasgow 1928-33. St Mirin's, Paisley 1933-40. Biggar 1940-41. St Stephen's, Dalmuir 1941-47. St Thomas's, Glasgow 1947-49. St Anne's, Glasgow 1949-67. Died Glasgow 19 Aug 1967.

WATTERS, JAMES F: Born Glasgow 1905. Educated Blairs 1922-26; Scots College, Rome 1926-33. Ordained Rome 1932. St Patrick's, Greenock 1933-58; thus moving to Paisley diocese. Clarkston 1958-61. St Peter's, Paisley 1961-74. Died Glasgow 9 Sept 1974.

WEBB, CHARLES: Born Brighton 1860. Educated Apostolic School, Kelvedon, Essex; St Joseph's College, Mill Hill 1884-87; St Peter's 1887-89. Ordained Glasgow 1889. St Patrick's, Coatbridge 1889. Glasgow Cathedral 1889-93. Carluke 1893-1900. Carfin 1900-08. Cardowan 1908-21. Died Cardowan 24 April 1921.

WELSH, ANTHONY: Ordained 1970. St Constantine's, Glasgow 1973-77. St Robert's, Glasgow 1977-80. St Michael's, Glasgow 1980-.

WHITE, DANIEL B: Born and educated Ireland. Ordained Glasgow 1936. Glasgow Cathedral 1936. St Mirin's, Paisley 1936. Burnbank 1936-50; thus moving to Motherwell diocese. St Columbkille's, Rutherglen 1950-55. Strathaven 1955-59. Caldercruix 1959-61. Larkhall 1961-65. Shotts 1965-72. Newarthill 1972-84. Retired 1984. (Canning)

WHITE, JOSEPH: Born and educated Ireland. Ordained Castletown-Kilpatrick 1924. Lent to Glasgow. St Peter's, Glasgow 1924. Returned to Ireland 1924 and died there 17 Nov 1950. (Canning)

WHITE (Whyte), JUSTIN: Born Ireland. Educated St Peter's. Ordained Glasgow 1901. St John's, Glasgow 1901-14. Renfrew 1914-18. Johnstone 1918-23. St Mirin's, Paisley 1923-37. Died Paisley 8 Oct 1937. (Canning)

WHITE, WILLIAM: Born Ireland. Educated Ireland, St Peter's. Ordained Glasgow 1936. St Anne's, Glasgow 1936-38. Our Holy Redeemer, Clydebank 1938-43. St Roch's, Glasgow 1943-44. Forces chaplain 1944-47. St Bride's, Cambuslang 1947-54; thus moving to Motherwell diocese. St Luke's, Motherwell 1954-61. St Bridget's, Baillieston 1961-62. Died Moffat 26 Aug 1962. (Canning)

WHITTY, KEVIN: Born Glasgow 1905. Educated St Aloysius' College, Glasgow; Blairs 1919-24; St Peter's 1924-26; Scots College, Rome 1926-31. Ordained Rome 1931. St Patrick's, Coatbridge 1931-37. St Mirin's, Paisley 1937-47. Clarkston 1947-55. Died Glasgow 16 Jan 1955.

WILKINSON, JOSEPH (James): Born Glasgow 1925. Educated Blairs; St Peter's; Scots College, Rome. Ordained Glasgow 1948. Further studies, Rome 1948-50. St Patrick's, Glasgow 1950-67. St Robert's, Glasgow 1967-73. St Joseph's, Woodside, Glasgow 1973-76. St James's, Glasgow 1976-79. St Patrick's, Glasgow 1979-.

WILSON, JOHN F (1931): Born Glasgow 1907. Educated St Aloysius' College; Blairs 1922-25; St Peter's 1925-31. Ordained St Peter's College 1931. Airdrie 1931-33. No further entries.

WILSON, JOHN JOSEPH (1933): Born Glasgow 1910. Educated St Aloysius' College, Glasgow 1922-27; St Peter's 1927-33. Ordained Glasgow 1933. St Mary's, Coatbridge 1933-34. St Teresa's, Glasgow 1934-42. Carfin 1942-44. Forces chaplain 1944-46. Our Lady and St Margaret's, Glasgow 1946-47. Helensburgh 1947-48. Sacred Heart, Glasgow 1948-55. St Gabriel's, Glasgow 1955-60. St Conval's, Glasgow 1960-78. Died Glasgow 8 Nov 1978.

WINNING, THOMAS: see Motherwell diocese

WOITYS, LOUIS: Ordained 1897. St John's, Glasgow 1900-03. No further entries.

WOODFORD, MICHAEL: Born Leicester 1950. Educated St Aloysius' College, Glasgow; Scots College, Rome. Ordained Glasgow 1974. Our Lady of Good Counsel, Glasgow 1974. Representative of Scottish Hierarchy for Holy Year in Rome 1974-75. St Robert's, Glasgow 1975-77. Lent to Dunkeld diocese: St Pius's, Dundee 1977-78. Professor, Blairs 1978-86. St Margaret Mary's, Glasgow 1986-88. St Mark's, Glasgow 1988-.

WOODS, ALPHONSUS THOMAS: Born and educated Ireland. Ordained Kilkenny for Glasgow 1943. St Joseph's, Woodside, Glasgow 1943-44. St Mary's, Glasgow 1944-46. Blantyre 1946-50; thus moving to Motherwell diocese. St Margaret's, Airdrie 1950-60. St Aidan's, Wishaw 1960-83. St Patrick's, Coatbridge 1983-87. Retired 1987. (Canning)

WOODS, JOHN NOEL: Born Glasgow 1933. Educated Blairs, St Peter's. Ordained Glasgow 1958. St John's, Glasgow 1958-72. Glasgow Cathedral 1972-81. St Catherine's, Glasgow 1981-84. Chaplain, Notre Dame 1984-.

WOODS, ROBERT CAMPBELL: Born Longriggend 1912. Educated Blairs 1927-32; St Peter's 1932-39. Ordained Glasgow 1939. Sacred Heart, Glasgow 1939-44. Forces chaplain 1944-65. Garelochhead 1965-69. St Helen's, Glasgow 1969-74. Retired to Yorkshire 1974.

WRIGHT, RODERICK: Born Glasgow 1940. Educated St Gerard's School, Glasgow; Blairs; St Peter's. Ordained Glasgow 1964. St Laurence's, Glasgow 1964-66. St Jude's, Glasgow 1966-69. Spiritual Director and Procurator, Blairs 1969-74. Transferred to Argyll diocese. Dunoon 1974-76. Fort William 1976-80. Ardkenneth 1980-86. Corpach 1986-. Nominated Bishop of Argyll 1990.

WYCHERLEY, PATRICK: Born Ireland. Educated Ireland, Blairs, St Peter's. Ordained Glasgow 1929. Our Lady and St Margaret's, Glasgow 1929-35. St Aloysius', Glasgow 1935-36. St Columba's, Glasgow 1936-47. Professor, St Peter's College 1947-55. St Anthony's, Glasgow 1955-60. Holy Cross, Glasgow 1960-64. Died Glasgow 31 Dec 1964. (Canning)

YOUNG, FRANCIS: Born Glasgow 1861. Educated Blairs 1878-81; Valladolid 1881-87. Ordained Valladolid 1887. Maryhill 1887-89. St Patrick's, Coatbridge 1889-93. Larkhall 1893-97. St Mirin's, Paisley 1897-1917. St Charles', Paisley 1917-19. Leave of absence 1919-20. St Anthony's, Glasgow 1920-22. Died St Leonards-on-Sea 7 Feb 1932.

Parishes

In 1948 the dioceses of Motherwell and Paisley were created. A number of Glasgow's parishes were transferred, either to these new dioceses, or to Galloway. Entries for such parishes are given below until the rearrangement. For subsequent entries the reader is referred to the relevant new diocese.

ARCHBISHOPS: 1869-1902 Charles Eyre (WD). 1902-20 John Maguire (WD). 1922-43 Donald Mackintosh (Argyll). 1945-63 Donald Campbell (Argyll). 1964-74 James D Scanlan (Westminster). 1974- Thomas J Winning (Motherwell).
Coadjutor Archbishop: 1912-19 Donald Mackintosh (WD).
Bishops Auxiliary: 1894-1902 John Maguire (WD). 1960-73 James Ward (Glasgow). 1971-74 Thomas J Winning (Motherwell). 1977- Charles Renfrew (Glasgow). 1977-83 Joseph Devine (Glasgow). 1984-88 John A Mone (Glasgow).

AIRDRIE – ST ALOYSIUS': see Chapelhall

AIRDRIE – ST MARGARET'S: moves to Motherwell diocese
Heads: 1867-93 James McIntosh (WD). 1893-1926 Hubert Van Stiphout (WD). 1926-36 Stephen A Thornton. 1936-37 vacant. 1937- James McKenna.
Assistants: 1877-83 John Hughes (WD). 1883-86 John Dougan. 1886-87 Timothy O'Hea. 1887-93 Theophilus Delbeke. 1893-96 Hugh J Kelly (1889). 1896-97 Martin Jansen. 1896-1924 Edward Doody. 1920-23

Joseph O'Leary. 1923-25 James J Scanlon. 1924-26 Matthew Doherty. 1925 James Menton. 1925-27 Thomas Kelly (1925) (2). 1926-27 Bartholomew Atkinson. 1927-31 Jeremiah O'Sullivan. 1927-32 Edward Bradley. 1931-33 John F Wilson (1931). 1932-34 John Rooney. 1933- Daniel McGlinchey (1932). 1934-35 James Fitzgibbon. 1935-44 John McGarry. 1943- Peter J Murphy (1943).

ALEXANDRIA
Heads: 1878-85 Robert Grant (WD). 1885-87 Thomas Kerr (WD). 1887-97 Emile de Backer (WD). 1897-1904 William Gallagher (WD). 1904-23 Michael McCabe (1889). 1923-29 Peter Murray. 1929-37 John A Lyons (1907). 1937-48 John J Murphy (1914). 1948-57 James Clune. 1957-66 James Traynor. 1966-70 Daniel O'Leary. 1970-75 James V Reilly. 1975-81 Thomas Maguire. 1981- Francis Courtney.
Assistants: 1887-88 James J Burke. 1891-97 Louis de Backer. 1897-99 David Murie. 1908-09 Patrick Loy. 1909-16 Mortimer J Galvin. 1913 Joseph Kennedy. 1916 Bartholomew Flynn. 1916-17 Peter F Walshe. 1917-21 Thomas Murray (1916). 1921-25 Michael Quinlan. 1924-30 Timothy P Feely. 1929-30 Francis Misset. 1930-33 Angus McLean (1929). 1933-34 John Rogan. 1934-47 Jeremiah O'Leary. 1942-45 John V Murray (1934). 1945-46 Joseph Nee. 1946-51 Bernard Magauran. 1947-60 William J Strickland. 1952-58 Jeremiah Lane. 1960-67 George Crawley. 1967-79 Eugene McGee. 1979-86 Francis McPartlin. 1986- James Doherty (1979).

ARDROSSAN: moves to Galloway diocese
Head: 1945- Archibald McSparran.
Assistant: 1946- Matthew Littleton.

BAILLIESTON – ST BRIDGET'S: moves to Motherwell diocese
Heads: 1878-79 Richard Edgcome (WD). 1879-1914 Peter H Terkin (WD). 1914-26 Daniel J Horgan (1898). 1926-28 Octavius Claeys. 1928-29 Thomas Healy (1899). 1929-34 Daniel Collins. 1934-41 John R Tennant. 1941-42 John McCrory. 1942- John Rooney.
Assistants: 1894-97 Gisbert J Hartmann. 1897-1903 William Orr. 1903-10 Eugene O'Connor. 1910-15 Bartholomew Flynn. 1915-19 Michael Hackett. 1919-20 Francis G Mangan. 1920-25 William McMullan. 1925-33 Michael Sweeney. 1929 John McLaughlin. 1929-32 Patrick Heaney. 1933-41 Charles Burns. 1939-40 William Duddy. 1940-43 Patrick J Brady. 1943- John Moss. 1943- George Fryer. 1945-47 Francis McFarlane (St A & E).

BAILLIESTON – CONVENT OF MERCY: CHAPLAINS (to Motherwell)
1946-49 Herbert G Rogers.

BALLOCH
Heads: 1951-59 Bernard Magauran. 1959-60 Hugh McCranor. 1960-70

Michael J Walsh. 1970-74 John Macdonald (1945). 1974-89 Denis Meechan. 1989- James Clancy.
Assistants: 1955 John Lightbody. 1955-59 John G O'Hara. 1959-63 William McDonald. 1963-76 Francis O'Rourke. 1976-79 Daniel McEwan. 1979-89 Joseph N Burke. 1989- James M Lawlor.

BARGEDDIE: moves to Motherwell diocese
1947- Charles Craigen.

BARRHEAD: moves to Paisley diocese
Heads: 1873-93 Thomas Carlin (WD). 1893-1912 Bernard Tracy (WD). 1912-26 Peter Hilgers. 1926-29 Francis Dougan. 1929-31 Peter Murray. 1931-37 John F Clark. 1937- James Troy.
Assistants: 1895 Andrew Lynch. 1895-98 Robert Grant. 1897-1913 Henry Edgar. 1902-05 Alphonsus Ooghe. 1905-12 Edmond Fitzgerald. 1912-17 Henry Synnott. 1913-21 Michael Harrington. 1917-23 Andrew J O'Keeffe. 1920-21 John McIntyre (1920). 1922-30 Hugh Delargey. 1923-41 Hugh Bogan. 1930-32 John J Cusick (1930). 1930-34 Peter Murie. 1932-34 Patrick Heaney. 1934-41 William J Molloy. 1934-42 John V Murray (1934). 1940-42 Christopher Condon. 1941-42 John Hamill. 1942-46 John Deans. 1942-47 Michael O'Carroll. 1942- Eugene Divney. 1946- James A O'Neill (1929). 1947- Thomas Grace.

BEARSDEN
Heads: 1967-78 Francis Murphy. 1978- Patrick J Henry.
Assistants: 1968-79 Henry Parkinson. 1979-81 James T Clancy. 1981-82 Robert J Hill. 1982-86 David Brown. 1986-87 John G Kay. 1987- Henry Farrell.

BEITH: moves to Galloway diocese
1947- Thomas A Kelly (1926)

BIGGAR: moves to Motherwell diocese
1937-40 Edward Molumby. 1940-41 Archibald Watt. 1941-45 Michael Ward. 1945-46 Patrick Cummins. 1946-47 Joseph McErlain. 1947- Thomas Egan.

BISHOPBRIGGS – ST DOMINIC'S: (Glasgow, St Dominic's)
Heads: 1973-87 Michael O'Keeffe (1948). 1987- Christopher Gilfedder.
Assistants: 1977-78 Hugh Cassidy. 1979-82 Denis Bradley. 1983-84 John Brannan. 1984-85 Brian Magee. 1985- Peter Murphy (1969).

BISHOPBRIGGS – ST MATTHEW'S: (Glasgow, St Matthew's)
Heads: 1946-52 Thomas J O'Kane. 1952-55 John G Quinn (1931). 1955-84 Hugh Kelly (1933). 1984- Eugene McGee.
Assistants: 1963-70 Romeo Coia. 1969-75 John Sheary (1969). 1970-74 Patrick J Byrne. 1975 Philip Tartaglia. 1975-81 Brian Morren. 1976

Philip Tartaglia. 1979-82 Dermot Healy. 1981-85 Michael D McCabe (1957). 1982-86 Edward Campbell. 1986- John A Hughes. 1989- Paul Gallacher.

BISHOPTON: moves to Paisley diocese
1946- Joseph Hamill.

BLACKWOOD: moves to Motherwell diocese
1896-1913 served by Benedictines. 1913-19 Anthony Mullins. 1919-23 Thomas Kearney (1903). 1923-29 Joseph Courtney. 1929-32 John F Stuart. 1932-34 Peter Boland. 1934-39 Daniel Harty. 1939-41 James Black. 1941-45 Patrick Coogan. 1945- Michael J Sweeney.

BLANTYRE (St Joseph's): moves to Motherwell diocese
Heads: 1877-80 Thomas Frawley (WD). 1880 Edmund Cantwell (WD). 1880-86 Peter Donnelly (WD). 1886-1921 Thomas Hackett. 1921-23 Peter Murray. 1923-45 Robert Paterson. 1945- John M Ashe.
Assistants: 1895-98 James McDonnell. 1898-1900 John McCready (1897). 1900-03 John J Fleming. 1903-07 James Smyth. 1903-14 Thomas Corley. 1907-12 John O'Grady. 1912-17 Thomas O'Hanlon. 1913 Edmund O'Hanlon. 1914-15 Michael Mulvey. 1917-21 Hugh Macdonald (1906). 1918-20 Michael Hanrahan. 1920-26 Michael Sheehan. 1921-30 Thomas O'Halloran. 1926-29 John McNair. 1929-37 James P Fennessy. 1930 (-31) Bernard Magauran. 1930- Bernard Keenan. 1937-45 Patrick Cummins. 1941-42 Alphonsus McMullan. 1942-46 James Quinn (1942). 1945- Thomas Barry. 1946- Alphonsus Thomas Woods. 1947- Henry Corr.

BONHILL: 1973-78 Patrick Tobin. 1978-81 Anthony McHugo. 1981-86 Thomas S Cunningham (1953). 1986- James O'Reilly.

BOTHWELL: moves to Motherwell diocese
Heads: 1911-18 John McMillan (1898). 1918-23 James Hughes. 1923-30 Patrick Hourigan. 1930-33 James Montgomery. 1933-40 Thomas McCann. 1940-45 Henry E Hart. 1945-47 John McCrory. 1947- Thomas Brooks.
Assistant: 1939-40 Vincent Cowley.

BOTHWELL – FRANCISCAN CONVENT: CHAPLAINS (to Motherwell)
1881-93 Peter Forbes (WD). 1896-97 Michael Ahern. 1899-1906 James O'Neill (1887). 1912-45 Patrick McMullen. 1945-49 Gerard M Rogers.

BURNBANK: moves to Motherwell diocese
Heads: 1893-1900 Peter Muller. 1900-18 Duncan Brown. 1918-26 Peter O'Connor. 1926-32 Daniel O'Sullivan (1895). 1932-33 Patrick J Loy. 1933-44 James Montgomery. 1944-46 Peter Morrison. 1946- James F Walsh (1924).

Assistants: 1904-08 Thomas Gourlay. 1908-15 Daniel Colvin. 1915-18 Dominick Casey. 1918-19 Patrick J O'Sullivan (1918), (possibly). 1919-20 Peter J MacFarlane. 1920-21 Michael Quinlan. 1921-22 Alphonsus Mullen. 1922-24 Michael O'Brien. 1924-27 Archibald Watt. 1927-32 John B McDermott (1927). 1927-36 John McKenna. 1931-32 Patrick S Brennan. 1936- Daniel B White. 1938-41 Francis Misset. 1941-48 Anthony McGurk.

BUSBY: see Clarkston

CADZOW (Hamilton, Our Lady and St Anne's): moves to Motherwell diocese
Heads: 1883-87 Emile de Backer (WD). 1887-91 Louis de Backer. 1891-95 Thomas Kerr (WD). 1895-1903 William McAvoy. 1903-13 Peter McConnachie. 1913-14 vacant. 1914-23 Stephen A Thornton. 1923-36 Denis Scannell. 1936-39 Patrick Plunkett. 1939-47 Matthew Quillinan. 1947- Patrick McGonagle.
Assistants: 1901-03 John J Murphy (1901). 1903-05 John Lagan. 1906-11 James Durkin. 1911-14 Gisbert Hartmann. 1914-17 James McGrory. 1917-18 Patrick Sheehan. 1918-19 Joseph Sieger. 1919-20 John Godfrey. 1920-21 Charles O'Riordan. 1921-31 William J Hayes. 1931-36 Denis McGrath (1927). 1932-33 John B McDermott (1927). 1933- John Bredin. 1936-40 Patrick Brennan. 1940-45 Francis Burns. 1945-48 Denis Lucey.

CAMBUSLANG (St Bride's): moves to Motherwell diocese
Heads: 1878-85 William Carmichael (WD). 1885-88 John Taylor. 1888-91 Thomas J Cunningham (1879). 1891-1900 James F Morrison. 1900-29 Gerald Stack. 1929- Hugh Macdonald (1906).
Assistants: 1896-99 Patrick Farrell. 1899-1901 Thomas Healy (1899). 1901-03 Jeremiah O'Driscoll. 1902-06 Patrick Cush. 1903-19 Thomas Kearney (1903). 1906-08 Daniel Colvin. 1908-17 George Galbraith. 1909-10 James Lagan. 1917-23 Jerome Dennehy. 1919-23 Edward McGennis. 1923 John J Murphy (1923). 1923-24 Patrick F Keating. 1923-24 Francis Meaney (Galloway). 1924-26 Patrick Kelly (1924). 1924-29 Hugh Macdonald (1906). 1926-28 Jeremiah F Ahern. 1928 Francis Meaney (Galloway). 1928-30 Francis Magauran. 1929-40 James Lillis. 1930- Robert Douglas. 1940-45 Michael J Sweeney. 1945-47 Albert Chandler. 1947- William White.

CARDONALD: see Glasgow, Our Lady of Lourdes

CARDOWAN (Stepps): moves to Motherwell diocese
Heads: 1875-86 Francis J Hughes (WD). 1886-89 Peter Fegan. 1889-93 John Dougan. 1893-1904 John Black (WD). 1904-08 Denis McBrearty. 1908-21 Charles Webb. 1921-32 Patrick J Diamond. 1932-36 John Boyle (1909). 1936- John O'Callaghan (1917).

Assistants: 1903-04 Bernard J Sweeney. 1912-18 Timothy O'Kelleher. 1918-19 Michael McKenna. 1919-27 Peter Bonnyman. 1927-44 Michael O'Connor (1927). 1944-47 Thomas A Grace.

CARDROSS: 1978-86 James O'Reilly. 1986-89 Thomas McAteer. 1989- George Gillespie.

CARFIN: moves to Motherwell diocese
Heads: 1891-96 Charles Cunningham. 1896-1900 Thomas Smith. 1900-08 Charles Webb. 1908-15 Denis McBrearty. 1915- Thomas N Taylor (1897).
Assistants: 1899-1900 Michael Ahern. 1901-04 John O'Dea. 1904-06 William Orr. 1906-11 Gisbert Hartmann. 1911-14 Francis Dougan. 1914-32 John J Murphy (1914). 1926-27 Thomas Gourlay. 1929-30 Samuel Kilpatrick. 1932-33 Neil McKnight. 1932-39 William Smith. 1933-34 Albert Chandler. 1936-41 Thomas Sharkey. 1938-41 Francis McLeod. 1939-42 Thomas Murray (1936). 1941-42 Michael McNicholas. 1941-42 Thomas Glen. 1942-44 Gerard Hart. 1942-44 John J Wilson (1933). 1942-45 Charles Vallely. 1944-45 John Branagan. 1945-46 Thomas Berry. 1945- William J Smith. 1946- John W Boyle (1946).

CARLUKE: moves to Motherwell diocese
1860-93 Mortimer Cassin (WD). 1893-1900 Charles Webb. 1900-03 Peter McConnachie. 1903 Alexander McCormick (1895). 1903-05 Charles E Fleming. 1905-21 Robert James McCluskey. 1921-26 James Durkin. 1926-30 Henry Corr. 1930 John Ryan (1913). 1930-37 Matthew Quillinan. 1937-43 James P Fennessy. 1943-47 Francis Magauran. 1947- John Roger.

CARNTYNE (Glasgow, St Mark's)
Note: From 1912-45 Carntyne was combined, as a single parish, with St Paul's, Shettleston. Priests are listed together under the one presbytery, and the Directories give no indication of which priest was attached to which church.
Heads: 1906-12 Robert Paterson. 1912-45 see Shettleston. 1945-46 Cornelius Dennehy. 1946-48 James Clune. 1948-55 William McGhee. 1955-56 Thomas Taylor (1934). 1956-67 John McCready (1935). 1967-70 Edward O'Hara. 1970-73 Donald MacKinnon. 1973-77 Edmund Budds. 1977-82 Michael Henretty. 1982-86 John McGinlay (1940). 1986- Thomas Holloran.
Assistants: 1906-12 Hugh Macdonald (1906). 1945-46 Joseph Connelly. 1945-46 Patrick Gilmartin. 1945-46 John Little. 1945-51 Michael Lyne. 1946-47 Hugh C Mahon. 1946-48 Joseph Gallacher. 1947-48 Edward O'Hara. 1948-49 Michael J Walsh. 1949-51 James Traynor. 1951-55 James McShane. 1951-60 Joseph Breen. 1955-68 John O'Hagan. 1960-69 Joseph Nee. 1968-70 Daniel Creedon. 1969-77 Michael Keating. 1977-78 Hugh J McEwan (1960). 1981-88 Desmond Gunning. 1988- Michael Woodford.

CARSTAIRS – ST CHARLES' INSTITUTE/HOSPITAL: CHAPLAINS (to Motherwell)
Note: priests serving Tarbrax were sometimes resident at Carstairs House.
Heads: 1926-28 William Bradley (1911). 1928-29 Daniel Collins. 1938-57 Samuel McIsaac (Argyll).
Assistant: 1942-43 Neil McKnight.
In addresses, but not listed under Institute: 1947-48 Angus MacKellaig.

CHAPELHALL (Airdrie, St Aloysius'): moves to Motherwell diocese
Heads: 1876-79 William Gallagher (WD). 1879-93 Hubert van Stiphout (WD). 1893-97 John Macdonald (WD). 1897-1907 William Carmichael (WD). 1907-32 Donald A McPherson (Argyll). 1932 Thomas Brady. 1932-41 Thomas Rourke. 1941- Peter Murie.
Assistants: 1921-23 James E Quinn (1917) (Dunkeld). 1923-27 Thomas Mulvihill. 1927-44 Clement McGowan. 1944-46 Malachy Finnegan. 1946-47 Francis McLeod.

CLARKSTON (Busby): moves to Paisley diocese
Heads: 1879-84 John Muller (WD). 1884-88 Thomas J Cunningham (1879). 1888-1900 Louis de Meulenaere. 1900-02 Peter O'Connor. 1902-12 Walter Kelly. 1912-21 Bartholomew Atkinson. 1921-28 William J Molloy. 1928-32 Eugene Murray. 1932-37 Joseph Kennedy. 1937-38 Thomas Egan. 1938-44 John J Scanlon. 1944-47 Thomas Keane. 1947- E.C. Kavanagh.
Assistants: 1938-44 John Branagan. 1940-47 Brendan Murphy. 1944-45 Albert Chandler. 1945-46 Kenneth Grant. 1946-47 Thomas Healy (1939). 1947- Kevin Whitty. 1947- Owen Traynor.

CLELAND: moves to Motherwell diocese
Heads: 1876-83 Thomas Moran (WD). 1883-92 John Hughes (WD). 1892-93 Michael Fuller. 1893-1902 Patrick Hackett (1887). 1902-06 Robert Paterson. 1906-21 Peter Murray. 1921-25 Thomas Doyle. 1925-29 James Mullin. 1929-30 Patrick A McCarthy. 1930-32 John Boyle (1909). 1932-37 James Dolan. 1937-44 John Boyle (1918). 1944- Patrick Clarke.
Assistants: 1890-91 John Cameron. 1906-11 Joseph J Crumly. 1911-12 Charles McGhee. 1912-13 Michael Hartington. 1913-14 Jerome Dennehy. 1914-15 Dominick Casey. 1919-30 Hugh O'Brien. 1937-39 Patrick J Gullane. 1939-46 Richard Fennessy. 1946- Dermott McMullan.

CLYDEBANK – OUR HOLY REDEEMER
Heads: 1889-90 Peter Evers (WD). 1890-1914 John Montgomery. 1914-38 Charles E Fleming. 1938-41 Thomas McEwan. 1941-45 James Dolan. 1945-48 Michael Ward. 1948-68 William McGoldrick. 1968-71 Patrick Smith. 1971-72 vacant. 1972-74 Bishop Thomas Winning. 1974-82 Peter McCann (1949). 1982-89 Bruno Renucci. 1989- Thomas McAteer.
Assistants: 1897-1905 Thomas Lyne. 1902-14 Denis Scannell. 1905-12 Michael Lavelle. 1906-09 Timothy Kelleher. 1912-22 John O'Hanlon.

1913-32 William Bradley (1913). 1919-25 Denis Power. 1922-24 John Joyce (St A & E). 1924-38 Michael Ward. 1925-28 Hugh Milligan (St A & E). 1928-29 Aeneas Macrae (Aberdeen). 1929-32 Patrick O'Flaherty. 1930-33 James Meehan. 1932-39 James Graham. 1932-40 Francis Rota. 1934-38 Daniel Kennedy. 1937-39 Charles Duffin. 1938-43 William White. 1939-40 Thomas Healy (1939). 1939-41 John Harkin. 1940-41 Henry O'Kane. 1940-54 William Morgan. 1942-44 Thomas Hearty. 1942-48 Philip O'Reilly. 1943-57 Martin Hughes. 1945-47 William J Strickland. 1947-49 Alexander Johnston. 1948-52 John M O'Sullivan (1946). 1949-50 William Coghlan. 1952-65 James Martin. 1954-61 James Keenaghan. 1955 Edward Kelly. 1956-57 John McElroy (Paisley). 1957 John J McCabe. 1957-67 Martin Quinlan (1942). 1961-67 Edward Higgins. 1965-68 Joseph Cairns. 1967-69 Philip Hastings. 1967-71 Alistair MacLellan. 1968-72 Gerald P McCallion. 1969-72 Peter Clinton. 1972-74 John Muldoon. 1972-75 Dominic Doogan. 1975-77 Hugh J McEwan (1960). 1977 Brian C Reilly. 1977-78 Daniel Friel. 1978-82 Bruno Renucci. 1983 John P Quinn (1983). 1984- Hugh Kearns.

CLYDEBANK – ST EUNAN'S
Heads: 1948-70 Patrick A Sheridan (1928). 1970-81 Thomas G Mannion (1945). 1981-87 John Fitzgibbon (1945). 1987- Michael O'Keeffe (1948).
Assistants: 1949-59 Neil A Johnstone. 1950-60 Robert Bradley. 1959-61 John Roberts. 1960-66 Bartholomew Burns (1960). 1961-67 Daniel McEwan. 1966-76 Hugh Boyle. 1967-77 Francis Courtney. 1976-85 Peter Sweeney. 1985-86 Joseph McAuley. 1987-89 Francis Meagher. 1989- George McGarrigle.

CLYDEBANK – ST MARGARET'S
Heads: 1969-77 Michael Gavagan. 1977- James McShane.
Assistants: 1970-75 Timothy McGlynn. 1974-76 William Monaghan. 1975-77 John Manning. 1976-81 Michael Conroy. 1978-81 George McGarrigle. 1981-83 Sabatino Tedeschi. 1981-85 Peter McBride. 1985- Brian C Reilly.

COATBRIDGE – HOLY TRINITY AND ALL SAINTS: see Coatdyke

COATBRIDGE – ST AUGUSTINE'S (Langloan): moves to Motherwell diocese
Heads: 1892-1900 John Hughes (WD). 1900-29 Peter Muller. 1929-38 James Mullin. 1938-40 Alfred J Gallaucher. 1940- Edmund Macdonald.
Assistants: 1892-94 Thomas Hopwell. 1894-1904 Charles Brown (WD). 1894-97 Richard Meskell. 1897-1900 Patrick A McCarthy. 1899-1904 John Crawford (WD). 1904-09 Joseph P Sweeney (1903). 1904-11 Daniel J O'Herlihy. 1909-11 Alfred J Gallaucher. 1911-14 William Keogh. 1911-30 William Stopani. 1914-32 James Dolan. 1919-22 Edward Kinane. 1924-25 James Menton. 1926-40 Francis Hamilton (1926). 1931-40 Francis Burns. 1932-35 Patrick McHugh. 1936-37 Thomas Reilly. 1937-

40 Robert Beattie. 1940-42 John McNair. 1940-44 John Gillen. 1940- Patrick Brennan. 1942-47 Edward O'Hara. 1944-47 James Dooley. 1947- Edward Doherty. 1947- Hugh Mahon.

COATBRIDGE – ST MARY'S (Whifflet): moves to Motherwell diocese
Heads: 1874-79 John van den Noort (WD). 1879-1902 Thomas Curran (WD). 1902-37 Patrick Hackett (1887). 1937- Eugene Murray.
Assistants: 1894-98 John A Hickson (Galloway). 1898-1904 Daniel J Horgan (1898). 1900-06 Patrick Cronin. 1906-23 Patrick Hourigan. 1923-33 Denis Flynn. 1929-33 Charles Burns. 1933-34 John J Wilson (1933). 1933-37 Michael J Sweeney. 1934-37 John O'Donnell (1918). 1937-42 Patrick J Lynch. 1937-47 John Roger. 1942-45 James Meechan. 1945-46 Robert Connolly. 1946-47 Patrick J Loy. 1947- Charles McKinley. 1947- George Mullen.

COATBRIDGE – ST PATRICK'S: moves to Motherwell diocese
Heads: 1847-93 Michael O'Keeffe (WD). 1893-1903 John McCay. 1903-31 John Geerty. 1931- Daniel Colvin.
Assistants: 1874-79 Hubert van Stiphout (WD). 1879-84 Thomas O'Reilly (WD). 1880-81 Michael O'Neill (WD). 1881-84 Thomas Kearney (1880). 1884-88 Daniel Browne. 1884-89 Thomas McEvoy. 1888-91 John McAlister (1888). 1889 Charles Webb. 1889-93 Francis Young. 1891-92 John Cameron. 1892-96 John Nyhan. 1893-1903 John Geerty. 1896-97 James Urquhart (Aberdeen). 1896-98 James Harris (ED). 1897 Henry Edgar. 1898-99 Anthony O'Neill. 1898-1901 Robert Grant (WD). 1899-1903 Patrick Smyth. 1901-06 James B Jennings (Galloway). 1901-08 Bartholomew Canavan. 1906-15 Christopher Hillee. 1908-09 James Moloney. 1909-10 George Lillis. 1910-11 Daniel O'Dea. 1911-13 Michael McKenna. 1913-18 James Slattery. 1915 Michael Kinnane. 1915-23 Denis Scannell. 1918-23 Peter O'Sullivan. 1920-31 James Black. 1923-24 Patrick Deeney. 1924-25 J Haggarty. 1924-28 Patrick J McElwee. 1925-27 James O'Connor (1924). 1927-48 Michael Dooley. 1928-29 Thomas P McGregor (St A & E). 1929-33 Daniel O'Sullivan (1929). 1931-37 Kevin Whitty. 1931-40 Patrick Kelly (1924). 1933-34 Thomas Cahill. 1937-44 Albert Chandler. 1938-39 Joseph Breen. 1940 John J Rogan. 1941 James Fisher. 1941-48 Francis Misset. 1944-45 Michael Gilroy. 1945-48 John V Murray (1934).

COATDYKE (Coatbridge, Holy Trinity and All Saints): moves to Motherwell diocese
Heads: 1902-07 Daniel Collins. 1907-26 Francis McCann. 1926-31 Daniel Colvin. 1931-36 Henry Corr. 1936-41 Hugh Delargey. 1941- Alexander McBride.
Assistants: 1904-07 William J Molloy. 1907-08 George Galbraith. 1908-09 John Walsh. 1908-09 William J Sheridan. 1909-11 Michael Mulvey. 1911 Thomas Farry. 1918-24 Patrick Reilly. 1924-25 John Colleran.

1925-32 Francis P Taggart. 1932-47 Thomas Brady. 1938-39 Matthew Kinsella. 1939-41 Michael J Walsh. 1947- James E Hallinan.

CONDORRAT
Heads: 1974- Joseph Mulhall.
Assistants: 1978-81 Charles Kane. 1981- William B Donnelly.

COVE: see Roseneath

CROY
Heads: 1902-07 Francis McCann. 1907-29 John M M Charleson. 1929-32 Archibald McSparran. 1932-37 Eugene Murray. 1937-41 James Dolan. 1941-45 John McIntyre (1920). 1945-54 John Ryan (1913). 1954-81 Charles Sheridan. 1981-86 Anthony Tansey. 1986- Sabatino Tedeschi.
Assistants: 1903-06 Octavius F Claeys. 1909-13 James McRory. 1914-17 Charles McGlinchey. 1917-18 Patrick Reilly. 1918-19 Bartholomew Flynn. 1919 John MacNeill (1918) (Argyll). 1919-20 Thomas Healy (1899). 1920-23 Joseph Doherty. 1923-26 Peter Devlin. 1926-28 Francis Magauran. 1928-29 Charles Doherty. 1929-31 Matthew Littleton. 1931-38 Hugh O'Brien. 1938-39 Gerard Dunn. 1938-44 John Gillespie. 1941-48 Patrick Sheary. 1944-51 Thomas Reilly. 1948-50 Adrian Kelly (Dunkeld). 1950-67 John Hanrahan. 1951-67 Michael Henretty. 1967-72 George Gillespie. 1967-74 Michael D McCabe (1957). 1972-81 William B Donnelly. 1977-79 William McLellan. 1978- William J Gavin. 1979-81 Hugh O'Donnell. 1982-84 Patrick Gahagan. 1987-88 George Gillespie.

CUMBERNAULD – SACRED HEART
Heads: 1958-60 Thomas Reilly. 1960-86 Francis Jaconelli. 1986- Patrick Osborne.
Assistants: 1964-65 Patrick G Fitzpatrick. 1965-66 Brian Morren. 1966-70 James Kirby. 1970-71 Joseph P Brady. 1971-82 Vincent Quinn. 1975-79 Terence Friel. 1977-85 Anthony Beckett. 1984-85 Owen Gallagher. 1985- Thomas J Hendry. 1988- Joseph L McAuley.

CUMBERNAULD – ST JOSEPH'S
Heads: 1967-74 James Quinn (1942). 1974-81 Desmond Strain. 1981-84 Thomas G Mannion (1945). 1984-85 vacant. 1985-88 John J McCabe. 1988-89 George Gillespie. 1989- Francis Meagher.
Assistants: 1968-76 John McGuire. 1975-81 Peter O'Farrell. 1976- Neil Donnachie. 1982-84 John G Kay. 1984-88 John Quinn (1983). 1988- Gerard F Barnes.

CUMBERNAULD – ST LUCY'S
Heads: 1973-78 Anthony McHugo. 1978-84 James V Reilly. 1984- Andrew Tolan.
Assistants: 1981-84 Daniel Toy. 1984-88 John J McGrorry. 1988-89 Francis Kennedy. 1989- Noel Colford.

DALMUIR – OUR LADY OF LORETO
Heads: 1975-78 Gerald P McCallion. 1978-79 vacant. 1979-83 John Boles. 1983-84 vacant. 1984- John Manning.
Assistants: 1978-79 Ignatius Kennedy. 1979-82 Daniel McEwan. 1982-86 Anthony Bancewicz. 1986- Stephen French.

DALMUIR – ST STEPHEN'S
Heads: 1907-36 John Brotherhood, 1936-41 Henry Corr. 1941-47 Archibald Watt. 1947-55 Gerald McDade. 1955-72 William M Mallon. 1972-73 vacant. 1973-83 Michael J Connolly. 1983-89 John Broderick. 1989- James A Burns.
Assistants: 1909-17 Peter MacFarlane. 1917-19 Henry Synnott. 1919-22 Thomas O'Hanlon. 1922-26 Michael Guiry. 1926-27 James Halley. 1927-30 William McFadyen. 1928-29 Matthew Shiels. 1929-40 Ferdinand Tritschler. 1930-31 John Conroy. 1935-41 Patrick Sheary. 1940-42 Patrick Kelly (1924). 1943-65 Charles Cush. 1945-49 James Reilly. 1949-50 Daniel McMahon. 1950-67 William Tobin. 1965-70 John Macdonald (1945). 1967-68 James W Bovill. 1968-70 John Brannan. 1970-77 William Clarke. 1970-88 Angus MacDonald. 1977-85 George Bradburn. 1985-88 Patrick G O'Brien (1984). 1988-89 Hugh Lowrie. 1988- Stephen Hannah.

DALRY: moves to Galloway diocese
Heads: 1877-81 John Crawford (WD). 1881-83 Donald McIntosh (WD). 1883-91 Michael Dempsey (WD). 1891-96 Thomas Smith. 1896-1904 Michael McCabe (1889). 1904-14 William C Brown (1897). 1914-21 Patrick Diamond. 1921-22 Patrick J Laydon. 1922-28 Joseph Sieger. 1928-37 James Troy. 1937-45 Peter Fitzpatrick. 1945-47 George Aylward. 1947- Joseph Duffy.
Assistants: 1934-45 Thomas Meikleham. 1938-39 Patrick Rice. 1945-46 Hugh C Mahon.

DUMBARTON – ST MICHAEL'S
Heads: 1946-50 Hugh Bogan. 1950-59 Jeremiah O'Leary. 1959-73 Bernard A Magauran. 1973-88 Hugh G McEwan (1948). 1988- Henry Parkinson.
Assistants: 1946-55 Joseph Nee. 1946-60 James Quinn (1942). 1948-67 Donal Burke. 1955-66 John Manning. 1960-74 James Simcox. 1966-70 Anthony Beckett. 1967-69 Richard Dunne. 1969-73 Hugh J McEwan (1960). 1970-76 John McLaren. 1973-77 John McAveety. 1974-77 Michael Henretty. 1976-85 Joseph Mills. 1977-84 Edward Kelly. 1978-83 John McNamara. 1983-86 Stephen J French. 1985- Brendan J Murtagh. 1986-88 Henry Parkinson. 1988- Andrew McKenzie.

DUMBARTON – ST PATRICK'S
Heads: 1878-89 Charles Brown (WD). 1889-92 Michael Hughes. 1892-93 Michael McNairney. 1893-1901 John Linster (WD). 1901-50 Hugh Kelly (1889). 1950-75 Hugh Bogan. 1975- Thomas Murray (1936).

Assistants: 1879-81 Herman van Baer (WD). 1881-85 John Taylor. 1885-86 Thomas J Fitzgerald. 1887-88 Thomas McGrath. 1888-90 Ronald Mortimer. 1890-91 James Carroll. 1890-95 William McAvoy. 1895-96 Michael P O'Connor (1895). 1895-1902 Alphonsus Ooghe. 1896-97 Charles Cunningham. 1897-1900 Thomas N Taylor (1897). 1900-03 James MacDonald. 1902-04 James Kearney. 1903-04 William Orr. 1904-05 Robert Cairns. 1904-05 John McIlvaine. 1905-08 William Holland (St A & E). 1905-08 Charles Byrne. 1908-09 Michael Mulvey. 1908-26 Archibald McSparran. 1909-15 William J Sheridan. 1913-28 Thomas McGrory. 1915-19 Charles J Treanor. 1919-20 William McGoldrick. 1919-21 William Delahunty. 1921-23 Norbert O'Leary. 1923-28 John D Daniel. 1926-28 John Power. 1927 Denis M McGrath (1927). 1928 Patrick F Casey. 1928-29 Patrick Loy. 1928-31 Patrick Kevany. 1928-37 John Boyle (1918). 1929-34 Daniel McGlinchey (1927). 1931-35 John Conroy. 1934-36 Albert Chandler. 1935-36 Gerard Rogers. 1936-39 Denis Lucey. 1936-39 James Horan. 1937-39 Gerard Rogers. 1939-44 Bernard Magauran. 1939-54 Richard O'Callaghan. 1939-56 John McCready (1935). 1944-46 John Bradley. 1946 James McGinley. 1954-74 John Gowans. 1956-66 Desmond Gunning. 1958-59 David McLachlan. 1960-67 Francis Meagher. 1967-74 Michael Henretty. 1974-75 Carlo Centra. 1974-83 James Ryan. 1983-85 Francis Balmer. 1985-86 Joseph Mills. 1986- Edward B McNaught.

DUMBARTON – ST PETER'S
Heads: 1966-73 Charles Vallely. 1973-87 Nicholas Rowan. 1987- Thomas O'Rourke.
Assistants: 1967-74 Gerard Nugent. 1974-87 John Muldoon. 1987-89 Dominic Doogan.

DUNTOCHER
Heads: 1878-81 Hugh McConville (WD). 1881-86 James Bird (ED). 1886-98 Robert J McCluskey. 1898-1905 James Mullen. 1905-14 Bernard Lynch. 1914-18 Edward Lawton. 1918-19 Joseph O'Leary. 1919-32 Bartholomew Flynn. 1932-46 John F Stuart. 1946-68 James J Hogan. 1968-86 Jeremiah O'Flynn. 1986- Thomas S Cunningham (1953).
Assistants: 1905-09 Patrick J Cullinan. 1909-10 Alexander Mackintosh. 1918-25 John Ashe. 1925-32 Simon Keane. 1932-51 Hugh Cassidy. 1934-36 Donald Bonnar. 1936-37 Aloysius McGurk. 1937-41 Gerald Lord. 1938-47 Thomas McCabe. 1945-46 Daniel O'Flynn. 1947-49 John Dennehy. 1949-57 Patrick J Brady. 1951-55 Thomas Reilly. 1955-60 Daniel Moore. 1957-69 Patrick Gahagan. 1960-68 John Brannan. 1968-74 John Hanrahan. 1969-74 Desmond Strain. 1974-86 Edward Higgins. 1976-78 Germain Fitzpatrick. 1981-84 Anthony Sweeney. 1984- Aidan Martin. 1986- William McGinley. 1989- Michael G P Gallagher.

EAGLESHAM: 1877-79 John Muller (WD). From 1879 served from Busby (Clarkston).

EAST KILBRIDE – ST BRIDE'S: moves to Motherwell diocese
1946- John C Battel.

FAIFLEY
Heads: 1957-80 Thomas Glen. 1980-84 John Tobin. 1984-85 vacant. 1985-
David Currie.
Assistants: 1959-71 Peter Garland. 1962-67 George Gillespie. 1967-71
William B Donnelly. 1971-73 Anthony Beckett. 1971-78 John J Sheary
(1965). 1973-79 Thomas Holloran. 1978-79 Colman McGrath. 1979-81
Anthony Sweeney. 1979- Terence Friel. 1981-85 Alistair D MacLellan.
1988-89 James T Clancy.

GARELOCHHEAD: Until 1965 served from Helensburgh. 1965-69 Robert
Woods. 1969-73 Richard Dunne. 1973- John Duffy.

GLASGOW – ST ANDREW'S CATHEDRAL
Heads: 1867-92 Alexander Munro (WD). 1892-93 vacant. 1893-1900 James
Mackintosh (WD). 1900-14 James W McCarthy. 1914-23 George Ritchie.
1923-25 James Mullin. 1925-47 William Daly. 1947-65 Joseph Daniel.
1965-67 Denis Meechan. 1967-80 John McGuckin. 1980-83 John
Brannan. 1983- Hugh N Boyle.
Assistants: 1875-79 John A Maguire (WD). 1878-81 Charles Duperier (WD).
1879-80 James Coghlan. 1879-82 John B Macluskey (WD). 1880-81
William Davidson (WD). 1881-82 Laurence Richen. 1881-85 Michael
Hughes. 1882-84 Edmund Cantwell (WD). 1882-84 Charles Duperier
(WD). 1883-90 Bernard Dawson. 1885-92 William Carmichael (WD).
1886-87 William McLachlan. 1887-88 Duncan Brown. 1888-89 William
P O'Brien. 1889-93 Charles Webb. 1890-91 William Sutton. 1891-92
John McAllister. 1891-95 Daniel Stewart. 1892-97 John Scannell. 1894-
95 John Doherty (Dunkeld). 1895-99 Henry Forbes. 1895-1903 James
Towie. 1897-1905 Florence McCarthy. 1899-1905 Bernard Lynch. 1903-
11 Thomas Farry. 1905-15 David Barry. 1905-16 John McIlvaine. 1907-
08 William J Sheridan. 1911-16 John A Lyons (1907). 1915-23 Patrick F
Keating. 1916-21 Thomas O'Connor. 1916-23 John McQuillan. 1921-22
Donald A Campbell (Argyll). 1922-24 Joseph Daniel. 1923-24 John
McKenna. 1923-25 Simon Keane. 1924-31 John McCrory. 1924-41
William McGhee. 1925-31 John Ashe. 1931-32 Thomas Frigerio. 1931-
39 John G Quinn (1931). 1931-47 Denis Meechan. 1934 Michael Little.
1936 Daniel B White. 1939-44 James Dooley. 1940 Joseph Power. 1941-
56 Desmond Gunning. 1944-49 Sydney McEwan (Argyll). 1947-54
Gerard Hart. 1949-52 Francis Coyle. 1952-59 Frederick Thompson.
1954 James Keenaghan (Paisley). 1954-62 William Morgan. 1955 William
Mone. 1956-69 Bernard Chalmers. 1957 Patrick Gahagan. 1958 Joseph
D Coyle. 1959-67 John Muldoon. 1962 Bernard Connell. 1962-66
Charles Vallely. 1966-71 Daniel Friel. 1967-69 Desmond Strain. 1969-70
James McMahon. 1969-70 Gerard C Hill. 1969-82 Peter Murphy (1969).
1970-77 John Brannan. 1971-72 John Broderick. 1972-81 John N

Woods. 1977-79 Christopher Gilfedder. 1979-82 Andrew Hosie. 1981-83 Patrick J Byrne. 1983- Brian Madden SDB. 1984 Joseph L McAuley. 1984-89 Joseph Boyle. 1985 Gerard Tartaglia. 1987 James Lawlor. 1988 Paul G Murray. 1989 Hugh Bradley (1989). 1989- John D Broderick.

GLASGOW – ALL SAINTS
Heads: 1969-81 John Fitzgibbon (1945). 1981-82 vacant. 1982-84 John McLaren. 1984- John Conway.
Assistants: 1971-72 James Kirby. 1972-73 Desmond J McGinty. 1973-74 Anthony Beckett. 1974-81 Patrick J Byrne. 1981-83 John Sheridan (1956). 1983-88 Michael Conroy (1974). 1988- John G McGinlay (1965).

GLASGOW – CHRIST THE KING
Heads: 1934-38 Cornelius Dennehy. 1938-45 John M Ashe. 1945-48 William McGhee. 1948-77 Samuel Kilpatrick. 1977-87 Joseph McElholm. 1987- James McMahon.
Assistants: 1936-46 Hugh Kelly (1933). 1939-40 Patrick Rice. 1940-59 Hugh McCranor. 1946 Kevin Barry. 1947-54 Thomas Cahill. 1954-67 Desmond Maguire. 1959-75 Terence Friel. 1967-68 John Hanrahan. 1968-76 Francis Goodfellow. 1975-83 Henry McKay. 1976-81 John McCabe. 1981 John G Kay. 1981-89 Patrick Currie. 1982 John J McGrorry. 1983-87 Anthony McLaren. 1984-89 Thomas Docherty. 1987- Allan P Cameron. 1989- Joseph N Burke.

GLASGOW – CORPUS CHRISTI
1969-78 Michael Mooney. 1978-82 Francis Murphy. 1982-84 James Meechan. 1984-86 Patrick Gahagan. 1986- Thomas Murphy (1948).
Assistant: 1972-79 Patrick Osborne.

GLASGOW – GOOD SHEPHERD
Heads: 1948-55 Vincent O'Sullivan. 1955-64 Gerald A Harvey. 1964-65 vacant. 1965-67 Thomas Maguire. 1967-72 George Burns. 1972-75 Robert Bradley.
Assistants: 1948-55 Edward O'Hara. 1949-55 Robert Ryan. 1953-60 James Simcox. 1955-65 Thomas Healy (1939). 1960-67 Michael McCabe (1957). 1965-66 John J Sheary (1965). 1966-72 J Noel Burke. 1968-70 Sean Rynn. 1970-72 William J Gavin. 1972-75 John Sheridan (1956).
Church closed 1975.

GLASGOW – HOLY CROSS
Heads: 1886-89 Peter Link. 1889-1930 William P O'Brien. 1930-59 Bishop Henry G Graham. 1959-60 vacant. 1960-64 Patrick Wycherley. 1964-65 vacant. 1965-73 Bishop James Ward (1929). 1973-84 John Gillespie. 1984- John Hanrahan.
Assistants: 1895-96 Joseph Laveth. 1896-1910 Thomas Carlin (WD). 1904-12 William Mangan. 1910-17 Patrick A Hackett (1910). 1912-18 Timothy Courtney. 1917-19 Alexander Hamilton. 1918-22 Alexander McCormick

(1918). 1919-20 Daniel J Horgan (1919). 1919-26 Patrick O'Brien (1918). 1922-27 Patrick O'Mahony. 1926-28 Denis Griffin. 1927-31 Michael McNicholas. 1928-29 John Stuart. 1928-29 John Fitzgibbon. 1928-48 Patrick A Sheridan (1928). 1929-30 John Little. 1929-38 Patrick Clark. 1930-40 James McGrory. 1931-33 Robert Doherty. 1937-51 Jeremiah O'Kane. 1938-39 James Black. 1939-46 Gerald McDade. 1940-41 Joseph Power. 1941-62 Gaetano Rossi. 1946-57 Hugh Deery. 1948-60 Michael O'Keeffe (1948). 1951-54 Hugh Cassidy. 1954-65 Norman Baird. 1957-69 Michael Mooney. 1959-84 Owen Gallagher. 1961-64 Richard Sewards. 1962-65 David Currie. 1965-70 Charles Kane. 1965-78 Jeremiah Carroll. 1969-75 Joseph Mills. 1970-72 John McAuley. 1974-76 Michael Conroy. 1976-82 David Brown. 1979-82 Brian C Reilly. 1980-82 Gerard McKay (Argyll). 1982-86 Peter M Gallacher. 1983-86 Stephen Holland. 1984-87 Francis Meagher. 1986 Joseph E Sullivan. 1986-88 Hugh Lowrie. 1986- Gerard Tartaglia. 1987- John Lyons (1980). 1988- Peter Clinton.

GLASGOW – HOLY NAME: 1975-78 James O'Reilly. 1978- Patrick J Kelly (1951)

GLASGOW – IMMACULATE CONCEPTION
Heads: 1858-1913 James Cameron (WD). 1913-17 Daniel Stewart. 1917-18 vacant. 1918-23 James Mullin. 1923-25 Bernard Lynch. 1925-26 vacant. 1926-41 Peter O'Connor. 1941-72 Patrick Torley. 1972-83 Robert G O'Kane. 1983- William Mone.
Assistants: 1876-79 Peter H Terken (WD). 1879-80 John O'Donovan. 1979-81 Emile de Backer (WD). 1880-81 Patrick Browne. 1881-82 James Conaghan (WD). 1881-84 Thomas J Cunningham (1879). 1882-86 James Rochead. 1884-87 James Morrison. 1886-87 Henry Kuppers. 1887-89 Gerald Stack. 1887-89 Francis Young. 1889-93 Patrick Hackett (1887). 1889-96 James Humble. 1893-97 Andrew J O'Brien. 1896-1900 James Macdonald. 1897-98 John McAllister (1891). 1898-1900 Peter O'Connor. 1900-02 Patrick A McCarthy. 1900-06 William Ahern. 1902-06 Daniel Colvin. 1903-08 John Meade. 1906-14 Jeremiah O'Donoghue. 1906-15 Patrick Cush. 1908-12 Paul McKenna. 1912-14 Martin Murphy. 1914-15 William Gillies (Argyll). 1914-23 Simon Keane. 1915-27 Michael O'Connor (1915). 1918-19 William McMullan. 1919-22 Thomas Farry. 1922-23 Peter McLachlan. 1923-30 John Murphy (1923). 1924-25 John Holmes. 1925-26 Thomas Keane. 1927-28 Jeremiah O'Leary. 1927-47 Charles Craigen. 1928 James C Ward (1928). 1928-29 Donald McMaster (Argyll). 1929-30 James Fitzgibbon. 1930-46 Patrick Rogers. 1931-32 Philip I Boyce. 1932-42 Thomas McGhie. 1942-44 George Mullen. 1944-47 James McGill. 1946-47 John Carter. 1947-52 Thomas Healy (1939). 1947-53 Thomas Brady. 1947-54 Martin Doherty. 1952-57 John J McKee. 1953-56 Charles Renfrew. 1954-68 John Conlan. 1956-60 James McGinley. 1957-74 John J McCabe. 1960-71 Francis McPartlin. 1968-73 John Gilmartin. 1973-79 Denis Bradley. 1974-76 Malachy

Bergin. 1978-79 Angus MacLean (1969). 1979-83 John O'Hagan. 1981-83 Stephen Holland. 1983-87 David Trainer. 1986 Joseph E Sullivan. 1986- Gerard M Bacon. 1987- John Sheary (1969).

GLASGOW – IMMACULATE HEART OF MARY
Heads: 1946-48 James K Elliot. 1948-57 James Fitzgibbon. 1957-75 Thomas Murray (1936). 1975-83 William Morgan. 1983-87 Francis Mallon. 1987- Duncan Kane.
Assistants: 1949-51 Patrick J McGovern (1947) (1). 1951-52 Edward Molumby. 1951-57 Edmund Budds. 1952 John D Broderick. 1952-56 Daniel O'Leary. 1956-63 Gerard O'Meara. 1957-67 Francis Murphy. 1963-68 Peter Marr. 1967-72 John O'Brien. 1968-70 Noel Colford. 1969 Angus E MacLean (1969). 1970-72 William O'Connell. 1972-82 Denis A Hurley. 1982-86 Joseph Coyle. 1986- Bernard Connell.

GLASGOW – OUR LADY OF THE ASSUMPTION
Heads: 1952-67 John Hickey. 1967-75 Thomas Maguire. 1975-78 Thomas Murphy (1948). 1978-82 John McGinlay (1940). 1982-89 John J N Burns. 1989- Gerard Nugent.
Assistants: 1953-67 Francis Gilfedder. 1955-63 John Conway (1955). 1963-65 John McAveety. 1965-77 David Tracey. 1967-76 Daniel McEwan. 1977-80 Bernard Connell. 1980-82 James Kirby. 1982-87 William McLellan. 1987-89 Alexander Johnston. 1989- William J Slavin.

GLASGOW – OUR LADY OF CONSOLATION
Heads: 1966-78 Frederick Rawlings. 1978- John J O'Brien.
Assistants: 1967-73 John McAveety. 1967-74 James Ryan. 1973-74 William McGinley. 1974-76 William O'Neil. 1974-80 Sean Fitzgerald. 1976-77 John O'Sullivan (1954). 1980-84 Francis Gallagher.

GLASGOW – OUR LADY OF FATIMA
Heads: 1950-59 James Meehan. 1959-73 John Gogarty. 1973-77 Joseph McElholm. 1977-81 Bernard V Devine. 1981-84 John Roberts. 1984-85 vacant. 1985-86 Michael D McCabe (1957). 1986-87 Edward Higgins. 1987- Anthony Gallagher.
Assistants: 1951-67 Bernard V Devine. 1954-70 John McLaren. 1967-74 Joseph Kerr. 1970-72 Patrick G Fitzpatrick. 1972-73 Philip Hastings. 1974-79 John O'Hagan. 1980- William Monaghan.

GLASGOW – OUR LADY OF GOOD COUNSEL
Heads: 1962-75 Hugh Deery. 1975-85 Michael J Walsh. 1985- Owen Gallagher.
Assistants: 1962-67 William McLellan. 1963-69 Sean Fitzgerald. 1967-70 Bernard Devlin. 1967-72 Eamon V Friel. 1969-77 Patrick Gahagan. 1971-74 George Crawley. 1974 Michael Woodford. 1974-78 Neil McDaid. 1977-83 Desmond Maguire. 1978-79 Edward B McNaught. 1984-85 Daniel Toy.

GLASGOW – OUR LADY OF LOURDES (Cardonald)
Heads: 1907-10 Hugh Gunther. 1910-13 Francis Joseph Laveth. 1913-22 Henry Edgar. 1922-26 Patrick Doyle. 1926-33 James Durkin. 1933-60 George Galbraith. 1960-76 Patrick Gilmartin. 1976-88 Brendan H Murphy. 1988- John J McCabe.
Assistants: 1921-26 Bernard Gallagher. 1924-25 Patrick Molloy. 1926-30 Peter Devlin. 1930 Sean J Kilpatrick. 1930-37 Edward Molumby. 1935-36 John Cummings. 1936-39 John Jennings. 1937-54 Charles Sheridan. 1940-41 Daniel O'Leary. 1940-50 John O'Riordan. 1941 William McDonald. 1941-57 Francis Murphy. 1950-51 Carlo Centra. 1951-74 Donal McMenamin. 1954-61 Christopher Gilfedder. 1957 William Clarke. 1957-70 Alexander Johnston. 1958-60 Francis McPartlin. 1961-67 John Roberts. 1967-68 Thomas Dolan. 1968-74 John O'Hagan. 1969-75 John Hay. 1974-75 William Murphy (1952). 1975-80 James McLaughlin (1973). 1975-82 Thomas Tierney. 1975-82 Dominic Doogan. 1980-81 Philip Tartaglia. 1981- Joseph Walsh. 1982-84 Dermot Healy. 1982-85 Desmond J McGinty. 1983-86 Thomas Holloran. 1985- Donald J Cumming. 1986-88 Edward Vesey. 1988- Joseph McNulty.

GLASGOW – OUR LADY OF PERPETUAL SUCCOUR
Heads: 1962-68 Patrick Smith. 1968-72 John Conlan. 1972-82 James Meechan. 1982-87 Christopher Gilfedder. 1987- Michael Mooney.
Assistants: 1964-65 Joseph Cairns. 1965-69 William J Slavin. 1969-72 Daniel J C Hart. 1972-79 Hugh O'Donnell. 1975-80 Thomas Hurley. 1979-82 John J N Burns. 1984-89 George McGarrigle. 1989- David Tracey.

GLASGOW – OUR LADY QUEEN OF PEACE: 1978-81 John O'Hara. 1981-85 John Loughlin. 1985-87 Noel Colford. Church closed 1987.

GLASGOW – OUR LADY AND ST GEORGE
Heads: 1949-54 Patrick F Casey. 1954-65 Denis Meechan. 1965-79 John Cawley. 1979- Robert Bradley.
Assistants: 1950-67 John Tobin. 1953-59 Thomas Maguire. 1959-62 David McLachlan. 1962-73 Michael O'Keeffe (1948). 1967-71 Eugene Connolly. 1969-72 Christopher J Ryan. 1972-73 Joseph N Burke. 1973-75 Christopher P Gilfedder. 1973-77 Francis Meagher. 1975-79 John Mone. 1975-81 Daniel Fitzgerald. 1977-80 James Durning. 1979 Peter M Gallacher. 1980- Alfred McKenzie. 1981-83 Hugh Lowrie. 1983-84 Patrick Osborne. 1984-86 Eamon V Friel.

GLASGOW – OUR LADY AND ST MARGARET
Heads: 1876-79 John B Macluskey (WD). 1879-1915 Donald A Mackintosh (WD). 1915-32 Patrick Gallacher. 1932-33 vacant. 1933-43 Patrick J Laydon. 1943-48 James P Kelly. 1948-67 Michael McCarthy (1909).

1967-82 John Hickey. 1982-83 Hugh J McEwan (1960). 1983-85 John J
McCabe. 1985-87 John Sheridan (1956). 1987- Donal Burke.
Assistants: 1878-79 Thomas O'Reilly (WD) (possibly; appears
simultaneously under two parishes). 1879-84 James McCarthy. 1880-
86 Peter Link. 1885-88 John Godley. 1886-91 Thomas Smith. 1888-90
Thomas Currie. 1890-96 John J Sheehy. 1891-94 Michael Dempsey
(WD). 1894-1901 Francis Cronin. 1896-99 Daniel Stewart. 1898-1900
Patrick Gallacher. 1899-1906 Hugh Gunther. 1900-11 William Daly.
1901-14 James Cowhey. 1906-17 Patrick Sheehan. 1909-26 Michael
McCarthy (1909). 1911-29 Patrick Plunkett. 1914 Malcolm MacKinnon
(Argyll). 1914-16 Thomas O'Connor. 1917-20 James McGrory. 1919-25
William L Cahill. 1920-21 John Macmillan (1903) (Argyll). 1921-23
Michael Collins (1921). 1925-26 Francis Magauran. 1926-29 Patrick
O'Loughlin. 1926-37 James Henry. 1927-30 John J Healy. 1929-30
James McChrystal. 1929-30 James C Ward (1928). 1929-35 Patrick
Wycherley. 1930-41 Timothy Feely. 1930-45 James Sweeney. 1935-46
Thomas E Frigerio. 1937-44 John McGuckin. 1941-66 Frederick
Rawlings. 1942-43 Thomas Fehily. 1945-46 John Macdonald (1945).
1945-52 John G Quinn (1931). 1946-47 John J Wilson (1933). 1946-55
Hugh Kelly (1933). 1947-48 Patrick Loy. 1948-50 Duncan Kane. 1950-52
Daniel McMahon. 1952-53 John O'Hara. 1952-67 Robert G O'Kane.
1953-57 John Carter. 1955-60 Joseph Kerr. 1957-70 William Clarke.
1960-65 James O'Reilly. 1966-71 John J Sheary (1965). 1967-73 Hugh
G McEwan (1948). 1970-78 Bruno Renucci. 1971-79 John Chalmers.
1978-82 Hugh J McEwan (1960). 1985-87 Daniel Toy.

GLASGOW – SACRED HEART
Heads: 1872-86 Edward Noonan (WD). 1886-1904 Francis J Hughes (WD).
1904-21 Michael Hughes. 1921-55 Anthony Mullins. 1955-67 Peter
Morrison. 1967-74 Denis Meechan. 1974-77 Daniel Moore. 1977-78
Patrick J Henry. 1978-82 Matthew Coakley. 1982- Joseph Murphy.
Assistants: 1876-79 Peter Donnelly (WD). 1879-81 Richard Edgcome (WD).
1880-86 Edward Doody. 1885-88 John G Foley (1885) (St A & E). 1886-
87 John O'Callaghan (1886). 1887-90 Thomas McCulla. 1888-93 Gerald
O'Connell. 1890 Edmund Cotter. 1890-1903 James Bird (ED). 1893-95
Thomas Carlin (WD). 1895-1904 Daniel O'Sullivan (1895). 1898-1902
Francis McElmail. 1902-15 James Nolan (1902). 1903-08 Denis Duggan
(1899). 1904-07 John McMillan (1898). 1907-21 Patrick Laydon. 1908-
18 Michael O'Kennedy. 1911-14 Thomas Farry. 1914-16 Thomas Kerr
(WD). 1915-16 Francis Hamilton (1915). 1916-29 Patrick J Flood. 1918-
23 James McChrystal. 1920-25 Michael Power. 1921-26 Edward Ryan.
1924-28 William Brennan. 1925-29 Richard Power. 1926-36 Cornelius
O'Leary. 1928-33 Patrick Dillon. 1928-48 Vincent O'Sullivan. 1929-43
James Butler. 1933-37 John B McDermott (1927). 1936-39 James
Fletcher. 1937-42 George Mullen. 1939-44 Robert Woods. 1942-54
Daniel Moore. 1943-54 William Forbes. 1944 John Rae. 1945-50 Richard
Dunne. 1948-55 John J Wilson (1933). 1951-55 Matthew Coakley. 1953-

56 Joseph Mahon. 1954-57 John O'Sullivan (1954). 1955-61 Gerard Philips SMA. 1955-62 Hugh Kearns. 1956-67 Thomas McKeown. 1957-72 Austin Ruane. 1962-72 James A Burns. 1967-73 John J Dunne. 1971-72 Dominic Doogan. 1972-77 Patrick J Henry. 1982-85 James Kirby. 1987- Daniel Toy.

GLASGOW - ST AGNES'

Heads: 1884-86 Aloysius Godfrey (WD). 1886-87 Edward Doody. 1887-1905 Patrick Houlihan. 1905-16 James Mullen. 1916-26 John McMenemy. 1926-37 William Flanagan. 1937-43 George Stuart. 1943-70 James P Fennessy. 1970-73 John Gillespie. 1973- Samuel J Lavery.

Assistants: 1895-99 John Crawford (WD). 1899-1903 Octavius F Claeys. 1901-13 Joseph Shinnick. 1903-05 Thomas Agnew. 1913-20 Edmund O'Hanlon. 1920-21 James E Quinn (1917) (Dunkeld). 1921-24 William Lynagh. 1924-30 Matthew Quillinan. 1930-33 Charles Gallacher. 1931-38 Herbert G Rogers. 1938-40 John O'Riordan. 1940-53 Thomas Maguire. 1943-47 Thomas McAteer. 1947-48 Daniel Kennedy. 1948-70 Daniel Clancy. 1953-55 John G O'Hara. 1955-67 John Lightbody. 1967-74 William McLellan. 1970-77 Joseph Murphy. 1977-82 John O'Sullivan (1954). 1982- Peter Marr.

GLASGOW - ST ALBERT'S

Heads: 1965- Patrick J Brady.

Assistants: 1975-78 Romeo Coia. 1978-83 Hugh N Boyle. 1984-86 Francis Gallagher. 1986- Robert J Hill.

GLASGOW - ST ALOYSIUS' (Springburn)

Heads: 1872-84 James P Conway (WD). 1884-96 John J Dyer (WD). 1896-1908 John L Murphy (1881). 1908-15 Patrick Ryan. 1915-46 Denis McBrearty. 1946-56 Cornelius Dennehy. 1956-57 Patrick Rogers. 1957-67 James Fitzgibbon. 1967-78 Thomas Meikleham. 1978-81 Patrick J McGovern (1947) (1). 1981- Noel Murray.

Assistants: 1882-85 Patrick Barton. 1886-88 Ronald Mortimer. 1888-89 James Bird (ED). 1889-92 David Morris. 1892-98 John Nagle. 1896-1910 Thomas Kerr (WD). 1898-99 Stephen A Thornton. 1899-1900 Alexander H Thomson (Aberdeen). 1900-04 Florence O'Driscoll. 1903-10 John J O'Callaghan (1900). 1904-05 James Hughes. 1905-10 John Lynch (1905). 1906-09 John Coyle. 1910-14 Richard Cronin. 1910-16 James McKenna. 1910-20 William Flanagan. 1914-16 Thomas Corley. 1916-24 John A Lyons (1907). 1916-24 Robert Devitt. 1920-26 James McNally. 1924 Francis G Mangan. 1924-26 James Phelan. 1924-30 Thomas Loftus. 1926-28 Simon Hegarty. 1926-33 Charles McFadden (1926). 1928-36 Bartholomew Burns (1928). 1930-32 Patrick J Loy. 1932-35 Thomas E Frigerio. 1933-36 Hugh Kelly (1933). 1935-36 Patrick Wycherley. 1936-39 Gerald McDade. 1936-39 Denis McGrath (1927). 1936-39 Edward McEllin. 1939-45 Denis Lucey. 1939-52 Thomas O'Friel. 1939-57 Patrick Smith. 1945-47 James Sweeney. 1946 Dermot

McMullan. 1946 Ferdinand Tritschler. 1947-49 Patrick McGovern (1947) (1). 1948-51 Edmund Budds. 1949-74 Joseph Mulhall. 1953-61 John Branagan. 1955-56 Patrick Rogers (administrator). 1957-62 Hugh Deery. 1962-70 John Loughlin. 1962-75 Peter O'Farrell. 1970-71 Anthony Beckett. 1971-74 Thomas Quinn. 1974-81 Noel Murray. 1975-78 Desmond J McGinty. 1978-81 Timothy McGlynn.

GLASGOW – ST ALPHONSUS'
Heads: 1877-90 Michael Maginn (WD). 1890-1930 Thomas P O'Reilly (WD). 1930-43 Patrick Hourigan. 1943-44 vacant. 1944-45 John Ryan (1913). 1945-47 John McIntyre (1920). 1947-59 Daniel O'Keeffe. 1959-76 Laurence Brady. 1976-78 Malachy Bergin. 1978-84 Jeremiah Carroll. 1984- Edward Kelly.
Assistants: 1878-84 Aloysius Godfrey (WD). 1884-86 Timothy O'Hea. 1886-90 John Montgomery. 1887-90 Henry Kuppers. 1890-91 Thomas Kerr (WD). 1890-92 Denis Frawley. 1891-97 Angus McEachen. 1892-94 Jeremiah Maher. 1893-98 John Murray (1893). 1897-98 Thomas Gavagan. 1898-1900 James Harris (ED). 1898-1901 Joseph E Conway. 1900-12 Daniel Scannell. 1901-06 John F Kelly. 1904-05 Frederick R Pirrie. 1905-08 Denis Hehir. 1906-12 Patrick McGonagle. 1908-10 Michael Gordon. 1912-14 Patrick Gaynor. 1912-18 James Hughes. 1914-30 Peter Boland. 1918-19 Patrick J O'Sullivan (1918) (possibly; he is given as being in two parishes simultaneously). 1918-26 John Boyle (1918). 1919-20 Thomas Daly. 1924 Edward Douglas. 1925-31 Daniel O'Keeffe. 1926-46 Joseph McErlain. 1931-33 James L Cullen. 1931-49 Patrick F Casey. 1933-50 William Mallon. 1946-67 Matthew Carney. 1949-55 Anthony Donnelly. 1950-52 Charles MacFadden (1950). 1952-62 William Murphy (1952). 1955-63 John Boles. 1957 John Loughlin. 1962 Alistair MacLellan. 1962-76 Joseph Coyle. 1963-83 Philip O'Reilly. 1967-69 Joseph Mills. 1969- Thomas J Chambers.

GLASGOW – ST ANNE'S
Heads: 1899-1900 Charles McGhee. 1900-17 Thomas Currie. 1917-23 Robert Paterson. 1923-41 John J Fleming. 1941-49 Joseph J Crumly. 1949-67 Archibald Watt. 1967-74 Gaetano Rossi. 1974-84 John Macdonald (1945). 1984- Daniel O'Leary.
Assistants: 1900-12 Bartholomew Atkinson. 1901-04 Mark McGrath. 1904-10 John A Waldron. 1910-20 John Roche (1910). 1912-17 Andrew J O'Keefe. 1913-14 James McRory. 1917-23 Joseph Courtney. 1920-23 Thomas Mulvihill. 1920-24 John Power. 1923-24 Edward McGennis. 1923-34 Daniel Harty. 1924-25 Bernard Plunkett. 1924-37 James Walsh (1924). 1925-32 Peter Sexton. 1932-36 Thomas Gannon (Dunkeld). 1933-44 Gerald A Harvey. 1936-38 William White. 1936-39 Donald Bonnar. 1937-39 Ian McLaughlin. 1938-41 Michael Ward. 1939-41 Samuel Lavery. 1939-42 James Walshe. 1941-47 Owen Traynor. 1941-49 Daniel McMahon. 1942-49 Robert O'Kane. 1944-47 Michael O'Connor (1927). 1947-49 James Sweeney. 1947-49 William Coghlan. 1949-50

Alexander Johnston. 1949-55 Daniel Toy. 1949-60 James Reilly. 1955-63 Jeremiah Carroll. 1960-66 William J Strickland. 1963-79 John Boles. 1966-72 Duncan Kane. 1972-74 John F Jordan. 1974-77 Bernard Connell. 1977-79 John Brannan. 1979-84 George Gillespie. 1983-85 Noel Colford. 1984-85 Peter Smith. 1985- Peter Sweeney.

GLASGOW – ST ANTHONY'S (Govan)

Heads: 1865-85 Walter Dixon (WD). 1885-1918 George McBrearty (WD). 1918-28 Daniel Collins. 1928-44 John Devine. 1944-45 vacant. 1945-48 Edward Douglas. 1948-50 Timothy Feely. 1950-51 vacant. 1951-55 James Graham. 1955-60 Patrick Wycherley. 1960-77 Edward Molumby. 1977-81 John Manning. 1981-87 Francis H Gilfedder. 1987- William McLellan.

Assistants: 1878-83 Michael Dempsey (WD). 1880-81 James Coghlan. 1881-82 Nicholas Power (1879). 1882-88 Louis de Meulenaere. 1883-89 John Foley (1883). 1888-94 James H Kirk. 1889 David Morris. 1889-99 Louis J C McIntyre (WD). 1894-99 Peter Fouhy. 1894-1902 Robert Paterson. 1899-1903 John McMillan (1898). 1899-1907 Martin Quinlan (1899). 1902-16 William O'Carroll. 1903-09 John Collins (1902). 1904-05 Alexander Taylor (1903). 1905 James P Prendergast (1904). 1905-09 Patrick Waldron. 1907-11 William Brown (1906). 1909-15 James A Mulvenna. 1909-26 Henry Corr. 1911-14 William Bradley (1911). 1914-18 Alexander McBride. 1915-20 Thomas Rourke. 1916-21 John P Kenneally. 1918 Denis Sheehan (1918). 1918-19 William M Kelly (1918). 1918-21 Thomas Dumphy. 1920-22 Francis Young. 1921-22 James Galbraith (Argyll). 1921-23 Patrick Mulholland (Galloway). 1922-23 Timothy O'Mahony. 1923-40 George Conlon. 1923-41 James Hogan. 1926-27 Michael Kearns. 1926-27 Edmund Ryan. 1926-45 John C Battel. 1927-36 John Cusick (1927). 1927-46 Joseph Sweeney (1927). 1936-48 Bartholomew Burns (1928). 1940-52 Michael Meechan. 1941-45 James Fisher. 1945-47 Daniel Kennedy. 1946-48 John M O'Sullivan (1946). 1947-50 Thomas McAteer. 1948-58 Philip O'Reilly. 1948-73 Joseph McElholm. 1951-55 John Boles. 1952-59 John Gillespie. 1955-56 Anthony Donnelly. 1956-63 Thomas Lafferty. 1959-71 Patrick Gunning. 1964-67 Eugene Connolly. 1967-72 John O'Halloran. 1972-77 David Currie. 1978-81 Robert J Hill.

GLASGOW – ST AUGUSTINE'S

Heads: 1953-82 Thomas Brady. 1982-83 vacant. 1983- Desmond Maguire.
Assistants: 1954-67 Denis A Hurley. 1956-69 Michael Keating. 1967-77 Bernard V Devine. 1970-71 Alexander Johnston. 1971-72 John D McGinley (1968). 1972-87 Lawrence McMahon. 1977-78 Eamon V Friel. 1978-80 John McAuley. 1980-86 Thomas Hurley. 1984 Michael Barrett. 1987- Peter Smith. 1989- William Kelly (1989).

GLASGOW – ST BARNABAS'

Heads: 1950-51 John O'Riordan. 1951-55 John Cusick (1927). 1955-58

Joseph Gallacher. 1958-70 Patrick Dineen. 1970-75 Thomas Healy (1939). 1975-78 James V Reilly. 1978-87 Michael Meechan. 1987- George Crawley.

Assistants: 1950-53 Duncan Kane. 1952-60 George Crawley. 1953-73 Patrick Tobin. 1960-68 Daniel Moore. 1968-71 Vincent Quinn. 1973-75 Philip Hastings. 1983 John P Quinn (1983).

GLASGOW – ST BARTHOLOMEW'S
Heads: 1955-72 Daniel Toy. 1972-87 Duncan Kane. 1987- Francis Mallon.

Assistants: 1956-64 Joseph P Brady. 1958-67 John B Byrne. 1964-78 Peter McCafferty. 1967-68 John Tobin. 1968-69 Joseph Cairns. 1969-74 Bernard Chalmers. 1974-77 Anthony Beckett. 1975-76 David Brown. 1976-80 William Monaghan. 1978-79 Joseph Dunne. 1979-83 Ignatius Kennedy. 1980/81-83 Hugh J McGinlay (1977). 1983- James Cosker. 1985-88 Peter McBride.

GLASGOW – ST BENEDICT'S
Heads: 1960-71 Brendan Moriarty. 1971-87 Daniel Clancy. 1987-88 Francis H Gilfedder. 1988- Peter Lennon.

Assistants: 1961-69 Hugh J McEwan (1960). 1968-73 John Tobin. 1969-89 Joseph Cairns. 1974-75 Daniel Fitzgerald. 1975-81 George Morgan. 1980-86 Edward Vesey.

GLASGOW – ST BERNADETTE'S
Heads: 1950-55 William M Mallon. 1955-65 John Cawley. 1965-78 John McGinlay (1940). 1978-89 Hugh A Deery. 1989- Colman McGrath.

Assistants: 1950-51 George Burns. 1951-52 John O'Hara. 1952-53 John O'Sullivan (1943). 1953-59 Sean O'Sullivan (1946). 1959-75 Thomas Tierney. 1975-80 John J McKee. 1981-83 George McGarrigle. 1983-85 Ignatius Kennedy. 1985- Charles Kane.

GLASGOW – ST BERNARD'S
Heads: 1960-67 Gerard Dunn. 1967-79 Matthew Carney. 1979-80 John Brannan. 1980-87 George Crawley. 1987- James Lafferty.

Assistants: 1962-68 William McGinley. 1968-73 John Conway (1955). 1972-78 John King. 1973-74 Maurice Ward. 1974-81 Michael D McCabe (1957). 1982-85 Alan Love.

GLASGOW – ST BONAVENTURE'S
Heads: 1952-60 Patrick Gilmartin. 1960-67 Michael Meechan. 1967-68 Michael Lyne. 1968-74 Daniel Moore. 1974-88 Joseph Breen. 1988- Francis H Gilfedder.

Assistants: 1952-53 Desmond Strain. 1953-57 Donald A Smith. 1953-68 Thomas S Cunningham (1953). 1957-65 Felix Beattie. 1965-70 Charles McFadden (1950). 1968-70 Germain Fitzpatrick. 1970-71 John King. 1971-74 Noel Murray.

GLASGOW – ST BRENDAN'S
Heads: 1946-59 Cornelius O'Leary. 1959-67 Thomas Meikleham. 1967-81 Thomas McKeown. 1981-89 Anthony McHugo. 1989- vacant
Assistants: 1946-47 Thomas P Mannion (1946). 1947-65 Daniel Gallagher. 1950-51 James McShane. 1951-67 George Burns. 1965-67 Gerald Fallon. 1967-69 Thomas J Chambers. 1968-70 Patrick G Fitzpatrick. 1968-71 Noel Murray. 1970-71 John McDermott (1964). 1971-74 Neil McDaid. 1971-74 Francis Kennedy. 1974-76 John Gowans. 1974-84 Andrew Tolan. 1976-77 Felix Beattie. 1977-80 Francis Courtney. 1980-81 Thomas S Cunningham (1953). 1981-86 William McGinley. 1984 Peter Smith. 1984-86 George Gillespie. 1986-89 Eamon V Friel. 1989- Joseph Mills. 1989- John McAuley.

GLASGOW – ST BRIGID'S
Heads: 1955-83 Patrick J Sheary. 1983- John O'Hagan.
Assistants: 1957-59 Francis Goodfellow. 1959-61 Neil A Johnstone. 1961-83 James Cosker. 1964-65 William J Slavin. 1966-78 Michael D O'Grady. 1978-87 Neil McDaid. 1985- Anthony Sweeney. 1987- Nicholas Rowan.

GLASGOW – ST CATHERINE LABOURE'S
Heads: 1950-54 William Lowery. 1954-72 Gerard Hart. 1972-81 Daniel Toy. 1981-87 Bernard V Devine. 1987-88 John McLaren. 1988-89 vacant. 1989- John J N Burns.
Assistants: 1953-67 Denis Bradley. 1956-60 Joseph Nee. 1961-74 Peter Lennon. 1967-73 Francis H Gilfedder. 1973-77 John Gilmartin. 1974-81 Patrick G Currie. 1977-84 Anthony Gallagher. 1981-84 John N Woods. 1984-86 Paul Budis. 1985- William Clarke. 1989- Alexander Johnston.

GLASGOW – ST CHARLES'
Note: From 1913-26 St Columba's was combined with St Charles'. Priests serving the two churches are listed under the one presbytery, so it is impossible to determine which priests were serving which church.
Heads: 1899-1913 Daniel Stewart. 1913-20 Edward Fitzgerald (1894). 1920-29 Patrick Cush. 1929-37 Daniel J Horgan (1898). 1937-55 John A Lyons. 1955-79 Vincent O'Sullivan. 1979- John Chalmers.
Assistants: 1899-1900 Alexander McCormick (1895). 1900-03 John J O'Callaghan (1900). 1903-08 John Roche (1903). 1903-09 Patrick Sheridan (1903). 1908-09 Mortimer J Galvin. 1909-28 Patrick Loy. 1909-28 Eugene Murray. 1913-22 John Devine. 1913-26 Edmund MacDonald. 1922-25 Michael J Murphy. 1925-26 Edmond Ryan. 1927-28 Daniel Molloy. 1928-29 James C Ward (1928). 1928-30 Edmund Macdonald. 1929-31 Daniel Molloy. 1929-48 James Ward (1929). 1930-31 Columba McGoldrick. 1931-42 Daniel O'Keefe. 1931-42 Thomas O'Neill. 1940 James E Hallinan. 1942-57 Thomas Glen. 1942-57 Martin Quinlan (1942). 1948-52 Guido Vaccaro. 1952-67 Francis Coyle. 1957-61 John McElroy (Paisley). 1957-68 Gerald P McCallion. 1961-67 Thomas Dolan.

1967-69 John Muldoon. 1967-72 Nicholas Rowan. 1968-73 William McGinley. 1969-72 John Sheridan (1956). 1972-77 Edward Kelly. 1973-74 Sean Fitzgerald. 1974-77 William McLellan. 1977-79 George F Gillespie.

GLASGOW – ST COLUMBA'S
Note: From 1913-26 see St Charles' above.
Heads: 1906-13 Edward Fitzgerald (1894). 1926-29 Francis A McCann. 1929-37 James McKenna. 1937-47 Denis Flynn. 1947-59 Thomas Keane. 1959-67 John McGuckin. 1967-84 John McCready (1935). 1984- John Roberts.
Assistants: 1906-13 John A Devine. 1926-27 Charles McKenna. 1926-28 Edmund Macdonald. 1927-47 Joseph Duffy. 1928-29 William Christie. 1929-32 Neil McKnight. 1932-36 Patrick S Brennan. 1936-47 Patrick Wycherley. 1942-82 Joseph Gutauskas. 1946-47 Vincent E Grace. 1947-48 James Fitzgibbon. 1947-65 Brendan Murphy. 1948-61 Malachy Finnegan. 1961-70 James P Corrigan. 1965-69 Felix Beattie. 1969-74 John A Collins (1969). 1970-77 John Loughlin. 1985- Patrick G Fitzpatrick. 1986-87 Paul Budis.

GLASGOW – ST CONSTANTINE'S
Note: From 1926-45 served from St Anthony's.
Heads: 1921-26 Daniel Colvin. 1945-67 James Fletcher. 1967-78 Michael Meechan. 1978- William Tobin.
Assistants: 1921-23 Michael Munnelly. 1923-26 Michael Kearns. 1945-46 John C Battel. 1946-50 Charles Duffin. 1946-51 Michael O'Sullivan. 1949-67 Malachy Bergin. 1950-57 James O'Reilly. 1951-52 Daniel O'Leary. 1952-55 Thomas Healy (1939). 1955-58 Thomas Reilly. 1957-67 Samuel McGinness. 1958-63 John McAveety. 1959-71 Sabatino Tedeschi. 1963-68 John Conway (1955). 1967-72 Anthony Donnelly. 1967-72 Denis A Hurley. 1968-69 Hugh McGinlay (1964). 1969-70 Angus MacLean (1969). 1970-73 Brendan Foley. 1971-80 James Lafferty. 1972-77 James A Burns. 1973-76 Peter C McKelvie. 1973-77 Anthony Welsh. 1977-80 George Crawley. 1977-81 John Loughlin. 1980-85 John A Collins (1969). 1981-84 Francis O'Rourke. 1981-84 James McLaughlin (1973). 1985-88 George Bradburn. 1985- Francis Balmer. 1988- John O'Neill.

GLASGOW – ST CONVAL'S
Heads: 1949-52 Patrick Conway. 1952-60 Edward Molumby. 1960-78 John J Wilson. 1978-86 Thomas Murphy (1948). 1986- Patrick Gahagan.
Assistants: 1949-51 Louis Knight. 1951-52 Robert G O'Kane. 1951-62 Patrick J Henry. 1952-59 William McDonald. 1959-63 John MacNeil (1957). 1962-65 Hugh Kearns. 1963-67 John McFaul. 1965-73 John Glynn. 1967-74 Malachy Bergin. 1972-74 Patrick G Fitzpatrick. 1974-76 Ewen McPhail. 1974-77 George Crawley. 1976-80 Edward Vesey. 1977-

79 Andrew Hosie. 1979-82 William McLellan. 1980- Robert McCann. 1984-89 David Tracey. 1989- Patrick Currie.

GLASGOW – ST DOMINIC'S: see Bishopbriggs, St Dominic's

GLASGOW – ST GABRIEL'S
Heads: 1955-60 John J Wilson (1933). 1960-74 Joseph Breen. 1974-82 James Quinn (1942). 1982- Richard Dunne.
Assistants: 1964-70 John McDermott (1964). 1970-71 James Fitzgerald (1940). 1971-78 Alistair D MacLellan. 1978-81 Francis H Gilfedder. 1981-89 Brian Morren. 1989- Hugh Lowrie.

GLASGOW – ST GREGORY'S
Heads: 1965-76 Brendan H Murphy. 1976- Daniel M Gallagher.
Assistants: 1965-67 William Donnelly. 1966-80 Thomas J Hendry. 1967-77 Desmond Maguire. 1974-76 Anthony Sweeney. 1976-79 William O'Neil. 1980-89 John McAuley. 1981-84 Brian Magee. 1984- Charles McElwee.

GLASGOW – ST HELEN'S
Heads: 1966-69 Desmond Gunning. 1969-74 Robert Woods. 1974-84 John Hanrahan. 1984- Daniel J C Hart.
Assistants: 1968-69 James McShane. 1970 Angus J MacDonald. 1970-71 George Crawley. 1971-73 Patrick Gunning. 1973-75 John A McKelvie. 1975-79 Francis McPartlin. 1979 Alfred McKenzie. 1979-83 Colman McGrath. 1980 Christopher J McElroy. 1981 Paul J Kierney. 1982 Aidan Martin. 1983-86 Hugh Lowrie. 1984 Charles J McElwee. 1986- David Brown.

GLASGOW – ST JAMES'
Heads: 1949-55 John Martin. 1955-67 Daniel Kennedy. 1967-76 Martin Quinlan (1942). 1976-79 Joseph Wilkinson. 1979-83 James Martin. 1983- Matthew Coakley.
Assistants: 1956-66 Daniel O'Leary. 1966-75 John Manning. 1968-69 Desmond J McGinty. 1969-82 Peter Marr. 1975-76 Joseph Dunne. 1976-82 John McLaren. 1982-88 Peter Clinton. 1984-87 Dermot Healy. 1988- Peter C McKelvie. 1989- Joseph Cairns.

GLASGOW – ST JOACHIM'S: 1954-63 John Noon. 1963-79 Joseph Gallacher. 1979-89 William Murphy (1952). 1989- Hugh J McEwan (1960).

GLASGOW – ST JOHN'S (St John the Evangelist)
Heads: 1855-82 Valentine Chisholm (WD). 1882-1920 John B Macluskey (WD). 1920-29 Patrick Ryan. 1929-32 Patrick Cush. 1932-45 Archibald McSparran. 1945-46 Henry Corr. 1946-67 John Boyle (1918). 1967-79 Charles Duffin. 1979-82 Joseph Kerr.
Assistants: 1875-79 Thomas Curran (WD). 1878-79 Thomas P O'Reilly (WD)

(possibly; appears simultaneously under two parishes). 1879-80 Peter Donnelly (WD). 1879-85 Joseph van Hecke. 1880-82 Edmund Cantwell (WD). 1881-86 John Murphy (1881). 1883-86 Bernard McGivney. 1885-89 Patrick Daly. 1886-92 Michael Fuller. 1888-90 William McAvoy. 1889-91 Thomas Hopwell. 1890-93 Michael Curtin. 1891-97 Peter Hilgers. 1892-99 Patrick Ryan. 1894-1901 Peter Murray. 1897-1900 John Cahill. 1898-1900 Vincent Warnagiris. 1899-1910 James Fitzgerald (1899). 1900-03 Louis Woitys. 1900-05 Stephen A Thornton. 1901-14 Justin Whyte. 1903-14 John J Fleming. 1905 Alexander Mackintosh. 1905-08 Patrick Loy. 1910-18 Alexander Mackintosh. 1914-16 Thomas Farry. 1914-16 Peter F Walshe. 1915-20 Patrick Ryan (administrator). 1916-24 Hugh J Bradley (1916). 1917-18 Thomas O'Hanlon. 1918-19 John MacNeil (1918) (Argyll). 1918-25 Denis Sheehan (1918). 1918-33 John O'Donnell (1918). 1919-23 Constantine Doherty. 1924-36 James Fletcher. 1925 Edmund Ryan. 1925-27 John Lynch (1925). 1926-37 Guido Toncker. 1927-29 Charles McKenna. 1929-33 Matthew Shiels. 1932 Martin Doherty. 1933-39 William Hart. 1933-50 James Meechan. 1936-46 Cornelius O'Leary. 1937-58 Patrick Dinneen. 1939-51 Joseph Breen. 1946-47 Charles McKinney (Argyll). 1947-67 Nicholas Rowan. 1950-57 John Ryan (1950). 1951 John G O'Hara. 1953-54 John Gowans. 1954 Christopher P Gilfedder. 1954-71 John Chalmers. 1957-60 Francis Molloy. 1958-72 John N Woods. 1960-61 James McGladrigan. 1962-65 David Tracey. 1967-73 Denis Bradley. 1972-75 Gerald P McCallion. 1980-81 William J Slavin.
Church closed 1982.

GLASGOW – ST JOHN OGILVIE'S (originally Blessed John Ogilvie's)
Heads: 1957-60 Jeremiah Healy. 1960-78 Thomas Reilly. 1978-89 Patrick Tobin. 1989- Eamon V Friel.
Assistants: 1959-61 Edward Higgins. 1961-69 John Fitzgibbon (1945). 1969-75 John J McKee. 1975-77 Brendan T Foley. 1977-78 Michael Keating. 1987-89 Noel Colford.

GLASGOW – ST JOSEPH'S, TOLLCROSS
Heads: 1893-94 Edward Doody. 1894-1909 James Kirk. 1909-26 Daniel O'Sullivan (1895). 1926-29 Daniel J Horgan (1898). 1929-38 Michael McCarthy (1909). 1938-45 Cornelius Dennehy. 1945-70 Alfred Joseph Gallaucher. 1970-79 Edward O'Hara. 1979-84 John Mone. 1984-87 Donald MacKinnon. 1987- Michael Meechan.
Assistants: 1899-1908 Matthew Hennessy. 1908-11 John A Lyons (1907). 1911-13 Michael Mulvey. 1911-14 Daniel F Crowe. 1913-24 Matthew Quillinan. 1914-33 Peter Fitzpatrick. 1924-26 Joseph O'Leary. 1925-26 Jeremiah F Ahern. 1926 James H Doherty (1911). 1926-29 Gerald McDade. 1929-50 William Lowery. 1933-42 Neil McKnight. 1942-43 John McGinlay (1940). 1943-50 Neil McKnight. 1950-57 Jeremiah O'Flynn. 1950-67 John O'Brien. 1957-59 Thomas Holloran. 1959-62 Francis Goodfellow. 1962-70 Patrick J Kelly (1951). 1967-74 William

Tobin. 1971-83 Frederick Thompson. 1974-76 Hugh Lowrie. 1976-78 Edward B McNaught. 1981-85 Charles Kane. 1983- Michael Sharkey. 1986-88 Alistair MacLellan. 1989- John J Carroll.

GLASGOW – ST JOSEPH'S, WOODSIDE
Served by Jesuits until 1930.

Heads: 1930-43 James P Kelly. 1943-48 George Stuart. 1948-55 Peter Morrison. 1955-62 John Martin. 1962-67 Gaetano Rossi. 1967-72 Robert G O'Kane. 1972-73 Francis Coyle. 1973-76 Joseph Wilkinson. 1976-84 Charles McFadden (1950).

Assistants: 1930-31 Edmond Mollumby (possibly: he is given under two parishes simultaneously). 1930-38 Francis Misset. 1930-38 John Scanlon. 1930-43 Samuel Kilpatrick. 1930/31-32 Bernard Magauran. 1931-36 Matthew Littleton. 1932 Thomas P Murphy (1932). 1936-41 Owen Traynor. 1938-40 John McNair. 1938-40 Bernard Feeney. 1940-41 Francis Hamilton (1926). 1940-47 Michael J O'Connell. 1941-45 William Coghlan. 1941-51 Daniel O'Leary. 1943-44 Thomas A Woods. 1944-52 Gerald A Harvey. 1945-54 Charles Vallely. 1947-48 John Carter. 1949-50 William Tobin. 1951-56 Michael Connolly. 1951-67 Michael Lyne. 1953-65 Andrew Burns. 1954-59 Felix McCarney (Paisley). 1959-67 Patrick Osborne. 1967-69 Patrick Tierney. 1967-70 George Crawley. 1970-71 Hugh McGinlay (1964). 1972-77 Hugh McGinlay (1964). 1972-84 Daniel J C Hart. 1976-78 John A McKelvie.

United with St Columba's in 1984.

GLASGOW – ST JUDE'S
Heads: 1954-82 Martin Doherty. 1982-86 Denis A Hurley. 1986- Thomas Hurley.

Assistants: 1956-65 Gerard Fallon. 1965-66 James O'Reilly. 1966-69 Roderick Wright. 1969-70 John F Ward. 1970-74 Charles McFadden (1950). 1974-79 Peter Lennon. 1980-81 Francis Courtney. 1981-84 Ewen McPhail. 1984-87 Anthony Gallagher.

GLASGOW – ST LAURENCE'S
Heads: 1954-57 William Forbes. 1957-67 Charles Duffin. 1967-70 Richard J O'Callaghan. 1970-75 Michael J Walsh. 1975-86 Michael O'Connell. 1986- David McLachlan.

Assistants: 1956-64 John McCarthy. 1957-60 James O'Reilly. 1960-67 James V Reilly. 1964-66 Roderick Wright. 1966-67 Francis Cowan MHM. 1967-72 James O'Hare. 1967-81 John Roberts. 1972-76 John D McGinley (1968). 1976-78 Joseph Dunne. 1977-82 William Clarke. 1981-82 Peter O'Farrell. 1982-86 James Doherty (1979). 1986-89 Joseph Mills.

GLASGOW – ST LEO THE GREAT
Heads: 1962-67 Richard J O'Callaghan. 1967-69 John McFaul. 1969-87 Joseph Nee. 1987- John Muldoon.

Assistants: 1979-80 Gerard McKay. 1983-85 John Sheridan (1956).

GLASGOW – ST LOUISE'S
Heads: 1973-80 Donal Burke. 1980- John J McKee.
Assistants: 1977-82 Joseph Murphy. 1982- Peter O'Farrell.

GLASGOW – ST LUKE'S
Heads: 1905-08 Patrick Ryan. 1908-15 Patrick Gallacher. 1915-18 William J McLaughlin. 1918-23 John McMillan (1898). 1923-38 James Nolan (1902). 1938-39 vacant. 1939-44 Peter Boland. 1944-46 John Boyle (1918). 1946-48 Peter Morrison. 1948-52 Patrick Gilmartin. 1952-69 Patrick Conway. 1969-81 John McFaul. 1981-82 John G O'Hara. 1982-84 Joseph Kerr. 1984- Francis O'Rourke.
Assistants: 1905-06 Patrick Griffin. 1905-09 John Crumly. 1906-08 Joseph Courtney. 1908-16 Joseph Doherty. 1909-13 Patrick Garvey. 1912-13 Francis Vasiliauskas. 1913-22 Hugh Delargey. 1914-20 Antony Shvaeistris. 1916-24 Francis Taggart. 1920-22 Charles Gallagher. 1922-23 James Galbraith (Argyll). 1922-28 James McGrory. 1924-25 Thomas Guinan. 1924-34 Peter Harte. 1927-33 Patrick Kelly (1927). 1928-37 William McGoldrick. 1933-34 William Forbes. 1934-35 Daniel O'Brien. 1934-37 Thomas Cahill. 1935-36 John O'Callaghan (1917). 1936-40 Joseph Regan. 1937-39 Thomas Murray (1936). 1937-42 James Walsh (1924). 1937-49 Daniel Toy. 1940-43 Peter McCann (1940). 1942-47 Joseph Sheary. 1943-49 Patrick J Brady. 1947-48 Michael J Walsh. 1948-53 Joseph Gallagher. 1949-51 Robert G O'Kane. 1949-67 John Dennehy. 1951-52 Thomas McCabe. 1952-60 John Brannan. 1953-57 Charles Duffin. 1957-70 Patrick J Byrne. 1961 James P Corrigan. 1967-71 Francis Meagher. 1971-72 Robert Bradley. 1972-75 John O'Brien. 1979-80 John Gilmartin. 1982- Philip Hastings.

GLASGOW – ST MARGARET MARY'S
Heads: 1957-70 Martin Hughes. 1970-78 Patrick Dineen. 1978-87 Michael Mooney. 1987- Bernard V Devine.
Assistants: 1957-65 Anthony Burke. 1960-65 John Glynn. 1962-64 Anthony Donnelly. 1965-72 James Martin. 1965-82 Anthony Bancewicz. 1968-70 Edward Gallagher. 1970-76 John Ward. 1972-78 Matthew Coakley. 1976-81 Sabatino Tedeschi. 1978-83 John A McKelvie. 1981- Lawrence Jamieson. 1982-84 Edward Lindsay. 1983-85 Hugh J McGinlay (1977). 1984-86 John Brannan. 1985-86 Alistair MacLellan. 1986-88 Michael Woodford. 1986- Francis Gallagher. 1988- John P Quinn (1983).

GLASGOW – ST MARK'S: see Carntyne

GLASGOW – ST MARIA GORETTI'S
Heads: 1953-63 Patrick Coogan. 1963-77 Joseph Connelly. 1977-82 Sean O'Neill. 1982- Michael Henretty.

Assistants: 1955-61 Daniel McEwan. 1958-71 William Coghlan. 1961-62 Gerard Philips SMA. 1962-63 Joseph Connelly. 1963-71 Neil McDaid. 1971-73 Neil Donnachie. 1972-77 George F Gillespie. 1973-81 John Conway (1955). 1978-79 James Wallace. 1980-82 Thomas Docherty. 1981-83 John McCabe. 1983-86 Frederick Thompson. 1983-86 Sabatino Tedeschi. 1986-88 Gerard F Barnes. 1986-89 James A Burns. 1989- John F Gannon.

GLASGOW – ST MARTIN'S
Heads: 1957-68 Jeremiah O'Flynn. 1968-72 Michael Lyne. 1972-73 John Conlan. 1973-82 Richard Dunne. 1982- Michael Keating.
Assistants: 1957-59 John McNeil (1957). 1959-65 Thomas Holloran. 1961-63 Maurice Ward. 1963-67 Peter McKelvie. 1965-67 James Quinn (1942). 1967-74 Bernard Connell. 1967-75 Henry McKay. 1974-80 John A Collins (1969). 1975-77 Joseph Boyle. 1977-84 David Tracey. 1980-85 James Lafferty. 1984- George Morgan. 1985-88 John McGinley (1985).

GLASGOW – ST MARY'S
Heads: 1872-96 Donald Carmichael (WD). 1896-1922 John J Dyer (WD). 1922-42 Edward Fitzgerald (1894). 1942-48 Peter Bonnyman. 1948-73 Michael Ward. 1973-75 Thomas Murphy (1948). 1975-78 John O'Brien.
Assistants: 1876-79 Frederick J Evertz (WD). 1877-81 Denis McCarthy (WD). 1878-84 Michael Benger (WD). 1879-81 John Linster (WD). 1881-83 Emile de Backer (WD). 1881-86 Daniel Donnelly (WD). 1881-86 Peter Fegan. 1883-85 Michael McCarthy (1882). 1884-89 Adrian van der Heyde. 1885-90 James Nolan (1885). 1886-93 Philip McColl. 1887 John Cameron. 1887-90 Aloysius Godfrey (WD). 1889-94 Robert Grant (WD). 1890-94 Jeremiah Burke. 1890-95 David Murie. 1893-98 Peter O'Connor. 1894 Francis Cronin. 1894-96 Michael Dempsey (WD). 1894-1900 Charles Haeger. 1895-96 Alexander McCormack (1895). 1895-98 Aloysius Reifenrath. 1896-1902 Edward Fitzgerald (1894). 1897-1905 Myles Ambrose. 1898-1907 John Brotherhood. 1900-07 Thomas Joyce (Galloway). 1902-14 Patrick Diamond. 1905-11 James P Prendergast (1904). 1907-24 Thomas McEwan. 1907-30 Angus McInnes (Aberdeen). 1910-11 Daniel Duane. 1911-18 James H Doherty (1911). 1914-22 Michael O'Brien. 1918-19 John O'Callaghan (1917). 1919-24 Patrick McRory. 1920-22 Edward Fitzgerald (1894) (administrator). 1922-26 Edward Kinane. 1924-27 John O'Donoghue. 1924-27 Michael O'Carroll. 1925-26 Thomas Griffin. 1926-32 Thomas McLoughlin. 1927-28 Patrick F Keating. 1927-32 Richard Fennessey. 1928-32 David L Power (1928). 1928-32 John Bredin. 1930-32 Peter Boland. 1932-37 Thomas Egan. 1932-37 Patrick Torley. 1932-46 James K Elliot. 1932-48 John Noon. 1935-36 Gerald Lord. 1936 James Horan. 1936-41 Hugh McKeague. 1937 Hugh McCranor. 1937-39 Joseph O'Hagan. 1937-44 Thomas Reilly. 1939-46 Gerald O'Callaghan. 1941-44 James McGill. 1944-46 Thomas A Woods. 1944-49 Patrick Conway. 1945-65 Jeremiah O'Connor. 1946-47 Robert Barclay. 1947-53 Thomas Sharkey. 1948-55

Patrick Sheary. 1949-51 Donald McDougall (Argyll). 1951-65 John Macdonald (1945). 1953-54 Felix Beattie. 1954-56 Michael Keating. 1955-63 Anthony Beckett. 1956-62 David Currie. 1963-65 Jeremiah Carroll. 1964-65 Noel Colford. 1965-66 Noel Joseph Burke. 1965-68 Charles Cush. 1965-73 Thomas Holloran. 1966-72 John McKelvie. 1968-71 John D McGinley (1968). 1969 John Hay. 1972-73 John McAuley. 1973-77 Anthony Gallagher.
From 1978 served by Carmelites.

GLASGOW – ST MARY IMMACULATE
Heads: 1861-80 Bernard Tracy (WD). 1880-99 James McNamara (WD). 1899-1900 James W McCarthy. 1900-16 James F Morrison. 1916-18 James Mullen. 1918-36 Emile de Backer (WD). 1936-48 Edward Lawton. 1948-64 James P Kelly. 1964-65 vacant. 1965-81 Joseph Daniel. 1981-Hugh O'Donnell.
Assistants: 1879-80 Edmund Cantwell (WD). 1880-84 James Mackintosh (WD). 1887-88 Owen McPolin. 1890-94 Thomas Currie. 1894-97 Francis A McCann. 1897-1902 Richard Meskell. 1902-04 George J Ryan. 1902-08 Charles A Cunningham. 1904-06 Daniel J Horgan (1898). 1906-22 Patrick Doyle. 1908-13 Denis Murrin. 1913 Charles McGhee. 1913-28 John Stuart. 1915-17 Achille van Wesemael CSsR. 1922-23 Joseph Byrne (St A & E). 1923-41 Patrick Coogan. 1928-39 Kenneth Grant (Argyll). 1933 Daniel McGlinchey (1932). 1933-34 John R Tennant. 1934-45 Thomas J Taylor (1934). 1936-37 John McCready (1935). 1939-44 Michael Gilroy. 1941-44 Daniel O'Doherty. 1942-43 Thomas McKeown. 1944-45 Hugh Mahon. 1944-57 Jeremiah Healy. 1945-48 Daniel Clancy. 1945-50 Thomas Meikleham. 1948-50 John Duffy. 1950-52 William Coghlan. 1950-67 Richard Dunne. 1952-55 Daniel Friel. 1955-70 Bruno Renucci. 1957-58 William Foran. 1958-69 Francis Mallon. 1967-70 James V Reilly. 1969-73 Sean Fitzgerald. 1970-73 Gerard C Hill. 1970-77 Patrick J Kelly (1951). 1973-74 Patrick G Currie. 1974-76 Joseph Kerr. 1976-81 Francis O'Rourke. 1977-81 William McGinley. 1981-87 Christopher McElroy. 1987-88 Joseph Dunne. 1988-Paul G Murray.

GLASGOW – ST MATTHEW'S: see Bishopbriggs, St Matthew's

GLASGOW – ST MICHAEL'S (Parkhead)
Heads: 1877-85 Thomas Kerr (WD). 1885-90 Arthur Beyaert. 1890-97 John Toner. 1894 Peter Murray (interim head). 1897-99 Michael McNairney. 1899-1900 John Ritchie. 1900-08 Ellis P Rogan. 1908-19 Martin Jansen. 1919-21 Anthony Mullins. 1921-22 Bartholomew Atkinson. 1922-33 Patrick J Laydon. 1933-52 James Durkin. 1952-67 Thomas J O'Kane. 1967-72 James Meechan. 1972- Michael Lyne.
Assistants: 1877-79 Emile de Backer (WD). 1880-81 Thomas J Cunningham (1879). 1881-83 Patrick Browne. 1883-84 Thomas

Brosnan. 1886-87 Aloysius Godfrey (WD). 1887-89 John Cameron. 1889-93 Edward Doody. 1894-95 Michael Dinan. 1895-96 Alexander Macdonald. 1896-97 Donald A McPherson (Argyll). 1897-99 Francis A McCann. 1898-1902 Maurice Fitzgibbon. 1899-1900 William C Brown (1897). 1900-05 Edmond Fitzgerald. 1902-03 Daniel Gillon. 1903-04 Thomas Barrett. 1903-05 Bernard Cunningham. 1904-10 Edward Vaughan. 1905-12 Robert Cairns. 1906 Patrick Doyle. 1907-09 James Troy. 1910-19 Peter Bonnyman. 1912-14 Michael Cannon. 1914-17 Jerome Dennehy. 1916-21 Timothy O'Sullivan (1899). 1919-28 Peter Murie. 1921-22 John Fahey. 1921-33 John McIntyre (1920). 1922-24 Thomas P Guinan. 1924-27 Robert Devitt. 1927-31 Denis McGrath (1927). 1928-40 John D Daniel. 1931-39 Alexander Fyfe. 1932 Hugh Cassidy. 1933-41 Michael McNicholas. 1938-39 Richard Fennessy. 1939-40 Patrick J Gullane. 1939-45 Thomas Kelly (1925) (2). 1940-43 Ferdinand Tritschler. 1941-44 Michael Walshe. 1941-52 Joseph Power. 1943-44 Michael Houlihan. 1944-57 Michael Mooney. 1945-47 John Branagan. 1945-48 William Hart. 1947-51 Edward Molumby. 1949 Gerald P McCallion. 1949-66 Michael O'Connell. 1951-52 Joseph Kerr. 1952-54 John Duffy. 1954-55 Michael Dunleavy. 1955-63 Francis O'Rourke. 1957-66 Edmund Budds. 1963-64 William McDonald. 1964-72 John Newman. 1966-69 William J Strickland. 1966-72 Bartholomew Burns (1960). 1969-75 William J Slavin. 1972-73 Denis Cronin CSsP. 1972-80 James Kirby. 1975-80 Francis Gallagher. 1980- Anthony Welsh.

GLASGOW – ST MONICA'S
Heads: 1969-76 William J Strickland. 1976-78 William Tobin. 1978-82 Thomas Reilly. 1982- John O'Sullivan (1954).
Assistants: 1974-76 William Tobin. 1986-88 Joseph McAuley.

GLASGOW – ST NICHOLAS'
Heads: 1949-51 William A Hart. 1951-59 Laurence Brady. 1959-61 Michael J McEleney. 1961-70 John Branagan. 1970-71 Daniel Clancy. 1971-74 Daniel M Gallagher. 1974-76 Donal MacMenamin. 1976-79 Joseph Kerr.
Assistants: 1950-57 Alexander Johnston. 1951-55 Patrick J Kelly (1951). 1954-60 Joseph Murphy. 1957-61 John Fitzgibbon (1945). 1960-64 Peter McCafferty. 1964-70 Joseph P Brady. 1970-72 Hugh O'Donnell.
Church closed 1979.

GLASGOW – ST NINIAN'S
Heads: 1927-41 Patrick Reilly. 1941-57 Thomas Rourke. 1957-63 Michael J Connolly. 1963-75 John Noon. 1975- John Bennett.
Assistants: 1930-37 Charles McKinley. 1937-50 Jeremiah O'Flynn. 1939-41 Peter Murie. 1940-42 Luke Brady. 1941-42 Angus MacKellaig. 1941-50 Charles Burns. 1948-51 Donal McMenamin. 1950-51 John Bradley. 1950-52 John Duffy. 1950-53 Charles Duffin. 1952-73 Thomas Murphy (1948). 1952-75 John Mone. 1953-55 Thomas Sharkey. 1956-63 Henry

Farrelly. 1963-78 Ignatius Kennedy. 1973-75 Desmond J McGinty. 1975-80 Lawrence Jamieson. 1978-82 Peter McCafferty. 1978-84 Francis Meagher. 1980-86 Bernard Connell. 1982-86 Noel Barry. 1984- Ewen McPhail. 1986-87 Stephen Holland. 1986-88 James T Clancy. 1987- John Campbell. 1988-89 Colman McGrath. 1989- Michael Duffy.

GLASGOW – ST PATRICK'S
Heads: 1867-85 John Dwyer (WD). 1885-1902 Michael Condon (WD). 1902-18 James Mullin. 1918-40 William J McLaughlin. 1940-43 Joseph Kennedy. 1943-44 vacant. 1944-73 Peter Boland. 1973-79 John Martin. 1979- Joseph Wilkinson.
Assistants: 1876-81 James Conaghan (WD). 1877-79 John Linster (WD). 1877-80 Michael O'Neill (WD). 1879-81 John Taylor. 1880-83 William Keating. 1881-82 Denis McCarthy (WD). 1881-82 Humphry O'Callaghan. 1882-85 Louis de Backer. 1882-86 Thomas Hackett. 1883-86 John Angland. 1885-86 William van Wyk. 1886-89 Patrick Buckley. 1886-91 Charles McGhee. 1888-89 Owen McPolin. 1889-90 David Murie. 1889-96 Michael McCabe (1889). 1890-94 Gisbert J Hartmann. 1891-93 John Black (WD). 1893-97 John Cameron. 1894-1901 Jeremiah O'Driscoll. 1896-97 William Orr. 1897-98 Matthew Burke. 1897-1901 John Toner (administrator). 1897-1901 Donald McPherson (Argyll). 1898-99 Angus Mackintosh. 1899-1905 Alexander Macdonald. 1899-1908 John McMenemey. 1901-02 James Mullin (administrator). 1901-04 Patrick Green (St A & E). 1901-06 Angus Mackintosh. 1901-14 Edward Lawton. 1903-09 James F Prendergast (1903). 1904-07 William J J Trainor (Galloway). 1904-17 James Kelly. 1906-36 Andrew Lynch. 1907-12 James C Coyne. 1908-11 John F Kenny. 1909-10 Peter Bonnyman. 1910-16 Charles R Brown (WD). 1911-15 Michael Hackett. 1912-13 Jerome Dennehy. 1913-16 Francis Taggart. 1914-18 John Ashe. 1915-19 Nicholas H Power (1914). 1916-17 Francis Hamilton (1915). 1916-26 Thomas McCann. 1917-26 David Quigley. 1917-31 James Clune. 1918-23 James J Scanlon. 1919 Bartholomew Flynn. 1919-29 Patrick Clarke. 1920-21 David Power (1920). 1923-26 John McDonald (1916) (Dunkeld). 1926-29 Hector McNeil (Dunkeld). 1926-30 Daniel J Donovan. 1926-34 James B Walsh (1925). 1929 Matthew Littleton. 1929-49 John Martin. 1929-51 Laurence Brady. 1930-34 James Fitzgibbon. 1931-53 Daniel Scullion. 1934-37 Daniel Toy. 1934-44 Joseph Brett. 1936-40 John Deans. 1937-40 John J Cusick (1930). 1940-46 Patrick Rice. 1940-52 John Gogarty. 1943-44 Jeremiah Lane. 1945-55 Thomas J Taylor (1934). 1946-55 Robert K Connolly. 1950-67 Joseph Wilkinson. 1951-65 Sean O'Neill. 1952-59 Thomas Tierney. 1953-59 John Roberts. 1955-68 Edward Lindsay. 1956-57 Francis Molloy. 1957 Michael D McCabe (1957). 1959-78 John O'Hara. 1967-73 Donal Burke. 1968-69 Peter Marr. 1969-72 Philip Hastings. 1978-79 John J N Burns. 1989- Dominic Doogan.

GLASGOW – ST PAUL'S (Shettleston): see Shettleston, St Paul's

GLASGOW – ST PAUL'S (Whiteinch)
Heads: 1903-05 Andrew Lynch. 1905-14 Alphonsus Ooghe. 1914-33 Angus
Mackintosh. 1933-42 Peter Bonnyman. 1942-59 David Quigley. 1959-72
Thomas Keane. 1972-80 Gerard Hart. 1980-87 James McMahon. 1987-
John Sheridan (1956).
Assistants: 1906-23 Joseph Murray. 1923-26 Constantine Doherty. 1926-
44 Thomas Keane. 1937-41 Thomas Glen. 1941-51 Samuel Lavery.
1944-59 John McGuckin. 1951-75 John Bennett. 1957-58 John
McAveety. 1959-60 Brendan Moriarty. 1959-62 Peter A Moran. 1960-67
Joseph Kerr. 1967-68 John B Byrne. 1968-73 David Trainer. 1973
Edward B McNaught. 1974-81 James Simcox. 1975-79 William Murphy
(1952). 1976-77 John D McGinley (1968). 1979-87 Joseph Dunne. 1982-
Andrew Hosie. 1984 John A Hughes. 1987- John G Kay.

GLASGOW – ST PETER'S
Heads: 1855-83 Daniel Gallaugher (WD). 1883-86 John A Maguire (WD).
1886-99 Angus MacFarlane (WD). 1899-1929 Michael McNairney. 1929-
38 James Clarke. 1938-48 James Mullin. 1948-59 George Stuart. 1959-
74 Cornelius O'Leary. 1974- Gaetano Rossi.
Assistants: 1878-82 Andrew Ryan (WD). 1879-81 William Hallinan (WD).
1882-86 Robert J McCluskey. 1883-87 Patrick Houlihan. 1886-91
Michael McNairney. 1887-90 Denis Frawley. 1890-96 Denis J Dennehy.
1891-98 James Mullen. 1894-99 James Rochead. 1896-1900 Denis
McBrearty. 1897-98 John McCready (1897). 1898-1902 Alphonsus
Ward. 1899-1900 William Byrne. 1899-1902 Francis McCann. 1900-07
John O'Shea. 1900-09 Maurice Ronayne. 1902-03 Thomas Corley. 1902-
04 William Gillespie. 1903-04 Michael McHugh. 1904-10 Charles R
Brown (WD). 1904-11 Edward Prendiville. 1906-10 John Cleary. 1907
James C Coyne. 1907-09 Michael Morris. 1909 John Walsh. 1909-15
James McBride. 1909-27 John Boyle (1909). 1910-11 Daniel O'Connell.
1910-18 David Power (1910). 1911-29 John Conlon. 1913-15 Thomas
Rourke. 1915-16 Michael Kinnane. 1915-20 Angus McEachen. 1915-21
Thomas A Murphy (1915). 1918-24 Edward Bradley. 1918-24 Francis
McIntyre. 1921-22 Michael Holloway. 1922-28 James P Close. 1924
Joseph White. 1924-26 Gerard Morris. 1925-45 Thomas P Reilly (1925)
(1). 1926-30 Joseph Hamill. 1927-31 John Rogan. 1928-33 Archibald
Watt. 1928-39 Roger McCauley. 1929-50 Donald Robertson. 1930 John
J Cusick (1930). 1930-38 Michael Brennan. 1931-38 James Black.
1938-39 Patrick Clarke. 1938-43 David McRoberts. 1938-47 Thomas A
Kelly (1926). 1939-45 Matthew Kinsella. 1943-54 John Conlan. 1945-57
John Fitzgibbon (1945). 1947-60 Francis Jaconelli. 1950-55 John
Cawley. 1954-61 Noel Murray. 1955-75 William Mone. 1956-61 Daniel J
Hart. 1957-73 Patrick J McGovern (1947) (1). 1961-66 James
McGladrigan. 1961-72 Lawrence McMahon. 1962-64 Peter A Moran.
1966-73 Edmund Budds. 1972-79 James Martin. 1973-76 Neil
Donnachie. 1975-77 Francis McManamon. 1976-79 Anthony Sweeney.
1977-82 Patrick Gahagan. 1979-82 James Doherty (1979). 1979-86

Henry Parkinson. 1982-84 Paul Budis. 1982-85 William Clarke. 1983 John P Quinn (1983). 1984- John Casey. 1985-89 Gerard J Conroy. 1986- Anthony Bancewicz. 1989- Joseph Mackle.

GLASGOW – ST PHILIP'S
Heads: 1954-68 Thomas Cahill. 1968-81 Charles Cush. 1981-84 John Manning. 1984- Edward Lindsay.
Assistants: 1955-67 Bernard Devlin. 1967-73 Peter McKelvie. 1973-75 Brendan T Foley. 1975-81 Philip Hastings. 1982 Stephen J French.

GLASGOW – ST PHILOMENA'S
Heads: 1940-48 William McGoldrick. 1948-50 James K Elliot. 1950-73 George Aylward. 1973- Francis Coyle.
Assistants: 1940-47 James E Hallinan. 1941-44 Denis Garrity. 1944-52 John Gillespie. 1946-48 John Duffy. 1947-56 Thomas McKeown. 1948-55 Daniel Kennedy. 1952-53 Guido A Vaccaro. 1953-81 Anthony Tansey. 1954-58 Francis Mallon. 1955-56 Joseph Nee. 1956-59 Joseph Mahon. 1956-63 John Sheridan (1956). 1958-59 William Foran. 1959-60 John Ryan (1950). 1960-73 Thomas Hurley. 1961-68 Thomas O'Rourke. 1963-66 Hugh Boyle. 1966- Anthony Burke. 1968-75 Francis Gallagher. 1973-76 Germain Fitzpatrick. 1975-78 Timothy McGlynn. 1978-81 Alistair MacLellan. 1981-82 Christopher Gilfedder. 1981-83 Michael Conroy. 1982-85 Peter Murphy (1969). 1985-87 James Lafferty. 1987-89 Gerard Nugent. 1989- Joseph Boyle.

GLASGOW – ST PIUS X
Heads: 1954-76 Hugh Cassidy. 1976- Martin Quinlan (1942).
Assistants: 1956-60 Andrew Tolan. 1957-58 Anthony Donnelly. 1958-62 Richard O'Callaghan. 1960 Peter McCafferty. 1961-71 James Lafferty. 1962-66 Patrick J Henry. 1966-73 Anthony McHugo. 1971-74 Sabatino Tedeschi. 1973-78 Francis Gilfedder. 1974-75 William McGinley. 1975-81 John Sheridan (1956). 1978-82 John Sheary (1969). 1982-83 Matthew Coakley. 1983-84 George McGarrigle. 1984-85 Anthony Sweeney. 1985- Sean Fitzgerald.

GLASGOW – ST ROBERT BELLARMINE'S
Heads: 1942-48 Timothy Feely. 1948-75 Bartholomew Burns (1928). 1975-80 John Dennehy. 1980-87 Donal Burke. 1987- Lawrence McMahon.
Assistants: 1946-48 Duncan Kane. 1948-49 William Colbert. 1948-52 Thomas Murphy (1948). 1949-67 Peter McCann (1949). 1952-65 Joseph Power. 1953-70 Hugh O'Donnell. 1954-57 Hugh Heslin (Paisley). 1957-62 John Loughlin. 1962-65 Lawrence Jamieson. 1965-67 Joseph Devine. 1965-69 George Bradburn. 1967-73 Joseph Wilkinson. 1967-75 James L Walsh (1960). 1969-72 Desmond McGinty. 1970-74 James P Corrigan. 1973-75 John Tobin. 1973-76 Patrick Gunning. 1975 Peter Sweeney. 1975-76 Joseph Mills. 1975-77 Michael Woodford. 1975-82 Anthony Donnelly. 1977-79 Gerard Meacher. 1977-80 Anthony Welsh. 1978-83

Gerard Nugent. 1980-85 Sean Fitzgerald. 1983-89 Michael Duffy. 1985-Leonard A Purcell.

GLASGOW – ST ROCH'S

Heads: 1907-18 Daniel Collins. 1918-36 Edward Lawton. 1936-65 John Boyle (1909). 1965-66 vacant. 1966-78 James G Traynor. 1978- Malachy Bergin.

Assistants: 1907-10 William Murphy (1907). 1907-11 William Molloy. 1907-12 Timothy O'Kelleher. 1911-12 Jeremiah A McGrath. 1911-20 Joseph J Crumly. 1912-15 Patrick F Keating. 1913-21 William J Hayes. 1916-17 John O'Mahony (1915). 1917-29 James P Fennessy. 1920-21 William Molloy. 1921-27 Charles Riordan. 1921-27 Francis O'Doherty. 1927-29 Patrick Heron. 1927-32 Henry McFaul. 1928-29 Peter Travers. 1929-33 Thomas McCann. 1929-33 Michael Rynn. 1932-33 Edward C Kavanagh. 1933-36 Daniel O'Sullivan (1929). 1933-38 Charles Gallagher. 1933-42 Gerald Hart. 1934-50 John Cawley. 1935-36 James Murphy (1935). 1936-43 Martin Hughes. 1937-39 John Cullen. 1937-43 Brendan Moriarty. 1938-43 Henry McWilliams. 1942-54 Thomas Murray (1936). 1943-44 William White. 1943-44 Malachy Finnegan. 1943-47 John Dennehy. 1944-45 John O'Donnell (1944). 1945-48 John Cusick (1927). 1945-54 Michael Gavagan. 1947-50 Thomas McCabe. 1948-49 John Carter. 1949-66 Anthony McHugo. 1951-55 John Manning. 1951-57 Patrick J McGovern (1947) (1). 1954-62 Charles Vallely. 1954-69 John J Burns. 1955-72 Matthew Coakley. 1962-67 Bernard Connell. 1966-71 Daniel M Gallagher. 1967-74 Edward Higgins. 1971-73 Joseph P Brady. 1972-79 James M O'Hare. 1973-78 Charles Kane. 1974-76 Dermot Healy. 1976-79 Francis Goodfellow. 1977 Gerard I Meacher. 1978-81 Eamon V Friel. 1979-85 Peter Lennon. 1980-87 James Wallace. 1981-84 John Conway (1955). 1984-87 Michael J Barrett. 1985- John Loughlin. 1987- Anthony McLaren. 1987- Stephen Connelly.

GLASGOW – ST SAVIOUR'S

Heads: 1897-1918 Emile de Backer (WD). 1918-25 William Daly. 1925-51 Thomas Doyle. 1951-55 William A Hart. 1955-75 John Cusick (1927). 1975-81 Desmond Gunning. 1981-83 Desmond Strain. 1983- James Martin.

Assistants: 1897-1919 Louis de Backer. 1913-25 John Donnelly. 1916-30 James L Cullen. 1924-38 Henry Laverty. 1928-30 Denis McGrath (1928). 1930-35 William McFadyen. 1930-52 John Hickey. 1935-52 Joseph Mahon. 1938-41 John Hamill. 1941-44 Thomas Sharkey. 1945-46 Thomas McGurk. 1946-57 James McMahon. 1952-60 Eugene McGee. 1953-55 Gerald A Harvey. 1955-65 Charles Kane. 1957-65 Patrick J Brady. 1958-59 Owen Gallagher. 1959 Sabatino Tedeschi. 1960-61 Richard Sewards. 1961-71 Frederick Thompson. 1962 James A Burns. 1965-67 David Currie. 1965-74 Sean O'Neill. 1967-70 Joseph Murphy. 1971-72 John Muldoon. 1972-82 Peter Clinton. 1974-76 Sabatino

Tedeschi. 1976-88 Peter C McKelvie. 1978 Thomas C Docherty. 1982-87 Peter McCafferty. 1988- Edward J Higgins.

GLASGOW – ST SIMON'S
Heads: 1945-47 Thomas Egan. 1947-50 George Aylward. 1950-72 Donald Robertson. 1972- Patrick Tierney.
Assistants: 1945-47 Edward Molumby. 1947-52 John Branagan. 1951-55 Jeremiah Carroll. 1952-65 Charles McFadden (1950). 1955-72 Edward Kelly.

GLASGOW – ST STEPHEN'S
Heads: 1968-75 John Dennehy. 1975-79 Robert Bradley. 1979-84 Eugene McGee. 1984- Charles McFadden (1950).
Assistants: 1972-75 Anthony Donnelly. 1976-77 William McGinley. 1977-87 John D McGinley (1968).

GLASGOW – ST TERESA'S
Heads: 1932-37 John Conlon. 1937-38 vacant. 1938-48 Michael McCarthy (1909). 1948-61 John J Murphy (1914). 1961-62 vacant. 1962-73 John Martin. 1973-84 Donald MacKinnon. 1984-87 John McLaren. 1987- Peter McCafferty.
Assistants: 1932-39 Bernard Magauran. 1932-46 Thomas P Murphy (1932). 1932-46 Thomas McGrory. 1934-42 John J Wilson (1933). 1937-38 Henry McWilliams. 1938-39 William Duddy. 1939-47 Thomas Cahill. 1942-48 Michael McNicholas. 1946-47 Edward McKay (St A & E). 1946-67 Donald McKinnon. 1947-52 William McDonald. 1947-60 John McFaul. 1948-53 Vincent J Cowley. 1952-71 John Broderick. 1953-59 Francis McLeod. 1959-63 Joseph Gallacher. 1960-67 Joseph Murphy. 1963-66 Anthony Beckett. 1966-75 James O'Reilly. 1967-68 John Dennehy. 1967-72 David Currie. 1968-69 Michael Gavagan. 1969-72 Patrick Tierney. 1971-75 Francis McPartlin. 1972-73 Bartholomew Burns (1960). 1973-76 Edward B McNaught. 1975-77 James Durning. 1975-83 William Mone. 1977-78 Francis Meagher. 1977-80/1 Hugh J McGinlay (1977). 1978 Joseph Walsh. 1978-84 Alexander Johnstone. 1983 Anthony McLaren. 1983-87 Gerard Nugent. 1983-89 John McNamara. 1987- Christopher J McElroy. 1989- Neil A M McGarrity.

GLASGOW – ST THOMAS APOSTLE
Heads: 1924-38 Thomas McEwan. 1938-47 Joseph Daniel. 1947-49 Archibald Watt. 1949-62 Joseph Brett. 1962-75 William Morgan. 1975- Carlo Centra.
Assistants: 1926-34 John Gallagher. 1929-44 James A O'Neill (1929). 1934-49 James G Traynor. 1934-53 Thomas Cassidy. 1936-40 John Haran. 1940-42 Gerard Rogers. 1942 Joseph Sheary. 1942-50 George Burns. 1944-47 William Colbert. 1949-63 Patrick Tierney. 1953-67 Francis Courtney. 1962-63 Colman McGrath. 1963-64 Eamon Friel. 1964-67 James F Walsh (1962). 1967-72 Patrick Osborne. 1967-74 Peter

McCann (1949). 1972-77 Daniel Friel. 1974-78 Gerard Nugent. 1977-86 James A Burns. 1978-79 Gerard McGuinness. 1979-81 Brian Magee. 1982 Gerard J Conroy. 1986- Edward Campbell. 1987-89 Luke O'Reilly (Columban Father). 1989- Joseph Doherty CSsR.

GLASGOW – ST VINCENT'S (Duke Street)
Heads: 1878-79 William J Cullen (WD). 1879-86 Frederick J Evertz (WD). 1886-1902 Charles G Duperier (WD).
Assistants: 1878-81 Thomas Dunne (WD). 1883-84 Donald McIntosh (WD). 1884-86 Michael Benger (WD). 1886-88 James Bird (ED). 1888-89 James J Burke. 1889-96 Martin Jansen. 1896-97 John McAllister (1891). 1897-1902 Charles A Cunningham. 1902 Patrick Diamond.
Church closed 1902.

GLASGOW – ST VINCENT DE PAUL'S (Thornliebank)
Heads: 1942-47 Daniel O'Keefe. 1947-54 Joseph McErlain. 1954-68 James Sweeney. 1968-86 Thomas Cahill. 1986- Joseph Coyle.
Assistants: 1946-47 Denis Garrity. 1947-49 Michael J O'Connell. 1949-57 Gerald McCallion. 1954-57 Joseph Quinn (Paisley). 1957-66 John O'Sullivan (1954). 1957-69 John J McKee. 1960-65 James Quinn (1942). 1965-66 Daniel M Gallagher. 1966-67 Patrick J Henry. 1966-80 Gerard Philips SMA. 1967-70 Donald McKinnon. 1969-78 John J Burns. 1970-71 Robert Bradley. 1971-73 Francis Meagher. 1978-83 Francis Mallon. 1983 Michael Sharkey. 1983-85 Gerard McCue OSB. 1988- Peter McBride.

GLASGOW – DIOCESAN OFFICE
Diocesan Secretaries: 1879-83 John A Maguire (WD). 1883-86 James McLachlan. 1886-89 Michael Hughes. 1900-29 John Ritchie.
Other Officials: 1950-65 James Ward (Vicar General, then Auxiliary Bishop). 1976-78 Hugh N Boyle (Chancellor).

GLASGOW – ARCHBISHOP'S ASSISTANTS
Chaplains: 1895-96 Daniel Stewart. 1896-99 Bernard Lynch. 1901-02 William Mullen.
Secretaries: 1899-1901 Angus Mackintosh. 1964-65 Joseph Devine. 1965-67 Hugh G McEwan (1948). 1967-72 Francis Coyle. 1972-76 John Broderick.

GLASGOW – NATIONAL VOCATIONS OFFICE. 1986- Angus MacLean.

GLASGOW – DIOCESAN CENTRE. 1976-82 Thomas O'Rourke.

GLASGOW – DIOCESAN PASTORAL CENTRE (St Peter's Pastoral Centre). 1983-88 Hugh J McEwan (1960). 1985-86 Patrick Osborne. 1988- Angus MacDonald.

GLASGOW – CATHOLIC CHILD CARE OFFICE. 1962-69 Peter J Murphy (1943) (director).

GLASGOW UNIVERSITY CHAPLAINS
Heads: 1930-45 William E Brown (1929). 1945-79 Jesuits. 1979- Michael J Conway (Motherwell)
Assistants: 1974-77 Joseph Devine. 1977-79 Michael J Conway (Motherwell). 1980-85 Thomas J Hendry. 1985- Brian Magee.

GLASGOW – STRATHCLYDE UNIVERSITY CHAPLAINS: 1977-78 William J Gavin (assistant). Otherwise served by Dominicans.

GLASGOW – ST ANDREW'S COLLEGE OF EDUCATION: CHAPLAINS
1983-84 John A McKelvie.

GLASGOW – BARLINNIE PRISON AND ST JOSEPH'S HOME: CHAPLAINS
Until 1898 served by Passionists. 1898-1900 Aloysius Reifenrath. 1900-07 Patrick B McMullen. 1907-11 John McMillan (1898). 1911-20 William J Molloy. 1920-23 Joseph J Crumly. 1923-26 James Montgomery. 1926-33 Michael O'Brien. 1933-44 Peter Morrison. 1944-49 Joseph Brett. 1949-54 James Sweeney. 1954-57 James Traynor. 1957-62 Patrick Smith. 1962-68 Michael Gavagan. 1968-82 Edward Lindsay. 1982- John McQuade.

GLASGOW – NOTRE DAME: CHAPLAINS
(Convent; also Teachers' Training college until 1981)
1923-25 Octavius Claeys. 1925-41 served by Benedictines. 1941-48 James Black. 1948-50 James Ward (1929). 1950-59 Thomas Meikleham. 1959-70 John Gillespie. 1970-73 Charles Kane. 1974-76 Felix Beattie. 1976-83 John D Broderick. 1983-84 John McKelvie. 1984- John N Woods.

GLASGOW – WEST THORN REFORMATORY: CHAPLAINS
Note: From 1902-38 the chaplaincy was combined with that of the Good Shepherd Convent, Dalbeth. The (two) chaplains lived at Dalbeth presbytery. It is impossible to determine how their duties were divided.
1878-80 Hugh McDonald (ND). 1880-81 served from St Michael's. 1881-82 Charles Duperier (WD). 1882-89 served from Good Shepherd Convent. 1889-91 Thomas McEvoy 1891-96 John Angland. 1896 Charles E Fleming. 1896-99 Alexander Macdonald. 1899-1900 Louis J McIntyre (WD). 1900-03 Alexander McCormick (1895). 1902-18 John Linster. 1903-06 Joseph Laveth. 1906-10 James McKenna. 1910-11 John Lynch (1905). 1911-12 Edward Fitzgerald (1909). 1912-16 Jeremiah McGrath. 1916-17 Daniel McLaughlin. 1917-25 Thomas Gourlay. 1918-19 Patrick O'Brien (1918). 1919-20 John Angland. 1920-23 Daniel Harty. 1923-24 Joseph O'Leary. 1924-29 Alfred J Gallaucher. 1925-38 John Proctor. 1929-32 Patrick J Flood. 1932-38 Richard Fennessy. From 1938 served from Good Shepherd Convent.

GLASGOW – GOOD SHEPHERD CONVENT: CHAPLAINS
1878-80 James Mackintosh (WD). 1880-89 Hugh McDonald (ND). 1889-91 John Black (WD). 1891-96 William Fraser (ND). 1896-97 James Slorach (Aberdeen). 1897-1900 Andrew J O'Brien. 1900-02 Charles Haeger. 1902-38 see Glasgow, West Thorn Reformatory. 1938-44 John Proctor. 1942-46 Charles Gallacher, with evacuees at Castle Huntly, Dundee. 1944-49 John McNair.

GLASGOW – HOSPITAL CHAPLAINS
Gartnaval: 1973-75 Thomas Hurley.
Stobhill: 1988 Paul G Murray.

GLASGOW – GLENGOWAN HOUSE: DIRECTORS. 1987-88 John King. 1988-89 James L Walsh (1960). 1989- John King.

GLASGOW – MARIST BROTHERS: CHAPLAINS. 1971-74 James Fitzgerald (1940). 1974-76 Patrick G Fitzpatrick. 1978-79 Patrick G Fitzpatrick.

GLASGOW – BON SECOURS CONVENT: CHAPLAINS. 1975-89 Charles Renfrew. 1989- Bruno Renucci.

GLASGOW – CARMILITE CONVENT: CHAPLAINS. 1951-64 Francis Taggart. 1964-69 William McDonald.

GLASGOW – FRANCISCAN CONVENT (Immaculate Conception):-CHAPLAINS.
1864-80 William Caven (WD). 1881-93 Peter Forbes (WD). 1897-99 Michael Ahern. 1899-1906 James O'Neill. 1906-07 Octavius Claeys. 1907-12 Patrick McMullen.

GLASGOW – ST HELEN'S CONVENT: CHAPLAINS. 1946-52 Charles Gallagher. 1953-70 Vincent Cowley. 1970-75 Romeo Coia.

GLASGOW – NAZARETH HOUSE: CHAPLAINS: 1906-07 Hugh Gunther.

GLASGOW – OUR LADY OF THE MISSIONS CONVENT: CHAPLAINS:
1969-72 John Boyle (1930).

GLENBOIG: moves to Motherwell diocese
Heads: 1902-19 Charles Haeger. 1919-30 Alexander Mackintosh. 1930 Joseph Hamill. 1930-34 John Ryan (1913). 1934-38 Francis J Laveth. 1938-39 vacant. 1939-40 Joseph Doherty. 1940-45 Edward Douglas. 1945-48 Hugh O'Brien.
Assistants: 1913-15 Patrick J Flood. 1915-18 Frederick R Pirrie. 1918-19 Alexander Mackintosh. 1933-34 Thomas McLoughlin. 1934-38 John

Rooney. 1937-40 Henry Kelly (Dunkeld). 1940-42 John Deans. 1942-44 John Hamill. 1944- John Gillen.

GOUROCK: moves to Paisley diocese
Until 1896 served from Greenock.
Heads: 1896-97 David Morris. 1897-1901 Peter Hilgers. 1901-05 Francis Cronin. 1905-08 Stephen A Thornton. 1908-18 Patrick A McCarthy. 1918-21 Daniel Colvin. 1921-22 Robert J McCluskey. 1922-28 John Devine. 1928-34 Francis Joseph Laveth. 1934-42 James Clune. 1942-43 James L Cullen. 1943-45 John D Daniel. 1945-47 Henry E Hart. 1947- Francis Magauran.
Assistants: 1941-42 Francis McLeod. 1945- Hugh Gallagher.

GOVAN: see Glasgow, St Anthony's

GREENGAIRS: 1897-1900 Angus MacEachen. From 1900 served from Whiterigg.

GREENOCK – ST JOSEPH'S: moves to Paisley diocese
Head: 1947- Robert H Barclay.
Assistant: 1947- Ferdinand Tritschler.

GREENOCK – ST LAURENCE'S: moves to Paisley diocese
Heads: 1859-85 Michael Condon (WD). 1885 Robert Grant (WD). 1885-90 Thomas P O'Reilly (WD). 1890-96 John L Murphy (1881). 1896-1906 Michael Fox (WD). 1906-45 William Horgan. 1945- John D Daniel.
Assistants: 1876-81 Alexander Bisset (ND). 1881-82 John Kearney. 1882-87 John Toner. 1887-89 Patrick Hackett (1887). 1889-92 Gerald Stack. 1892-98 Bernard J Dawson. 1895-96 David O'Connell. 1896-97 Matthew Fanning. 1897-1900 Thomas Meehan. 1898-1905 Matthew Carroll. 1900-04 William C Brown (1897). 1904-10 William Flanagan. 1905-14 Michael Macdonnell. 1910-13 John J O'Callaghan (1900). 1913-14 Michael Mulvey. 1914-18 Francis Dougan. 1914-20 Joseph Higgins. 1918-21 James Kennedy. 1920-22 James McGrory. 1921 David Power (1920). 1921-26 Teague McGinley. 1922-30 Charles Gallacher. 1926-29 Thomas Egan. 1929-34 Thomas O'Doherty. 1930-36 Alexander McBride. 1930-37 Robert Beattie. 1934-37 John J Cusick (1930). 1936-37 Albert Chandler. 1937-39 Hugh McCranor. 1937-40 Michael J Sweeney. 1937-47 John Boyle (1930). 1939-47 Florence O'Flynn. 1940- James M Lillis. 1947- Joseph Sheary. 1947- James Sheehan.

GREENOCK – ST MARY'S: moves to Paisley diocese
Heads: 1852-81 William Gordon (WD). 1881-1905 Alexander Taylor (WD). 1905-23 Patrick Houlihan. 1923-45 John McMillan (1898). 1945-47 William Horgan. 1947- Henry E Hart.
Assistants: 1868-81 Alexander Taylor (WD). 1878-79 Patrick Graham (WD). 1879-80 Thomas J Cunningham (1879). 1880-81 Humphry O'Callaghan.

1880-85 Patrick Gaule. 1881-83 John Angland. 1883-88 William P O'Brien. 1885-87 Louis de Backer. 1887-91 James F Morrison. 1888-90 Ellis P Rogan. 1890-95 Charles A de Monti. 1891-92 Ludger W Kuhler. 1892-96 David Morris. 1892-96 James Carroll. 1895-1900 Andrew Lynch. 1896-1901 Charles Mann (Aberdeen). 1896-1903 Charles E Fleming. 1900-11 Thomas Gibbons. 1901-05 Joseph O'Leary. 1903-08 James McDaid. 1905-10 William Browne. 1905-16 Michael O'Donoghue. 1908-12 William O'Connor (Galloway). 1910-20 Michael Fitzpatrick. 1911-19 Thomas Wall. 1912-15 William Ryan. 1914-15 William O'Connor (Galloway). 1915-21 Maurice O'Connor. 1916-17 Michael Roche. 1916-25 John Wall. 1917-19 Peter J MacFarlane. 1919-25 James Ronan. 1919-30 John Scanlon. 1920-24 Daniel J Horgan (1919). 1921-25 Michael Costello. 1925-26 Simon Hegarty. 1925-28 William Christie. 1925-34 Aloysius McGurk. 1926-27 James Phelan. 1927-29 Daniel McGlinchey (1927). 1928-29 Edward Dempsey (Dunkeld). 1929-31 Gerald McDade. 1929-43 John McLaughlin. 1930-33 William Mallon. 1931-33 Michael McNicholas. 1933-36 Gerald McDade. 1933-43 Francis Magauran. 1934-38 John O'Riordan. 1936-45 John Cusick (1927). 1938-40 Herbert G Rogers. 1939-41 John Ross (Dunkeld). 1942-46 Francis McLeod. 1943-47 Thomas Brooks. 1943-47 Thomas McKeown. 1945- James Fisher. 1946-47 Daniel Horgan (1927). 1946- John G Earley. 1947- Vincent E Grace.

GREENOCK – ST MUNGO'S: moves to Paisley diocese
Heads: 1934-44 John Ryan (1913). 1944- John J Scanlan.
Assistants: 1935-36 Owen Traynor. 1936-42 Vincent Grace. 1937-42 James Aylward. 1942-43 William Burke. 1942- Luke Brady. 1943- James Murphy (1943).

GREENOCK – ST PATRICK'S: moves to Paisley diocese
Heads: 1924-30 James P Kelly. 1930- Joseph Courtney.
Assistants: 1925-27 Patrick J Molloy. 1927-32 Edward C Kavanagh. 1928 Patrick Dillon. 1930 William Mallon. 1932-45 Peter Sexton. 1933- James F Watters. 1941-46 Joseph O'Leary. 1945- Matthew Kinsella.

GREENOCK – LITTLE SISTERS OF THE POOR: CHAPLAINS: moves to Paisley diocese.
1924-43 Gisbert Hartmann. 1943-46 John P Conway (1914). 1946- Richard Fennessy.

HAMILTON – OUR LADY AND ST ANNE'S: see Cadzow

HAMILTON – ST MARY'S: moves to Motherwell diocese
Heads: 1859-86 James Donaher (WD). 1886-1902 Peter Donnelly (WD). 1902-03 vacant. 1903-32 William McAvoy. 1932- Bartholomew Flynn.
Assistants: 1891-92 Thomas Hopwell. 1898-1903 Patrick O'Halloran. 1903-14 John J Murphy (1901). 1906-07 John Czuberkis. 1906-18 Joseph

Sieger. 1908 Bartholomew Canavan. 1914-24 John P Conway (1914). 1916-17 Thomas Murray (1916). 1918-19 John Godfrey. 1919-22 Joseph Sieger. 1922-24 Joseph Ivory. 1924-26 William Lynagh. 1924-26 James Leyne. 1926-28 Timothy Marnane. 1926-37 Dominic McGlynn. 1928-29 Michael Teehan. 1928-34 Jeremiah O'Leary. 1929-33 William Hart. 1934-37 John Rogan. 1934- Anthony Kilcoyne. 1937-40 Patrick J O'Sullivan (1937). 1937-48 Philip Boyce. 1940-46 John P Earley. 1946- Michael Houlihan.

HARTHILL: moves to Motherwell diocese
1924-27 Patrick Reilly. 1927-30 John Boyle (1909). 1930-32 Thomas Rourke. 1932-33 Francis P Taggart. 1933-38 Michael O'Brien. 1938-45 Thomas Egan. 1945- Peter Sexton.

HELENSBURGH
Heads: 1878-89 Louis MacIntyre (WD). 1889-93 John Foley. 1893-1901 Theophilus Delbeke. 1901-02 John A Hickson (Galloway). 1902-06 Edward Fitzgerald (1894). 1906-14 Angus Mackintosh. 1914-30 William C Brown (1897). 1930-34 William J Molloy. 1934-37 Simon Keane. 1937-40 Joseph Kennedy. 1940-45 John F O'Donnell (1918). 1945-53 Patrick Coogan. 1953-56 David Scullion. 1956-57 Michael J Connolly. 1957-65 John G Carter. 1965-66 vacant. 1966-87 James Meehan. 1987- Maurice Ward.
Assistants: 1900 Edmund Fitzgerald. 1928-29 James Montgomery. 1929-30 Michael Teehan. 1936-37 John Cummings. 1937-44 Daniel O'Sullivan (1929). 1941-47 William McDonald. 1944-52 Jeremiah Lane. 1947-48 John J Wilson (1933). 1949-57 Austin Ruane. 1957-60 Michael McCabe (1957). 1960-62 Michael O'Keeffe (1948). 1962-65 David McLachlan. 1965-67 James L Walsh (1960). 1967-72 Joseph Devine. 1972-74 Lawrence Jamieson. 1974-76 John J McCabe. 1976-82 Joseph Coyle. 1982-87 John Sheary (1969). 1987- John Clohesy MHM.

HOUSTON: moves to Paisley diocese
Heads: 1867-79 Eugene Small (WD). 1879-80 served from Johnstone. 1880-81 Angus MacFarlane (WD). 1881-84 Alexander Bisset (ND). 1884-86 Charles G Duperier (WD). 1886-91 John Angland. 1891-99 Charles McGhee. 1899-1905 William Horgan. 1905-27 James Macdonald. 1927-33 Peter Bonnyman. 1933-42 James L Cullen. 1942-46 James Clune. 1946- Patrick Cummins.
Assistants: 1915-16 Bartholomew Flynn. 1916-17 Joseph Courtney. 1934-35 John McGarry. 1939-40 Hugh McCranor. 1940-43 Henry S Leonard. 1943-44 Angus MacKellaig. 1944-46 Denis Garrity.

JOHNSTONE (St Margaret's): moves to Paisley diocese
Heads: 1859-81 Hugh Chisholm (WD). 1881-86 Angus MacFarlane (WD). 1886-89 James Rochead. 1889-1903 William Davidson (WD). 1903-17 John Nyhan. 1917-18 vacant. 1918-23 Justin White. 1923-24 Michael

McCabe (1889). 1924-45 Aloysius Reifenrath. 1945- John O'Donnell (1918).

Assistants: 1877-80 William Davidson (WD). 1879 John Taylor. 1880-81 Donald McIntosh (WD). 1881-82 Richard Boyle. 1882-83 James McLachlan. 1883-84 Thomas McEvoy. 1884-90 Peter Muller. 1890-91 J Fitzgerald. 1891-95 Aloysius Reifenrath. 1895-97 David Murie. 1896-98 Joseph Laveth. 1897-1900 Andrew Lalor. 1900-02 Daniel Gillon. 1902-03 Thomas Healy (1899). 1902-05 William Mullen. 1903-05 James MacDonald. 1905-06 Bernard Cunningham. 1905-09 John McIntyre (1905). 1906-08 Joseph Doherty. 1908-16 Joseph Courtney. 1909-25 David Morris. 1920-27 Daniel V Sheehan. 1925-45 George Aylward. 1927-28 Michael O'Carroll. 1927-45 Daniel Horgan (1927). 1928-42 Thomas McVann. 1942-45 John Mackay. 1945-46 Gerald Maher. 1945- Donald Bonnar. 1945- James Jackson. 1946-47 Kevin Barry. 1947- John Boyle (1930).

KILBIRNIE: moves to Galloway diocese

Heads: 1877-81 Peter Forbes (WD). 1881-90 James Milne (WD). 1890-92 Bernard J Dawson. 1892-93 Denis Frawley. 1893-94 Charles Brown (WD). 1894-1919 Thomas Hopwell. 1919-20 vacant. 1920-29 James Clarke. 1929-36 Patrick Plunkett. 1936-41 Denis Scannell. 1941-45 Henry Corr. 1945-48 James Dolan.

Assistants: 1921-22 Patrick Donagher (Dunkeld). 1922-25 Thomas Daly. 1925-27 Clement McGowan. 1926-32 James K Elliot. 1932-33 John Bredin. 1933-48 Michael Rynn. 1938-41 Edward Doherty. 1941-47 Francis Jaconelli.

KILCREGGAN: see Roseneath

KILWINNING: moves to Galloway diocese:

1945-48 Peter Fitzpatrick

KIRKINTILLOCH – HOLY FAMILY AND ST NINIAN

Heads: 1875-90 James Bonnyman (WD). 1890-97 Arthur Beyaert. 1897-1901 James Mullin. 1901-19 Theophilus Delbeke. 1919-41 Martin Jansen. 1941-55 John R Tennant. 1955-77 William McGhee. 1977-86 Michael Gavagan. 1986- Denis A Hurley.

Assistants: 1894 Francis Cronin. 1895-96 Thomas Kerr (WD). 1898-99 Joseph Laveth. 1899-1901 Patrick Green (St A & E). 1901-02 Thomas Healy (1899). 1902-10 John Nolan. 1905-07 John Charleson. 1907-08 Thomas Joyce (Galloway). 1908-11 Thomas Gourlay. 1911-16 James O'Connor (1911). 1911-19 Daniel Duane. 1916-18 Thomas R Griffith. 1918-32 Patrick Torley. 1919-22 George Galbraith. 1922-25 Patrick Barrett. 1925-26 James B Walsh (1925). 1926-37 David Quigley. 1932-35 David L Power (1928). 1935-39 Patrick McHugh. 1937-39 John McCready (1935). 1938-43 Robert Connolly. 1939-46 Joseph Hamill. 1939-60 Gerard Dunn. 1943-65 John McGinlay (1940). 1946-48

Malachy Finnegan. 1952-55 Joseph Kerr. 1955-67 Edward O'Hara. 1960-67 Eugene McGee. 1965-68 Andrew Burns. 1967-70 Robert Bradley. 1968-80 Thomas S Cunningham (1953). 1970-78 Angus E MacLean (1969). 1972-73 Austin Ruane. 1978-82 Michael Keating. 1980-81 James Durning. 1981-82 Noel Barry. 1982-87 Thomas O'Rourke. 1983-88 Michael Savage. 1987- David Trainer. 1988- Joseph E Sullivan.

KIRKINTILLOCH – ST FLANNAN'S
Heads: 1948-51 James Graham. 1951-58 John Little. 1958-59 vacant. 1959-66 James Meehan. 1966-75 Michael O'Connell. 1975-78 Hugh A Deery. 1978- Daniel Friel.
Assistants: 1948-53 Patrick Tobin. 1953-66 Duncan Kane. 1956-62 Joseph Connelly. 1962-66 Gerard Philips SMA. 1966-76 John O'Sullivan (1954). 1969-70 Patrick Toher. 1970 Brendan T Foley. 1970-83 Noel Colford. 1976-77 Joseph McAndrew SMA. 1978-81 Alan Love. 1981-86 James Durning. 1983- Henry McKay. 1986-88 Joseph E Sullivan. 1988- Michael Savage.

LANGBANK CHILDREN'S HOME – CHAPLAINS: moves to Paisley diocese
1920-23 Thomas B Rourke. 1923-26 James H Doherty (1911). 1926-41 Joseph O'Leary. 1946-51 Joseph O'Leary.

LARGS: moves to Galloway diocese
Heads: 1873-79 Herman van Baer (WD). 1879 Thomas O'Reilly (WD). 1879-97 William Gallagher (WD). 1897-1901 Gisbert J Hartmann. 1901-06 Peter Murray. 1906-08 Patrick McCarthy. 1908-15 John McMenemy. 1915-18 Daniel Colvin. 1918-23 James Kearney. 1923-33 Joseph Doherty. 1933-39 Michael O'Connor (1915). 1939-44 Patrick Clarke. 1944- Clement McGowan.
Assistant: 1946-48 Thomas P Murphy (1932).

LARKHALL: moves to Motherwell diocese
Heads: 1878-85 Paul Pies (WD). 1885-93 Patrick Gaule. 1893-97 Francis Young. 1897-1904 John Scannell. 1904-26 Francis A Steven. 1926-29 Michael McCarthy (1909). 1929-31 Alfred J Gallaucher. 1931-38 William J Hayes. 1938- Michael O'Brien.
Assistants: 1880-81 Thomas Kearney (1880). 1881-84 John Crawford (WD). 1907 Henry G Graham. 1938-45 Hugh O'Brien. 1945-47 William Coghlan. 1945-47 Cornelius Burke. 1947- James McGill.

LINWOOD: moves to Paisley diocese
1898-1908 William Shaw (Aberdeen). 1908-10 Charles A Cunningham. 1910-15 Daniel Gillon. 1915-20 James Clarke. 1920-28 Thomas Healy (1899). 1928-30 William J Molloy. 1930-33 Cornelius Dennehy. 1933-37

Denis Flynn. 1937-42 David Quigley. 1942-46 James Walsh (1924). 1946- Francis Hamilton (1926).

LONGRIGGEND: moves to Motherwell diocese
Heads: 1881-93 John Linster (WD). 1893-96 Michael Fox (WD). 1896-1903 John Nyhan. 1903-05 Jeremiah O'Driscoll. 1905-15 Myles Ambrose. 1915-17 Henry G Graham. 1917 David Quigley. 1917-24 James Kelly. 1924-28 James Troy. 1928-30 William Bradley (1911). 1930-36 Hugh Delargey. 1936-41 Alexander McBride. 1941-45 Hugh Bogan. 1945- Thomas P Kelly (1925) (1).
Assistants: 1890-92 John Nyhan. 1892-96 John McAllister (1891). 1923-24 William Boyce. 1924-26 Thomas Moore (St A & E). 1926-28 Thomas P McGregor (St A & E). 1928-29 Patrick Casey. 1928-30 Peter Murie. 1929-30 James Meehan. 1934-35 John O'Callaghan (1917).

MARYHILL: see Glasgow, Immaculate Conception

MILLPORT (Garrison Church): moves to Galloway diocese
1939-48 Alexander Fyfe.

MILNGAVIE
Heads: 1877-81 James Bird (ED). 1881-89 William Davidson (WD). 1889-91 George W Ritchie. 1891-92 Michael McNairney. 1892-93 vacant. 1893-97 Michael McNairney. 1897-1900 Martin Jansen. 1900-04 Andrew J O'Brien. 1904-09 Daniel O'Sullivan (1895). 1909-11 James H Kirk. 1911-16 William Daly. 1916-26 James McKenna. 1926-61 Patrick Doyle. 1961-70 Michael J McEleney. 1970-76 Vincent J Cowley. 1976-86 Thomas McAteer. 1986- Michael D McCabe (1957).
Assistants: 1943-48 Samuel Kilpatrick. 1948-54 John Noon. 1954-62 Michael Gavagan. 1962-67 Alistair MacLellan. 1967-72 Patrick J Henry. 1977-79 John Gilmartin. 1979-81 Christopher Gilfedder. 1981-84 George Morgan. 1984-86 Bryan Cunningham. 1986- Noel Barry.

MOSSEND: moves to Motherwell diocese
Heads: 1871-81 James Milne (WD). 1881-92 Michael Fox (WD). 1892-1904 Michael Hughes. 1904-07 John Scannell. 1907-18 Francis Cronin. 1918-26 Duncan Brown. 1926-36 John McMenemy. 1936-37 vacant. 1937- William Flanagan.
Assistants: 1895-1900 Charles Daly. 1898-1901 Michael McCormack. 1900-05 Patrick Griffin. 1901-13 Benjamin Kenneally. 1904-05 John P Czuberkis. 1905-06 Antony Racewicz. 1905-09 Michael Collins (1905). 1907-09 John P Czuberkis. 1909-15 Timothy Kelleher. 1910-12 Francis Vasiliauskas. 1912-20 Joseph Norbut. 1913-28 Joseph Kennedy. 1915-18 William Bradley (1911). 1918-24 Daniel McLaughlin. 1920-34 Joseph Petranskis. 1924-27 Denis F MacDaid. 1927-43 Thomas Brooks. 1928-29 William Brennan. 1929-34 Samuel McIsaac (Argyll). 1934 Joseph Gallacher. 1934-36 Aloysius McGurk. 1934-42 Joseph Gutauskas. 1935-

37 James Kilpatrick. 1936-38 Bernard Feeney. 1937-42 David L Power (1928). 1938-49 Stephen A Keane (Aberdeen). 1943- James Butler. 1943- Thomas Fehily.

MOTHERWELL (Our Lady of Good Aid): moves to Motherwell diocese
Heads: 1877-88 James Glancy (WD). 1888-1917 John Taylor. 1917-35 Thomas Currie. 1935-46 Bartholomew Atkinson. 1946-47 vacant. 1947- Denis Flynn.
Assistants: 1879-82 Arthur Beyaert. 1882-84 Laurence Richen. 1884-85 John Crawford (WD). 1884-86 Ronald Mortimer. 1885-88 George McDonnell. 1887-89 Thomas Kerr (WD). 1888-93 Duncan Brown. 1893-1902 Daniel Collins. 1898-1901 John Greed. 1901-07 Donald A McPherson (Argyll). 1902-06 Patrick A McCarthy. 1905-14 Joseph O'Leary. 1906-18 William Orr. 1907-15 Henry G Graham. 1914-16 Alexander Hamilton. 1916-21 Denis M Sheehan (1915). 1916-25 Joseph Doherty. 1918-23 Nicholas Tangney. 1921-23 Thomas O'Connor. 1923-40 Henry Hart. 1924-27 Patrick F Keating. 1925-37 Patrick Cummins. 1927-33 Michael O'Connor (1915). 1930-31 Edmund Mollumby (possibly). 1930-32 Patrick McHugh. 1932-39 Edward Bradley. 1933-47 Edward C Kavanagh. 1937-39 James Walshe. 1939-40 John Carter. 1939-48 Ian McLaughlin. 1940-41 Francis Jaconelli. 1940-47 Francis Rota. 1941-47 Edward Docherty. 1947-48 Henry McGinn. 1947- James Dooley.

MUIRHEAD: moves to Motherwell diocese
1947- Michael O'Connor (1927).

NEILSTON: moves to Paisley diocese
1863-80 James McNamara (WD). 1880-93 Bernard Tracy (WD). 1893-1900 Duncan Brown. 1900-24 Aloysius Reifenrath. 1924-31 John F Clark. 1931-38 John Ashe. 1938-41 Joseph Costeur. 1941-46 James Hogan. 1946-47 Gerard McDade. 1947- Daniel McGlinchey (1927).

NEWMAINS: moves to Motherwell diocese
Heads: 1896-1903 James Humble. 1903-16 James Bird (ED). 1916-21 William O'Carroll. 1921-24 Hugh Macdonald (1906). 1924-29 John A Lyons (1907). 1929-30 Joseph Courtney. 1930-37 William Stopani. 1937-40 John F O'Donnell (1918). 1940-41 John McIntyre (1920). 1941-45 William McGhee. 1945- Thomas Kelly (1925) (2).
Assistants: 1935-36 Daniel Logue (St A & E). 1936-37 Joseph O'Hagan.

NEW STEVENSTON: moves to Motherwell diocese
Head: 1946- Dominic McGlynn.
Assistant: 1947- Patrick B McGovern (1947) (1).

NEWTON: moves to Motherwell diocese
Heads: 1894-1900 Thomas Currie. 1900-09 Louis de Meulenaere. 1909-15

Angus MacEachen. 1915-23 James Nolan (1902). 1923-25 Joseph Murray. 1925-26 John Power. 1926-33 George Galbraith. 1933-40 Edmund Macdonald. 1940-45 Alfred Gallaucher. 1945-46 Hugh Bogan. 1946- Thomas J Murray (1916).
Assistants: 1904-08 Thomas J Doyle. 1908-09 James A Mulvenna. 1929-46 Michael O'Sullivan. 1946- Gerald O'Callaghan.

OLD KILPATRICK: 1946-48 Patrick Gilmartin. 1948-51 John Cusick (1927). 1951-75 John O'Riordan. 1975-80 John Tobin. 1980-82 Felix Beattie. 1982- Sean O'Neill.

PAISLEY – ST CHARLES': moves to Paisley diocese
Heads: 1898 Charles Culligan. 1898-1917 John McAllister (1891). 1917-19 Francis Young. 1919-23 Frederick R Pirrie. 1923-29 Thomas Kearney (1903). 1929-41 Joseph J Crumly. 1941- Joseph Costeur.
Assistants: 1918-19 Patrick Deeney. 1920-28 William McGoldrick. 1928-34 Joseph Brett. 1930-34 John O'Riordan. 1934-40 Joseph Gallagher. 1934-47 Daniel McGlinchey (1927). 1940-44 John Carter. 1941 James Black. 1944- Thomas Hearty. 1947- Kevin Barry.

PAISLEY – ST MARY'S: moves to Paisley diocese
Heads: 1877-1903 John McDonald (WD). 1903-27 William Davidson (WD). 1927- Frederick R Pirrie.
Assistants: 1882-85 Arthur Beyaert. 1885-87 James J Burke. 1887-89 William Dawson [OMI]. 1889-93 Hugh J Kelly (1889). 1892-99 William Horgan. 1894-96 Edward Fitzgerald (1894). 1897-99 Peter Tracy. 1899-1900 Angus McInnes (Aberdeen). 1899-1903 Denis Duggan (1899). 1900-11 William Walsh. 1903-07 Daniel Nyhan. 1906 William Brown (1906). 1907-09 Patrick Sreenan. 1910-11 James Lagan. 1911-15 Thomas Gourlay. 1911-18 Michael J Murray. 1915-24 Philip Fogarty. 1918-21 Thomas O'Halloran. 1920-22 Patrick Lyons. 1923-26 Peter McLachlan. 1923-27 Frederick R Pirrie (administrator). 1924-26 Michael O'Brien. 1925 John Holmes. 1925-28 Michael O'Riordan. 1926-28 William Mahon. 1926-34 James McVann. 1928-29 Michael O'Carroll. 1928-29 Michael Rynn. 1928-38 Patrick Conway. 1929-32 James Graham. 1932-37 John Boyle (1930). 1934-36 Vincent Grace. 1936-38 Francis McFadden. 1937-43 Dominic McGlynn. 1938-39 Charles Lawn. 1939-40 John Gillen. 1939-48 James McEwan. 1940-46 Robert Beattie. 1943-45 James Bannon. 1945-46 Daniel Horgan (1927). 1946-47 Frederick Tritschler. 1946-47 Daniel M Gallagher. 1947-48 Daniel Horgan (1927). 1947- Thomas Mannion (1946). 1947- Patrick Durcan.

PAISLEY – ST MIRIN'S: moves to Paisley diocese
Heads: 1874-81 Michael Fox (WD). 1881-1908 Hugh Chisholm (WD). 1908-14 Ellis P Rogan. 1914-23 Alphonsus Ooghe. 1923-37 Justin White. 1937-47 John F Clark. 1947- John McIntyre (1920).
Assistants: 1877-79 Edmund Cantwell (WD). 1879-81 Nicholas Power

(1879). 1881-82 James Coghlan. 1882-85 Michael O'Keeffe (1882). 1883-86 John Montgomery. 1886-89 John Dougan. 1886-91 Charles A Cunningham. 1889-93 Charles R Brown (WD). 1891-97 James Mullin. 1893-1900 Peter McConnachie. 1896-99 Casper Grau. 1897-1917 Francis Young. 1899-1908 William McLaughlin. 1900-03 Michael Ahern. 1903-10 Bartholomew Flynn. 1908-12 Patrick Keenan (Aberdeen). 1908-24 John F Clark. 1910-18 John O'Mahony (1910). 1913-30 Cornelius Dennehy. 1917-19 Hugh Curley. 1918-22 Hugh J Keane. 1919-25 Nicholas Walsh. 1919-30 Joseph Costeur. 1922-27 Francis Davin. 1922-33 Peter Morrison. 1924-26 James McVann. 1925-27 Michael Quinlan. 1926-29 Thomas McCann. 1927-28 Thomas O'Doherty. 1927-29 Richard Barclay. 1927-37 John Roger. 1929-38 John McNair. 1929-44 Hugh Barclay. 1930-37 John Little. 1930- Michael Teehan. 1933-40 Archibald Watt. 1936 Daniel B White. 1937-47 Kevin Whitty. 1937- James A E Nevin. 1938-42 John Rooney. 1940- John Haran. 1942-48 Vincent J Cowley. 1944- John Fox. 1947- Francis Hopkins.

PARKHEAD: see Glasgow, St Michael's

POLLOKSHAWS: see Glasgow, St Mary Immaculate

PORT GLASGOW – HOLY FAMILY: moves to Paisley diocese
Head: 1946- Joseph Sweeney.
Assistant: 1946- Patrick Rice.

PORT GLASGOW – ST JOHN THE BAPTIST'S: moves to Paisley diocese
Heads: 1872-84 Daniel Conway (WD). 1884-99 James W McCarthy. 1899-1930 Philip McColl. 1930-37 James P Towie. 1937- Simon Keane.
Assistants: 1882-89 George Ritchie. 1889-90 John Cameron. 1890-92 John Scannell. 1891-92 James Carroll. 1892-97 William Carmichael (WD). 1895-96 Bernard Lynch. 1897-98 William Shaw (Aberdeen). 1897-1905 Timothy O'Shea. 1898-1900 Charles Culligan. 1900-01 James Austin. 1901-13 Anthony Mullins. 1905-09 Patrick Murphy. 1909-29 George Stuart. 1913-30 John Ryan (1913). 1929-31 Patrick Heron. 1929-31 Patrick F Casey. 1930-31 Hugh O'Brien. 1930-35 James McChrystal. 1931-33 Gerald McDade. 1931-48 Jeremiah O'Sullivan. 1933-40 John McIntyre (1920). 1935-39 James McEwan. 1939-40 Gaetano Rossi. 1939-44 Patrick Conway. 1940-46 Matthew Littleton. 1940-46 Thomas Healy (1939). 1945-46 Hugh McGurk. 1946-48 Daniel O'Flynn. 1946- James Donnelly. 1947- James Murphy (1947).

RENFREW (St James'): moves to Paisley diocese
Heads: 1877-89 Peter Evers (WD). 1889-90 James Bird (ED). 1890-91 served from St Mirin's, Paisley. 1891-99 Thomas McEvoy. 1899-1905 Robert J McCluskey. 1905-14 Charles E Fleming. 1914-18 Justin White. 1918-26 Francis Dougan. 1926-28 James McKenna. 1928-30 Bernard

Atkinson. 1930-31 Henry Corr. 1931-38 Alfred J Gallaucher. 1938-William J Hayes.

Assistants: 1920-22 Thomas Daly. 1922-23 Patrick Donagher (Dunkeld). 1923-27 Michael Collins (1921). 1930 Lawrence Fischer (Galloway). 1930-32 John Boyle. 1935-37 David L Power (1928). 1937-47 Martin Doherty. 1947- Albert Chandler.

RENTON

Heads: 1899-1900 David Murie. 1900-08 Martin Jansen. 1908-14 Stephen A Thornton. 1914-23 John J Fleming. 1923-29 Joseph J Crumly. 1929-37 George Stuart. 1937-39 Matthew Quillinan. 1939-47 Edward Bradley. 1947-50 Jeremiah O'Leary. 1950-51 Charles Burns. 1951-74 Michael O'Sullivan. 1974-76 Daniel M Gallagher. 1976-81 Donal McMenamin. 1981- James Simcox.

Assistants: 1910-11 Hugh Gunther. 1928 Dominic McKellaig (Argyll). 1928-30 Joseph N Maxwell (Galloway). 1930-32 Thomas McGhie. 1932-37 Philip I Boyce. 1941-45 James Jackson. 1945-47 Patrick McHugh. 1947-48 William Colbert. 1948-49 Anthony McHugo. 1949-53 John Carter. 1953-55 Joseph Gallacher. 1955-62 Patrick J Kelly (1951). 1962-74 William Murphy (1952). 1982-87 Dominic Doogan.

ROSENEATH (Kilcreggan, Cove)

1951-68 John P Conway. 1968-73 Samuel J Lavery. 1973-76 Thomas McAteer. 1976-77 Hugh Cassidy. 1977-78 Patrick J Kelly (1951). 1978-86 Patrick Dinneen. 1986- Francis McPartlin.

RUTHERGLEN (St Columbkille's): moves to Motherwell diocese

Heads: 1851-85 John Shaw (WD). 1885-86 Michael Hughes. 1886-99 Denis McCarthy (WD). 1899-1901 Angus MacFarlane (WD). 1901-14 John Toner. 1914-33 John Montgomery. 1933-39 Angus Mackintosh. 1939-Patrick J Plunkett.

Assistants: 1884-85 Thomas Fitzgerald. 1886-87 Owen McPolin. 1887-88 John O'Callaghan (1886). 1889-90 James Rochead. 1890-93 John MacDonald (WD). 1893-97 Timothy O'Sullivan (1893). 1897-99 William C Brown (1897). 1898-1907 Denis Duggan (1898). 1899-1903 James Rochead. 1903-09 Angus McEachen. 1907-08 James E Mulvenna. 1908-18 Thomas J Doyle. 1909-24 James Troy. 1918-30 Alexander McBride. 1924-27 Cornelius Brew. 1927-36 John Crerand. 1930-39 Joseph Hamill. 1936-40 Matthew Littleton. 1937 John McCready (1935). 1938-45 Daniel Kennedy. 1939- Patrick Hoey. 1940-42 John McGinlay (1940). 1942- Thomas McGhie. 1945-48 John O'Donnell (1944).

SALTCOATS (Our Lady Star of the Sea): moves to Galloway diocese

Heads: 1878-84 William H Bergemann (WD). 1884-93 James Mackintosh (WD). 1893-99 Philip McColl. 1899-1905 Patrick Ryan. 1905-07 Francis Cronin. 1907-14 William Carmichael (WD). 1914-23 Bernard Lynch.

1923-26 Stephen A Thornton. 1926-32 Francis A Steven. 1932-33 vacant. 1933-39 Joseph Doherty. 1939- Michael O'Connor (1915).
Assistants: 1901-11 William Keogh. 1910-14 James Montgomery. 1911-24 Alfred J Gallaucher. 1914-20 John Power. 1920-24 Francis G Mangan. 1924-27 John McKenna. 1924-32 John Rooney. 1927 Jeremiah O'Sullivan. 1927-39 Thomas Kelly (1925) (2). 1932-37 Martin Doherty. 1937-39 Thomas Cahill. 1938 Charles Lawn. 1938-40 Thomas McGuire. 1939-40 Rodger McCauley. 1939-41 Michael J Connolly. 1940-42 Herbert G Rogers. 1940-46 Hugh Deery. 1941-47 John McFaul. 1942- Daniel Brennan. 1947- Cornelius Burke.

SHETTLESTON (St Paul's)
Note: combined with Carntyne 1912-45.
Heads: 1871-85 George McBrearty (WD). 1885-93 Joseph van Hecke. 1893-1902 Patrick Gaule. 1902-04 Peter O'Connor. 1904-23 Andrew J O'Brien. 1923-45 James Kearney. 1945-70 George Conlon. 1970-84 Daniel O'Leary. 1984- Jeremiah Carroll.
Assistants: 1891-92 William Fitzgerald. 1900-05 John Cahill. 1903 John Collins (1902). 1903-04 John McMillan (1898). 1905-09 David Morris. 1909-17 Michael B Morrissey. 1912-17 Hugh MacDonald (1906). 1913-14 John Power. 1914-23 James Montgomery. 1917-19 Thomas Farry. 1917-20 Daniel Harty. 1919-20 William McMullen. 1920-22 Patrick Fahey. 1920-26 Peter J MacFarlane. 1922-26 Patrick J Creedon. 1923-29 James McLaughlin (1923). 1924-25 James O'Connor (1924). 1926-29 James Graham. 1926-45 Patrick Gilmartin. 1929-34 Michael O'Carroll. 1929-37 James A E Nevin. 1934-35 John McCrory. 1934-42 Michael J McEleney. 1935-39 James Fitzgibbon. 1937-45 John Little. 1939-45 Joseph Connelly. 1942-45 Michael Lyne. 1946-50 Joseph Connelly. 1946-51 John Little. 1947-52 Francis McLeod. 1950-56 John Deans. 1951-74 Carlo Centra. 1952-60 John Glynn. 1956-57 Richard O'Callaghan. 1957-59 John Ryan (1950). 1959-70 James Fitzgerald (1940). 1960-74 Andrew Tolan. 1970-71 James Kirby. 1974-75 Lawrence Jamieson. 1974-77 Sean O'Neill. 1975-76 William McGinley. 1976-81 Ewen McPhail. 1977-85 David Currie. 1985- James Kirby.

SHIELDMUIR (Wishaw, St Patrick's): moves to Motherwell diocese
Served from Motherwell until 1891.
Heads: 1891-1914 George W Ritchie. 1914-19 Ellis P Rogan. 1919-29 Theophilus Delbeke. 1929-30 vacant. 1930-35 Bartholomew Atkinson. 1935- Alexander Hamilton.
Assistants: 1894-1902 Walter Kelly. 1896 Casper P Grau. 1896-99 Alexander McCormick (1895). 1899 George P Shaw (Aberdeen). 1899-1902 William Scanlan. 1902-11 Francis Dougan. 1902-15 James Clarke. 1911-21 James Durkin. 1915 John R Tennant. 1915-17 Thomas Gourlay. 1917-18 Daniel McLaughlin. 1917-23 Denis Flynn. 1918-19 William Bradley (1911). 1921 John McIntyre (1920). 1921-25 David Power (1920). 1923-30 Thomas Rourke. 1925-30 Columba McGoldrick.

1929 Gerard Lord. 1930-38 Joseph Costeur. 1930-48 James C Ward
(1928). 1933-37 Charles Sheridan. 1937-40 Henry Leonard. 1938-42
William Burke. 1940-41 William Coghlan. 1941-46 Francis Hamilton
(1926). 1945-47 Thomas G Mannion (1945). 1946- Thomas J O'Neill.

SHOTTS
Heads: 1878-84 John Sutherland (WD). 1884-85 Thomas P O'Reilly (WD).
   1885-89 Robert Grant (WD). 1889-90 Thomas Kerr (WD). 1890-93 Peter
   Muller. 1893-96 Peter Forbes (WD). 1896-1901 Hugh Kelly (1889). 1901-
   12 Peter Hilgers. 1912-17 Robert Paterson. 1917-34 John McAllister
   (1891). 1934-39 Peter Boland. 1939- Daniel Harty.
Assistants: 1894 Francis A McCann. 1900-04 Denis McBrearty. 1904-18
   James Kearney. 1918-19 Thomas O'Hanlon. 1919-21 Alphonsus Mullen.
   1921-23 Thomas Dumphy. 1923-26 Patrick O'Loughlin. 1926-28 John
   Boyle (1918). 1928-29 Thomas O'Doherty. 1929-32 Thomas Egan. 1932-
   33 Thomas McLoughlin. 1933-34 John O'Donnell (1918). 1933-34 Peter
   J Moore. 1934-48 Michael Little.

SPRINGBURN: see Glasgow, St Aloysius'

STEVENSTON: moves to Galloway diocese
Heads: 1905-06 William Horgan. 1906-15 James O'Neill (1887). 1915-16
   John McMenemy. 1916-18 William Daly. 1918-29 Patrick A McCarthy.
   1929-32 John Conlon. 1932-43 William Bradley (1913). 1943- John
   McQuillan.
Assistants: 1934-36 John McMahon (Dunkeld). 1937-40 John Gogarty.
   1940-45 John J Cusick (1930). 1945- James Bannon.

STRATHAVEN: moves to Motherwell diocese
1878-80 Patrick T O'Gorman (WD). 1880-84 served from Larkhall. 1884-85
   William Hallinan (WD). 1885-86 Herman van Baer (WD). 1886-97 Daniel
   Donnelly (WD). 1897-98 John Cameron. 1898-1901 John A Hickson
   (Galloway). 1901-06 Gisbert Hartmann. 1906-14 Daniel J Horgan (1898).
   1914-18 Joseph O'Leary. 1918-21 Thomas Doyle. 1921-26 Robert
   Cairns. 1926-29 Archibald McSparran. 1929-30 James Montgomery.
   1930-33 Edmund Macdonald. 1933-37 Peter Fitzpatrick. 1937-40
   William McGoldrick. 1940-43 John Daniel. 1943-48 Patrick Kelly (1924).

SYMINGTON (Land Scheme): 1931-36 John McQuillan. 1936 John
   Crerand.

TARBRAX: 1922-26 George Galbraith. 1926-28 James Montgomery. 1928-
   32 Joseph Kennedy. 1932-34 Simon Keane. 1934-38 Samuel McIsaac
   (Argyll). From 1938 served from Biggar.

TOLLCROSS: see Glasgow, St Joseph's (Tollcross)

TWECHAR: 1945-56 James L Cullen. 1956-59 John Deans. 1959-65 Thomas Maguire. 1965-70 Thomas Healy (1939). 1970-72 James McMahon. 1972-73 Nicholas Rowan. 1973-78 Patrick J McGovern (1947) (1). 1978- Thomas Meikleham.

UDDINGSTON – ST COLUMBA'S: moves to Motherwell diocese
Head: 1940- Thomas McCann.
Assistants: 1940-42 Vincent Cowley. 1942-43 Patrick Kelly (1924). 1943- John McLaughlin. 1946-48 Richard Lillis.

UDDINGSTON – ST JOHN THE BAPTIST'S: moves to Motherwell diocese
Heads: 1882-86 Denis McCarthy (WD). 1886-90 John L Murphy (1881). 1890-97 Ronald Mortimer. 1897-1907 Arthur Beyaert. 1907-30 James P Towie. 1930- Patrick McCarthy.
Asistants: 1898-1900 Matthew Burke. 1900-01 Edward Mollumby. 1901-08 John Walsh. 1902-06 James McKenna. 1907-08 Michael O'Boyle. 1908-17 Patrick Reilly. 1909-11 Edward Fitzgerald (1909). 1914-15 William Bradley (1911). 1917-18 Charles McGlinchey. 1918-22 Michael Ahearne. 1922-26 Michael Barron. 1926-34 Daniel O'Brien. 1927-28 Archibald Watt. 1928-30 James McGrory. 1934-43 William Forbes. 1934- Patrick Heaney. 1943- Peter McCann (1940).

VIEWPARK: see Uddingston, St Columba's

WEST KILBRIDE: moves to Galloway diocese
1947- Michael O'Carroll.

WHIFFLET: see Coatbridge, St Mary's

WHITERIGG: moves to Motherwell diocese
Heads: 1900-03 Angus McEachen. 1903-07 James P Towie. 1907-08 Denis Duggan (1898). 1908-15 William J McLaughlin. 1915-20 Patrick Cush. 1920-26 William Flanagan. 1926-31 Peter J MacFarlane. 1931-32 John McCrory. 1932-37 John J Murphy (1914). 1937-41 Patrick Torley. 1941- Patrick F Keating.
Assistants: 1940-42 Michael O'Carroll. 1942- Christopher Condon.

WISHAW – ST IGNATIUS': moves to Motherwell diocese
Heads: 1860-93 John McCay (WD). 1893-1927 Joseph van Hecke. 1927-29 vacant. 1929- Thomas Kearney (1903).
Assistants: 1878-79 John Crocius (WD). 1887-89 John Black (WD). 1889-91 Ludger W Kuhler. 1890-93 Edmund Cotter. 1894-96 Edward Doody. 1898-1900 Thomas Dooley. 1900-12 James Leonard. 1905-08 George Lillis. 1911-12 Patrick Gaynor. 1912-19 Patrick Hallinan. 1912-21 Robert Cairns. 1919-23 Patrick Deeney. 1921-33 Thomas Murray (1916). 1924-27 Edward Bradley. 1927-28 Bernard Atkinson. 1927-46 Thomas

O'Kane. 1928 Octavius Claeys. 1933-36 Alexander Mackintosh. 1936-44 Jeremiah Healy. 1944- Daniel O'Doherty. 1946-47 John Deans. 1947- Denis Garrity.

WISHAW – ST PATRICK'S: see Shieldmuir

INDUSTRIAL/APPROVED SCHOOLS- CHAPLAINS
Note: Although some of these schools were situated outwith the Archdiocesan boundaries they came within its remit.

KENMURE INDUSTRIAL SCHOOL (St Mary's Boys' School)
1906-10 Joseph Laveth. 1910-14 Thomas Kerr (WD). 1914-18 Gisbert Hartmann. 1918-21 James Doherty (1911). 1921-26 William Bradley (1911). 1926-31 Patrick Kelly (1924). 1931-32 John Rogan. 1932-34 John McCrory. 1934-40 Michael O'Carroll. 1940-64 Joseph Doherty. 1976-77 Dermot Healy.

ST MUNGO'S APPROVED SCHOOL (Mauchline)
1942-46 Herbert G Rogers. 1946-56 Thomas McGrory.

ST NINIAN'S APPROVED SCHOOL (Kirkconnel, Gartmore)
1946-47 Angus McKellaig. 1947-50 John Deans. 1950-56 Joseph Connelly. 1956-65 Thomas McGrory. 1965-68 Jeremiah O'Connor.

WEST THORN REFORMATORY: see Glasgow, West Thorn.

Diocese of Motherwell

Secular Clergy

ALLISON, HENRY J: Born and educated Ireland. Ordained Wexford for Motherwell 1958. Chapelhall 1958. St Bartholomew's, Coatbridge 1958-67. St Ninian's, Hamilton 1967-70. Bothwell 1970-82. St Leonard's, East Kilbride 1982-87. St Anthony's, Rutherglen 1987-. (Canning)

ASHE, JAMES JOSEPH: Born and educated Ireland. Ordained All Hallows College for Motherwell 1953. St Ignatius', Wishaw 1953-57. Caldercruix 1957-58. Sacred Heart, Bellshill 1958-71. Moodiesburn 1971-75. St Benedict's, Easterhouse 1975-81. St Brendan's, Motherwell 1981-. (Canning)

ASHE, JOHN: see Glasgow Archdiocese.

BARRY, THOMAS: see Glasgow Archdiocese.

BATTELL, JOHN CHARLES: see Glasgow Archdiocese.

BEATTIE, HUGH: Born Dumbarton 1928. Educated Priory College, Bishop's Waltham; St Peter's. Ordained Glasgow 1955. Burnbank 1955-59. Sacred Heart, Bellshill 1959-61. Forces chaplain 1961-.

BOGAN, GERARD: Born Carfin 1960. Educated Our Lady's High School, Motherwell; Valladolid. Ordained Newarthill 1985. St Patrick's, Wishaw 1985-87. St Bride's, East Kilbride 1987-.

BOYCE, PHILIP: see Glasgow Archdiocese.

BOYD, GEORGE: Born Mossend 1924. Educated Blairs, St Peter's. Ordained Motherwell 1948. St Patrick's, Wishaw 1948-54. St Mary's, Coatbridge 1954-62. Chapelhall 1962-69. St Thomas's, Wishaw 1969-77. St Bernadette's, Motherwell 1977-.

411

BOYLE, JAMES: Ordained 1968. St Leonard's, East Kilbride 1970-76. Mossend 1976-80. Moodiesburn 1980-81. St Clare's, Easterhouse 1981-83. C/o Diocesan Centre 1983-.

BOYLE, JOHN A (1959): Ordained 1959. Possibly an ex-Redemptorist Father. St James', Coatbridge 1971-73. No other entries. (A John Boyle C.Ss.R, ordained 1959, appears under Kinnoull in CD 1971.)

BOYLE, JOHN WATTERS (1946): see Glasgow Archdiocese.

BOYLE, WILLIAM: Born Coatbridge 1919. Educated Glasgow University; Scots College, Rome. Ordained Rome 1952. Sacred Heart, Bellshill 1953. Died Bellshill 23 Aug 1953.

BRADLEY, WILLIAM (1911): see Glasgow Archdiocese.

BRADY, JOHN CHARLES: Born Carfin 1930. Educated Our Lady's High School, Motherwell; Scots College, Rome, returning home following rheumatic fever; St Peter's. Ordained Motherwell 1956. St Mary's, Hamilton 1956. Larkhall 1956-61. St Joseph's, Blantyre 1961-68. St Benedict's, Easterhouse 1968-70. St Anthony's, Rutherglen 1970-78. Lent to Aberdeen Diocese: Tomintoul 1978-79; Dingwall 1979-82; Aviemore 1982. Died Aviemore 8 Dec 1982.

BRADY, THOMAS JOSEPH: Born Bellshill 1954. Educated Langbank, Blairs, Valladolid. Ordained Cardowan 1978. St Bride's, East Kilbride 1978-82. St James', Coatbridge 1982-86. St Bridget's, Baillieston 1986-.

BRANNIGAN, JOSEPH: Born Airdrie 1954. Educated St Patrick's High School, Coatbridge; Blairs; St Peter's; Drygrange. Ordained Airdrie 1978. St Monica's, Coatbridge 1978-80. Shotts 1980-83. Professor, Blairs 1983-86. St Leonard's, East Kilbride 1986-88. Our Lady and St Anne's, Hamilton 1988-.

BREDIN, JOHN: see Glasgow Archdiocese.

BRENNAN, PATRICK: see Glasgow Archdiocese.

BRESLIN, JOHN FRANCIS: Born Carfin 1929. Educated Our Lady's High School, Motherwell; Scots College, Rome. Ordained Rome 1953. St Joseph's, Blantyre 1953-61. Chaplain, Franciscan Convent, Bothwell 1961-65. Bothwell 1965-69. Chaplain, Sisters of Mercy Convent, Baillieston 1969-74. St Bride's, Cambuslang 1974-.

BRESLIN, RAYMOND JOHN: Born Bellshill 1965. Educated Langbank; Blairs; Scots College, Rome. Ordained Shotts 1989. Our Lady and St Anne's, Hamilton 1989-.

BRIODY, MICHAEL: Born Glasgow 1954. Educated Langbank, Blairs, Valladolid. Ordained Bellshill 1977. St Monica's, Coatbridge 1977-78. St Bartholomew's, Coatbridge 1978-86. St James', Coatbridge 1986-.

BROOKS, THOMAS: see Glasgow Archdiocese.

BROSNAN, PATRICK: Born and educated Ireland. Ordained Kilkenny for Motherwell 1953. Halfway 1953-59. Carfin 1959-62. St Andrew's, Airdrie 1962-69. St Bartholomew's, Coatbridge 1969-73. St Bernard's, Coatbridge 1973-81. Our Lady of Lourdes, East Kilbride 1981-87. St Patrick's, Coatbridge 1987-. (Canning)

BROSNAN, TIMOTHY: Born and educated Ireland. Ordained Kilkenny for Motherwell 1957. Garthamlock 1957-60. St Margaret's, Airdrie 1960-71. Sacred Heart, Bellshill 1971-76. Chapelhall 1976-81. St Benedict's, Easterhouse 1981-84. St Gerard's, Bellshill 1984-. (Canning)

BURNS, JOHN JOSEPH: Born Glasgow 1932. Educated St Joseph's College, Dumfries; Scots College, Rome. Ordained Rome 1956. Motherwell Cathedral 1956-70. St Brendan's, Motherwell 1970-79. Director, Religious Education Centre 1979-83. St Aidan's, Wishaw 1983-.

BUTLER, JAMES: see Glasgow Archdiocese

CAHILL, HUGH: see Glasgow Archdiocese.

CANNON, BARTHOLOMEW: Born Glasgow 1960. Educated St Aloysius' College, Glasgow; Glasgow University; Drygrange. Ordained Cadzow 1986. St Vincent de Paul's, East Kilbride 1986-89. St Andrew's, Airdrie 1989-.

CAREY, NOEL F: Born and educated Ireland. Ordained Carlow for Motherwell 1953. St Mary's, Coatbridge 1953-56. Carfin 1956-58. Muirhead 1958-67. New Stevenston 1967-68. Carfin 1968-73. St Brendan's, Motherwell 1973-81. Motherwell Cathedral 1981-. (Canning)

CARLIN, NEAL PHELIM: Born and educated Ireland. Ordained Wexford for Motherwell 1964. Burnbank 1964-68. St Luke's, Motherwell 1968-70. C/o Diocesan Office 1970-71 (St Mary's College, Strawberry Hill-Canning). Plains 1971-72. New Stevenston 1972-75. From 1975 serving in Ireland. (Canning)

CHROMY, GERARD: Born Glasgow 1953. Educated Holy Cross High School, Hamilton; St Peter's. Ordained Cambuslang 1976. St Patrick's, Wishaw 1976-82. Bothwell 1982-88. Motherwell Cathedral 1988-.

CLARKE, PATRICK: see Glasgow Archdiocese.

CLEMENTS, JOSEPH: Born Calderbank 1938. Educated Blairs, Valladolid. Ordained Valladolid 1962. Carfin 1962-68. St Aidan's, Wishaw 1968-70. St Bride's, East Kilbride 1970-77. Motherwell Cathedral 1977-87. St Thomas's, Wishaw 1987-.

COLVIN, DANIEL: see Glasgow Archdiocese.

COMERFORD, JAMES: Born and educated Ireland. Ordained Kilkenny for Motherwell 1952. Shotts 1952-55. Carfin 1955-65. St Joseph's, Blantyre 1965-68. Left priesthood 1968. (Canning)

CONDON, CHRISTOPHER: see Glasgow Archdiocese.

CONNELLY, LAWRENCE F: Born Carfin 1930. Educated Blairs, St Peter's. Ordained Glasgow 1954. St Bartholomew's, Coatbridge 1954-60. All Saints', Coatdyke 1960-64. Died Glasgow 3 Oct 1964.

CONNELLY, THOMAS ANTHONY: Born Edinburgh 1933. Educated Holy Cross Academy, Edinburgh; St Sulpice. Ordained Portobello 1962. St Margaret's, Airdrie 1962-64. St Bernadette's, Motherwell 1964-73. St Benedict's, Easterhouse 1973-78. Halfway 1978-.

CONROY, JOHN: see Glasgow Archdiocese.

CONWAY, MICHAEL JOSEPH: Born and educated Ireland. Ordained Kilkenny for Motherwell 1963. St James', Coatbridge 1963-65. Plains 1965-67. Newarthill 1967-70. C/o Diocesan Office 1970-75. St Monica's, Coatbridge 1975-77. Went to Glasgow Archdiocese: Chaplain, Glasgow University 1977-. (Canning)

CORLESS, THOMAS JOSEPH: Born and educated Ireland. Ordained Wexford for Motherwell 1951. Larkhall 1951-56. St John the Baptist's, Uddingston 1956-60. New Stevenston 1960-65. St Patrick's, Wishaw 1965-68. On mission in Sierra Leone 1968-74. Mossend 1974-76. St Clare's, Easterhouse 1976-82. Uddingston 1982-. (Canning)

CORR, HENRY: see Glasgow Archdiocese.

CORRY, MICHAEL THOMAS: Born and educated Ireland. Ordained Carlow for Motherwell 1952. St Bridget's, Baillieston 1952-55. Glenboig 1955-61. Halfway 1961-63. St Mary's, Whifflet 1963-64. No further entries. (Canning)

COSGROVE, JOHN: Ordained 1935. St Margaret's, Airdrie 1950-53. Longriggend 1953-54. Baillieston (not attached to parish) 1954-55. Chaplain, Sisters of Mercy, Baillieston, 1955-68. Blackwood 1968-72. Serving in Ireland 1972-.

COSTELLO, DENIS: Born and educated Ireland. Ordained Maynooth 1949. Lent to Motherwell diocese. Shotts 1949-50. Resumed his vocation in Ireland, and also serving in Peru, from 1950. (Canning)

COYLE, ANTHONY: Born Coatbridge 1948. Educated St Patrick's High School, Coatbridge; Valladolid. Ordained Coatbridge 1973. St Columbkille's, Rutherglen 1973-77. Burnbank 1977-78. Society of St James the Apostle, Boston, USA, 1978-89. No further entries.

CRAIGEN, CHARLES: see Glasgow Archdiocese.

CULLEN, DAVID JAMES: Born and educated Ireland. Ordained Wexford for Motherwell 1954. Burnbank 1954-57. Mossend 1957-58. No further entries. (Canning)

CUNNANE, MICHAEL ALOYSIUS: Born and educated Ireland. Ordained Wexford for Motherwell 1961. St Bride's, East Kilbride 1961-67. Mossend 1967-74. Halfway 1974-76. Burnbank 1976-77. St Martin's Church, La Mesa, California 1977-89. No further entries. (Canning)

CURLEY, ROBERT: Born Chapelhall 1939. Educated Our Lady's High School, Motherwell; Blairs; St Peter's. Ordained Motherwell 1962. St Benedict's, Easterhouse 1962-67. Plains 1967-72. St Augustine's, Coatbridge 1972-77. St Bride's, East Kilbride 1977-83. Carfin 1983-85. St Aidan's, Wishaw 1985-87. St Clare's, Easterhouse 1987-.

CUSHLEY, JOHN: Born Coatbridge 1941. Educated St Patrick's High School, Coatbridge; Valladolid. Ordained Motherwell 1967. St Bride's, East Kilbride 1967-70. St Edward's, Airdrie 1970-72. Garthamlock 1972-73. No further entries.

CUSHLEY, LEO W: Born Wester Moffat 1961. Educated Holy Cross High School, Hamilton; Blairs; Scots College, Rome. Ordained Uddingston 1985. Further studies, Rome 1985-87. Motherwell Cathedral 1987-88. St Serf's, Airdrie 1988-.

CUSICK, JOHN J (1930): see Glasgow Archdiocese.

D'ARCY, AIDAN: Born and educated Ireland. Ordained Thurles for Motherwell 1957. St James', Coatbridge 1957-66. Our Lady of Lourdes, East Kilbride 1966-72. St Serf's, Airdrie 1972-81. St Bernard's, Coatbridge 1981-86. St Joseph's, Blantyre 1986-. (Canning)

DARROCH, FRANCIS F: Born Uddingston 1930. Educated Our Lady's High School, Motherwell; Blairs; St Peter's; St Sulpice. Ordained Motherwell 1956. Newarthill 1956-65. St Peter's, Hamilton 1965-66. St

Joseph's, Blantyre 1966-72. St Ninian's, Hamilton 1972-79. Our Lady and St Anne's, Hamilton 1979-.

DAVIDSON, JAMES: Born Coatbridge 1952. Educated St Patrick's High School, Coatbridge; St Peter's; Drygrange. Ordained Coatbridge 1977. Cambuslang 1977-82. Carfin 1982-83. St Anthony's, Rutherglen 1983-85. St Andrew's, Airdrie 1985-87. Sacred Heart, Bellshill 1987-88. No further entries.

DELANEY, JOHN JOSEPH: Born Govan 1928. Educated St Patrick's College, Armagh; St Patrick's College, Carlow. Ordained Carlow for Motherwell 1954. St Mary's, Whifflet 1954-59. Burnbank 1959-60. Caldercruix 1960-63. Carfin 1963-65. Sacred Heart, Bellshill 1965-73. St Stephen's, Coatbridge 1973-84. Bargeddie 1984-.

DEMPSEY, NICHOLAS: Born Ireland. Educated England and Scots College, Rome. Ordained Wexford for Motherwell 1971. St Joseph's, Blantyre 1971-82. Sacred Heart, Bellshill 1982-87. San Diego, California from 1987. (Canning)

DEMPSEY, RAYMOND: Born Bellshill 1959. Educated Our Lady's High School, Motherwell; Drygrange. Ordained Bellshill 1984. St Leonard's, East Kilbride 1984-.

DEVANNY, ALEXANDER SUTHERLAND: Born Shieldmuir 1935. Educated Our Lady's High School, Motherwell; Blairs; St Peter's. Ordained Motherwell 1959. St Columba's, Viewpark 1959. St Monica's, Coatbridge 1959-68. New Stevenston 1968-72. Our Lady of Lourdes, East Kilbride 1972-80. St Mary's, Hamilton 1980-.

DEVINE, (Thomas) GERARD: Born Hamilton 1953. Educated Langbank, Blairs, St Peter's, Drygrange. Ordained Hamilton 1977. St James', Coatbridge 1977-82. Our Lady of Lourdes, East Kilbride 1982-86. St Ignatius', Wishaw 1986-.

DEVLIN, GERARD: Born Motherwell 1960. Educated Our Lady's High School, Motherwell; Drygrange. Ordained Motherwell 1985. St Augustine's, Coatbridge 1985-89. C/o Diocesan Office 1989-.

DOCHERTY, HENRY NOEL: Born Glasgow 1930. Educated St Mungo's Academy, Glasgow; Scots College, Rome. Ordained Rome 1955. Completing studies in Rome 1955-56. St James', Coatbridge 1956-59. St Patrick's, Wishaw 1959-67. St Bartholomew's, Coatbridge 1967-68. St Augustine's, Coatbridge 1968-69. St Brendan's, Motherwell 1969-70. Chaplain, Notre Dame College of Education 1970-78. St Serf's, Airdrie 1978-79. Sacred Congregation for the Doctrine of the Faith, Rome, 1979-87. Secretary, Bishops' Conference of Scotland, 1987-.

DOHERTY, CHARLES JOSEPH: Born and educated Ireland. Ordained Kilkenny for Motherwell 1957. St Mark's, Rutherglen 1957-61. Mossend 1961-65. On mission in Peru 1965-68. Rockledge, Florida 1968-69. St Columba's, Viewpark 1969-73. Uddingston 1973-76. Serving in Ireland 1976-78. St Mary's, Hamilton 1978-80. St Peter's, Hamilton 1980-82. Died Ireland 23 April 1982. (Canning)

DOHERTY, EDWARD: see Glasgow Archdiocese.

DOHERTY, JOHN: Born Motherwell 1942. Educated Blairs, Valladolid. Ordained Motherwell 1967. St Andrew's, Airdrie 1967-73. St James', Coatbridge 1973-74. Cleland 1974-75. St Clare's, Easterhouse 1975-81. Muirhead 1981-83. St Ignatius', Wishaw 1983-87. St Patrick's, Wishaw 1987-88. Newmains 1988-.

DONALDSON, GEORGE: Born Baillieston 1937. Educated Our Lady's High School, Motherwell; Blairs; Scots College, Rome. Ordained Rome 1961. Motherwell Cathedral 1961-69. St Mary's, Coatbridge 1969-72. Professor, St Peter's College 1972-85. Professor, Chesters College 1985-.

DONNELLY, ANTHONY: see Glasgow Archdiocese.

DONNELLY, BRIAN: Born Motherwell 1936. Educated Our Lady's High School, Motherwell; Blairs; Valladolid; St Peter's. Ordained Motherwell 1960. St Clare's, Easterhouse 1960-65. St Augustine's, Coatbridge 1965-68. St Bridget's, Baillieston 1968-70. St Columba's, Viewpark 1970-73. St Clare's, Easterhouse 1973-82. Uddingston 1982-85. St Vincent de Paul's, East Kilbride 1985-.

DOOLEY, JAMES: see Glasgow Archdiocese.

DOOLEY, MICHAEL: see Glasgow Archdiocese.

DORNAN, CHARLES CAMPBELL: Born Glasgow 1956. Educated St Patrick's High School, Coatbridge; Notre Dame College of Education. Teaching career. Educated for priesthood Valladolid, Salamanca. Ordained Coatbridge 1989. St Vincent de Paul's, Coatbridge 1989-.

DOUGLAS, DOMINIC SAVIO: Born Glasgow 1960. Educated Langbank; Blairs; Scots College, Rome. Ordained Cambuslang 1984. Carluke 1984. Completing studies, Rome 1984-85. St Bride's, East Kilbride 1985-87. St Andrew's, Airdrie 1987-89. St Bartholomew's, Coatbridge 1989-.

DOUGLAS, EDWARD: see Glasgow Archdiocese.

DOUGLAS, ROBERT: see Glasgow Archdiocese.

DUDDY, JAMES: Born Craigneuk 1950. Educated Our Lady's High School, Motherwell; St Patrick's College, Buchlyvie; St Peter's; Drygrange. Ordained Wishaw 1977. St Patrick's, Coatbridge 1977. St Benedict's, Easterhouse 1977-80. St Bernadette's, Motherwell 1980-88. St Joseph's, Blantyre 1988-.

DUDDY, WILLIAM: see Glasgow Archdiocese.

DUNNACHIE, WILLIAM: Born Motherwell 1940. Educated Our Lady's High School, Motherwell; Valladolid. Ordained Glasgow 1964. St Bartholomew's, Coatbridge 1964-70. St Mary's, Hamilton 1970-71. C/o Diocesan Office 1971-72. Plains 1972-78. St Mary's, Coatbridge 1978-87. Our Lady of Lourdes, East Kilbride 1987-.

EGAN, THOMAS: see Glasgow Archdiocese.

FARNIN, JOSEPH: Born Viewpark 1935. Educated Our Lady's High School, Motherwell; Blairs; St Peter's. Ordained Motherwell 1959. St Mary's, Whifflet 1959-60. All Saints, Airdrie 1960-66. C/o Diocesan Office 1966-71. No further entries.

FARRELL, JOHN BERNARD: Born Dublin 1942. Entered Congregation of Christian Brothers. Taught in their schools in Ireland, Africa, England and Scotland. Entered St Patrick's College, Maynooth and was ordained Dublin 1987. St Bridget's, Baillieston 1987-88. Sacred Heart, Bellshill 1988-.

FEHILY, THOMAS: see Glasgow Archdiocese.

FISHER, JAMES: Ordained 1924. St Patrick's, Wishaw 1972-78. No further entries.

FITZPATRICK, JOSEPH: Born Cambuslang 1940. Educated Blairs; Scots College, Rome. Ordained Rome 1964. Our Lady of Lourdes, East Kilbride 1964-66. Further studies, Cambridge University 1966-69. Professor, Blairs 1969-70. No further entries.

FLACK, HERBERT: Born and educated Ireland. Ordained All Hallows for Motherwell 1952. Chapelhall 1952-58. St Bridget's, Baillieston 1958-65. Halfway 1965-70. Harthill 1970-72. Stepps 1972-. (Canning)

FLANAGAN, PHILIP: Born Baillieston 1913. Educated St Aloysius' College, Glasgow; Scots College, Rome 1929-35. Ordained Rome for Glasgow 1935. Further studies, Rome 1935-38. Vice-rector, Scots College, Rome 1938-40. Professor, Blairs 1940-46. Vice-rector, Scots College, Rome 1946-52. Joined Motherwell diocese. Rector, Valladolid 1952-60. Rector, Scots College, Rome 1960-67. Sacred Heart, Bellshill 1967-78. Chapelhall 1978-83. Died Glasgow 22 Nov 1983.

FLANAGAN, WILLIAM: see Glasgow Archdiocese.

FLYNN, BARTHOLOMEW: see Glasgow Archdiocese.

FLYNN, DENIS: see Glasgow Archdiocese.

FLYNN, JAMES: Born and educated Ireland. Ordained Thurles for Motherwell 1957. St Columba's, Viewpark 1957-58. Shotts 1958-68. On mission in Brazil 1968-74. Our Lady and St Anne's, Hamilton 1974-82. St Clare's, Easterhouse 1982-84. St Stephen's, Coatbridge 1984-85. Died Ireland 11 April 1985. (Canning)

FOLEY, JAMES: Born Glasgow 1931. Educated Scots College, Rome. Ordained Rome 1955. Motherwell Cathedral 1955-56. Continuing studies, Rome 1956-59. Ripetitore, Scots College, Rome 1959-65. Professor, St Peter's College 1965-77. St Mary's, Coatbridge 1977-85. St Augustine's, Coatbridge 1985-.

FRYER, GEORGE: see Glasgow Archdiocese.

GALLACHER, JOHN FRANCIS: Born Coatbridge 1927. Educated St Aloysius' College, Glasgow; St Sulpice. Ordained Motherwell 1951. Chapelhall 1951-52. Carluke 1952-57. Burnbank 1957-61. St Mark's, Rutherglen 1961-68. Mossend 1968-70. Carluke 1970-82. St Joseph's, Blantyre 1982-86. St Bernard's, Coatbridge 1986-.

GARRITY, DENIS: see Glasgow Archdiocese.

GAULT, THOMAS MURRAY: Born Cambuslang 1956. Educated Langbank; Blairs; Scots College, Rome. Ordained Cambuslang 1980. Our Lady of Lourdes, East Kilbride 1980. Completing studies, Rome 1980-81. Our Lady and St Anne's, Hamilton 1981-86. Motherwell Cathedral 1986-.

GIBBONS, THOMAS: Born Motherwell 1930. Educated Blairs, St Peter's. Ordained Glasgow 1954. St Bride's, East Kilbride 1954. Cambuslang 1954-58. St Margaret's, Airdrie 1958-61. Uddingston 1961-69. Glasgow, no parish, 1969-81. St Monica's, Coatbridge 1981-.

GILHOOLEY, DAMIEN JAMES: Born Cambuslang 1944. Educated Our Lady's High School, Motherwell; Valladolid. Ordained Motherwell 1968. St James', Coatbridge 1968-71. St Benedict's, Easterhouse 1971-75. St Andrew's, Airdrie 1975-80. Our Lady of Lourdes, East Kilbride 1980-83. St Bartholomew's, Coatbridge 1983-88. Halfway 1988-.

GILLEN, JOHN: see Glasgow Archdiocese.

GIVENS, JOHN FRANCIS: Born Airdrie 1926. Educated Valladolid, St Sulpice. Ordained Shieldmuir 1955. Mossend 1955-57. St Bride's, East Kilbride 1957-65. St Bridget's, Baillieston 1965-66. St James', Coatbridge 1966-68. St Mark's, Rutherglen 1968-76. St Gabriel's, Viewpark 1976-84. St Clare's, Easterhouse 1984-87. St Leonard's, East Kilbride 1987-.

GLACKIN, EDWARD: Born Motherwell 1934. Educated Our Lady's High School, Motherwell; Blairs; Valladolid. Ordained Valladolid 1958. St Ninian's, Hamilton 1958-67. C/o Diocesan Office 1967-68. St Mary's, Coatbridge 1968-69. Spiritual Director, Valladolid 1969-73. Newmains 1973-83. St Columba's, Viewpark 1983-.

GORMAN, PETER: Born Airdrie 1939. Educated Blairs, St Sulpice, St Peter's. Ordained Motherwell 1965. Newmains 1965-68. St Joseph's, Blantyre 1968-74. Chapelhall 1974-76. St Bernadette's, Motherwell 1976-79. St Columbkille's, Rutherglen 1979-86. Died Rutherglen 15 Sept 1986.

GRANT, JAMES ANTHONY: Born Baillieston 1959. Educated St Patrick's High School, Coatbridge; Valladolid. Ordained Calderbank 1983. Shotts 1983-89. Our Lady of Lourdes, East Kilbride 1989-.

HALAVAGE, FRANCIS: Born Coatbridge 1942. Educated St Patrick's High School, Coatbridge; St Augustine's School, Coatbridge; St Peter's. Ordained Coatbridge 1975. Motherwell Cathedral 1975. Our Lady of Lourdes, East Kilbride 1975-78. St Margaret's, Airdrie 1978-85. St Serf's, Airdrie 1985-88. St Columbkille's, Rutherglen 1988-.

HALLINAN, JAMES E: see Glasgow Archdiocese.

HAMILTON, ALEXANDER: see Glasgow Archdiocese.

HARTY, DANIEL: see Glasgow Archdiocese.

HAYES, NIALL PATRICK: Born and educated Ireland. Ordained All Hallows for Motherwell 1949. Sacred Heart, Bellshill 1949-58. St Ignatius', Wishaw 1958-65. St Anthony's, Rutherglen 1965-81. St Thomas's, Wishaw 1981-85. New Stevenston 1985-. (Canning)

HAYES, VIVIAN MARTIN: Born and educated Ireland. Ordained All Hallows for Motherwell 1955. St Columbkille's, Rutherglen 1955-62. St Joseph's, Blantyre 1962-64. St Edward's, Airdrie 1964-70. St Bartholomew's, Coatbridge 1970-74. St Columba's, Viewpark 1974-77. St Francis of Assisi's, Baillieston 1977-. (Canning)

HEALEY, ROBERT JOSEPH: Born Hamilton 1951. Educated Holy Cross High School, Hamilton; University of Strathclyde; Valladolid. Ordained

Cadzow 1978. Professor, Blairs College 1978-84. Newarthill 1984-86. St Monica's, Coatbridge 1986-88. St Peter's, Hamilton 1988-89. Shotts 1989-.

HEALY, JOHN BERNARD: Born and educated Ireland. Ordained Kilkenny for Motherwell 1954. Newmains 1954-65. St Bernadette's, Motherwell 1965-70. Motherwell Cathedral 1970-75. Holytown 1975-83. Sacred Heart, Bellshill 1983-. (Canning)

HEANEY, PATRICK JOSEPH: see Glasgow Archdiocese.

HENNESSY, DANIEL J: Born and educated Ireland. Ordained Waterford for Motherwell 1948. St Patrick's, Coatbridge 1948-55. St Bernadette's, Motherwell 1955-64. Strathaven 1964-68. St Benedict's, Easterhouse 1968-75. St Bridget's, Baillieston 1975-. (Canning)

HENNESSY, PATRICK ANTHONY: Born and educated Ireland. Ordained Waterford for Motherwell 1969. St Columbkille's, Rutherglen 1969-74. St James', Coatbridge 1974-77. Professor, Langbank 1977-78. Professor, Blairs 1978-86. Our Lady and St Anne's, Hamilton 1986-88. On mission in Peru 1988-. (Canning)

HICKEY, THOMAS C: Born and educated Ireland. Ordained Maynooth 1950. Lent to Motherwell diocese. Burnbank 1950-53. Resumed his vocation in Ireland 1953. (Canning)

HIGGINS, RICHARD: Born and educated Ireland. Ordained Wexford for Motherwell 1958. St Columbkille's, Rutherglen 1958-61. St Columba's, Viewpark 1961-69. Our Lady and St Anne's, Hamilton 1969-77. In hospital in Ireland 1977-85. No further entries. (Canning)

HOBAN, DENIS: Born Craigneuk, Wishaw 1926. Educated St Patrick's School, Shieldmuir; St Aloysius' College, Glasgow; Our Lady's High School, Motherwell; Blairs; St Peter's. Interrupted his studies at St Peter's during the war to work in the mines. Ordained Motherwell 1953. St Columbkille's, Rutherglen 1953. Newmains 1953-54. Bargeddie 1954-57. Army Chaplain 1957-60. St Columba's, Viewpark 1960-61. Joined the South African mission for the sake of his health 1961. Died Port Elizabeth 6 July 1962.

HOEY, PATRICK: see Glasgow Archdiocese.

HOULIHAN, MICHAEL: see Glasgow Archdiocese.

HUGHES, COLIN THOMAS: Born Shotts 1956. Educated St Aidan's High School, Wishaw; Bell College, Hamilton; Notre Dame College of Education; Drygrange. Ordained Shotts 1986. Carfin 1986. Our Lady of Lourdes, East Kilbride 1986-89. St Patrick's, Coatbridge 1989-.

HUNTER, PATRICK: Ordained 1972. St Clare's, Easterhouse 1972-73. St Monica's, Coatbridge 1973-74. No further entries.

HYNES, PATRICK: Born Airdrie 1955. Educated St Margaret's High School, Airdrie; St Patrick's High School, Coatbridge; Scots College, Rome. Ordained Airdrie 1981. Completing studies, Rome 1981-82. St Peter's, Hamilton 1982-83. Sacred Heart, Bellshill 1983-85. St Joseph's, Blantyre 1985-86. C/o Diocesan Office 1986-.

KANE, ROBERT: Born Hamilton 1948. Educated Holy Cross High School, Hamilton; Scots College, Rome. Ordained Hamilton 1971. Our Lady of Lourdes, East Kilbride 1972-75. Professor, Langbank 1975-78. Further studies, Cambridge University 1978-80. Professor, Blairs 1980-83. St Joseph's, Blantyre 1983-85. St Columbkille's, Rutherglen 1985-88. St Aidan's, Wishaw 1988-.

KEANE, DENIS: Born and educated Ireland. Ordained Wexford for Motherwell 1949. Newton 1949-51. Shotts 1951-53. All Saints, Airdrie 1953-58. St Patrick's, Coatbridge 1958-65. St Brendan's, Motherwell 1965-73. St Columba's, Viewpark 1973-82. Burnbank 1982-. (Canning)

KEANE, STEPHEN ALOYSIUS: see Aberdeen diocese.

KEARNEY, THOMAS (1903): see Glasgow Archdiocese.

KEATING, PATRICK F: see Glasgow Archdiocese.

KEEGAN, JAMES JOSEPH: Born and educated Ireland. Ordained Carlow 1952. Longriggend 1952-53. St Margaret's, Airdrie 1953-58. St Columba's, Viewpark 1958-60. St Patrick's, Wishaw 1960-69. St Mary's, Coatbridge 1969-70. St Luke's, Motherwell 1970-77. Strathaven 1977-86. St Patrick's, Wishaw 1986-. (Canning)

KEENAN, BERNARD: see Glasgow Archdiocese.

KELLY, FRANCIS: Born Motherwell 1930. Educated Our Lady's High School, Motherwell; Scots College, Rome. Ordained Rome 1954. Muirhead 1954-55. St Bridget's, Baillieston 1955-61. Larkhall 1961-65. St Patrick's, Coatbridge 1965-66. Spiritual Director, Scots College, Rome 1966-69. Chapelhall 1969-74. Cleland 1974-82. St Mark's, Rutherglen 1982-85. St Mary's, Coatbridge 1985-.

KELLY, HUGH PATRICK: Born Stirling 1941. Educated Our Lady's High School, Motherwell; St Peter's. Ordained Motherwell 1967. Motherwell Cathedral 1967-73. Sacred Heart, Bellshill 1973-78. St Ninian's, Hamilton 1978-82. St Patrick's, Wishaw 1982-85. St Bridget's, Baillieston 1985-86. St Bartholomew's, Coatbridge 1986-.

KELLY, JOHN: Born Shieldmuir 1940. Educated Blairs, Issy, Valladolid. Ordained Glasgow 1964. St Clare's, Easterhouse 1964-69. Our Lady of Lourdes, East Kilbride 1969-72. Spiritual Director, St Peter's College 1972-78. St Bernadette's, Motherwell 1978-80. Motherwell Cathedral 1980-81. St Thomas's, Wishaw 1981-85. Newmains 1985-88. St James', Coatbridge 1988-.

KELLY, MARTIN JOSEPH: Born and educated Ireland. Ordained Carlow for Motherwell 1965. St Columba's, Viewpark 1965-74. On foreign missions 1974-77. Guayaquil, Ecuador 1977-80. St Columbkille's, Rutherglen 1980-85. On foreign missions 1985-. (Canning)

KELLY, PATRICK (1924): see Glasgow Archdiocese.

KELLY, THOMAS PATRICK (1925) (1): see Glasgow Archdiocese.

KELLY, THOMAS (1925) (2): see Glasgow Archdiocese.

KENNY, LAWRENCE (Laurence): Born and educated Ireland. Ordained Carlow for Motherwell 1957. Halfway 1957-65. St Clare's, Easterhouse 1965-66. St Bridget's, Baillieston 1966-69. St Ninian's, Hamilton 1969-72. St Monica's, Coatbridge 1972-81. St Edward's, Airdrie 1981-. (Canning)

KILCOYNE, ANTHONY: see Glasgow Archdiocese.

KILCOYNE, PATRICK EMMET: Born Glasgow 1929. Educated Clongowes Wood College, Co. Kildare; All Hallows College, Dublin. Ordained All Hallows for Motherwell 1955. Our Lady and St Anne's, Hamilton 1955-65. Carfin 1965-70. Newarthill 1970-76. Biggar 1976-82. St Columba's, Viewpark 1982-83. St James', Coatbridge 1983-.

KILPATRICK, JAMES: see Glasgow Archdiocese.

KILPATRICK, JOSEPH: see Fitzpatrick, Joseph. (Error in 1965 Directory)

LAMB, BRIAN JAMES: Born Bellshill 1963. Educated St Margaret's High School, Airdrie; Scots College, Rome. Ordained Plains 1988. St Peter's, Hamilton 1988. Our Lady of Lourdes, East Kilbride 1988-.

LAVERTY, EDWARD: Born Shieldmuir 1923. Educated Fort Augustus; Blairs 1938-44; St Peter's 1944-48. Ordained Motherwell 1948. St Mary's, Hamilton 1948-49. St Anne's, Cadzow 1949-53. Mossend 1953-56. Larkhall 1956. St Mary's, Whifflet 1956-58. Retired in bad health to a convent in Yorkshire. Died there 5 April 1958.

LAVERY, JOHN: Born Coatbridge 1930. Educated Blairs, St Peter's. Ordained Glasgow 1955. St Bernadette's, Motherwell 1955-65. St Benedict's, Easterhouse 1965-68. St Joseph's, Blantyre 1968-75. Carfin 1975-77. St Luke's, Motherwell 1977-78. No further entries.

LAWSON, GEORGE: Ordained 1946. Garthamlock 1971-73. No further entries.

LILLIS, RICHARD: see Glasgow Archdiocese.

LITTLE, MICHAEL: see Glasgow Archdiocese.

LOCKHART, VINCENT GERARD: Born Baillieston 1952. Educated Langbank; Holy Cross High School, Hamilton; St Peter's; Focolare House, Rocca di Papa, Italy; Drygrange; Notre Dame College of Education. Ordained Hamilton 1983. With Focolare Movement in Cameroon 1983-.

LOGUE, BRIAN: Born and educated Ireland. Ordained Wexford for Motherwell 1961. St Luke's, Motherwell 1961-68. Shotts 1968-73. St Bernadette's, Motherwell 1973-78. St Vincent de Paul's, East Kilbride 1978-85. Carfin 1985-. (Canning)

LOUGHRAN, PATRICK JOSEPH: Born Airdrie 1940. Educated Blairs, St Peter's. Ordained Motherwell 1963. St Mark's, Rutherglen 1963-65. Motherwell Cathedral 1965-66. Halfway 1966-70. C/o Diocesan Office 1970-71. St Benedict's, Easterhouse 1971-72. No further entries.

LUCEY, DENIS: see Glasgow Archdiocese.

LYNCH, PATRICK: Born Hamilton 1933. Educated Blairs; St Sulpice; Catholic Institute, Paris. Ordained Motherwell 1956. Carluke 1956-60. Professor, Blairs 1960-67. C/o Diocesan Office 1967-68. Professor, Blairs 1968-72. St Monica's, Coatbridge 1972-73. No further entries.

McALISTER, THOMAS ANTHONY: Born Bellshill 1943. Educated Our Lady's High School, Motherwell; St Joseph's College, Dumfries; St Peter's. Ordained Motherwell 1968. St Columbkille's, Rutherglen 1968-71. St James', Coatbridge 1971-73. St Andrew's, Airdrie 1973-75. No further entries.

McBRIDE, ALEXANDER: see Glasgow Archdiocese.

McCANN, PETER (1940): see Glasgow Archdiocese.

McCANN, THOMAS: see Glasgow Archdiocese.

McCARTHY, MICHAEL A: Born and educated Ireland. Ordained Waterford for Motherwell 1953. St Monica's, Coatbridge 1953. St Margaret's,

Airdrie 1953-59. St Mary's, Hamilton 1959-70. Uddingston 1970-73. St Leonard's, East Kilbride 1973-82. Carluke 1982-. (Canning)

McCARTHY, PATRICK A: see Glasgow Archdiocese.

McCAULEY, AUGUSTINE HUGH: Born and educated Ireland. Ordained Maynooth 1950. Lent to Motherwell diocese. Sacred Heart, Bellshill 1950-55. St Bride's, Cambuslang 1955-56. Resumed his vocation in Ireland 1956. (Canning)

McCLUSKEY, ALEXANDER: see Paisley diocese.

McCOLGAN, GERARD: Born Mossend 1928. Educated Our Lady's High School, Motherwell; Blairs; St Peter's. Ordained Motherwell 1953. St Augustine's, Coatbridge 1953-57. St Bride's, East Kilbride 1957-58. Caldercruix 1958-60. St Thomas's, Wishaw 1960-67. St Peter's, Hamilton 1967-69. Bothwell 1969-70. Moodiesburn 1970-71. St Margaret's, Airdrie 1971-72. Craigend 1972-83. St Serf's, Airdrie 1983-87. Died Bellshill 25 Jan 1987.

McCONNELL, JOHN BERNARD: Born Blantyre 1939. Educated Our Lady's High School, Motherwell; Blairs; St Peter's. Ordained Motherwell 1965. Garthamlock 1965-72. Cambuslang 1972-75. No further entries.

McCRORY, JOHN: see Glasgow Archdiocese.

McDEVITT, KEVIN: Ordained 1968. St Joseph's, Blantyre 1974-75. No further entries.

MACDONALD, EDMUND: see Glasgow Archdiocese.

MACDONALD, HUGH (1906): see Glasgow Archdiocese.

McGEEVER, KEVIN: Born Hamilton 1956. Educated Langbank; Blairs; Scots College, Rome. Ordained Cambuslang 1980. St Patrick's, Wishaw 1980. Completing studies, Rome 1980-81. St Patrick's, Wishaw 1981-82. St Bride's, East Kilbride 1982-84. St Peter's, Hamilton 1984-88. Catholic Chaplaincy, Hull 1988-.

McGHIE, THOMAS: see Glasgow Archdiocese.

McGILL, GEORGE PHILIP: Born Bargeddie 1943. Educated Blairs, St Peter's. Ordained Coatbridge 1969. St Patrick's, Wishaw 1969-73. Garthamlock 1973-75. C/o Diocesan Office 1975-77. No further entries.

McGILL, JAMES: see Glasgow Archdiocese.

McGINN, HENRY: see Glasgow Archdiocese.

McGLINCHEY, DANIEL (1932): see Glasgow Archdiocese.

McGLINCHEY, JAMES: Born and educated Ireland. Ordained Kilkenny for Motherwell 1959. St Benedict's, Easterhouse 1959-65. Larkhall 1965-66. Carluke 1966-72. St Ignatius', Wishaw 1972-83. Craigend 1983-. (Canning)

McGLYNN, DOMINIC: see Glasgow Archdiocese.

McGONAGLE, PATRICK: see Glasgow Archdiocese.

McGOVERN, PATRICK B (1947) (1): see Glasgow Archdiocese.

McGURK, ANTHONY: see Glasgow Archdiocese.

McGURK, HUGH: see Glasgow Archdiocese.

McGURK, THOMAS: see Glasgow Archdiocese.

McHALE, EAMONN: Born and educated Ireland. Ordained Carlow for Motherwell 1962. St Patrick's, Coatbridge 1962. St Mary's, Whifflet 1962-69. Left the priesthood. (Canning)

McHUGH, PATRICK: see Glasgow Archdiocese.

McINTYRE, JOHN: Born Airdrie 1937. Educated St Aloysius' College, Glasgow; Scots College, Rome. Ordained Rome 1961. St Monica's, Coatbridge 1961-63. Uddingston 1963-68. Langbank 1968-69. Professor, Blairs 1969-83. Vice-rector, Blairs 1983-85. Rector, Blairs 1985-86. St Bride's, East Kilbride 1986-89. Rector, Scots College, Rome 1989-.

McISAAC, SAMUEL: see Argyll diocese.

MACKELLAIG, ANGUS: see Glasgow Archdiocese.

McKENNA, JAMES: see Glasgow Archdiocese.

McKINLEY, CHARLES: see Glasgow Archdiocese.

MACKLE, GERARD: Born Blantyre 1923. Educated Blairs, St Peter's. Ordained Motherwell 1948. Holy Trinity and All Saints, Coatbridge 1948-53. Plains 1953-65. Harthill 1965-69. Garthamlock 1969-75. Plains 1975-86. St Luke's, Motherwell 1986-.

McLAREN, ISAAC: Born Chapelhall 1935. Educated Our Lady's High School, Motherwell; Blairs; Valladolid. Ordained Valladolid 1960. Cleland 1960-67. St Benedict's, Easterhouse 1967-68. St Augustine's, Coatbridge 1968-69. St Bride's, Cambuslang 1969-77. St Mary's, Hamilton 1977-78. St James', Coatbridge 1978-83. St Andrew's, Airdrie 1983-85. St Stephen's Coatbridge 1985-.

McLAUGHLIN, IAN: see Glasgow Archdiocese.

McLAUGHLIN, JOHN: see Glasgow Archdiocese.

McMULLAN, DERMOTT: see Glasgow Archdiocese.

McMURRAY, JOHN: Born Coatbridge 1932. Educated Our Lady's High School, Motherwell; St Peter's. Ordained Motherwell 1958. Muirhead 1958-59. St Columbkille's, Rutherglen 1959-66. St Peter's, Hamilton 1966-67. Bargeddie 1967-68. St Ignatius', Wishaw 1968-72. St Mary's, Hamilton 1972-74. On foreign missions 1974-77. Not in Catholic Directory 1977-85. Sacred Heart, Bellshill 1985-86. Newarthill 1986-.

MACNAMEE, MICHAEL FRANCIS: Born and educated Ireland. Ordained Thurles for Motherwell 1959. St Mary's, Hamilton 1959-69. St Peter's, Hamilton 1969-73. St Columbkille's, Rutherglen 1973-80. Muirhead 1980-81. St Leonard's, East Kilbride 1981-83. Moodiesburn 1983-. (Canning)

McQUADE, JOHN: Born and educated Ireland. Ordained Carlow 1950. Further studies, Rome 1950-53. Uddingston 1953-59. Motherwell Cathedral 1959-65. Carluke 1965-70. St Monica's, Coatbridge 1970-72. President, Scottish Catholic Tribunal 1972-82. Glasgow, no parish (retired?) 1982-. (Canning)

McROBERTS, DAVID: see Glasgow Archdiocese.

MAGILL, GERARD WILLIAM: Born Hamilton 1951. Educated Langbank; Blairs; Scots College, Rome. Ordained Hamilton 1975. Garthamlock 1975. Completing studies, Rome 1975-76. Professor, Drygrange 1976-85. St Anthony's, Rutherglen 1985-86. On sabbatical 1986-89. St Louis, USA 1989-.

MAGILL, THOMAS FRANCIS: Born Hamilton 1953. Educated Langbank; Blairs; Scots College, Rome. Ordained Hamilton 1976. Completing studies, Rome 1976-78. Motherwell Cathedral 1978-79. Vice-rector, Scots College, Rome 1979-83. St Bride's, East Kilbride 1983-85. Professor, Chesters College 1985-89. St Mary's, Coatbridge 1989-.

MAHER, BERNARD: see Maher, Michael (1939).

MAHER, GERALD: see Glasgow Archdiocese.

MAHER, MICHAEL (1939): Born Bellshill 1912. Educated St Francis Xavier School, Carfin; Our Lady's High School, Motherwell; Blairs; St Peter's. Joined Cistercians at Mount Melleray 1933 and was ordained for them 1939. Left the Order for health reasons and joined Motherwell diocese 1950. Newmains 1950-53. Newton 1953-57. St Augustine's, Coatbridge 1957-65. St Ignatius', Wishaw 1965-67. Cambuslang 1967-69. Harthill 1969-70. Died Bangour Hospital 2 Feb 1970.

MAHER, MICHAEL (1950): Born and educated Ireland. Ordained Maynooth 1950. Lent to Motherwell diocese. St Patrick's, Coatbridge 1950-52. Chapelhall 1952. Resumed his vocation in Ireland 1952. (Canning)

MAHER, MICHAEL (1968): Born Bellshill 1944. Educated Blairs, Valladolid. Ordained Motherwell 1968. St Mary's, Whifflet 1968-73. St Patrick's, Wishaw 1973-76. St Leonard's, East Kilbride 1976-86. St Bride's, East Kilbride 1986-87. Biggar 1987-.

MAHON, HUGH: see Glasgow Archdiocese.

MAHONEY, BERNARD: Born Coatbridge 1926. Educated Blairs, St Peter's. Ordained Motherwell 1949. Carfin 1949-53. Our Lady and St Anne's, Hamilton 1953-65. Larkhall 1965-68. St Bridget's, Baillieston 1968-75. Moodiesburn 1975-77. St Paul's, Hamilton 1977-.

MANNION, JOHN C: Born and educated Ireland. Ordained Wexford for Motherwell 1955. St Joseph's, Blantyre 1955-60. St Patrick's, Coatbridge 1960-70. All Saints, Airdrie 1970-77. St Thomas's, Wishaw 1977-81. Uddingston 1981-82. Died Uddingston 10 March 1982. (Canning)

MARTIN, JOSEPH: Born and educated Ireland. Ordained All Hallows for Motherwell 1951. St Columbkille's, Rutherglen 1951-52. St Joseph's, Blantyre 1952-62. St Columba's, Viewpark 1962-70. Our Lady and St Anne's, Hamilton 1970-79. Shotts 1979-88. St Bride's, Cambuslang 1988-. (Canning)

MARTIN, MICHAEL: Born Glasgow 1941. Educated Our Lady's High School, Motherwell; Blairs; Valladolid. Ordained Glasgow 1964. Sacred Heart, Bellshill 1964-66. Our Lady of Lourdes, East Kilbride 1966-69. C/o Diocesan Office 1969-70. No further entries.

MEEHAN, JAMES: Born and educated Ireland. Ordained Maynooth 1950. Lent to Motherwell diocese. St Columba's, Viewpark 1950-54. Resumed his vocation in Ireland 1954. (Canning)

MILLAR, DANIEL JUDE: Born Bellshill 1946. Educated Our Lady's High School, Motherwell; Blairs; St Peter's; Scots College, Rome. Ordained Bellshill 1970. St Clare's, Easterhouse 1970-72. All Saints, Airdrie 1972-74. C/o Diocesan Office 1974-77. No further entries.

MILLAR, THOMAS: Born Stepps 1954. Educated St Patrick's High School, Coatbridge; Langbank; Blairs; St Peter's; Drygrange. Ordained Cardowan 1978. Sacred Heart, Bellshill 1978-83. St Serf's, Airdrie 1983-85. St Bride's, Cambuslang 1985-.

MILLIGAN, ROBERT: Born Motherwell 1936. Educated Our Lady's High School, Motherwell; Blairs; St Peter's. Ordained Motherwell 1960. Mossend 1960-61. St Andrew's, Airdrie 1961-62. St Joseph's, Blantyre 1962-65. Shotts 1965-67. Burnbank 1967-69. No further entries.

MISSET, FRANCIS THOMAS: see Glasgow Archdiocese.

MONAGHAN, JAMES: Born and educated Ireland. Ordained All Hallows for Motherwell 1952. St Bartholomew's, Coatbridge 1952-54. St Patrick's, Wishaw 1954-65. St Bride's, East Kilbride 1965-70. St Francis', Baillieston 1970-77. Died Glasgow 13 Nov 1977. (Canning)

MORRIS, CHARLES: Born 1949. Educated St Patrick's High School, Coatbridge; St Peter's; Drygrange. Ordained Airdrie 1977. St Columbkille's, Rutherglen 1977-78. Shotts 1978-82. St Columba's, Viewpark 1982-83. St Bride's, Cambuslang 1983-87. St Joseph's, Blantyre 1987-88. Went to Dunkeld diocese: Auchterarder 1988-.

MORRIS, JAMES: Born Airdrie 1949. Educated St Patrick's High School, Coatbridge; Blairs; Scots College, Rome. Ordained Airdrie 1973. Completing studies, Rome 1973-74. St Bride's, East Kilbride 1974-78. St Ignatius', Wishaw 1978-83. St Columba's, Viewpark 1983-.

MORRIS, THOMAS COLM: Born and educated Ireland. Ordained Carlow for Motherwell 1953. St Monica's, Coatbridge 1953-65. Newarthill 1965-67. Cambuslang 1967-72. St Clare's, Easterhouse 1972-76. Newmains 1976-85. Halfway 1985-88. Retired in Ireland 1988-. (Canning)

MORTON, PAUL: Born Glasgow 1960. Educated St Bride's High School, East Kilbride; Scots College, Rome. Ordained East Kilbride 1985. St Mary's, Hamilton 1985-89. St Augustine's, Coatbridge 1989-.

MOSS, JOHN: see Glasgow Archdiocese.

MOSS, PATRICK J: Born and educated Ireland. Ordained Kilkenny 1950. Glenboig 1950-55. Muirhead 1955-58. St Columbkille's, Rutherglen 1958-67. St Gerard's, Bellshill 1967-77. St James', Coatbridge 1977-81. St Anthony's, Rutherglen 1981-87. Blackwood 1987-. (Canning)

MULDOON, LEO: Born and educated Ireland. Ordained Wexford for Motherwell 1964. Garthamlock 1964-65. Completing studies, Rome 1965-66. Sacred Heart, Bellshill 1966-67. Shotts 1967-74. St Bartholomew's, Coatbridge 1974-83. Our Lady of Lourdes, East Kilbride 1983-88. St Peter's, Hamilton 1988-. (Canning)

MULLEN, GEORGE: see Glasgow Archdiocese.

MURIE, PETER ALOYSIUS: see Glasgow Archdiocese.

MURPHY, DAMIAN MICHAEL: Born Ireland. Educated Ireland; Scots College, Rome. Ordained Dublin 1976. Newmains 1976. Completing studies, Rome 1976-77. St Columba's, Viewpark 1977-82. St Joseph's, Blantyre 1982-83. Burnbank 1983-. (Canning)

MURPHY, MICHAEL J: Born and educated Ireland. Ordained Maynooth 1950. Lent to Motherwell diocese. Longriggend 1950-51. St Joseph's, Blantyre 1951-53. Resumed his vocation in Ireland 1953. (Canning)

MURPHY, PETER JOSEPH (1943): see Glasgow Archdiocese.

MURRAY, EUGENE: see Glasgow Archdiocese.

MURRAY, JOHN VINCENT (1934): see Glasgow Archdiocese.

MURRAY, THOMAS J (1916): see Glasgow Archdiocese

NAUGHTON, JAMES JOSEPH: Born and educated Ireland. Ordained Thurles for Motherwell 1965. St Monica's, Coatbridge 1965-72. Catechetical Centre, Dundalk 1972-73. St Mary's, Coatbridge 1973-86. Newmains Pastoral Centre 1986-. (Canning)

NICOL, JAMES GERARD: Born Coatbridge 1954. Educated St Patrick's High School, Coatbridge; Blairs; Scots College, Rome. Ordained Coatbridge 1978. St Columbkille's, Rutherglen 1978. Completing studies, Rome 1978-79. Motherwell Cathedral 1979-80. Sacred Heart, Bellshill 1980-82. St Bridget's, Baillieston 1982-85. St Vincent de Paul's, East Kilbride 1985-86. St Anthony's, Rutherglen 1986-.

NIVEN, DAVID: Born Glasgow 1962. Educated Langbank, Blairs, Valladolid. Ordained Baillieston 1986. St Joseph's, Blantyre 1986-.

NOLAN, WILLIAM: Born Motherwell 1954. Educated Langbank; Blairs; Scots College, Rome. Ordained Motherwell 1977. St Bridget's, Baillieston 1977. Completing studies, Rome 1977-78. Our Lady of Lourdes, East Kilbride 1978-80. Plains 1980-83. Vice-rector, Scots College, Rome 1983-.

OATES, BERNARD MICHAEL: Born and educated Ireland. Ordained Carlow for Motherwell 1954. St Augustine's, Coatbridge 1954. St Columbkille's, Rutherglen 1954-58. St Augustine's, Coatbridge 1958-65. St Benedict's, Easterhouse 1965-73. St Peter's, Hamilton 1973-88. Died Glasgow 31 July 1988. (Canning)

O'BRIEN, HENRY: Born Annathill 1957. Educated St Patrick's High School, Coatbridge; St Peter's; Drygrange. Ordained Moodiesburn 1981. St Joseph's, Blantyre 1981-83. Further studies, Rome 1983-88. St Mark's, Rutherglen 1988-89. St Mark's, Rutherglen in addresses, but not under parishes, 1989-.

O'BRIEN, MICHAEL: see Glasgow Archdiocese.

O'CALLAGHAN, GERALD: see Glasgow Archdiocese.

O'CALLAGHAN, JOHN (1917): see Glasgow Archdiocese.

O'CONNOR, MICHAEL (1927): see Glasgow Archdiocese.

O'DOHERTY, DANIEL: see Glasgow Archdiocese.

O'DOHERTY, KEVIN: Born and educated Ireland. Ordained Wexford for Motherwell 1963. St Augustine's, Coatbridge 1963-64. St Mary's, Coatbridge 1964-68. C/o Diocesan Office 1968-77. Ireland 1977-84. St Brendan's, Motherwell 1984-87. C/o Diocesan Centre 1987-. (Canning)

O'DONNELL, EDWARD: Born Glasgow 1963. Educated Trinity High School, Cambuslang; Langbank; Blairs; Valladolid. Ordained Cambuslang 1987. Sacred Heart, Bellshill 1987. St Bride's, East Kilbride 1987-.

O'DONNELL, JOHN (1944): see Glasgow Archdiocese.

O'DONOGHUE, PATRICK: Born and educated Ireland. Ordained Carlow for Motherwell 1950. Bargeddie 1950-54. Motherwell Cathedral 1954-55. Shotts 1955-65. New Stevenston 1965-69. Glenboig 1969-82. Cleland 1982-. (Canning)

O'FARRELL, KIERAN: Born and educated Ireland. Ordained Kilkenny for Motherwell 1950. Carfin 1950-55. Sacred Heart, Bellshill 1955-59. Motherwell Cathedral 1959-66. St Leonard's, East Kilbride 1966-73. St Patrick's, Wishaw 1973-86. Strathaven 1986-. (Canning)

O'GRADY, MARTIN: Born and educated Ireland. Ordained Carlow for Motherwell 1952. St Augustine's, Coatbridge 1952-53. Carfin 1953-56. Cambuslang 1956-64. On mission in Peru 1964-. (Canning)

O'HARA, JAMES: Born Carluke 1937. Educated Campion House, Osterley; St Peter's. Ordained Motherwell 1968. St Benedict's, Easterhouse 1968-71. St Columbkille's, Rutherglen 1971-74. Army chaplain 1974-.

O'HARE, PATRICK: Born and educated Ireland. Ordained Carlow for Motherwell 1953. Muirhead 1953-58. Cambuslang 1958-67. St Clare's, Easterhouse 1967-71. St Paul's, Hamilton 1971-77. St Gerard's, Bellshill 1977-84. Harthill 1984-. (Canning)

O'HARE, THOMAS: Born Motherwell 1935. Educated Our Lady's High School, Motherwell; Blairs; St Peter's. Ordained Motherwell 1959. St Margaret's, Airdrie 1959-60. Glenboig 1960-69. New Stevenston 1969-72. St Mary's, Hamilton 1972-84. St Benedict's, Easterhouse 1984-86. St Serf's, Airdrie 1986-.

O'KEEFFE, MARTIN: Born Ireland. Educated Ireland, St Sulpice. Ordained Waterford for Motherwell 1954. St Columba's, Viewpark 1954-65. Mossend 1965-67. Garthamlock 1967-70. Halfway 1970-74. St Vincent de Paul's, East Kilbride 1974-85. St Margaret's, Airdrie 1985-. (Canning)

O'LEARY, CORNELIUS FRANCIS: Born and educated Ireland. Ordained Carlow for Motherwell 1962. St James', Coatbridge 1962-71. Burnbank 1971-76. Uddingston 1976-80. St Monica's, Coatbridge 1980-86. St Benedict's, Easterhouse 1986-88. Shotts 1988-. (Canning)

O'LEARY, MICHAEL CHRISTOPHER: Born and educated Ireland. Ordained All Hallows for Motherwell 1956. St Joseph's, Blantyre 1956-62. St Bridget's, Baillieston 1962-68. Chapelhall 1968-69. Uddingston 1969-70. No further entries. (Canning)

O'MAHONY, HUMPHREY: Born and educated Ireland. Ordained Waterford for Motherwell 1961. St Columbkille's, Rutherglen 1961-69. Newmains 1969-73. Shotts 1973-75. St Peter's, Hamilton 1975-76. Sacred Heart, Bellshill 1976-80. Uddingston 1980-82. Chapelhall in addresses, but not under parishes, 1982-83. St Ignatius', Wishaw 1983-85. St Mark's, Rutherglen 1985-. (Canning)

O'NEILL, MICHAEL: Born Bellshill 1941. Educated Blairs; Scots College, Rome. Ordained Rome 1965. St Joseph's, Blantyre 1965-66. St Mary's, Coatbridge 1966-68. C/o Diocesan Office 1968-70. No further entries.

O'NEILL, THOMAS J: see Glasgow Archdiocese.

O'NEILL, VINCENT: Born Airdrie 1939. Educated Blairs; Scots College, Rome. Ordained Rome 1963. St Ninian's, Hamilton 1964-65. New Stevenston 1965-66. C/o Diocesan Office 1966-67. Professor, Blairs 1967-68. St Clare's, Easterhouse 1968-73. Our Lady and St Anne's, Hamilton 1973-74. No further entries.

O'REGAN, BARTHOLOMEW: Born and educated Ireland. Ordained Carlow for Motherwell 1956. New Stevenston 1956-65. Our Lady and St Anne's, Hamilton 1965-70. In Ireland 1970-75. Shotts 1975-76. St Peter's, Hamilton 1976-80. Harthill 1980-84. St Gabriel's, Viewpark 1984-. (Canning)

O'REGAN, DAVID WILLIAM: Born and educated Ireland. Ordained 1961. Lent to Motherwell diocese. St James', Coatbridge 1961-62. Resumed his vocation in Ireland 1962. (Canning)

O'RIORDAN, EDWARD: Born and educated Ireland. Ordained Maynooth 1949. Lent to Motherwell diocese. Larkhall 1949-51. Resumed his vocation in Ireland 1951. (Canning)

O'RIORDAN, JEREMIAH: Born and educated Ireland. Ordained Kilkenny for Motherwell 1960. Garthamlock 1960-65. St Clare's, Easterhouse 1965-66. St Patrick's, Coatbridge 1966-72. St Margaret's, Airdrie 1972-77. Carfin 1977-82. St Ninian's, Hamilton 1982-83. St Aidan's, Wishaw 1983-85. St Thomas's, Wishaw 1985-87. Sick leave 1987-. (Canning)

O'SHEA, SEAN: Born and educated Ireland. Ordained Kilkenny for Motherwell 1949. Carluke 1949-52. St Patrick's, Wishaw 1952-58. RAF chaplain 1958-75. Ireland 1976-. (Canning)

O'SULLIVAN, PATRICK: Born and educated Ireland. Ordained All Hallows for Motherwell 1955. St Peter's, Hamilton 1955-65. All Saints, Airdrie 1965-70. St Mary's, Whifflet 1970-77. St John Ogilvie's, Blantyre 1977-83. St Andrew's, Airdrie 1983-. (Canning)

O'SULLIVAN, TIMOTHY: Born and educated Ireland. Ordained Carlow 1952. Lent to Motherwell diocese. Burnbank 1952-54. St Columba's, Viewpark 1954-57. Resumed his vocation in Ireland 1957. (Canning)

O'SULLIVAN, WILLIAM: Born and educated Ireland. Ordained Carlow for Motherwell 1957. St Thomas's, Wishaw 1957-60. Burnbank 1960-67. Cleland 1967-70. St Bride's, East Kilbride 1970-74. On foreign missions 1974-75. St Joseph's, Blantyre 1975-82. St Andrew's, Airdrie 1982-83. Muirhead 1983-. (Canning)

PLUNKETT, PATRICK: see Glasgow Archdiocese.

POWER, DENIS AUGUSTINE: Born Abbington, Co Limerick 1926. Educated St Patrick's College, Thurles. Ordained Thurles for Motherwell 1951. St Augustine's, Coatbridge 1951-54. Motherwell Cathedral 1954-59. Halfway 1959-61. Burnbank 1961-65. St Monica's, Coatbridge 1965-68. St Serf's, Airdrie 1968-83. Sick leave 1983-84. Newarthill 1984-.

PRIESTLEY, JOHN: Born Calderbank 1931. Educated Blairs; Scots College, Rome. Ordained Rome 1955. St Patrick's, Wishaw 1955-59. St Mary's, Coatbridge 1959-66. St Aidan's, Wishaw 1966-68. St Patrick's, Wishaw 1968-70. No further entries.

QUIN, JAMES: Born Motherwell 1923. Educated Blairs; St Peter's; Scots College, Rome. Ordained Rome 1947. Continuing studies, Rome 1947-50. St Mary's, Coatbridge 1950-51. Professor, St Peter's College 1951-72. St Ninian's, Hamilton 1972-83. Retired 1983-.

QUINN, DOMINIC: Born Glasgow 1963. Educated St Bride's High School, East Kilbride; Blairs; Scots College, Rome. Ordained East Kilbride 1988. St Monica's, Coatbridge 1988-.

REEN, ANDREW: Born and educated Ireland. Ordained Wexford for Motherwell 1953. Longriggend 1953-54. Caldercruix 1954-57. St Ignatius', Wishaw 1957-68. Bargeddie 1968-69. St Mary's, Hamilton 1969-72. Plains 1972-75. Garthamlock 1975-84. Bothwell 1984-. (Canning)

RODGERS, RICHARD JOHN: Born Coatbridge 1936. Educated Our Lady's High School, Motherwell; St Peter's. Ordained Motherwell 1960. Carluke 1960-66. St Clare's, Easterhouse 1966-67. Motherwell Cathedral 1967-70. St Clare's, Easterhouse 1970-75. St Leonard's, East Kilbride 1975-81. St Serf's, Airdrie 1981-83. St Augustine's, Coatbridge 1983-84. Carluke 1984-85. St Ignatius', Wishaw 1985-86. Plains 1986-.

ROGER, JOHN: see Glasgow Archdiocese.

ROGERS, GERARD: see Glasgow Archdiocese.

ROGERS, HERBERT G: see Glasgow Archdiocese.

ROGERS, JAMES KEVIN: Born and educated Ireland. Ordained Carlow for Motherwell 1953. Burnbank 1953-54. Mossend 1954-56. St Columbkille's, Rutherglen 1956-59. St Margaret's, Airdrie 1959-67. Muirhead 1967-72. Harthill 1972-80. St Bride's, East Kilbride 1980-86. Died East Kilbride 25 May 1986. (Canning)

ROONEY, DANIEL: Born Bellshill 1948. Educated Breakspeare College, Herts; St Peter's. Ordained Cadzow 1972. St Benedict's, Easterhouse 1972-75. Motherwell Cathedral 1975-78. St Columbkille's, Rutherglen 1978-88. St Bernadette's, Motherwell 1988-.

ROONEY, GERARD: Born Bridgeton, Glasgow 1946. Educated Holy Cross High School, Hamilton; Blairs; St Peter's. Ordained East Kilbride 1971.

St Luke's, Motherwell 1971. St Anne's, Cadzow 1971-73. C/o Diocesan Office 1973-75. No further entries.

ROONEY, JOHN A: see Glasgow Archdiocese.

RYAN, MICHAEL: Born and educated Ireland. Ordained Thurles for Motherwell 1959. Our Lady of Lourdes, East Kilbride 1959-66. Our Lady and St Anne's, Hamilton 1966-69. C/o Diocesan Office 1969-70. St Bernadette's, Motherwell 1970-76. Newarthill 1976-84. Garthamlock 1984-. (Canning)

SCOTT, WALTER: Born Motherwell 1930. Educated Our Lady's High School, Motherwell; Scots College, Rome. Ordained Rome 1960. St Andrew's, Airdrie 1960-61. Sacred Heart, Bellshill 1961-65. St Mark's, Rutherglen 1965-88. Retired 1988-.

SEXTON, PETER: see Glasgow Archdiocese.

SHEAHAN, ANDREW CHRISTOPHER: Born and educated Ireland. Ordained Carlow for Motherwell 1961. Glenboig 1961-63. St Serf's, Airdrie 1963-68. Corpus Christi College, London 1968-69. St Monica's, Coatbridge 1969-70. St Augustine's, Coatbridge 1970-74. C/o Diocesan Office 1974-77. No further entries. (Canning)

SHEEHAN, THOMAS GERARD: Born and educated Ireland. Ordained Kilkenny for Motherwell 1953. St Andrew's, Airdrie 1953-67. St Patrick's, Wishaw 1967-72. Blackwood 1972-75. Died Ireland 16 Jan 1975. (Canning)

SHERIDAN, HUGH: Born and educated Ireland. Ordained Maynooth 1955. Served in Ireland 1955-73. Came to Motherwell diocese 1973. Halfway 1973-74. St Bartholomew's, Coatbridge 1974-78. St Benedict's, Easterhouse 1978-86. Sacred Heart, Bellshill 1986-87. Retired 1987-. (Canning)

SHERIDAN, JOHN A (1931): see Glasgow Archdiocese.

SHIELS, JAMES: Born and educated Ireland. Ordained Derry for Motherwell 1973. St Columba's, Viewpark 1973-75. St Benedict's, Easterhouse 1975-78. Returned to Ireland 1978. (Canning)

SMALL, JAMES: Born Shotts 1935. Educated Our Lady's High School, Motherwell; Blairs; Valladolid. Ordained Valladolid 1960. St Mary's, Whifflet 1960-63. Moodiesburn 1963-70. Cleland 1970-74. St Mary's, Hamilton 1974-77. Santiago, Chile 1977-83. St Peter's, Hamilton 1983-84. Ireland 1984-.

SMITH, BRENDAN: Born Ireland. Educated Ireland, St Peter's. Ordained Motherwell 1956. All Saints, Coatdyke 1956. Lent to St A & E: St Cuthbert's, Edinburgh 1956-58. St Andrew's, Airdrie 1958-59. Muirhead 1959-67. St Thomas's, Wishaw 1967-72. St Patrick's, Coatbridge 1972-78. St Luke's, Motherwell 1978-86. Sick leave 1986-. (Canning)

SMITH, WILLIAM J: see Glasgow Archdiocese.

SPROUL, WILLIAM PATRICK: Born and educated Ireland. Ordained Kilkenny for Motherwell 1958. Mossend 1958-68. Burnbank 1968-70. Carfin 1970-75. St Bridget's, Baillieston 1975-82. Biggar 1982-83. St Ninian's, Hamilton 1983-. (Canning)

STEWART, PAUL: Born Glasgow 1951. Educated Holyrood School, Glasgow; St Peter's. Ordained East Kilbride 1974. Shotts 1974-80. St Benedict's, Easterhouse 1980-87. Sacred Heart, Bellshill 1987-.

SULLIVAN, MICHAEL J: Born and educated Ireland. Ordained Carlow for Motherwell 1955. Garthamlock 1955-67. St Columbkille's, Rutherglen 1967-73. Motherwell Cathedral 1973-77. Died Motherwell 12 May 1977. (Canning)

SWEENEY, EAMONN JUDE: Born and educated Ireland. Ordained Wexford for Motherwell 1969. St Bridget's, Baillieston 1969-75. St Columba's, Viewpark 1975-76. St Mark's, Rutherglen 1976-82. St Ninian's, Hamilton 1982-85. St Thomas's, Wishaw 1985-. (Canning)

SWEENEY, MICHAEL J: see Glasgow Archdiocese.

TAYLOR, CHRISTOPHER GABRIEL: Born Glasgow 1953. Educated Langbank, Blairs, Valladolid. Ordained East Kilbride 1977. St Bride's, East Kilbride 1977. St Augustine's, Coatbridge 1977-85. Uddingston 1985-.

TAYLOR, JOHN: Born Holytown 1931. Educated St Mary's College, Aberystwyth; St Peter's. Ordained Newarthill 1972. St Edward's, Airdrie 1972-73. St James', Coatbridge 1973-78. Plains 1978-80. Our Lady of Lourdes, East Kilbride 1980-82. Cambuslang 1982-85. St Ninian's, Hamilton 1985-87. St Patrick's, Wishaw 1987-.

TAYLOR, MAURICE: Born Hamilton 1926. Educated Blairs 1942-44; military service 1944-47; Scots College, Rome 1947-51. Ordained Rome 1950. St Bartholomew's, Coatbridge 1951-52. Further studies, Rome 1952-54. St Bernadette's, Motherwell 1954-55. Professor, St Peter's College 1955-65. Rector, Valladolid 1965-74. Our Lady of Lourdes, East Kilbride 1974-81. Consecrated Bishop of Galloway 1981.

TAYLOR, THOMAS N (1897): see Glasgow Archdiocese.

THOMSON, FRANCIS: see Archdiocese of St Andrew's and Edinburgh.

THOMSON, JAMES: Born Bellshill 1960. Educated Langbank, Blairs, Drygrange, Glengowan House (social work), St Peter's, Chesters. Ordained Baillieston 1988. St Columbkille's, Rutherglen 1988-.

TOWEY, DOMINIC MICHAEL: Born and educated Ireland. Ordained Wexford for Motherwell 1970. St Benedict's, Easterhouse 1970-71. St Mary's, Hamilton 1971-72. St Thomas's, Wishaw 1972-78. Burnbank 1978-83. St Joseph's, Blantyre 1983-. (Canning)

TRENCH, THOMAS COLUMBANUS: Born and educated Ireland. Ordained Wexford for Motherwell 1967. St Ignatius', Wishaw 1967-77. St Margaret's, Airdrie 1977-78. St Patrick's, Coatbridge 1978-89. 1989-C/o Diocesan Office. (Canning)

TUNN, ANDREW: Born Saltcoats 1902. Educated St Mungo's Academy. Worked for a railway company. Later joined the Society for African Missions and studied in Holland, Belgium and France. Ordained 1930. Served in Ghana 1930-44. RAF chaplain 1944-48. Left the Society and joined Motherwell diocese. St Margaret's, Airdrie 1951. St Patrick's, Wishaw 1951-56. Mossend 1956-58. All Saints, Airdrie 1958-60. St Bartholomew's, Coatbridge 1960-66. St Patrick's, Coatbridge 1966-75. Died Coatbridge 7 Aug 1975.

WALSH, JAMES F (1924): see Glasgow Archdiocese.

WALSH, MICHAEL: Born and educated Ireland. Ordained Carlow for Motherwell 1959. St Bernadette's, Motherwell 1959-60. Chapelhall 1960-63. Halfway 1963-66. All Saints, Airdrie 1966-72. Muirhead 1972-80. St Andrew's, Airdrie 1980-83. Chapelhall 1983-. (Canning)

WALSH, PATRICK: Born and educated Ireland. Ordained Wexford for Motherwell 1949. St Mary's, Hamilton 1949-52. St Bride's, East Kilbride 1952-57. Chaplain, St Charles' Institute, Carstairs 1957-63. St Monica's, Coatbridge 1963-65. Cardowan 1965-72. Holy Trinity and All Saints, Coatdyke 1972-. (Canning)

WARD, JAMES CUTHBERT (1928): see Glasgow Archdiocese.

WARD, JOHN L: Born and educated Ireland. Ordained Wexford for Motherwell 1957. St Mary's, Hamilton 1957-60. St Patrick's, Wishaw 1960-61. Calderbank 1961-63. Caldercruix 1963-67. St Bartholomew's, Coatbridge 1967-68. Newmains 1968-69. St Augustine's, Coatbridge 1969-70. St Serf's, Airdrie 1970-73. London 1973-78. St Thomas's, Wishaw 1978-80. Sick leave 1980-. (Canning)

WHITE, DANIEL B: see Glasgow Archdiocese.

WHITE, WILLIAM (1936): see Glasgow Archdiocese.

WHITE, WILLIAM (1953): Born and educated Ireland. Ordained Waterford for Motherwell 1953. Sacred Heart, Bellshill 1953-65. St Augustine's, Coatbridge 1965-72. St Edward's, Airdrie 1972-81. St James', Coatbridge 1981-88. Glenboig 1988-. (Canning)

WINNING, THOMAS JOSEPH: Born Wishaw 1925. Educated Blairs; St Peter's; Scots College, Rome. Ordained Rome 1948. Chapelhall 1949-50. Continuing studies, Rome 1950-53. St Mary's, Hamilton 1953-57. Motherwell Cathedral 1957-58. Chaplain, Franciscan Convent, Bothwell 1958-61. Spiritual Director, Scots College, Rome 1961-66. St Luke's, Motherwell 1966-70. President, Scottish Catholic Marriage Tribunal 1970-71. Consecrated Bishop Auxiliary of Glasgow Archdiocese 1971. Our Holy Redeemer, Clydebank 1972-74. Consecrated Archbishop of Glasgow 1974.

WOODS, THOMAS ALPHONSUS (or Alphonsus T): see Glasgow Archdiocese.

Parishes

In 1948 Glasgow Archdiocese was split into three, with two new dioceses, Motherwell and Paisley, being formed. The following lists of parishes are mainly a continuation of lists found under Glasgow Archdiocese.

BISHOPS: 1948-54 Edward Douglas (Glasgow). 1955-64 James Scanlan (Westminster, Dunkeld). 1965-82 Francis Thomson (St A & E). 1983- Joseph Devine (Glasgow).

AIRDRIE - ALL SAINTS': (Airdrie, Holy Trinity and All Saints 1976; Coatbridge, Holy Trinity and All Saints 1977).
Heads: 1941-51 Alexander McBride. 1951-52 John McCrory. 1952-57 Thomas J Murray. 1957-61 Hugh Cahill. 1961-65 Patrick Brennan. 1965-72 Hugh McGurk. 1972- Patrick Walsh.
Assistants: 1947-53 James Hallinan. 1948-53 Gerard Mackle. 1953-56 John Gillen. 1953-58 Denis Keane. 1956 Brendan Smith. 1956-60 Dermot McMullan. 1958-60 Andrew Tunn. 1960-64 Lawrence Connelly. 1960-66 Joseph Farnin. 1965-70 Patrick O'Sullivan. 1966-72 Michael Walsh. 1970-77 John Mannion. 1972-74 Daniel Millar.

AIRDRIE - ST ANDREW'S
Heads: 1950-58 Patrick McHugh. 1958-65 George Mullen. 1965-82 George Fryer. 1982-83 William O'Sullivan. 1983- Patrick O'Sullivan.

Assistants: 1953-67 Thomas Sheehan. 1958-59 Brendan Smith. 1960-61 Walter Scott. 1961-62 Robert Milligan. 1962-69 Patrick Brosnan. 1967-73 John Doherty. 1973-75 Thomas McAlister. 1975-80 Damien Gilhooley. 1980-83 Michael Walsh. 1983-85 Isaac McLaren. 1985-87 James Davidson. 1987-89 Dominic Douglas. 1989- Bartholomew Cannon.

AIRDRIE – ST EDWARD'S
Heads: 1960-72 Thomas Barry. 1972-81 William White (1953). 1981- Lawrence Kenny.
Assistants: 1964-70 Vivian Hayes. 1970-72 John Cushley. 1972-73 John Taylor. 1973-81 Edward Doherty.

AIRDRIE – ST MARGARET'S
Heads: 1937-49 James McKenna. 1949-67 Thomas McCann. 1967-77 John Sheridan. 1977-85 William Duddy. 1985- Martin O'Keeffe.
Assistants: 1933-49 Daniel McGlinchey. 1943-53 Peter J Murphy. 1949-50 John Sheridan. 1950-53 John Cosgrove. 1950-60 Alphonsus T Woods. 1951 Andrew Tunn. 1951-54 Charles McKinley. 1953-58 James J Keegan. 1953-59 Michael McCarthy. 1958-61 Thomas Gibbons. 1959-60 Thomas O'Hare. 1959-67 James K Rogers. 1960-71 Timothy Brosnan. 1962-64 Thomas Connelly. 1971-72 Gerard McColgan. 1972-77 Jeremiah O'Riordan. 1977-78 Thomas Trench. 1978-85 Francis Halavage.

AIRDRIE – ST SERF'S
Heads: 1961-72 Richard Lillis. 1972-83 Denis Power. 1983-86 Gerald B McColgan. 1986- Thomas O'Hare.
Assistants: 1963-68 Andrew Sheahan. 1968-72 Denis Power. 1970-73 John Ward. 1972-81 Aidan D'Arcy. 1978-79 Henry Docherty. 1981-83 Richard Rodgers. 1983-85 Thomas Millar. 1985-88 Francis Halavage. 1988- Leo Cushley.

BAILLIESTON – ST BRIDGET'S
Heads: 1942-50 John Rooney. 1950-51 vacant. 1951-55 Alexander McBride. 1955-61 John Sheridan. 1961-62 William White (1936). 1962-68 John McCrory. 1968-75 Bernard Mahoney. 1975- Daniel Hennessy.
Assistants: 1943-51 George Fryer. 1943-58 John Moss. 1951-52 Hugh Cahill. 1952-55 Michael Corry. 1955-61 Francis Kelly. 1958-65 Herbert Flack. 1961-62 Denis Garrity. 1962-68 Michael O'Leary. 1965-66 John F Givens. 1966-69 Lawrence Kenny. 1968-70 Brian Donnelly. 1969-75 Eamonn Sweeney. 1975-82 William Sproul. 1977 William Nolan. 1982-85 James Nicol. 1985-86 Hugh Kelly. 1986- Thomas Brady. 1987-88 John B Farrell.

BAILLIESTON – ST FRANCIS OF ASSISI: 1970-77 James Monaghan. 1977- Vivian Hayes.

BAILLIESTON – CONVENT OF MERCY: CHAPLAINS
1949-54 William Bradley. 1955-68 John Cosgrove. 1969-74 John F Breslin.

BARGEDDIE
Heads: 1947-53 Charles Craigen. 1953-58 Patrick Heaney. 1958-61 William Duddy. 1961-65 Philip Boyce. 1965-69 Thomas McGurk. 1969-84 James Dooley. 1984- John J Delaney.
Assistants: 1949-50 Richard Lillis. 1950-54 Patrick O'Donoghue. 1954-57 Denis Hoban. 1960 William Smith. 1967-68 John McMurray. 1968-69 Andrew Reen.

BELLSHILL – SACRED HEART
Heads: 1949-58 James Butler. 1958-67 Patrick Heaney. 1967-78 Philip Flanagan. 1978-83 Thomas McGurk. 1983- John B Healy.
Assistants: 1949-58 Niall Hayes. 1950-55 Augustine McCauley. 1953 William Boyle. 1953-65 William White (1953). 1955-59 Kieran O'Farrell. 1958-71 James Ashe. 1959-61 Hugh Beattie. 1961-65 Walter Scott. 1964-66 Michael Martin. 1965-73 John Delaney. 1966-67 Leo Muldoon. 1971-76 Timothy Brosnan. 1973-78 Hugh Kelly. 1976-80 Humphrey O'Mahoney. 1978-83 Thomas Millar. 1980-82 James Nicol. 1982-87 Nicholas Dempsey. 1983-85 Patrick Hynes. 1985-86 John V McMurray. 1986-87 Hugh Sheridan. 1987 Edward O'Donnell. 1987-88 James Davidson. 1987- Paul Stewart. 1988- John B Farrell.

BELLSHILL – ST GERARD'S: 1967-77 Patrick Moss. 1977-84 Patrick J O'Hare. 1984- Timothy Brosnan.

BIGGAR: 1947-49 Thomas Egan. 1949-50 Patrick Heaney. 1950-58 served by Xaverian Fathers. 1958-65 John J Cusick. 1965-66 vacant. 1966-71 Gerald O'Callaghan. 1971-72 vacant. 1972-75 Francis Murray CSSp. 1975-76 Daniel O'Doherty. 1976-82 Patrick Kilcoyne. 1982-83 William Sproul. 1983-87 Bishop Francis Thomson. 1987- Michael Maher (1968).

BLACKWOOD
Heads: 1945-50 Michael Sweeney. 1950-53 Patrick Heaney. 1953-54 William Smith. 1954-55 Michael Little. 1955-59 Patrick Hoey. 1959-68 Michael Houlihan. 1968-72 John Cosgrove. 1972-75 Thomas Sheehan. 1975-77 Francis Murray CSSp. 1977-87 Thomas Fehily. 1987- Patrick Moss.
Assistant: 1959 Peter Murphy.

BLANTYRE – ST JOHN OGILVIE'S
Heads: 1977-83 Patrick O'Sullivan. 1983- Peter McCann.
Assistant: 1983- Dominic Towey.

BLANTYRE – ST JOSEPH'S
Heads: 1945-58 John Ashe. 1958-69 John Battel. 1969-82 Anthony McGurk. 1982-86 John F Gallacher. 1986- Aidan D'Arcy.

Assistants: 1930-51 Bernard Keenan. 1945-55 Thomas Barry. 1946-50 Alphonsus T Woods. 1946-51 Henry Corr. 1950-52 John Sheridan. 1951-53 Michael Murphy. 1952-62 Joseph Martin. 1953-56 Christopher Condon. 1953-61 John Breslin. 1955-60 John Mannion. 1956-62 Michael O'Leary. 1961-68 John Brady. 1962-64 Vivian Hayes. 1962-65 Robert Milligan. 1964-65 Thomas McGurk. 1965-66 Michael O'Neill. 1965-68 James Comerford. 1966-72 Francis Darroch. 1968-74 Peter Gorman. 1968-75 John Lavery. 1972-82 Nicholas Dempsey. 1974-75 Kevin McDevitt. 1975-82 William O'Sullivan. 1981-83 Henry O'Brien. 1982-83 Damian Murphy. 1983-85 Robert Kane. 1985-86 Patrick Hynes. 1986- David Niven. 1987-88 Charles Morris. 1988- James Duddy.

BOTHWELL
Heads: 1947-49 Thomas Brooks. 1949-55 Thomas Egan. 1955-58 George Mullen. 1958-61 Daniel O'Doherty. 1961-68 John Boyle (1946). 1968-84 Michael Houlihan. 1984- Andrew Reen.
Assistants: 1965-69 John Breslin. 1969-70 Gerard McColgan. 1970-82 Henry J Allison. 1982-88 Gerard Chromy.

BOTHWELL – FRANCISCAN CONVENT: CHAPLAINS
1945-49 Gerard Rogers. 1950-58 John J Cusick. 1958-61 Thomas Winning. 1961-65 John F Breslin.

BURNBANK
Heads: 1946-65 James Walsh. 1965-82 Bernard Keenan. 1982- Denis Keane.
Assistants: 1936-50 Daniel White. 1940-48 Anthony McGurk. 1948-54 Angus McKellaig. 1950-53 Thomas Hickey. 1952-54 Timothy O'Sullivan. 1953-54 James Rogers. 1954-55 Patrick Hoey. 1954-57 David Cullen. 1955-59 Hugh Beattie. 1957-61 John Gallacher. 1959-60 John Delaney. 1960-67 William O'Sullivan. 1961-65 Denis Power. 1964-68 Neal Carlin. 1967-69 Robert Milligan. 1968-70 William Sproul. 1969-71 John Buckley SPS. 1971-76 Cornelius O'Leary. 1976-77 Michael Cunnane. 1977-78 Anthony Coyle. 1978-83 Dominic Towey. 1983- Damian Murphy.

CADZOW: see Hamilton, Our Lady and St Anne's

CALDERBANK
Heads: 1948-59 Michael Dooley. 1959-62 Peter Murphy. 1962-69 Patrick McGovern. 1969-82 James McGill. 1982-89 Anthony McGurk. 1989- Thomas Barry.
Assistants: 1955-59 Michael Houlihan. 1961-63 John Ward.

CALDERCRUIX
Heads: 1954-59 Bernard Keenan. 1959-61 Daniel White. 1961-71 Daniel O'Doherty. 1971- Christopher Condon.

Assistants: 1954-57 Andrew Reen. 1957-58 James Ashe. 1958-60 Gerard McColgan. 1960-63 John Delaney. 1963-67 John Ward.

CAMBUSLANG – ST BRIDE'S
Heads: 1929-50 Hugh McDonald. 1950-57 John Rooney. 1957-74 Thomas Murray. 1974- John Breslin.
Assistants: 1930-49 Robert Douglas. 1947-54 William White (1936). 1950-55 Richard Lillis. 1954-58 Thomas Gibbons. 1955-56 Augustine McCauley. 1956-64 Martin O'Grady. 1958-67 Patrick O'Hare. 1964-67 Angus McKellaig. 1967-69 Michael B Maher (1939). 1967-72 Thomas Morris. 1969-77 Isaac McLaren. 1972-75 John B McConnell. 1975-83 Michael Gallagher SPS. 1977-82 James Davidson. 1982-85 John Taylor. 1983-87 Charles Morris. 1985- Thomas Millar.

CAMBUSLANG – ST CADOC'S: see Halfway

CARDOWAN: see Stepps

CARFIN
Heads: 1915-63 Thomas Taylor. 1963-65 vacant. 1965-85 George Mullen. 1985- Brian Logue.
Assistants: 1945-53 William Smith. 1946-49 John W Boyle (1946). 1949-53 Bernard Mahoney. 1950-55 Kieran O'Farrell. 1953-56 Martin O'Grady. 1953-59 Peter Murphy. 1955-65 James Comerford (administrator from 1960). 1956-58 Noel Carey. 1959-62 Patrick Brosnan. 1962-68 Joseph Clements. 1963-65 John Delaney. 1965-70 Patrick Kilcoyne. 1968-73 Noel Carey. 1970-75 William Sproul. 1975-77 John T Lavery. 1977-82 Jeremiah O'Riordan. 1982-83 James Davidson. 1983-85 Robert Curley. 1986 Colin T Hughes.

CARLUKE
Heads: 1947-49 John Roger. 1949-53 John Bredin. 1953-54 Peter Murie. 1954-55 Anthony Kilcoyne. 1955-59 Edward Doherty. 1959-65 George Fryer. 1965-70 John McQuade. 1970-82 John F Gallacher. 1982- Michael A McCarthy.
Assistants: 1949-52 Sean O'Shea. 1952-57 John Gallacher. 1956-60 Patrick Lynch. 1960-66 Richard J Rodgers. 1966-72 James McGlinchey. 1984 Dominic Douglas. 1984-85 Richard J Rodgers.

CARSTAIRS – ST CHARLES' INSTITUTE/HOSPITAL: CHAPLAINS
Heads: 1938-57 Samuel McIsaac (Argyll). 1957-63 Patrick Walsh. 1963-72 David McRoberts. 1972-80 John Mackay (Glasgow). 1980-83 Hugh Kearns (Glasgow).
Assistant: 1948-49 Richard Lillis.

CHAPELHALL – ST ALOYSIUS'
Heads: 1941-52 Peter Murie. 1952-62 John McCrory. 1962-69 George

Boyd. 1969-78 John Battel. 1978-83 Philip Flanagan. 1983- Michael
Walsh.

Assistants: 1949-50 Thomas Winning. 1951-52 John Gallacher. 1952
Michael Maher (1950). 1952-58 Herbert Flack. 1958 Henry J Allison.
1958-59 William Smith. 1960-63 Michael Walsh. 1968-69 Michael
O'Leary. 1969-74 Francis Kelly. 1974-76 Peter Gorman. 1976-81
Timothy Brosnan.

CLELAND

Heads: 1944-69 Patrick Clarke. 1969-74 James Hallinan. 1974-82 Francis
Kelly. 1982- Patrick O'Donoghue.

Assistants: 1946-49 Dermot McMullan. 1949-59 James McGill. 1959-60
William Smith. 1960-67 Isaac McLaren. 1967-70 William O'Sullivan.
1970-74 James Small. 1974-75 John Doherty.

COATBRIDGE – HOLY TRINITY AND ALL SAINTS: see Airdrie, All Saints

COATBRIDGE – ST AUGUSTINE'S (Langloan)

Heads: 1940-63 Edmund MacDonald. 1963-64 vacant. 1964-71 Denis
Lucey. 1971-72 vacant. 1972-85 John Moss. 1985- James Foley.

Assistants: 1940 -52 Patrick Brennan. 1947-50 Edward Doherty. 1947-58
Hugh Mahon. 1951-54 Denis Power. 1952-53 Martin O'Grady. 1953-57
Gerard McColgan. 1954 Bernard Oates. 1957-58 James Kilpatrick.
1957-65 Michael Maher (1939). 1958-65 Bernard Oates. 1963-64 Kevin
O'Doherty. 1965-68 Brian Donnelly. 1965-72 William White (1953).
1968-69 Henry Docherty. 1969-70 John Ward. 1970-74 Andrew
Sheahan. 1972-77 Robert Curley. 1977-85 Christopher Taylor. 1983-84
Richard J Rodgers. 1985-89 Gerard Devlin. 1989- Paul Morton.

COATBRIDGE – ST BARTHOLOMEW'S

Heads: 1950-65 Thomas McGhie. 1965-69 Thomas Brooks. 1969-77
Patrick McGovern. 1977-89 Thomas Barry. 1989- Hugh Kelly.

Assistants: 1951-52 Maurice Taylor. 1952-54 James Monaghan. 1954-58
Angus McKellaig. 1954-60 Lawrence Connelly. 1958-67 Henry Allison.
1960-66 Andrew Tunn. 1964-70 William Dunnachie. 1967-68 Henry
Docherty. 1967-68 John Ward. 1968-69 Isaac McLaren. 1969-73 Patrick
Brosnan. 1970-74 Vivian Hayes. 1974-78 Hugh Sheridan. 1974-83 Leo
Muldoon. 1978-86 Michael Briody. 1983-88 Damian Gilhooley. 1986-89
Hugh Kelly. 1989- Dominic Douglas.

COATBRIDGE – ST BERNARD'S: 1973-81 Patrick Brosnan. 1981-86 Aidan
D'Arcy. 1986- John F Gallacher.

COATBRIDGE – ST JAMES'

Heads: 1956-68 Peter McCann. 1968-77 John W Boyle (1946). 1977-81
Patrick J Moss. 1981-88 William White (1953). 1988- John Kelly.

Assistants: 1956-59 Henry Docherty. 1957-66 Aidan D'Arcy. 1959-61 John

W Boyle (1946). 1961-62 David O'Regan. 1962-71 Cornelius O'Leary. 1963-65 Michael Conway. 1966-68 John F Givens. 1968-71 Damien Gilhooley. 1971-73 John A Boyle (1959). 1971-73 Thomas McAlister. 1973-74 John Doherty. 1973-78 John Taylor. 1974-77 Patrick Hennessy. 1977-82 Thomas Devine. 1978-83 Isaac McLaren. 1982-86 Thomas Brady. 1983- Patrick Kilcoyne. 1986- Michael Briody.

COATBRIDGE – ST MARY'S
Heads: 1937-53 Eugene Murray. 1953-66 Charles Craigen. 1966-77 Ian McLaughlin. 1977-85 James Foley. 1985- Francis Kelly.
Assistants: 1947-49 Charles McKinley. 1947-53 George Mullen. 1949-54 Patrick Hoey. 1950-51 James Quin. 1953-56 Noel Carey. 1954-59 John Delaney. 1954-62 George Boyd. 1956-58 Edward Laverty. 1959-60 Joseph Farnin. 1959-66 John Priestley. 1960-63 James Small. 1962-69 Eamonn McHale. 1963-64 Michael Corry. 1964-68 Kevin O'Doherty. 1966-68 Michael O'Neill. 1968-69 Edward Glackin. 1968-73 Michael Maher (1968). 1969-70 James J Keegan. 1969-72 George Donaldson. 1970-77 Patrick O'Sullivan. 1973-86 James Naughton. 1978-87 William Dunnachie. 1989- Thomas F Magill.

COATBRIDGE – ST MONICA'S
Heads: 1950-69 Thomas Kelly (1925) (1). 1969-70 vacant. 1970-72 John McQuade. 1972-81 Denis Garrity. 1981- Thomas Gibbons.
Assistants: 1953 Michael McCarthy. 1953-62 Patrick McGovern. 1953-65 Thomas Morris. 1959-68 Alexander Devanny. 1962-63 John McIntyre. 1963-65 Patrick Walsh. 1965-68 Denis Power. 1965-72 James Naughton. 1968-72 Cornelius McDonnell SM. 1969-70 Andrew Sheahan. 1972-73 Patrick Lynch. 1972-81 Lawrence Kenny. 1973-74 Patrick Hunter. 1975-77 Michael J Conway. 1977-78 Michael Briody. 1978-80 Joseph Brannigan. 1980-86 Cornelius O'Leary. 1986-88 Robert Healey. 1988-89 John McCluskey SJ. 1988- Dominic Quinn.

COATBRIDGE – ST PATRICK'S
Heads: 1931-51 Daniel Colvin. 1951-52 vacant. 1952-58 John Battel. 1958-59 vacant. 1959-62 Peter Sexton. 1962-77 William Duddy. 1977-83 Peter McCann. 1983-87 Alphonsus T Woods. 1987- Patrick Brosnan.
Assistants: 1927-48 Michael Dooley. 1947-50 Patrick McHugh. 1948-55 Daniel Hennessy. 1948-58 Anthony McGurk. 1950-52 Michael Maher (1950). 1955-60 Richard Lillis. 1958-65 Denis Keane. 1960-70 John Mannion. 1962 Eamonn McHale. 1965-66 Francis Kelly. 1966-72 Jeremiah O'Riordan. 1966-75 Andrew Tunn. 1972-78 Brendan Smith. 1977 James Duddy. 1978-89 Thomas Trench. 1989- Colin Hughes.

COATBRIDGE – ST STEPHEN'S: 1973-84 John J Delany. 1984-85 James Flynn. 1985- Isaac McLaren.

COATDYKE: see Airdrie, All Saints

CRAIGEND: 1972-83 Gerard McColgan. 1983- James McGlinchey.

EASTERHOUSE – ST BENEDICT'S
Heads: 1958-62 Angus McKellaig. 1962-68 Henry McGinn. 1968-75 Daniel Hennessy. 1975-81 James J Ashe. 1981-84 Timothy Brosnan. 1984-86 Thomas O'Hare. 1986-88 Cornelius O'Leary.
Assistants: 1959-65 James McGlinchey. 1962-67 Robert Curley. 1965-68 John Lavery. 1965-73 Bernard Oates. 1967-68 Isaac McLaren. 1968-70 John Brady. 1968-71 James O'Hara. 1970-71 Dominic Towey. 1971-72 Patrick J Loughran. 1971-75 Damien Gilhooley. 1972-75 Daniel J Rooney. 1973-78 Thomas Connelly. 1975-78 James Shiels. 1977-80 James Duddy. 1978-86 Hugh Sheridan. 1980- 87 Paul Stewart.
From 1988 served by Salesians.

EASTERHOUSE – ST CLARE'S
Heads: 1959-65 Edward Doherty. 1965-66 vacant. 1966-72 John Moss. 1972-76 Thomas C Morris. 1976-82 Thomas Corless. 1982-84 James Flynn. 1984-87 John F Givens. 1987- Robert Curley.
Assistants: 1960-65 Brian Donnelly. 1964-69 John Kelly. 1965-66 Lawrence Kenny. 1965-66 Jeremiah O'Riordan. 1966-67 Richard Rodgers. 1967-71 Patrick O'Hare. 1968-73 Vincent O'Neill. 1970-75 Richard Rodgers. 1971-72 Daniel Millar. 1972-73 Patrick Hunter. 1973-82 Brian Donnelly. 1975-81 John Doherty. 1981-83 James Boyle.

EAST KILBRIDE – OUR LADY OF LOURDES
Heads: 1958-69 Anthony McGurk. 1969-74 John Gillen. 1974-81 Maurice Taylor. 1981-87 Patrick Brosnan. 1987- William Dunnachie.
Assistants: 1959-66 Michael Ryan. 1964-66 Joseph Kilpatrick. 1966-69 Michael Martin. 1966-72 Aidan D'Arcy. 1969-72 John Kelly. 1972-75 Robert Kane. 1972-80 Alexander Devanny. 1975-78 Francis Halavage. 1978-80 William Nolan. 1980 Thomas Gault. 1980-82 John Taylor. 1980-83 Damien Gilhooley. 1982-86 Thomas Devine. 1983-88 Leo Muldoon. 1986-89 Colin Hughes. 1988- Brian Lamb. 1989- James A Grant.

EAST KILBRIDE – ST BRIDE'S
Heads: 1946-52 John Battel. 1952-55 Thomas Brooks. 1955-59 Anthony Kilcoyne. 1959-71 James Kilpatrick. 1971-80 Gerald Maher. 1980-86 James K Rogers. 1986-89 John McIntyre. 1989- Michael Ryan.
Assistants: 1949-52 John W Boyle (1946). 1952-57 Patrick Walsh. 1954 Thomas Gibbons. 1954-57 William Smith. 1957-58 Gerard McColgan. 1957-65 John Givens. 1961-67 Michael Cunnane. 1965-70 James Monaghan. 1967-70 John Cushley. 1970-74 William O'Sullivan. 1970-77 Joseph Clements. 1974-78 James Morris. 1977 Christopher Taylor. 1977-83 Robert Curley. 1978-82 Thomas Brady. 1982-84 Kevin McGeever. 1983-85 Thomas Magill. 1985-87 Dominic Douglas. 1986-87 Michael Maher (1968). 1987- Gerard Bogan. 1987- Edward O'Donnell.

EAST KILBRIDE – ST LEONARD'S
Heads: 1966-73 Kieran O'Farrell. 1973-82 Michael McCarthy. 1982-87 Henry J Allison. 1987- John F Givens.
Assistants: 1968-69 Henry Bradley SPS. 1969-75 Michael Gallagher SPS. 1970-76 James Boyle. 1975-81 Richard Rodgers. 1976-86 Michael Maher (1968). 1981-83 Michael MacNamee. 1982 James McGill. 1984- Raymond Dempsey. 1986-88 Joseph Brannigan.

EAST KILBRIDE – ST VINCENT DE PAUL'S
Heads: 1974-85 Martin O'Keeffe. 1985- Brian Donnelly.
Assistants: 1978-85 Brian Logue. 1985-86 James G Nicol. 1986-89 Bartholomew Cannon. 1989- Charles Dornan.

GARTHAMLOCK
Heads: 1954-59 John Murray. 1959-69 Thomas O'Neill. 1969-75 Gerard Mackle. 1975-84 Andrew Reen. 1984-89 Michael Ryan.
Assistants: 1955-67 Michael Sullivan. 1957-60 Timothy Brosnan. 1960-65 Jeremiah O'Riordan. 1964-65 Leo Muldoon. 1965-72 John McConnell. 1967-70 Martin O'Keeffe. 1971-73 George Lawson. 1972-73 John Cushley. 1973-75 George P McGill. 1975 Gerard W Magill. 1975-80 Joseph Ryce WF.
From 1989 served from Craigend.

GLENBOIG
Heads: 1948-53 Patrick Kelly. 1953-60 John Bredin. 1960-69 John V Murray. 1969-82 Patrick O'Donoghue. 1982-88 George Fryer. 1988- William White (1953).
Assistants: 1944-50 John Gillen. 1950-55 Patrick Moss. 1955-61 Michael Corry. 1960-69 Thomas O'Hare. 1961-63 Andrew Sheahan.

HALFWAY (Cambuslang, St Cadoc's)
Heads: 1949-69 Robert Douglas. 1969-75 Thomas O'Neill. 1975-76 vacant. 1976-85 Daniel O'Doherty. 1985-88 Thomas C Morris. 1988- Thomas Connelly.
Assistants: 1953-59 Patrick Brosnan. 1957-65 Laurence Kenny. 1959-61 Denis Power. 1961-63 Michael Corry. 1963-66 Michael Walsh. 1965-70 Herbert Flack. 1966-70 Patrick Loughran. 1970-74 Martin O'Keeffe. 1973-74 Hugh Sheridan. 1974-76 Michael Cunnane. 1978-88 Thomas Connelly. 1988- Damian Gilhooley.

HAMILTON – OUR LADY AND ST ANNE'S (Cadzow)
Heads: 1947-70 Patrick McGonagle. 1970-79 Joseph Martin. 1979- Francis Darroch.
Assistants: 1933-49 John Bredin. 1948-49 Francis Misset. 1949-50 Charles McKinley. 1949-53 Edward Laverty. 1950-55 Edward Docherty. 1953-65 Bernard Mahoney. 1955-65 Patrick Kilcoyne. 1965-66 Gerald Maher. 1965-70 Bartholomew O'Regan. 1966-69 Michael Ryan. 1969-77

Richard Higgens. 1971-73 Gerard Rooney. 1973-74 Vincent O'Neill. 1974-82 James Flynn. 1981-86 Thomas Gault. 1986-88 Patrick Hennessy. 1988- Joseph Brannagan. 1989- Raymond J Breslin.

HAMILTON – ST MARY'S

Heads: 1932-49 Bartholomew Flynn. 1949-71 Alexander Hamilton. 1971-72 vacant. 1972-83 Hugh Cahill. 1983- Alexander Devanny.

Assistants: 1934-49 Anthony Kilcoyne. 1946-52 Michael Houlihan. 1948-49 Edward Laverty. 1948-54 John Murray. 1949-52 Patrick Walsh. 1952-59 John W Boyle (1946). 1953-57 Thomas Winning. 1956 John Brady. 1957-60 John Ward. 1959-69 Michael MacNamee. 1959-70 Michael McCarthy. 1969-72 Andrew Reen. 1970-71 William Dunnachie. 1971-72 Dominic Towey. 1972-74 John McMurray. 1972-84 Thomas O'Hare. 1974-77 James Small. 1977-78 Isaac McLaren. 1978-80 Charles Doherty. 1980-83 Alexander Devanny. 1985-89 Paul Morton.

HAMILTON – ST NINIAN'S

Heads: 1955-66 Ian McLaughlin. 1966-72 Denis Garrity. 1972-83 James Quin. 1983- William Sproul.

Assistants: 1958-67 Edward Glackin. 1964-65 Vincent O'Neill. 1966-69 Edward Docherty. 1967-70 Henry Allison. 1969-72 Lawrence Kenny. 1972-79 Francis Darroch. 1978-82 Hugh Kelly. 1982-83 Jeremiah O'Riordan. 1982-85 Eamonn Sweeney. 1985-87 John Taylor.

HAMILTON – ST PAUL'S: 1954-60 Denis Lucey. 1960-66 John Moss. 1966-71 Gerald Maher. 1971-77 Patrick J O'Hare. 1977- Bernard Mahoney

HAMILTON – ST PETER'S

Heads: 1953-64 Daniel McGlinchey. 1964-69 James McGill. 1969-73 Edward Doherty. 1973-88 Bernard Oates. 1988- Leo Muldoon.

Assistants: 1955-65 Patrick O'Sullivan. 1965-66 Francis Darroch. 1966-67 John McMurray. 1967-69 Gerard McColgan. 1969-73 Michael MacNamee. 1973-75 Thomas Hamill SMM. 1975-76 Humphrey O'Mahoney. 1976-80 Bartholomew O'Regan. 1980-82 Charles Doherty. 1982-83 Patrick Hynes. 1983-84 James Small. 1984-88 Kevin McGeever. 1988 Brian J Lamb. 1988-89 Robert Healey.

HARTHILL: 1945-50 Peter Sexton. 1950-51 John McLaughlin. 1951-52 vacant. 1952-55 Patrick Brennan. 1955-58 William Duddy. 1958-59 Denis Garrity. 1959-61 Philip Boyce. 1961-65 Hugh McGurk. 1965-69 Gerald Mackle. 1969-70 Michael B Maher (1939). 1970-72 Herbert Flack. 1972-80 James K Rogers. 1980-84 Bartholomew O'Regan. 1984- Patrick J O'Hare.

HOLYTOWN: 1975-83 John B Healy. 1983- Thomas McGurk.

LANGLOAN: see Coatbridge, St Augustine's

LARKHALL
Heads: 1938-55 Michael O'Brien. 1955-61 Patrick Brennan. 1961-65 Daniel White. 1965-68 Bernard Mahoney. 1968- Henry McGinn.
Assistants: 1947-49 James McGill. 1949-51 Edward O'Riordan. 1951-56 Thomas Corless. 1956 Edward Laverty. 1956-61 John Brady. 1961-65 Francis Kelly. 1965-66 James McGlinchey.

LONGRIGGEND
Heads: 1945-50 Thomas Kelly. 1950-51 John McCrory. 1951-54 Bernard Keenan.
Assistants: 1950-51 Michael Murphy. 1952-53 James Keegan. 1953-54 Andrew Reen. 1953-54 John Cosgrove.
From 1954 served from Caldercruix.

MOODIESBURN
Heads: 1960-71 Hugh Mahon. 1971-75 James J Ashe. 1975-77 Bernard Mahoney. 1977-83 Patrick B McGovern. 1983- Michael MacNamee.
Assistants: 1963-70 James Small. 1970-71 Gerald McColgan. 1980-81 James Boyle.

MOSSEND – HOLY FAMILY
Heads: 1937-52 William Flanagan. 1952-53 Peter Murie. 1953-69 Patrick Kelly. 1969-80 Robert Douglas. 1980- Gerald Maher.
Assistants: 1938-49 Stephen Keane (Aberdeen). 1943-49 James Butler. 1943-53 Thomas Fehily. 1949-54 Anthony Kilcoyne. 1953-56 Edward Laverty. 1954-56 James Rogers. 1955-57 John Givens. 1956-58 Andrew Tunn. 1957-58 David Cullen. 1958-60 Hugh Mahon. 1958-68 William Sproul. 1960-61 Robert Milligan. 1961-65 Charles Doherty. 1965-67 Martin O'Keeffe. 1967-74 Michael Cunnane. 1968-70 John F Gallacher. 1974-76 Thomas J Corless. 1976-80 James Boyle.

MOTHERWELL – OUR LADY OF GOOD AID CATHEDRAL
Heads: 1947-56 Denis Flynn. 1956-60 Gerard Rogers. 1960-81 John Conroy. 1981- Noel Carey.
Assistants: 1947-48 Henry McGinn. 1947-51 James Dooley. 1948-54 Michael Little. 1948-54 Denis Lucey. 1948-56 John O'Donnell. 1951-59 George Fryer. 1954-55 Patrick O'Donoghue. 1954-59 Denis Power. 1955-56 James Foley. 1956-70 John J Burns. 1957-58 Thomas Winning. 1959-61 Hugh McGurk. 1959-65 John McQuade. 1959-66 Kieran O'Farrell. 1961-69 George Donaldson. 1965-66 Patrick Loughran. 1966-67 Anthony Donnelly. 1967-70 Richard Rodgers. 1967-73 Hugh Kelly. 1970-75 John B Healy. 1973-77 Michael J Sullivan. 1975 Francis Halavage. 1975-78 Daniel Rooney. 1977-87 Joseph Clements. 1978-79 Thomas Magill. 1979-80 James Nicol. 1980-81 John Kelly. 1986- Thomas Gault. 1987-88 Leo Cushley. 1988- Gerard Chromy.

MOTHERWELL – ST BERNADETTE'S
Heads: 1950-59 Peter Sexton. 1959-60 John V Murray. 1960-77 John Bredin. 1977- George Boyd.
Assistants: 1950-55 William Duddy. 1952-54 Michael Houlihan. 1954-55 Maurice Taylor. 1955-64 Daniel J Hennessy. 1955-65 John Lavery. 1959-60 Michael Walsh. 1964-73 Thomas Connelly. 1965-70 John B Healy. 1970-76 Michael Ryan. 1973-78 Brian Logue. 1976-79 Peter Gorman. 1978-80 John Kelly. 1980-88 James Duddy. 1988- Daniel Rooney.

MOTHERWELL – ST BRENDAN'S
Heads: 1965-73 Denis Keane. 1973-81 Noel Carey. 1981- James Ashe.
Assistants: 1969-70 Henry Docherty. 1970-79 John J Burns. 1984-87 Kevin O'Doherty.

MOTHERWELL – ST LUKE'S
Heads: 1954-61 William White (1936). 1961-62 William Duddy. 1962-66 Denis Garrity. 1966-70 Thomas Winning. 1970-77 James J Keegan. 1977-78 John T Lavery. 1978-86 Brendan Smith. 1986- Gerard Mackle.
Assistants: 1961-68 Brian Logue. 1968-70 Neal Carlin. 1971 Gerard Rooney.

MOTHERWELL – DIOCESAN POSTS (no parish):
1949-56 Gerard Rogers, Diocesan Office, Vicar General.
1969-78 Thomas McGurk, Religious Education Centre.
1979-83 John J Burns, Religious Education Centre.
1986- James Naughton, Pastoral Centre, Newmains.

MUIRHEAD
Heads: 1947-55 Michael O'Connor. 1955-60 Michael Little. 1960-64 Denis Lucey. 1964-72 Daniel McGlinchey. 1972-83 Anthony Kilcoyne. 1983- William O'Sullivan.
Assistants: 1953-58 Patrick O'Hare. 1954-55 Francis Kelly. 1955-58 Patrick Moss. 1958-59 John McMurray. 1958-67 Noel Carey. 1959-67 Brendan Smith. 1960-61 Denis Garrity. 1967-72 James K Rogers. 1972-80 Michael Walsh. 1980-81 Michael MacNamee. 1981-83 John Doherty.

NEWARTHILL
Heads: 1956-69 John Gillen. 1969-72 John V Murray. 1972-84 Daniel B White. 1984- Denis Power.
Assistants: 1956-65 Francis Darroch. 1965-67 Thomas Morris. 1967-70 Michael J Conway. 1970-76 Patrick Kilcoyne. 1976-84 Michael Ryan. 1984-86 Robert Healey. 1986- John V McMurray.

NEWMAINS
Heads: 1945-52 Thomas Kelly (1925) (2). 1952-57 Hugh Cahill. 1957-67 John O'Donnell. 1967-76 Angus MacKellaig. 1976-85 Thomas C Morris. 1985- John W Boyle (1946).

Assistants: 1949 William Bradley. 1950-53 Michael Bernard Maher (1939). 1953-54 Denis Hoban. 1954-65 John Healy. 1965-68 Peter Gorman. 1968-69 John Ward. 1969-73 Humphrey O'Mahoney. 1973-83 Edward Glackin. 1976 Damian Murphy. 1985-88 John Kelly. 1988- John Doherty.

NEW STEVENSTON
Heads: 1946-61 Dominic McGlynn. 1961-72 Hugh Cahill. 1972-77 Thomas Barry. 1977-85 John W Boyle (1946). 1985- Niall Hayes.
Assistants: 1947-53 Patrick McGovern. 1953-55 George Mullen. 1955-60 Thomas Barry. 1956-65 Bartholomew O'Regan. 1960-65 Thomas Corless. 1965-66 Vincent O'Neill. 1965-69 Patrick O'Donoghue. 1966-67 Andrew Laverty CRIC. 1967-68 Noel Carey. 1968-72 Alexander Devanny. 1969-72 Thomas O'Hare. 1972-75 Neal Carlin.

NEWTON
Heads: 1946-52 Thomas Murray. 1952-55 John Sheridan. 1955-73 Thomas Egan. 1973-74 vacant.
Assistants: 1946-53 Gerard O'Callaghan. 1949-51 Denis Keane. 1953-57 Michael Bernard Maher (1939).
From 1974 served from St Bride's, Cambuslang.

PLAINS (Whiterigg)
Heads: 1941-49 Patrick Keating. 1949-52 Thomas Brooks. 1952-59 Thomas O'Neill. 1959-72 Patrick Hoey. 1972-75 Andrew Reen. 1975-86 Gerard Mackle. 1986- Richard Rodgers.
Assistants: 1942-49 Christopher Condon. 1949-53 Denis Garrity. 1953-65 Gerard Mackle. 1965-67 Michael Conway. 1967-72 Robert Curley. 1971-72 Neal Carlin. 1972-78 William Dunnachie. 1978-80 John Taylor. 1980-83 William Nolan. 1983- Michael Gallagher SPS.

RUTHERGLEN – ST ANTHONY'S
Heads: 1965-81 Niall Hayes. 1981-87 Patrick J Moss. 1987- Henry Allison.
Assistants: 1970-78 John C Brady. 1983-85 James Davidson. 1985-86 Gerard Magill. 1986- James G Nicol.

RUTHERGLEN – ST COLUMBKILLE'S
Heads: 1939-57 Patrick Plunkett. 1957-74 John Rooney. 1974- John Gillen.
Assistants: 1939-49 Patrick Hoey. 1942-50 Thomas McGhie. 1948-54 Henry McGinn. 1949-56 Dermot McMullan. 1950-55 Daniel White. 1951-52 Joseph Martin. 1953 Denis Hoban. 1953-58 Denis Garrity. 1954-58 Bernard Oates. 1955-62 Vivian Hayes. 1956-59 James Rogers. 1958-61 Richard Higgins. 1958-67 Patrick Moss. 1959-66 John McMurray. 1961-69 Humphrey O'Mahoney. 1966-68 Alexander McCluskey. 1967-73 Michael J Sullivan. 1968-71 Thomas McAlister. 1969-74 Patrick Hennessy. 1971-74 James O'Hara. 1973-77 Anthony

Coyle. 1973-80 Michael MacNamee. 1977-78 Charles Morris. 1978 James G Nicol. 1978-88 Daniel Rooney. 1979-86 Peter Gorman. 1980-85 Martin Kelly. 1985-88 Robert Kane. 1987- Angus McLaughlin OP. 1988-89 Francis Halavage. 1988- James Thomson.

RUTHERGLEN – ST MARK'S
Heads: 1956-71 Christopher Condon. 1971-82 James Kilpatrick. 1982-85 Francis Kelly. 1985- Humphrey O'Mahoney.
Assistants: 1957-61 Charles Doherty. 1961-68 John F Gallacher. 1963-65 Patrick J Loughran. 1965-88 Walter Scott. 1968-76 John F Givens. 1976-82 Eamonn Sweeney. 1988-89 Henry O'Brien.

RUTHERGLEN – CHILDREN'S REFUGE, BELLVUE HOUSE: CHAPLAINS
1950-59 Philip Boyce.

SHIELDMUIR: see Wishaw, St Patrick's

SHOTTS
Heads: 1939-49 Danicl McHarty. 1949-55 John O'Callaghan. 1955-65 Thomas Brooks. 1965-72 Daniel B White. 1972-79 Hugh McGurk. 1979-88 Joseph Martin. 1988- Cornelius O'Leary.
Assistants: 1933-48 Michael Little. 1948-55 Ian McLaughlan. 1949-50 Denis Costello. 1951-53 Denis Keane. 1952-55 James Comerford. 1953-57 James Hallinan. 1955-65 Patrick O'Donoghue. 1957-58 William Smith. 1958-68 James Flynn. 1965-67 Robert Milligan. 1967-74 Leo Muldoon. 1968-73 Brian Logue. 1973-75 Humphrey O'Mahoney. 1974-80 Paul Stewart. 1975-76 Bartholomew O'Regan. 1978-82 Charles Morris. 1980-83 Joseph Brannigan. 1983-89 James A Grant. 1989- Robert Healey.

STEPPS (Cardowan): 1936-49 John O'Callaghan. 1949-58 John Roger. 1958-65 Gerald O'Callaghan. 1965-72 Patrick Walsh. 1972- Herbert Flack.

STRATHAVEN: 1948-55 James Ward. 1955-59 Daniel White. 1959-64 James McGill. 1964-68 Daniel Hennessy. 1968-77 Peter McCann. 1977-86 James J Keegan. 1986- Kieran O'Farrell.

UDDINGSTON – ST JOHN THE BAPTIST'S
Heads: 1930-59 Patrick McCarthy. 1959-65 Bernard Keenan. 1965-81 Philip Boyce. 1981-82 John Mannion. 1982- Thomas Corless.
Assistants: 1934-49 Patrick Heaney. 1943-56 Peter McCann. 1949-53 Daniel McGlinchey. 1949-58 Patrick Keating. 1953-57 John McQuade. 1956-60 Thomas Corless. 1957-59 John McQuade (administrator). 1960-61 Richard Lillis. 1961-69 Thomas Gibbons. 1963-68 John McIntyre. 1969-70 Michael O'Leary. 1970-73 Michael McCarthy. 1973-

76 Charles Doherty. 1976-80 Cornelius O'Leary. 1980-82 Humphrey O'Mahoney. 1982-85 Brian Donnelly. 1985- Christopher Taylor.

VIEWPARK – ST COLUMBA'S
Heads: 1940-49 Thomas McCann. 1949-58 Patrick Keating. 1958-59 James Kilpatrick. 1959-73 Michael Dooley. 1973-82 Denis Keane. 1982-83 Patrick Kilcoyne. 1983- Edward Glackin.

Assistants: 1943-50 John McLaughlin. 1946-48 Richard Lillis. 1948-50 Philip Boyce. 1950-53 John Gillen. 1950-54 James Meehan. 1953-54 Gerard O'Callaghan. 1954-57 Timothy O'Sullivan. 1954-62 Henry McGinn. 1954-65 Martin O'Keeffe. 1957-58 James Flynn. 1958-60 James Keegan. 1959 Alexander Devanny. 1960-61 Denis Hoban. 1961-69 Richard Higgins. 1962-70 Joseph Martin. 1965-74 Martin J Kelly. 1969-73 Charles Doherty. 1970-73 Brian Donnelly. 1973-75 James Shiels. 1974-77 Vivian Hayes. 1975-76 Eamonn Sweeney. 1977-82 Damian Murphy. 1982-83 Charles Morris. 1983- James Morris.

VIEWPARK – ST GABRIEL'S: 1976-84 John F Givens. 1984- Bartholomew O'Regan.

WHIFFLET: see Coatbridge, St Mary's

WHITERIGG: see Plains

WISHAW – ST AIDAN'S
Heads: 1960-83 Alphonsus T Woods. 1983- John J Burns.
Assistants: 1966-68 John Priestley. 1968-70 Joseph Clements. 1970-72 Patrick McAnally SMA. 1983-85 Jeremiah O'Riordan. 1985-87 Robert Curley. 1988- Robert Kane.

WISHAW – ST IGNATIUS'
Heads: 1929-66 Thomas Kearney. 1966-67 vacant. 1967-83 John O'Donnell. 1983- Patrick B McGovern.
Assistants: 1944-58 Daniel O'Doherty. 1947-49 Denis Garrity. 1949-53 Christopher Condon. 1953-57 James Ashe. 1957-68 Andrew Reen. 1958-65 Niall Hayes. 1965-67 Michael B Maher (1939). 1967-77 Thomas Trench. 1968-72 John McMurray. 1972-83 James McGlinchey. 1978-83 James Morris. 1983-85 Humphrey O'Mahoney. 1983-87 John Doherty. 1985-86 Richard Rodgers. 1986- Thomas Devine.

WISHAW – ST PATRICK'S (Shieldmuir)
Heads: 1935-49 Alexander Hamilton. 1949-56 Daniel Harty. 1956-59 Denis Flynn. 1959-72 Anthony Kilcoyne. 1972-73 Richard Lillis. 1973-86 Kieran O'Farrell. 1986- James J Keegan.
Assistants: 1929-48 James Ward. 1946-52 Thomas O'Neill. 1948-54 George Boyd. 1949-51 Francis Misset. 1951-56 Andrew Tunn. 1952-58 Sean O'Shea. 1954-65 James Monaghan. 1955-59 John Priestly. 1958-60

John Moss. 1959-67 Henry Docherty. 1960-61 John Ward. 1960-69 James J Keegan. 1965-68 Thomas Corless. 1967-72 Thomas Sheehan. 1968-70 John Priestley. 1969-73 George McGill. 1972-78 James Fisher. 1973-76 Michael Maher (1968). 1976-82 Gerard Chromy. 1980 Kevin McGeever. 1981-82 Kevin McGeever. 1982-85 Hugh Kelly. 1985-87 Gerard Bogan. 1987-88 John Doherty. 1987- John Taylor.

WISHAW – ST THOMAS'S
Heads: 1957-69 James Hallinan. 1969-77 George Boyd. 1977-81 John Mannion. 1981-85 Niall Hayes. 1985-87 Jeremiah O'Riordan. 1987- Joseph Clements.

Assistants: 1957-60 William O'Sullivan. 1960-67 Gerard McColgan. 1967-72 Brendan Smith. 1972-78 Dominic Towey. 1978-80 John Ward. 1981-85 John Kelly. 1985- Eamonn Sweeney.

WISHAW – HELPERS OF HOLY SOULS CONVENT: CHAPLAINS
1949-50 John J Cusick.

Diocese of Paisley

Secular Clergy

ADAMS, JAMES ANTHONY: Born Johnstone 1936. Educated St Mirin's Academy, Paisley; Blairs; St Peter's. Ordained Paisley 1960. Clarkston 1960-68. C/o Bishop's House 1968-69. C/o Diocesan Office 1969-75. No further entries.

ALEXANDER, JOSEPH GERARD: Born Crosshill, Glasgow 1930. Educated St Aloysius' College, Glasgow; Campion House, Osterley; St Peter's. Ordained Paisley 1962. Linwood 1962-69. St Mungo's, Greenock 1969-75. St Mary's, Greenock 1975-83. St James', Renfrew 1983-.

BARCLAY, ROBERT HUGH: see Glasgow Archdiocese.

BARRY, KEVIN: see Glasgow Archdiocese.

BECKETT, ANTONY: see Glasgow Archdiocese.

BEECHER, JOHN: Born and educated Ireland. Ordained Waterford 1949. St Mary's, Paisley 1949-61. Chaplain, Royal Navy 1961-76. Laicised 1977. (Canning)

BERRY, DESMOND JAMES: Born Glasgow 1951. Educated St Aloysius' College, Glasgow; Blairs; St Peter's. Ordained Clarkston 1976. St Andrew's, Greenock 1976-77. Paisley Cathedral 1977-85. Barrhead 1985-.

BONNAR, DONALD: see Glasgow Archdiocese.

BOYD, DAVID: Born Johnstone 1961. Educated St Stephen's High School, Port Glasgow; St Peter's; Chesters. Ordained Port Glasgow 1985. St Patrick's, Greenock 1985-89. Clarkston 1989-.

BOYLE, EUGENE AMBROSE: Born Philadelphia, USA 1923. Educated St Columb's College, Derry; St Patrick's, Maynooth. Ordained Ballybrack, Co Donegal 1948. St Fergus's, Paisley 1948-50. No further entries.

BOYLE, JOHN (Jun) (1930): see Glasgow Archdiocese.

BOYLE, THOMAS HUGH: Born Govan 1962. Educated St Brendan's High School, Linwood; Strathclyde University; St Patrick's College, Thurles. Ordained Linwood 1986. St Columba's, Renfrew 1986-.

BRADLEY, FRANCIS ANTHONY: Born and educated Ireland. Ordained Wexford for Paisley 1955. St James', Renfrew 1955. Neilston 1955-59. Bishopton 1959-60. Forces Chaplain 1960-67. St Paul's, Paisley 1967-68. St Andrew's, Greenock 1968-69. Retired to Dublin 1969. (Canning)

BRADY, JOSEPH P: see Glasgow Archdiocese.

BRADY, LUKE: see Glasgow Archdiocese.

BRANNAN, PATRICK: Born Paisley 1939. Educated St Peter's. Ordained Paisley 1969. St Paul's, Paisley 1969-70. St Andrew's, Greenock 1970-78. Gourock 1978-88. St John the Baptist's, Port Glasgow 1988-.

BRENNAN, GERARD: Born and educated Ireland. Ordained Kilkenny for Paisley 1958. St Margaret's, Johnstone 1958-72. St Joseph's, Greenock 1972-80. St James', Renfrew 1980-83. St John the Baptist's, Port Glasgow 1983-88. Clarkston 1988-. (Canning)

BURKE, PATRICK J: Born and educated Ireland. Ordained Carlow for Paisley 1951. Holy Family, Port Glasgow 1951-60. St Charles', Paisley 1960-68. St Laurence's, Greenock 1968-75. St Joseph's, Greenock 1975-85. St Charles', Paisley 1985-. (Canning)

BURNS, CHARLES VINCENT: Born Glasgow 1933. Educated St Aloysius' College, Glasgow; Blairs; St Peter's. Ordained Paisley 1957. St Peter's, Paisley 1957. Went to Rome to continue his studies in 1957, and stayed on there to work in the Vatican Archives.

BYERS, JAMES ANTHONY: Born Glasgow 1947. Educated St Aloysius' College, Glasgow; St Peter's. Ordained Paisley 1971. St Mary's, Paisley 1971-73. Professor, Langbank 1973-78. St Patrick's, Greenock 1978-87. Bishopton 1987-88. Newton Mearns 1988-.

CAMERON, EDWARD DEEHAN: Born Johnstone 1961. Educated St Aelred's High School and St Mirin's & St Margaret's High School, Paisley; St Peter's; Chesters. Ordained Paisley 1985. Holy Family, Port Glasgow 1985-.

CANNING, BERNARD J: Born and educated Ireland. Ordained Derry 1956. St James', Renfrew 1956-68. St Fergus's, Paisley 1968-74. St Laurence's, Greenock 1974-86. Howwood 1986-. (Canning)

CARLIN, DENIS EDWARD: Born Barrhead 1950. Educated St Mirin's Academy, Paisley; Langbank; Blairs; Scots College, Rome. Ordained Paisley 1974. St Andrew's, Greenock 1974. Completing studies, Rome 1974-75. Barrhead 1975. Linwood 1975-78. St Andrew's, Greenock 1978-85. Professor, Chesters 1985-.

CARROLL, ANDREW: Born Barrhead 1942. Educated St Mirin's Academy, Paisley; St Peter's. Ordained Barrhead 1974. St Mary's, Paisley 1974-87. St Patrick's, Greenock 1987-88. Director, St Vincent's Centre, Langbank 1988-.

CASSIDY, VINCENT: Born Nitshill, Glasgow 1941. Educated Blairs, St Peter's. Ordained Paisley 1966. Holy Family, Port Glasgow 1966-69. St Laurence's, Greenock 1969-74. St Fergus's, Greenock 1974-78. No further entries.

CAVANAGH, CHARLES: Ordained 1963. St Fergus's, Paisley 1965-69. Holy Family, Port Glasgow 1969-78. St Charles', Paisley 1978-86. St Peter's, Paisley 1986-.

CHANDLER, ALBERT: see Glasgow Archdiocese.

CONNOLLY, FELIX: Born and educated Ireland. Ordained Carlow for Paisley 1949. St Patrick's, Greenock 1949-68. Barrhead 1968-73. Howwood 1973-85. Retired 1985. (Canning)

COPPINGER, MICHAEL: see Archdiocese of St Andrew's and Edinburgh.

COSTELLO, EDWARD GERARD: Born Houston 1923. Educated Blairs, St Peter's. Ordained Paisley 1948. St John's, Port Glasgow 1948-68. St Patrick's, Greenock 1968-71. Holy Family, Port Glasgow 1971-77. St Fergus's, Paisley 1977-87. Retired 1987.

COSTEUR, JOSEPH: see Glasgow Archdiocese.

COURTNEY, JOSEPH: see Glasgow Archdiocese.

CRAWFORD, WILLIAM: Born Blantyre 1937. Educated Our Lady's High School, Motherwell; St Mary's College, Aberystwyth; St Peter's. Ordained Paisley 1974. St Charles', Paisley 1974-85. St Aidan's, Johnstone 1985-86. St Laurence's, Greenock 1986-89. St Mary's, Paisley 1989-.

CREAN, PATRICK: Born and educated Ireland. Ordained Kilkenny 1950. Paisley Cathedral 1950-68. St John's, Port Glasgow 1968-73. St Patrick's, Greenock 1973-74. St John Bosco's, Erskine 1974-80. St James', Paisley 1980-. (Canning)

CUMMINS, PATRICK: see Glasgow Archdiocese.

CUNNEY, JOHN GERARD: Born and educated Ireland. Ordained Carlow for Paisley 1955. St James', Renfrew 1955-63. St Patrick's, Greenock 1963-75. St John's, Port Glasgow 1975-83. St Bernadette's, Erskine 1983-. (Canning)

CUNNINGHAM, JAMES DOHERTY: Born Paisley 1936. Educated Blairs; Scots College, Rome. Ordained Paisley 1960. Rome, continuing studies 1960-63. St Patrick's, Greenock 1963-64. St Mary's, Greenock 1964-69. Spiritual Director, Scots College, Rome 1969-75. St Francis', Port Glasgow 1975-86. Clarkston 1986-89. St James', Renfrew 1989-.

CUNNINGHAM, JOHN: Born Paisley 1938. Educated Blairs; St Peter's; Scots College, Rome. Ordained Paisley 1961. Rome, continuing studies 1961-64. Bishopton 1964-69. Chaplain, Franciscan Convent, Paisley 1969-74. St Columba's, Renfrew 1974-86. Glasgow from 1986, no parish, presumably retired.

CUNNINGHAM, THOMAS JAMES: Born East Orange, New Jersey, USA 1931. Educated Blairs; Scots College, Rome. Ordained Rome 1956. St Charles', Paisley 1956-57. St Mungo's, Greenock 1957-60. Clarkston 1960-66. Newton Mearns 1966-71. St James', Renfrew 1971-75. St Peter's, Paisley 1975-86. St Anthony's, Johnstone 1986-.

DANIEL, JOHN D: see Glasgow Archdiocese.

DIAMOND, WILLIAM: Born Paisley 1931. Educated Blairs, St Peter's. Ordained Paisley 1955. St Mungo's, Greenock 1955. St Andrew's, Greenock 1955-61. Chaplain, Convent of Our Lady of the Missions, Cathcart 1961-69. Bishopton 1969-80. Holy Family, Port Glasgow 1980-85. Howwood 1985-86. St James', Renfrew 1986-89. St Margaret's, Johnstone 1989-.

DILLON, MATTHEW: Born and educated Ireland. Ordained Newry for Paisley 1949. St Charles', Paisley 1949-51. St Mary's, Greenock 1951-58. Linwood 1958-61. Forces Chaplain 1961-63. Left Paisley Diocese to serve in Ireland 1963. (Canning)

DIVNEY, EUGENE: see Glasgow Archdiocese.

DOHERTY, JOHN: Born Port Glasgow 1935. Educated Blairs; St Peter's. Ordained Paisley 1962. St Charles', Paisley 1962-63. St James', Renfrew 1963-69. Linwood 1969-75. St Patrick's, Greenock 1975-85. St Andrew's, Greenock 1985-89. St Joseph's, Greenock 1989-.

DONNELLY, JAMES: see Glasgow Archdiocese.

DORNAN, JAMES: Born Greenock 1954. Educated Langbank; Blairs; St Columba's High School, Greenock; Glasgow University; Notre Dame College of Education; taught for four years; Scots College, Rome. Ordained Greenock 1986. Houston 1986. St Margaret's, Johnstone 1986. Rome, studying canon law 1986-87. St Mary's, Paisley 1987-89. St Margaret's, Johnstone 1989-.

DOW, JOSEPH JOHN: Born Greenock 1945. Educated Osterley, St Peter's. Ordained Greenock 1973. Paisley Cathedral 1973-76. Holy Family, Port Glasgow 1976-80. St Andrew's, Greenock 1980-83. Clarkston 1983-85. St Fergus's, Paisley 1985-87. St Joseph's, Greenock 1987-.

DOWDS, BRIAN JOSEPH: Born Greenock 1950. Educated St Columba's School, Greenock; Blairs; Valladolid. Ordained Greenock 1974. St Laurence's, Greenock 1974. St Peter's, Paisley 1974-77. St Andrew's, Greenock 1977-78. No further entries.

DRUMMOND, EAMONN J: Born Howwood 1937. Educated Blairs, St Peter's. Ordained Paisley 1960. St Mary's, Greenock 1960. St John's, Port Glasgow 1960-68. Paisley Cathedral 1968-73. C/o Diocesan Office 1973-75. No further entries.

DUFFIN, NEIL: Born Paisley 1933. Educated St Mirin's Academy, Paisley; Blairs; St Peter's. Ordained Paisley 1958. St Mary's, Greenock 1958-66. C/o Bishop's House 1966-69. St Laurence's, Greenock 1969-78. St James', Renfrew 1978-80. St Andrew's, Greenock 1980-83. St Joseph's, Greenock 1983-88. Elderslie 1988-.

DURCAN, PATRICK: see Glasgow Archdiocese.

EARLEY, JOHN THOMAS: see Glasgow Archdiocese.

FARRELLY, HENRY: see Glasgow Archdiocese.

FENNESSY, RICHARD: see Glasgow Archdiocese.

FERGUSON, JAMES ROBERTSON: Born Paisley 1936. Educated Campion House, Osterley; St Peter's. Ordained Paisley 1965. St Patrick's, Greenock 1965-72. St Mungo's, Greenock 1972-84. Monastery of Jesus, Bridge of Weir, 1984-87. No further entries.

FISHER, JAMES: see Glasgow Archdiocese.

FITZGERALD, RICHARD: Born and educated Ireland. Ordained Thurles 1952. Lent to Paisley diocese. Barrhead 1952-55. Resumed his vocation in Ireland 1955. (Canning)

FITZSIMMONS, JOHN: Born Paisley 1939. Educated Blairs; Scots College, Rome. Ordained Rome 1963. Further studies, Rome 1963-66. St Mary's, Greenock 1966-67. Professor, St Peter's College 1967-79. Vice-rector, St Peter's College 1979-82. Clarkston 1982-86. Rector, Scots College, Rome 1986-89. St Patrick's, Greenock 1989-.

FORAN, WILLIAM: Born Paisley 1924. Educated St Peter's. Ordained Paisley 1956. No further entries.

FOX, COLUMBA (COLM): Born and educated Ireland. Ordained Carlow for Paisley 1955. Clarkston 1955-57. St Laurence's, Greenock 1957-69. St Mary's, Paisley 1969-77. Barrhead 1977-85. Houston 1985-88. C/o Diocesan Office 1988-. (Canning)

FOX, SEAN (John Edward): see Glasgow Archdiocese.

FRENEY, GERARD OLIVER: Born Cashel 1961. Educated Christian Brothers' School, Thurles; St Patrick's College, Thurles. Ordained Thurles for Paisley 1986. Holy Family, Port Glasgow 1986-87. St Mungo's, Greenock 1987-.

GALLACHER, (Gerard) KIERAN: Born Coatbridge 1929. Educated St Aloysius' College, Glasgow; St Peter's. Ordained Paisley 1954. St Charles', Paisley 1954-56. Linwood 1956-58. Chaplain, Franciscan Convent, Paisley 1958-69. Paisley Cathedral 1969-76. St Paul's, Paisley 1976-89. St John the Baptist's, Port Glasgow 1989-.

GALLAGHER, GERARD JAMES: Born Glasgow 1960. Educated Langbank; Blairs; Scots College, Rome. Ordained Greenock 1984. St Charles', Paisley 1984. Rome, completing studies 1984-85. St Andrew's, Greenock 1985-.

GALLAGHER, HUGH: see Glasgow Archdiocese.

GRACE, THOMAS: see Glasgow Archdiocese.

GRACE, VINCENT E: see Glasgow Archdiocese.

HAMILL, JOSEPH: see Glasgow Archdiocese.

HAMILTON, FRANCIS (1926): see Glasgow Archdiocese.

HARAN, JOHN: see Glasgow Archdiocese.

HARKINS, WILLIAM RAYMOND: Born Port Glasgow 1933. Educated St Columba's High School, Greenock; Campion House, Osterley; Scots College, Rome. Ordained Rome 1960. Rome, completing studies 1960-61.

St Andrew's, Greenock 1961-72. St Margaret's, Johnstone 1972-85. St Charles', Paisley 1985-89. St Paul's, Paisley 1989-.

HART, HENRY E: see Glasgow Archdiocese.

HAYES, WILLIAM J: see Glasgow Archdiocese.

HEALY, BRENDAN: Born and educated Ireland. Ordained Carlow for Paisley 1954. St James', Paisley 1954-70. Paisley Cathedral 1970-78. St Anthony's, Johnstone 1978-86. Linwood 1986-. (Canning)

HEARTY, THOMAS: see Glasgow Archdiocese.

HEFFERNAN, JOHN M: Born Ireland. Educated Ireland, St Peter's. Ordained Paisley 1954. Paisley Cathedral 1954-68. St Joseph's, Greenock 1968-71. St Charles', Paisley 1971-74. C/o Diocesan Office 1974-. (Canning)

HERRIOTT, GEORGE: Born Greenock 1940. Educated Valladolid. Ordained Valladolid 1966. Holy Family, Port Glasgow 1966. St Charles', Paisley 1966-70. St Aidan's, Johnstone 1970-71. C/o Diocesan Office 1971-73. No further entries.

HESLIN, HUGH: Born Newark, New Jersey, USA 1924. Educated Blairs, St Sulpice. Ordained Paisley 1954. Lent to Glasgow Archdiocese: St Robert's, Glasgow 1954-57. St Patrick's, Greenock 1957-67. Lent to Argyll diocese: Chaplain, Sisters of St Joseph of Newark, Isle of Bute 1967-71. St Andrew's, Greenock 1971-75. St Fergus's, Paisley 1975-77. St Andrew's, Greenock 1977-79. Retired in bad health to St Vincent's Home, Kingussie 1977 and died Inverness 10 Jan 1982.

HOPKINS, FRANCIS: see Glasgow Archdiocese.

HORGAN, DANIEL (1927): see Glasgow Archdiocese.

JACKSON, JAMES A: see Glasgow Archdiocese

JAMIESON, THOMAS: Born Paisley 1929. Educated Blairs, St Peter's. Ordained Paisley 1954. St Joseph's, Greenock 1954-68. St James', Renfrew 1968-71. Newton Mearns 1971-80. St Laurence's, Greenock 1980-.

KAVANAGH, EDWARD C: see Glasgow Archdiocese.

KEANE, SIMON: see Glasgow Archdiocese.

KEATING, LAWRENCE: Born Glasgow 1934. Educated Holyrood School, Glasgow; Blairs; St Peter's. Ordained Paisley 1958. St Andrew's, Greenock 1958-70. Gourock 1970-76. Barrhead 1976-77. C/o Diocesan Office 1977-78. No further entries.

KEAVENEY, LAWRENCE: Born and educated Ireland. Ordained Ballybrack 1948. Lent to Paisley diocese. Bishopton 1948-50. Paisley Cathedral 1950. Resumed his vocation in Ireland 1950. (Canning)

KEENAGHAN, JAMES: Born and educated Ireland. Ordained Kilkenny for Paisley 1954. Lent to Glasgow Archdiocese: Glasgow Cathedral 1954; Holy Redeemer, Clydebank 1954-61. St Mary's, Paisley 1961-68. St Mungo's, Greenock 1968-72. St Aidan's, Johnstone 1972-78. Houston 1978-85. St Joseph's, Greenock 1985-. (Canning)

KENNEDY, JAMES: Born Johnstone 1964. Educated St Cuthbert's High School, Johnstone; Paisley College of Technology; nursing training; St Patrick's College, Thurles; Maynooth. Ordained Johnstone 1989. St Joseph's, Greenock 1989-.

KILPATRICK, ARTHUR JOSEPH: Born Greenock 1936. Educated St Columba's High School, Greenock; Scots College, Rome; St Peter's. Ordained Paisley 1960. St Mary's, Paisley 1960. St Paul's, Paisley 1960-69. Gourock 1969-70. C/o Diocesan Office 1970-71. Paisley Cathedral 1971-73. Clarkston 1973-78. St Paul's, Paisley 1978-80. Lima, Peru 1980-81. Chaplain, Franciscan Convent, Paisley 1981-83. St Joseph's, Greenock 1983-88. St Fergus's, Paisley 1988-.

KINSELLA, MATTHEW: see Glasgow Archdiocese.

LEONARD, HENRY STEPHEN: see Glasgow Archdiocese.

LILLIS, JAMES MARTIN: see Glasgow Archdiocese.

LOGUE, JOSEPH: Born Johnstone 1924. Educated St Peter's. Ordained Paisley 1953. Paisley Cathedral 1953-69. St Mary's, Greenock 1969-75. St Anthony's, Johnstone 1975-78. Bishopton 1978-.

McCAHILL, PETER: Born Port Glasgow 1931. Educated St Columba's High School, Greenock; Campion House, Osterley; Valladolid; St Peter's. Ordained Paisley 1964. St Aidan's, Johnstone 1964-72. St Joseph's, Greenock 1972-83. Linwood 1983-.

McCARNEY, FELIX: Born and educated Ireland. Ordained Monaghan for Paisley 1954. Lent to Glasgow Archdiocese: St Joseph's, Woodside, Glasgow 1954-59. St Andrew's, Greenock 1959-74. St Charles', Paisley 1974-78. St Francis', Port Glasgow 1978-. (Canning)

McCLUSKEY, ALEXANDER: Born Greenock 1940. Educated St Columba's High School, Greenock; Campion House, Osterley. Ordained Paisley 1966. Lent to Motherwell diocese: St Columbkille's, Rutherglen 1966-68. St Fergus's, Paisley 1968-85. St Laurence's, Greenock 1985-87. Died Greenock 23 June 1987.

McDADE, WILLIAM: Born Paisley 1937. Educated St Aloysius' College, Glasgow; Scots College, Rome. Ordained Rome 1962. St Joseph's, Greenock 1962-72. St Patrick's, Greenock 1972-73. Holy Family, Port Glasgow 1973-76. St Gabriel's, Middlesex 1976-77. C/o Craiglockhart College of Education 1977-78. Livingston, not serving a parish 1978-88. Bishopton 1988-.

McDERMOTT, VINCENT P J: Born Ireland. Educated Blairs, St Peter's. Ordained Paisley 1957. St Patrick's, Greenock 1957-63. Went to an English diocese in 1963 and was later laicised. (Canning)

McELROY, JOHN: Born and educated Ireland. Ordained Carlow for Paisley 1956. Lent to Glasgow Archdiocese: Holy Redeemer, Clydebank 1956-57; St Charles', Glasgow 1957-61. St Mary's, Greenock 1961-72. St Paul's, Paisley 1972-77. St Mungo's, Greenock 1977-87. St Fergus's, Paisley 1987-88. Eaglesham 1988-. (Canning)

McFADDEN, ANDREW: Born Glasgow 1964. Educated Langbank; Blairs; Scots College, Rome. Ordained Gourock 1989. St Mary's, Greenock 1989. St Andrew's, Greenock 1989-.

McGARRY, PETER: Born Greenock 1954. Educated Langbank; Blairs; Scots College, Rome. Ordained Greenock 1978. Paisley Cathedral 1978. Rome, completing studies 1978-79. Paisley Cathedral 1979-88. St Patrick's, Greenock 1988-.

McGEE, BRIAN: Born Greenock 1965. Educated Langbank; Blairs; St Patrick's College, Thurles; Maynooth. Ordained Greenock 1989. St Charles', Paisley 1989-.

McGHEE, JAMES A: Born Port Glasgow 1939. Educated Blairs, Valladolid. Ordained Valladolid 1962. Paisley Cathedral 1962-63. Professor, Langbank 1963-75. St James', Renfrew 1975-78. Clarkston 1978-83. St Mary's, Greenock 1983-.

McGLINCHEY, DANIEL: see Glasgow Archdiocese.

McGRADY, SYLVESTER: Born Ireland. Educated Ireland, St Peter's. Ordained Paisley 1952. St John's, Port Glasgow 1952-57. Chaplain, Royal Navy 1957-61. Linwood 1961-62. Serving in Ireland 1962-74. Died Ireland 14 Feb 1974. (Canning)

McGRATH, DENIS MICHAEL (1927): see Glasgow Archdiocese.

McGRORY, NEIL: Born Paisley 1930. Educated Blairs; St Peter's; Scots College, Rome. Ordained Paisley 1953. Rome, completing studies 1953-54. St Peter's, Paisley 1954-75. St Patrick's, Greenock 1975-80. Clarkston 1980-88. Paisley Cathedral 1988-.

McINTYRE, JOHN (1920): see Glasgow Archdiocese.

McKILLOP, DENIS: Born Coatbridge 1921. Educated St Sulpice. Ordained Paisley 1956. Gourock 1956-68. St James', Paisley 1968-69. Neilston 1969-71. Clarkston 1971-73. Paisley Cathedral 1973-76. Linwood 1976-82. Died Glasgow 8 Jan 1983.

McLOUGHLIN, DANIEL JOSEPH: Born Paisley 1955. Educated St Mirin's Academy, Paisley; Blairs; Valladolid; St Patrick's College, Thurles; Maynooth. Ordained Paisley 1982. St Paul's, Paisley 1982-83. St Andrew's, Greenock 1983-85. St Margaret's, Johnstone 1985-.

McMAHON, MICHAEL MAURICE: Born Glasgow 1961. Educated St Columba's High School, Gourock; Langbank; Blairs; Scots College, Rome. Ordained Port Glasgow 1985. Barrhead 1985. Rome, continuing studies 1985-88. Paisley Cathedral 1988-.

McNELLIS, GERARD: Born Greenock 1963. Educated Langbank, Blairs, St Peter's, Chesters. Ordained Port Glasgow 1987. St Laurence's, Greenock 1987-.

McNICHOLAS, MICHAEL: see Glasgow Archdiocese.

MAGAURAN, FRANCIS BERNARD: see Glasgow Archdiocese.

MAHON, THOMAS A: Born Ireland. Educated Ireland, St Peter's. Ordained Paisley 1951. Barrhead 1951-58. St Fergus's, Paisley 1958-68. St John's, Port Glasgow 1968-75. Died Longford 31 May 1975. (Canning)

MANNION, THOMAS (1946): see Glasgow Archdiocese.

MAXWELL, JAMES FRANCIS: see Archdiocese of St Andrew's and Edinburgh.

MOLLOY, FRANCIS: see Glasgow Archdiocese.

MOLONEY, PATRICK B: Born Ireland. Entered Cistercians and was ordained 1922. Left Order, and offered his services to Paisley diocese 1950. St Mary's, Greenock 1950-75. Retired to Dublin 1975 and died there 14 Feb 1978. (Canning)

MONAGHAN, THOMAS JOHN: Born Paisley 1944. Educated St Mirin's Academy, Paisley; Campion House, Osterley. Ordained Paisley 1969. Linwood 1969-76. Paisley Cathedral 1976-83. Director of Diocesan Centre 1983-88. Barrhead 1988-.

MOONEY, HENRY: Born Port Glasgow 1923. Educated Blairs; St Peter's; Scots College, Rome. Ordained Glasgow 1947. Rome, continuing studies 1947-50. Bishopton 1950-51. St Fergus's, Paisley 1951-68. Paisley Cathedral 1968-70. St James', Paisley 1970-74. St James', Renfrew 1974-86. St Peter's, Paisley 1986-.

MORRIS, RICHARD JOSEPH: Born Birkenhead, Cheshire 1933. Educated St Columba's High School, Greenock; St Peter's. Ordained Paisley 1958. Barrhead 1958-60. Professor, Blairs 1960-67. Clarkston 1967-68. Glasgow, no parish, 1968-70. No further entries.

MORROW, JAMES: Born Paisley 1934. Educated St Mirin's Academy, Paisley; Scots College, Rome. Ordained Rome 1958. Studying at Glasgow University 1958-59. Chaplain, Convent of Our Lady of the Missions, Cathcart 1959-61. Professor, Langbank 1961-68. Linwood 1968-69. Professor, Blairs 1969-80. Went to Aberdeen Diocese: Braemar 1980-90. Braemar, no parish, 1990-.

MURPHY, JAMES (1943): see Glasgow Archdiocese.

MURPHY, JAMES (1947): see Glasgow Archdiocese.

MURPHY, PETER: Born Stevenston 1923. Educated Blairs, St Peter's. Ordained Paisley 1948. St James', Paisley 1948-68. St Joseph's, Greenock 1968-72. St Columba's, Renfrew 1972-.

MURRAY, NOEL: see Glasgow Archdiocese.

NEVIN, JAMES E A: see Glasgow Archdiocese.

NEW, KEVIN: Born Johnstone 1958. Educated St Cuthbert's Secondary School, Johnstone; St Mirin's Academy, Paisley; worked in the motor industry; St Peter's; Chesters. Ordained Johnstone 1986. St Charles', Paisley 1986. St Mary's, Paisley 1986-.

NOLAN, THOMAS: Born and educated Ireland. Ordained Kilkenny for Paisley 1954. Clarkston 1954-60. St Mungo's, Greenock 1960-66. Barrhead 1966-76. Gourock 1976-78. Linwood 1978-85. Paisley Cathedral 1985-. (Canning)

O'CONNELL, JAMES: Born and educated Ireland. Ordained Waterford 1948. St Mary's, Paisley 1948-49. St Laurence's, Greenock 1949-68.

Clarkston 1968-71. Larkfield 1971-77. St Margaret's, Johnstone 1977-89. Barrhead 1989-. (Canning)

O'CONNOR, THOMAS: Born and educated Ireland. Ordained Waterford for Paisley 1953. Paisley Cathedral 1953-71. Barrhead 1971-75. Wemyss Bay 1975-77. St Francis's, Port Glasgow 1977-78. Sick leave 1978. Linwood 1978-88. Retired 1988. (Canning)

O'DONNELL, JOHN F (1918): see Glasgow Archdiocese.

O'DWYER, JOHN: Born and educated Ireland. Ordained Waterford for Paisley 1950. Holy Family, Port Glasgow 1950-68. St Charles', Paisley 1968-74. St Mungo's, Greenock 1974-. (Canning)

O'KEEFFE, BENEDICT: Born and educated Ireland. Ordained Carlow for Paisley 1960. Barrhead 1960-71. St Joseph's, Greenock 1971-75. St John's, Port Glasgow 1975. Spiritual Director, Blairs 1975-79. St Andrew's, Greenock 1979-80. Newton Mearns 1980-88. Houston 1988-. (Canning)

O'LEARY, JOSEPH: see Glasgow Archdiocese.

O'NEILL, JAMES A (1929): see Glasgow Archdiocese.

O'SULLIVAN, JEREMIAH: see Glasgow Archdiocese.

PIRRIE, FREDERICK R: see Glasgow Archdiocese.

QUINN, JAMES: Born and educated Ireland. Ordained Thurles for Paisley 1954. Lent to Archdiocese of St A & E: St Margaret Mary's, Edinburgh 1954-58. St John the Baptist's, Port Glasgow 1958-70. St Charles', Paisley 1970-85. Died Newmarket on Fergus 24 Feb 1985. (Canning)

QUINN, JOSEPH: Born and educated Ireland. Ordained Thurles for Paisley 1954. Lent to Glasgow Archdiocese: St Vincent de Paul's, Glasgow 1954-57. St Peter's, Paisley 1957-74. St Andrew's, Greenock 1974-77. Holy Family, Port Glasgow 1977-. (Canning)

REEN, DENIS: Born and educated Ireland. Ordained Kilkenny for Paisley 1950. St Fergus's, Paisley 1950-65. St Margaret's, Johnstone 1965-68. Holy Family, Port Glasgow 1968-73. Clarkston 1973-80. Died Barrhead 10 Oct 1980. (Canning)

REID, ANDREW: Born Paisley 1927. Educated Blairs, St Peter's. Ordained Paisley 1951. St Mungo's, Greenock 1951-69. St James', Paisley 1969-75. St Fergus's, Paisley 1975-77. St Andrew's, Greenock 1977-.

REILLY, PATRICK THOMAS: Born Dublin 1956. Educated St Dhulaigh's College, Dublin; St Patrick's College, Thurles. Ordained Thurles for Paisley 1988. St John's, Port Glasgow 1988. Gourock 1988-.

RICE, PATRICK: see Glasgow Archdiocese.

ROBERTSON, JOHN: see Dunkeld Diocese.

RYAN, THOMAS: Born Johnstown, Co Kilkenny 1925. Educated St Kieran's College, Kilkenny. Ordained Kilkenny 1950. St Laurence's, Greenock 1950-68. St Mary's, Paisley 1968-74. Elderslie 1974-88. Monastery of Jesus, Bridge of Weir 1988-89. St Bernadette's, Erskine 1989-.

SCAHILL, PATRICK J: Born Ireland. Educated Ireland, St Peter's. Ordained Paisley 1953. St Andrew's, Greenock 1953. St Joseph's, Greenock 1953-62. Got exeat to Dromore, Ireland 1962. (Canning)

SCANLON, JOHN J: see Glasgow Archdiocese.

SHANKLAND, DAVID ARNOLD: Born Paisley 1951. Educated Johnstone High School; Scots College, Rome. Ordained Johnstone 1986. Paisley Cathedral 1986-87. Holy Family, Port Glasgow 1987-.

SHARP, JAMES: Born Greenock 1942. Educated Valladolid. Ordained Paisley 1967. Professor, Blairs 1967-69. C/o Diocesan Office 1969-75. St Margaret's, Johnstone 1975-78. Society of St James the Apostle, Boston, Massachusetts 1978-79. Santiago, Chile 1979-.

SHARP, NEIL: Born Greenock 1945. Educated St Columba's High School, Greenock; St Peter's. Ordained Greenock 1970. St Margaret's, Johnstone 1970-75. St Patrick's, Greenock 1975-78. Society of St James the Apostle, Boston, Massachusetts, 1978-79. Santiago, Chile 1979-.

SHEAHAN, DENIS J: Born and educated Ireland. Ordained Kilkenny for Paisley 1955. Barrhead 1955-56. St Margaret's, Johnstone 1956-70. St Paul's, Paisley 1970-73. Barrhead 1973-85. Linwood 1985-86. St Francis', Port Glasgow 1986-. (Canning)

SHEARY, JOSEPH: see Glasgow Archdiocese.

SHEEHAN, JAMES: see Glasgow Archdiocese.

SHERIDAN, MICHAEL GERARD: Born Glasgow 1931. Educated St Aloysius' College, Glasgow; St Mary's College, Aberystwyth; St Peter's. Ordained Paisley 1960. St Margaret's, Johnstone 1960. St Aidan's, Johnstone 1960-64. St Mungo's, Greenock 1964-71. St Patrick's,

Greenock 1971-78. Holy Family, Port Glasgow 1978-86. Bishopton 1986-87. St Mary's, Greenock 1987-.

SMITH, GERARD CHRISTOPHER: Born Paisley 1956. Educated Langbank; Blairs; Scots College, Rome. Ordained Paisley 1980. St Peter's, Paisley 1980. Rome, completing studies, 1980-81. St Laurence's, Greenock 1981-85. Barrhead 1985-88. St Joseph's, Greenock 1988-89. No further entries.

SWEENEY, JOSEPH (1927): see Glasgow Archdiocese.

TEEHAN, MICHAEL: see Glasgow Archdiocese.

TORMEY, JOHN: Born Greenock 1957. Educated Langbank; Blairs; Scots College, Rome. Ordained Greenock 1981. Paisley Cathedral 1981. Rome, continuing studies 1981-82. Paisley Cathedral 1982-84. Dean of Studies, Scots College, Rome 1984-.

TRAYNOR, OWEN: see Glasgow Archdiocese.

TRITSCHLER, FERDINAND C: see Glasgow Archdiocese.

TROY, JAMES: see Glasgow Archdiocese.

WATTERS, JAMES F: see Glasgow Archdiocese.

WHITTY, KEVIN: see Glasgow Archdiocese.

WOODS, PATRICK: Born Greenock 1930. Educated St Peter's. Ordained Paisley 1953. St Fergus's, Paisley 1953-58. Holy Family, Port Glasgow 1958-68. St Mary's, Paisley 1968-71. Linwood 1971-74. St Mungo's, Greenock 1974-77. Wemyss Bay 1977-.

Parishes

In 1948 Glasgow Archdiocese was split into three, with two new dioceses, Motherwell and Paisley, being created. The following lists of parishes are therefore largely a continuation of lists found under Glasgow Archdiocese.

BISHOPS: 1948-68 James Black (Glasgow). 1968- Stephen McGill (Argyll).

BARRHEAD
Heads: 1937-56 James Troy. 1956-76 Michael Teehan. 1976-89 Luke Brady. 1989- James O'Connell.
Assistants: 1942-50 Eugene Divney. 1946-51 James O'Neill. 1947-68 Thomas Grace. 1950-66 Joseph Sheary. 1951-58 Thomas Mahon. 1952-

55 Richard Fitzgerald. 1955-56 Denis Sheahan. 1958-60 Richard J Morris. 1960-71 Benedict O'Keeffe. 1966-76 Thomas Nolan. 1968-73 Felix Connolly. 1971-75 Thomas B O'Connor. 1973-74 Thomas Hearty. 1973-85 Denis Sheahan. 1975 Denis E Carlin. 1975-77 Donald MacIntyre MHM. 1976-77 Laurence Keating. 1977-85 Colm Fox. 1985 Michael McMahon. 1985-88 Gerard C Smith. 1985- Desmond Berry. 1988- Thomas Monaghan.

BISHOPTON
Heads: 1946-56 Joseph Hamill. 1956-61 John Boyle. 1961-64 James Fisher. 1964-66 Henry Leonard. 1966-73 James Jackson. 1973-78 James Murphy (1943). 1978- Joseph Logue.
Assistants: 1948-50 Lawrence Keaveney. 1950-51 Henry Mooney. 1950-59 John Haran. 1959-60 Francis Bradley. 1960-62 James Donnelly. 1964-69 John Cunningham. 1969-80 William Diamond. 1980-86 Donald MacIntyre MHM. 1986-87 Michael G Sheridan. 1987-88 James A Byers. 1988- William McDade.

BISHOPTON – CONVENT OF THE GOOD SHEPHERD: CHAPLAINS
1962-63 James Donnelly. 1963-69 Albert Chandler.

CATHCART – SISTERS OF OUR LADY OF THE MISSIONS: CHAPLAINS
1961-69 William Diamond. 1969-72 John Boyle.

CLARKSTON
Heads: 1947-58 Edward C Kavanagh. 1958-61 James F Watters. 1961-66 Patrick Rice. 1966-73 Thomas Hearty. 1973-80 Denis Reen. 1980-88 Neil C McGrory. 1988- Gerard Brennan.
Assistants: 1947-54 Owen Traynor. 1947-55 Kevin Whitty. 1954-60 Thomas Nolan. 1955-57 Columba Fox. 1957-60 Luke Brady. 1960-66 Thomas J Cunningham. 1960-68 James Adams. 1967-68 Richard Morris. 1968-71 James O'Connell. 1971-73 Denis McKillop. 1973-78 Arthur J Kilpatrick. 1978-83 James A McGhee. 1982-86 John Fitzsimmons. 1983-85 Joseph Dow. 1986-89 James Cunningham. 1989- David Boyd.

EAGLESHAM: Until 1985 served from Clarkston. 1985-88 Henry Farrelly. 1988- John McElroy.

ELDERSLIE: 1969-74 Albert Chandler. 1974-88 Thomas Ryan. 1988- Neil Duffin.

ERSKINE – ST BERNADETTE'S: 1983- John G Cunney.

ERSKINE – ST JOHN BOSCO'S: 1974-80 Patrick Crean. 1980- Thomas Hearty.

GOUROCK
Heads: 1947-51 Francis Magauran. 1951-69 Daniel McGlinchey. 1969-75 Eugene Divney. 1975- Patrick Durcan.
Assistants: 1945-56 Hugh Gallagher. 1956-68 Denis McKillop. 1968-69 Thomas Grace. 1969-70 Arthur J Kilpatrick. 1970-76 Laurence Keating. 1976-78 Thomas Nolan. 1978-88 Patrick Brannan. 1988- Patrick T Reilly.

GREENOCK – ST ANDREW'S
Heads: 1951-61 James A O'Neill. 1961-71 Matthew Kinsella. 1971-77 James O'Connell. 1977- Andrew Reid.
Assistants: 1953 Patrick J Scahill. 1953-59 Vincent Grace. 1955-61 William Diamond. 1958-70 Laurence Keating. 1959-74 Felix McCarney. 1961-72 William R Harkins. 1968-69 Francis Bradley. 1970-78 Patrick Brannan. 1971-75 Hugh Heslin. 1974 Denis Carlin. 1974-77 Joseph Quinn. 1976-77 Desmond Berry. 1977-78 Brian Dowds. 1977-79 Hugh Heslin. 1978-85 Denis Carlin. 1979-80 Benedict O'Keeffe. 1980-83 Neil Duffin. 1980-83 Joseph Dow. 1983-85 Daniel J McLoughlin. 1985-89 John Doherty. 1985- Gerard Gallagher. 1989- Andrew McFadden.

GREENOCK – ST JOSEPH'S
Heads: 1947-59 Robert Barclay. 1959-75 Ferdinand Tritschler. 1975-85 Patrick Burke. 1985-89 James Keenaghan. 1989- John Doherty.
Assistants: 1947-51 Ferdinand Tritschler. 1951-53 Sean Fox. 1953-62 Patrick Scahill. 1954-68 Thomas Jamieson. 1962-72 William McDade. 1968-71 John Heffernan. 1968-72 Peter Murphy. 1971-75 Benedict O'Keeffe. 1972-80 Gerard Brennan. 1972-83 Peter McCahill. 1983-88 Neil Duffin. 1983-88 Arthur J Kilpatrick. 1987- Joseph Dow. 1988-89 Gerard C Smith. 1989- James Kennedy.

GREENOCK – ST LAURENCE'S
Heads: 1945-59 John Daniel. 1959-61 Robert Barclay. 1961-78 Daniel Horgan. 1978-80 James Murphy (1943). 1980- Thomas Jamieson.
Assistants: 1940-50 James Lillis. 1947-50 Joseph Sheary. 1947-57 James Sheehan. 1949-68 James O'Connell. 1950-66 Eugene Divney. 1950-68 Thomas Ryan. 1957-69 Colm Fox. 1968-69 James Murphy (1947). 1968-75 Patrick Burke. 1969-74 Vincent Cassidy. 1969-78 Neil Duffin. 1974 Brian Dowds. 1974-86 Bernard Canning. 1978-80 Donald MacIntyre MHM. 1981-85 Gerard C Smith. 1985-87 Alexander McCluskey. 1986-89 William Crawford. 1987- Gerard McNellis.

GREENOCK – ST MARY'S
Heads: 1947-59 Henry Hart. 1959-72 John Daniel. 1972- Hugh Gallagher.
Assistants: 1945-61 James Fisher. 1946-51 John Earley. 1947-50 Vincent Grace. 1950-75 Patrick B Moloney. 1951-58 Matthew Dillon. 1958-66 Neil Duffin. 1960 Eamonn Drummond. 1961-72 John McElroy. 1964-69 James Cunningham. 1966-67 John Fitzsimmons. 1969-75 Joseph

Logue. 1975-83 Joseph G Alexander. 1983- James A McGhee. 1987-
Michael G Sheridan.

GREENOCK – ST MUNGO'S
Heads: 1944-49 John Scanlon. 1949-50 vacant. 1950-57 Joseph Costeur.
1957-61 Daniel Horgan. 1961-69 John Boyle. 1969-74 Thomas A Grace.
1974- John O'Dwyer.
Assistants: 1942-57 Luke Brady. 1943-64 James Murphy (1943). 1951-69
Andrew Reid. 1955 William Diamond. 1957-60 Thomas J Cunningham.
1960-66 Thomas Nolan. 1964-71 Michael Sheridan. 1968-72 James
Keenaghan. 1969-75 Joseph G Alexander. 1972-84 James Ferguson.
1974-77 Patrick Woods. 1977-87 John McElroy. 1987- Gerard Freney.

GREENOCK – ST PATRICK'S
Heads: 1930-49 Joseph Courtney. 1949-57 John Scanlon. 1957-66 Joseph
Costeur. 1966-68 Vincent E Grace. 1968-72 Donald Bonnar. 1972-75
John Haran. 1975-80 Neil McGrory. 1980- James J Sheehan.
Assistants: 1933-58 James Watters. 1945-57 Matthew Kinsella. 1949-68
Felix Connolly. 1957-63 Vincent McDermott. 1957-67 Hugh Heslin.
1963-64 James Cunningham. 1963-75 John Cunney. 1965-72 James
Ferguson. 1968-71 Edward G Costello. 1971-78 Michael G Sheridan.
1972-73 William McDade. 1973-74 Patrick Crean. 1975-78 Neil Sharp.
1975-85 John Doherty. 1978-87 James A Byers. 1985-89 David Boyd.
1987-88 Andrew Carroll. 1988- Peter McGarry. 1989- John Fitzsimmons.

GREENOCK – LITTLE SISTERS OF THE POOR: CHAPLAINS
1946-51 Richard Fennessey. 1951-57 Ferdinand Tritschler. 1957-64 John
Scanlon. 1964-69 Hugh Gallagher.

HOUSTON
Heads: 1946-50 Patrick Cummins. 1950-57 Daniel Horgan. 1957-59
Ferdinand Tritschler. 1959-61 Patrick Rice. 1961-72 John Haran. 1972-
79 Kevin Barry. 1979-85 James Keenaghan. 1985-88 Columba Fox.
1988- Benedict O'Keeffe.
Assistants: 1978-79 James Keenaghan (administrator). 1986 James
Dornan.

HOWWOOD: 1948-50 Daniel Horgan. 1950-59 James Lillis. 1959-66
Vincent E Grace. 1966-68 Joseph Sheary. 1968-73 James Murphy
(1943). 1973-85 Felix Connolly. 1985-86 William Diamond. 1986-
Bernard Canning.

JOHNSTONE – ST AIDAN'S
Heads: 1960-86 John T Earley. 1986- Thomas Grace.
Assistants: 1960-64 Michael Sheridan. 1964-72 Peter McCahill. 1970-71
George Herriott. 1972-78 James Keenaghan. 1985-86 William Crawford.

JOHNSTONE – ST ANTHONY'S: 1969-72 Kevin Barry. 1972-75 Patrick Rice. 1975-78 Joseph Logue. 1978-86 Brendan Healy. 1986- Thomas J Cunningham.

JOHNSTONE – ST MARGARET'S

Heads: 1945-68 John O'Donnell. 1968-77 Edward Kavanagh. 1977-89 James O'Connell. 1989- William Diamond.

Assistants: 1945-51 James Jackson. 1945-59 Donald Bonnar. 1947-56 John Boyle. 1951-60 John Earley. 1956-70 Denis Sheahan. 1958-72 Gerard Brennan. 1960 Michael G Sheridan. 1960-69 Kevin Barry. 1965-68 Denis Reen. 1970-75 Neil Sharp. 1972-85 William R Harkins. 1975-78 James Sharp. 1985- Daniel J McLoughlin. 1986 James Dornan. 1989- James Dornan.

LANGBANK – ST VINCENT'S: CHAPLAINS

Note: St Vincent's began as a country home for children. In 1961 it became the National Preparatory Junior Seminary (see under 'Colleges'). When the seminary closed in 1978 St Vincent's was turned into a holiday home, retreat centre and conference centre.

Home: 1951-52 Denis McGrath. 1956-59 Albert Chandler. 1959-61 John Haran.

Centre – Heads: 1978-80 Maurice Ward (Glasgow). 1980-88 John Gilmartin (Glasgow). 1988- Andrew Carroll.

Centre – Assistants: 1983-84 Thomas Docherty (Glasgow). 1984-85 John P King (Glasgow).

LINWOOD

Heads: 1946-49 Francis Hamilton. 1949-56 Michael Teehan. 1956-63 Joseph Hamill. 1963-64 vacant. 1964-77 James Fisher. 1977-78 vacant. 1978-85 Thomas Nolan. 1985-86 Denis Sheahan. 1986- Brendan Healy.

Assistants: 1956-58 Kieran Gallacher. 1958-61 Matthew Dillon. 1961-62 Sylvester McGrady. 1962-69 Joseph Alexander. 1968-69 James Morrow. 1969-75 John Doherty. 1969-76 Thomas Monaghan. 1971-74 Patrick Woods. 1975-78 Denis Carlin. 1976-82 Denis McKillop. 1978-88 Thomas B O'Connor. 1983- Peter McCahill.

NEILSTON

Heads: 1947-51 Daniel McGlinchey. 1951-59 Richard Fennessey. 1959-68 Donald Bonnar. 1968-71 Vincent E Grace. 1971-80 James Sheehan. 1980- James Murphy (1943).

Assistants: 1955-59 Francis Bradley. 1959-63 Albert Chandler. 1963-64 Hugh Gallagher. 1964-68 James Murphy (1943). 1969-71 Denis McKillop.

NEWTON MEARNS

Heads: 1966-69 Eugene Divney. 1969-73 James Murphy (1947). 1973- James Jackson.

Assistants: 1966-71 Thomas J Cunningham. 1971-80 Thomas Jamieson. 1980-88 Benedict O'Keeffe. 1988- James A Byers.

PAISLEY – ST MIRIN'S CATHEDRAL
Heads: 1947-61 John McIntyre. 1961-71 Robert Barclay. 1971-88 Matthew Kinsella. 1988- Neil McGrory.
Assistants: 1930-49 Michael Teehan. 1937-54 James Nevin. 1940-50 John Haran. 1944-51 John Fox. 1947-51 Francis Hopkins. 1950 Lawrence Keaveney. 1950-68 Patrick Crean. 1951-68 James Murphy (1947). 1953-69 Joseph Logue. 1953-71 Thomas O'Connor. 1954-68 John Heffernan. 1962-63 James McGhee. 1968-70 Henry Mooney. 1968-73 Eamonn Drummond. 1969-76 Kieran Gallacher. 1970-78 Brendan Healy. 1971-73 Arthur J Kilpatrick. 1973-76 Denis McKillop. 1973-76 Joseph Dow. 1976-83 Thomas Monaghan. 1977-85 Desmond Berry. 1978 Peter McGarry. 1979-88 Peter McGarry. 1981 John Tormey. 1982-84 John Tormey. 1985- Thomas Nolan. 1986-87 David Shankland. 1988- Michael McMahon.

PAISLEY – ST CHARLES'
Heads: 1941-50 Joseph Costeur. 1950-58 Patrick Cummins. 1958-68 Edward C Kavanagh. 1968-78 James Lillis. 1978-79 vacant. 1979-85 James Quinn. 1985- Patrick Burke.
Assistants: 1944-66 Thomas Hearty. 1947-60 Kevin Barry. 1949-51 Matthew Dillon. 1951-54 James Maxwell (St A & E). 1954-56 Kieran Gallacher. 1956-57 Thomas J Cunningham. 1957-71 James Sheehan. 1960-68 Patrick Burke. 1962-63 John Doherty. 1966-70 George Herriott. 1968-74 John O'Dwyer. 1970-79 James Quinn. 1971-74 John Heffernan. 1974-78 Felix McCarney. 1974-85 William Crawford. 1976-86 Charles Cavanagh. 1984 Gerard Gallagher. 1985-89 William R Harkins. 1986 Kevin New. 1989- Brian McGee.

PAISLEY – ST FERGUS'S
Heads: 1948-59 Jeremiah O'Sullivan. 1959-68 James Lillis. 1968-69 Joseph Sheary. 1969-75 Patrick Durcan. 1975-77 Andrew Reid. 1977-87 Edward G Costello. 1987-88 John McElroy. 1988- Arthur J Kilpatrick.
Assistants: 1948-50 Eugene Boyle. 1948-51 Denis McGrath. 1950-65 Denis Reen. 1951-68 Henry Mooney. 1953-58 Patrick Woods. 1958-68 Thomas Mahon. 1965-69 Charles Cavanagh. 1968-74 Bernard Canning. 1968-85 Alexander McCluskey. 1974-78 Vincent Cassidy. 1975-77 Hugh Heslin. 1985-87 Joseph Dow.

PAISLEY – ST JAMES'
Heads: 1948-59 Michael McNicholas. 1959-70 Richard Fennessy. 1970-74 Henry Mooney. 1974-80 Thomas Hearty. 1980- Patrick Crean.
Assistants: 1948-68 Peter Murphy. 1954-70 Brendan Healy. 1968-69 Denis McKillop. 1969-75 Andrew Reid.

PAISLEY – ST MARY'S
Heads: 1923-57 Frederick Pirrie. 1957-58 vacant. 1958-74 Francis Magauran. 1974-75 vacant. 1975-76 Eugene Divney. 1976-77 vacant. 1977- Thomas Mannion.
Assistants: 1947-68 Thomas Mannion. 1947-69 Patrick Durcan. 1948-49 James O'Connell. 1949-61 John Beecher. 1960 Arthur J Kilpatrick. 1961-68 James Keenaghan. 1968-71 Patrick Woods. 1968-74 Thomas Ryan. 1969-77 Colm Fox. 1971-73 James A Byers. 1974-87 Andrew Carroll. 1986- Kevin New. 1987-89 James Dornan. 1989 Andrew McFadden. 1989- William Crawford.

PAISLEY – ST PAUL'S
Heads: 1960-76 Luke Brady. 1976-89 Kieran Gallacher. 1989- William R Harkins.
Assistants: 1960-69 Arthur J Kilpatrick. 1969-70 Patrick Brannan. 1970-73 Denis Sheahan. 1972-77 John McElroy. 1977-78 Donald McIntyre MHM. 1978-80 Arthur J Kilpatrick. 1982-83 Daniel J McLoughlin.

PAISLEY – ST PETER'S
Heads: 1954-61 James Nevin. 1961-74 James Watters. 1974-86 Thomas A Grace. 1986- Henry Mooney.
Assistants: 1954-75 Neil McGrory. 1957 Charles Burns. 1957-74 Joseph Quinn. 1974-77 Brian Dowds. 1975-86 Thomas J Cunningham. 1980 Gerard C Smith. 1986- Charles Cavanagh.

PAISLEY – FRANCISCAN CONVENT: CHAPLAINS
1958-69 Kieran Gallacher. 1969-74 John Cunningham. 1974-78 Albert Chandler. 1981-83 Arthur J Kilpatrick.

PORT GLASGOW – HOLY FAMILY
Heads: 1946-66 Joseph Sweeney. 1966-71 Patrick Rice. 1971-77 Edward G Costello. 1977- Joseph Quinn.
Assistants: 1946-51 Patrick Rice. 1950-68 John O'Dwyer. 1951-60 Patrick Burke. 1958-68 Patrick Woods. 1960-66 James Jackson. 1966 George Herriott. 1966-69 Vincent Cassidy. 1968-69 Thomas Mannion. 1968-73 Denis Reen. 1969-78 Charles Cavanagh. 1973-76 William McDade. 1976-80 Joseph Dow. 1978-86 Michael G Sheridan. 1980-85 William Diamond. 1985- Edward D Cameron. 1986-87 Gerard Freney. 1987- David Shankland.

PORT GLASGOW – ST FRANCIS'
Heads: 1969-77 Thomas Mannion. 1977-78 Thomas B O'Connor. 1978- Felix McCarney.
Assistants: 1975-86 James Cunningham. 1986- Denis Sheahan.

PORT GLASGOW – ST JOHN THE BAPTIST'S
Heads: 1937-50 Simon Keane. 1950-51 vacant. 1951-58 Francis

Magauran. 1958-72 Patrick Cummins. 1972-73 vacant. 1973-89 James Murphy (1947). 1989- Kieran Gallacher.

Assistants: 1947-51 James Murphy (1947). 1947-60 James Donnelly. 1948-68 Edward Costello. 1951-53 Hugh McGonagle. 1952-57 Sylvester McGrady. 1957-58 Owen Traynor. 1958-70 James Quinn. 1960-68 Eamonn Drummond. 1968-73 Patrick Crean. 1968-75 Thomas Mahon. 1975 Benedict O'Keeffe. 1975-83 John G Cunney. 1983-88 Gerard Brennan. 1988 Patrick T Reilly. 1988- Patrick Brannan.

RENFREW – ST COLUMBA'S
Heads: 1969-72 Hugh Gallagher. 1972- Peter Murphy.
Assistants: 1974-86 John Cunningham. 1986- Thomas H Boyle.

RENFREW – ST JAMES'
Heads: 1938-49 William Hayes. 1949-74 Francis Hamilton. 1974-86 Henry Mooney. 1986-89 William Diamond. 1989- James Cunningham.
Assistants: 1947-56 Albert Chandler. 1955 Francis Bradley. 1955-63 John Cunney. 1956-68 Bernard Canning. 1963-69 John Doherty. 1968-71 Thomas Jamieson. 1971-75 Thomas J Cunningham. 1975-78 James McGhee. 1978-80 Neil Duffin. 1980-83 Gerard Brennan. 1983- Joseph G Alexander.

WEMYSS BAY: 1968-69 Hugh Gallagher. 1969-71 served from St Andrew's, Greenock. 1971-75 Vincent E Grace. 1975-77 Thomas B O'Connor. 1977- Patrick Woods.

Scottish Colleges and Seminaries

In the following lists only secular priests who were full-time residential members of staff are listed.

SCOTS COLLEGE, ROME

Rectors: 1878-97 James A Campbell (WD). 1897-1913 Robert Fraser (Aberdeen). 1913-22 Donald Mackintosh (Argyll). 1922-40 William R Clapperton (Aberdeen). 1940-46 closed during war. 1946-60 William R Clapperton (Aberdeen). 1960-67 Philip Flanagan (Motherwell). 1967-73 Daniel P Boyle (1940) (St A & E). 1973-81 Sean O'Kelly (St A & E). 1981-86 James Clancy (Glasgow). 1986-89 John Fitzsimmons (Paisley). 1989- John McIntyre (Motherwell).

Vice-rectors: 1885-86 Alexander Stuart (St A & E). 1886-91 William E Rooney (St A & E). 1901-13 Donald Mackintosh (Argyll). 1915-22 William R Clapperton (Aberdeen). 1923-30 David Paterson (Aberdeen). 1930-33 Francis Magauran (Glasgow). 1933-38 John A Sheridan (1931) (Glasgow). 1938-40 Philip Flanagan (Motherwell). 1946-52 Philip Flanagan (Motherwell). 1952-59 John Gogarty (Glasgow). 1959-65 Hugh McEwan (1948) (Glasgow). 1965-73 Sean O'Kelly (St A & E). 1973-75 Hugh J McEwan (1960) (Glasgow). 1975-78 John Sheary (1969) (Glasgow). 1978-79 Philip Tartaglia (Glasgow). 1979-83 Thomas Magill (Motherwell). 1983- William Nolan (Motherwell.

Spiritual Directors: 1933-34 John Coogan (Dunkeld). 1934-40 Thomas Gillon (St A & E). 1947-54 Denis Meechan (Glasgow). 1954-57 Thomas Murray (1936) (Glasgow). 1957-61 Matthew Kinsella (Glasgow). 1961-66 Thomas Winning (Motherwell). 1966-69 Francis Kelly (Motherwell). 1969-75 James Cunningham (Paisley). 1975-77 John Ramsay (St A & E). 1977-85 William R T Anderson (St A & E). 1985-88 Peter Lennon (Glasgow). 1988- George Bradburn (Glasgow).

Ripetitore: 1946-51 Michael Connolly (Glasgow). 1951-59 Hugh McEwan (1948) (Glasgow). 1959-65 James Foley (Motherwell). 1965-70 Lawrence Jamieson (Glasgow).

Deans of Studies: 1980-84 James MacNeil (Argyll). 1984- John Tormey (Paisley).

VALLADOLID (Royal Scots College): transferred to SALAMANCA 1988.

Rectors: 1873-79 John Cowie (ED). 1879-1903 David MacDonald (WD). 1903-09 John Woods (Galloway). 1909-46 James Humble (Glasgow). 1946-52 James Connolly (St A & E). 1952-60 Philip Flanagan (Motherwell). 1960-65 Daniel P Boyle (1940) (St A & E). 1965-74 Maurice Taylor (Motherwell). 1974-81 John Walls (Galloway). 1981-87 John McGee (Galloway). 1987- Ian Murray (St A & E).

Vice-rectors: 1873-79 David MacDonald (WD). 1879-88 James MacDonald (ND). 1888-89 Augustine McDermott (ED). 1889-94 James McGinnes (ED). 1897-99 Donald Easson (St A & E). 1903-09 James Humble (Glasgow). 1909-11 Patrick McDaniel (Dunkeld). 1911-18 Francis Cronin (Aberdeen). 1919-46 James Connolly (St A & E). 1948-49 William Hart (Glasgow). 1956-63 Hugh Gallagher (Glasgow). 1963-70 Ian Murray (St A & E). 1970-74 John Walls (Galloway). 1974-81 John McGee (Galloway). 1981-84 John K Brown (Galloway). 1984- Donald J MacKay (Argyll).

Professors: 1875-79 James MacDonald (ND). 1886-90 James J Dawson (Argyll). 1887-88 Augustine McDermott (ED). 1889-92 Augustine McDermott (ED). 1891-94 John Docherty (Dunkeld). 1894-1902 William McMaster (Argyll). 1894-1903 Francis A Steven (Glasgow). 1897-99 Donald Easson (St A & E). 1909-11 Peter J Burns (St A & E).

Spiritual Directors: 1950-52 Daniel P Boyle (1940) (St A & E). 1952-60 Michael Meechan (Glasgow). 1960-63 John McFaul (Glasgow). 1963-69 John Sheridan (1956) (Glasgow). 1969-73 Edward Glackin (Motherwell). 1973-79 Joseph N Burke (Glasgow). 1979-83 Thomas Holloran (Glasgow). 1983- Jame Ryan (Glasgow).

BLAIRS COLLEGE: National Minor Seminary (closed 1986)

Presidents: 1864-90 Peter J Grant (ND). 1890-99 Aeneas Chisholm (ND).

Rectors: 1899-1928 James McGregor (Aberdeen). 1928-39 Francis Cronin (Aberdeen). 1939-47 Patrick McGonagle (Glasgow). 1947-51 Gordon Gray (St A & E). 1951-60 Stephen McGill (Argyll). 1960-64 Francis Thomson (St A & E). 1964-65 vacant. 1965-67 Daniel P Boyle (1940) (St A & E). 1967-74 James Brennan (St A & E). 1974-80 Benjamin Donachie (Dunkeld). 1980-85 Keith O'Brien (St A & E). 1985-86 John McIntyre (Motherwell).

Vice-rectors: 1891-97 William Shaw (Aberdeen). 1914-15 Frederick Pirrie (Glasgow). 1918-19 Frederick Pirrie (Glasgow). 1978-83 John A Macdonald (Argyll). 1983-85 John McIntyre (Motherwell). 1985-86 Peter Moran (Glasgow).

Headmasters: 1942-46 John Breen (St A & E). 1946-49 John Sheridan (Glasgow).

Procurators: 1852-91 Andrew Fleming (ND). 1951-57 James Kilpatrick (Glasgow). 1957-61 Charles Renfrew (Glasgow). 1975-77 Desmond Lynagh (St A & E). From 1977 post was combined with rectorship.

Spiritual Directors: 1913-32 Peter Butti (ED). 1933-41 Joseph C Long (St A & E). 1941-51 Stephen McGill (Argyll). 1951-54 Duncan Stone (Aberdeen). 1954-57 Denis O'Connell (St A & E). 1975-79 Benedict O'Keeffe (Paisley). 1979-86 Angus MacLean (1969) (Glasgow).

Procurator and Spiritual Director (combined post): 1961-66 James K Brennan (St A & E). 1966-69 James Friel (St A & E). 1969-74 Roderick Wright (Glasgow). 1974-75 John A MacMillan (Argyll).

Archivist: 1957-58 William J Anderson (Westminster).

Professors: 1867-90 James A Smith (ED). 1876-82 Alexander Bisset (ND). 1879-82 Matthew Brady (ED). 1882-83 John Doherty (Dunkeld). 1882-91 William Shaw (Aberdeen). 1883-97 Robert Fraser (Aberdeen). 1890-92 Donald A Chisholm (Aberdeen). 1891-94 Patrick Green (St A & E). 1892-1905 Thomas Welsh (Dunkeld). 1894-1905 Thomas Miley (St A & E). 1897-1907 Andrew Murdoch (Aberdeen). 1897-1910 John McBain (Aberdeen). 1899-1905 Joseph McHardy (Galloway). 1905-12 James Hughes (Glasgow). 1905-14 Frederick Pirrie (Glasgow). 1905-16 John Noonan (Dunkeld). 1906-13 Robert G Russell (Dunkeld). 1908-23 John McKee (1906) (St A & E). 1910-18 Alexander Bennett (Aberdeen). 1912-39 Patrick McGonagle (Glasgow) (prefect of studies 1934-39). 1913-19 Alexander J Gillies (Argyll). 1915-33 John R Tennant (Glasgow). 1916-24 Alexander O'Donoghue (St A & E). 1918-31 William S Watson (Aberdeen). 1919-33 John MacNeil (1918) (Argyll). 1919-34 John O'Callaghan (1917) (Glasgow). 1923-29 James McChrystal (Glasgow). 1924-40 Edward Douglas (Glasgow). 1927-35 John Cummings (Glasgow). 1927-37 Bernard O'Hanlon (St A & E). 1929-33 William Brennan (Glasgow). 1931-40 Joseph McGee (Dunkeld). 1933-37 Angus McLean (1929) (Glasgow). 1933-41 Ewen MacInnes (Argyll). 1934-42 John J Donnelly (St A & E). 1935-41 John McCrory (Glasgow). 1937-47 Charles McKinley (Glasgow). 1937-51 James Kilpatrick (Glasgow). 1938-42 John Breen (St A & E). 1940-41 Stephen McGill (Argyll). 1940-46 Hugh Cahill (Glasgow). 1940-46 Philip Flanagan (Motherwell). 1940-50 William Duddy (Glasgow). 1940-54 John McKee (1936) (St A & E). 1941-43 James O'Hanlon (St A & E). 1941-46 John Sheridan (1931) (Glasgow). 1941-46 Michael Connolly (Glasgow). 1941-55 Francis Duffy (Galloway). 1942-43 Edward Quigley (St A & E). 1943-49 Daniel P Boyle (1940) (St A & E). 1943-56 Matthew J Donoghue (St A & E). 1944-46 Angus MacKellaig (Glasgow). 1946-53 Walter P Crampton (St A & E). 1946-54 James O'Hanlon (St A & E). 1946-56 James McGinley (Glasgow). 1946-59 Hugh McGurk (Glasgow). 1947-70 Thomas Mannion (1945) (Glasgow). 1949-60 Michael Walsh (Glasgow). 1949-65 Gerald Maher (Glasgow). 1950-64 Thomas McGurk (Glasgow). 1952-60 Daniel P Boyle (1940) (St A & E). 1953-59 Desmond Strain (Glasgow). 1954-55 Karl Kruger (St A & E). 1954-57 Felix Beattie (Glasgow). 1955-66 Daniel Friel (Glasgow) 1956-57 Charles Renfrew (Glasgow). 1956-61 James Friel (St A & E). 1957-61 John Symon (Aberdeen). 1957-64 John Kane (Galloway). 1957-73 David P Brown (St A & E). 1958-74 Benjamin Donachie (Dunkeld). 1959-63 Romeo Coia

(Glasgow). 1960-67 Patrick Lynch (Motherwell). 1960-67 Richard J Morris (Paisley). 1961-69 Daniel J C Hart (Glasgow). 1961-69 William R T Anderson (St A & E). 1961-73 Christopher Gilfedder (Glasgow). 1963-78 Colman McGrath (Glasgow). 1964-85 Peter Moran (Glasgow). 1965-67 Eamon V Friel (Glasgow). 1967-68 Vincent O'Neill (Motherwell). 1967-69 James Sharp (Paisley). 1967-79 James T Clancy (Glasgow). 1968-72 Patrick Lynch (Motherwell). 1969-70 Joseph Fitzpatrick (Motherwell). 1969-75 Desmond Lynagh (St A & E). 1969-80 James Morrow (Paisley). 1969-83 John McIntyre (Motherwell). 1970-75 Joseph Boland (Galloway). 1972-77 Eamon V Friel (Glasgow). 1973-76 Francis Kennedy (Dunkeld). 1973-78 John McAuley (Glasgow). 1974-77 James Henry (St A & E). 1975-78 John A MacDonald (Argyll). 1976-81 Donald MacKinnon (Argyll). 1977-84 Joseph Boyle (Glasgow). 1977-86 Michael H Johnston (St A & E). 1978-81 Hugh Lowrie (Glasgow). 1978-83 David Trainer (Glasgow). 1978-83 Archibald Brown (Galloway). 1978-84 Robert Healy (Motherwell). 1978-86 Patrick Hennessy (Motherwell). 1978-86 Michael Woodford (Glasgow). 1979-86 Edward B McNaught (Glasgow). 1980-83 Robert Kane (Motherwell). 1981-86 Stephen Robson (St A & E). 1982-86 Robert Hill (Glasgow). 1983-86 Joseph Brannigan (Motherwell). 1983-86 Joseph Toal (Argyll). 1984-86 John Kay (Glasgow). 1985-86 William R T Anderson (St A & E).

LANGBANK: Junior School for Blairs 1961-78

Rectors: 1961-74 Charles Renfrew (Glasgow). 1974-78 Maurice Ward (Glasgow).

Professors: 1961-63 John Archibald (St A & E). 1961-66 James Friel (St A & E). 1961-68 James Morrow (Paisley). 1961-70 James McGhee (1961) (Glasgow). 1963-68 Francis Crowley (Galloway). 1963-73 Maurice Ward (Glasgow). 1963-75 James McGhee (1962) (Paisley). 1966-75 Brian Morren (Glasgow). 1968-69 John McIntyre (Motherwell). 1968-76 Thomas O'Rourke (Glasgow). 1969-77 George Bradburn (Glasgow). 1970-73 Germain Fitzpatrick (Glasgow). 1971-76 Donald Mackinnon (Argyll). 1973-78 David Trainer (Glasgow). 1973-78 James A Byers (Paisley). 1975-78 Robert Kane (Motherwell). 1975-78 Archibald Brown (Galloway). 1976-77 Donald J MacKay (Argyll). 1976-78 Hugh Lowrie (Glasgow). 1977-78 Patrick Hennessy (Motherwell).

ST PETER'S COLLEGE: Major Seminary – Province of Glasgow 1874-1985.

Note: Priests are from Glasgow Archdiocese unless otherwise stated.

Rectors: 1878-80 Angus MacFarlane (WD). 1880-96 William Caven (WD). 1896-1902 Donald Carmichael (WD). 1902-14 Archbishop John Maguire (WD). 1914-45 Henry Forbes. 1945-63 Charles J Treanor. 1963-72 Michael J Connolly. 1972-80 James McMahon. 1980-85 Maurice Ward.

Vice-rectors: 1899-1914 Henry Forbes. 1923-24 James Hughes. 1925-35 John Donnelly. 1947-60 John Conroy. 1979-82 John Fitzsimmons (Paisley).

Spiritual Directors: 1933-46 Thomas Murray (1916). 1946-55 Patrick Rogers. 1955-57 Robert Ryan. 1957-69 James McMahon. 1969-71 John Muldoon. 1971-72 Daniel Friel. 1972-78 John Kelly (Motherwell). 1978-79 John J Sheary (1965). 1979-83 Patrick Osborne. 1983-85 Colman McGrath.

Professors: 1878-84 John J Dyer (WD). 1881-99 John Ritchie. 1884-87 Laurence Richen. 1887-90 John Toner. 1890-1900 Ellis P Rogan. 1892-1900 Gerald Stack. 1895-1900 Charles A de Monti. 1897-98 Stephen Thornton. 1900-03 Andrew Lynch. 1900-08 Patrick Gallacher. 1900-15 Thomas N Taylor (1897). 1903-10 Daniel Gillon. 1907-17 Octavius Claeys. 1910-17 Michael Gordon. 1915-16 Patrick J Flood. 1916-17 Alexander Hamilton. 1918-23 Octavius Claeys. 1919-35 Alexander Hamilton. 1919-45 Charles J Trainor. 1923-31 John McQuillan. 1924-38 Joseph Daniel. 1931-34 James Clune. 1934-40 Hugh Cahill. 1935-47 John Conroy. 1938-43 John McQuillan. 1943-63 David McRoberts. 1945-72 John MacKay. 1946-51 Hugh Cahill. 1947-55 Patrick Wycherley. 1948-59 John Rae. 1948-67 James Meechan. 1951-72 James Quin (Motherwell). 1955-65 Maurice Taylor (Motherwell). 1955-67 James McShane. 1959-67 Desmond Strain. 1960-67 Robert Bradley. 1963-67 Patrick Tierney. 1965-77 James Foley (Motherwell). 1967-77 James F Walsh (1962). 1967-79 John Fitzsimmons (Paisley). 1972-74 Joseph Devine. 1972-85 George Donaldson (Motherwell). 1973-85 Gerard C Hill. 1974-83 Francis Kennedy. 1977-82 Martin Drysdale (Dunkeld). 1979-80 Philip Tartaglia. 1981-85 Philip Tartaglia. 1982-85 Brian C Reilly. 1982-85 Paul Kierney. 1983-85 Paul Conroy.

CHESTERS COLLEGE: Major Seminary (all dioceses except St A & E and Aberdeen) founded 1985.

Note: Glasgow priests except where otherwise stated.

Rectors: 1985-87 Maurice Ward. 1987- Philip Tartaglia.

Vice-rectors: 1985-87 Philip Tartaglia. 1987- Gerard Hill.

Spiritual Directors: 1985-88 Colman McGrath. 1988- Michael Conroy.

Pastoral Director: 1985- Denis Carlin (Paisley).

Professors: 1985-87 Gerard C Hill. 1985-89 Thomas Magill (Paisley). 1985- Paul Conroy. 1985- Paul Kierney. 1986- Peter M Gallacher. 1989- Gerard Conroy.

DRYGRANGE COLLEGE: Major Seminary (Archdiocese of St Andrews & Edinburgh) 1953-86.

Note: Priests belong to St A & E unless otherwise stated.

Rectors: 1953-60 Roger Gallagher. 1960-77 John C Barry. 1977-84 Gordon Brown. 1984-86 James Henry.

Bursars: 1962-63 John Cullen. 1963-66 Henry Reid.

Spiritual Directors: 1964-70 John Dalrymple. 1978-80 Keith O'Brien. 1980-86 Patrick Fallon.

Professors: 1953-55 Walter P Crampton. 1953-60 John C Barry. 1953-60 Francis Thomson. 1955-57 John Dalrymple. 1955-68 Thomas Hanlon. 1957-70 Karl Kruger. 1960-64 John Dalrymple. 1960-71 Vincent Moffat. 1961-72 John Symon (Aberdeen). 1966-70 Daniel Boyd. 1968-72 Peter J Nelson. 1968-79 Hugh G White. 1970-77 Gordon Brown. 1970-78 Charles Barclay. 1971-81 Robert Hendrie. 1972-86 Bernard Doonan. 1974-82 William Conway. 1976-85 Gerard Magill (Motherwell). 1977-84 James Henry. 1979-86 Gerard Hand. 1981-82 Gerard Rooney. 1982-86 Philip Kerr. 1984-86 Patrick Boylan.

GILLIS COLLEGE: Major Seminary (St A & E and Aberdeen) founded 1986.

Note: Priests belong to St A & E unless otherwise stated.

Rectors: 1986-87 James Henry. 1987- Anthony McNally.

Vice-rectors: 1986- Philip Kerr.

Spiritual Directors: 1986-88 Patrick Fallon. 1988- Leo Glancy.

Pastoral and Vocations Director: 1986- David Gemmell.

Professor: 1986- Gerard Hand.

NOTE: The Scots Colleges in Paris and Douay closed at the time of the French Revolution. The revenues were recovered after the Napoleonic Wars and were used to establish bursaries whereby boys could be educated in France. The colleges most frequently used by the Scottish hierarchy were the English Benedictine College of St Edmund's, Douay, and the Sulpician colleges of Issy (philosophy) and St Sulpice (theology). The College of Propaganda in Rome also had bursaries for Scots boys. Late vocations generally studied at the Beda College in Rome. If no places were available in Scots Colleges or on Scots bursaries, boys could be sent to colleges in England or Ireland.

Selective Bibliography

It would be impossible to list all the material consulted during the compilation of these lists. Printed sources, for instance, included parish centenary brochures, English Catholic directories and panegyrics. Many were used only in connection with a single individual; not all were helpful.

The indispensable printed sources are given below. They were supplemented by manuscript material found in the Scottish Catholic Archives and by information supplied by the priests themselves.

The Catholic Directory for Scotland, published annually.

Bernard J Canning: *Irish-Born Secular Priests in Scotland, 1829-1979*, Inverness 1979.

James Darragh: *The Catholic Hierarchy of Scotland*, Glasgow 1986.

Christine Johnson: 'Scottish Secular Clergy, 1830-1878: The Northern and Eastern Districts', *Innes Review*, XL 1989.

Christine Johnson: 'Scottish Secular Clergy, 1830-1878: The Western District', *Innes Review* XL 1989.

Maurice Taylor: *The Scots College in Spain*, Valladolid 1971.

Index of Clergy

The following is an index to biographical notes on clergy. It gives name, date of ordination and diocese under which notes are to be found. Priests of the same surname and Christian name are listed chronologically by ordination date. Middle initials are not taken into account.

Bennett, George: 1898 St A & E. 3
Bennett, John J: 1951 Glasgow. 213
Bennett, Peter: 1934 St A & E. 3
Bergin, Malachy: 1949 Glasgow. 213
Berkery, William: 1881 St A & E. 3
Bermingham, Patrick: 1944 St A & E. 3
Berry, Desmond J: 1976 Paisley. 455
Berry, Thomas F: 1945 Glasgow. 213
Beveridge, John: 1977 Aberdeen. 96
Beyaert, Arthur: 1879 Glasgow. 213
Birnie, James K: 1937 St A & E. 3
Birnie, Patrick: 1893 St A & E. 4
Birrell, James M: 1979 Aberdeen. 96
Black, James: 1920 Glasgow. 213
Blake, Edward: 1902 St A & E. 4
Blake, Matthew: 1914 Dunkeld. 144
Blee, Bernard: 1934 St A & E. 4
Bogan, Gerard: 1985 Motherwell. 411
Bogan, Hugh: 1923 Glasgow. 213
Bohan, William: 1901 Galloway. 175
Boilson, Thomas: 1881 St A & E. 4
Boland, Joseph: 1969 Galloway. 175
Boland, Peter: 1914 Glasgow. 213
Boles, John: 1951 Glasgow. 213
Bonnar, Donald: 1934 Glasgow. 214
Bonner, James: 1915 St A & E. 4
Bonnyman, James: 1941 Aberdeen. 96
Bonnyman, Peter: 1909 Glasgow. 214
Bourke, Jeremiah: 1944 St A & E. 4
Bovill, James W: 1967 Glasgow. 214
Bowden, Thomas: 1937 St A & E. 4
Bowie, William: 1932 Aberdeen. 96
Boyce, Philip: 1931 Glasgow. 214
Boyce, William: 1923 Glasgow. 214
Boyd, Daniel: 1961 St A & E. 4
Boyd, David: 1985 Paisley. 455
Boyd, George: 1948 Motherwell. 411
Boyd, Joseph V: 1957 Galloway. 175
Boyd, William H: 1984 Galloway. 175
Bolyan, Patrick: 1977 St A & E. 4
Boyle, Anthony: 1962 Dunkeld. 144
Boyle, Daniel Joseph: 1940 St A & E. 4
Boyle, Daniel Patrick: 1940 St A & E. 5
Boyle, Eugene A: 1948 Paisley. 455
Boyle, Hugh N: 1962 Glasgow. 214
Boyle, James: 1968 Motherwell. 412
Boyle, John: 1909 Glasgow. 214
Boyle, John: 1918 Glasgow. 214
Boyle, John: 1930 Glasgow. 215
Boyle, John W: 1946 Glasgow. 215
Boyle, John A: 1959 Motherwell. 412
Boyle, Joseph: 1975 Glasgow. 215
Boyle, Liam: 1954 St A & E. 5
Boyle, Richard: 1881 Glasgow. 215
Boyle, Thomas H: 1986 Paisley. 456
Boyle, William: 1952 Motherwell. 412
Bracelin, John: 1927 St A & E. 5

Bradburn, George C: 1965 Glasgow. 215
Bradley, Denis: 1953 Glasgow. 215
Bradley, Edward: 1918 Glasgow. 215
Bradley, Francis A: 1955 Paisley. 456
Bradley, Hugh J: 1916 Glasgow. 215
Bradley, Hugh: 1989 Glasgow. 215
Bradley, John: 1944 Glasgow. 216
Bradley, Robert: 1947 Glasgow. 216
Bradley, Stephen G: 1973 Galloway. 175
Bradley, William: 1911 Glasgow. 216
Bradley, William: 1913 Glasgow. 216
Brady, Hugh: 1935 St A & E. 5
Brady, John I: 1893 Galloway. 176
Brady, John C: 1956 Motherwell. 412
Brady, Joseph P: 1956 Glasgow. 216
Brady, Laurence: 1929 Glasgow. 216
Brady, Luke: 1940 Glasgow. 216
Brady, Patrick: 1889 Dunkeld. 144
Brady, Patrick J: 1940 Glasgow. 216
Brady, Patrick: 1965 St A & E. 5
Brady, Philip: 1943 Galloway. 176
Brady, Thomas: 1932 Glasgow. 217
Brady, Thomas J: 1978 Motherwell. 412
Branagan, John: 1938 Glasgow. 217
Brannan, Christopher: 1983 Aberdeen. 96
Brannan, John: 1952 Glasgow. 217
Brannan, Patrick: 1969 Paisley. 456
Brannigan, Joseph: 1978 Motherwell. 412
Bredin, John: 1928 Glasgow. 217
Bredin, Patrick J: 1931 St A & E. 5
Breen, John: 1928 St A & E. 5
Breen, Joseph: 1938 Glasgow. 217
Breen, Lawrence: 1933 Galloway. 176
Breen, Patrick: 1947 St A & E. 5
Bremner, Alexander: 1957 St A & E. 6
Brennan, Daniel: 1942 Glasgow. 217
Brennan, Gerard: 1958 Paisley. 456
Brennan, James: 1934 St A & E. 6
Brennan, James: 1945 St A & E. 6
Brennan, James: 1947 St A & E. 6
Brennan, Michael: 1930 Glasgow. 217
Brennan, Patrick: 1931 Glasgow. 217
Brennan, Timothy: 1897 Argyll. 121
Brennan, William: 1924 Glasgow. 218
Brennan, William: 1962 St A & E. 6
Breslin, John F: 1953 Motherwell. 412
Breslin, Raymond J: 1989 Motherwell. 412
Brett, James C: 1913 St A & E. 6
Brett, Joseph: 1928 Glasgow. 218
Brew, Cornelius: 1924 Glasgow. 218
Briody, Michael: 1977 Motherwell. 413
Broderick, John D: 1952 Glasgow. 218
Brodie, Charles: 1946 St A & E. 6
Broeders, Severinus: 1906 Dunkeld. 144
Brooks, Thomas: 1927 Motherwell. 218
Brophy, Thomas: 1884 Dunkeld. 144
Brosnan, Patrick: 1953 Motherwell. 413

Coogan, Patrick: 1923 Glasgow. 230
Cooper, Norman P: 1980 St A & E. 11
Copland, John F: 1946 Aberdeen. 97
Coppinger, Michael: 1954 St A & E. 11
Corcoran, Thomas: 1930 St A & E. 11
Corduff, James: 1937 St A & E. 11
Corless, Thomas J: 1951 Motherwell. 414
Corley, Thomas: 1902 Glasgow. 230
Corr, Henry: 1908 Glasgow. 230
Corrigan, James P: 1961 Glasgow. 231
Corry, Michael T: 1952 Motherwell. 414
Cosgrove, John: 1935 Motherwell. 414
Cosker, James: 1961 Glasgow. 231
Costello, Denis: 1949 Motherwell. 415
Costello, Edward G: 1948 Paisley. 457
Costello, Michael: 1920 Glasgow. 231
Costello, (-): 1897 St A & E. 11
Costeur, Joseph: 1919 Glasgow. 231
Costigan, William P: 1886 St A & E. 11
Cotter, Edmund: 1890 Glasgow. 231
Courtney, Francis: 1953 Glasgow. 231
Courtney, Joseph: 1906 Glasgow. 231
Courtney, Timothy: 1911 Glasgow. 231
Couttenier, Octave: 1893 St A & E. 11
Cowhey, James: 1901 Glasgow. 231
Cowley, Vincent J: 1939 Glasgow. 232
Cox, Kenneth C: 1943 St A & E. 12
Coyle, Andrew: 1968 Argyll. 123
Coyle, Anthony: 1973 Motherwell. 415
Coyle, Francis: 1947 Glasgow: 232
Coyle, James: 1942 Galloway. 178
Coyle, John: 1906 Glasgow. 232
Coyle, Joseph D: 1958 Glasgow. 232
Coyle, Raymond: 1977 Aberdeen. 98
Coyne, James C: 1906 Glasgow. 232
Craigen, Charles: 1927 Glasgow. 232
Crampton, Patrick: 1940 St A & E. 12
Crampton, Walter P: 1940 St A & E. 12
Crawford, William: 1974 Paisley. 457
Crawley, George: 1952 Glasgow: 232
Crean, Patrick: 1950 Paisley. 457
Creanor, John: 1965 St A & E. 12
Creedon, Daniel: 1937 Glasgow. 232
Creedon, Patrick J: 1922 Glasgow. 232
Creegan, Joseph: 1966 Dunkeld. 146
Crerand, John: 1927 Glasgow. 232
Cronin, Francis: 1894 Glasgow. 233
Cronin, Francis: 1903 Aberdeen. 98
Cronin, Patrick: 1900 Glasgow. 233
Cronin, Richard: 1910 Glasgow. 233
Crotty, Patrick: 1887 Dunkeld. 146
Crowe, Daniel F: 1911 Glasgow. 233
Crowley, Francis D: 1956 Galloway. 178
Crowley, John: 1955 Galloway. 178
Crumley, John: 1905 Glasgow. 233
Crumly, Joseph J: 1906 Glasgow. 233
Cuffe, Philip J: 1932 Dunkeld. 146

Culhane, George: 1888 Dunkeld. 146
Culhane, Stephen: 1884 St A & E. 12
Cullen, David J: 1954 Motherwell. 415
Cullen, James L: 1916 Glasgow. 233
Cullen, John: 1936 Glasgow. 233
Cullen, John: 1960 St A & E. 12
Cullerton, Peter: 1937 Dunkeld. 146
Culley, Alexander J: 1986 Argyll. 123
Culligan, Charles: 1898 Glasgow. 233
Cullinan, Patrick J: 1905 Glasgow. 233
Cumming, Donald J: 1982 Glasgow. 234
Cummings, John: 1927 Glasgow. 234
Cummins, James: 1942 St A & E. 12
Cummins, Patrick: 1925 Glasgow. 234
Cummins, Thomas: 1933 Galloway. 178
Cunnane, Michael A: 1961 Motherwell. 415
Cunney, John G: 1955 Paisley. 458
Cunningham, Bernard: 1903 Glasgow. 234
Cunningham, Charles A: 1885 Glasgow. 234
Cunningham, James D: 1960 Paisley. 458
Cunningham, John: 1955 Aberdeen. 98
Cunningham, John: 1961 Paisley. 458
Cunningham, Michael: 1881 Galloway. 178
Cunningham, Patrick: 1940 St A & E. 12
Cunningham, Thomas J: 1879 Glasgow. 234
Cunningham, Thomas: 1953 Glasgow. 234
Cunningham, Thomas J: 1956 Paisley. 458
Curley, Hugh: 1917 Glasgow. 234
Curley, Robert: 1962 Motherwell. 415
Curran, Henry: 1945 St A & E. 12
Curran, John D: 1967 St A & E. 13
Currie, David: 1956 Glasgow. 234
Currie, Patrick G: 1973 Glasgow. 235
Currie, Thomas: 1888 Glasgow. 235
Curtin, Michael: 1890 Glasgow. 235
Cush, Charles: 1943 Glasgow. 235
Cush, Patrick: 1902 Glasgow. 235
Cushley, John: 1967 Motherwell. 415
Cushley, Leo W: 1985 Motherwell. 415
Cusick, John: 1927 Glasgow. 235
Cusick, John J: 1930 Glasgow. 235
Czuberkis, John: 1897 Glasgow. 235

Daine, John: 1878 Aberdeen. 98
Dalrymple, Jock J: 1986 St A & E. 13
Dalrymple, John: 1954 St A & E. 13
Dalton, Joseph: 1977 Aberdeen. 98
Daly, Charles: 1895 Glasgow. 236
Daly, Charles: 1914 St A & E. 13
Daly, Charles A: 1916 Dunkeld. 146
Daly, Eugene: 1947 St A & E. 13
Daly, Patrick: 1885 Glasgow. 236
Daly, Thomas: 1919 Glasgow. 236
Daly, William: 1900 Glasgow. 236

Daniel, John D: 1923 Glasgow. 236
Daniel, Joseph F: 1922 Glasgow. 236
D'Arcy, Aidan: 1957 Motherwell. 415
Darroch, Francis F: 1956 Motherwell. 415
Davidson, James: 1977 Motherwell. 416
Davin, Francis: 1922 Glasgow. 236
Davis, Wilfrid: 1930 Aberdeen. 98
Davison, Laurence: 1943 St A & E. 13
Davitt, Thomas: 1926 St A & E. 13
Dawson, Bernard J: 1883 Glasgow. 236
Dawson, James J: 1881 Argyll. 123
Dawson, Justin: 1942 St A & E. 13
Dawson, Peter: 1889 Dunkeld. 147
Day, Aidan J: 1951 St A & E. 13
Deans, John: 1935 Glasgow. 236
De Backer, Louis: 1881 Glasgow. 236
Deeney, Patrick: 1918 Glasgow. 237
Deery, Hugh A: 1939 Glasgow. 237
Deery, Leo: 1947 St A & E. 13
Delahunty, William: 1919 Glasgow. 237
Delaney, John J: 1954 Motherwell. 416
Delaney, Patrick: 1937 St A & E: 14
Delaney, Richard: 1912 St A & E. 14
Delargey, Hugh: 1913 Glasgow. 237
Delbeke, Theophilus: 1887 Glasgow. 237
De Meulenaere, Louis: 1882 Glasgow. 237
De Monti, Charles: 1889 Glasgow. 237
Dempsey, Edward: 1928 Dunkeld. 147
Dempsey, Nicholas: 1971 Motherwell. 416
Dempsey, Raymond: 1984 Motherwell. 416
Dennehy, Cornelius: 1913 Glasgow. 237
Dennehy, Denis: 1890 Glasgow. 238
Dennehy, Jerome: 1912 Glasgow. 238
Dennehy, John: 1943 Glasgow. 238
Dennis, James K: 1934 St A & E. 14
De Souza, Achilles: 1968 St A & E. 14
Devane, Michael J: 1941 St A & E. 14
Devaney, Patrick: 1889 Galloway. 178
Devaney, Thomas: 1930 St A & E. 14
Devanny, Alexander S: 1959 Motherwell. 416
Devine, Bernard V: 1951 Glasgow. 238
Devine, Gerard: 1977 Motherwell. 416
Devine, John A: 1906 Glasgow. 238
Devine, John: 1925 Dunkeld. 147
Devine, Joseph: 1960 Glasgow. 238
Devlin, Bernard: 1955 Glasgow. 238
Devlin, Brian: 1985 St A & E. 14
Devlin, Gerard: 1946 St A & E. 14
Devlin, Gerard: 1985 Motherwell. 416
Devlin, Peter: 1923 Glasgow. 238
Devitt, Robert: 1916 Glasgow. 238
Diamond, Patrick: 1902 Glasgow. 239
Diamond, William: 1955 Paisley. 458
Dick, Barrington D: 1892 Galloway. 178
Dillon, Matthew: 1949 Paisley. 458
Dillon, Patrick: 1928 Glasgow. 239

Dillon, Thomas J: 1942 Dunkeld. 147
Dinan, Michael: 1894 Glasgow. 239
Dinneen, Patrick: 1937 Glasgow. 239
Dinneen, William: 1943 Argyll. 123
Divney, Eugene: 1942 Glasgow. 239
Dobrina, Vincent: 1939 St A & E. 14
Docherty, Henry N: 1955 Motherwell. 416
Docherty, Joseph: 1906 Glasgow. 239
Docherty, Thomas C: 1978 Glasgow. 239
Doherty, Charles: 1924 Glasgow. 239
Doherty, Charles J: 1957 Motherwell. 417
Doherty, Constantine: 1919 Glasgow. 239
Doherty, Daniel: 1983 Galloway. 178
Doherty, Edward: 1938 Glasgow. 240
Doherty, Francis J: 1951 St A & E. 14
Doherty, James H: 1911 Glasgow. 240
Doherty, James J: 1979 Glasgow. 240
Doherty, John: 1881 Dunkeld. 147
Doherty, John: 1962 Paisley. 458
Doherty, John: 1967 Motherwell. 417
Doherty, Joseph: 1916 Glasgow. 240
Doherty, Martin: 1932 Glasgow. 240
Doherty, Matthew: 1923 Glasgow. 240
Doherty, Patrick: 1889 St A & E. 15
Doherty, Philip: 1955 St A & E. 15
Doherty, Robert: 1931 Glasgow. 240
Dolan, James: 1914 Glasgow. 240
Dolan, Thomas: 1961 Glasgow. 241
Donachie, Benjamin: 1958 Dunkeld. 147
Donagher, Patrick: 1920 Dunkeld. 147
Donaghue, Alexander: 1912 St A & E. 15
Donaldson, George: 1961 Motherwell. 417
Donati, Peter: 1930 St A & E. 15
Donlevy, Joseph: 1887 St A & E. 15
Donnachie, Neil: 1971 Glasgow. 241
Donnelly, Anthony: 1949 Glasgow. 241
Donnelly, Brian: 1960 Motherwell. 417
Donnelly, James: 1908 Galloway. 179
Donnelly, James: 1938 Glasgow. 241
Donnelly, John: 1913 Glasgow. 241
Donnelly, John J: 1932 St A & E. 15
Donnelly, John: 1946 Galloway. 179
Donnelly, Philip: 1938 Dunkeld. 148
Donnelly, William B: 1965 Glasgow. 241
Donoghue, James: 1939 St A & E. 15
Donoghue, Matthew J: 1939 St A & E. 15
Donovan, Daniel: 1926 Glasgow. 241
Donworth, Robert: 1889 Galloway. 179
Doody, Edward: 1880 Glasgow. 241
Doogan, Dominic: 1971 Glasgow. 242
Dooley, James: 1939 Glasgow. 242
Dooley, Michael: 1927 Glasgow. 242
Dooley, Thomas: 1898 Glasgow. 242
Doonan, Bernard: 1969 St A & E. 15
Dornan, Charles: 1989 Motherwell. 417
Dornan, James: 1986 Paisley. 459
Dorrian, Gerald: 1930 St A & E. 15

Dougan, Francis: 1902 Glasgow. 242
Dougan, John: 1883 Glasgow. 242
Douglas, Archibald: 1876 Galloway. 179
Douglas, Dominic S: 1984 Motherwell. 417
Douglas, Edward: 1924 Glasgow. 242
Douglas, Robert: 1929 Glasgow. 242
Dow, Joseph J: 1973 Paisley. 459
Dowds, Brian J: 1974 Paisley. 459
Dowling, George: 1872 St A & E. 16
Dowling, James: 1881 Dunkeld. 148
Downey, Michael: 1921 St A & E. 16
Doyle, Alistair: 1962 Aberdeen. 98
Doyle, Martin: 1914 Galloway. 179
Doyle, Patrick: 1906 Glasgow. 242
Doyle, Patrick: 1926 St A & E. 16
Doyle, Thomas J: 1904 Glasgow. 243
Drummond, Eamonn J: 1960 Paisley. 459
Drysdale, Martin: 1975 Dunkeld. 148
Duane, Daniel: 1910 Glasgow. 243
Duddy, James: 1977 Motherwell. 418
Duddy, William: 1937 Glasgow. 243
Duffin, Charles: 1936 Glasgow. 243
Duffin, Neil: 1958 Paisley. 459
Duffy, Anthony L: 1973 St A & E. 16
Duffy, Augustine: 1942 St A & E. 16
Duffy, Francis O: 1938 Galloway. 179
Duffy, James: 1879 Argyll. 123
Duffy, John: 1886 Galloway. 179
Duffy, John: 1946 Glasgow. 243
Duffy, Joseph: 1927 Glasgow. 243
Duffy, Michael: 1983 Glasgow. 243
Duffy, Vincent: 1944 St A & E. 16
Duggan, Denis: 1898 Glasgow. 243
Duggan, Denis: 1899 Glasgow. 244
Dumphy, Thomas: 1918 Glasgow. 244
Dunleavy, Michael: 1934 Glasgow. 244
Dunn, Gerard: 1938 Glasgow. 244
Dunnachie, William: 1964 Motherwell. 418
Dunne, John J: 1967 Glasgow. 244
Dunne, Joseph: 1975 Glasgow. 244
Dunne, Richard: 1945 Glasgow. 244
Durand, Richard A: 1919 Dunkeld. 148
Durcan, Patrick: 1947 Glasgow. 244
Durkin, Edward: 1956 Dunkeld. 148
Durkin, James: 1906 Glasgow. 244
Durning, James: 1975 Glasgow. 244
Duthie, Charles J: 1890 St A & E. 16

Eardley, Bernard: 1899 St A & E. 16
Eardley, Stanislaus: 1936 St A & E. 16
Earley, John: 1940 Glasgow. 245
Easson, Donald: 1887 St A & E. 17
Edgar, Henry: 1897 Glasgow. 245
Edie, Mark T: 1983 St A & E. 17
Egan, Daniel P: 1921 St A & E. 17
Egan, Patrick G: 1917 Dunkeld. 148

Egan, Thomas: 1916 Glasgow: 245
Elliot, James K: 1926 Glasgow. 245
Engelen, Thomas: 1943 St A & E. 17
English, Patrick: 1891 Galloway. 179
English, William: 1883 Galloway. 180

Fahey, John: 1921 Glasgow. 245
Fahey, Patrick: 1920 Glasgow. 245
Fahy, John: 1919 Dunkeld. 148
Fahy, Michael J: 1915 Dunkeld. 148
Fairlie, Gilbert: 1922 Dunkeld. 148
Falconer, James P: 1950 St A & E. 17
Fallon, Gerard J: 1956 Glasgow. 245
Fallon, Michael: 1977 St A & E. 17
Fallon, Patrick M: 1968 St A & E. 17
Fanning, Matthew: 1895 Glasgow. 245
Farnin, Joseph: 1959 Motherwell. 418
Farrell, Henry: 1987 Glasgow. 245
Farrell, John B: 1987 Motherwell. 418
Farrell, Patrick: 1896 Glasgow. 246
Farrelly, Henry: 1956 Glasgow. 246
Farrington, Michael: 1970 Galloway. 180
Farry, Thomas: 1903 Glasgow. 246
Feely, Timothy P: 1924 Glasgow. 246
Feeney, Bernard: 1936 Glasgow. 246
Fegan, Peter: 1881 Glasgow. 246
Fehily, Thomas: 1942 Glasgow. 246
Fennessy, James P: 1917 Glasgow. 246
Fennessy, Richard: 1927 Glasgow. 246
Ferguson, Alexander: 1914 Aberdeen. 98
Ferguson, James R: 1965 Paisley. 459
Ferguson, William: 1957 St A & E. 18
Ferrari, James: 1960 St A & E. 18
Ferrigan, Thomas: 1906 St A & E. 18
Finnegan, Malachy: 1943 Glasgow. 247
Finnegan, Thomas: 1903 Galloway. 180
Finnigan, James I: 1927 St A & E. 18
Fischer, Lawrence W: 1930 Galloway. 180
Fisher, James: 1924 Motherwell. 418
Fisher, James: 1941 Glasgow. 247
Fitzgerald, Daniel: 1939 Glasgow. 247
Fitzgerald, Edmond: 1900 Glasgow. 247
Fitzgerald, Edward: 1894 Glasgow. 247
Fitzgerald, Edward: 1909 Glasgow. 247
Fitzgerald, James: 1899 Glasgow. 247
Fitzgerald, James: 1940 Glasgow. 247
Fitzgerald, J: 1890 Glasgow. 247
Fitzgerald, Richard J: 1905 St A & E. 18
Fitzgerald, Richard: 1952 Paisley. 459
Fitzgerald, Sean M: 1963 Glasgow. 248
Fitzgerald, Thomas: 1883 Glasgow. 248
Fitzgerald, William: 1890 Glasgow. 248
Fitzgibbon, James: 1928 Glasgow. 248
Fitzgibbon, John: 1928 Glasgow. 248
Fitzgibbon, John: 1945 Glasgow. 248
Fitzgibbon, Maurice: 1898 Glasgow. 248

Garvey, Patrick: 1909 Glasgow. 254
Gaule, Patrick: 1880 Glasgow. 254
Gault, Thomas M: 1980 Motherwell. 419
Gavagan, Michael: 1945 Glasgow. 255
Gavagan, Thomas: 1897 Glasgow. 255
Gavin, William J: 1969 Glasgow. 255
Gaynor, Patrick: 1911 Glasgow. 255
Geary, Patrick J: 1913 St A & E. 21
Geddes, Aeneas: 1905 Aberdeen. 99
Geerty, John: 1893 Glasgow. 255
Gemmel, Roderick: 1941 St A & E. 21
Gemmell, David: 1978 St A & E. 22
Gettins, Wilfrid: 1896 Argyll. 124
Gibbons, Daniel: 1925 Argyll. 124
Gibbons, John: 1955 St A & E. 22
Gibbons, Thomas: 1900 Glasgow. 255
Gibbons, Thomas: 1954 Motherwell. 419
Gilbride, Patrick M: 1942 St A & E. 22
Gilchrist, Edward T: 1938 St A & E. 22
Gilfedder, Christopher P: 1954 Glasgow. 255
Gilfedder, Francis: 1953 Glasgow. 255
Gilhooley, Damien J: 1968 Motherwell. 419
Gillan, Ian T: 1953 St A & E. 22
Gillen, John: 1939 Glasgow. 255
Gillespie, George F: 1961 Glasgow. 256
Gillespie, John: 1938 Glasgow. 256
Gillespie, William: 1901 Glasgow. 256
Gillies, Alexander J: 1913 Argyll. 124
Gillies, Iain: 1948 Argyll. 124
Gillies, William: 1911 Argyll. 124
Gillon, Daniel: 1900 Glasgow. 256
Gillon, Thomas: 1903 St A & E. 22
Gilmartin, John: 1968 Glasgow. 256
Gilmartin, Patrick: 1926 Glasgow. 256
Gilroy, Michael: 1939 Glasgow. 256
Givens, John F: 1955 Motherwell. 420
Glackin, Edward: 1958 Motherwell. 420
Glackin, John: 1927 St A & E. 22
Glancey, Lawrence A: 1943 St A & E. 22
Glancy, Leo: 1963 St A & E. 22
Glancy, Walter J: 1938 St A & E. 23
Glasheen, Michael: 1880 St A & E. 23
Glass, Charles: 1946 St A & E. 23
Gleeson, Henry: 1901 Glasgow. 256
Gleeson, John: 1889 Dunkeld. 150
Glen, Thomas: 1937 Glasgow. 257
Glendinning, Joseph: 1980 Galloway. 181
Glynn, John: 1952 Glasgow. 257
Godfrey, John: 1918 Glasgow. 257
Godley, John: 1885 Glasgow. 257
Gogarty, John: 1936 Glasgow. 257
Goodfellow, Francis P: 1957 Glasgow. 257
Gordon, Eric: 1940 St A & E. 23
Gordon, Hugh: 1937 St A & E. 23
Gordon, John: 1965 St A & E. 23
Gordon, Michael: 1907 Glasgow. 257

Gorman, Peter: 1965 Motherwell. 420
Gouldbourn, Francis L: 1946 St A & E. 23
Gourlay, Thomas P: 1904 Glasgow. 257
Gowans, John: 1953 Glasgow. 257
Grace, Pierce: 1939 St A & E. 23
Grace, Thomas: 1944 Glasgow. 258
Grace, Vincent E: 1934 Glasgow. 258
Grady, Patrick: 1944 Aberdeen. 99
Grady, Patrick J: 1945 St A & E. 24
Graham, Edward: (-) Dunkeld. 150
Graham, Henry G: 1906 Glasgow. 258
Graham, James: 1926 Glasgow. 258
Grant, Andrew: 1894 Aberdeen. 99
Grant, George: 1900 Aberdeen. 100
Grant, James A: 1983 Motherwell. 420
Grant, Kenneth: 1927 Argyll. 125
Grant, William: 1901 St A & E. 24
Gration, Joseph G: 1965 Aberdeen. 100
Grau, Casper P: 1896 Glasgow. 258
Gray, Gordon J: 1935 St A & E. 24
Gray, John: 1901 St A & E. 24
Gray, John A: 1902 St A & E. 24
Greed, John: 1898 Glasgow. 258
Green, Patrick: 1891 St A & E. 24
Green, Patrick: 1942 Galloway. 181
Greenan, Thomas: 1980 St A & E. 24
Griffin, Denis: 1926 Glasgow. 258
Griffin, Patrick: 1900 Glasgow. 259
Griffin, Patrick: 1927 St A & E. 24
Griffin, Thomas: 1925 Glasgow. 259
Griffith, Thomas R: 1915 Glasgow. 259
Grogan, James: 1950 Galloway. 181
Guinan, Joseph: 1904 Dunkeld. 150
Guinan, Thomas P: 1922 Glasgow. 259
Guiry, Michael: 1922 Glasgow. 259
Gullane, Patrick J: 1937 Glasgow. 259
Gunning, Desmond: 1941 Glasgow. 259
Gunning, Patrick J: 1939 Galloway. 181
Gunning, Patrick J: 1959 Glasgow. 259
Gunther, Hugh: 1899 Glasgow. 259
Gutauskas, Joseph: 1924 Glasgow. 259

Hackett, Michael: 1911 Glasgow. 260
Hackett, Patrick: 1887 Glasgow. 260
Hackett, Patrick A: 1910 Glasgow. 260
Hackett, Thomas: 1882 Glasgow. 260
Haegar, Charles: 1894 Glasgow. 260
Haggarty, J: 1924 Glasgow. 260
Hainey, Daniel B: 1968 Galloway. 181
Halavage, Francis: 1975 Motherwell. 420
Halley, James: 1926 Glasgow. 260
Hallinan, James E: 1940 Glasgow. 260
Hallinan, Patrick: 1912 Glasgow. 260
Hallinan, William: 1935 Dunkeld. 150
Halloran, Brian: 1959 St A & E. 25
Hamill, John: 1938 Glasgow. 260

Hamill, Joseph: 1926 Glasgow. 261
Hamilton, Alexander: 1914 Glasgow. 261
Hamilton, Francis: 1915 Glasgow. 261
Hamilton, Francis: 1926 Glasgow. 261
Hamilton, William D: 1948 St A & E. 25
Hand, Gerard R: 1973 St A & E. 25
Hanlon, John B: 1957 Dunkeld. 150
Hanlon, Robert: 1983 Galloway. 181
Hanlon, Thomas: 1952 St A & E. 25
Hannah, Stephen: 1988 Glasgow. 261
Hannan, Joseph: 1879 St A & E. 25
Hannan, Michael: 1899 Galloway. 181
Hanrahan, John: 1950 Glasgow. 261
Hanrahan, Michael: 1918 Glasgow. 261
Haran, John: 1936 Glasgow. 261
Harbison, Stanislaus: 1953 Galloway. 181
Harkin, John: 1939 Glasgow. 261
Harkin, John J: 1958 Galloway. 182
Harkin, Peter: 1930 St A & E. 25
Harkins, William R: 1960 Paisley. 460
Harold, James G: 1922 St A & E. 25
Harrington, Michael: 1912 Glasgow. 262
Hart, Daniel J: 1956 Glasgow. 262
Hart, Dominic: 1906 St A & E. 25
Hart, Gerard: 1933 Glasgow. 262
Hart, Henry E: 1923 Glasgow. 262
Hart, James: 1916 St A & E. 26
Hart, William: 1929 Glasgow. 262
Harte, Peter: 1924 Glasgow. 262
Hartigan, Patrick: 1889 St A & E. 26
Hartmann, Gisbert J: 1890 Glasgow. 262
Harty, Daniel: 1917 Glasgow. 262
Harty, John: 1975 Dunkeld. 150
Harvey, Gerald A: 1932 Glasgow. 263
Hassett, Edmond: 1889 Dunkeld. 150
Hastings, Philip: 1967 Glasgow. 263
Hay, John: 1969 Glasgow. 263
Hayes, Niall P: 1949 Motherwell. 420
Hayes, Thomas A: 1901 Galloway. 182
Hayes, Vivian M: 1955 Motherwell. 420
Hayes, William J: 1913 Glasgow. 263
Healey, Robert J: 1978 Motherwell. 420
Healy, Brendan: 1954 Paisley. 461
Healy, Dermot: 1974 Glasgow. 263
Healy, Jeremiah: 1936 Glasgow. 263
Healy, John J: 1925 Glasgow. 263
Healy, John B: 1954 Motherwell. 421
Healy, Joseph: 1930 St A & E. 26
Healy, Liam: 1956 St A & E. 26
Healy, Thomas: 1899 Glasgow. 263
Healy, Thomas: 1939 Glasgow. 264
Heaney, James: 1911 St A & E. 26
Heaney, Patrick J: 1928 Glasgow. 264
Heaphy, Daniel: 1887 Galloway. 182
Hearty, Thomas: 1942 Glasgow. 264
Heelan, Edward: 1873 Galloway. 182
Heffernan, John M: 1954 Paisley. 461

Heffron, Samuel A: 1918 Galloway. 182
Hegarty, Simon: 1924 Glasgow. 264
Hehir, Denis: 1905 Glasgow. 264
Henderson, James: 1891 Aberdeen. 100
Hendrie, Robert: 1962 St A & E. 26
Hendry, Charles: 1955 Dunkeld. 150
Hendry, Ronald J: 1947 Argyll. 125
Hendry, Thomas J: 1966 Glasgow. 264
Henery, William W: 1948 St A & E. 26
Hennessy, Daniel J: 1948 Motherwell. 421
Hennessy, Francis: 1937 St A & E. 26
Hennessy, Matthew: 1899 Glasgow. 264
Hennessy, Patrick: 1938 Galloway. 182
Hennessy, Patrick A: 1969 Motherwell. 421
Hennessy, Thomas: 1959 St A & E. 26
Henretty, Michael: 1951 Glasgow. 264
Henry, David: 1962 St A & E. 27
Henry, James: 1926 Glasgow. 265
Henry, James: 1970 St A & E. 27
Henry, Patrick J: 1951 Glasow. 265
Heron, Patrick: 1925 Glasgow. 265
Herriott, George: 1966 Paisley. 461
Heslin, Hugh: 1954 Paisley. 461
Hession, Michael J: 1921 St A & E. 27
Hickey, John: 1930 Glasgow. 265
Hickey, Michael P: 1884 Galloway. 182
Hickey, Thomas C: 1950 Motherwell. 421
Hickson, John A: 1880 Galloway. 182
Higgins, Edward J: 1959 Glasgow. 265
Higgins, Jeremiah: 1932 Dunkeld. 150
Higgins, John: 1866 Galloway. 182
Higgins, Joseph: 1914 Glasgow. 265
Higgins, Peter G: 1931 St A & E. 27
Higgins, Richard: 1958 Motherwell. 421
High, James H: 1986 Dunkeld. 151
Hilgers, Peter: 1891 Glasgow. 265
Hill, Gerard C: 1968 Glasgow. 265
Hill, Robert J: 1977 Glasgow. 265
Hillee, Christopher: 1906 Glasgow. 266
Hoban, Denis: 1953 Motherwell. 421
Hoban, Frederick: 1886 St A & E. 27
Hodgson, Reginald J: 1940 St A & E. 27
Hoey, Patrick: 1938 Motherwell. 266
Hogan, James J: 1923 Glasgow. 266
Hogan, Joseph: 1888 Galloway. 182
Hogan, Richard: 1897 St A & E. 27
Hogan, Thomas: 1943 St A & E. 27
Holden, Francis: 1939 St A & E. 27
Holden, Patrick: 1934 St A & E. 28
Holland, Stephen D: 1981 Glasgow. 266
Holland, William: 1902 St A & E. 28
Holloran, Thomas: 1957 Glasgow. 266
Holloway, Michael: 1921 Glasgow. 266
Holmes, John: 1924 Glasgow. 266
Holohan, John J: 1940 St A & E. 28
Holton, Michael: 1937 Dunkeld. 151
Holuka, Ryszard: 1974 St A & E. 28

Hopkins, Francis: 1946 Glasgow. 266
Hopwell, Thomas: 1889 Glasgow. 266
Horan, James: 1936 Glasgow. 267
Horgan, Daniel J: 1898 Glasgow. 267
Horgan, Daniel J: 1919 Glasgow. 267
Horgan, Daniel: 1927 Glasgow. 267
Horgan, Patrick: 1910 St A & E. 28
Horgan, William: 1892 Glasgow. 267
Horne, Iain: 1985 St A & E. 28
Hosie, Andrew C: 1977 Glasgow. 267
Houlihan, Michael: 1943 Glasgow. 267
Houlihan, Patrick: 1882 Glasgow. 267
Hourigan, John: 1883 Galloway. 182
Hourigan, Patrick R: 1906 Glasgow. 268
Howard, James: 1944 Dunkeld. 151
Hughes, Colin T: 1986 Motherwell. 421
Hughes, James: 1904 Glasgow. 268
Hughes, John: 1926 Galloway. 183
Hughes, John A: 1984 Glasgow. 268
Hughes, Martin: 1936 Glasgow. 268
Hughes, Michael: 1881 Glasgow. 268
Humble, James: 1889 Glasgow. 268
Hunkin, Andrew: 1974 Aberdeen. 100
Hunter, Patrick: 1972 Motherwell. 422
Hurley, Denis A: 1954 Glasgow. 268
Hurley, Patrick: 1898 Dunkeld. 151
Hurley, Thomas A: 1960 Glasgow. 268
Hutchison, Douglas: 1985 Galloway. 183
Hyland, Edward: 1940 St A & E. 28
Hynes, Patrick: 1981 Motherwell. 422

Ireland, Jerome: 1940 Argyll. 125
Ireland, Walter: 1940 Argyll. 125
Ivory, Joseph: 1922 Glasgow. 268

Jackson, James A: 1941 Glasgow. 269
Jackson, Michael: 1943 St A & E. 28
Jaconelli, Francis: 1939 Glasgow. 269
Jamieson, Lawrence: 1962 Glasgow. 269
Jamieson, Thomas: 1954 Paisley. 461
Jansen, Martin H: 1889 Glasgow. 269
Jennings, James B: 1898 Galloway. 183
Jennings, John: 1936 Glasgow. 269
Johnston, Alexander: 1947 Glasgow. 269
Johnston, Michael H: 1975 St A & E. 28
Johnstone, Neil A: 1949 Glasgow. 269
Jordan, John Francis: 1972 Glasgow. 270
Joyce, John: 1896 St A & E. 28
Joyce, John B: 1899 St A & E. 29
Joyce, Kiernan: 1919 St A & E. 29
Joyce, Thomas: 1897 Galloway. 183
Judge, Stephen: 1958 St A & E. 29

Kane, Charles: 1955 Glasgow. 270
Kane, Duncan: 1946 Glasgow. 270
Kane, John: 1951 Galloway. 183
Kane, Robert: 1971 Motherwell. 422

Kavanagh, Edward C: 1927 Glasgow. 270
Kay, John G: 1981 Glasgow. 270
Kaye, Peter: 1936 Dunkeld. 151
Keane, Denis: 1949 Motherwell. 422
Keane, Hugh J: 1917 Glasgow. 270
Keane, Simon: 1914 Glasgow. 270
Keane, Stephen A: 1929 Aberdeen. 100
Keane, Thomas: 1925 Glasgow. 270
Kearney, James: 1902 Glasgow. 271
Kearney, John: 1880 Glasgow. 271
Kearney, Patrick: 1890 Dunkeld. 151
Kearney, Thomas: 1880 Glasgow. 271
Kearney, Thomas: 1903 Glasgow. 271
Kearns, Hugh: 1955 Glasgow. 271
Kearns, Michael: 1923 Glasgow. 271
Keating, Lawrence: 1958 Paisley. 462
Keating, Michael F: 1954 Glasgow. 271
Keating, Patrick F: 1912 Glasgow. 271
Keating, William: 1880 Glasgow. 272
Keaveney, Lawrence F: 1948 Paisley. 462
Keegan, Gerard: 1941 Dunkeld. 151
Keegan, James J: 1952 Motherwell. 422
Keegans, Patrick: 1970 Galloway. 183
Keenaghan, James: 1954 Paisley. 462
Keenan, Bernard: 1930 Glasgow. 272
Keenan, Joseph: 1901 Dunkeld. 151
Keenan, Patrick: 1903 Aberdeen. 100
Keith, David: 1948 Aberdeen. 100
Kelleher, Timothy: 1906 Glasgow. 272
Kelly, Adrian J: 1926 Dunkeld. 151
Kelly, Anthony: 1930 St A & E. 29
Kelly, Bernard: 1934 St A & E. 29
Kelly, Charles J: 1941 St A & E. 29
Kelly, Daniel: 1912 St A & E. 29
Kelly, Declan: 1969 Galloway. 183
Kelly, Edward: 1955 Glasgow. 272
Kelly, Francis: 1954 Motherwell. 422
Kelly, Henry: 1937 Dunkeld. 152
Kelly, Hugh J: 1889 Glasgow. 272
Kelly, Hugh: 1933 Glasgow. 272
Kelly, Hugh P: 1967 Motherwell. 422
Kelly, James: 1903 Glasgow. 272
Kelly, John F: 1901 Glasgow. 272
Kelly, John: 1964 Motherwell. 423
Kelly, Martin J: 1965 Motherwell. 423
Kelly, Michael: 1928 St A & E. 30
Kelly, Patrick: 1908 Glasgow. 273
Kelly, Patrick: 1924 Glasgow. 273
Kelly, Patrick: 1927 Glasgow. 273
Kelly, Patrick J: 1951 Glasgow. 273
Kelly, Patrick: 1959 St A & E. 30
Kelly, Paul: 1985 St A & E. 30
Kelly, Thomas (1): 1925 Glasgow. 273
Kelly, Thomas (2): 1925 Glasgow. 273
Kelly, Thomas A: 1926 Dunkeld. 152
Kelly, Walter: 1894 Glasgow. 273
Kelly, William M: 1918 Glasgow. 273

Kelly, William R: 1939 St A & E. 30
Kelly, William J: 1989 Glasgow. 273
Kenneally, Benjamin: 1901 Glasgow. 274
Kenneally, John P: 1916 Glasgow. 274
Kennedy, Alistair: 1901 Aberdeen. 100
Kennedy, Daniel: 1934 Glasgow. 274
Kennedy, Francis: 1970 Dunkeld. 152
Kennedy, Francis: 1970 Glasgow. 274
Kennedy, Ignatius: 1963 Glasgow. 274
Kennedy, James: 1917 Glasgow. 274
Kennedy, James: 1989 Paisley. 462
Kennedy, John: 1936 St A & E. 30
Kennedy, Joseph: 1913 Glasgow. 274
Kennedy, Patrick: 1959 Argyll. 125
Kennedy, Stephen: 1941 Galloway. 183
Kenny, Harry: 1907 St A & E. 30
Kenny, John F: 1908 Glasgow. 274
Kenny, John: 1936 St A & E. 30
Kenny, Lawrence: 1957 Motherwell. 423
Keogh, Daniel: 1893 Galloway. 184
Keogh, William: 1901 Glasgow. 274
Kerr, Alexander: 1926 Dunkeld. 152
Kerr, Alexander S: 1962 Aberdeen. 101
Kerr, Edward N: 1953 St A & E. 30
Kerr, Francis: 1937 St A & E. 30
Kerr, Francis: 1970 St A & E. 31
Kerr, George G: 1933 Aberdeen. 101
Kerr, John: 1933 St A & E. 31
Kerr, John: 1964 Galloway. 184
Kerr, Joseph: 1936 Galloway. 184
Kerr, Joseph: 1951 Glasgow. 274
Kerr, Philip J: 1979 St A & E. 31
Kerrin, Daniel: 1885 Galloway. 184
Kerrisk, John M: 1943 St A & E. 31
Kevany, Patrick: 1928 Glasgow. 275
Kielt, Bernard: 1932 St A & E. 31
Kiernan, Anthony: 1946 St A & E. 31
Kiernan, Francis A: 1948 Galloway. 184
Kierney, Paul J: 1981 Glasgow. 275
Kilcoyne, Anthony: 1934 Glasgow. 275
Kilcoyne, Patrick E: 1955 Motherwell. 423
Kilcullen, John: 1895 Dunkeld. 152
Kilpatrick, Arthur J: 1960 Paisley. 462
Kilpatrick, James: 1935 Glasgow. 275
Kilpatrick, Joseph: 1964 Motherwell. 423
Kilpatrick, Samuel J: 1929 Glasgow. 275
Kilroy, Thomas: 1930 St A & E. 31
Kinane, Edward: 1919 Glasgow. 275
King, John P: 1970 Glasgow. 275
King, Kenneth: 1966 Dunkeld. 152
Kinnane, Louis: 1935 Dunkeld. 152
Kinnane, Michael: 1914 Glasgow. 275
Kinsella, Matthew: 1938 Glasgow. 276
Kinsler, John: 1965 Galloway. 184
Kirby, James: 1966 Glasgow. 276
Kirk, James H: 1888 Glasgow. 276
Kirke, Terence: 1931 St A & E. 31

Klein, Augustine A: 1955 Dunkeld. 152
Knight, Louis: 1949 Glasgow. 276
Kruger, Karl H: 1949 St A & E. 31
Kuhler, Ludger W: 1889 Glasgow. 276
Kuppers, Henry: 1886 Glasgow. 276

Lafferty, James: 1961 Glasgow. 276
Lafferty, Thomas: 1956 Glasgow. 276
Lagan, James: 1909 Glasgow. 276
Lagan, John: 1902 Glasgow. 276
Lalor, Andrew: 1897 Glasgow. 277
Lamb, Brian J: 1988 Motherwell. 423
Lamont, Joseph: 1928 Aberdeen. 101
Lane, Jeremiah: 1943 Glasgow. 277
Langley, Henry: 1893 Galloway. 184
Larkin, Richard: 1950 Aberdeen. 101
Laughton, Herbert R: 1890 St A & E. 32
Lavelle, Michael: 1887 Dunkeld. 152
Lavelle, Michael: 1905 Glasgow. 277
Laverty, Edward: 1948 Motherwell. 423
Laverty, Henry S: 1882 Galloway. 184
Laverty, Henry: 1924 Glasgow. 277
Lavery, John: 1955 Motherwell. 424
Lavery, Samuel J: 1939 Glasgow. 277
Laveth, Francis J: 1895 Glasgow. 277
Lawless, Edward: 1888 Aberdeen. 101
Lawlor, James M: 1987 Glasgow. 277
Lawn, Charles: 1937 Glasgow. 277
Lawson, Alistair: 1966 St A & E. 32
Lawson, George: 1946 Motherwell. 424
Lawton, Edward: 1901 Glasgow. 277
Laydon, Patrick: 1906 Glasgow. 277
Lea, Michael: 1944 Argyll. 125
Leahy, James W: 1925 St A & E. 32
Leckie, James: 1946 St A & E. 32
Lee, John: 1882 Galloway. 184
Lee, Thomas: 1886 St A & E. 32
Leen, John: 1942 Galloway. 184
Leen, Michael: 1947 Galloway. 185
Leggatt, Matthew: 1979 Dunkeld. 153
Leitchman, George: 1938 Dunkeld. 153
Lennon, Peter: 1961 Glasgow. 278
Leonard, Henry S: 1937 Glasgow. 278
Leonard, James: 1900 Glasgow. 278
Leverage, Thomas: 1960 Galloway. 185
Leyden, Charles: 1931 St A & E. 32
Leyne, James: 1924 Glasgow. 278
Lightbody, John: 1955 Glasgow. 278
Lillis, George: 1905 Glasgow. 278
Lillis, James M: 1929 Glasgow. 278
Lillis, Richard: 1946 Glasgow. 278
Lindsay, Edward: 1955 Glasgow. 278
Link, Peter: 1879 Glasgow. 279
Little, John: 1929 Glasgow. 279
Little, Michael: 1934 Glasgow. 279
Littleton, Matthew: 1929 Glasgow. 279

McCarthy, Sean: 1954 St A & E. 36
McCarville, Thomas: 1940 St A & E. 36
McCaulay, Rodger: 1928 Glasgow. 285
McCauley, Augustine H: 1950 Motherwell. 425
McCauley, James: 1947 St A & E. 36
McChrystal, James J: 1917 Glasgow. 285
McClafferty, Manus: 1933 St A & E. 36
McClelland, William: 1934 St A & E. 36
McClement, Frederick: 1890 Argyll. 126
McCluskey, Alexander: 1966 Paisley. 463
McCluskey, Martin: 1959 Galloway. 186
McCluskey, Robert J: 1882 Glasgow. 285
McClymont, Bernard: 1890 Argyll. 126
McClymont, Frederick: 1890 Argyll. 126
McColgan, Edward: 1943 St A & E. 36
McColgan, Gerard: 1953 Motherwell. 425
McColl, Philip: 1886 Glasgow. 285
McConnachie, George: 1899 St A & E. 36
McConnachie, Peter: 1893 Glasgow. 285
McConnell, John B: 1965 Motherwell. 425
McConnell, Michael: 1924 Glasgow. 285
McConville, Timothy B: 1987 St A & E. 36
McCormack, James: 1899 Dunkeld. 154
McCormack, Michael: 1898 Glasgow. 285
McCormack, Patrick: 1929 St A & E. 37
McCormick, Alexander: 1895 Glasgow. 285
McCormick, Alexander: 1918 Glasgow. 285
MacCormick, John: 1939 Argyll. 126
McCranor, Hugh: 1937 Glasgow. 286
McCready, John: 1897 Glasgow. 286
McCready, John: 1935 Glasgow. 286
McCrory, John: 1924 Glasgow. 286
McCruden, James R: 1988 Dunkeld. 154
McCulla, Thomas: 1887 Glasgow. 286
McCullagh, Francis: 1881 Argyll. 126
McCullagh, Michael C: 1947 St A & E. 37
McCurrach, George: 1939 Aberdeen. 101
McCurrach, William: 1899 Dunkeld. 154
McDade, Gerald S: 1926 Glasgow. 286
McDade, William: 1962 Paisley. 463
MacDaid, Denis F: 1924 Glasgow. 286
McDaid, James: 1903 Glasgow. 287
McDaid, Neil F: 1963 Glasgow. 287
McDaniel, John: 1897 Dunkeld. 154
McDaniel, Patrick: 1899 Dunkeld. 154
McDaniel, Peter: 1887 St A & E. 37
McDermott, Francis J: 1943 Dunkeld. 154
McDermott, Henry J: 1952 Galloway. 186
MacDermott, James: 1898 St A & E. 37
McDermott, John B: 1927 Glasgow. 287
McDermott, John P: 1964 Glasgow. 287
McDermott, Joseph: 1941 St A & E. 37
McDermott, Patrick J: 1918 Galloway. 186
McDermott, Vincent P: 1957 Paisley. 463
McDevitt, Kevin: 1968 Motherwell. 425
MacDonald, Alexander: 1895 Glasgow. 287

McDonald, Allan: 1882 Argyll. 126
MacDonald, Angus: 1883 Argyll. 126
MacDonald, Angus J: 1970 Glasgow. 287
MacDonald, Bernard G: 1948 Aberdeen. 101
MacDonald, Brian A: 1982 Aberdeen. 102
MacDonald, Charles: 1891 Aberdeen. 102
MacDonald, Colin: 1923 Aberdeen. 102
McDonald, David: 1882 Aberdeen. 102
MacDonald, Edmund: 1913 Glasgow. 287
MacDonald, Hugh: 1906 Glasgow. 287
McDonald, James V: 1887 Dunkeld. 154
MacDonald, James: 1896 Glasgow. 287
MacDonald, James: 1903 St A & E. 37
McDonald, James: 1914 Argyll. 126
McDonald, James: 1940 St A & E. 37
MacDonald, James: 1989 St A & E. 37
McDonald, John: 1889 Aberdeen. 102
McDonald, John: 1916 Dunkeld. 154
MacDonald, John: 1945 Glasgow. 288
MacDonald, John A: 1970 Argyll. 127
MacDonald, Michael J: 1978 Argyll. 127
MacDonald, Patrick: 1914 Argyll. 127
McDonald, Robert A: 1952 Aberdeen. 102
MacDonald, Roderick: 1949 Argyll. 127
MacDonald, Samuel: 1894 Argyll. 127
MacDonald, Thomas: 1891 Aberdeen. 102
MacDonald, William C: 1889 Argyll. 127
McDonald, William: 1941 Glasgow. 288
McDonell, Archibald J: 1873 Argyll. 127
McDonna, Thomas: 1894 St A & E. 37
McDonnell, George: 1885 Glasgow. 288
McDonnell, James: 1895 Glasgow. 288
MacDonnell, Michael: 1904 Glasgow. 288
MacDougall, Alexander: 1890 Argyll. 127
MacDougall, Donald: 1949 Argyll. 127
McEachen, Angus: 1891 Glasgow. 288
McEleney, Michael J: 1934 Glasgow. 288
McElhenney, Joseph: 1927 St A & E. 38
McElholm, Joseph: 1948 Glasgow. 288
McEllin, Edward: 1936 Glasgow. 288
McElmail, Francis: 1894 Glasgow. 289
MacElmail, John: 1883 Argyll. 128
McElroy, Christopher: 1980 Glasgow. 289
McElroy, John: 1956 Paisley. 463
McElwee, Charles J: 1984 Glasgow. 289
McElwee, Patrick J: 1923 Glasgow. 289
McErlain, Joseph: 1926 Glasgow. 289
McEvoy, Michael: 1943 Dunkeld. 155
MacEvoy, Thomas: 1883 Glasgow. 289
McEwan, Daniel: 1955 Glasgow. 289
McEwan, Hugh G: 1948 Glasgow. 289
McEwan, Hugh J: 1960 Glasgow. 289
McEwan, James: 1934 Glasgow. 290
MacEwan, Sydney: 1944 Argyll. 128
McEwan, Thomas: 1906 Glasgow. 290
McEwan, William J: 1946 St A & E. 38

McFadden, Andrew: 1989 Paisley. 463
McFadden, Charles: 1926 Glasgow. 290
McFadden, Charles: 1950 Glasgow. 290
McFadden, Francis: 1936 Glasgow. 290
McFadden, Patrick: 1955 St A & E. 38
McFadden, William R: 1985 Galloway. 186
McFadyen, William: 1927 Glasgow. 290
McFarlane, Francis J: 1928 St A & E. 38
McFarlane, Henry J: 1967 Galloway. 186
MacFarlane, Malcolm W: 1943 St A & E. 38
MacFarlane, Peter: 1908 Glasgow. 290
MacFarlane, Peter: 1931 St A & E. 38
McFaul, Henry: 1927 Glasgow. 290
McFaul, John: 1941 Glasgow. 290
McGarrigle, George: 1978 Glasgow. 291
McGarrigle, Robert G: 1968 St A & E. 38
McGarrity, Neil A: 1989 Glasgow. 291
McGarry, Alexander: 1958 Galloway. 187
McGarry, Gerard: 1938 St A & E. 38
McGarry, John: 1934 Glasgow. 291
McGarry, Peter: 1978 Paisley. 463
McGarry, William: 1938 St A & E. 39
McGarvey, Thomas: 1925 St A & E. 39
McGee, Brian: 1989 Paisley. 463
McGee, Eugene: 1952 Glasgow. 291
McGee, James E: 1955 St A & E. 39
McGee, John A: 1970 Galloway. 187
McGee, Joseph: 1929 Dunkeld. 155
McGeever, Kevin: 1980 Motherwell. 425
McGennis, Edward: 1919 Glasgow. 291
McGeown, John: 1933 St A & E. 39
McGeown, John: 1938 St A & E. 39
McGettigan, John: 1928 St A & E. 39
McGettigan, Patrick: 1893 St A & E. 39
McGhee, Charles: 1886 Glasgow. 291
McGhee, Edward: 1972 Galloway. 187
McGhee, James: 1961 Glasgow. 291
McGhee, James A: 1962 Paisley. 463
McGhee, William: 1924 Glasgow. 291
McGhie, James: 1957 Dunkeld. 155
McGhie, Thomas: 1930 Glasgow. 291
McGill, George P: 1969 Motherwell. 425
McGill, James: 1941 Glasgow. 292
McGill, Stephen: 1936 Argyll. 128
McGilligan, John: 1915 Galloway. 187
McGinlay, Hugh: 1964 Glasgow. 292
McGinlay, Hugh J: 1977 Glasgow. 292
McGinlay, John J: 1940 Glasgow. 292
McGinley, James: 1946 Glasgow. 292
McGinley, John D: 1968 Glasgow. 292
McGinley, John G: 1985 Glasgow. 292
McGinley, Teague: 1921 Glasgow. 293
McGinley, William: 1962 Glasgow. 293
McGinn, Henry: 1947 Glasgow. 293
McGinness, Samuel: 1956 Glasgow. 293
McGinty, Desmond J: 1968 Glasgow. 293
McGivney, Bernard: 1882 Glasgow. 293

McGladrigan, James: 1960 Glasgow. 293
McGlinchey, Charles: 1914 Glasgow. 293
McGlinchey, Daniel: 1927 Glasgow. 293
McGlinchey, Daniel: 1932 Glasgow. 294
McGlinchey, James: 1959 Motherwell. 426
McGloin, Patrick: 1934 St A & E. 39
McGlynn, Dominic: 1926 Glasgow. 294
McGlynn, James: 1909 St A & E. 40
McGlynn, Timothy: 1970 Glasgow. 294
McGoldrick Columba: 1925 Glasgow. 294
McGoldrick William: 1919 Glasgow. 294
McGonagle, Patrick: 1906 Glasgow. 294
McGovern, Matthew: 1977 St A & E. 40
McGovern, Michael: 1935 St A & E. 40
McGovern, Patrick B (1): 1947 Glasgow. 294
McGovern, Patrick J (2): 1947 Glasgow. 295
McGowan, Clement: 1925 Glasgow. 295
McGrady, Sylvester: 1952 Paisley. 463
McGrail, John: 1925 St A & E. 40
McGrail, Joseph P: 1898 St A & E. 40
McGrain, John: 1911 St A & E. 40
McGrath, Alphonsus B: 1942 St A & E. 40
McGrath, Charles: 1948 Galloway. 187
McGrath, Colman: 1962 Glasgow. 295
McGrath, Denis M: 1927 Glasgow. 295
McGrath, Denis: 1928 Glasgow. 295
McGrath, Jeremiah A: 1910 Glasgow. 295
McGrath, John P: 1944 St A & E. 40
McGrath, Mark: 1901 Glasgow. 295
McGrath, Thomas: 1886 Glasgow. 295
McGread, Thomas J: 1952 Galloway. 187
McGregor, Charles: 1954 Aberdeen. 102
McGregor, James: 1883 Aberdeen. 103
McGregor, Thomas P: 1926 St A & E. 40
McGrorry, John J: 1982 Glasgow. 295
McGrory, James J: 1914 Glasgow. 296
McGrory, John: 1924 Glasgow. 296
McGrory, Neil: 1953 Paisley. 464
McGrory, Thomas: 1913 Glasgow. 296
McGuckin, John: 1937 Glasgow. 296
McGuigan, Patrick: 1947 St A & E. 41
McGuinness, Daniel: 1949 St A & E. 41
McGuire, James: 1968 Dunkeld. 155
McGuire, John: 1968 Glasgow. 296
McGuire, Thomas: 1938 Glasgow. 296
McGurk, Aloysius: 1925 Glasgow. 296
McGurk, Anthony: 1940 Glasgow. 296
McGurk, Hugh: 1945 Glasgow. 296
McGurk, Thomas: 1945 Glasgow. 297
McHale, Eamonn: 1962 Motherwell. 426
McHardy, Joseph: 1899 Galloway. 187
McHardy, Walter: 1912 Aberdeen. 103
McHugh, Francis P: 1956 Galloway. 187
McHugh, Ignatius: 1909 St A & E. 41
McHugh, James: 1959 Galloway. 187

Maguire, Thomas: 1938 Glasgow. 307
Maher, Bernard: 1939 Motherwell. 427
Maher, Gerald: 1945 Glasgow. 307
Maher, Jeremiah: 1892 Glasgow. 307
Maher, Michael: 1939 Motherwell. 428
Maher, Michael: 1950 Motherwell. 428
Maher, Michael: 1968 Motherwell. 428
Mahon, Hugh C: 1944 Glasgow. 307
Mahon, Joseph: 1935 Glasgow. 307
Mahon, Michael: 1926 Glasgow. 307
Mahon, Thomas A: 1951 Paisley. 464
Mahon, William: 1926 Glasgow. 308
Mahoney, Bernard: 1949 Motherwell. 428
Malaney, Hugh: 1947 Aberdeen. 105
Malaney, James: 1945 Dunkeld. 157
Malcolm, John: 1884 Dunkeld. 157
Mallon, Francis J: 1954 Glasgow. 308
Mallon, William: 1929 Glasgow. 308
Malloy, John B: 1926 Dunkeld. 157
Mancini, Ralph: 1954 Galloway. 189
Manders, William: 1912 Aberdeen. 105
Mangan, Francis G: 1918 Glasgow. 308
Mangan, William: 1904 Glasgow. 308
Mann, Andrew: 1980 Aberdeen. 105
Mann, Charles: 1886 Aberdeen. 105
Mann, Robert: 1938 Aberdeen. 105
Manning, James: 1945 Galloway. 189
Manning, John: 1951 Glasgow. 308
Mannion, John C: 1955 Motherwell. 428
Mannion, Thomas G: 1945 Glasgow. 308
Mannion, Thomas: 1946 Glasgow. 308
Marnane, Timothy: 1926 Glasgow. 308
Marr, James: 1917 Aberdeen. 105
Marr, Peter: 1963 Glasgow. 309
Martin, Aidan: 1982 Glasgow. 309
Martin, Donald: 1905 Argyll. 133
Martin, James: 1952 Glasgow. 309
Martin, John J: 1929 Glasgow. 309
Martin, Joseph: 1951 Motherwell. 428
Martin, Michael: 1964 Motherwell. 428
Martin, Thomas: 1936 St A & E. 46
Mason, George: 1891 St A & E. 46
Matheson, Donald: 1899 Aberdeen. 105
Matheson, John A: 1925 Aberdeen. 105
Mathews, Eugene: 1946 Galloway. 189
Matthews, Charles: 1952 Galloway. 189
Matthews, James: 1919 Dunkeld. 157
Maugaruan, Bernard: 1918 Glasgow. 309
Maxwell, James F: 1927 St A & E. 46
Maxwell, Joseph: 1928 Galloway. 189
Meacher, Gerard I: 1977 Glasgow. 309
Meade, John L: 1892 St A & E. 47
Meade, John: 1903 Glasgow. 309
Meagher, Francis: 1960 Glasgow. 309
Meagher, Jeremiah: 1884 Dunkeld. 158
Meagher, Martin: 1901 Galloway. 189
Meaney, Francis: 1917 Galloway. 189

Meany, John C: 1887 Aberdeen. 106
Meechan, Denis: 1931 Glasgow. 309
Meechan, James: 1942 Glasgow. 310
Meechan, Michael: 1939 Glasgow. 310
Meehan, James: 1929 Glasgow. 310
Meehan, James: 1950 Motherwell. 428
Meehan, Thomas: 1897 Glasgow. 310
Meehan, William: 1925 St A & E. 47
Meikleham, Thomas: 1934 Glasgow. 310
Mellon, Edward: 1908 St A & E. 47
Mellon, William H: 1902 St A & E. 47
Melloy, Darby: 1930 Dunkeld. 158
Menton, James: 1924 Glasgow. 310
Meskell, Richard: 1894 Glasgow. 310
Mifsud, Joseph: 1970 St A & E. 47
Miley, Edward I: 1897 St A & E. 47
Miley, Thomas: 1894 St A & E. 47
Millar, Daniel J: 1970 Motherwell. 429
Millar, Thomas: 1978 Motherwell. 429
Milligan, Hugh: 1924 St A & E. 47
Milligan, Robert: 1960 Motherwell. 429
Mills, Joseph P: 1967 Glasgow. 310
Milton, Michael J: 1988 Dunkeld. 158
Minnagh, Hugh: 1920 Galloway. 190
Misset, Francis T: 1929 Glasgow. 311
Mitchell, Alexander J: 1968 St A & E. 48
Moffatt, Vincent: 1960 St A & E. 48
Mohan, Edward: 1932 St A & E. 48
Molloy, Daniel: 1925 Glasgow. 311
Molloy, Francis: 1956 Glasgow. 311
Molloy, Patrick J: 1923 Glasgow. 311
Molloy, William J: 1904 Glasgow. 311
Mollumby, Edmond: 1930 Glasgow. 311
Mollumby, Edward: 1896 Glasgow. 311
Moloney, James: 1907 Glasgow. 311
Moloney, Patrick B: 1922 Paisley. 464
Moloney, Philip: 1906 St A & E. 48
Molumby, Edward: 1930 Glasgow. 312
Monaghan, Andrew G: 1964 St A & E. 48
Monaghan, James: 1940 St A & E. 48
Monaghan, James: 1952 Motherwell. 429
Monaghan, Thomas M: 1882 St A & E. 48
Monaghan, Thomas J: 1969 Paisley: 465
Monaghan, William: 1974 Glasgow. 312
Mone, John: 1952 Glasgow. 312
Mone, William: 1955 Glasgow. 312
Montgomery, James: 1910 Glasgow. 312
Montgomery, John: 1883 Glasgow. 312
Moonan, Lawrence: 1960 St A & E. 48
Mooney, Henry: 1947 Paisley. 465
Mooney, Michael: 1944 Glasgow. 312
Moore, Daniel: 1942 Glasgow. 312
Moore, Francis P: 1960 Galloway. 190
Moore, James: 1877 Aberdeen. 106
Moore, Peter J: 1932 Glasgow. 313
Moore, Thomas J: 1919 St A & E. 48
Moran, Peter: 1959 Glasgow. 313

Morgan, Frederick: 1957 St A & E. 49
Morgan, George: 1975 Glasgow. 313
Morgan, Vaughan F: 1957 St A & E. 49
Morgan, William: 1939 Glasgow. 313
Moriarty, Brendan: 1937 Glasgow. 313
Moriarty, Francis: 1954 St A & E. 49
Moriarty, Myles P: 1935 Galloway. 190
Morren, Brian: 1965 Glasgow. 313
Morris, Charles: 1977 Motherwell. 429
Morris, David: 1889 Glasgow. 313
Morris, Gerard: 1924 Glasgow. 313
Morris, James: 1973 Motherwell. 429
Morris, Michael: 1906 Glasgow. 313
Morris, Richard J: 1958 Paisley. 465
Morris, Thomas C: 1953 Motherwell. 429
Morrison, Donald: 1900 Argyll. 133
Morrison, Edward: 1916 St A & E. 49
Morrison, James F: 1884 Glasgow. 314
Morrison, John: 1938 Argyll. 133
Morrison, Malcolm: 1935 Argyll. 133
Morrison, Patrick: 1895 Argyll. 134
Morrison, Peter: 1922 Glasgow. 314
Morrissey, Michael B: 1909 Glasgow. 314
Morrow, James: 1958 Paisley. 465
Mortimer, Ronald: 1884 Glasgow. 314
Morton, Paul: 1985 Motherwell. 429
Moss, John: 1943 Glasgow. 314
Moss, Patrick J: 1950 Motherwell. 429
Muldoon, John: 1959 Glasgow. 314
Muldoon, Leo: 1964 Motherwell. 430
Mulhall, Joseph: 1949 Glasgow. 314
Mulhern, James: 1905 St A & E. 49
Mulholland, Patrick: 1915 Galloway. 190
Mullan, George: 1886 St A & E. 49
Mullan, James: 1917 St A & E. 49
Mullan, John D: 1946 St A & E. 49
Mullen, Alphonsus: 1919 Glasgow. 314
Mullen, George: 1937 Glasgow. 314
Mullen, Ian: 1978 Dunkeld. 158
Mullen, James: 1891 Glasgow. 315
Mullen, Thomas: 1977 St A & E. 49
Mullen, William: 1901 Glasgow. 315
Muller, Peter: 1884 Glasgow. 315
Mulligan, William: 1904 Aberdeen. 106
Mullin, James: 1890 Glasgow. 315
Mullins, Anthony: 1901 Glasgow. 315
Mullins, Denis: 1940 St A & E. 49
Mullins, Richard F: 1879 Galloway. 190
Mulvenna, Hugh: 1934 Galloway. 190
Mulvenna, James A: 1907 Glasgow. 315
Mulvey, Michael: 1908 Glasgow. 315
Mulvey, Michael: 1908 St A & E. 50
Mulvihill, Thomas: 1892 St A & E. 50
Mulvihill, Thomas: 1920 Glasgow. 315
Munnelly, Michael: 1921 Glasgow. 316
Murdoch, Andrew: 1897 Aberdeen. 106
Murdoch, Charles: 1894 St A & E. 50

Murdoch, William: 1924 Aberdeen. 106
Murie, David: 1889 Glasgow. 316
Murie, Peter A: 1919 Glasgow. 316
Murnin, Michael: 1927 St A & E. 50
Murphy, Alexander C: 1956 St A & E. 50
Murphy, Brendan: 1940 Glasgow. 316
Murphy, Damian M: 1976 Motherwell. 430
Murphy, Daniel: 1914 St A & E. 50
Murphy, Edward J: 1945 St A & E. 50
Murphy, Edward A: 1966 Argyll. 134
Murphy, Francis: 1941 Glasgow. 316
Murphy, James: 1935 Glasgow. 316
Murphy, James: 1943 Glasgow. 316
Murphy, James: 1947 Glasgow. 316
Murphy, John: 1880 St A & E. 50
Murphy, John L: 1881 Glasgow. 316
Murphy, John J: 1901 Glasgow. 317
Murphy, John N: 1903 Galloway. 190
Murphy, John: 1908 Galloway. 190
Murphy, John J: 1914 Glasgow. 317
Murphy, John J: 1923 Glasgow. 317
Murphy, John J: 1924 St A & E. 50
Murphy, John: 1954 Galloway. 191
Murphy, John G: 1965 Dunkeld. 158
Murphy, Joseph: 1954 Glasgow. 317
Murphy, Martin: 1912 Glasgow. 317
Murphy, Michael: 1907 Aberdeen. 106
Murphy, Michael J: 1922 Glasgow. 317
Murphy, Michael J: 1950 Motherwell. 430
Murphy, Nicholas F: 1945 Galloway. 191
Murphy, Patrick: 1880 Galloway. 191
Murphy, Patrick: 1905 Glasgow. 317
Murphy, Peter J: 1943 Glasgow. 317
Murphy, Peter: 1948 Paisley. 465
Murphy, Peter: 1969 Glasgow. 317
Murphy, Philip: 1920 St A & E. 50
Murphy, Sean: 1948 Galloway. 191
Murphy, Thomas A: 1915 Glasgow. 317
Murphy, Thomas P: 1932 Glasgow. 317
Murphy, Thomas: 1943 Galloway. 191
Murphy, Thomas: 1948 Glasgow. 318
Murphy, William: 1907 Glasgow. 318
Murphy, William: 1919 St A & E. 51
Murphy, William: 1952 Glasgow. 318
Murray, Eugene: 1909 Glasgow. 318
Murray, Ian: 1956 St A & E. 51
Murray, John: 1893 Glasgow. 318
Murray, John V: 1934 Glasgow. 318
Murray, Joseph: 1906 Glasgow. 318
Murray, Joseph: 1974 St A & E. 51
Murray, Michael: 1889 Dunkeld. 158
Murray, Michael J: 1911 Glasgow. 318
Murray, Noel: 1954 Glasgow. 318
Murray, Paul G: 1988 Glasgow. 318
Murray, Peter: 1894 Glasgow. 319
Murray, Thomas J: 1916 Glasgow. 319
Murray, Thomas: 1936 Glasgow. 319

O'Farrell, Peter: 1962 Glasgow. 325
O'Farrell, Thomas: 1889 Galloway. 192
O'Flaherty, James: 1917 St A & E. 53
O'Flaherty, Patrick: 1929 Glasgow. 325
O'Flynn, Daniel: 1945 Glasgow. 326
O'Flynn, Florence: 1939 Glasgow. 326
O'Flynn, Jeremiah: 1936 Glasgow. 326
O'Freil, Thomas: 1939 Glasgow. 326
Ogilvie, Maxwell: 1918 Dunkeld. 159
O'Gorman, Benedict: 1942 Galloway. 192
O'Grady, John: 1906 Glasgow. 326
O'Grady, Martin: 1952 Motherwell. 431
O'Grady, Michael D: 1966 Glasgow. 326
O'Hagan, John: 1955 Glasgow. 326
O'Hagan, Joseph: 1936 Glasgow. 326
O'Halloran, John: 1962 Glasgow. 326
O'Halloran, Patrick: 1898 Glasgow. 326
O'Halloran, Thomas: 1918 Glasgow. 326
O'Hanlon, Bernard: 1920 St A & E. 53
O'Hanlon, Edmund: 1913 Glasgow. 327
O'Hanlon, James: 1937 St A & E. 53
O'Hanlon, John: 1906 Galloway. 192
O'Hanlon, John: 1912 Glasgow. 327
O'Hanlon, Thomas: 1912 Glasgow. 327
O'Hara, Edward: 1942 Glasgow. 327
O'Hara, James: 1968 Motherwell. 432
O'Hara, John G: 1951 Glasgow. 327
O'Hare, James M: 1967 Glasgow. 327
O'Hare, Patrick: 1953 Motherwell. 432
O'Hare, Thomas: 1959 Motherwell. 432
O'Hea, Jeremiah: 1882 Dunkeld. 159
O'Hea, Timothy: 1884 Glasgow. 327
O'Herlihy, Daniel J: 1904 Glasgow. 327
O'Kane, Edmund: 1880 St A & E. 53
O'Kane, Henry: 1938 Glasgow. 327
O'Kane, Jeremiah: 1937 Glasgow. 327
O'Kane, Robert: 1942 Glasgow. 327
O'Kane, Thomas J: 1927 Glasgow. 328
O'Keefe, Andrew J: 1912 Glasgow. 328
O'Keefe, Daniel: 1924 Glasgow. 328
O'Keefe, Thomas: 1911 St A & E. 53
O'Keeffe, Benedict: 1960 Paisley. 466
O'Keeffe, Martin: 1954 Motherwell. 432
O'Keeffe, Michael: 1882 Glasgow. 328
O'Keeffe, Michael: 1948 Glasgow. 328
O'Kelleher, Timothy: 1907 Glasgow. 328
O'Kelly, Sean: 1962 St A & E. 53
O'Kennedy, Michael: 1907 Glasgow. 328
O'Leary, Cornelius: 1926 Glasgow. 328
O'Leary, Cornelius F: 1962 Motherwell. 432
O'Leary, Daniel: 1940 Glasgow. 328
O'Leary, Jeremiah: 1927 Glasgow. 329
O'Leary, Joseph: 1901 Glasgow. 329
O'Leary, Michael: 1909 St A & E. 53
O'Leary, Michael C: 1956 Motherwell. 432
O'Leary, Norbert: 1920 Glasgow. 329
O'Leary, Patrick: 1932 St A & E. 53

Oliver, Leonard A: 1976 St A & E. 54
O'Loughlin, Patrick: 1923 Glasgow. 329
O'Mahony, Humphrey: 1961 Motherwell. 432
O'Mahony, John: 1910 Glasgow. 329
O'Mahony, John: 1915 Glasgow. 329
O'Mahony, Liam: 1951 St A & E. 54
O'Mahony, Patrick: 1922 Glasgow. 329
O'Mahony, Timothy: 1922 Glasgow. 329
O'Malley, Charles J: 1889 Galloway. 192
O'Meara, Gerard J: 1956 Glasgow. 329
O'Meara, Maurice: 1936 St A & E. 54
Ommer, Francis G: 1960 Galloway. 192
O'Neil, William J: 1974 Glasgow. 329
O'Neill, Anthony: 1898 Glasgow. 330
O'Neill, Henry: 1933 St A & E. 54
O'Neill, James: 1887 Glasgow. 330
O'Neill, James A: 1892 Argyll. 134
O'Neill, James A: 1929 Glasgow. 330
O'Neill, John: 1884 Dunkeld. 159
O'Neill, John: 1988 Glasgow. 330
O'Neill, Michael: 1965 Motherwell. 432
O'Neill, Sean V: 1951 Glasgow. 330
O'Neill, Thomas J: 1931 Glasgow. 330
O'Neill, Vincent: 1963 Motherwell. 432
Ooghe, Alphonsus: 1895 Glasgow. 330
O'Raw, William: 1900 St A & E. 54
O'Regan, Bartholomew: 1956 Motherwell. 433
O'Regan, David W: 1961 Motherwell. 433
O'Regan, Patrick: 1930 Argyll. 134
O'Reilly, Daniel: 1930 St A & E. 54
O'Reilly, Dermot: 1916 Galloway. 193
O'Reilly, Francis: 1891 St A & E. 54
O'Reilly, James T: 1938 St A & E. 54
O'Reilly, James: 1950 Glasgow. 330
O'Reilly, Michael: 1939 St A & E. 54
O'Reilly, Philip: 1941 Glasgow. 330
O'Riordan, Charles: 1920 Glasgow. 331
O'Riordan, Edward: 1949 Motherwell. 433
O'Riordan, Jeremiah: 1960 Motherwell. 433
O'Riordan, John: 1929 Glasgow. 331
O'Riordan, Michael L: 1925 Glasgow. 331
O'Rorke, Thomas: 1933 Aberdeen. 107
O'Rourke, Francis: 1955 Glasgow. 331
O'Rourke, Thomas: 1914 Dunkeld. 160
O'Rourke, Thomas: 1961 Glasgow. 331
Orr, William: 1896 Glasgow. 331
Osborne, Patrick: 1959 Glasgow. 331
Osei-Bonsu, Joseph: (-) Aberdeen. 107
O'Shea, John: 1899 Glasgow. 331
O'Shea, Sean: 1949 Motherwell. 433
O'Shea, Thomas E: 1918 Dunkeld. 160
O'Shea, Timothy: 1897 Glasgow. 331
O'Sullivan, Basil: 1956 Dunkeld. 160
O'Sullivan, Daniel: 1895 Glasgow. 332

Redmond, Charles B: 1944 Aberdeen. 107
Reen, Andrew: 1953 Motherwell. 434
Reen, Denis: 1950 Paisley. 466
Regan, Joseph: 1936 Glasgow. 336
Regan, Matthew: 1934 St A & E. 58
Regan, Michael B: 1982 St A & E. 58
Regan, William: 1931 St A & E. 58
Reid, Andrew: 1951 Paisley. 466
Reid, Henry: 1961 St A & E. 58
Reid, Robert: 1965 Galloway. 194
Reifenrath, Aloysius: 1891 Glasgow. 336
Reilly, Brian C: 1977 Glasgow. 336
Reilly, James V: 1945 Glasgow. 337
Reilly, Owen J: 1986 Dunkeld. 161
Reilly, Patrick: 1908 Glasgow. 337
Reilly, Patrick T: 1988 Paisley. 467
Reilly, Thomas: 1936 Glasgow. 337
Renfrew, Charles: 1953 Glasgow. 337
Renucci, Bruno: 1954 Glasgow. 337
Reynolds, Robert: 1908 St A & E. 58
Rhatigan, Thomas: 1947 St A & E. 59
Rice, Patrick: 1924 St A & E. 59
Rice, Patrick: 1938 Glasgow. 337
Richen, Laurence: 1879 Glasgow. 337
Rigg, George: 1891 Argyll. 134
Riordan, Charles: 1920 Glasgow. 337
Riordan, James: 1924 St A & E. 59
Ritchie, George: 1882 Glasgow. 338
Ritchie, John: 1880 Glasgow. 338
Ritter, Henry F: (-) Aberdeen. 107
Roberts, John: 1953 Glasgow. 338
Robertson, David: 1895 St A & E. 59
Robertson, Donald: 1929 Glasgow. 338
Robertson, James K: 1937 Aberdeen. 107
Robertson, John: 1958 Dunkeld. 161
Robinson, John G: 1972 St A & E. 59
Robson, James G: 1953 Aberdeen. 108
Robson, Stephen: 1979 St A & E. 59
Roche, Alfred P: 1878 St A & E. 59
Roche, Alphonsus: 1906 Dunkeld. 161
Roche, John: 1899 Dunkeld. 161
Roche, John: 1903 Glasgow. 338
Roche, John: 1910 Glasgow. 338
Roche, Joseph: 1899 Dunkeld. 161
Roche, Michael: 1915 Glasgow. 338
Roche, Richard: 1923 St A & E. 59
Roche, Stephen: 1915 Galloway. 194
Roche, Thomas: 1888 Dunkeld. 161
Rochead, James: 1882 Glasgow. 338
Rodgers, George E: 1969 St A & E. 59
Rodgers, Richard J: 1960 Motherwell. 434
Rogan, Ellis P: 1887 Glasgow. 338
Rogan, John: 1927 Glasgow. 338
Roger, John: 1903 Aberdeen. 108
Roger, John: 1927 Glasgow. 339
Rogers, Gerard: 1931 Glasgow. 339
Rogers, Herbert G: 1930 Glasgow. 339

Rogers, James K: 1953 Motherwell. 434
Rogers, Patrick: 1930 Glasgow. 339
Rogerson, John: 1947 St A & E. 60
Ronan, James: 1919 Glasgow. 339
Ronayne, Maurice: 1900 Glasgow. 339
Rooney, Andrew J: 1956 Dunkeld. 161
Rooney, Charles: 1931 Galloway. 194
Rooney, Daniel: 1972 Motherwell. 434
Rooney, Gerard: 1971 Motherwell. 434
Rooney, Gerard P: 1974 St A & E. 60
Rooney, John A: 1924 Glasgow. 339
Rooney, William: 1884 St A & E. 60
Ross, John: 1939 Dunkeld. 161
Ross, William: 1913 Aberdeen. 108
Rossi, Gaetano: 1939 Glasgow. 340
Rota, Francis: 1913 Glasgow. 340
Rourke, Patrick J: 1941 St A & E. 60
Rourke, Thomas B: 1913 Glasgow. 340
Rowan, Nicholas: 1947 Glasgow. 340
Ruane, Austin: 1949 Glasgow. 340
Russell, Robert G: 1901 Dunkeld. 162
Ryan, Christopher J: 1968 Glasgow. 340
Ryan, Edmund J: 1886 Galloway. 194
Ryan, Edmund: 1925 Glasgow. 340
Ryan, Edward: 1921 Glasgow. 340
Ryan, George J: 1901 Glasgow. 340
Ryan, James: 1885 Dunkeld. 162
Ryan, James: 1919 St A & E. 60
Ryan, James: 1967 Glasgow. 341
Ryan, John: 1913 Glasgow. 341
Ryan, John: 1944 St A & E. 60
Ryan, John: 1950 Glasgow. 341
Ryan, Michael: 1924 St A & E. 60
Ryan, Michael: 1959 Motherwell. 435
Ryan, Patrick: 1892 Glasgow. 341
Ryan, Peter: 1927 Dunkeld. 162
Ryan, Robert: 1949 Glasgow. 341
Ryan, Thomas: 1950 Paisley. 467
Ryan, William: 1912 Glasgow. 341
Rynn, Michael: 1928 Glasgow. 341
Rynn, Sean: 1965 Glasgow. 341

Saddler, Brian W: 1969 St A & E. 60
Saunderson, William: 1906 St A & E. 60
Savage, Michael C: 1983 Glasgow. 341
Savage, Thomas: 1944 St A & E. 60
Scahill, Patrick J: 1953 Paisley. 467
Scanlan, Edward: 1934 Galloway. 194
Scanlan, William: 1899 Glasgow. 341
Scanlon, James J: 1918 Glasgow. 342
Scanlon, John J: 1919 Glasgow. 342
Scannell, Daniel: 1900 Glasgow. 342
Scannell, Denis: 1902 Glasgow. 342
Scannell, John: 1890 Glasgow. 342
Scott, Bryan: 1942 St A & E. 61
Scott, James: 1919 St A & E. 61

Scott, Walter: 1960 Motherwell. 435
Scullion, Daniel: 1931 Glasgow. 342
Sewards, Richard H: 1960 Glasgow. 342
Sexton, Peter: 1925 Glasgow. 342
Shaffrey, Patrick: 1881 Galloway. 195
Shaffrey, Patrick: 1881 Argyll. 134
Shankland, David A: 1986 Paisley. 467
Shannon, Hugh D: 1970 St A & E. 61
Sharkey, Alphonsus: 1934 Dunkeld. 162
Sharkey, Michael: 1983 Glasgow. 342
Sharkey, Thomas: 1935 Glasgow. 343
Sharp, James: 1967 Paisley. 467
Sharp, Neil: 1970 Paisley. 467
Sharpley, Charles: 1925 St A & E. 61
Shaw, George P: 1899 Aberdeen. 108
Shaw, William: 1882 Aberdeen. 108
Shaw, William: 1911 Aberdeen. 108
Sheahan, Andrew C: 1961 Motherwell. 435
Sheahan, Denis J: 1955 Paisley. 467
Sheahan, Maurice: 1871 Dunkeld. 162
Sheahan, Philip: 1889 St A & E. 61
Sheary, John J: 1965 Glasgow. 343
Sheary, John: 1969 Glasgow. 343
Sheary, Joseph: 1942 Glasgow. 343
Sheary, Patrick J: 1935 Glasgow. 343
Sheehan, Daniel V: 1920 Glasgow. 343
Sheehan, Denis M: 1915 Glasgow. 343
Sheehan, Denis: 1918 Glasgow. 343
Sheehan, James: 1947 Glasgow. 343
Sheehan, Michael: 1879 Argyll. 134
Sheehan, Michael: 1920 Glasgow. 344
Sheehan, Patrick: 1906 Glasgow. 344
Sheehan, Thomas G: 1953 Motherwell. 435
Sheehy, John: 1884 Galloway. 195
Sheehy, John J: 1890 Glasgow. 344
Sheehy, Patrick: 1898 Dunkeld. 162
Sheridan, Charles: 1933 Glasgow. 344
Sheridan, Hugh: 1943 Aberdeen. 108
Sheridan, Hugh: 1955 Motherwell. 435
Sheridan, John A: 1931 Glasgow. 344
Sheridan, John: 1956 Glasgow. 344
Sheridan, Michael G: 1960 Paisley. 467
Sheridan, Patrick: 1903 Glasgow. 344
Sheridan, Patrick A: 1928 Glasgow. 344
Sheridan, William J: 1907 Glasgow. 344
Shields, Thomas J: 1989 Dunkeld. 162
Shiels, Andrew: 1954 St A & E. 61
Shiels, James: 1973 Motherwell. 435
Shiels, Matthew: 1928 Glasgow. 345
Shine, James: 1908 Dunkeld. 162
Shinnick, Joseph: 1901 Glasgow. 345
Shivers, Patrick: 1883 St A & E. 61
Shvaeistris, Antony: 1906 Glasgow. 345
Sieger, Joseph: 1906 Glasgow. 345
Simcox, James: 1953 Glasgow. 345
Simpson, Daniel: 1955 St A & E. 61
Simpson, John: 1900 Aberdeen. 108

Sinnott, Gerald: 1926 St A & E. 61
Sinnott, John: 1926 St A & E. 61
Slattery, James: 1912 Glasgow. 345
Slattery, John: 1907 St A & E. 62
Slavin, William J: 1964 Glasgow. 345
Sloan, Michael: 1974 St A & E. 62
Slorach, James: 1894 Aberdeen. 109
Small, James: 1960 Motherwell. 435
Smith, Alexander M: 1947 Aberdeen. 109
Smith, Anthony: 1938 St A & E. 62
Smith, Bernard A: 1912 St A & E. 62
Smith, Brendan: 1956 Motherwell. 436
Smith, Donald A: 1943 Glasgow. 345
Smith, Gerard C: 1980 Paisley. 468
Smith, James: 1989 St A & E. 62
Smith, John: 1896 Galloway. 195
Smith, John: 1973 St A & E. 62
Smith, Patrick: 1939 Glasgow. 345
Smith, Peter: 1940 St A & E. 62
Smith, Peter: 1984 Glasgow. 345
Smith, Stanislaus J: 1952 St A & E. 62
Smith, Thomas: 1886 Glasgow. 346
Smith, William J: 1932 Glasgow. 346
Smith-Steinmetz, Alfred: 1905 St A & E. 62
Smith-Steinmetz, Alistair: 1903 St A & E. 62
Smyth, James: 1902 Glasgow. 346
Smyth, Kevin A: 1944 Dunkeld. 162
Smyth, Patrick: 1899 Glasgow. 346
Smyth, Peter: 1944 St A & E. 63
Somers, Richard: 1945 St A & E. 63
Sproul, William P: 1958 Motherwell. 436
Sreenan, Hugh J: 1962 Dunkeld. 163
Sreenan, Patrick: 1906 Glasgow. 346
Stack, Gerald: 1887 Glasgow. 346
Stanley, Charles: 1960 Aberdeen. 109
Staples, Francis: 1947 St A & E. 63
Steven, Francis A: 1894 Glasgow. 346
Stewart, Colin J: 1982 Aberdeen. 109
Stewart, Daniel: 1891 Glasgow. 346
Stewart, Paul: 1974 Motherwell. 436
Stone, Duncan: 1942 Aberdeen. 109
Stopani, William: 1911 Glasgow. 346
Strain, Desmond: 1949 Glasgow. 347
Stretch, Walter R: 1903 Dunkeld. 163
Strickland, William J: 1945 Glasgow. 347
Stuart, Alexander: 1883 St A & E. 63
Stuart, Douglas G: 1929 Aberdeen. 109
Stuart, George: 1908 Glasgow. 347
Stuart, Hamish: 1936 Dunkeld. 163
Stuart, John L: 1895 St A & E. 63
Stuart, John: 1896 Dunkeld. 163
Stuart, John: 1913 Glasgow. 347
Stuart, Robert L: 1953 Aberdeen. 109
Stuart, William: 1879 Aberdeen. 109
Sullivan, Alexander D: 1929 Aberdeen. 110
Sullivan, Joseph E: 1986 Glasgow. 347

Sullivan, Michael J: 1955 Motherwell. 436
Sutton, William: 1890 Glasgow. 347
Sweeney, Anthony A: 1974 Glasgow. 347
Sweeney, Antony: 1894 Dunkeld. 163
Sweeney, Bernard J: 1903 Glasgow. 347
Sweeney, Eamonn Jude: 1969 Motherwell. 436
Sweeney, James: 1930 Glasgow. 347
Sweeney, Joseph P: 1903 Glasgow. 348
Sweeney, Joseph: 1927 Glasgow. 348
Sweeney, Joseph: 1935 St A & E. 63
Sweeney, Michael J: 1925 Glasgow. 348
Sweeney, Peter: 1975 Glasgow. 348
Symon, John: 1953 Aberdeen. 110
Synnott, Henry: 1912 Glasgow. 348

Tabone, Loreto: 1974 St A & E. 63
Taggart, Francis P: 1913 Glasgow. 348
Tangney, Nicholas: 1918 Glasgow. 348
Tansey, Anthony: 1953 Glasgow. 348
Tartaglia, Gerard: 1985 Glasgow. 348
Tartaglia, Philip: 1975 Glasgow. 349
Taylor, Alexander: 1903 Glasgow. 349
Taylor, Charles: 1910 St A & E. 63
Taylor, Christopher G: 1977 Motherwell. 436
Taylor, John: 1879 Glasgow. 349
Taylor, John: 1972 Motherwell. 436
Taylor, Maurice: 1950 Motherwell. 436
Taylor, Thomas N: 1897 Glasgow. 349
Taylor, Thomas J: 1934 Glasgow. 349
Tedeschi, Sabatino: 1959 Glasgow. 349
Teehan, Michael: 1928 Glasgow. 349
Templeton, Iain: 1986 Aberdeen. 110
Tennant, John R: 1914 Glasgow. 349
Terry, Joseph: 1949 Argyll. 134
Thain, Charles: 1927 Aberdeen. 110
Thompson, Frederick: 1952 Glasgow. 350
Thompson, George: 1989 Galloway. 195
Thomson, Alexander: 1899 Aberdeen. 110
Thomson, Andrew: 1879 Aberdeen. 110
Thomson, Francis: 1946 St A & E. 64
Thomson, James: 1963 St A & E. 64
Thomson, James: 1988 Motherwell. 437
Thomson, Joseph: 1895 Aberdeen. 110
Thornhill, Richard: 1914 St A & E. 64
Thornton, Stephen A: 1896 Glasgow. 350
Tierney, Patrick: 1947 Glasgow. 350
Tierney, Thomas: 1952 Glasgow. 350
Toal, James A: 1965 Galloway. 195
Toal, Joseph: 1980 Argyll. 134
Tobin, John: 1950 Glasgow. 350
Tobin, Patrick: 1948 Glasgow. 350
Tobin, William: 1949 Glasgow. 350
Toher, Patrick: 1951 Glasgow. 350
Tolan, Andrew: 1956 Glasgow. 351

Tollan, William M: 1986 Dunkeld: 163
Toman, Sidney: 1922 Aberdeen. 110
Toncher, Guido: 1909 Glasgow. 351
Toner, John: 1882 Glasgow. 351
Toner, Stephen D: 1983 St A & E. 64
Tonner, James F: 1908 St A & E. 64
Torley, Patrick: 1918 Glasgow. 351
Tormey, John: 1981 Paisley. 468
Torsney, Nicholas: 1950 St A & E. 64
Tosh, Alistair G: 1963 Galloway. 195
Towey, Dominic: 1970 Motherwell. 437
Towie, James: 1895 Glasgow. 351
Toy, Daniel: 1934 Glasgow. 351
Tracey, David: 1962 Glasgow. 351
Tracey, James G: 1988 St A & E. 64
Tracy, Peter: 1897 Glasgow. 351
Trainer, David: 1968 Glasgow. 351
Trainor, William J: 1903 Galloway. 195
Travers, Peter: 1928 Glasgow. 352
Traynor, Edward P: 1985 Aberdeen. 110
Traynor, James G: 1934 Glasgow. 352
Traynor, Owen: 1934 Glasgow. 352
Treanor, Charles J: 1914 Glasgow. 352
Trench, Thomas C: 1967 Motherwell. 437
Tritschler, Ferdinand C: 1929 Glasgow. 352
Troy, James: 1907 Glasgow. 352
Tully, Edward: 1941 Galloway. 195
Tunn, Andrew: 1930 Motherwell. 437
Turner, James: 1937 St A & E. 64
Turner, Michael J: 1879 St A & E. 64
Tweedie, John G: 1949 St A & E. 65

Urquhart, James: 1896 Aberdeen. 111
Urquhart, John: 1959 St A & E. 65

Vaccaro, Guido: 1948 Glasgow. 352
Vallely Charles: 1941 Glasgow. 352
Van der Heyde, Adrian: 1884 Glasgow. 353
Van Hecke, Joseph: 1879 Glasgow. 353
Van Wyk, William: 1881 Glasgow. 353
Vasiliauskas, Francis: 1893 Glasgow. 353
Vaughan, Edward: 1904 Glasgow. 353
Vaughan, Kieran S: 1957 Galloway. 195
Vesey, Edward: 1962 Glasgow. 353
Vignoles, Reginald: 1886 Galloway. 195

Waldron, John A: 1903 Glasgow. 353
Waldron, Patrick: 1905 Glasgow. 353
Waleczek, Aloysius: 1939 Aberdeen. 111
Walker, Vincent: 1941 Galloway. 196
Wall, John: 1916 Glasgow. 353
Wall, Thomas: 1911 Glasgow. 353
Wallace, James: 1957 Glasgow. 353
Walls, John: 1961 Galloway. 196

Walls, Michael J: 1935 St A & E. 65
Walls, Ronald J: 1977 Aberdeen. 111
Walsh, Andrew: 1939 St A & E. 65
Walsh, Frank: 1925 Aberdeen. 111
Walsh, James: 1924 Glasgow. 354
Walsh, James B: 1925 Glasgow. 354
Walsh, James B: 1939 St A & E. 65
Walsh, James L: 1960 Glasgow. 354
Walsh, James F: 1962 Glasgow. 354
Walsh, John: 1901 Glasgow. 354
Walsh, John: 1947 St A & E. 65
Walsh, John: 1950 Galloway. 196
Walsh, Joseph: 1978 Glasgow. 354
Walsh, Michael J: 1938 Glasgow. 354
Walsh, Michael: 1947 St A & E. 65
Walsh, Michael: 1959 Motherwell. 437
Walsh, Nicholas: 1919 Glasgow. 354
Walsh, Patrick: 1949 Motherwell. 437
Walsh, Thomas: 1933 St A & E. 65
Walsh, William: 1900 Glasgow. 354
Walshe, Austin: 1899 Argyll. 134
Walshe, James: 1937 Glasgow. 355
Walshe, Maurice: 1951 St A & E. 65
Walshe, Peter F: 1914 Glasgow. 355
Ward, Alphonsus: 1898 Glasgow. 355
Ward, David F: 1962 Dunkeld. 164
Ward, Dolty: 1930 St A & E. 65
Ward, James C: 1928 Glasgow. 355
Ward, James: 1929 Glasgow. 355
Ward, James: 1945 Dunkeld. 164
Ward, John: 1927 St A & E. 65
Ward, John: 1934 St A & E. 66
Ward, John L: 1957 Motherwell. 437
Ward, John F: 1969 Glasgow. 355
Ward, Joseph A: 1922 St A & E. 66
Ward, Maurice: 1960 Glasgow. 355
Ward, Michael: 1924 Glasgow. 355
Warnagiris, Vincent: 1886 Glasgow. 355
Warran, John T: 1904 Dunkeld. 164
Watson, William S: 1918 Aberdeen. 111
Watt, Archibald: 1924 Glasgow. 356
Watt, Thomas: 1938 St A & E. 66
Watters, James F: 1932 Glasgow. 356
Webb, Charles: 1889 Glasgow. 356

Webb, James: 1913 Argyll. 135
Welsh, Anthony: 1970 Glasgow. 356
Welsh, Francis: 1981 St A & E. 66
Welsh, Thomas: 1893 Dunkeld. 164
Welsh, Walter: 1912 St A & E. 66
Wheeler, William: 1936 Galloway. 196
Whelahan, Michael: 1917 St A & E. 66
White, Anthony: 1958 Galloway. 196
White, Daniel B: 1936 Glasgow. 356
White, Hugh G: 1963 St A & E. 66
White, James: 1932 St A & E. 67
White, Joseph: 1924 Glasgow. 356
White, Justin: 1901 Glasgow. 356
White, William: 1936 Glasgow. 356
White, William: 1953 Motherwell. 438
Whitty, Kevin: 1931 Glasgow. 356
Whitty, Thomas J: 1884 Argyll. 135
Wiggans, Robert: 1936 St A & E. 67
Wilkinson, Joseph: 1948 Glasgow. 357
Wilson, Alan J: 1977 Galloway. 196
Wilson, John F: 1931 Glasgow. 357
Wilson, John J: 1933 Glasgow. 357
Wilson, William: 1934 St A & E. 67
Winning, Thomas J: 1948 Motherwell. 438
Wiseman, George: 1895 Aberdeen. 111
Woitys, Louis: 1897 Glasgow. 357
Wood, John D: 1903 St A & E. 67
Woodford, Michael: 1974 Glasgow. 357
Woods, Alphonsus T: 1943 Glasgow. 357
Woods, Henry: 1881 St A & E. 67
Woods, John: 1879 Galloway. 196
Woods, John: 1942 St A & E. 67
Woods, John N: 1958 Glasgow. 357
Woods, Patrick: 1953 Paisley. 468
Woods, Robert C: 1939 Glasgow. 357
Wright, Roderick: 1964 Glasgow. 358
Wrightson, Arthur: 1915 Galloway. 196
Wycherley, Patrick: 1929 Glasgow. 358
Wynne, Stephen: 1958 St A & E. 67
Wynne, Thomas: 1957 Argyll. 135

Young, Francis: 1887 Glasgow. 358
Young, Patrick: 1938 Galloway. 197

Index of Places

The following is an index to the diocesan parish lists.